# EXPLORING EDUCATION

## An Introduction to the Foundations of Education

Alan R. Sadovnik
Peter W. Cookson, Jr.
Susan F. Semel

All of Adelphi University

**Allyn and Bacon**

Boston  London  Toronto  Sydney  Tokyo  Singapore

*Series Editor*: Virginia Lanigan
*Editorial Assistant*: Nicole DePalma
*Production Administrator*: Annette Joseph
*Production Coordinator*: Holly Crawford
*Editorial-Production Service*: Lynda Griffiths/TKM Productions
*Cover Administrator*: Linda K. Dickinson
*Composition Buyer*: Linda Cox
*Manufacturing Buyer*: Louise Richardson

**Library of Congress Cataloging–in–Publication Data**

Sadovnik, Alan R.
    Exploring education: an introduction to the foundations of
education / Alan R. Sadovnik, Peter W. Cookson, Jr., Susan F. Semel.
        p.    cm.
    Includes bibliographical references (p. ) and index.
    ISBN 0-205-14191-9
    1. Education--United States.    2.  Educational sociology--United
States.  3.  Education--United States--Philosophy.   I. Cookson,
Peter W.   II. Semel, Susan F.   III. Title.
LB17.S113   1994
370'.973--dc20                                              93-34996
                                                               CIP

Printed in the United States of America

10  9  8  7  6  5  4  3  2  1      99  98  97  96  95  94

*For Our Children:*
*Sasha and Aram Cookson*
*and*
*Margaret and John Semel*

*And to the Memory of Carla Hernandez*

# Contents

Preface    xiii

Acknowledgments    xv

Chapter 1    The Limits and Promises of Education: Toward
Reflective Practitioners    1

**Educational Problems    6**
The Crisis in Urban Education    6
The Decline of Literacy    9
Assessment Issues    11

**Understanding Education: The Foundations Perspective    12**
The History of Education    13
The Philosophy of Education    14
The Politics of Education    15
The Sociology of Education    16

**The Foundations Perspective: A Multidisciplinary
and Interdisciplinary Approach    17**

**Critical Literacy and Empowerment: Toward the Active
Voice of Teachers    17**

**Chapter 1 References    19**

**Suggested Readings    20**

Chapter 2    Perspectives on Education: Conservative, Liberal,
and Radical Visions    21

**The Purposes of Schooling    22**

**Political Perspectives    23**
General Issues: Conservative, Liberal, and Radical Perspectives    24
Traditional and Progressive Visions of Education    27

The Role of the School    28
Explanations of Unequal Educational Performance    30
Definition of Educational Problems    30
Educational Policy and Reform    31
Education and the American Dream    33

**From Political Perspectives to the Politics of Education    34**

**Readings:**
*The Drive for Excellence: Moving Towards a Public Consensus*    39
Chester E. Finn, Jr.

*Popular Schooling*    45
Lawrence A. Cremin

*Building a New Agenda*    59
Anne Bastian, Norm Fruchter, Marilyn Gittel, Colin Greer, and
Kenneth Haskins

**Chapter 2 References    64**
**Suggested Readings    64**

**Chapter 3    The History of Education    67**
**Old World and New World Education: The Colonial Era    68**
**The Age of Reform: The Rise of the Common School    72**
Opposition to Public Education    73
Education for Women and African Americans    74
**Urbanization and the Progressive Impetus    75**
Education for All: The Emergence of the Public High School    78
**The Post–World War II Era: 1945–1980    80**
Cycles of Reform: Progressive and Traditional    80
Equality of Opportunity    82
**Educational Reaction and Reform: 1980s–1990s    87**
**Understanding the History of U.S. Education: Different
Historical Interpretations    88**
The Democratic-Liberal School    89
The Radical-Revisionist School    90
Conservative Perspectives    91
**Conclusion    92**

**Readings:**
*Broken Promises: School Reform in Retrospect*    95
Samuel Bowles and Herbert Gintis

*Forgetting the Questions: The Problem of Educational Reform*    123
Diane Ravitch

**Chapter 3 References    132**
**Suggested Readings    133**

**Chapter 4     The Sociology of Education     137**

    **The Uses of Sociology for Teachers     138**

    **The Relation between School and Society     139**
        Theoretical Perspectives     140
        Functional Theories     140
        Conflict Theories     141
        Interactional Theories     143

    **Effects of Schooling on Individuals     144**
        Knowledge and Attitudes     144
        Employment     145
        Education and Mobility     146

    **Inside the Schools     147**
        Teacher Behavior     148
        Student Peer Groups and Alienation     149

    **Education and Inequality     150**
        Inadequate Schools     151
        Tracking     151
        De Facto Segregation     151
        Gender     152

    **Sociology and the Current Educational Crisis     153**

    **Readings:**
    *Functional and Conflict Theories of Educational Stratification*     155
    Randall Collins

    *On Understanding the Processes of Schooling: The Contributions of Labeling Theory*     175
    Ray C. Rist

    *Closing the Rift between Scholarship and Practice: The Need to Revitalize Educational Research*     189
    Peter W. Cookson, Jr.

    **Chapter 4 References     194**
    **Suggested Readings     195**

**Chapter 5     Philosophy of Education and Its Significance
           for Teachers     197**

    **The Perspective of Philosophy of Education     197**
        What Is Philosophy of Education?     198
        The Meaning of Philosophical Inquiry     198

    **Particular Philosophies of Education     199**
        Idealism     199
        Realism     201
        Pragmatism     205
        Existentialism and Phenomenology     210
        Neo-Marxism     212

**Conclusion    215**

**Readings:**
*My Pedagogic Creed    217*
John Dewey

*Wide-Awakeness and the Moral Life    221*
Maxine Greene

*Reproduction and Resistance in Radical Theories of Schooling    229*
Stanley Aronowitz and Henry Giroux

**Chapter 5 References    238**
**Suggested Readings    239**


**Chapter 6    Schools as Organizations and Teacher Professionalization    243**

**The Structure of U.S. Education    244**
Governance    244
Size and Degree of Centralization    245
Student Composition    246
Degree of "Openness"    246
Private Schools    247
Conclusion    248

**International Comparisons    248**
Great Britain    249
France    250
The Former Soviet Union    250
Japan    252
Conclusion    252

**School Processes and School Cultures    253**

**Teachers, Teaching, and Professionalization    256**
Who Become Teachers?    256
The Nature of Teaching    257
Teacher Professionalization    259

**Readings:**
*Organizational Tensions and Authority in Public Schools    263*
Mary Haywood Metz

*Contradictions of Reform    275*
Linda M. McNeil

*What Is a Teacher's Job?: An Examination of the Social and Legal Causes of Role Expansion and Its Consequences    287*
Judith H. Cohen

**Chapter 6 References    300**
**Suggested Readings    301**

**Chapter 7     Curriculum, Pedagogy, and the Transmission of Knowledge     303**

What Do the Schools Teach?     303

The History and Philosophy of the Curriculum     304

The Politics of the Curriculum     309

The Sociology of the Curriculum     315

Pedagogic Practices: How the Curriculum Is Taught     319

The Philosophy of Teaching: Differing Views on Pedagogic Practices     319

The Stratification of the Curriculum     322

The Effects of the Curriculum: What Is Learned in Schools?     324

Conclusion     326

**Readings:**

*The Text and Cultural Politics*     *327*
Michael W. Apple

*The Mimetic and the Transformative: Alternative Outlooks on Teaching*     *343*
Philip W. Jackson

*Taking Women Students Seriously*     *353*
Adrienne Rich

Chapter 7 References     359

Suggested Readings     362

**Chapter 8     Equality of Opportunity and Educational Outcomes     365**

Calculating Educational and Life Outcomes     366

    Class     369
    Race     370
    Gender     370
    Conclusion     371

School Differences and Educational Outcomes     371

    The Coleman Study (1966)     372
    The Coleman Study (1982)     374
    Conclusion     375

Educational Attainment and Economic Achievement     375

Education and Inequality: Mobility or Reproduction?     377

**Readings:**

*Inferences from Studies of Public/Private School Differences*     *381*
John F. Witte

*A Black Student's Reflection on Public and Private Schools*     *387*
Imani Perry

*Chartering and Bartering: Elite Education and Social Reproduction*   393
Caroline Hodges Persell and Peter W. Cookson, Jr.

*The Effects of Community Colleges: Aid or Hindrance to Socioeconomic Attainment?*   411
Kevin Dougherty

**Chapter 8 References**   435
**Suggested Readings**   435

**Chapter 9     Explanations of Educational Inequality     439**
**Explanations of Educational Inequality     440**
**Student-Centered Explanations     443**
    Genetic Differences     444
    Cultural Deprivation Theories     445
    Cultural Difference Theories     446
**School-Centered Explanations     449**
    School Financing     449
    Effective School Research     452
    Between-School Differences: Curriculum and Pedagogic Practices     454
    Within-School Differences: Curriculum and Ability Grouping     456
    Gender and Schooling     458
**Do Schools Reproduce Inequality?     460**

**Readings:**
*Building 860*     465
Christian Neira

*Females + Mathematics = A Complex Equation*     471
Karen Karp

*Keeping Track, Part 1: The Policy and Practice of Curriculum Inequality*     485
Jeannie Oakes

*Social Class Differences in Family-School Relationships: The Importance of Cultural Capital*     495
Annette Lareau

**Chapter 9 References**     513
**Suggested Readings**     516

**Chapter 10     Educational Reform and School Improvement     521**
**Effective Teachers     522**
**Educational Reform in the 1980s     523**
    School Choice     525
    School-Business Partnerships     528

School-Based Management and Teacher Empowerment     528
The Effective School Movement     530
Teacher Education     532

**Educational Reform in the 1980s: Major Themes     534**
The Reform of Actors and Their Roles     534
Excellence and Equity     535
The Redefinition of Good Education     535
The Creation of an Educational Marketplace     536
Redefining the Role of the Teacher     537

**Education in the 1990s     538**

**A Theory of Educational Problems and Reforms     540**

**Readings:**
*Reinventing Teaching     545*
Deborah Meier

*Better Schools     557*
Theodore Sizer

**Chapter 10 References     571**

**Suggested Readings     573**

**Index     575**

# Preface

*Exploring Education: An Introduction to the Foundations of Education* developed out of our dissatisfaction with the textbooks available for foundations of education courses. None of us is a strong advocate of traditional textbooks, as they often simplify complex material to the point of distortion and, more importantly, they do too much work for students. One of the reasons many undergraduate and graduate students cannot read in a critical and analytical mode is that they have been educated, in part, through reading textbooks that summarize everything for them. As firm believers in the use of primary sources, we have written a book that will provide students with material that will encourage them to read, write, and think critically.

Originally, we wanted to compile a reader in the foundations of education. Once we began, however, the project evolved into a combined text/reader in a number of ways. First, in testing the readings in our classes, we found that many of our students required a context to help them make sense of the readings. Thus, we concluded that a book that combined our own text with illustrative readings made more pedagogical sense. As we moved along, we began to realize that our writings should not simply be an introduction to the readings; rather, each chapter should include our own analysis of the material, with a set of readings at the end of each chapter to illuminate the major concepts. This formula, we believed, would provide the necessary balance between text and primary sources.

Moreover, in thinking about our own textual material, we concluded that we wanted to present our point of view about the value of the foundations of education and their application to understanding education. Further, we wanted to argue that a "foundations perspective," as we call it, is a useful tool in helping to improve schools and schooling.

Thus, the final product is the result of considerable thinking about the importance of the foundations of education for teachers and prospective teachers and about how best to present the foundations of education to students. Our book is nontraditional in that it combines our own analysis with primary source readings. We have chosen to include a smaller number of complete or near-complete readings, rather than a larger number of shorter, excerpted readings. We believe strongly that students need to read complete sources to develop their critical reading, writing, and thinking skills.

The purpose of *Exploring Education* is to provide prospective and practicing teachers with an introduction to the foundations of education: history, philosophy, politics, and sociology of education. We also draw on the research of anthropologists of education in a number of places. Chapters 1 through 5 provide a basic introduction to the value of the foundations perspective and to the politics, history, sociology, and philosophy of education. Chapters 6 through 10 apply the foundations of education to particular educational issues, including school organization and teaching, curriculum and pedagogic practices, education and inequality, and school reform and improvement. Our approach is not meant to be exhaustive. Rather, we have attempted to provide a research and theory-based approach that demonstrates the usefulness of the foundations lens for thinking critically about and, hopefully, solving educational problems.

This book has truly been a collaborative effort. Although each of us was responsible for writing a number of chapters (Sadovnik: Chapters 2, 7, and 9; Cookson: Chapters 4, 6, and 8; Semel: Chapters 3 and 5; Sadovnik, Cookson, and Semel: Chapter 1; Semel, Cookson, and Sadovnik: Chapter 10), each of us edited all of the chapters, and the final product is the outcome of our joint efforts. We have attempted to create a consistency in style throughout.

Finally, we hope this book provides teachers and prospective teachers with a tool for understanding schools and a belief in their ability to help improve schooling. Although this book conveys a realistic portrayal of the societal and institutional factors that inhibit meaningful educational change, we believe that teachers, long the forgotten voice in educational reform, need to be part of such change. We believe that the foundations perspective is an important tool in school improvement and change, and hope our book provides its readers with both a realistic picture of educational problems and a sense of hope that they can contribute to change.

# Acknowledgments

A number of individuals have contributed to the publication of this book. At Allyn and Bacon, Sean Wakely, our original editor, Virginia Lanigan, our editor, and Nicole DePalma, our editorial assistant, provided essential advice and support. Sean Wakely believed in this project from the outset and had the vision to sign a nontraditional textbook. Virginia Lanigan, who took over the project when Sean left Allyn and Bacon, provided strong and sound guidance in the completion of the manuscript and production stages. Nicole DePalma provided assistance during all phases of the project. Our thanks, too, to Lynda Griffiths, of TKM Productions.

This book could not have been completed without the assistance of a number of people at Adelphi University. Betty Hendry and Janet Murphy provided essential secretarial support. A number of graduate assistants over the past four years provided indispensable assistance. These include Lavita Nadkarny, Judy Malone, Linda Bunting, Linda DeVreis, Carla Hernandez, and Claudia Grinberg. A special thanks to Claudia Grinberg, who provided skilled copyediting, typing, and bibliographic assistance in the final stages of manuscript preparation. Without her able assistance, we could not have met our deadlines.

Seven reviewers provided thoughtful, critical, and insightful comments on the manuscript: They are Justine C. Baker (West Chester University), William M. Britt (University of North Carolina–Charlotte), Joseph C. Bronars (Queens College), Richard C. Jacobs (California State Polytechnic University–Pomona), John McFadden (California State University–Sacramento), David N. Mielke (Appalachian State University), and Harry White (State University of New York–New Paltz). We hope the book reflects many of their suggestions and we believe it is a better book because of their input. We are, however, responsible for whatever shortcomings remain.

This book has been used in a variety of forms at Adelphi University over the past three years. In addition to our own foundations of education classes, at both the undergraduate and graduate levels, it was field tested by Professors Diana Feige and Dale Snauwaert. Professors Feige and Snauwaert provided their own personal comments and that of their students. Their help is greatly appreciated. Our students at Adelphi University have provided the most critical input, as they constantly kept us aware of what worked and what needed revision. Many of the readings included are here because they proved to be pedagogically successful; many others were eliminated because they were not. Most importantly, our students served as constant reminders of our intended audience.

In July 1993, Carla A. Hernandez died; she was 24 years old. Carla was an undergraduate and graduate student of ours at Adelphi University; she was also our graduate assistant and, after graduation, was Peter W. Cookson, Jr.'s assistant. She was a gifted teacher and, at the time of her death, was the coordinator of Adelphi University's Off-Campus Education Program in Huntington, New York. Carla's contributions to this book and to our work were profound. She not only provided expert editorial assistance but also contributed many insights and observations about the nature of education and the possibilities of teaching. Carla was a lover of life and true educator; few people have left such a deep impression in such a short period of time.

CHAPTER **1**

# The Limits and Promises
# of Education:
# Toward Reflective Practitioners

Americans have always placed a great deal of faith in education. Schools have been viewed as providers of opportunities for social mobility, as places that nurture and develop the hearts and minds of children, as antidotes for ignorance and prejudice, and as solutions to myriad social problems. Throughout this country's history, countless Americans have regarded schools as a symbol of the American dream—that each successive generation, through hard work and initiative, could achieve more than their parents' generation.

This is not to say that Americans have not been critical of their educational system—quite the contrary! Throughout history, schools have been the subject of intense controversy and debate. Questions concerning teaching methods, politics, curricula, racial desegregation, equality of educational opportunity, and countless other issues have constantly defined the educational arena. It is precisely because Americans believe so passionately in education and expect so much from their schools that the educational system has never been free of disagreements and, at times, heated disputes.

Throughout the twentieth century, educational leaders, teachers, parents, and students have disagreed about the fundamental goals of education and the educational practices occurring within classrooms. As the educational system steadily expanded and as the society of which it is a part became more complex, the role of schools also became more diverse, if not more diffuse. As prospective teachers, you are about to enter a profession that has both exciting possibilities and serious challenges. It is also a profession that is constantly subject to criticism and reform efforts. A look at the last 20 years provides a small but poignant glimpse of some of these reform movements.

Once again, today, there is a crisis in education. To historians of education, however, the existence of a crisis is by no means new and the meaning of *crisis* is by no means clear. In the early 1970s, *crisis in education* referred to the inequalities of educational opportunity, the allegedly authoritarian and oppressive nature of the schools, and the way in which classroom practices thwarted the personal development of students. The phrases of the day emphasized *relevance, equity, freedom,* and *individualism.* In the 1980s, however, the emphasis shifted and the crisis was attributed to the decline of standards and authority, which was thought to be linked to the erosion of U.S. economic superiority in the world. The phrases of the day talked about *excellence, standards, back to basics,* and *cultural literacy.*

In these cycles of educational reform, teachers are often seen as both scapegoats and saviors. They are scapegoats in that if students do not know enough, it is because their teachers have not taught them enough or, worse still, do not know enough to teach them. Or, if children are not developing their individual creative abilities, it is because their teachers may have been more concerned with classroom control than individualized instruction. Teachers are saviors, on the other hand, in that they are mandated to implement the recommendations of each new wave of reforms.

As prospective teachers, you are thinking about a career in education for a variety of reasons. Some of them may include your love of children, the effects your own teachers had on you, the desire to make a difference and contribute to society, and your desire to help children develop both emotionally and intellectually. Some of you may have some less noble reasons, including the perception—however inaccurate—that teachers have easy schedules (home by 3:00 and summers off). Whatever your specific motives, we are sure that you are entering the profession to make a positive contribution to the lives of children and to gain internal satisfaction from witnessing educational success. Although we strongly believe that teachers can and do make a difference, we also recognize that you will be entering an educational system that has many problems. These problems often limit teachers in the fulfillment of their goals.

It is not our intention to depress you with pictures of educational problems nor to create an unrealistic portrait of an educational panacea that does not exist. Rather, we wish to produce a balanced tapestry of the world of schools—a world filled with both promise and limits, hope and despair. But most important, the purpose of this book is to help you understand this world of education: how it works, the factors that affect it, and your role as a teacher in making it better.

The following vignettes present the two poles of the teaching experience. The first, the poignant story of a teacher in an urban public school system, represents the underside of this country's schools and the frustration of a teacher caught in the middle of political, social, and educational problems:

My experience as a school teacher, both as a high school English teacher and an elementary school teacher, has been one of disappointment, frustration, anger and anxiety. I chose secondary English for a number of reasons, two primary ones being my love of literature and my comfortable familiarity with the school setting. Nothing in my college training gave me even an inkling that literature would not be the focus of my teaching, or that my future students would have values, outlooks and attitudes that were totally unfamiliar to me....

Imagine my shock, then, when I walked into a classroom the following fall as a newly licensed teacher, and encountered surly, hostile, disinterested, below-grade-level students!...They had been reared on failure and low expectations, and consequently regarded school and teachers as enemies....

As shocked and repulsed as I was initially, I was still determined to make a difference in the lives of my students. I thought I could plough through the poverty, illness, abuse, neglect and defeatism of their lives and get them to respond to Shakespeare's language, to Hawthorne's characters, to Hardy's themes. How foolishly unrealistic I was. My successes were scant and infrequent, my failures numerous and daily. I rarely knew the feeling that some teachers profess to experience when they "reach even one child." I was too numbed by a sense of futility to feel any sense of success....

Over the years, I became cynical and resentful and even contemptuous of some of my students. When colleagues praised my teaching and my management ability, I felt as though I were fooling the world—a guilty feeling. Why would people think I was a good teacher when I knew that most of my students were bored, that they were making little if any progress and that I was not being dynamic or even enthusiastic in my approach? The answer is that none of those things mattered. As long as there was order in the room and notes on the chalkboard, everyone was satisfied. Record-keeping and keeping control of the kids were all that seemed important to administrators. You clocked in and clocked out and got paid, regardless of what you did in the intervening hours. Good teachers got no more recognition than poor ones, and poor ones could not be weeded out once they were tenured. It all seemed so pointless and hopeless.

...My current school has classrooms that are converted closets, lacks paper and other integral supplies, employs an assistant principal whose job was given to him by a politician, allows hoards of children to simply watch cartoons in the auditorium and calls that a "media lesson," is overrun with mice and roaches, has gaping holes in ceilings and walls, has toilets and water fountains that are non-functioning, and promotes children who are practically illiterate. Security breeches abound, with intruders walking in and out of the building at will; instruction is interrupted sometimes ten or fifteen times in one hour by announcements blaring over the intercom; innovative ideas that certain teachers toil to create in an effort to improve the school are almost always ignored by a principal who is resistant to change. Teachers live for 3 o'clock dismissals, for holidays, for summer vacations. A snow storm that closes the school for a day is viewed as one of nature's blessings.

What happened to the joys and rewards of teaching and learning? After eighteen years of seeking the answer and trying to buck the system, I've given up. It's been said that one good teacher can influence a child's entire life. I've never seen that happen personally. I've seen students come back to visit favorite teachers, I've heard students thank and praise helpful teachers, and I've known students who'll work harder for one teacher than he has for others. But I've never met an inner-city student who claimed that the course of his life had been shaped by one particular teacher, or who was inspired enough by that teacher's values and ideals to rethink his own. Maybe I expected too much from the profession; maybe I should be satisfied when one or two children out of thirty improve their reading comprehension or math skills each year. But I'm not; it isn't enough for me! (Katz, 1988)*

The difficulties experienced by this teacher are not representative of what all or even most teachers face, but they do indicate that the educational systems that you will enter are often beset with problems that are not solely educational.

On the other hand, this second vignette speaks passionately and lovingly about the positive effects of teachers and describes the kind of teacher we all want to be. Written by Fred Hechinger in *The New York Times* and entitled "Gift of a Great Teacher," this tribute captures the ways in which teachers make a significant difference in the lives of students:

Tessie is different from the other teachers, a 9-year-old boy told his parents....When he was asked how she was different, he replied, "Tessie knows how we children think."

Tessie, the boy's fourth-grade teacher at [a school in New York City], was Theresa Ross, who taught elementary and middle school classes for nearly 60 years.... Last June Tessie, who was affectionately known by that name to children and adults alike, died at the age of 83....

The only way to describe great teaching, a rare art, is to study great teachers like Tessie. When her pupils recognized that she knew how they thought, it did not mean that she herself thought childishly or indulgently about them. To write about her is not to celebrate a person but to try to define some qualities of exceptional teaching.

It has been said that education is what you remember when you have forgotten what you learned. Often, that means remembering one's great teachers more vividly than any particular lesson. Anyone who has never had at least one such teacher is truly deprived. To expect many is unreasonable.... As a teacher, [Tessie's] only doctrine was to make education come to life. When she taught history, her favorite subject, she took the children back with her into antiquity. She believed that even fourth-graders could deal with the universe.

[A former student teacher] in Tessie's class...recalls how Tessie used all the children's experiences to teach them—street games, the previous night's television programs, great myths.

She would do "weird" things.... To make children understand the evil consequences of a hostile invasion, she once had her pupils "invade" another classroom. As expected, the result was often bedlam, and she asked the children to report on the experience.

Great teachers are strong enough to dare being unconventional, even controversial, and this was an example. Actually,...Tessie had second thoughts about the experiment and never repeated it. Still, both she and the children had learned from the experience.

*Reprinted by permission of the author.

...Great teachers develop their own ways, without relying on prescribed lesson plans. Tessie said: "The child needs a framework within which to find himself; otherwise, he is an egg without a shell. The adult is there to guide and teach. If a child asks how to do something, you don't tell him just to go and find out; you say, 'Come, let's work it out together.'"

...Once, a picnic in the park that she and her fourth-graders had prepared was rained out, to universal groans. Tessie's response was to have the desks and chairs pushed aside, turning the classroom floor into a substitute picnic ground.

Tessie tried to get children to understand the nature of leadership without lecturing about it. She might start with baseball or with the news, and then move on to Julius Caesar.

...When Tessie died, even the youngest children who had known her sensed a sharp loss. Some felt guilty, said one teacher who met with them to talk about Tessie's life and to help them cope with her death. Perhaps, the teacher thought, as Tessie got older and a little forgetful, the children thought they might not have been sufficiently thoughtful and appreciative. A more plausible explanation may be that the children instinctively recognized an extraordinary teacher, and mourned the loss. (Hechinger, 1987)*

How do you balance the extremes of these portraits? On the one hand, you see an educational system beset with insurmountable problems; on the other hand, you see a world in which individual teachers have the power to influence countless children in a positive way. Moreover, what is the relationship between the two? That is, how do the problems within schools limit teachers' abilities to make a difference? And how do teachers who do make a difference help solve some of the problems?

As a person entering the teaching profession, you will ultimately find yourself in a curious quandary—responsible for educational problems and their solutions, but often without the necessary knowledge and perspective for understanding the complexity of these problems and the intricacies of their solutions. Furthermore, although teacher education programs do a respectable job at providing teachers with teaching methods, research on teacher education as well as a number of reform proposals indicates that programs are less effective in providing teachers with a social and intellectual context for understanding the educational world in which these methods will be employed. This understanding is crucial to the development of teachers, who must be an integral part of the problem-solving process if schools are to fulfill their promise.

In his classic book, *The Sociological Imagination*, C. Wright Mills (1959) outlined the value of a sociological perspective for understanding the society in which we live. The sociological imagination, according to Mills, allows individuals to transcend the often narrow boundaries of their lives and to see the world from the broader context of history and society. Adopting the sociological imagination permits the user to connect his or her own life with the social, cultural, and historical events that have affected it, and ultimately enables the individual to understand how and why these forces are instrumental in shaping human existence. The promise of sociology, then, is its ability to provide a powerful understanding of society and ourselves (Sadovnik, Persell, Baumann, & Mitchell, 1987, p. 3). In light of the

---

significant social, political, economic, and moral questions of his time, Mills argued that "the sociological imagination [is] our most needed quality of mind" (Mills, 1959, p. 3).

In a similar vein, contemporary American education, as we have argued, is beset by problems. The following section provides a brief overview of some of these.

## EDUCATIONAL PROBLEMS

During the 1980s, educational problems became the focus of national attention. The issues of educational standards, excellence, and the decline of U.S. educational superiority in the international arena became central concerns. To a lesser extent, although of equal importance, the topic of equity, with particular attention to the crisis in urban education and the plight of children in the United States, received significant discussion. Although subsequent chapters will look at these issues more completely, this section briefly outlines two of the significant educational problems of our times and some of the policies and programs aimed at treating them.

### The Crisis in Urban Education

This nation's urban public schools are in crisis. Over the past 20 years, as central cities have become increasingly poor and populated by minorities, the schools reflect the problems endemic to urban poverty. Although there are similar problems in rural schools and in many suburban schools, urban educational problems represent perhaps the nation's most serious challenge. A high proportion of urban schools are ineffective by most measures of school quality, a large percentage of urban students perform below national standards, and high school dropout rates in many large cities are over 40 percent. Despite these dismal data, there are policies and programs— including school restructuring programs, effective school models, and school choice and magnet programs—that many believe display significant potential for improvement. Clear national, state, and local policies are needed that emphasize excellence with equity and funding for programs.

*Trends.* Urban schools reflect the demographic characteristics of the urban environment. As large cities have become increasingly poor and populated by minorities, their schools reflect the problems of urban poverty. Low student achievement, high dropout rates, and high levels of school ineffectiveness characterize many urban school districts.

- The United States has witnessed a significant increase in the percentage of poor and minority children and youth living in the central cities of the country. In 1971, 17 percent of the children and youth between the ages of 6 and 17 in large central cities were both poor and minority; by 1983, this percentage increased to 28 percent and continued to increase throughout the 1980s (Levine & Havighurst, 1989, p. 75).
- Urban schools reflect social stratification and segregation. Due to the concentration of poor and minority populations in large urban areas, urban public

schools have significantly higher percentages of low socioeconomic status (SES) and minority students than neighboring suburban school districts. In Milwaukee, the average percentage of low SES students in 1984 was 30 percent, compared to 6 percent in its surrounding suburbs; the average percentage of minority students in the city was 57 percent, compared to 4 percent for the suburban schools (Levine & Havighurst, 1989, pp. 80–84). In 1989, 48.6 percent of the children in New York City were from low-income families; 80.1 percent were black, Hispanic, or Asian. Increasingly, affluent white families in cities send their children to private schools (New York City Board of Education, 1989).

- In urban schools, the relationship between socioeconomic status and academic attainment and achievement reflects overall national patterns. Students from lower SES families attain lower levels of academic attainment and performance than students from higher SES backgrounds. For example, in New York City districts with 50 percent or more students from low-income families, 38.9 percent are reading at or above grade level; in districts with less than 50 percent of students from low-income families, 57.4 percent are reading at or above grade levels (New York City Board of Education, 1989). In addition, urban school dropout rates reflect this pattern. For example, the dropout rate in East Los Angeles is 60 percent; Boston, 50 percent; and Washington, D.C., 45 percent. In other cities, such as Detroit, Pittsburgh, Chicago, New York, Cleveland, and Baton Rouge, high school dropout rates are also very high (between 30 and 45 percent) (Levine & Havighurst, 1989, pp. 55–58).

- Many urban public schools do not provide their students with a minimally adequate education. For example, in New York City, 47.2 percent of the public schools are rated ineffective by New York State Department of Education standards. In addition, only 47.8 percent of its students are reading at or above grade levels, and only 56.2 percent of its students are at or above grade level in mathematics. These data reflect national patterns for public schools in large urban areas (New York City Board of Education, 1989).

*Policy Issues.* There is considerable disagreement among researchers and policy makers as to how to improve urban schools. There is little consensus about school choice (giving parents the right to choose their children's schools), desegregation, and school financing policies. What is clear, however, is that policies that are aimed at the schools alone, without addressing the significant social and economic problems of urban areas, are doomed to failure.

- Inequities in school financing exacerbate the problems faced by urban school systems. Because school financing is based on state funding formulas and local property taxes, most urban districts spend significantly less per pupil than wealthier suburban districts. Recent lawsuits in New Jersey, New York, and other states have sought to remedy these inequalities with varying degrees of success.
- Demographic realities make urban schools increasingly segregated both by race and social class. Although the evidence on the effects of school desegregation

on academic achievement is not conclusive, many policy makers argue that there are moral imperatives requiring school desegregation.

- The difficult problems within urban schools have, in part, resulted in a crisis in staffing. Many urban school systems face a continual teacher shortage and witness significant teacher turnover. Most important, in many cities there is a crucial shortage of minority teachers to serve as role models for the increasingly minority student population (Educational Priorities Panel, 1987).
- Policy makers disagree about how to improve urban schools. Some studies propose a radical overhaul of public education, including a voucher system, a free market competition between public and private schools, and unlimited parental choice in school selection (Chubb & Moe, 1990). Other studies suggest that such policies will increase the ability of high-income families to improve their children's education and ultimately continue to penalize low-income families.

*Programmatic Issues.*   Research suggests that there are programs that will improve urban schools. Effective school models, magnet programs (specialized schools), school choice programs, and parental community involvement all indicate promise. Funding for successful programs is needed to encompass a larger urban population.

- Effective school research has indicated that there are programmatic ways to improve urban schools. For example, the following characteristics have been identified with unusually effective schools in general and in urban settings: a safe and orderly environment; a clear school mission; instructional leadership by a principal or school head; a climate of a high expectations; a concentration on instructional tasks; monitoring of student progress; and positive home-school relations (cited in Gartner & Lipsky, 1987, p. 389). School restructuring efforts based on these principles suggest promise. For instance, the work of Deborah Meier, principal of Central Park East Secondary School in New York City, and James Comer, at Yale Medical School, in the New Haven Schools, are striking examples. Meier has successfully implemented progressive school restructuring in an urban school with a mostly black and Latino population. Comer has sucessfully implemented a school-university cooperative program for mostly low-income black students.
- Compensatory education programs (programs aimed at providing equality of opportunity for disadvantaged students) have resulted in academic improvement for children from low SES and disadvantaged backgrounds. Although the overall research on the effects of compensatory programs is mixed, there are studies that indicate that effective compensatory programs result in positive academic and social results (Natriello, McDill, & Pallas, 1990). Many policy makers believe that programs such as Head Start (a preschool program for children from low-income families), dropout prevention programs, and many bilingual education programs need to be funded, not eliminated.
- School choice programs may help to improve the education of urban children. Although there is disagreement about the extent of parental choice, many researchers believe that some combination of school choice and magnet school programs will improve urban education problems. In a number of urban

settings, such as Minneapolis and District 4 in New York City, there have been significant improvements. In addition, studies of magnet schools indicate significant educational possibilities.

- The paucity of minority teachers and the lack of multicultural curricula are significant problems in urban school systems. Many experts believe that given the student populations of most urban schools, it is imperative that programs are developed to attract and train minority teachers and to develop more multicultural curriculum projects.

## The Decline of Literacy

During the 1980s, critics of U.S. public education pointed to the failure of schools to teach children basic literacy skills in reading, writing, and mathematics and basic knowledge in history, literature, and the arts. Although there has been significant controversy over the value of such skills and knowledge, and whether such a decline is related to the decline in U.S. economic superiority, it is apparent that schools have become less effective in transmitting skills and knowledge.

*Trends.* Most experts agree that U.S. student achievement in terms of basic skills and knowledge has declined in the past two decades Although there are some problems with using standardized tests, comparisons of U.S. students to students from other countries, SAT scores, and other data indicate problems in literacy.

- U.S. high school students performed less well than their counterparts in other industrialized nations in mathematics, science, history, and literature. Studies by the International Association for the Evaluation of Educational Achievement (IAEEA) reflect this trend. In a mathematics test given to twelfth-grade students who ranked in the top 5 percent, the United States had an average score of 52.2, compared to the average score of all nations tested of 57.1. Canadian students scored 58.3; British students 55.5; and Japanese students 65.0. In tests of biology, twelfth-grade U.S. students enrolled in science courses scored 37.9. Japanese students scored 46.2; British students 63.4; and Canadian students 45.9. Although the validity of such comparisons is questionable, since they often compare students in an open system (United States) to students in more selective elite systems, nonetheless these data suggest problems in the U.S. educational system (U.S. Department of Education, Center for Education Statistics, 1989).
- U.S. high school students continued to score lower on the SAT verbal and mathematic tests in the 1980s than in previous decades. For example, in 1967–1968, the average verbal SAT score was 466 and the average mathematics score was 492. In 1977–1978, the average scores were 429 and 468, respectively; and in 1987–1988, the average scores were 428 and 476, respectively (U.S. Department of Education, Center for Education Statistics, 1989). Again, the validity of these scores is questionable, since more students attended college and thus took the SATs in the 1980s (therefore, a larger number of students from the lower achievement tracks in high school took the SATs), but these

data point to problems in the U.S. schools. In addition, U.S. high school students do not score particularly well on standardized tests of culturally valued knowledge in history and literature. For example, in *What Do Our Seventeen Year Olds Know?* Ravitch and Finn (1988) argued that 17-year-old high school students have abysmal knowledge of basic information in history and literature. Although there is general controversy over the intrinsic value of such knowledge, New York State high school performance on these tests may indicate a problem in U.S. schools in transmitting this form of cultural knowledge to its students.

- The curriculum in many public and private high schools is "watered down" and provides far too many elective courses of suspect value and too little of substance. The National Commission on Excellence report *(A Nation at Risk)* and other reports pointed to the absence of a core curriculum of required courses for all students. In addition, critics suggest that, because most states require only the fulfillment of credit hours (that is, four years of English, three years of mathematics, etc.), specific knowledge in curriculum areas is rarely uniformly required. In addition, some critics point to the absence of a national curriculum and standards, commonplace in many countries (e.g., France), as a major shortcoming in U.S. education. Although there has been significant controversy over many of these claims, there is an agreement that the curriculum in most U.S. high schools needs significant attention.
- The U.S. literacy (and illiteracy rate) is shocking. Jonathan Kozol, in *Illiterate America* (1986), indicated that there are over 25 million functionally illiterate Americans. This record is well below the literacy rates of other industrialized nations and is a serious indictment of our educational system.

*Policy Issues.*   There is little agreement about policy regarding standards and curriculum. Given the constitutional authority granted to states and localities for educational policies, many people argue against any federal governmental role. Others, such as Chester Finn, Jr., propose the adoption of national standards in curriculum, knowledge, and skills (Finn, 1989). Finally, many are concerned with the need to balance higher standards with the guarantee that all students are given an equal opportunity to meet these standards.

- The adoption of national standards in curriculum, knowledge, and skills is a controversial proposal. The creation of nationally prescribed norms of what should be taught, what students should learn and know, and what students should be able to do is favored by some and opposed by others. Those in opposition believe that such norms should be locally determined or that such norms are impossible to develop.
- The balancing of higher standards and the ability of all students, particularly disadvantaged students, to meet these standards is an important issue. With dropout rates over 50 percent in many urban school districts, many fear that simply raising standards will exacerbate an already problematic situation.
- The development of core curriculum for graduation from high school, which would include the same academic subjects and knowledge for all students,

poses significant issues about what the curriculum would include. Proponents of core curriculum, such as Diane Ravitch, Chester Finn, Jr., and E. D. Hirsch, suggest that the curriculum should include the canons of Western civilization as its starting point. Critics of this view suggest that a more multicultural curriculum needs to be developed.

- Policies aimed at raising standards and improving curriculum need to look at the effects of curriculum tracking policies. Curriculum tracking at the high school level and ability grouping (with the same or different curricula) at the K–12 level is a controversial policy. Proponents point to the functional necessity and benefits of homogeneous groups; critics, such as Jeannie Oakes (1985), point to the inequities of such arrangements. Because research is inconclusive, policies concerning tracking need to be carefully addressed.

*Programmatic Issues.* In the past few years, many states and localities have implemented programs to raise academic achievement. At the federal level, the Goals 2000 legislation (before the Congress in 1993) seeks to define a national set of learning goals for all students.

- Programs at the state and local levels to define what students should know and be able to do are well underway. Taking their initial cue from the National Commission on Excellence report, *A Nation at Risk,* many states and districts have increased curriculum requirements for graduation and have instituted core curriculum requirements. One fear is that such programmatic reforms may be artificial and raise scores simply by having teachers teach to tests. Another concern is that such standardization of curriculum may reduce innovation.
- Many states have initiated minimum performance requirements for promotion (grades 4, 8, 10) and graduation (grade 12). There is a concern with the use of standardized tests as the inclusive evaluation tool, and many states and local districts are experimenting with portfolios and other more qualitative evaluations.
- Effective school research indicates that schools that place student learning as the most important school goal are effective in improving learning. The application of effective school models, especially in urban areas, is necessary to ensure equity.
- Compensatory education programs and dropout prevention programs are essential if higher standards are not to become one more barrier for disadvantaged students. With literacy rates lowest with at-risk children and poor adults, both in urban and rural settings, literacy programs aimed at these populations are required.

## Assessment Issues

For both educational problems—the crisis in urban education and the decline of literacy—there are a number of assessment issues that need to be addressed. More empirical evidence on school effectiveness, especially qualitative studies on school processes, is needed. New assessment measures that eliminate class, racial, and cultural bias must be developed.

- Large-scale educational studies have provided important data on school and student outcomes. More studies on the process of schooling, including ethnographic studies, are needed to understand the factors within schools that affect student achievement.
- Effective school research has provided significant understanding of the relationship between school organization and processes and academic achievement. Research that assesses the implementation of effective school models based on this research is needed.
- More research on the relationship between family, culture, community, and school is needed. Although there are many theoretical analyses of these issues, far more empirical research is needed.
- New assessment techniques are needed to evaluate teacher and student performance and curriculum design. Studies indicate that traditional assessment devices may be culturally and racially biased. In addition to different quantitative measures, many researchers and educators believe that qualitative approaches such as portfolios should be considered (Martin-Kniep & Kniep, 1992).

The preceding discussion is a brief overview of two of the many problems addressed more fully in this book. The presentation of trends, policy issues, programmatic issues, and assessment issues provides only a glimpse into the complexity of the problems and their solutions. In subsequent chapters, the specific issues will be explored in greater detail. For our purposes here, it is important to recognize that, as teachers, you will face many of these problems and will need a perspective for grappling with them. We believe that the foundations perspective is an important tool in understanding and solving such difficult educational dilemmas.

## UNDERSTANDING EDUCATION: THE FOUNDATIONS PERSPECTIVE

As you can see, there is no shortage of critiques and there are a plethora of reform proposals. New teachers need a quality of mind—the kind of perspective that the sociological imagination advocated by Mills (1959) offers—in order to place the educational system in a context. Such a context or framework is necessary to understand the schools and the teacher's place within them, to understand how the schools relate to other aspects of society, and to see how educational problems are related to larger societal dilemmas. Finally, seeing the schools in their context will enhance the understanding of how the schools today reflect the historical evolution of reform efforts as well as how current debates frame what the schools will look like for each successive generation of teachers and students.

What do we propose that you, as prospective teachers, need in order to understand and answer these questions? Quite simply, we call it a *foundations perspective*. The foundations perspective is a lens for viewing the schools analytically from a variety of approaches that, taken together, provide the viewer with an understanding of the connections between teacher, student, school, and society. The foundations perspective also serves to relate educational organization and processes, and educational theory and practice. Most importantly, it links the understanding of these relationships to meaningful activity—the improvement of this nation's schools.

The foundations perspective consists of four interrelated approaches: historical, philosophical, political, and the sociological. Through the use of the insights of the history of education, the philosophy of education, the politics of education, and the sociology of education, you will be better able to comprehend the educational system you are about to enter as teachers.

The history, philosophy, politics, and sociology of education, or what are commonly referred to as the *foundations of education,* are by no means separate and distinct perspectives. On one hand, they represent the unique vantage points of the separate disciplines of history, philosophy, political science, and sociology. On the other hand, historians, philosophers, political scientists, and sociologists rarely write from their own disciplines alone; more often than not, they tend to view the world from interdisciplinary and multidisciplinary perspectives. Therefore, although the following discussion presents the insights of each as a separate entity, please keep in mind that ultimately the foundations perspective seeks to combine all four disciplinary approaches and to look at the relationships between their central areas of concern. What, then, are the central areas of concern? And what is their value for teachers? We begin with the first question.

## The History of Education

In *The Culture of Narcissism,* Christopher Lasch (1983) bemoaned what he termed the "waning of a sense of history." Lasch argued that contemporary Americans had lost their understanding of the past and therefore could neither understand the complexities of the present nor look to a better future. For Lasch, the historical perspective is essential not only because it gives one a grasp of one's heritage but also because it empowers one to envision the possibilities of the future.

All of you will enter an educational system that looks the way it does today because of historical processes and events. The debates, controversies, and reforms of the past are not unimportant footnotes for historians to mull over in their scholarly work. Rather, they are the pieces in the historical puzzle that comprise the educational world that you as teachers will inherit. Likewise, you in turn will become the next generation to place its stamp and have an impact on what the schools of tomorrow will be like.

In *The Eighteenth Brumaire of Louis Bonaparte,* Karl Marx (1963) wrote, "Men make their own history, but they do not make it just as they please; they do not make it under circumstances chosen by themselves, but under circumstances directly encountered, given, and transmitted from the past." History, then, provides people not only with a chronicle of the past but with a deep understanding of how and why the world has come to be. Such an understanding helps individuals to see both the limits and the possibilities for the future.

The schools look and work the way they do because of complex historical events and processes. To understand the educational problems of today, you must first have a perspective from which to comprehend these historical processes. This is the value and purpose of the history of education.

It is often said that people who do not understand history are doomed to repeat the mistakes of the past. Although we do not claim that the study of the history of education will make educators capable of eliminating mistakes altogether, and although the history of education suggests that people indeed tend to repeat some mistakes, we nonetheless believe that an ignorance of the past is a major barrier to educational improvement. Thus, the insights of the history of education are crucial to a foundations perspective.

This book will introduce you to the events that have defined the evolution of the U.S. educational system and to the significant debates between historians of education regarding the meaning of these events. First, you will look at the major historical periods in U.S. educational history: the colonial period, the common school era, the progressive era, and the modern era. Through an examination of what historians have written about each period, you will come to understand the relationship between each period and the debates and issues that characterized it, and you will be able to see how each educational reform set the stage for successive reform and reaction. Second, the readings in this book will also explore the controversies in the history of education about the interpretation of these events. That is, even when historians agree about the facts of educational development, they often passionately disagree about why things happened as they did. Over the past 25 years, for example, democratic liberal historians, who believe the history of U.S. education represents the increasing success of the schools in providing equality of opportunity for all citizens, and revisionist historians, who believe that the history of U.S. education represents a series of broken promises and the triumph of social and economic elites, have raised significant questions about the role of schools and the groups that have power to shape the educational system. Through an exploration of the writings of historians from both of these perspectives, you may see that our schools are indeed the product of a variety of related factors and that the present debates are inherited from the past and influenced by its triumphs and defeats. To understand this is to understand the complexity of the present.

## The Philosophy of Education

In order to comprehend fully the world of schooling that they are about to enter, future teachers must possess a social and intellectual context (the foundations perspective). An understanding of the philosophy of education is essential in building this perspective.

Students often wonder why philosophy is considered to be an integral part of the foundations perspective, arguing that education is shaped by practice rather than by theory. They argue that teachers are called on to make situational decisions and that the methods employed by teachers at any given moment are based on their instincts or feelings. Students object to the study of philosophy on the grounds that it is an elite discipline that has little practical value. Why, then, do we contend that philosophy is an important component of both comprehending and negotiating the world of schooling?

We begin to answer this question by establishing the relationship between educational practices and philosophy. As is customary in the discipline of philosophy, issues are often resolved by posing questions and offering answers, which in turn usually lead to more questions. This method, established centuries ago by the ancient Greeks, is known as the *dialectic method*. Thus, we begin by posing the first of two questions to our students: What is your practice?—that is, What will you do with your own classes when you become practitioners? After our students describe, define, or clarify what they intend, we pose a second question: Why will you do what you have just described? By asking you to reflect on the "what" and "how" as you go about teaching in your classrooms, we may help you realize that your decisions and actions are shaped by a host of human experiences firmly rooted in our culture.

For example, why do some of you prefer informal classroom settings to formal ones? Why might some of you lean toward the adoption of the project method—an interdisciplinary curriculum approach developed during the progressive era? We suggest that your feelings might be articulated in the work of John Dewey, or that a preference for adopting the spiral curriculum may best be articulated through Jerome Bruner's work on curriculum. In other words, the choices that you, as prospective teachers, make and the preferences you have may best be clarified and expressed through the study of the philosophy of education.

As educators, we believe certain fundamentals exist within the human experience that color the choices we make as human beings and as teachers in the classroom. We suggest that as prospective teachers, you begin your reflective quest for these fundamentals by examining thought patterns and ideas within the discipline of philosophy.

This brings us to our second point: the uniqueness of the study of the philosophy of education, as distinct from philosophy. An interdisciplinary approach is called for in order to seek out the theoretical foundations upon which practice will be built. As students of the philosophy of education, it is important that you read selections from literature, psychology, sociology, and history, as well as philosophy. Through a thorough examination of thought patterns within the different disciplines, you will be sufficiently empowered to effect your own personal syntheses of the human experience, reflect on your world views, and make your own intensely personal choices as to what sort of practitioners you will be. Ultimately, the philosophy of education will allow you to examine *what ought to be* and thus enable you to envision the type of teachers you want to be and the types of schools that ought to exist.

## The Politics of Education

Throughout history, schools have been the subject of considerable conflict about goals, methods, curriculum, and other important issues. Decisions about educational policies are rarely made in a smooth consensual manner, but rather are often the result of battles between various interest groups. U.S. schools are a contested terrain in which groups attempt to use political strategies to shape the educational system to best represent their interests and needs.

Political science helps educators understand power relations and the way interest groups use the political process to maximize their advantages within organizations. A political science perspective focuses on the politics of education—on power relations; on the relationship between the local, state, and federal governments and education; on school financing and law; and on the question of who controls the schools.

One of the major questions political scientists ask is How democratic are our schools?—that is, To what extent are educational policies shaped by the pluralistic input of many groups, or To what extent are they the result of domination by political elites? The political science approach to education will allow you to examine the complexities of questions such as these, while also providing important insights into education policy and change.

Another issue of importance, especially for teachers, is the organizational politics within schools. How do educational interest groups within schools—including administrators, teachers, students, and parents—arrive at policy? Which groups have the power to shape educational decisions for their own benefit? What are the patterns of political conflict and consensus? How do the relationships between these groups help define the educational debates of today? Through a close look at the politics of education, you will become aware of how these group interactions are essential for understanding schools and, more importantly, the ability of teachers to shape and change the educational system.

## The Sociology of Education

The discipline of sociology developed at the end of the nineteenth century amidst the turmoil and promise of industrialization, urbanization, and a growing faith in democracy and education. As more and more children were required to attend schools, questions arose about the relationship between school and society. As the institution of education grew, there was a perception among many thinkers that schools would help usher in a modern era in which merit and effort would replace privilege and inheritance as the criteria for social and occupational success.

Sociologists of education generally shared in this optimism. They began to explore the ways in which students were socialized for adult status, they examined the school as a social system, and they analyzed the effects of education on students' life chances. They believed that they could improve education through the application of social scientific theory and research. Because of their scientific orientation, sociologists of education are more apt to ask *what is* rather than *what ought to be*. They want to know what really goes on in schools and what the measurable effects of education are on individuals and on society. The hallmark of the sociological approach to education is empiricism, or the collection and analysis of social facts within a theoretical context that allows researchers to build a coherent set of findings. Thus, sociologists of education are interested in collecting data and they try to avoid abstract speculation.

The sociological method is particularly useful when educational practices are related to educational outcomes. For example, in a recent study of public, Catholic, and other private schools, sociologists Coleman, Hoffer, and Kilgore (1982) were able to compare learning outcomes in these three types of schools by using survey analysis techniques. A practitioner or policy maker interested in school improvement can have some confidence that these results are valid and generalizable, and not simply opinion or wishful thinking. Of course, results are always subject to interpretation because all knowledge is, in a sense, the result of competing interpretations of events and ideas.

In sum, the methods of sociology are useful tools for understanding how schools actually interact with society. Although social science has no monopoly on wisdom or knowledge, it is based on an honest attempt to be objective, scientific, and empirical. Like history, sociology grounds us in the social context and tempers our educational inquiries by contrasting the real with the ideal. The sociological approach is fundamental to the foundations perspective because it keeps one's observations focused and testable. Without knowing *what is,* one cannot make the *ought to be* a reality.

## THE FOUNDATIONS PERSPECTIVE: A MULTIDISCIPLINARY AND INTERDISCIPLINARY APPROACH

The history, philosophy, politics, and sociology of education are separate disciplines; they are rarely used in isolation and are most often combined to ask the type of questions we have discusssed. Although the selections in this book are often written from one of the perspectives, they generally use more than one of the disciplinary approaches. In fact, they are usually multidisciplinary and/or interdisciplinary (i.e., integrating more than one discipline). Moreover, the foundations perspective is a way of viewing schools that uses each of the approaches—the historical, the philosophical, the political and the sociological—in an integrative manner. Therefore, although Chapters 2 through 5 of this book are organized around each discipline, the remainder is thematically arranged. Each theme is looked at through a variety of foundations approaches, each reflecting the critical applications of a foundations perspective to education.

## CRITICAL LITERACY AND EMPOWERMENT: TOWARD THE ACTIVE VOICE OF TEACHERS

Teachers' voices have long been silent in discussions of educational reform. On one hand, administrators, college professors, politicians, and other educational experts all write about what is wrong with schools, but often without the practical experiential foundation of what it is like in the classroom. On the other hand, teachers often criticize these writings because the experts lack an understanding of what is termed "life in the trenches." However, many teachers show the same kind of oversight when they criticize the experts—they sometimes believe that the voice of experience is sufficient to describe, understand, and change schools. What is needed is a perspective that relates theory and practice so that teachers can combine their experiential knowledge with a broader, more multidimensional analysis of the context in which their experiences occur. The foundations perspective provides a theoretical and empirical base, but it alone is similarly insufficient as a tool for optimal understanding and effective change. When combined with the experiential voice of teachers, however, the foundations perspective becomes a powerful tool for teachers in the development of their active voice about educational matters.

In the view of C. Wright Mills (1959), the individual does not have the ability to understand the complex social forces that affect him or her and make up a society simply by virtue of living in the society. Likewise, teachers, solely by virtue of their classroom experiences, do not have the tools to make sense of the world of education. In fact, some teachers are too close and subjectively involved to have the emotional distance that is required for critical analysis. We are not suggesting that a teacher's experience is unimportant. We are saying that the theoretical and empirical insights of the foundations of education must comprise a crucial part of a teacher's perspective on education and thereby contribute to critical literacy. *Critical literacy* in education is simply the ability to connect knowledge, theory, and research evidence to the everyday experiences of teaching. Through the use of a foundations perspective, teachers can develop this essential ability and become, in Donald Schön's (1983) words, "reflective practitioners."

Recent criticisms of teacher education programs suggest that teachers do not receive a sufficiently intellectually rigorous education. Reports by the Carnegie Task Force (1986) and the Holmes Group (1986) state that teacher education programs, especially those at the undergraduate level, place too much emphasis on methodology and do not provide a solid knowledge base in the traditional disciplines that education students will eventually teach. The overemphasis on process at the expense of depth and breadth of knowledge and intellectual demands has, according to these critics, resulted in teachers who do not possess the intellectual tools needed to educate their students successfully. Thus, the cycle of educational decline in terms of knowledge and skills is reproduced. These reports propose the elimination of undergraduate education programs. In their place, the Commission recommends the requirement that prospective teachers complete professional training at the graduate level after attaining a liberal arts baccalaureate degree.

Although these criticisms are somewhat simplistic in that they often scapegoat teachers for educational problems that go well beyond the shortcomings of teacher education programs, we do believe that teachers should be more liberally and critically educated. The emphasis on knowledge, however, is not sufficient. The cultural literacy envisioned by the educational reformers of the 1980s and championed by writers such as E. D. Hirsch, Allan Bloom, and Diane Ravitch will not by itself provide teachers with the analytical and critical tools needed for understanding the schools. Although cultural literacy is important (even though the question of what constitutes the knowledge that teachers and students ought to have is a crucial dilemma), teachers need critical literacy in their ongoing attempt to make their voices heard and to effect meaningful change.

Students and teachers often ask us how critical literacy will help them solve problems. Are we suggesting that teachers equipped with the ability to understand the educational system will improve it easily? Of course not! Understanding the schools and improving them are two different matters. Without changes in the factors that affect the schools, as well as changes in the structure and processes within the schools, it is highly unlikely that large-scale change or even significant improvement will take place. What we are saying, however, is that teachers must be part of the ongoing dialogue focused on improving schools, and in order to contribute meaningfully to this dialogue they need more than their own experiences. They need the knowledge, confidence, and authority that are products of critical literacy.

Developing critical literacy is a first and necessary step toward bringing the active voice of teachers into the educational debates so that, together with other professionals, teachers can become intimately involved in the development of a better educational world. It will not be easy. As sociologists, philosophers, and historians of education, we do not pretend that the record suggests that we should be overly optimistic; neither does it suggest, however, that we should lose hope. It is our profound desire that the readings in this book will give you the tools to become part of this ongoing effort—the quest for better schools, better teachers, and a more humane and intelligent society!

## CHAPTER 1 REFERENCES

Carnegie Task Force on Teaching as a Profession. (1986). *A nation prepared: Teachers for the 21st century.* Washington, DC: Carnegie Forum on Education and the Economy.

Chubb, J., & Moe, T. (1990). *Politics, markets, and America's schools.* Washington, DC: Brookings Institution.

Coleman, J., Hoffer, T., & Kilgore, S. (1982). *High school achievement.* New York: Basic Books.

Educational Priorities Panel. (1987). *A teacher for the apple: Why New York City can't staff its schools.* New York: Educational Priorities Panel.

Finn, C. (1989). Presentation at *Forum on National Standards.* Teachers College, Columbia University.

Gartner, A., & Lipsky, D. K. (1987). Beyond special education: Toward a quality system for all students. *Harvard Educational Review, 57,* 367–395.

Hechinger, F. (1987, November 10). Gift of a great teacher. *New York Times.*

Holmes Group. (1986). *Tomorrow's teachers.* East Lansing, MI: The Holmes Group.

Katz, J. (1988). Unpublished commentary on New York City education.

Kozol, J. (1986). *Illiterate America.* New York: New American Library.

Lasch, C. (1983). *The culture of narcissism.* New York: Norton.

Levine, D. U., & Havighurst, R. J. (1989). *Society and education* (7th ed.). Boston: Allyn and Bacon.

Martin-Kniep, G. & Kniep, W. M. (1992). Alternative assessment: Essential, not sufficient for systematic change. *Holistic Education Review, 9*(4), 4–13.

Marx, K. (1963). *The eighteenth brumaire of Louis Bonaparte.* New York: International Publishing Company. (Original work published 1852)

Mills, C. W. (1959). *The sociological imagination.* New York: Oxford University Press.

National Commission on Excellence in Education. (1983). *A nation at risk.* Washington, DC: U.S. Government Printing Office.

Natriello, G., McDill, E., & Pallas, A. (1990). *Schooling disadvantaged students: Racing against catastrophe.* New York: Teachers College Press.

New York City Board of Education. (1989). *Human relations task force: Final report.* New York: New York City Board of Education.

Oakes, J. (1985). *Keeping track: How schools structure inequality.* New Haven: Yale University Press.

Ravitch, D., & Finn, C. E., Jr. (1988). *What do our seventeen year olds know?* New York: Basic Books.

Sadovnik, A. R., Persell, C., Bauman, E., & Mitchell, R., Jr. (1987). *Exploring society.* New York: Harper and Row.

Schön, D. A. (1983). *The reflective practitioner: How professionals think in action.* New York: Basic Books.

U.S. Department of Education, Center for Education Statistics. (1989). *Digest of education Statistics, 1989.* Washington, DC: Government Printing Office.

## SUGGESTED READINGS

Austin, G. R. (Ed.). (1982). *The rise and fall of national test scores.* New York: Academic Press.

Borman, K. M., & Spring, J. H. (1984). *Schools in central cities.* New York: Longman.

Farkas, G., et al. (1990). Cultural resources and school success: Gender, ethnicity, and poverty groups within an urban school district. *American Sociological Review, 55,* 127–142.

Fine, M. (1986). Why urban adolescents drop into and out of public high school. *Teachers College Record, 87,* 393–409.

Hammack, F. M. (1986). Large school systems: Dropout reports: An analysis of definitions, procedures and findings. *Teachers College Record, 87,* 324–342.

Hodgkinson, H. L. (1985). *All one system: Demographics of education, kindergarten through graduate school.* Washington, DC: Institute for Educational Leadership.

Inkeles, A. (1979). National differences in scholastic performance. *Comparative Education Review, 23,* 386–407.

Kingston, P. W. (1986, Fall). Theory at risk: Accounting for the excellence movement. *Sociological Forum, 1,* 632–656.

LeCompte, M. D. (1987). The cultural context of dropping out: Why remedial programs don't solve the problems. *Education and Urban Society, 19,* 232–249.

U.S. Department of Education, Center for Education Statistics. (1989a). *The condition of education, 1989 edition.* Washington, DC: Government Printing Office.

U.S. Department of Education, Center for Education Statistics. (1989b). *Digest of education statistics, 1989.* Washington, DC: Government Printing Office.

Weis, L. (Ed.). (1988). *Class, race and gender in American education.* Albany: State University of New York Press.

CHAPTER 2

# Perspectives on Education: Conservative, Liberal, and Radical Visions

Too often, teachers and prospective teachers look at educational issues within the narrow context of the schools. That is, they treat what goes on inside classrooms and in the school at large as unrelated to the larger society of which it is a part. Schools are institutions that are rarely immune from external influences such as the economy, the political system, the family, and so on. Moreover, schools in every society exist for specific reasons, not all of which are educational. It is essential, then, that you understand the diverse and often conflicting purposes of schooling, as these goals are often at the heart of disagreements about education.

The terms *education* and *schooling* are sometimes used interchangeably when in fact they refer to somewhat different but related processes. Lawrence Cremin, the distinguished historian of U.S. education, defined *education* as

> the deliberate, systematic, and sustained effort to transmit, evoke, or acquire knowledge, attitudes, skills, or sensibilities, as well as any outcomes of that effort.... The definition projects us beyond the schools and colleges to the multiplicity of individuals and institutions that educate—parents, peers, siblings, and friends, as well as families, churches, synagogues, libraries, museums, summer camps, benevolent societies, agricultural fairs, settlement houses, factories, publishers, radio stations, and television networks. (1977, pp. 135–136)

Cremin's definition looks at education in the broadest possible sense to include all processes in a society that transmit knowledge, skills, and values, and educational institutions as all the places in which these activities occur.

*Schooling* is a more narrow process, as it is concerned with the activities that occur in schools. Therefore, where education is the most general societal activity, schooling is a particular example of the ways in which education occurs within the schools. Clearly from these definitions, schools are educational institutions. Why do they exist and what are their purposes?

In the broadest sense, schools have political, social, economic, and intellectual purposes. On a philosophical level, however, the purposes of education speak to what the political scientist Amy Gutmann refers to as "that portion of education most amenable to our influence; the conscious efforts of men and women to inform the intellect and to shape the character of less educated men and women. And we naturally begin by asking what the purposes of human education should be—what kind of people should human education create" (1987, p. 19). Therefore, the purposes of education, in general, and schooling, in particular, are concerned with the type of society people wish to live in and the type of people we wish to live in it. Ultimately, the purposes of education are directed at conceptions of what constitutes the "good life" and a "good person"—questions that have been at the center of philosophical inquiry from Plato to Aristotle, Marx, Freud, and Dewey.

As you will read throughout this book, there is little agreement about these difficult questions. Although men and women have different ideas about what society and individuals ought to look like, every society attempts to transmit its conception on these matters to its citizens. Education is crucial to this process.

## THE PURPOSES OF SCHOOLING

The specific purposes of schooling are intellectual, political, social, and economic (Bennett & LeCompte, 1990, pp. 5–21). These purposes refer to their role within any existing society—for our purposes, U.S. society. As you will read later in this chapter and in Chapter 4, one often must make the distinction between what the purposes of schooling are and what they ought to be. For example, those who support the goals of a society believe that schools should educate citizens to fit into that society; those who disagree with its goals believe that schools should educate citizens to change the society. As you can see, differing visions of education relate back to differing conceptions of what constitutes a good society.

The *intellectual* purposes of schooling are to teach basic cognitive skills such as reading, writing, and mathematics; to transmit specific knowledge (e.g., in literature, history, the sciences, etc.); and to help students acquire higher-order thinking skills such as analysis, evaluation, and synthesis.

The *political* purposes of schooling are to inculcate allegiance to the existing political order (patriotism); to prepare citizens who will participate in this political order (e.g., in political democracies); to help assimilate diverse cultural groups into a common political order; and to teach children the basic laws of the society.

The *social* purposes of schooling are to help to solve social problems; to work as one of many institutions, such as the family and the church (or synagogue) to ensure social cohesion; and to socialize children into the various roles, behaviors, and values of the society. This process, referred to by sociologists as *socialization,* is a key ingredient to the stability of any society.

The *economic* purposes of education are to prepare students for their later occupational roles and to select, train, and allocate individuals into the division of labor. The degree to which schools directly prepare students for work varies from society to society, but most schools have at least an indirect role in this process.

As you will read in Chapter 4, these purposes sometimes contradict each other. For example, the following question underscores the clash between the intellectual and political purposes of the school: If it is the intellectual purpose of the school to teach higher-order thinking skills, such as critical thinking and evaluation, then can it simultaneously engender patriotism and conformity to society's rules? Lawrence Cremin pointed out:

> Schooling, like education in general—never liberates without at the same time limiting. It never empowers without at the same time constraining. It never frees without at the same time socializing. The question is not whether one or the other is occurring in isolation but what the balance is, and to what end, and in light of what alternatives. (1977, p. 37)

This dialectic, or the tension between schooling's role in maintaining the status quo and its potential to bring about change, is at the heart of differing conceptions of education and schooling. As we pointed earlier, those who support the society tend to stress the school's role in helping to maintain it; those who believe the society is in need of improvement or change stress its role in either improving or transforming it. In the following sections, you will read about how different political perspectives on education view not only the purposes of schooling but a variety of related issues.

## POLITICAL PERSPECTIVES

Debates about educational issues often focus on different views concerning the goals of schools and their place within our society. From the inception of the U.S. republic through the present, there have been significantly different visions of U.S. education and the role of schools in society. Although many of the views are complex, it is helpful to simplify them through the use of a political typology. In its most simple form, the different visions of U.S. education can be discussed in terms of conservative, liberal, and radical perspectives. Although the nature of these approaches has changed over time, what follows is a contemporary model of how each perspective views a number of related educational issues. In the following sections, we will explore each perspective in terms of its view of U.S. society, its view of the role of the school in relation to equality and the "American dream," its explanation of student failure and underachievement in schools, its definition of educational problems in the 1980s and 1990s, and its educational policy and reform proposals.

### General Issues: Conservative, Liberal, and Radical Perspectives

Political perspectives on education have rarely been used consistently. One of the problems in using labels or typologies is that there is often little agreement about what constitutes the basic principles of any particular perspective. Furthermore, there have been historical changes in the meanings of each of the approaches under consideration: the conservative, the liberal, and the radical. In addition, as many educators have used the terms *traditional* and *progressive* to denote similar approaches, there is often considerable confusion over matters of terminology. In this section, we will define each of the perspectives and relate them to progressive and traditional perspectives. In subsequent sections, the specific features of the conservative, liberal, and radial perspectives will be delineated.

A *perspective* is a general model for looking at something—in this case, a model for understanding, analyzing, and solving educational problems. As you will see throughout this book, there has been and continues to be little agreement about the nature, causes, and solutions to educational problems. In order to understand the ways in which various authors look at educational issues, it is necessary to understand how they approach the problems—that is, to understand where they are coming from (their perspective, its assumptions, etc.).

The conservative, liberal, and radical perspectives all look at educational issues and problems from distinctly different, although at times overlapping, vantage points. Although there are areas of agreement, they each have distinctly different views on education and its role in U.S. society. Moreover, they each have fundamentally different viewpoints on social problems and their solution in general, and their analysis of education is a particular application of this more general world view.

*The Conservative Perspective.*   The conservative view has its origins in nineteenth-century social Darwinist thought (see Gordon, 1977) that applied the evolutionary theories of Charles Darwin to the analysis of societies. This perspective, developed originally by the sociologist William Graham Sumner, looks at social evolution as a process that enables the strongest individuals and/or groups to survive, and looks at human and social evolution as adaptation to changes in the environment. From this point of view, individuals and groups must compete in the social environment in order to survive, and human progress is dependent on individual initiative and drive.

A second feature of the conservative viewpoint is the belief that the free market or market economy of capitalism is both the most economically productive economic system as well as the system that is most respectful of human needs (e.g., for competition and freedom). Based in part on the eighteenth-century writings of the British political economist Adam Smith and applied to twentieth-century economic policy by the Nobel laureate economist Milton Freidman, conservatism argues that free market capitalism allows for the maximization of economic growth and individual liberty with competition ensuring that potential abuses can be minimized. Central to this perspective is the view that individuals are rational actors who make decisions on a cost/benefit scale.

Thus, the conservative view of social problems places its primary emphasis on the individual and suggests that individuals have the capacity to earn or not earn their place within a market economy, and that solutions to problems should also be addressed at the individual level. The presidency of Ronald Reagan represented the political ascendancy of this viewpoint. Reagan championed a free market philosophy and argued that welfare state policies (government intervention in the economy) were at the heart of an American malaise. His presidency (1980–1988) was characterized by supply side economics (a form of free market capitalism), the elimination of many governmental regulations, and the curtailment of many social programs. The Reagan philosophy stressed individual initiative and portrayed the individual as the only one capable of solving his or her own problems. Whereas conservatives lauded Reagan's policies and credited him with restoring U.S. economic growth, both liberals and radicals were very critical.

*The Liberal Perspective.* The liberal view has its origins in the twentieth century, in the works of the U.S. philosopher John Dewey, and, historically, in the progressive era of U.S. politics from the 1880s to the 1930s. Perhaps more important, the liberal view became politically dominant during the administration of Franklin Delano Roosevelt (1932–1945) and what is often referred to as the *New Deal era.*

The liberal perspective, although accepting the conservative belief in a market capitalist economy, believes that the free market, if left unregulated, is prone to significant abuses, particularly to those groups who are disadvantaged economically and politically. Moreover, the liberal view, based on the economic theories of John Maynard Keynes, believes that the capitalist market economy is prone to cycles of recession that must be addressed through government intervention. Thus, the liberal perspective insists that government involvement in the economic, political, and social arenas is necessary to ensure fair treatment of all citizens and to ensure a healthy economy. The impact of such liberal policies is evident throughout the twentieth century, from the New Deal initiatives of FDR (including the Social Security Act and the Works Progress Administration, a federally funded jobs program) to the New Frontier proposals of John F. Kennedy, to the Great Society programs of Lyndon Baines Johnson to (although he probably would take issue with this) George W. Bush's savings and loan bailout.

The liberal perspective, then, is concerned primarily with balancing the economic productivity of capitalism with the social and economic needs of the majority of people in the United States. Because liberals place a heavy emphasis on issues of equality, especially equality of opportunity, and because they believe that the capitalist system often gives unfair advantages to those with wealth and power, liberals assert that the role of the government is to ensure the fair treatment of all citizens, to ensure that equality of opportunity exists, and to minimize exceedingly great differences in the life chances and life outcomes of the country's richest and poorest citizens. Moreover, liberals believe that individual effort alone is sometimes insufficient and that the government must sometimes intercede on behalf of those in need. Finally, the liberal perspective on social problems stresses that groups rather than individuals are affected by the structure of our society, so solutions to social problems must address group dynamics rather than individuals alone.

*The Radical Perspective.* The radical perspective, in contrast to both the conservative and liberal perspectives, does not believe that free market capitalism is the best form of economic organization, but rather believes that democratic socialism is a fairer political-economic system. Based on the writings of the nineteenth-century German political economist and philosopher Karl Marx (1818–1883), the radical viewpoint suggests that the capitalist system, although undeniably the most productive form of economic organization, also produces fundamental contradictions that ultimately will lead to its transformation into socialism.

Although the economic analysis of these contradictions are complex and unnecessary to the level of understanding required here, it is important to note that the central contradiction pointed out by radicals is between the accumulation laws of capitalism (i.e., that wealth is both accumulated and controlled privately) and the general social welfare of the public. That is, radicals (Gordon, 1977; Bowles & Gintis, 1976, 1986) assert that, at this stage in capitalist development, U.S. society has the productive capacity to ensure a minimally acceptable standard of living, including food and shelter for all its citizens. Thus, radicals believe a socialist economy that builds on the democratic political system (and retains its political freedoms) would more adequately provide all citizens with a decent standard of living. What is essential to the radical perspective is the belief that social problems such as poverty and the educational problems of the poorest citizens are endemic to capitalism and cannot be solved under the present economic system. Rather, radicals assert that only a transformation of capitalism into democratic socialism will ensure that the social problems that disproportionately affect the disadvantaged in U.S. society will be addressed.

Radicals believe that the capitalist system is central to U.S. social problems. They also recognize that the capitalist system is not going to change easily and, furthermore, that most Americans fervently support it. Therefore, most radicals place their primary emphasis on the analysis of inequality under capitalism, the economic and power relationships that are central to the perpetuation of inequalities, and policies that seek to reduce these inequities under the existing capitalist system. Thus, while theoretically and politically supporting change, the radical perspective often agrees with those liberal programs aimed at issues concerning equity.

Finally, the radical perspective believes that social problems are structural in nature—that is, that they are caused by the structure of U.S. society and therefore the solutions must be addressed to this structure, not at individuals. To argue that social problems are caused by deficits in individuals or groups is to "blame the victim," according to the radical perspective (Ryan, 1971).

The collapse of the communist (state socialism) world in Eastern Europe and the former Soviet Union has resulted in serious challenges in the United States to the claims of the radical perspective. Conservatives and many liberals argue that the events in the former Soviet Union and Eastern Europe signal the death of communism, as well as socialism, and denote historical evidence for the superiority of capitalism. Although it is clear that state socialism as practiced in the former Soviet Union and Eastern Europe has failed, radicals do not agree that its failure denotes either the bankruptcy of socialism or the final moral victory of capitalism. Rather, radicals suggest that socialism failed in these cases for a number of reasons.

First, without a capitalist economic base to build on (a prerequisite for socialism in Marx's original theory), socialist economies in communist societies could not efficiently produce sufficient goods and services. Second, without a democratic political base, communist societies denied the necessary human freedoms essential to a healthy society. Furthermore, radicals suggest that the collapse of state socialist economies does not preclude the ability of socialism to succeed in democratic-capitalist societies. Finally, radicals argue that the collapse of communism in no way eliminates the problems endemic to Western capitalist societies, particularly those related to extremes of inequality. Therefore, although conservatives view recent events with great satisfaction, radicals point to the social problems in U.S. society. Liberals, to some degree, believe that these events point to the power of their point of view: that the collapse of socialist economies in communist societies indicates the strength of the capitalist economy, while the significant social problems that remain in U.S. society suggest the importance of further liberal responses.

The three perspectives, then, have overlapping but distinctly different views on the nature of U.S. society and its social problems. The conservative perspective is a positive view of U.S. society and believes that capitalism is the best economic system, as it ensures maximum productivity with the greatest degree of individual freedom. Social problems, from its vantage point, are caused by individuals and groups, and it must be individuals and groups that solve them on their own, with little or no direct government intervention.

The liberal perspective is also positive about U.S. society, albeit with reservations. Liberals also believe that capitalism is indeed the most productive economic system, but they suggest that, if left unrestrained, capitalism often creates far too much political and economic disparity between citizens. Thus, liberals believe the state (government) must intercede to ensure the fair treatment of all and that social problems are often the result of societal rather than individual or group forces.

Finally, the radical perspective, unlike the other two, is negative about U.S. society. It recognizes the productive capacity of its capitalist economic system, but it argues that the society structurally creates vast and morally indefensible inequalities between its members. Radicals, who favor significantly greater equality of outcomes between citizens, believe that U.S. social problems cannot be solved under the existing economic system. They favor a movement toward democratic socialism: a society that, according to radicals, would combine democratic political principles (including representative government, civil liberties, and individual freedom) with a planned economic system—one that is planned for the satisfaction of the human needs of all of its citizens.

## Traditional and Progressive Visions of Education

Discussions of education often refer to *traditional* and *progressive* visions. Although these terms have a great deal in common with the conservative, liberal, and radical perspectives discussed earlier, they are sometimes used interchangeably or without clear definitions, and therefore there is often confusion concerning terminology. For our purposes, we will use the terms *traditional* and *progressive* as the most general representations of views about education. Traditional visions tend to view the schools as necessary to the transmission of the traditional values of U.S. society, such as hard work, family unity, individual initiative, and so on. Progressive visions tend to view the schools as central to solving social problems, as a vehicle for upward mobility, as essential to the development of individual potential, and as an integral part of a democratic society.

In a nutshell, traditionalists believe the schools should pass on the best of what was and what is, and progressives believe the schools should be part of the steady progress to make things better. In relation to the conservative, liberal, and radical perspectives, there is significant overlap. If we use a political continuum from left to right, with the left signifying the radical pole and the right the conservative pole (mirroring the political terminology of *left* and *right wing*), we suggest the following relationship:

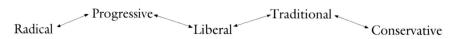

Thus, progressive visions encompass the left liberal to the radical spectrums; traditional vision encompass the right liberal to the conservative spectrums. Obviously, as with all typologies, this is somewhat of a simplification. Although many theories that we will discuss and illustrate in subsequent chapters may have significantly more overlap, this typology is, nonetheless, a useful tool for understanding different visions about education.

The discussion so far has concentrated on the general approach to U.S. society and social problems taken by each perspective. The next section looks specifically at how each perspective analyzes education and educational problems.

**The Role of the School**

The role of the school is a central focus of each of the perspectives and is at the heart of their differing analyses. The school's role in the broadest sense is directly concerned with the aims, purposes, and functions of education in a society.

The conservative perspective sees the role of the school as providing the necessary educational training to ensure that the most talented and hard-working individuals receive the tools necessary to maximize economic and social productivity. In addition, conservatives believe that schools socialize children into the adult roles necessary to the maintenance of the social order. Finally, they see the school's function as one of transmitting the cultural traditions through what is taught (the curriculum). Therefore, the conservative perspective views the role of the school as essential to both economic productivity and social stability.

The liberal perspective, while also stressing the training and socializing function of the school, sees these aims a little differently. In line with the liberal belief in equality of opportunity, it stresses the school's role in providing the necessary education to ensure that all students have an equal opportunity to succeed in society. Whereas liberals also point to the school's role in socializing children into societal roles, they stress the pluralistic nature of U.S. society and the school's role in teaching children to respect cultural diversity so that they understand and fit into a diverse society. On the political level, liberals stress the importance of citizenship and participation in a democratic society and the need for an educated citizenry in such a society. Finally, the liberal perspective stresses individual as well as societal needs and thus sees the school's role as enabling the individual to develop his or her talents, creativity, and sense of self.

Therefore, the liberal perspective sees the role of education as balancing the needs of society and the individual in a manner that is consistent with a democratic and meritocratic society. That is, liberals envision a society in which citizens participate in decision making, in which adult status is based on merit and achievement, and in which all citizens receive a fair and equal opportunity for economic wealth, political power, and social status.

Diane Ravitch, historian of education, eloquently summarizes the liberal view of education:

> To believe in education is to believe in the future, to believe in what may be accomplished through the disciplined use of intelligence, allied with cooperation and good will. If it seems naively American to put so much stock in schools, colleges, universities, and the endless prospect of self-improvement and social improvement, it is an admirable, and perhaps even a noble flaw. (1983, p. 330)

The radical perspective, given its vastly differing view on U.S. society, likewise has a significantly different view of what the school's role is. According to radicals, the school's role is to reproduce the unequal economic conditions of the capitalist economy and to socialize individuals to accept the legitimacy of the society. Through what radicals term *social and cultural reproduction,* the school's role is to perpetuate the society and to serve the interests of those with economic wealth and political power. Most important, through a vastly unequal educational system, radicals believe that schools prepare children from different social backgrounds for different roles within the economic division of labor. The radical perspective, unlike the liberal, views equality of opportunity as an illusion and as no more than an ideology used to convince individuals that they have been given a fair chance, when in fact they have not. Therefore, the radical perspective argues that schools reproduce economic, social, and political inequality within U.S. society.

In Chapter 1, we discussed the U.S. belief in education and the view that schooling is an essential component of the American dream of social mobility and equality of opportunity. Conservatives, liberals, and radicals have differing views on the role of the school in meeting these goals.

The conservative perspective believes that schools should ensure that all students have the opportunity to compete individually in the educational marketplace and that schools should be meritocratic to the extent that individual effort is rewarded. Based on the belief that individuals succeed largely on their own accord, conservatives argue that the role of the school is to provide a place for individual merit to be encouraged and rewarded.

Liberals believe that schools should ensure that equality of opportunity exists and that inequality of results be minimized. Based on the historical record, the liberal perspective indicates that although schools have made a significant difference in the lives of countless Americans and have provided upward mobility for many individuals, there remain significant differences in the educational opportunities and achievement levels for rich and poor.

Radicals believe that schools should reduce inequality of educational results and provide upward social mobility, but that historically the schools have been ineffective in attaining these noble goals. Moreover, the radical perspective argues that under capitalism schools will remain limited, if not wholly unsuccessful, vehicles for addressing problems of inequality—problems that radicals suggest are structurally endemic to capitalism.

### Explanations of Unequal Educational Performance

If, as radicals and many liberals suggest, schooling has not sufficiently provided a reduction in inequality of results, and as educational achievement is closely related to student socioeconomic backgrounds (as was indicated in Chapter 1), then the explanation of why certain groups, particularly from lower socioeconomic backgrounds, perform less well in school is a crucial one. Conservatives argue that individuals or groups of students rise and fall on their own intelligence, hard work, and initiative, and that achievement is based on hard work and sacrifice. The school system, from this vantage point, is designed to allow individuals the opportunity to succeed. If they do not, it may be because they are, as individuals, deficient in some manner or because they are members of a group that is deficient.

The liberal perspective argues that individual students or groups of students begin school with different life chances and therefore some groups have significantly more advantages than others. Therefore, society must attempt through policies and programs to equalize the playing field so that students from disadvantaged backgrounds have a better chance.

Radicals, like liberals, believe that students from lower socioeconomic backgrounds begin schools with unequal opportunities. Unlike liberals, however, radicals believe that the conditions that result in educational failure are caused by the economic system, not the educational system, and can only be ameliorated by changes in the political-economic structure.

### Definition of Educational Problems

Until this point, we have focused on the role of the school and, in particular, its relationship to equality of opportunity and results. Although these are certainly significant issues, the ways in which each perspective addresses specific educational problems of the 1980s and 1990s, and consequently how each sees solutions to these, is of the utmost importance. We will begin with a discussion of the definition of educational problems.

The conservative perspective argues the following points:

1. In their response to liberal and radical demands for greater equality in the 1960s and 1970s, schools systematically lowered academic standards and reduced educational quality. Conservatives often refer to this problem as the *decline of standards.*

2. In their response to liberal and radical demands for multicultural education (i.e., education that responds to the needs of all cultural groups), schools

watered down the traditional curriculum and thus weakened the school's ability to pass on the heritage of American and Western civilizations to children. Conservatives often define this problem as the *decline of cultural literacy*.

3. In their response to liberal and radical demands for cultural relativism (i.e., that every culture's values and ideas are equally valid), schools lost their traditional role of teaching moral standards and values. Conservatives often refer to this problem as the *decline of values or of civilization*.

4. In their response to liberal and radical demands for individuality and freedom, schools lost their traditional disciplinary function and often became chaotic. Conservatives often refer to this problem as the *decline of authority*.

5. Because they are state controlled and are immune from the laws of a competitive free market, schools are stifled by bureaucracy and inefficiency.

Liberals have significantly different viewpoints on the major educational problems of our times. The liberal perspective argues the following points:

1. Schools have too often limited the life chances of poor and minority children and therefore the problem of underachievement by these groups is a critical problem.

2. Schools place too much emphasis on discipline and authority, thus limiting their role in helping students develop as individuals.

3. The differences in quality and climate between urban and suburban schools and, most specifically, between schools with students of low socioeconomic backgrounds and high socioeconomic backgrounds is a central problem related to inequalities of results.

4. The traditional curriculum leaves out the diverse cultures of the groups that comprise the pluralistic society.

The radical perspective, although often similar in its analysis to the liberal viewpoint, is quite different in its tone. The radical perspective argues the following points:

1. The educational system has failed the poor, minorities, and women through classist, racist, and sexist policies.

2. The schools have stifled critical understanding of the problems of American society through a curriculum and teaching practices that promote conformity.

3. The traditional curriculum is racist, sexist, and classist and leaves out the culture, history, and voices of the oppressed.

4. In general, the educational system promotes inequality of both opportunity and results.

## Educational Policy and Reform

Defining educational problems is the first step toward the construction of solutions. During the 1980s and into the 1990s, proponents of each perspective have supported specific educational reform and policy recommendations. The following brief discussion outlines the policies and programs of each without going into any detail. (A more detailed analysis will be provided in Chapters 3, 6, and 10.)

Conservatives support the following:

1. Return to basics (often referred to as *back to basics*), including the strengthening of literacy skills, such as reading and writing, and other forms of traditional learning.
2. Return to the traditional academic curriculum, including history, literature, and the canons of Western civilization.
3. Introduce accountability measures for students and schools, including minimum standards of performance and knowledge—that is, create minimum standards for what students should know and for the skills they should possess at specific grade levels (e.g., fourth, eighth, and twelfth grades).
4. Introduce free market mechanisms in the educational marketplace, including tuition tax credits and vouchers for parents who wish to send their children to private schools and public school choice programs (allowing parents to choose among different public schools). This is often referred to as *school privatization.*

Liberals support the following:

1. Policies should combine a concern for quality for all students with equality of opportunity for all. This is sometimes referred to as *quality with equality.*
2. Policies should lead to the improvement of failing schools, especially urban schools. Such programs should include school-based management and teacher empowerment (decentralized control of individual schools with teachers having a significant voice in decision making), effective school programs (programs that are based on what is called the *effective school research*—research that indicates "what works"), and public school choice programs. Whereas liberals support parental choice of public schools, they rarely support conservative proposals for complete privatization, tuition tax credits, and vouchers, as these are seen as threatening public education and creating increasingly unfair advantages for parents who are already economically advantaged.
3. Programs should enhance equality of opportunity for disadvantaged groups, including Head Start (a preschool program for students from lower socioeconomic backgrounds), affirmative action programs, compensatory higher education programs (college programs for disadvantaged students), and so forth.
4. A curriculum should balance the presentation of the traditions of Western civilization with the treatment of other groups within the culturally diverse society.
5. A balance should be maintained between setting acceptable performance standards and ensuring that all students can meet them.

Radicals support the following:

1. On a general level, radicals do not believe that educational reform alone will solve educational problems, as they see their causes outside the purview of the educational system. Short of what most radicals see is necessary but unrealistic

large-scale societal change—they support most liberal reform programs as long as they lead to greater equality of educational results.

2. Programs should result in greater democratization of schools—that is, give teachers, parents, and students a greater voice in decision making. Examples of these are teacher empowerment, school-based management, school decentralization, and school-community cooperation efforts.

3. Curriculum and teaching methods should involve "critical pedagogy" (Giroux, 1988)—that is, radicals support educational programs that enable teachers and students to understand social and educational problems and to see potential solutions (radical) to these.

4. Curriculum and teaching methods should be multicultural, antiracist, antisexist, and anticlassist—that is, radicals support educational programs that include curricular treatment of the diverse groups that comprise U.S. society and that are pedagogically aimed at sensitizing students to racism, sexism, and classism.

Radicals, although often supporting many of the liberal educational reform proposals, are less sanguine about their potential effectiveness. In fact, as Samuel Bowles pointed out, the failure of liberal reforms may prove successful in a very different political context:

> Educational equality cannot be achieved through changes in the school system alone. Nonetheless, attempts at educational reform may move us closer to that objective if, in their failure, they lay bare the unequal nature of our school system and destroy the illusion of unimpeded mobility through education. Successful educational reforms—reducing racial and class disparities in schooling, for example, may also serve the cause of equality of education, for it seems likely that equalizing access in schooling will challenge the system to make good its promise of rewarding educational attainment or find ways of coping with mass disillusionment with the great panacea. (1977, p. 149)

## Education and the American Dream

The next chapter will focus directly on the ways in which educational reform evolved in U.S. history. Although our discussion thus far has looked at the last 30 years, it is essential to understand that the present debates and crises are outcomes of a much longer historical time span in which the disagreements about educational issues helped shape the present educational system. It is also important to note that all three perspectives have different views on U.S. educational history, especially with regard to the school's success in living up to the democratic promise discussed in Chapter 1.

Conservatives argue that the U.S. schools have succeeded in providing a quality education for those who are capable and have taken advantage of it, and that, until the 1960s and 1970s, schools were responsible for U.S. superiority in economic and technological realms. On one hand, conservatives argue that the system has provided a meritocratic selection process that has ensured that the most talented and motivated individuals are rewarded by the schools and later in life. This mechanism historically has successfully guaranteed that the important roles and occupations are filled with those individuals capable of handling them. On the other hand, conservatives believe that the progressive reforms of the twentieth century (to be discussed in Chapter 3), especially those occurring in the 1960s and 1970s, eroded the quality of the schools, their curriculum, and what students learned. Thus, the U.S. educational system, from this point of view, is found wanting, especially in relation to its role in economic development and competitiveness.

The liberal perspective is more concerned with the social and political functions of schooling than the economic. As such, liberals believe that schools have been successful in extending public education to the masses and providing more opportunity for mobility than any other system in the world. Moreover, liberals believe that U.S. education has been essential in the long, slow, and flawed march toward a more democratic and meritocratic society—a society where one's individual achievement is more important than one's family background, a society that is more just and humane, and a society where tolerance of others who are different is an important value. Despite these successes, liberals argue that the educational system has been an imperfect panacea (Perkinson, 1977) and has yet to provide sufficient access, opportunity, and success for all citizens, and thus must continue to improve.

The radical perspective is far less optimistic about the historical success than either the liberal or conservative viewpoints. According to radicals, the U.S. schools have been unsuccessful in providing equality of opportunity or results to the majority of citizens. Although it is true that the United States has educated more people for longer periods of time than any other nation in the world, radicals believe the overall outcomes have reproduced rather than reduced social and economic inequalities. According to this perspective, the historical record suggests that, although educational opportunities expanded throughout the twentieth century, students from different class backgrounds were offered different types of education (e.g., middle- and upper middle-class students in an academic program in the public high school and poor students in a vocational program; middle- and upper middle-class students in a four-year baccalaureate college education and poor students a two-year community college education). Therefore, according to radicals, the history of U.S education has been the story of false promises and shattered dreams.

In the next chapter, you will have the opportunity to explore the events, conflicts, debates, and reforms that comprise this history and to judge for yourself the extent to which the history of U.S. education supports one or more of these political interpretations.

## FROM POLITICAL PERSPECTIVES TO THE POLITICS OF EDUCATION

As you have read, there is considerable disagreement among the three perspectives. In the world of education, these disagreements play themselves out in conflicts. These conflicts involve different groups, parents, teachers, administrators, legislators, business people, and so on, and are central to understanding educational decision making. As you will read in Chapter 3, the history of education in the United States has rarely been a smooth one. It has involved the conflict between groups with opposing values and interests, groups all seemingly interested in the same thing—the best education for our children—but with significantly different perceptions of what that constitutes and how to go about it.

Sometimes these conflicts have been about curriculum and pedagogy (e.g., the conflicts about vocational versus academic education in the 1930s and 1940s or traditional versus child-centered teaching at the turn of the twentieth century); sometimes they have been about values and morality (e.g., as in the textbook and book-banning controversies of the last 15 years or over the question of prayer in schools); and sometimes they have been about civil rights and racial issues (e.g., the violent battles over school desegregation in Little Rock, Arkansas, in the late 1950s and in Boston, Massachusetts, in the 1970s).

Sometimes these conflicts are external to the school and involve the federal, state, and local governments, the courts, and the business community. Sometimes they are internal to the schools and involve parents, teachers and teacher unions or organizations, students, and administrators.

Whatever the specific nature of the conflicts, they all involve power and power relationships. Political scientists are concerned with understanding how power relationships (i.e., which groups have power and which do not) affect educational decision making and organizational outcomes. As our discussion in Chapter 3 about the history of education will reveal, struggles about education rarely involve equals, but rather involve groups with disparate degrees of power. Therefore, these struggles often involve the attempts to maximize political advantage and to minimize that of opposing groups.

Whereas political scientists are concerned with who controls our schools (Kirst, 1984), political philosophers are concerned with who ought to control them and for what end. In her brilliant book *Democratic Education*, Gutmann (1987) outlined the philosophical dimensions of this political question. She argued that there are four different conceptions of who should have the authority to determine educational matters, the family state, the state of families, the state of individuals, and the democratic state (pp. 19–47). Each perspective answers the question, Who should have the authority over educational decisions in a different manner?

The family state viewpoint is derived from Plato's theories of education (to be discussed more fully in Chapter 5). This approach sees the purpose of education as creating a socially stable society committed to the good life and justice. The definition of a just society, however, is determined by an elite—what Plato referred to as the *philosopher kings* (or in Gutmann's gender equal terminology, *philosopher queens*). It is this elite that defines the just society and it is through education that citizens learn to accept this view of society and are thereby able to contribute to its smooth functioning. In terms of educational authority, it is a small and hopefully just elite that should determine educational decisions.

The second viewpoint, the state of families, is derived from the eighteenth-century English political philosopher John Locke. Based on the Lockean view that parents are the best guardians of their children's rights and interests, it suggests that families should have the final authority in educational decision making.

The third position, the state of individuals, is derived from the work of the nineteenth-century British philosopher John Stuart Mill. Based on the nineteenth-century liberal notion that the state should not impose its will on individuals nor threaten their individual liberties, it suggests that educational authorities should not "bias the choices of children toward some disputed or controversial ways of life and away from others" (Gutmann, 1987, p. 34). Thus, educational authority ought to provide opportunity for choice among competing conceptions of the good life and neutrality among them (Gutmann, 1987, p. 34). In this manner, individuals have authority over educational matters to the extent that they are given the freedom to choose among the widest possible options about the kind of lives they wish to live.

Gutmann provided an exhaustive criticism of these three perspectives, suggesting that the family state leaves one at the tyranny of the state, the state of families at the tyranny of families, and the state of individuals without a clear way to reproduce what a society believes is responsible for its citizens. Each perspective, she argued, is flawed because it fails to provide a compelling rationale for either its view of a good society or who should define it.

Gutmann proposed a fourth perspective: the democratic state of education. In this view,

> Educational authority must be shared among parents, citizens, and professional educators even though such sharing does not guarantee that power will be wedded to knowledge (as in the family state), that parents can successfully pass their prejudices on to their children (as in the state of families), or that education will be neutral among competing conceptions of the good life (as in the state of individuals). (1987, p. 42)

Recognizing that a democratic state has built-in problems, including the tyranny of the many over the few, Gutmann argued that there must be two limitations on such a state: nonrepression and nondiscrimination. Nonrepression does not permit the state or groups to use the educational system for eliminating choice between different alternatives of a just society; nondiscrimination requires that all children receive an adequate education—one that will enable them to participate in the democratic deliberations of their society (1987, p. 46).

As you can see, the question of educational authority is a complex one and has been at the center of educational conflict. Throughout this book, you will read about different educational viewpoints and different recommendations for solutions to educational problems. In this chapter, we have tried to make you aware that such conflicts rest on different assumptions about society, the purposes of education, and who should determine these important matters.

In the following readings, the perspectives on education are illustrated. In the first article, "The Drive for Excellence: Moving Towards a Public Consensus," educator Chester E. Finn, Jr., the former Assistant Secretary of Education during the Reagan administration, discusses the national reform efforts during the 1980s for increased educational standards. This drive for excellence, accountability, and a standardized core curriculum is at the center of conservative educational policy.

The second article, "Popular Schooling," written by the late historian of education Lawrence A. Cremin, discusses the historical dissatisfaction with U.S. education and the possibility of achieving the American dream of a quality education for all. The liberal vision of education is illustrated through a historical analysis of the popularization of the U.S. educational system.

The third article, "Building a New Agenda," by Anne Bastian, Norm Fruchter, Marilyn Gittel, Colin Greer, and Kenneth Haskins, argues for radical public reconstruction of our educational aims. The authors, all educators and activists, provide a critique of the conservative agenda of the 1980s and call for an educational system dedicated to democracy and equality.

# The Drive for Excellence: Moving Towards a Public Consensus

## CHESTER E. FINN, JR.

If a shroud could somehow be thrown over the nation's capital and another draped over most of the education profession, much of the news about American education in recent months would be heartening to those who have been looking for signs of heightened concern for the quality of teaching and learning in our schools and colleges.

That is not to suggest that fiscal woes and enrollment shortfalls have vanished—to the contrary—that every educational institution has suddenly burst into intellectual bloom. But if one steps back and asks not what it is like to run a school or teach in a university in 1983 but, rather, what the concerned citizen ought to think about the direction in which our educational system is generally headed, there is reason for encouragement.

What one sees in Washington today, on the whole, are missed opportunities, stalemated controversies and partisan bickering. What one hears from most of the organized education interest groups is the endless repetition of the same old fiscal and programmatic mantras. And what one witnesses in much of the profession are weariness and bitterness, a sense that something is fundamentally wrong with the course that American education is following and a feeling of powerlessness to do much about it, leading in many cases to the discouraging suspicion that perhaps one chose the wrong profession.

But if we look instead to a growing number of state capitals, school boards, popular magazines, newspaper editorials, citizens'

task force reports, pronouncements of business leaders, and even books proffered by major commercial publishers, we glimpse something altogether different: fresh ideas, renewed commitment to educational standards, rising expectations for teacher competence and student performance, impatience with trendy innovations and flabby practices, and a hot, bright faith in the importance of high quality education for the individual and the nation alike.

At the risk of overstatement, I suggest that our society and culture are in the throes of an educational reform movement of epochal proportions. But for the first time in memory, this is an educational reform movement that draws its force neither from the federal government nor from the profession. It is very nearly a populist movement, led primarily by self-interested parents and employers and by elected officials responding to overt and implicit signals from the voting, tax-paying public. Although the manifestations of this are untidy, sometimes clumsy, and occasionally simplistic, they are evolving into actual changes in educational policy and practice in many parts of the land.

I will sketch six general categories into which these changes may usefully be grouped, acknowledging at the outset that they are fuzzy and overlapping tendencies, rather than tight analytic compartments. First, in a number of states and communities, new—or newly enforced—*standards have been established for student achievement in the*

*Source: Change Magazine,* pp. 14–22, April 1983. Reprinted with permission of the Helen Dwight Reid Educational Foundation. Published by Heldref Publications, 1319 Eighteenth St., N.W., Washington D.C. 20036-1802. Copyright © 1983.

*public schools.* In simplest form, these stipulate that a child must show that he or she has acquired certain skills and knowledge before proceeding to the next grade or educational level. Typical examples are "proficiency tests" that students must pass before obtaining high school diplomas (some form of which are already in place or under development in most states) and "promotional gates" programs that serve to retain primary school youngsters in their school grades until they have mastered the prescribed learning objectives. These practices stand in sharp contrast to the "social promotion" policies that have been in effect in many schools for some time, and to the habit of conferring a high school diploma on any student who enrolled in the requisite courses for the appropriate number of years whether or not the student learned anything.

The new policies have their shortcomings, to be sure, and can create fresh problems even as they help solve old ones. Still, the emergence (in many places in reemergence) of such policies is clear evidence of popular insistence that diplomas come to signify actual accomplishment and that school be a place where a youngster learns, not just where he or she passes time. Moreover, the popularity of this view is shown by the fact that these policies have been formulated by state legislatures, governors, elected boards of education, and citizens' commissions far more frequently than by school professionals, panels of educational experts, or the facilities of teacher colleges.

Second, *college and university entrance requirements are being stiffened,* particularly on the campuses of public institutions that must heed the wishes of state officials, and high school graduation requirements are being toughened alongside them. A survey conducted in the summer of 1982 by the National Association of Secondary School Principals revealed that the major public universities in twenty-seven of the fifty states had recently "increased their admissions requirements or currently have admissions requirements under major review." More than the "flagship campuses" are involved. The *Chronicle of Higher Education* reported in September 1982 that even some community colleges "are establishing admission standards for the first time" and "are also tightening academic-program requirements and suspending or dismissing students who continue to fail courses."

Many of these changes entail the adumbration of more courses that applicants must take while in high school—typically in math, history, English, and science—while others include greater attention to class rank, grade point average, or test scores. This development is altogether remarkable, given the difficulty that many colleges now face in filling their classrooms and dorms, the ardor with which college "recruiters" go about their work, and the assumption, widespread in higher education, that shrinkage of the traditional college-age population is causing many institutions to slacken if not actually abandon all admissions standards. Some states, to be sure, may be making a marriage of convenience between fiscal exigency and educational quality, raising standards partly in order to shrink enrollments and thereby save money. But the motive may not matter so much as the result. And the motives, in any case, are often mixed. As explained by Harry M. Snyder of the Kentucky Council for Higher Education,

> The reasons institutions are imposing higher standards and will not be as wide open in their 'open door' admissions policies are partly financial, partly a matter of stating identity.... We have to impose higher standards or be forced to deal with kids who shouldn't be in college in the first place. We have some kids who can't do college-level work. We wonder how they ever did high-school level work.

His colleague to the north, Chancellor Edward Q. Moulton of the Ohio Board of

Regents, is even blunter: "We have just passed through a permissive period. Our lower admissions standards simply meant that more students could flunk out."

The tie between college entrance expectations and high school requirements is firm. "In our study," reports Ernest L. Boyer of the Carnegie Foundation for the Advancement of Teaching, "we found that the single most important activity that could cause overnight change in the high school curriculum would be if colleges announce their standards." And although the current round of changes in college standards is too new to have had a measurable effect, bountiful anecdotal evidence suggests that it will have. *Education Week* reported in November 1982 that "an informal survey of education officials and guidance counselors in several states indicates that the most dramatic changes will result from the growing number of students taking higher-level courses to keep their options for college training open. The need for more academic work in required fields of study, state officials and guidance counselors say, will prod many students to become more serious about their schoolwork." Moreover, a number of individual high schools, school systems, and entire states are boosting high school requirements on their own, or promulgating "model curricula" with meatier content and loftier standards. The Ohio State Board of Education recently added a second year of math to the high school graduation requirements. The Tennessee Board, encouraged by a blue-ribbon task force, is on the verge of adding 2½ "Carnegie units" to the current requirements. The "model curriculum" recently drafted by the California State Board includes four years of English, three of math, two of science, two of foreign language, and three of social studies.

Third, concern for deteriorating teacher quality has prompted a number of communities and states *to stiffen their intellectual norms for school teachers,* at least for those being licensed (or hired) for the first time.

Some twenty states have recently imposed new requirements or are developing them. In contrast to the historic pattern of teacher licensure, in which anyone graduating from an "approved" teacher education program or displaying the requisite course labels on his or her transcript would automatically be certified to teach, the new requirements characteristically insist that candidates demonstrate actual intellectual attainment or pedagogical prowess, such as by achieving a minimum score on the National Teachers Examination or by displaying classroom competence in evaluations conducted during an apprenticeship or probationary period.

The most sweeping such reform on a statewide basis was recently proposed by Tennessee Governor Lamar Alexander. His scheme entails reshaping the entire teaching occupation in Tennessee into a four-tiered edifice, in which an individual can move from a prolonged apprenticeship through "professional teacher" status, to "senior teacher," and ultimately to the rank of "master teacher," with substantially increased responsibilities and pay at each level, and with movement determined by demonstrated knowledge and actual classroom performance rather than by paper credentials, longevity, or friendship with the principal.

Fourth, an astonishing number of states are *developing comprehensive school improvement strategies* that may include but are not limited to achievement standards for students and licensure requirements for teachers. "As if some great dam had broken," reported *Education USA* in late December, "state policymakers are flooding public education institutions with proposals, and in some cases mandates, for higher standards." Some of these are the direct work of constitutional authorities, such as governors and state boards of education; some are the product of task forces, panels, and advisory commissions established for the purpose by government leaders seeking comprehensive counsel; and some are the result of similar efforts by citizens' groups, business and labor organizations, "good government" watchdog units, and kindred bodies that may not wait for an "official" request to advise government on how to get into better shape but whose advice, once proffered, is often taken seriously.

These statewise strategies are as varied in content as the auspices under which they are generated. The Commission on Secondary Schools appointed by Governor Bob Graham of Florida understandably concentrated on the reform of high school education, but took a long view that included teacher education and licensure, graduation requirements, funding formulae, statewide testing programs, and the creation of new institutional forms. Governor Winter of Mississippi, on the other hand, addressed himself to such elemental reforms as the establishment of kindergartens, the enforcement of compulsory attendance laws (which had lapsed in Mississippi in recent years), and the improvement of teacher compensation. Tennessee's Comprehensive Education Task Force ranged from new guidelines for in-service teacher training across the governance structure of public higher education to the scholastic standards of state-run dental and veterinary schools. The Governor's Task Force on Effective Schooling, appointed by former Alaska Governor Jay Hammond, developed dozens of recommendations covering the role of the principal as instructional leader, the proportion of time during the school day that is actually devoted to academic instruction, etc. And the Minnesota Citizens League, which has no direct governmental links, recently proposed a comprehensive restructuring of elementary and secondary education that would decentralize authority, deregulate the schools, and foster parental choice.

While it is too early to venture a general "impact statement," no one who follows education news could fail to note that the accounts of recommendations *to* policymakers

are beginning to be rivaled in frequency by reports of proposals by governors to legislatures, of laws enacted, of new regulations and procedures adopted, and of changes in long-established practice.

Fifth, though most of the actual policy changes are at the state and local levels, dozens of *school reform commissions, study groups and projects have been at work on the national level, as well.* Most of these are foundation-supported, and a large proportion have been concentrating on the high school, which for the last several years has been the institutional darling of education improvers. Some of these projects are small, some quite ambitious. A few emphasize the strengthening of basic structural relationships, such as the College Board-sponsored effort to improve the articulation of college entrance expectations and high school curricular requirements. Others, such as the Ford Foundation's project of cash awards to individual high schools, envision short-range changes at the building level. Still others, such as the large inquiries led by Ernest Boyer and Theodore Sizer, are searching reappraisals of the high school's role in society. The fastest-moving and perhaps the bravest of them all is the National Task Force on Education for Economic Growth; cochaired by two governors (Hunt of North Carolina and duPont of Delaware) and a major industrialist (Cary of IBM), which contains very few professional educators but—perhaps not coincidentally—is on the brink of making some very bold and far-reaching recommendations that would effectively restructure formal education in the United States. While these multiple ventures are predictably variegated, virtually all are addressed to improvements in the cognitive outcomes of schooling, and practically none is concerned with the role of the federal government in bringing about such improvements. Even the one pertinent venture *by* the federal government, Secretary Bell's National Commission on Excellence in Education, is expected to pay little attention to "the federal role."

Sixth, and least palpable but perhaps most consequential of all, the beginnings of a *major shift* in the cultural, intellectual, and political mainstream are becoming visible *with respect to the society's ideas and values about education in general and schooling in particular.* Concern for educational standards, the acquisition of skills and knowledge, the development of fundamental values and the strengthening of character are no longer confined to the ruminations of "conservative" publications, reactionary organizations, and oppositional groups. They are appearing with some regularity in the editorial admonitions of leading newspapers and journals of opinion, and even in the campaign statements of successful candidates for local, state, and national office. Major commercial publishers no longer assume that the only kinds of books about education that people will buy are the radical nostrums of Jonathan Kozol, Ivan Illich, Herbert Kohl, and John Holt, in which schools are excoriated for crippling the psyches of the young and molding them into the tools of a repressive capitalist society. Instead, one finds Harcourt Brace Jovanovich publishing Theodore Black's commonsensical *Straight Talk About American Education;* Basic Books issuing James Coleman's scholarly analysis of the educational efficacy of public and private high schools; Macmillan promoting Adler's clarion *Paideia Proposal,* and a splendid treatise on basic education by Gilbert Sewall; and McGraw-Hill venturing into the bold analyses of *Compelling Belief* by Stephen Arons.

A few swallows do not necessarily signal a change of climate, and it is possible that the recent warming trend will not last. Certainly it is premature to conclude that all is now well with American education. Average Scholastic Aptitude Test scores may have ticked upward this year—or they may have "bottomed out"; in any case there's quite a distance to go before years of decline in SAT and ACT averages are recouped. The findings of the National Assessment of Education Progress continue to show deterioration, particularly in the acquisition of advanced cognitive skills. A sobering new report by the Center for Public Resources shows that even the most basic skills remain in grave disrepair, particularly as viewed from the perspective of employers. One still picks up the newspaper and encounters such dispiriting findings as the recent report by the New Jersey board of higher education that only 11 percent of the public college freshmen in the Garden State "appeared to be proficient" in algebra and that "there is no evidence to indicate any meaningful improvement over the past five years."

Yet the fact that such information is deemed newsworthy in a sense attests to the nation's deepening seriousness of purpose about education. So does the large number of students recently put on academic probation by the vigorous new president of the University of the District of Columbia, Benjamin Alexander, who insists that students at his (predominantly black) institution come to value the college degree as a mark of actual educational accomplishment. Indeed, one of the most encouraging developments of all is the public acknowledgement by some of the more reflective civil rights leaders of a reality that most have long since accepted with respect to the education of their own children, namely that long-term success for minority youngsters entails the acquisition of high quality education. It will no longer do to excuse poor results with talk of prejudice. Though some minority educators resist the imposition of uniform educational standards—the most visible recent instance being the outcry by black college presidents against the NCAA-ACE academic requirements for varsity athletes—at least as many are quietly passing the word that all students must clear the same intellectual hurdles, regardless of race, gender, or whatever.

## MORE FROM LESS

Most remarkable of all is the fact that the qualitative reforms now underway in American education coincide with a period of grave financial distress for many schools and colleges, and for the state and local governments that support them. Adjusted for inflation, per pupil expenditures in the nation's schools *declined* in 1980 for the first time since the National Center for Education Statistics began tracking such figures in 1968. Severe program cutbacks and stringent budgetary constraints are the order of the day in one community and institution after another. And it is not only academic frills and extracurricular activities that are suffering. For the first time in recent history, some colleges and universities are discharging tenured faculty members in basic academic disciplines solely because there is no money with which to pay their salaries. Nor is there any reason to expect the gloomy fiscal picture to brighten in the near future. The *Wall Street Journal* reported in January 1983 that the latest state revenue-and-expenditure projections for fiscal 1983 indicate an aggregate two-billion-dollar deficit, as anticipated income to the states falls almost eight billion below estimates made just six months earlier. The consequences—due primarily to the economic recession, but also to faltering federal assistance budgets, rising demands on welfare programs, and the like—in many jurisdictions are draconian austerity moves that affect schools and colleges along with other public agencies and services.

How, one may ask, is it possible to witness all these signs of educational revitalization even when so many of our schools and colleges are in such straitened fiscal circumstances? The explanation, it turns out, is both straightforward and in its way refreshing, at least to those who are not trying to make institutional ends meet. The society appears to have shelved the long-established notion that doing something better necessarily means doing it more expensively. We have grown so accustomed to additive reform of our public institutions, services, and agencies, so acclimated to "external funds"—often furnished by Washington—supplying the incentive or motivation to make a change, and so habituated to the view that every improvement costs money, that we tended to forget how much can be achieved simply through the intelligent application of energy, resolve, and common sense. Now we are remembering.

# Popular Schooling

## LAWRENCE A. CREMIN

> Every nation, and therefore every national system of education, has the defects of its qualities.—Sir Michael Sadler, "Impressions of American Education"

The popularization of American schools and colleges since the end of World War II has been nothing short of phenomenal, involving an unprecedented broadening of access, an unprecedented diversification of curricula, and an unprecedented extension of public control. In 1950, 34 percent of the American population twenty-five years of age or older had completed at least four years of high school, while 6 percent of that population had completed at least four years of college. By 1985, 74 percent of the American population twenty-five years of age or older had completed at least four years of high school, while 19 percent had completed at least four years of college. During the same thirty-five year period, school and college curricula broadened and diversified tremendously, in part because of the existential fact of more diverse student bodies with more diverse needs, interests, abilities, and styles of learning; in part because of the accelerating growth of knowledge and new fields of knowledge; in part because of the rapid development of the American economy and its demands on school systems; and in part because of the transformation of America's role in the world. The traditional subjects could be studied in a greater range of forms; the entry of new subjects into curricula provided a greater range of choice; and the effort to combine subjects into new versions of general education created a greater range of requirements. Finally, the rapid increase in the amount of state and federal funds invested in the schools and colleges, coupled with the rising demand for access on the part of segments of the population traditionally held at the margins, brought a corresponding development of the instruments of public oversight and control—local community boards, state coordinating boards, court-appointed masters and monitors, and federal attorneys with the authority to enforce federal regulations. In the process, American schools became at the same time both more centralized and more decentralized.[1]

It was in many ways a remarkable achievement, of which Americans could be justifiably proud. Yet it seemed to bring with it a pervasive sense of failure. During the 1970s, there was widespread suspicion that American students were failing behind in international competition, that while more people were going to school for ever longer periods of time, they were learning less and less. And in the 1980's, that suspicion seemed to be confirmed by the strident rhetoric of the National Commission on Excellence in Education. Recall the commission's charges in *A Nation at Risk*:

> We report to the American people that while we can take justifiable pride in what our schools and colleges have historically accomplished and contributed to the United States and the well-being of its people, the educational foundations of our society are presently being eroded by a rising tide of mediocrity that threatens our very future as a Nation and a people. What was unimaginable a genera-

tion ago has begun to happen—others are matching and surpassing our educational attainments.

If an unfriendly power had attempted to impose on America the mediocre educational performance that exists today, we might well have viewed it as an act of war. As it stands, we have allowed this to happen to ourselves.[2]

Now, there have always been critics of the schools and colleges. From the very beginning of the public school crusade in the nineteenth century, there were those who thought that popular schooling was at best a foolish idea and at worst a subversive idea. The editor of the Philadelphia *National Gazette* argued in the 1830s that free universal education was nothing more than a harebrained scheme of social radicals, and claimed that it was absolutely illegal and immoral to tax one part of the community to educate the children of another. And beyond such wholesale opposition, even those who favored the idea of universal education thought that the results were unimpressive. The educator Frederick Packard lamented that the schools were failing dismally in even their most fundamental tasks. He charged on the basis of personal visits to classrooms that nine out of ten youngsters were unable to read a newspaper, keep a simple debit and credit account, or draft an ordinary business letter. The writer James Fenimore Cooper was ready to grant that the lower schools were developing a greater range of talent than was the case in most other countries, but he pointed to what he thought was the superficiality of much of the work of the colleges and bemoaned the absence of genuine accomplishment in literature and the arts. And the French commentator Alexis de Tocqueville, echoing the English critic Sydney Smith, observed that America had produced few writers of distinction, no great artists, and not a single first-class poet. Americans were a practical people, he concluded, but not very speculative. They could boast many lawyers but no jurists, many good workers but few imaginative inventors.[3]

By the early years of the twentieth century, as some elementary education was becoming nearly universal and as secondary education was beginning to be popularized, the critisism became broader and sharper. A writer in *Gunton's Magazine* charged that as schooling had spread it had been made too easy and too entertaining. "The mental nourishment we spoonfeed our children," he observed, "is not only minced but peptonized so that their brains digest it without effort and without benefit and the result is the anaemic intelligence of the average American schoolchild." And a Maryland farmer named Francis Livesey became so outraged at the whole idea of free universal education that he organized a society called the Herbert Spencer Education Club with two classes of membership—one for those seeking the complete abolition of public schooling and one for those willing to settle for the repeal of all compulsory attendance laws.[4]

With respect to secondary and higher education, critics such as Irving Babbitt, Abraham Flexner, and Robert Hutchins leveled blast after blast against the relaxation of language requirements, the overcrowding of curricula with narrow technical courses, and the willingness to permit students to work out their own programs of study. The spread of educational opportunity in the United States, they observed, reflected less a spirit of democratic fairness than a willingness to prolong adolescence. The result was an inferior educational product at every level—high school programs were too watered down and fragmented; the colleges were graduating men and women unable to write and spell a decent English and pitifully ignorant of mathematics, the sciences, and modern languages; and the graduate schools were crowded with students of mediocre ability who lacked the slightest appreciation of higher culture.[5]

Even those foreign observers who were prone to admire the American commitment to popular schooling wrung their hands at what they saw as the widespread absence of high intellectual expectations, particularly at the high school and college levels. Thus, Sir Michael Sadler, the director of the Office of Special Inquiries and Reports of the British government, and a great friend of the United States, noted an absence of intellectual discipline and rigor in American schools—too much candy and ice cream, he liked to say, and not enough oatmeal porridge. And Erich Hylla, a member of the German ministry of education who had spent a year in residence at Teachers College, Columbia University, and who translated Dewey's *Democracy and Education* into German, lamented what he perceived as the disjointedness and superficiality of secondary and undergraduate study and the resultant poor achievement of American students.[6]

As popularization advanced at every level of schooling after World War II, the drumbeat of dissatisfaction grew louder. Arthur Bestor and Hyman Rickover argued during the 1950s and 1960s that popular schooling had been literally subverted by an interlocking directorate of education professors, state education officials, and professional association leaders; they charged that the basics had been ignored in favor of a trivial curriculum parading under the name of Life Adjustment Education and that as a result American freedom was in jeopardy. Robert Hutchins continued his mordant criticisms of the 1930s, contending that the so-called higher learning purveyed by the colleges and universities was neither higher nor learning but rather a collection of trade school courses intended to help young people win the material success that Americans prized so highly. And again, even those foreign observers who were disposed to admire the American commitment to popular education now made it something of a litany to comment on what they perceived to be the low standards and mediocre achievements of American students. The English political economist Harold Laski noted the readiness of American parents to expect too little of their youngsters and the readiness of the youngsters to see interest in abstract ideas as somewhat strange at best, with the result that American college graduates seemed to him to be two to three years less intellectually mature than their English or French counterparts. And the Scottish political scientist D. W. Brogan was quite prepared to grant that the American public school had been busy Americanizing immigrants for several generations at least—he liked to refer to the public school as "the formally unestablished national church of the United States"—but he saw the price of that emphasis on social goals as an insufficient attention to intellectual goals. For all their talk of preparing the young for life, Brogan maintained, Americans were not being realistic about what life would actually demand during the second half of the twentieth century.[7]

Within such a context, Paul Copperman's allegations of the late 1970s that Americans of that generation would be the first whose educational skills would not surpass or equal or even approach those of their parents, which the National Commission on Excellence in Education quoted approvingly in *A Nation at Risk*, and Allan Bloom's assertions of the late 1980s that higher education had failed democracy and impoverished the souls of American students were scarcely surprising or even original. Why all the fuss, then? How, if at all, did the criticisms of the 1980s differ from those that had come before? I believe they differed in three important ways: they were more vigorous and pervasive; they were putatively buttressed by data from cross-national studies of educational achievement; and, coming at a time when Americans seemed to be feeling anxious about their place in the world, they gave every indication of being potentially more dangerous and destructive.[8]...

The 1980s brought another shift in the climate of educational opinion, this one exemplified by the two reports that have already been alluded to, the reports of the National Commission on Excellence in Education entitled *A Nation at Risk,* and of the Study Group on the State of Learning in the Humanities in Higher Education entitled *To Reclaim a Legacy.*

The National Commission had been created in 1981 by President Reagan's first secretary of education, Terrel Bell—the same Terrel Bell, incidentally, who in the 1970s had introduced the report of the USOE's National Panel on High School and Adolescent Education with a glowing foreword referring to the report as a major contribution to the public discussion of secondary education. The membership of the commission included educators, scientists, businesspeople, and politicians, with David P. Gardner, president of the University of Utah, as chair (Gardner subsequently became president of the University of California) and Yvonne W. Larsen, immediate past president of the San Diego school board, as vice-chair. The commission held hearings, took testimony, and visited schools in various parts of the country through much of 1982 and then reviewed various quite different drafts of the report during the first months of 1983. The final report—terse, direct, and unqualified in its assertions—was largely the work of the scientists on the panel. In effect, it put forward a severe indictment of American education and proposed a fundamental set of reforms. The report cited rates of adult illiteracy (as many as 23 million functionally illiterate Americans), declining scores on the Scholastic Aptitude Test (an almost unbroken decline from 1963 to 1980), and deficiencies in knowledge on the part of seventeen-year-olds as revealed by international tests of achievement (American students never ranked first or second on any of nineteen academic tests). From this and other "dimensions of the risk before us," the commission concluded that "the educational foundations of our society are presently being eroded by a rising tide of mediocrity that threatens our very future as a Nation and a people."[9]

As remedies, the commission put forward five recommendations: (1) that, as a minimum, all students seeking a high school diploma be required to complete during the four years of high school the following work in the "new basics"—four years of English, three years of mathematics, three years of science, three years of social studies, and a half year of computer science; (2) that schools, colleges, and universities adopt higher expectations of their students and that four-year colleges and universities raise their requirements for admission; (3) that significantly more time be devoted to teaching and learning the new basics, and that this be achieved through more effective use of the existing school day, a lengthened school day, or a lengthened school year; (4) that the preparation of teachers be strengthened and teaching be made a more rewarding and more respected profession; and (5) that citizens throughout the nation require their elected officials to support these reforms and to provide the money necessary to achieve them. Interestingly, the report mentioned a role for the federal government in defining the national interest in education, but it assigned to state and local officials the primary responsibility for initiating and carrying out the recommendations. Beyond that, it ended with a word to parents and students, asking the parents to raise their expectations of their children, and asking students to work harder in school.[10]

During the next few years there followed in the wake of *A Nation at Risk* a score of reports on the problems of the schools, each putting forth its own particular agenda for reform. A task force organized by the Twentieth Century Fund stressed the need for English as the language of schooling, through the grades and across the country. A commission organized by the National Science

Board stressed the need for all young Americans to have a firm grounding in mathematics, science, and technology. A task force organized by the Education Commission of the States stressed the relationship of more intense schooling to the maintenance of America's economic competitiveness in the world. A panel organized by the National Academy of Sciences stressed the need for academic competence in the kind of workplace that was coming into being in the United States. A task force organized by the Committee for Economic Development stressed the need for businesspeople to be interested and involved in the work of the schools. And Ernest Boyer, writing on behalf of the Carnegie Foundation for the Advancement of Teaching, stressed the need for a coherent curriculum core at the heart of any worthy secondary education. All in one way or another re-sounded the themes of *A Nation at Risk*—the need for emphasis on a new set of basics, the need for a more intensive school experience for all young people, and the need for a better trained teaching profession in the nation's schools.[11]

In addition, several major reports dealing with higher education also followed the publication of *A Nation at Risk*, notably, William J. Bennett's report on behalf of the National Endowment for the Humanities Study Group, entitled *To Reclaim a Legacy;* the report of a Select Committee of the Association of American Colleges, entitled *Integrity in the College Curriculum;* and a report of Ernest Boyer, again writing on behalf of the Carnegie Foundation for the Advancement of Teaching, entitled *College: The Undergraduate Experience in America.* All three lamented the absence of a clear vision of the educated person at the heart of undergraduate education, one that would call for all students to undertake fundamental studies in the humanities (Bennett), the natural sciences, and the social sciences (the AAC Select Committee and Boyer); all three lamented the concentration on research and the inattention to teaching in the preparation and careers of college professors; all three called for a renewed effort to develop an integrated core of required subjects that would be taught to all candidates for the bachelor's degree, whatever their majors or professional goals; and all three called for a new emphasis on imaginative and informed teaching in the nation's colleges and universities.[12]

Yet again, let us examine the grand story implicit and explicit in these reports, the ideas they present about how education works, why it goes wrong, and how it can be set right. For the various commissions of the early 1980s, the popularization of education has been an utter and complete failure, because popularization has brought with it declension and degradation. For the National Commission on Excellence in Education, the educational foundations of society are being eroded by a rising tide of mediocrity; in the National Commission's view, Paul Copperman is correct in his assertion that for the first time in the history of the United States the educational achievement of the present generate on will not surpass, equal, or even approach the educational achievement of its parents. For the AAC Select Committee, a century-long decline of undergraduate education into disarray and incoherence has accompanied the rise of academic specialization associated with the research universities, and that decline has been accelerated by the upsurge of higher education enrollments since World War II. In effect, the decline and degradation have occurred because education is essentially the study of the liberal arts—what Conant called general education, what the National Commission called the new basics, what Ernest Boyer called the integrated core. The liberal arts were at the heart of education during the nineteenth and early twentieth centuries, and popularization has brought a vitiation of their formative power in favor of narrow specialization and crass vocationalism. How can education be set right? By requiring study of the liberal arts of all students, and by popularizing education without permitting it to be vulgarized, that is, by universalizing precisely the education that was formerly preserved for the few and making it mandatory for all. The popularization of education involves an increase in the size of the clientele, not a transformation in the nature of the curriculum.

Nowhere was the grand story of the early 1980s more dramatically presented than in Allan Bloom's *The Closing of the American Mind*. The educational and political crisis of twentieth-century America is essentially an intellectual crisis, Bloom asserted. It derives, he continued, from the university's lack of central purpose, from the students' lack of fundamental learning, from the displacement of the traditional classical humanistic works that long dominated the curriculum—the works of Plato and Aristotle and Augustine and Shakespeare and Spinoza and Rousseau—by specialized electives and courses in the creative arts, and from the triumph of relativism over perennial humanistic values. How can the crisis be resolved? Clearly, by a restoration of true learning in the schools and colleges through the traditional disciplines and the works of the Western canon. Could that restoration be compatible with further popularization of higher education? Almost certainly not!

My friend Richard Heffner once asked me on his television program, *The Open Mind*, whether the ideal of popular education was not an impossible ideal, whether it not only was not working but in the end could not work. I maintained that no ideal is ever completely achievable; if it is, it is not an ideal. What an ideal does hold out is a goal, which people can then approach more or less successfully. And I argued that the ideal of popular education, at least as it had developed in the United States, was one of the most radical ideals in the Western world, that we had made great progress in moving toward the ideal, but that the attainment had been want-

ing in many domains, and that the institutions we had established to further that attainment had been flawed in many respects. We had, to be blunt, a long way to go, but it was worth trying to get there.

After we were off the air, I asked Heffner if he was not really asking whether the phrase popular education is an oxymoron, a contradiction, in its very nature flawed and unachievable. He protested not. But I think many people believe that the contradiction is there, that education in its true meaning is an elite phenomenon, just as such people would argue that culture in its true meaning is an elite phenomenon, and that as soon as education begins to be transformed by popularization—by popular interest, popular demand, popular understanding, and popular acceptance—it is inevitably vulgarized. In essence, these people would argue that there is no more possibility of a popular education than there is of a popular culture. What results when education is popularized is an educational version of what the critic Dwight Macdonald once labeled "masscult" or "midcult." I believe this is the explicit message of Allan Bloom's book. And I would trace the most fundamental and abiding discontent with popular education in the United States to the sense that it is not only an impossible ideal but in the end a hopeless contradiction.[13]

To argue in favor of popular education is not to deny the tremendous difficulties inevitably involved in achieving it. On the one side, there are the inescapable political problems of determining the nature, content, and values of popular education. Legislators want the schools to teach the advantages of patriotism and the dangers of substance abuse: parents want the schools to teach character and discipline; employers want the schools to teach diligence and the basic skills; arts advocates want the schools to teach painting, drama, music, and dance; academics want the schools to teach more of what they know—historians want more history, mathematicians more mathematics, and economists more economics; students want the schools to equip them to go on to college if they wish, to prepare them to obtain and hold a job with a future, and to offer them opportunities to enjoy sports, hobbies, and a decent social life; and a host of organized citizens' groups want the schools to attend to their special concerns, which range from civil liberties to fire prevention. Out of a process that involves all three branches of government at the state and federal levels as well as thousands of local school boards, a plethora of private interests ranging from publishers to accrediting agencies, and the variety of professionals who actually operate the schools emerges what we call the curriculum, with its requirements, its electives, its informal activities, and its unacknowledged routines. It is that curriculum, in various versions, that is supposed to be offered to all the children of all the people. On the other side, there are the demands of the children, with their almost infinite variety of needs, wants, and values, deriving from extraordinary differences in their family backgrounds, their rates and patterns of development, their learning styles, and their social, intellectual, and vocational aspirations.

The resulting dilemmas are as difficult philosophically as they are insistent politically. Will the increased stringency of academic requirements stimulated by the report of the National Commission on Excellence in Education create a rise in the dropout rate at the same time that it encourages more capable students to higher levels of academic performance? The dropout rate has indeed gone up, but we do not know whether that testifies to the inability (or unwillingness) of students to master the newly required material or the difficulties teachers face in teaching the newly required material with sufficient versatility, or both. However that may be, the loss to the American polity, economy, and society, and to the individual youngsters who drop out, is prodigious. Meanwhile, the

Japanese, though admittedly a less heterogeneous people than the Americans, are mandating even more difficult material for their high school students, with a lower dropout rate. Will the effort to advance racial integration by insisting upon comprehensive high schools cause white flight that in the end leads to increased segregation and lower academic performance? There are those who say that it will, and there are communities where the effort to maintain comprehensive high schools has been correlated with white flight, increased segregation, and lower academic performance. Meanwhile, the Swedes seem to be managing to maintain comprehensive high schools in an increasingly heterogeneous society without lowering academic performance. Do the traditions of competitive individualism lead American parents, teachers, and students to assume that some young people must inevitably fall? The data from John Goodlad's study of schooling provide evidence that such assumptions are rampant. Yet there have long been experimental schools in the United States and abroad in which the school class as a whole has been made responsible for the performance of individual members, with the result that students end up helping one another to succeed. In sum, does the success of popular education ultimately depend upon the values of the society it is meant to nurture and sustain, which in the American case involves a penchant for utility, an ambivalence toward book learning, and a preoccupation with individual success? Do such values by their very nature compromise the success of popular education?[14]

Furthermore, there are the patent flaws in the system of institutions Americans have created to realize the ideal of popular education. One might note in the first place the undetermined number of children in the United States who are simply not in school at any given time for one reason or another and who are not even known to be not in school. When the Children's Defense Fund did its pioneering study of *Children Out of School in America* during the early 1970s, it found, quite beyond the United States census statistic of nearly two million children between the ages of seven and seventeen out of school, thousands of children who had been expelled or suspended for disciplinary reasons, countless truants who had managed to elude census enumerators and attendance officers, and undetermined numbers of children who had fallen through the cracks of the system for reasons of pregnancy, poverty, mental retardation, or emotional disability. In addition, it found even greater numbers of children who were technically in school but who might just as well have been counted as out of school—youngsters of recent immigrant families sitting uncomprehendingly in classrooms conducted in English, youngsters misdiagnosed as retarded who were really deaf, youngsters so alienated by real or perceived indifference, condescension, or prejudice that they had long since stopped profiting from anything the schools had to offer.[15]

One might go on to note the flaws in individual institutions—elementary schools where children do not learn to read because they are not taught; high schools where young men and women from working-class backgrounds are denied access to the studies of languages and mathematics that would make it possible for them to become engineers or scientists; junior colleges where recent immigrants with aspirations to undergraduate degrees cannot find the guidance they require to choose the proper academic courses and hence end up locked into narrow occupational programs; and four-year colleges where students graduating with a melange of "gut" courses find themselves with a worthless credential and few prospects of decent employment. One might note, too, the flaws in whole systems of schooling, especially the overbureaucratized and underfinanced systems of many of our central cities, heavily populated by the poor, the nonwhite, and the recently arrived, those most in need of

carefully and expertly delivered educational services and least likely to receive them.

Popular education, then, is as radical an ideal as Americans have embraced. It is by its very nature fraught with difficulty, and the institutions we have established to achieve it are undeniably flawed. Yet it is important to be aware of what has been accomplished in the movement toward popular education and of the possibilities for the future. I believe the predicament of American schooling during the early 1980s was not nearly so dire as the report of the National Commission suggested. As Lawrence Stedman and Marshall Smith pointed out in a detailed examination of the evidence cited in the report, the academic achievement of young Americans in the early 1980s was far more mixed than the commission alleged. There were definite improvements in the performance of younger children, reflecting, I believe, the additional educational services made available by Title I/Chapter I federal funds. These were coupled with a patently uneven performance on the part of adolescents, a performance marked by relatively good showings in literature and the social studies and rather poor showings in foreign languages, mathematics, and the natural sciences as well as in the development of the higher order skills associated with critical thinking. Everyone agreed that the results should have been better—in fact, there were data in John Goodlad's study of schooling suggesting that significant numbers of the students themselves believed they might have been working harder and more effectively. Moreover, given the extraordinary percentage of young Americans who were continuing on to postsecondary education, the results would likely have been better in comparison with other countries had the tests been administered at age nineteen or twenty instead of seventeen or eighteen. However that may be, there was surely no evidence to support the commission's affirmation of Paul Copperman's claim that the present generation would be the first in

American history whose educational skills would not equal or even approach those of its parents.[16]

Furthermore, we know that standardized tests measure at best only a fraction of what young people have learned in school, and they measured that imperfectly, so that if one were to venture past the test scores to examine what was actually happening in the schools of the early 1980s, a cluster of studies by scholars like John Goodlad, Philip Jackson, Sara Lawrence Lightfoot, Mary Haywood Metz, Vito Perrone, Arthur Powell, and others revealed a far more complex picture of what was going on. They indicated that, overall, there was strong emphasis in school curricula on the English language and literature; that considerable importance was being placed on social studies, mathematics, the natural sciences, the arts, physical education, and, in the upper grades, so-called career education but that foreign languages were receiving limited attention at best; that teachers were mindful of their responsibility to inculcate discipline and nurture civic and social skills; that most schools were orderly places where teachers and students went about the diurnal business of education in a systematic and mutually respectful fashion; that many schools were contending thoughtfully and effectively with the prodigious problems of integrating vastly diverse clienteles into the American polity and economy; that students in general were learning what their parents and teachers thought it was important for them to learn; and that there were significant numbers of students who excelled, by any reasonable standard, in literature, the sciences, the fine and performing arts, and athletics. But they also indicated that students spent less time in school each year and less time at home doing schoolwork than their counterparts in a number of other countries; that teachers, particularly at the elementary level, were poorly trained in mathematics and the natural sciences and that their poor training was a key factor in the relatively low

achievement of students in those subjects; that far too much teaching was uninspired and unimaginative, with consistent overreliance on lectures, drills and workbooks and underreliance on a wide range of alternative pedagogies and technologies; that teachers felt severely constrained in their daily work by bureaucratic rules and procedures; and, most important, that the greatest failures and most serious unsolved problems of the system were those relating to the education of poor children from minority populations in the schools of the central cities.[17]

The reports on higher education during the 1980s, with their emphasis on the loss of an integrated core in undergraduate education and the deleterious effects of that loss, were also at best distorted in their diagnosis of the current situation. Whatever core there might have been in the liberal arts institutions of the seventeenth and eighteenth centuries had already begun to disintegrate in the nineteenth century in the face of rising enrollments and expanding commitments, and with the exception of its presence in a few elite colleges and universities, that core as traditionally defined has not been much seen in the twentieth century. The explosion of knowledge that marked the rise of the research university necessitated not only the extensive choice embodied in the elective system but also the kind of continuing redefinition of any integrated core by college and university faculties that would inevitably lead to various versions of general and liberal education. Allan Bloom's Western canon is one of those versions, but only one. There are other versions that derive from different definitions of the educated person.

That variety of definitions holds the key, it seems to me, to the current situation in American education. Americans have traditionally assigned a wide range of responsibilities to their schools and colleges. They want the schools and colleges to teach the fundamental skills of reading, writing, and arithmetic; to nurture critical thinking; to convey a general fund of knowledge; to develop creativity and aesthetic perception; to assist students in choosing and preparing for vocations in a highly complex economy; to inculcate ethical character and good citizenship; to develop physical and emotional well-being; and to nurture the ability, the intelligence, and the will to continue on with education as far as any particular individual wants to go. And this catalogue does not even mention such herculean social tasks as taking the initiative in racial desegregation and informing the population about the dangers of drug abuse and AIDS. Americans have also maintained broad notions of the active intellect and informed intelligence required to participate responsibly in the affairs of American life. One associates these notions with the inclusive definitions of literacy that make the role of literacy in everyday life central and with the plural definitions of intelligence that embrace musical and kinesthetic intelligence as well as logical, linguistic. and mathematical intelligence—the sorts of definitions that Howard Gardner has advanced in *Frames of Mind* (1983). And they have not only countenanced but urged a wide-ranging curriculum that goes far beyond the "new basics" or the "integrated core" or the "Western canon" of the recent policy reports—those are at best somewhat narrow, academicist versions of American education. As with all latitudinarianism, such definitions can permit triviality to enter the curriculum, and triviality is not difficult to find in American schools and colleges. But on balance I believe such broad definitions have served the American people well.[18]

If there is a crisis in American schooling, it is not the crisis of putative mediocrity and decline charged by the recent reports but rather the crisis inherent in balancing this tremendous variety of demands Americans have made on their schools and colleges—of crafting curricula that take account of the needs of a modern society at the same time that they make provision for the extraordinary diversity of America's young people; of designing institutions where well-prepared teachers can teach under supportive conditions, and where *all* students can be motivated and assisted to develop their talents to the fullest; and of providing the necessary resources for creating and sustaining such institutions. These tough problems may not make it into the headlines or onto television, and there is no quick fix that will solve them; but in the end they constitute the real and abiding crisis of popular schooling in the United States.

In thinking about the search for solutions, it is well to bear in mind that there remain some 15,000 school districts in the United States that sponsor about 59,000 elementary schools and 24,000 secondary schools, and that there are also almost 21,000 private elementary schools and 8,000 private secondary schools. In addition, there are around 3,000 institutions of higher education, of which fully a third are two-year community colleges. Given this multitude of institutions organized into fifty state systems—some highly centralized, some loosely decentralized—programs of education will differ, and local as well as cosmopolitan influences will prevail. For all the centralizing tendencies in American schooling—from federal mandates to regional accrediting association guidelines to standardized tests and textbooks—the experience students have in one school will differ from the experience they have in another, whatever the formal curriculum indicates might be going on; and the standards by which we judge those experiences will derive from local realities, clienteles, faculties, and aspirations as well as from cosmopolitan knowledge, norms, and expectations. The good school, as Sara Lightfoot has argued, is good in its context.[19]

It is that point, I believe, that the high school reports of the 1970s were trying to make, when they recommended the further differentiation of curricula and the brokering by the schools of educational opportunities for youngsters in libraries, museums, workplaces, government agencies, and community organizations. It is that point, too, that the Carnegie Commission was trying to make when it recommended a vast expansion of enrollments and a further diversification of curricula in the first two years of postsecondary education. Where I would quarrel with the Carnegie Commission (and later the Carnegie Council on Policy Studies in Higher Education) would be in its insistence on confining the expansion and diversification to the junior college and on protecting the four-year colleges from the demands and effects of popularization. In my own view, the commission drew far too great a distinction between the programs of two-year and four-year colleges and invested far too much energy in trying to preserve the imagined distinctions. For one thing, there is tremendous overlap in the character of the two kinds of institutions. For another, both need adjustment to facilitate the easy transfer of students from the former to the latter, which was envisioned by President Truman's Commission on Higher Education, but which has not come to pass.

More important, however, I believe there is need for a far greater sense of unity in the American school system, one that envisions the system whole, extending from nursery schools through the so-called doctorate-granting institutions, with individuals making their way through the system according to their own lights and aspirations and institutions creating their clienteles competitively, much as they do today. I would abandon the constraint the Carnegie Commission preached when it expressed the hope that the two-year colleges would be discouraged from trying to become four-year undergraduate institutions. Sir Eric Ashby, who prepared the immensely incisive monograph *Any Person, Any Study* for the Carnegie Commission—the title bespoke Sir Eric's sense of the openness of American higher education—observed that while the Soviet Union maintained a diversity of higher education institutions stratified according to subjects the United States maintained a diversity of higher education institutions stratified according to quality. He defined quality, of course, in terms of what Martin Trow had called the "autonomous" functions of higher education—with the elite universities devoted primarily to research at the top, with the comprehensive universites dividing their efforts between research and teaching at a somewhat lower status, and with the colleges and universites devoting their efforts primarily to teaching occupying an even lower status. I would alter Ashby's aphorism to argue that while the Soviet Union maintains a diversity of higher education institutions stratified according to subjects the United States maintains a diversity of higher education institutions organized according to missions, missions that vary considerably. And I think that kind of organization is part of the genius of American education—it provides a place for everybody who wishes one, and in the end yields one of the most educated populations in the world.[20]

## NOTES

1. Thomas D. Snyder, *Digest of Education Statistics, 1987* (Washington, D.C.: Government Printing Office, 1987), 13.
2. National Commission on Excellence in Education. *A Nation at Risk: The Imperative for Educational Reform* (Washington, D.C.: GPO, 1983), 5.
3. Philadelphia *National Gazette*, July 10, 1830, 2; [Frederick Adolphus Packard], *The Daily Public School in the United States* (Philadelphia: Lippincott, 1866), 10–11; J. F. Cooper, *Notions of the Americans* (2 vols.; London: Henry Colburn, 1828), 2:122, 127; and Alexis de Tocqueville, *Democracy in America,* edited by Phillips Bradley (2 vols.; New York: Knopf, 1945), 1:315.
4. Lys d'Aimée, "The Menace of Present Educational Methods," *Gunton's Magazine,* 19

(September 1900):263; and Lawrence A. Cremin and Robert M. Weiss, "Yesterday's School Critic," *Teachers College Record,* 54 (November 1952):77–82.

5. Irving Babbitt, *Literature and the American College: Essays in Defense of the Humanities* (Boston: Houghton Mifflin, 1908), chap. 3; Abraham Flexner, *A Modern College and a Modern School* (Garden City, N.Y.: Doubleday, Page, *1923), Do Americans Really Value Education?* (Cambridge, Mass.: Harvard University Press, 1927), and *Universities: American, English, German* (New York: Oxford University Press, 1930); and Robert Maynard Hutchins, *The Higher Learning in America* (New Haven: Yale University Press, 1936).

6. Michael E. Sadler, "Impressions of American Education," *Educational Review,* 25 (March 1903):228; and Erich Hylla, *Die Schule der Demokratie, Ein Aufriss des Bildungswesens der Vereinigten Staaten* (Langensalza: Verlag von Julius Beltz, 1928), chap. 3.

7. Arthur Bestor, *The Restoration of Learning: A Program for Redeeming the Unfulfilled Promise of American Education* (New York: Knopf, 1955): H. G. Rickover, *Education and Freedom* (New York: Dutton, 1959); Hutchins, *Higher Learning in America;* Harold J. Laski, *The American Democracy: A Commentary and an Interpretation* (New York: Viking, 1948), chap. 8; and D. W. Brogan, *The American Character* (New York: Knopf, 1944), 137.

8. Paul Copperman, *The Literacy Hoax: The Decline of Reading, Writing, and Learning in the Public Schools and What We Can Do About It* (New York: Morrow, 1978), and "The Achievement Decline of the 1970's," *Phi Delta Kappan,* 6o (June 1979):736–739; National Commission on Excellence in Education, *A Nation at Risk,* 11; and Allan Bloom, *The Closing of the American Mind* (New York: Simon and Schuster, 1987).

9. *National Commission on Excellence in Education, A Nation at Risk,* 8–11, 5.

10. *Ibid.,* 24–33.

11. Twentieth Century Fund Task Force on Federal Elementary and Secondary Education Policy, *Making the Grade* (New York: The Twentieth Century Fund, 1983); National Science Board Commission on Precollegiate Education in Mathematics, Science, and Technology, *Educating Americans for the 21st Century: A Plan of Action for Improving Mathematics, Science, and Technology Education for All American Elementary and Secondary Students So That Their Achievement Is the Best in the World by 1995* (Washington, D.C.: National Science Foundation, 1983); Education Commission of the States, Task Force on Education for Economic Growth, *Action for Excellence: A Comprehensive Plan to Improve Our Nation's Schools* (Washington, D.C., Education Commission of the States, 1983); National Academy of Sciences, Committee on Science, Engineering, and Public Policy, Panel on Secondary School Education for the Changing Workplace, *High Schools and the Changing Workplace: The Employers' View* (Washington, D.C.: National Academy Press, 1984); Committee for Economic Development, Research and Policy Committee, *Investing in Our Children: Business and the Public Schools* (New York: Committee for Economic Development, 1985); and Ernest L. Boyer, *High School: A Report on Secondary Education in America* (New York: Harper & Row, 1983).

12. William J. Bennett, *To Reclaim a Legacy: A Report on the Humanities in Higher Education* (Washington, D.C.: National Endowment for the Humanities, 1984); Association of American Colleges, Project on Defining the Meaning and Purpose of Baccalaureate Degrees, *Integrity in the College Curriculum: A Report to the Academic Community* (Washington, D.C.: Association of American Colleges, 1985); and Ernest L. Boyer, *College: The Undergraduate Experience in America* (New York: Harper & Row, 1987).

13. Dwight Macdonald, *Against the American Grain* (New York: Random House, 1962), part 1.

14. With respect to the prodigious costs of continuing high dropout rates, one might note the argument of Margaret D. LeCompte and Anthony Gary Dworkin: "Given the indirect link between education and poverty, we believe that a significant measure of the success of an educational innovation, whether enriching or compensatory, is not whether the stu-

dent test scores rise, but whether it improves the retention of an entire cohort of students and faculty," in "Educational Programs: Indirect Linkages and Unfulfilled Expectations," in Harrell R. Rodgers, Jr., ed., *Beyond Welfare: New Approaches to the Problem of Poverty in America* (Armonk, N.Y.: Sharpe, 1988), 136. For some of the Goodlad evidence, see Kenneth A. Tye, *The Junior High: School in Search of a Mission* (Lankam, Md.: University Press of America, 1985), 1–2.

15. Children's Defense Fund, *Children out of School in America* (Washington, D.C.: Children's Defense Fund, 1974).

16. Lawrence C. Stedman and Marshall S. Smith, "Recent Reform Proposals for American Education," *Contemporary Education Review,* 2 (Fall 1983):85–104. See also Ralph W. Tyler, "The U.S. vs. the World: A Comparison of Educational Performance," *Phi Delta Kappan,* 62 (January 1981): 307–310. Gilbert R. Austin and Herbert Garber, eds., *The Rise and Fall of National Test Scores* (New York: Academic Press, 1982), and, for a later summary of the test data, U. S. Congress, Congressional Budget Office, *Trends in Educational Achievement* (April 1986) and *Educational Achievement: Explanations and Implications of Recent Trends* (August 1987). John I. Goodlad, *A Place Called School Prospects for the Future* (New York: McGraw-Hill, 1984), chap. 3 and *passim,* and Barbara Benham Tye, *Multiple Realities: A Study of 13 American High Schools* (Lanham, N.Y.: University Press of America, 1985), chap. 4 and *passim.*

17. Goodlad, *A Place Called School:* Stephen R. Graubard, ed., "America's Schools: Portraits and Perspectives." *Daedalus,* 110 (Fall 1981); Sara Lawrence Lightfoot, *The Good High School: Portraits of Character and Culture* (New York: Basic Books, 1983); Mary Haywood Metz, *Different by Design: The Context and Character of Three Magnet Schools* (New York: Routledge & Kegan Paul, 1986); Jeannie Oakes, *Keeping Track: How Schools Structure Inequality* (New Haven: Yale University Press, 1985); Vito Perrone et al., *Portraits of High Schools* (Princeton, N.J.: The Carnegie Foundation for the Advancement of Teaching, 1985); Barbara Benham Tye, *Multiple Realities;* Kenneth A. Tye, *The Junior High,* and Arthur G. Powell, Eleanor Farrar, and David K. Cohen, *The Shopping Mall High School: Winners and Losers in the Educational Marketplace* (Boston: Houghton Mifflin, 1985).

For an early warning against using the international studies of education achievement as some kind of "international contest," see Torsten Husen, ed., *International Study of Achievement in Mathematics: A Comparison of Twelve Countries* (2 vols.; New York: Wiley, 1967), 2:288, and *passim.* For a review of the uses and limitations of standardized paper-and-pencil tests as instruments for assessing what is learned in school, see Bernard R. Gifford. ed., *Test Policy and Test Performance: Education, Language, and Culture* (Boston: Kluwer, 1989), Bernard R. Gifford and M. Catherine O'Connor, eds., *New Approaches to Testing: Rethinking Aptitude, Achievement, and Assessment* (Boston: Kluwer, 1990), and other publications reporting the work of the National Commission on Testing and Public Policy.

18. The list of responsibilities assigned to the schools and colleges is based on John I. Goodlad's study of schooling, as reported in *What Schools Are For* (Bloomington, Ind.: Phi Delta Kappa Educational Foundation, 1979) and *A Place Called School* and Ernest L. Boyer's study of the undergraduate experience, as reported in *College.*

19. Lightfoot, *The Good High School.*

20. Eric Ashby, *Any Person, Any Study: An Essay on Higher Education in the United States* (New York: McGraw-Hill, 1971); and Martin Trow, "Reflections on the Transition from Mass to Universal Higher Education," *Daedalus,* 99 (Winter 1970):1–7.

# Building a New Agenda

ANNE BASTIAN

NORM FRUCHTER

MARILYN GITTEL

COLIN GREER

KENNETH HASKINS

This article has surveyed a broad range of issues that are important to progessive directions in school change. We have tried to treat the subject comprehensively, with the sense that we must grasp the whole even while we address its distinct parts, we must have a long view even while we take small steps. We want to stress that isolated reforms, adjusting one or another aspect of the education system, will not go far in altering the instructional environment or institutional politics of schooling. Yet we are not suggesting that solutions can only be pursued in an all-or-nothing fashion. Rather, we suggest that any design for school improvement should lead us to ask: Does the proposal treat the symptom or the disease—does it locate the problem in individual or in institutional performance? Does it assume a hierarchy of merit or recognize that schools must teach all children according to their needs? Does it narrow our goals for achievement or broaden our concepts of what students can and should learn in order to function in society? We must also ask: Does a given reform preempt the empowerment of school constituents or enlarge their capacity to shape school policy and practice? Does it lower expectations for students and for schools or raise expectations and demands? Does it reinforce elitist goals for education or advance the democratic school mission?

In terms of what to do tomorrow, there are a number of immediate policy issues that call for alternative responses. We have argued throughout the book that most current reform initiatives can be framed in ways that either support or undermine the spirit of democratic schooling. For the most part, today's popular reforms are put forward as universally beneficial panaceas, while in practice they function as elitist prescriptions. Struggles around reform designs can alter this direction and change the focus of public concern.

One example is the merit pay concept, which is being constracted largely as a competitive mechanism for teacher motivation, but could be reconstructed as a fund to reward collective efforts for school improvement and to support collaborative teacher development programs. Another example is school-based management, which can be utilized to increase the authority of local administrators or can be a vehicle for teacher and parent empowerment as well. Business partnerships, which are now the central strategy for school-to-work linkages, raise serious questions of creaming, vocational tracking, and corporate intervention in public education. But school partnerships can be broadened to focus on a diverse range of community activities, including public services, which strengthen the school as a community institution.

*Source: Choosing Equality,* © 1985, 1986 by Temple University. Reprinted by permission of Temple University Press.

The issues of standards—curriculum, time, and testing—are most often raised in quantitative terms, with the call for "more" opposed to the notion of "less." But standards should be concerned with quality, with setting goals for school performance without rigidly dictating teaching approaches or rigidly labeling students. There are similar dual approaches to entitlement programs, which too often end up as mechanisms for segregating and stigmatizing special needs students, but can be designed to redress social inequities, introduce more innovative and individualized teaching practices, and offer new resources to mainstream education.

We have also pointed out two sides of the voucher or optional enrollment issue. Where option systems function as open markets with scarce resources, all students will not have an equal or comparable range of choices and the results will be a greater stratification of schools and students. Where option systems are constructed to add resources to deficient schools and to accommodate equally all levels of need—and where they are accessible to parent and community involvement—they may well promote diversity and responsiveness. In another example, the Effective Schools movement illustrates the dual potentials of a school improvement methodology that, if imposed as a static prescription, will have minimal impact but, if pursued through a participatory and collaborative process, can make enduring changes in the learning environment.

Any programmatic issue can reproduce the tension between democratic and elitist approaches, posing choices of design and implementation that serve either tendency. Certainly, there are structural reforms that are more conducive to democratic or to elitist goals; and there are different priorities in each agenda. But when we look at the issues, whether in response to the neo-conservative agenda or in advancing our own, the critical questions are not just about intentions or objectives. We must also evaluate the institutional structures and political processes that any given reform will operate within or will itself generate. These are the qualitative issues, implicit in any concrete program, which this book has attempted to draw out and debate. In doing so, we have come to a number of conclusions that we feel represent the case for democratic schooling:

**1.** The crisis of achievement in American education is twofold: there is a crisis of inequality and a crisis of citizenship. Our primary concern should lie with the acute failure to provide a vast number of low-income and minority students with decent schools and skills. We also need to recognize a chronic failure to enhance all children's capacities to think critically and to acquire social knowledge.

**2.** Massive school failure is primarily the long-term consequence of meritocratic school practices, which have created distinctly different conditions in elite and mass education. Moreover, meritocracy rationalizes school failure by attributing it to individual deficiencies, rather than to schools that do not serve children well. Today, as in the past, school resources, expectations, and services are highly unequal, both absolutely and relative to student needs. Competitive standards and methods of achievement compound social and educational advantages and disadvantages, and force unfair trade-offs between different kinds of need. Our school system has thus reproduced the prevailing pattern of social stratification, not transcended it.

**3.** Today's schools are not suffering an erosion of quality due to excessive egalitarian reform: the problem is not that schools have shortchanged those on the top, but that schools have so completely underserved those on the bottom. Overall, the equity reforms of the 1960s and 1970s accomplished a shift from exclusive meritocracy, which shut many students out, to inclusive meritocracy, which granted students access but not the resources to achieve. In the 1980s, even inclusion is being undermined, as elitist get-tough prescriptions erect new barriers and push more students out of school.

**4.** Economic realities do not justify the claim that a more competitive school regime will raise productivity and widely enhance job opportunities. The growing polarization of the workforce into a small professional strata and a large pool of low-wage, de-skilled service and production workers indicates that education will mean more for a few and less for many in terms of economic reward. The logic of today's marketplace is to lower expectations and limit chances for the majority of children, and elitist schooling reinforces this logic.

**5.** Schools do not have to mirror economic imperatives; they can also respond to social imperatives. If education were constructed around the social needs of children, families, communities, and a democratic society, the priority would be to endow all children with the basic and higher-order skills needed to fulfill personal and citizenship roles. The mission of schooling would be individual and social empowerment, which itself would promote more equitable chances of survival in the labor market. We believe schools can make a difference in our quality of life, but realizing this potential will require different schools.

**6.** School improvement and effective instruction cannot be legislated by quantitatively raising requirements, by imposing reward-and-punish systems of performance, or by singling out aspects of school practice that can be technically manipulated. More of the same is not better, when traditional practice has contributed to both school failure and alienation. Successful approaches to improving performances recognize the need to qualitatively change the environmental context—the school culture—that conditions the learning process. Effective reform must be multi-dimensional, must address structural, organizational, and managerial issues, and must account for the quality of relationships among staff and students.

**7.** In the debate over instructional reform, the differences between democratic and elitist approaches to improving instruction cannot be reduced to false choices between permissiveness and authority, or low and high standards. The differences represent conflicts over what constitutes achievement and who should achieve. These conflicts are expressed in general terms as the opposition between universal or selective access; between inclusive or exclusive advancement; between supportive or punitive motivation; between cooperative or competitive achievement; between collaborative or hierarchic management; between bottom-up and top-down change processes.

**8.** The approaches that constitute democratic education are known to promote school improvement in deprived and deficient schools; they can also work to make all schools more engaging, more attuned to individual potential, more collectively rewarding. Likewise, the conditions of educational achievement found in advantaged schools—such as better staffing ratios, greater community accountability, more resources for enrichment and supportive services—are conditions that can be provided in all schools. Equality does not dictate mediocrity any more than quality depends on privilege. Since we know a great deal about what makes all kinds of schools more effective, the issue is why we use that knowledge for some and not all children.

**9.** Addressing the crises in public education thus necessitates a challenge to the priorities we have set and to the way we set priorities. Progressive change must include reforming the political processes that determine our choices, both within the institution and in government. Today, the grassroots constituents of education—parents, teachers, community members—are increasingly distanced from the centers of power. As in other social institutions, control over school policy and practice is concentrated in the hands of administrative and professional bureaucrats, special interests, and political elites.

**10.** Progressive reform therefore requires empowering the constituents of schooling as both essential elements of school culture and indispensable agents for change. Progressive reform also requires renewing our conception of the school as a community institution, both drawing on and adding to community resources. The conception that schools should be socially responsive does not detract from their primary function of instruction; on the contrary, schools must respond to the societal conditions that influence them in order to perform well for all students.

**11.** Promoting constituent activism around school needs both generates and requires new power relationships. In advocating the construction of progressive federalism in education, we are calling for all levels of government to play a redistributive role in regard to governance as well as funding. The local governance of local schools is a core issue of school improvement and constituent empowerment, but will occur only with major policy shifts at the state level, an arena of education politics where progressives must direct new energy. Locating basic decision-making power at the school site also means that power-sharing mechanisms and equity standards must be more, not less, rigorously promoted at the state and federal levels. Alongside the policy goals of progressive federalism, it is necessary to renew our national sense of public ownership in education, defending schools as public institutions through which citizens rightfully assert social needs and priorities for their children and communities.

There is one more argument to add to these conclusions and to our debate with the new elitists. The emphasis they place on standardization and technique has been used on occasion to imply that financial resources are not at the heart of the school crisis, except perhaps in regard to teacher pay and shortages. Yet nearly every progressive measure that we have identified requires a higher level of fiscal support, as well as a redistribution of funding to those who are currently underserved. If the majority of American school children cannot rely on either meritocracy or the marketplace to secure their right to productive knowledge, if education can only advance through its democratic mission, then we have far to go in fulfilling our commitments. Democratic education can be pursued, but it cannot be achieved without substantially increasing funding to education —funding for equity, for innovation, for participatory institutions linked to community and social needs. Money is never a solution, but it is an essential means to an end. To those who argue that equality of results simply costs too much, Tom Bethell offers the best reply: "Compared to what?"[1]...

There are countless community, parent, and teacher groups engaged in intense struggles around schooling. These localized campaigns identify a wide range of concerns about quality and equality, representation and participation, that can spark citizen action and create new constituencies for reform. Across the country, struggles are being waged against regressive school boards, against the dismantling of entitlement programs, against discriminatory discipline, against punitive testing and tracking, and against many other barriers to educational equity. Struggles are being waged for early childhood programs, for the appointment of new school administrators, for a school bond issue or tax allocation, for the survival of the local schoolhouse, for academic freedom, and a host of other needs.

Some of these grassroots efforts receive supportive resources, such as legal assistance or organizer training; many are on their own. Some of these efforts represent passing campaigns; others are the work of ongoing organizations. Some are initiated by multi-issue citizens' groups, where school improvement is part of a larger social justice agenda. Some school struggles launch those broader organizations and agendas. It is clear, however, that too many school reform initiatives at the community level are not well connected to parallel struggles in other communities, states, and regions. And there is not yet an overarching national movement expressing the vitality and urgency of citizen demands for democratic education.

A critical step forward will be the creation of new alliances among school constituencies at state and local levels—alliances that draw together parents, frontline educators, community activists, and education advocates. The potential for grassroots alliances is based on profound common interests in better conditions for schooling but realizing this potential will require each constituency to overcome a regrettable history of isolation and misplaced blame. A further necessary step will be linking educational alliances to broader political movements and reasserting the priority of public education as an empowerment issue.

Prospects for the renewal of progressive coalition politics are emerging, even as conditions of inequality grow more extreme. Opportunities to develop an education agenda exist in the vast network of community organizing that has taken root over the past decade. Opportunities exist in the growing electoral participation of minorities and women, in the shifting alignments of urban poitics, embryonic "rainbow" alliances. There is new opportunity in the emergence of citizens coalitions deeply engaged in state legislative politics and begining to influence issues such as environmental protection, tax reform, consumer rights, and economic development. And there are opportunities on the national level, with the coalescence of social movements against federal cutbacks, such as the unprecedented effort mounted to save Chapter 1 and Head Start funding.

The revival of a public education movement may be aided by fresh analysis of the many complex issues of schooling, but finally a renewed movement will develop from concern that generates activism and activism that generates new vehicles and strategies for struggle, new expectations and visions for the school mission. If we accept that reform is a demanding process, which cannot be advanced through technocratic formulas or token commitments then we have already gotten past what the meritocrats are telling us about school change.

Every American has a stake in the success of public education as a universal right and a social institution. Schools are part of the promise of a democratic society because schools are capable of endowing all our children with the knowledge and reason to function as fully enfranchised citizens. Schools are part of the promise of a democratic society because they belong to the people they serve and can be directed to meet their needs. The persistence of unequal resources and narrow achievement in today's schools tells us that education must contend with powerful forces of economic stratification and social injustice. But this reality also signals the potential importance of schools as countervailing public institutions, as correctives for inequality, and as springboards for social change.

The opportunities now before us to reform education are also opportunities to recover democratic aspirations and prepare ourselves and our children to build a more decent society. The necessity of democratic reform lies in the millions of lives diminished and the millions of dreams deferred by continuing school failure. The possibility of democratic reform lies with citizens who choose equality as the standard of social progress and the measure of their own empowerment.

## ENDNOTE

1. Thomas N. Bethell, "Now Let's Talk About Jobs Again," *Rural Coalition Report,* Number 10, December 1984, p. 11.

## CHAPTER 2 REFERENCES

Bennett, K. P., & LeCompte, M. D. (1990). *How schools work*. New York: Longman.

Bowles, S. (1977). Unequal education and the reproduction of the social division of labor. In J. Karabel & A. H. Halsey (Eds.), *Power and ideology in education* (pp. 137–152). New York: Oxford University Press.

Bowles, S., & Gintis, H. (1976). *Schooling in capitalist America: Educational reform and the contradictions of economic life*. New York: Basic Books.

Bowles, S., & Gintis, H. (1986). *Democracy and capitalism*. New York: Basic Books.

Cremin, L. A. (1977). *Traditions of American education*. New York: Basic Books.

Giroux, H. (1988). *Teachers as intellectuals*. Granby, MA: Bergin and Garvey.

Gordon, D. (1977). *Problems in political economy: An urban perspective*. Boston: D. C. Heath.

Gutmann, A. (1987). *Democratic education*. Princeton, NJ: Princeton University Press.

Kirst, M. W. (1984). *Who controls our schools?* New York: W. H. Freeman.

Perkinson, H. (1977). *The imperfect panacea: American faith in education, 1865–1968*. New York: McGraw Hill.

Ravitch, D. (1983). *The troubled crusade*. New York: Basic Books.

Ryan, W. (1971). *Blaming the victim*. New York: Random House.

## SUGGESTED READINGS

Aronowitz, S., & Giroux, H. (1985). *Education under siege*. South Hadley, MA: Bergin and Garvey.

Bastian, A., Fruchter, N., Gittell, M., Greer, C., & Haskins, K. (1985). *Choosing equality: The case for democratic schooling*. Philadelphia: Temple University Press.

Bennett, K. P., & LeCompte, M. D. (1990). *How schools work*. New York: Longman.

Bluestone, B., & Harrison, B. (1982). *The de-industrialization of America*. New York: Basic Books.

Bowles, S., & Gintis, H. (1976). *Schooling in capitalist America: Educational reform and the contradictions of economic life*. New York: Basic Books.

Domhoff, G. W. (1967). *Who rules America?* Englewood Cliffs, NJ: Prentice Hall.

Gordon, D. (1977). *Problems in political economy: An urban perspective*. Boston: D. C. Heath.

Gutmann, A. (1987). *Democratic education*. Princeton, NJ: Princeton University Press.

Hacker, A. (1992). *Two nations: Black and white, separate, hostile, unequal*. New York: Scribners.

Hochschild, J. (1984). *The new American dilemma: Liberal democracy and school desegregation*. New Haven, CT: Yale University Press.

Hochschild, J. (1986). *What's fair? American beliefs about distributive justice*. Cambridge, MA: Harvard University Press.

Jencks, C. S. (1992). *Rethinking social policy: Race, poverty, and the underclass*. New York: HarperPerennial.

Katz, M. B. (1990). *The undeserving poor: From the war on poverty to the war on welfare.* New York: Pantheon Books.

Kirst, M. W. (1984). *Who controls our schools?* New York: W. H. Freeman.

Murray, C. (1989). *In pursuit of happiness and good government.* New York: Touchstone Books.

Orfield, G., & Ashkinaze, C. (1991). *The closing door: Conservative policy and black opportunity.* Chicago: University of Chicago Press.

Phillips, K. P. (1990). *The politics of rich and poor: Wealth and the American electorate in the Reagan aftermath.* New York: Random House.

Rogers, D. (1968). *110 Livingston Street: Politics and bureaucracy in the New York City schools.* New York: Random House.

Weir, M., Orloff, A., & Skocpol, T. (1988). *The politics of social policy in the United States.* Princeton, NJ: Princeton University Press.

# CHAPTER 3

# The History of Education

Our discussion of the history of education in the United States begins with the introduction of schooling in colonial America when Europeans settled in the colonies and began to devise systematic and deliberate forms of education for their children. Other forms of education existed in North America prior to European settlement. Native Americans educated their children within the structure of their communities and acculturated them into the rituals, obligations, and roles necessary for the maintenance and continuity of community life. Although such forms of education were extremely important, the development of U.S. schooling was heavily influenced by the European colonists as they adapted to life in North America.

There are many interpretations as to why education was so important to the early settlers and why it continues to be an important issue in contemporary society. Historians, such as Bernard Bailyn (1960), have attributed the use of the school to the failure of particular institutions such as the family, church, and community to provide the necessary tools demanded by the conditions of the new emerging society. Historian Merle Curti (1959) attributed the use of formal schooling to the interests of the colonists in protecting freedoms such as thought, religion, and press—freedoms necessary for the maintenance of a democratic society. Regardless of the motives and intentions, it is important to look at the early versions of schools in order to understand how the present-day school evolved. What will become increasingly apparent are three ideas:

1. From its very inception, the school was charged with assuming roles that once were the province of family, church, and community.
2. The school continues to serve as a focal point in larger issues of societal needs.
3. There is little consensus on the motives for school reforms.

## OLD WORLD AND NEW WORLD EDUCATION: THE COLONIAL ERA

Our discussion of the history of U.S. education begins with the settlers who brought their ideas about education to the New World. In general, the society of the Old World was highly stratified and the view most Europeans held was that only the sons of the rich required an education since they would be the future ruling class. Thus, early affluent settlers such as planters and townsmen, particularly in the southern colonies, hired tutors for their sons and sent their sons back to England, if they could afford it, for their university educations.

It is interesting to note, however, that many of the wealthy colonists' sons did remain in the United States for their higher education, since nine institutions of higher learning were founded prior to the American Revolution. These were Harvard University (1636), College of William and Mary (1693), Yale University (1701), University of Pennsylvania (1740), Princeton University (1746), Columbia University (1754), Brown University (1764), Rutgers University (1766), and Dartmouth College (1769). However, the colleges themselves were not at all revolutionary. They taught most of the same subjects found at Oxford or Cambridge, and Greek and Latin were required subjects.

What becomes increasingly apparent in the history of U.S. education is that even before education began to formalize and acquire certain specific patterns, there emerged distinctly different themes regarding the purpose of education. For example, as just noted, the upper-class planter aristocracy and wealthy merchants saw education as a means of perpetuating the ruling class. Religious, utilitarian, and civic motives also emerged over time.

The religious impetus to formalize instruction can best be exemplified by the Puritans in New England who, early in 1642 and 1647, passed school laws commonly referred to as the *Old Deluder Laws*. The first law chastised parents for not attending to their children's "ability to read and understand the principles of religion and capital laws of this country" and fined them for their children's "wanton" and "immodest" behavior. Thus, the first law pointed to a problem among the young, to which the parents failed to attend.

The second law was far more specific regarding formalized schooling. To keep the "old deluder" Satan away, the Massachusetts School Law of 1647 provided that every town that had "50 household" would appoint one person to teach all children, regardless of gender, to read and write. Furthermore, the town was required to pay the wages of the teacher. Towns that numbered "100 families or household" had to set up a grammar school (equivalent to a secondary school today) to prepare students for university studies. Towns that failed to comply were subject to fines. Thus, early in the nation's history, the theme of literacy as a means of teaching a Christian life was articulated.

The Old Deluder Law was not very popular throughout New England. Often, towns simply neglected to provide the education for their youth, as dictated by law. However, it remains a landmark in the history of U.S. education, for it established a precedent for public responsibility for education.

The theme of utilitarianism as the purpose of education can best be seen through an examination of the ideas of Benjamin Franklin, who, in 1749, published "Proposals Related to the Education of Youth in Pennsylvania." Franklin called for an education for youth based on secular and utilitarian courses of study rather than on the traditional studies of religion and classics. However, as Bailyn (1960) pointed out, Franklin did not define education along narrowly defined utilitarian principles. Rather, Franklin believed that "the purpose of schooling was to provide in systematic form what he had extemporized, haphazardly feeling his way" (p. 35). Thus, Franklin believed that students should pursue a course of study that would allow them mastery of process rather than rote learning. Reading, writing, public speaking, and art as a means of understanding creative expression would be integral components of the curriculum.

Utilitarian components of the curriculum would be practical aspects of mathematics, such as accounting and natural history (biology). Additionally, students would study history, geography, and political studies. Languages such as Latin and Greek would be available to students who wished to enter the ministry. Others, who sought commerce and trade as careers, might study more modern languages such as French, Italian, German, and Spanish.

Perhaps because of his own life experience, Benjamin Franklin fervently believed in the ability of people to better themselves. His faith in self-improvement through education and in an education that reflected practical concerns was not explored again until the nineteenth century. Franklin's proposal for an academy became the prototype for private secondary education in the United States. It was not until the second half of the nineteenth century, however, that public support for Franklin's ideas became a reality.

The civic motive for education is best illustrated through the ideas of the prominent American statesman, Thomas Jefferson, who fervently believed that the best safeguard for democracy was a literate population. It was Jefferson who proposed to the Virginia Legislature in 1779, a "Bill for the More General Diffusion of Knowledge," which would provide free education to *all* children for the first three years of elementary school. Jefferson, a product of enlightenment thinking, was optimistic enough to think that if citizens possessed enough education to read newspapers and thus inform themselves of pressing public issues, they would make intelligent, informed decisions at the polls.

Jefferson's bill also provided for a limited meritocracy within the educational structure. After the initial three years of reading, writing and "common arithmetic," all students could advance to 1 of 20 grammar schools within the state of Virginia, contingent on their payment of tuition. However, Jefferson proposed that each elementary school send one scholarship student to a grammar school. After two to three years of rigorous, classical studies (Latin, Greek, English grammar, geography, mathematics), the most promising scholarship student from among this group of 20 students would be selected for another funded four years of study, while the remaining group would be dismissed.

Finally, each grammar school would have the task of selecting 10 of its best students who would receive three-year scholarships to the College of William and Mary. Thus, Jefferson set forth in his bill a proposal for an aristocracy of talent, which would be nurtured and supported through a statewide educational structure. Unfortunately, Jefferson was ahead of his time; the majority of the state legislators agreed that the state should not be involved in educating its inhabitants and that, in any event, Jefferson's proposal required funds far beyond those possessed by the state of Virginia at that time. Therefore, through most of the first half the nineteenth century, schooling remained in the private sector.

The schools that were established in the United States during the colonial period varied greatly in the quality of instruction. In Puritan New England, often an elderly housewife (usually a widow) heard lessons, which consisted of recitations. These schools became known as *dame schools*. Elementary education, in the New England *town school,* established by the Old Deluder Law, consisted of such basic subjects as reading, writing, and religion. Students were taught by learning the alphabet: letters first, syllables and words next, and then sentences. There were few supplies and textbooks, except for the famous *New England Primer.* This book, sometimes referred to as the "Little Bible of New England," combined the teaching of reading with religious education, obedience, and citizenship. For example, in teaching the first letter of the alphabet, children would be treated to an illustration of Adam and Eve, the latter holding an apple given to her by a serpent, wrapped around a tree that was separating the couple, with the accompanying words: "A: "In Adam's Fall/We Sinned, All." This book, which appeared about 1690, sold more than 3,000,000 copies during the 1700s (Gutek, 1991).

Students were taught content mastery through memorization. They were taught writing skills by copying directly from the printed page or by taking dictation from the schoolmaster. Classes were ungraded; all students were housed in the same room and taught by a teacher who might have been either an indentured servant, a divinity student, or a village preacher. Strict disciplinary methods prevailed, which might be considered overly harsh by today's standards, perhaps influenced by the Puritan predilection to the "authoritarian temperament" of leadership (Button & Provenzano, 1989).

Secondary education, as it evolved in New England, was not coeducational, as was the elementary school; rather, it was for the sons of the elite who were usually tutored at home rather than receiving their primary schooling at the local town school. This school was called the *Latin Grammar School,* as the curriculum emphasized the teaching of Latin and Greek—languages of the educated elite in Europe. Ultimately, it served as a sorting device through which the newly formed Puritan elite in the United States could reproduce itself. Male students entered the Latin Grammar School at eight years of age and studied there for another eight years. They read classical texts, such as Cicero and Caesar in Latin, and Homer and Hesiod in Greek. Clearly, the emphasis here was not on a utilitarian education as later articulated by Franklin; rather, students were being "taught by example" from classical literature, which hopefully would enable them to function effectively as leaders in the Puritan oligarchy.

Education in the middle colonies was far more diverse than in Puritan New England, as the schools that emerged there reflected the vast religious and cultural differences of the region. Generally, education was the province of the colonies' numerous religious denominations, such as Dutch Reformed, Quaker, Roman Catholic, and Jewish. New York was dominated by the Dutch Reformed Church, which, like the Puritans, espoused the importance of literate congregations. When the English took over New York, they established charity schools, which were controlled by the Anglican Church. These schools emphasized reading, writing, arithmetic, catechism, and religion. In Pennsylvania, where English Quakers dominated the political and economic life of the colony, they also controlled education. However, in keeping with their humane attitude toward human life, the Quakers rejected the harsh treatment of children prevalent in the other colonies and paid more attention to individual children as they mastered reading, writing, arithmetic, and religion (Gutek, 1991).

Education in the South was largely confined to the upper class and took place at home on the plantation, since the vastness of these economic units made the construction of formal schools virtually impossible. Education was provided by tutors who might have been indentured servants, divinity students, impoverished second sons of European aristocrats, or convicts. Indeed, before the American Revolution, one observer reported that "two-thirds of the schoolmasters in Maryland were either indentured servants or convicts" (Wright, 1957, p. 101).

Both male and female children were educated on an aristocratic model: Classical studies were emphasized for boys, whereas dancing and music lessons were emphasized for girls. Although some Southern women may have shared their brothers' tutors, learning to master the social graces took precedence over Caesar in aristocratic Southern households. Occasionally, boys were sent away to school, most likely to England. Plantation management was learned by both sexes according to gender-specific roles. Girls were expected to master the domestic side of plantation management from their mothers, while boys learned the practical aspects from their fathers. Southern planters often sent their sons north to colonial colleges or to Europe to complete their education.

On the eve of the American Revolution, almost all of the African-American population of one-half million were slaves. As Gutek (1991) observed:

> In being uprooted from their native Africa, the blacks were torn from their own culture and thrust into an environment not merely inhospitable, but completely alien. As slaves the African blacks were undergoing induction into a society vastly different from that of their homeland. (p. 10)

Few members of this group could read or write. Those who could, more often than not, had received their instruction outside of existing formal schools, for "it appears that only a handful attended school along with the whites" (Cremin, 1970, pp. 194–195). Schools that did exist for African-Americans were usually sponsored by church groups, in particular Anglicans and Quakers (Button & Provenzo, 1989). Few slave owners were willing to support formal education for their slaves, since literacy was not directly connected to their work. Moreover, many feared that literate slaves would be more likely to lead insurrections. Although African Americans were kept illiterate as part of their subordinate position both on plantations and in the cities, some managed to learn skills as artisans, working as carpenters, coopers, wainwrights, farriers, coachmen, and skilled domestics.

Formal schooling for Native Americans was largely confined to missionary activities. In Virginia, the colonists at first attempted to establish "friendly" relations with their Native American neighbors. However, after hostilities broke out in 1622, they decided that "the way of conquering them is much more easy than of civilizing them by fair means" (Cremin, 1970, p. 194). There were some mildly successful educative endeavors in New England, particularly in Cambridge and Roxbury, which were directed by individual schoolmasters to prepare Native Americans for the Indian College that was established at Harvard University in approximately 1653. This Indian College, as Wright (1957) noted, was brought about largely due to the misguided belief held by some educated whites that "Indians were merely awaiting the opportunity to embrace classical scholarship and learn Cicero's orations" (p. 116). Ultimately, this experiment resulted in failure and was the first example of attempting to educate Native Americans by assimilating them into European culture. As in the case of African Americans, this period represents the beginning of the marginalization of Native Americans with respect to formal schooling.

## THE AGE OF REFORM: THE RISE OF THE COMMON SCHOOL

Historians point to the period from 1820 to 1860 in the United States as one in which enormous changes took place with unprecedented speed. The Industrial Revolution, which began in the textile industry in England, crossed the Atlantic Ocean and brought its factory system with its new machinery to urban areas, particularly in the North. Urban clusters grew more dense as migrants from agricultural areas and immigrants from Europe flocked to the factories, looking for work. By 1850, these immigrants included a significant group of Roman Catholics who were escaping starvation in Ireland. Westward expansion, aided in part by the revolution in transportation and in part by the land hunger of pioneers, extended to settlements in Oregon and California by 1850.

By 1828, when Andrew Jackson was elected president, all men (except slaves and emotionally disturbed persons) had obtained the right to vote. Thus, the founding fathers' visions of a political democracy were increasingly becoming a reality.

In the decades following 1815, groups of reformers—quite different from such archetypes of rationalism as Franklin and Jefferson—emerged. These men and women often lacked higher education and did not hold public office but often articulated their ideas with the fervor of evangelical Christianity. However, their ultimate goals were secular in nature. America, once seen as the New Jerusalem by the Puritans, would become a secular paradise created by the new reformers.

Ralph Waldo Emerson, a New England essayist and philosopher, wrote of this age, "We are all a little wild here with numberless projects of social reform."

Although the reform movement attempted to address such diverse societal problems as slavery, mental illness, intemperance, and pacificism, many reformers generally believed that the road to secular paradise was through education.

By 1820, it had become evident to those interested in education that the schools that had been established by the pre-war generation were no longer functioning effectively. Although Webster's *New England Primer* had been secularized so that the first line "In Adam's Fall/We Sinned, All" was replaced by "A was an Apple Pie made by the Cook" (Malone & Rauch, 1960, p. 491), few children had access to the reader. The vast majority of Americans were, not surprisingly, illiterate. Even in New England, with its laws specifying common schools, towns neglected or evaded their duties. In other parts of the country, charity schools provided the only opportunities for disadvantaged children to obtain an education.

The struggle for free public education was led by Horace Mann of Massachusetts. Abandoning a successful career as a lawyer, Mann lobbied for a state board of education, and when the Massachusetts legislature created one in 1837, Horace Mann became its first secretary, an office he occupied for 11 years. His annual reports served as models for public school reforms throughout the nation and, partly due to Mann's efforts, the first state *normal school,* or teacher training school was established in Lexington, Massachusetts, in 1839.

Mann's arguments for the establishment of the *common school,* or free publicly funded elementary schools, reflects both the concern for stability and order and the concern for social mobility—both of which were to be addressed through free public education.

Admittedly, Mann could not have been immune to the waves of different immigrant groups that were changing the cultural composition of the cities. Nor could he fail to be immune to the goals of his audiences, often the wealthy factory owners, who had to be convinced to support public education. Thus, he spoke of school as preparation for citizenship as well as the "balance wheel"—"the great equalizer of the conditions of men."

Although many historians, particularly liberals and conservatives, view Mann as one of America's greatest educational reformers, radicals take issue with his arguments, pointing to the common school as a pernicious device for teaching skills such as hygiene, punctuality, and rudimentary skills that would create docile, willing workers. Whatever interpretation one chooses, Mann's belief that schools can change the social order and that education can foster social mobility are beliefs responsible for the faith and support many people give to U.S. public schools.

## Opposition to Public Education

Not all groups subscribed to the idea of the common school. The same arguments made today by people without children or people who send their children to private schools in opposition to public support of schools were articulated against the common school Horace Mann envisioned. For example, taxation for public education, was viewed as "unjust" by nonrecipients. Roman Catholics, who viewed the common school as dominated by a Protestant ethos, founded their own schools.

However, by 1860, public support of elementary schools was becoming prevalent throughout the United States. Education beyond the elementary level, however, was primarily a province of private academies.

## Education for Women and African Americans

Traditionally the role of women in Western society has been that of helpmate or homemaker to the male, who assumed the role of provider. This role for women was vividly described by Jean-Jacques Rousseau in *Emile,* written in the eighteenth century. Rousseau, in his tract on education, created the female character, Sophie, who was to be the companion of the central male character, Emile, the recipient of a nontraditional but rigorous education. Sophie was encouraged to eat sweets, learn womanly arts, and be a supportive, loving helpmate to Emile.

This prescriptive role for women held sway throughout the nineteenth century and, for some, into the twentieth century as well. Generally, education for women was viewed as biologically harmful or too stressful. Thus, through the first half of the nineteenth century, educational opportunities for women were severely limited. Few females achieved an education other than rudimentary literacy and numeracy.

By the middle of the nineteenth century, however, a significant number of girls attended elementary schools and many were admitted to private academies, which functioned as secondary schools. By 1820, the movement for education for women in the Unites States was making important inroads.

In 1821, Emma Hart Willard opened the Troy Female Seminary in Troy, New York. The curriculum at this female seminary included so-called serious subjects of study, such as mathematics, science, history, and geography. Modeled on the curriculum of single-sex male academies, Troy Female Seminary sought to deliver an education to females, that was similar to that of their male counterparts. In subsequent years, other female reformers dedicated to education for women, such as Catherine Esther Beecher and Mary Lyon, opened schools for females. A pioneer in postsecondary education for women, Mary Lyon, founded Mount Holyoke College in 1837. Entry requirements (with the exception of a foreign language) and level of instruction were the same for women as for men at their institutions of higher learning.

Higher education for women did not remain the exclusive domain of Eastern reformers; the movement for female education spread quickly through the midwest. In 1834, Oberlin Collegiate Institute in Ohio opened its doors to women as well as African Americans. In 1856, the University of Iowa became the first state university to admit women.

Although educational opportunities for women were expanding during the period preceding the Civil War, education for African Americans was severely limited. After Nat Turner's Revolt in 1831, southerners believed more than ever that literacy bred both insubordination and revolution. Thus, they forbade the teaching of reading and writing to the slave population. In the North, education for African Americans was usually of inferior quality and separate from the mainstream public school, if provided at all by the public.

This dismal picture of schooling for African Americans prompted African-American parent, Benjamin Roberts, to file a legal suit in Boston in 1846 over the requirement that his daughter attend a segregated school. In a precedent-setting case, *Roberts* v. *City of Boston,* the court ruled that the local school committee had the right to establish separate educational facilities for whites and blacks. As a result of this ruling, African Americans were encouraged to establish their own schools. These were usually administered by their churches and aided in part through funds from abolitionists. The problem of equality of opportunity, in general, and school segregation, in particular, continued to be a significant issue throughout the remainder of the nineteenth and twentieth centuries (Anderson, 1988).

## URBANIZATION AND THE PROGRESSIVE IMPETUS

The beginning of the nineteenth century ushered in the First Industrial Revolution—immigration and urbanization of unprecedented proportions. Accordingly, the conditions created by these events were met with responses from social reformers whose concerns were far reaching and who attempted to address and redress the evils in U.S. life.

If the beginning of the nineteenth century seemed problematic to Americans, the close of the century must have been even more so. Again, there was a revolution in industry, referred to as the Second Industrial Revolution, this time involving steam-driven and electric-powered machinery. Factories had given way to gigantic corporations, under the control of such captains of industry as Andrew Carnegie, John D. Rockefeller, and Cornelius Vanderbilt. Significantly, immigrant labor played an essential role in this revolution.

At the beginning of the nineteenth century, the largest number of immigrants to the United States came from the northwestern part of Europe—namely, Great Britain, Scandinavia, Germany, and the Netherlands. After 1890, an increasingly large number of immigrants came from southern and eastern Europe. These immigrants' languages, customs, and living styles were dramatically different from those of the previous group. They settled in closely crowded substandard living quarters in urban areas and found work in factories. Thus, by the turn of the century, U.S. cities contained enormous concentrations of both wealth and poverty. Indeed, the gap between rich and poor had never been as great as it was at the close of the nineteenth century.

Thus far in this chapter, we have argued that the purpose of education has been seen in a variety of ways: religious, utilitarian, civic, and, with Mann, social mobility. The common school was born of an age of reform in this country that was unprecedented until the period between 1900 and 1914 in which a new reform movement, the Progressive Movement, would sweep the country. Progressive reformers insisted on government regulation of industry and commerce, as well as government regulation and conservation of the nation's natural resources. Moreover, progressive reformers insisted that government at national, state, and local levels be responsive to the welfare of its citizens rather than to the welfare of corporations. Significantly, progressive reforms had a sweeping agenda, ranging from secret ballot to schooling. As reformers, such as Horace Mann, in the nineteenth century had looked to schools as a means of addressing social problems, so reformers once again looked to schools as a means of preserving and promoting democracy within the new social order.

An important U.S. philosopher whose influence on schooling is still very much with us today was John Dewey (1859–1952). Dewey was a contemporary of such reformers as "Fighting Bob La Follette," governor of Wisconsin and architect of the "Wisconsin Idea," which harnessed the expertise of university professors to the mechanics of state government; settlement workers, such as Jane Addams and Lillian Wald; and municipal reformers and labor leaders, such as Henry Bruere and John Golden. Thus, progressive education, the movement with which John Dewey has become associated, can best be understood, as both historians Lawrence Cremin and Richard Hofstadter remind us, as part of "a broader program of social and political reform called the Progressive Movement" (Cremin, 1961, p. 88).

Just as the schools today are undergoing a transformation due in part to rapidly changing technology, altered life-styles and new, massive waves of immigrants, it could be argued that the schools at the turn of the century were undergoing a similar transformation in their time. In 1909, for example, 57.8 percent of the children in schools in 37 of the largest cities in the United States were foreign born (Cremin, 1961, p. 72). Suddenly, teachers were faced with problems of putative uncleanliness (bathing became part of the school curriculum in certain districts), and teachers began to teach basic socialization skills. Just how these socialization skills have come to be interpreted, whether malevolently by radical historians or benevolently by liberal and conservative historians, is not our concern here. What we do need to consider is how Dewey proposed to meet these challenges through education and how his ideas were interpreted by progressive disciples in such a way as to alter the course of schooling in this country.

John Dewey was born and raised in Vermont. By 1894, he had become thoroughly enmeshed in the problems of urbanization as a resident of Chicago and Chair of the Department of Philosophy, Psychology, and Pedagogy at the University of Chicago. Distressed with the abrupt dislocation of families from rural to urban environments, concerned with the loss of traditional ways of understanding the maintenance of civilization, and anxious about the effects unleashed individualism and rampant materialism would have on a democratic society, Dewey sought answers in pedagogic practice (see Westbrook, 1991, for an in-depth biography).

Dewey argued in *My Pedagogic Creed* (1897), *The School and Society* (1899), and *The Child and the Curriculum* (1902) for a restructuring of schools along the lines of "embryonic communities." He advocated the creation of a curriculum that would allow for the child's interests and developmental level while introducing the child to "the point of departure from which the child can trace and follow the progress of mankind in history, getting an insight also into the materials used and the mechanical principles involved" (Dworkin, 1959, p. 43).

Dewey believed that the result of education was growth, which was firmly posited within a democratic society. Thus, school for Dewey was "that form of community life in which all those agencies are concentrated that will be most effective in bringing the child to share in the inherited resources of the race, and to use his own powers for social ends" (Dworkin, 1959, p. 22).

To implement his ideas, Dewey created the Laboratory School at the University of Chicago. There, children studied basic subjects in an integrated curriculum since, according to Dewey, "the child's life is an integral, a total one" and therefore, the school should reflect the "completeness" and "unity" of "the child's own world" (Dworkin, 1959, p. 93). Dewey advocated active learning, starting with the needs and interests of the child; he emphasized the role of experience in education and introduced the notion of teacher as facilitator of learning rather than the font from which all knowledge flows. The school, according to Dewey, was a "miniature community, an embryonic society" (Dworkin, 1959, p. 41) and discipline was a tool that would develop "a spirit of social cooperation and community life" (Dworkin, 1959, p. 40).

That John Dewey made important contributions to both philosophy of education and pedagogic practice is undisputable, especially if one examines what happened to education in the wake of Dewey's early work. It is important to keep in mind just how rapidly education had expanded in this period. For example, in 1870, about 6.5 million children from ages 5 through 18 attended school; in 1880, about 15.5 million children attended school—a significant increase, indeed. No less than 31 states by 1900 had enacted compulsory education laws. Thus, what occurred in schools throughout this nation was to influence large numbers of Americans.

Although few can dispute Dewey's influence upon educational reformers, many believe that Dewey was often misread, misunderstood, and misinterpreted. Thus, Dewey's emphasis on the child's impulses, feelings, and interests led to a form of progressive education that often became synonymous with permissiveness, and his emphasis on vocations ultimately led the way for "life adjustment" curriculum reformers.

Psychologists as well as philosophers became actively involved in educational reform. In fact, two distinctly different approaches to progressive educational reforms became apparent: the child-centered pedagogy of G. Stanley Hall and the social efficiency pedagogy of Edward L. Thorndike.

G. Stanley Hall (1844–1924), once referred to as "the Darwin of the mind" (Cremin, 1961, p. 101), believed that children, in their development, reflected the stages of development of civilization. Thus, according to Hall, schools should tailor their curriculums to the stages of child development. Hall argued that traditional schools stifled the child's natural impulses, and he suggested that schools individualize instruction and attend to the needs and interests of the children they educate. This strand of progressive reform became known as child-centered reform.

On the opposite side of child-centered reform was social engineering reform, proposed by Edward L. Thorndike. Thorndike (1874–1949) placed his emphasis on the organism's response to its environment. Working with animals in the laboratory, he came to the conclusion that human nature could be altered for better or worse, depending on the education to which it was subjected. Ultimately, Thorndike came to believe that schools could change human beings in a positive way and that the methods and aims of pedagogy to achieve this would be scientifically determined (Cremin, 1961, p. 114).

Thorndike's work, Frederick Winslow Taylor's work in scientific management, and that of other progressive thinkers encouraged educators to be "socially efficient" in the ways they went about educating students. In particular, this thinking led to a belief that schools should be a meaningful experience for students and that schools should prepare students to earn a living. It also suggested that schools might begin to educate students based on their abilities or talents. In particular, a leading proponent of this view was educational reformer Franklin Bobbitt. An issue of particular importance, although never resolved, was Bobbitt's scientific approach to curriculum design (a curriculum designer, according to Bobbitt, was like a "great engineer"). The purpose of curriculum design was to create a curriculum that would include the full range of human experience and prepare students for life.

### Education for All: The Emergence of the Public High School

Prior to 1875, fewer than 25,000 students were enrolled in public high schools. Most adolescents who were engaged in some form of secondary education attended private academies that were either traditional, college preparatory schools or vocational schools (such as Franklin had proposed a century earlier). These academies taught not only academic subjects but also vocational ones. Yet, between 1880 and 1920, 2,382,542 students attended public high schools (Gutek, 1991, p. 122), probably outnumbering those who attended academies, and by 1940, about 6.5 million students attended public high school (*Digest of Education Statistics,* 1989, p. 45). In a scant 40 years or so, a structure for the high school had to be put in place and debates had to be resolved regarding the purpose of secondary education.

One of the great changes that has affected high school attendance is that "whereas once it was altogether voluntary, and for this reason quite selective, it is now, at least for those sixteen and under, compulsory and unselective" (Hofstadter, 1966, p. 326). Compulsory school laws grew steadily. In 1890, 27 states had them; by 1918, all states followed suit, encouraged by court cases, such as the one in Kalamazoo, Michigan, in 1874, which paved the way for the school districts' right to levy taxes to support public high schools.

In examining the evolution of the high school, what becomes immediately apparent is the tension in society over the meaning and purpose of education—a debate that began with the ideas of Jefferson and Franklin, that was augmented by the arguments of Horace Mann, and that was made even more complex with the ideas of progressive educators.

Historian Diane Ravitch has pointed to four themes in particular that were troubling high school educators at the turn of the century. The first was the tension between classical subjects, such as Latin and Greek, and modern subjects, such as science, English literature, and foreign languages. The second was the problem of meeting college entrance requirements, since different colleges required different courses of study. The third involved educators who believed that students should study subjects that would prepare them for life, as opposed to traditional academic subjects. And the fourth, inextricably linked to the other three, was whether all students should pursue the same course of study or whether the course of study should be determined by the interests and abilities of the students (Ravitch, 1983, pp. 136–137).

In order to address the reality that by the 1890s "the high school curriculum had begun to resemble a species of academic jungle creeper, spreading thickly and quickly in many directions at once" (cited in Powell, Farrar, & Cohen, 1985, p. 240) and to clarify the purpose of a high school education, a Committee of Ten was formed by the National Education Association, headed by Harvard University President Charles Eliot. The committee issued its report in 1893, supporting the academic purpose of secondary education and dismissing curricula differentiation. It argued that the purpose of secondary education was to prepare students for "the duties of life" ( quoted in Ravitch, 1983, p. 138). Furthermore, the committee recommended that modern academic subjects be awarded the same stature as traditional ones. It proposed five model curricula, including classical and modern languages, English, mathematics, history, and science—in essence, a liberal arts curriculum. Finally, the committee recommended that all students should be taught in the same manner; it was conspicuously silent on the subject of vocational education.

The Committee of Ten's recommendations were subsequently reinforced in two ways. The first was through the National Education Association's (NEA's) newly established committee on college entrance requirements, which recommended that all high school students study a core of academic subjects. The second was through the Carnegie Foundation for the Advancement of Teaching's adoption of the same core courses, which became known as Carnegie units and which were implemented in high schools throughout the country.

Not to be ignored was the progressive response to the Committee of Ten. In 1918, the NEA's Commission on the Reorganization of Secondary Schools made its report, which became known as the Cardinal Principles of Secondary Education. These principles, harkening back to the work of men such as G. Stanley Hall and supported by the "neutral measurement" work of Edward F. Thorndike, opened the door to a curriculum less academically demanding and far more utilitarian than the one proposed by Charles Eliot's Committee of Ten. Essentially, the Cardinal Principles, or the main goals of secondary education, were:

1. Health
2. Command of fundamental processes
3. Worthy home-membership
4. Vocation
5. Citizenship
6. Worthy use of leisure
7. Ethical character (Ravitch, 1983, p. 146)

For many educators, these Cardinal Principles helped to resolve the difficulty of educating students who were not college bound (at this time, only a small group of students in U.S. high schools expected to attend college). Educational historian David Cohen stated:

> Americans quickly built a system around the assumption that most students didn't have what it took to be serious about the great issues of human life, and that even if they had the wit, they had neither the will nor the futures that would support heavy-duty study. (cited in Powell et al., 1985, p. 245)

The final curriculum reform and a logical conclusion to the direction educational reform took during the period preceding the Second World War was the

"Education for Life Adjustment" movement, first proposed in a lecture at Harvard University by Charles Prosser in 1939. Concerned with the failure of educators to effect any meaningful changes during the Depression years, Prosser proposed a curriculum for the nation's high schools, which addressed the practical concerns of daily living. Prosser's ideas were not entirely new; in fact, they could be said to be the logical conclusion of educators who believed, in the final analysis, that not all students were able to master serious academic subject matter.

However, Prosser and his apostles sought life adjustment courses, not just for those at the bottom of the educational ladder but for all high school students. As Hofstader (1966) aptly observed, "American utility and American democracy would now be realized in the education of all youth" (p. 353). Students who once studied chemistry might study "the testing of detergents; not physics, but how to drive and service a car; not history, but the operation of the local gas works" (p. 356). As historians, Richard Hofstadter and David Cohen are quick to point out, this phase in educational reform exemplifies both the unbridled faith Americans have in education and the ambivalent feelings they harbor toward the life of the mind.

## THE POST–WORLD WAR II ERA: 1945–1980*

During the post-World War II period, the patterns that emerged during the Progressive Era were continued. First, the debate about the goals of education (i.e., academic, social, or both) and whether all children should receive the same education remained an important one. Second, the demand for the expansion of educational opportunity became perhaps the most prominent feature of educational reform. Whereas the Common School era opened access to elementary education and the Progressive era to secondary education, the post-World War II years were concerned with expanding opportunities to the postsecondary level. They were also directed at finding ways to translate these expanded opportunities into more equal educational outcomes at all levels of education. As in the first half of the twentieth century, so too in the second half, the compatibility of expanded educational opportunity with the maintenance of educational standards would create significant problems. Thus, the tensions between equity and excellence became crucial in the debates of this period.

### Cycles of Reform: Progressive and Traditional

The post-World War II years witnessed the continuation of the processes that defined the development of the comprehensive high school. The debates over academic issues, begun at the turn of the century, may be defined as the movement between pedagogical progressivism and pedagogical traditionalism. This movement continues a pattern that originated at the turn of the century and focuses not only on

*Material on pages 80 to 88 is adapted from Susan F. Semel, Peter W. Cookson, Jr., and Alan R. Sadovnik, "United States," in Peter W. Cookson, Jr., Alan R. Sadovnik, and Susan F. Semel (Eds.), *International Handbook of Educational Reform* (pp. 445–469). © 1992 by Peter W. Cookson, Jr., Alan R. Sadovnik, and Susan F. Semel. Westport, CT: Greenwood Press, 1992, an imprint of Greenwood Publishing Group. Inc., Westport, CT. Reprinted with permission.

the process of education but on its goals. At the center of these debates are the questions regarding the type of education children should receive and whether all children should receive the same education. Although many of these debates focused on curriculum and method, they ultimately were associated with the question of equity versus excellence.

Perhaps these debates can be best understood by examining reform cycles of the twentieth century that revolved between progressive and traditional visions of schooling. On one hand, traditionalists believed in knowledge-centered education, a traditional subject-centered curriculum, teacher-centered education, discipline and authority, and the defense of academic standards in the name of excellence. On the other hand, progressives believed in experiential education, a curriculum that responded to both the needs of students and the times, child-centered education, freedom and individualism, and the relativism of academic standards in the name of equity. Although these poles and educational practices rarely were in only one direction, the conflicts over educational policies and practices seemed to move back and forth between these two extremes. From 1945 to 1955, the progressive education of the previous decades was critically attacked.

These critics, including Mortimer Smith, Robert Hutchins, and Arthur Bestor, assailed progressive education for its sacrificing of intellectual goals to social ones. They argued that the life adjustment education of the period, combined with an increasingly antiintellectual curriculum, destroyed the traditional academic functions of schooling. Arthur Bestor, a respected historian and a graduate of the Lincoln School (one of the early progressive schools in New York City) argued that it was "regressive education," not progressive education, that had eliminated the school's primary role in teaching children to think (Ravitch, 1983, p. 76). Bestor, like the other critics, assailed the schools for destroying the democratic vision that all students should receive an education that was once reserved for the elite. He suggested that the social and vocational emphasis of the schools indicated a belief that all students could not learn academic material. In an ironic sense, many of the conservative critics were agreeing with the radical critique that the Progressive Era distorted the ideals of democratic education by tracking poor and working-class children into nonacademic vocational programs.

Throughout the 1950s the debate between progressives who defended the social basis of the curriculum and critics who demanded a more academic curriculum raged on. What was often referred to as "the great debate" (Ravitch, 1983, p. 79) ended with the Soviet launching of the space satellite *Sputnik*. The idea that the Soviets would win the race for space resulted in a national commitment to improve educational standards in general and to increase mathematical and scientific literacy in particular. From 1957 through the mid-1960s, the emphasis shifted to the pursuit of excellence, and curriculum reformers attempted to redesign the curricula in ways that would lead to the return of academic standards (although many doubted that such a romantic age ever existed).

By the mid-1960s, however, the shift in educational priorities moved again toward the progressive side. This occurred in two distinct but overlapping ways. First, the Civil Rights movement, as we will discuss, led to an emphasis on equity issues. Thus, federal legislation, such as the Elementary and Secondary Education Act of 1965, emphasized the education of disadvantaged children. Second, in the context of the antiwar movement of the times, the general criticism of U.S. society, and the persistent failure of the schools to ameliorate problems of poverty and of racial minorities, a "new progressivism" developed that linked the failure of the schools to the problems in society. Ushered in by the publication of A. S. Neill's *Summerhill* in 1960—a book about an English boarding school with few, if any, rules and that was dedicated to the happiness of the child—the new progressivism provided an intellectual and pedagogical assault on the putative sins of traditional education, its authoritarianism, its racism, its misplaced values of intellectualism, and its failure to meet the emotional and psychological needs of children.

Throughout the 1960s and early 1970s, a variety of books provided scathing criticism of U.S. education. These included Jonathon Kozol's *Death at an Early Age* (1967), which assailed the racist practices of the Boston public schools; Herbert Kohl's *36 Children* (1967), which demonstrated the pedagogical possibilities of open education; and Charles S. Silberman's *Crisis in the Classroom* (1970), which attacked the bureaucratic, stultifying mindlessness of U.S. education. These books, along with a series of articles by Joseph Featherstone and Beatrice and Ronald Gross on British progressive education (or open education), resulted in significant experimentation in some schools. Emphasis on individualism and relevant education, along with the challenge to the unquestioned authority of the teacher, resulted in alternative, free (or open) education—schooling that once again shifted attention away from knowledge (product) to process.

Although there is little evidence to suggest that the open classroom was a national phenomenon, and as the historian Larry Cuban noted in his history of teaching, *How Teachers Taught* (1984), there has been surprisingly little variation in the twentieth century in teacher methods. (That is, despite the cycles of debate and reform, most secondary teachers still lecture more than they involve students.) Nonetheless, the period from the mid-1960s to the mid-1970s was a time of great turmoil in the educational arena. A time marked by two simultaneous processes: (1) the challenge to traditional schooling and (2) the attempt to provide educational opportunity for the disadvantaged. In order to understand the latter, one must look back to the origins of the concerns for equity.

## Equality of Opportunity

The demand for equality of opportunity, as we have noted, has been a central feature of U.S. history. From the Jeffersonian belief in a meritocratic elite, to Mann's vision of schooling as a "great equalizer," to Dewey's notion that the schools would be a "lever of social progress," U.S. reformers have pointed to the schools as capable of solving problems of inequality. More importantly, as Lawrence Cremin (1990) pointed out, Americans have expected their schools to solve social, political, and economic problems and have placed on the schools "all kinds of millennial hopes and expectations" (p. 92). While this has been true throughout our history, the translation of this view into concrete policy has defined the post-war years and has helped explain the increasing politicization of the educational conflicts.

Immediately following the Second World War, the issue of access to educational opportunity became an important one. The GI Bill of Rights offered 16 million servicemen and -women the opportunity to pursue higher education. Ravitch (1983, pp. 12–13) pointed out that the GI Bill was the subject of considerable controversy over the question of access and excellence. On one hand, veterans groups, Congress, and other supporters believed the bill provided both a just reward for national service and a way to avoid massive unemployment in the postwar economy. Further, although aimed at veterans, it was part of the growing policy to provide access to higher education to those who, because of economic disadvantage and/or poor elementary and secondary preparation, had heretofore been denied the opportunity to attend college. On the other hand, critics such as Robert Maynard Hutchins, chancellor at the University of Chicago, and James Conant, president of Harvard University, feared that the policy would threaten the traditional meritocratic selection process and result in the lowering of academic standards (Ravitch, 1983, p. 13).

Despite these criticisms, the GI Bill, according to Ravitch (1983), was "the most ambitious venture in mass higher education that had ever been attempted by any society" (p. 14). Furthermore, she noted that the evidence does not suggest a decline in academic standards but rather a refreshing opening of the elite postsecondary education system. Historians and policymakers may disagree about the success of the GI Bill, but it is clear that it represented a building block in the post-World War II educational expansion. This expansion was similar to previous expansions, first in the Common School Era to compulsory elementary education, second in the Progressive Era to the high school, and in the post-World War II years to postsecondary education. The same types of questions left unresolved, especially from the Progressive Era, as to whether mass public education was possible, would become central points of controversy in the coming years.

Although the GI Bill set an important precedent, the issue of educational inequality for the poor and disadvantaged, in general, and for African Americans, in particular, became the focus of national attention and debate during this period. From the years immediately following the Second World War to the present, the questions of equality of opportunity at all levels have been significant areas of concern. In the late 1940s and 1950s, the relationships between race and education and the question of school segregation were at the forefront of political, educational, and moral conflicts.

Race, as much as any other single issue in U.S history, has challenged the democratic ethos of the American dream. The ideals of equality of opportunity and justice have been contradicted by the actual practices concerning African Americans and other minorities. Although legally guaranteed equal protection by the Fourteenth Amendment, African Americans continued to experience vast inequities. Nowhere was this more evident than in education.

The post-Civil War Reconstruction period, despite the constitutional amendments enacted to guarantee equality of treatment before the law, had little positive effect on African Americans, especially in the South. During the latter years of the nineteenth century, the Supreme Court successfully blocked civil rights legislation. In the famous 1896 decision relating to education, *Plessy* v. *Ferguson*, the Court upheld a Louisiana law that segregated railway passengers by race. In what is commonly referred to as its "separate but equal" doctrine, the Court upheld the constitutionality of segregated facilities. In his famous dissenting opinion, Justice John Marshall Harlan stated:

> In view of the Constitution, in the eye of the law, there is in this country no superior, dominant, ruling class of citizens. There is no caste here. Our constitution is color blind, and neither knows nor tolerates classes among citizens. In respect of civil rights, all citizens are equal before the law. The humblest is the peer of the most powerful. The law regards man as man, and takes no account of his surroundings or of his color when his civil rights guaranteed by the supreme law of the land are involved. (cited in Ravitch, 1983, p. 120)

Despite Justice Harlan's interpretation that the Constitution guaranteed a color-blind treatment of all citizens, the *Plessy* v. *Ferguson* decision remained the precedent through the first half of the twentieth century. In the 1930s and 1940s, the National Association for the Advancement of Colored People (NAACP) initiated a campaign to overthrow the law, with school segregation a major component of its strategy.

The unequal and separate education of African Americans in the South became a focal point of the civil rights movements of the 1930s, 1940s, and 1950s. Although the *Plessy* decision supported separate and equal, it was apparent to civil rights advocates that the schools were anything but equal. Furthermore, in terms of both educational opportunities and results, African Americans in both the North and South received nothing approximating equal treatment.

After a series of minor victories, the advocates of civil rights won their major victory on May 17, 1954, when, in its landmark decision in *Brown* v. *Topeka Board of Education,* the Supreme Court ruled that state imposed segregation of schools was unconstitutional. Chief Justice Earl Warren wrote:

> It is doubtful that any child may reasonably be expected to succeed in life if he is denied the opportunity of education. Such an opportunity, where the state has undertaken to provide it, is a right that must be made available to all on equal terms. (cited in Ravitch, 1983, p. 127)

Thus, the Supreme Court reversed the "separate but equal" doctrine enshrined in the *Plessy* case, and stated that separate educational institutions are unequal in and of themselves.

Although there would be considerable conflict in the implementation of the ruling, and although many legal scholars criticized both the basis and scope of the decision, the *Brown* decision marked both a symbolic and concrete affirmation of the ethos of democratic schooling. Although a compelling victory, *Brown* served to underscore the vast discrepancies between what Myrdal (1944) pointed to as the American belief in equality and the American reality of inequality. In the coming years, the fight for equality of opportunity for African Americans and other minorities would be a salient feature of educational reform. The *Brown* decision may have provided the legal foundation for equality, but the unequal results of schooling in the United States did not magically change in response to the law.

In the years following the *Brown* decision, the battle for equality of opportunity was fought on a number of fronts with considerable conflict and resistance. The attempt to desegregate schools in the South first, and later in the North, resulted in confrontation and, at times, violence. For example, in Little Rock, Arkansas, President Eisenhower sent federal troops to enforce desegregation in 1957. When Arkansas Governor Orval Faubus responded to the Supreme Court's refusal to delay desegregation by closing Little Rock's high schools, the federal courts declared the Arkansas school closing laws unconstitutional. Thus, events in Little Rock made it clear that the federal government would not tolerate continued school segregation. Although protests continued in the South into the 1960s, it was apparent that the segregationists would lose their battle to defend a Southern tradition.

The issue of school desegregation, however, was not an exclusively Southern matter. In the Northern cities and metropolitan area suburbs, where housing patterns resulted in segregated schools, the issue of *de jure* (segregation by law) segregation was often less clear. Where *de facto* segregation existed (that is, the schools were not segregated intentionally by law but by neighborhood housing patterns), the constitutional precedent for desegregation under *Brown* was shaky. Nonetheless, the evidence in the North of unequal educational opportunities based on race was clear. Thus, civil rights advocates pressed for the improvement of urban schools and for their desegregation.

The desegregation conflicts in Boston, every bit as embittered as in the South, demonstrated the degree to which the issue divided its citizens. As recently as the 1970s and early 1980s, the Boston School Committee was under judicial mandate to desegregate its schools. Judge Arthur Garrity ruled that the school committee knowingly, over a long period of time, conspired to keep schools segregated and thus limited the educational opportunity of African-American children. For a period of over five years, the citizens of Boston were torn apart by the Garrity desegregation order. Groups of white parents opposed, sometimes violently, the forced busing that was imposed. As J. Anthony Lukas, in his Pulitzer Prize-winning account *Common Ground* (1986) noted, the Boston situation became a symbol of frustration as it signified how a group of families, all committed to the best education for their children, could have such significantly different visions of what that meant. Judge Garrity stood resolute in his interpretation of the Constitution. Over time, the violence subsided. Many white Bostonians who could afford to do so either sent their children to private schools or moved to the suburbs. Thus, the Boston school system moved into an uneasy "cease fire" committed, at least publicly, to the improvement of education for all.

The Boston desegregation wars, like the conflicts a decade earlier in the South, revealed that U.S. society, although moving to ameliorate problems of racial inequality, was nonetheless a society in which racist attitudes changed slowly. Moreover, the Boston schools were a microcosm of the U.S. educational system—a system in which inequalities of race and class were salient features. Educational reforms of the 1960s and 1970s were directed at their elimination.

An important concurrent theme was the question of unequal educational outcomes based on socioeconomic position. From the late 1950s, the findings of social scientists, including James Coleman, author of the 1966 report *Equality of Educational Opportunity,* focused national attention on the relationship between socioeconomic position and unequal educational outcomes. Furthermore, as part of Presidents John F. Kennedy's and Lyndon Baines Johnson's social programs, Americans were sensitized to the idea of ameliorating poverty. Since schools were, in Horace Mann's vision, the lever of social reform, it was only natural that schools once again became the focal point.

During the 1960s and 1970s, a series of reform efforts were directed at providing equality of opportunity and increased access at all levels of education. Based on the Coleman report findings that unequal minority student educational achievement was caused more by family background than differences in the quality of schools attended, federally funded programs, such as Project Head Start, were aimed at providing early preschool educational opportunities for the disadvantaged. Although many radicals criticized the assumption of cultural deprivation implicit in these efforts, many reform efforts were aimed at the family and the school rather than the school itself.

Nowhere was the conflict over these liberal reforms more clearly demonstrated than in the area of higher education. During the 1960s, educational reformers placed significant emphasis on the need to open access to postsecondary education to students who were traditionally underrepresented at colleges and universities—namely, minority groups and the disadvantaged. Arguing that college was a key to social mobility and success, reformers concluded that college was a right rather than a privilege for all (see Lavin, Alba, & Silberstein, 1981). Defenders of the traditional admissions standards argued that postsecondary education would be destroyed if admissions standards were relaxed (see Sadovnik, 1993).

By the late 1960s, many colleges and universities adopted the policy of open enrollment. The City University of New York, long a symbol of quality education for the working class and poor, guaranteed a place for all graduating New York City high school students in either its four-year colleges (for students with high school averages of 80 and above) or its community college system (for students with averages below 80). Similar open admissions systems were introduced in other public university systems. Furthermore, federal financial aid funds were appropriated for students from low-income families. The results were a dramatic increase in the numbers of students participating in U.S. higher education and a growing debate over the efficacy of such liberal reforms.

Conservatives bemoaned the decline of standards and warned of the collapse of the intellectual foundations of Western civilization. Radicals suggested that more often than not students were given "false hopes and shattered dreams" as they were sometimes underprepared, given their unequal educational backgrounds, for the rigors of college education. Liberals, agreeing that the new students were often underprepared, suggested that it was now the role of the college to provide remedial services to turn access into success (see Sadovnik, 1993).

During the 1970s, colleges took on the task, however reluctantly, of providing remediation for the vast number of underprepared students, many of whom were first-generation college students. The City University of New York became perhaps the largest experiment in compensatory higher education. Its efforts symbolized both the hopes and frustrations of ameliorating unequal educational achievement. Although there is significant disagreement as to the success of these higher-education reforms (which we will examine more closely later in this book), it is important to recognize that this period did result in the significant expansion of higher education.

We have looked at two related processes that define the post-World War II history of education. The first is the continued debate between progressives and traditionalists about the proper aims, content, and methods of schooling. The second is the struggle for equality of opportunity and the opening of access to higher education. The educational history of the 1980s, as you will see, was characterized by the perceived failure of the reforms of this period, most particularly those of the 1960s and 1970s.

## EDUCATIONAL REACTION AND REFORM: 1980s–1990s

By the late 1970s, conservative critics began to react to the educational reforms of the 1960s and 1970s. They argued that liberal reforms in pedagogy and curriculum and in the arena of educational opportunity had resulted in the decline of authority and standards. Furthermore, the critics argued that the preoccupation with using the schools to ameliorate social problems, however well intended, not only failed to do this but was part of an overall process that resulted in mass mediocrity. What was needed was nothing less than a complete overhaul of the U.S. educational system. While radical critics also pointed to the failure of the schools to ameliorate problems of poverty, they located the problem not so much in the schools but in the society at large. Liberals defended the reforms of the period by suggesting that social improvement takes a long time, and a decade and a half was scarcely sufficient to turn things around.

In 1983, the National Commission on Excellence, founded by President Reagan's Secretary of Education, Terrel Bell, issued its now famous report, *A Nation at Risk*. This report provided a serious indictment of U.S. education and cited high rates of adult illiteracy, declining SAT scores, and low scores on international comparisons of knowledge by U.S. students as examples of the decline of literacy and standards. The committee stated that "the educational foundations of our society are presently being eroded by a rising tide of mediocrity that threatens our very future as a Nation and a people" (p. 5). As solutions, the commission offered five recommendations: (1) that all students graduating from high school complete what was termed the "new basics"—four years of English, three years of mathematics, three years of science, three years of social studies, and a half year of computer science; (2) that schools at all levels expect higher achievement from their students and that four-year colleges and universities raise their admissions requirements; (3) that more time be devoted to teaching the new basics; (4) that the preparation of teachers be strengthened and that teaching be made a more respected and rewarded profession; and (5) that citizens require their elected representatives to support and fund these reforms (cited in Cremin, 1990, p. 31).

The years following this report were characterized by scores of other reports that both supported the criticism and called for reform. During the 1980s, significant attention was given to the improvement of curriculum, the tightening of standards, and a move toward the setting of academic goals and their assessment. A coalition of U.S. governors took on a leading role in setting a reform agenda; business leaders stressed the need to improve the nation's schools and proposed partnership programs; the federal government, through its Secretary of Education (under Ronald Reagan), William Bennett took an active and critical role but continued to argue that it was not the federal government's role to fund such reform; and educators, at all levels, struggled to have a say in determining the nature of the reforms.

As we have pointed out in Chapter 2, the politics of the reform movement were complex and multidimensional. Conservatives wanted to restore both standards and the traditional curriculum; liberals demanded that the new drive for excellence not ignore the goals for equity; radicals believed it was another pendulum swing doomed to failure (one that sought to reestablish *excellence* as a code word for *elitism*).

In the 1990s, we appear at the crossroad of this most recent cycle of educational reform. At the present, there are a number of reforms that have the most visibility. Although they all purport to balance equity and excellence as their goal, it is not clear how effective they will be. In Chapter 10, we will discuss them more fully; in this section, we will describe them briefly.

First, school-based management is a reform that many believe holds promise. This reform shifts the control of schools from highly bureaucratic and centralized boards of education to the school itself, where teachers, parents, and administrators work cooperatively in decision making. Second, teacher empowerment, a reform closely related to school-based management, seeks to give teachers far more authority in decision making. Third, the school choice movement seeks to give parents the right to choose the public school to send their children, rather than the traditional method in which one's school was based on neighborhood zoning patterns. The choice movement is divided into those who support public school choice only (that is, giving parents the right to choose from public schools) to those who would include intersectional choice policies, including private schools. Such an intersectional choice program is now being tested in Milwaukee where low-income parents receive tuition vouchers to send their children to private schools. There is significant controversy over this plan, with supporters stating it is the key to equity and critics arguing that it means the death of public education.

It is too early to assess these reforms, but it is apparent that they are part of the recurring debate in U.S. educational history about the efficacy of mass public education and the compatibility of excellence and equity. Throughout history, these themes have been crucial as the preceding historical discussion delineates; the answer to the questions is a matter of both historical interpretation and empirical investigation.

## UNDERSTANDING THE HISTORY OF U.S. EDUCATION: DIFFERENT HISTORICAL INTERPRETATIONS

The history of education in the United States, as we have illustrated, has been one of conflict, struggle, and disagreement. It has also been marked by a somewhat ironic pattern of cycles of reform about the aims, goals, and purpose of education on one hand, and little change in actual classroom practice on the other (Cuban, 1984). Moreover, as we pointed out in Chapter 2, one's view of U.S. educational history and the effectiveness of the schools in meeting their democratic aspirations depends on one's interpretation of the historical trends and events. In the following sections, we outline the different schools of historical interpretation.

The different interpretations of U.S. Educational history revolve around the tensions between equity and excellence, between the social and intellectual functions of schooling, and over differing responses to the questions, Education in whose interests? Education for whom? The U.S. school system has expanded to serve more students for longer periods of time than any other system in the modern world. This occurred, first, by extending primary school to all through compulsory education laws during the Common School Era; second, by extending high school education to the majority of adolescents by the end of the Progressive Era; and third, by extending postsecondary education to the largest number of high school graduates in the world by the 1990s. However, historians and sociologists of education disagree about whether this pattern of increased access means a pattern of educational success. Moreover, these disagreements concern the questions of the causes of educational expansion (that is, who supported the reforms), who benefited from them, and which types of goals have been met and/or sacrificed.

### The Democratic-Liberal School

Democratic-liberals believe that the history of U.S. education involves the progressive evolution, albeit flawed, of a school system committed to providing equality of opportunity for all. Democratic-liberal historians suggest that each period of educational expansion involved the attempts of liberal reformers to expand educational opportunities to larger segments of the population and to reject the conservative view of schools as elite institutions for the meritorious (which usually meant the privileged). Historians such as Ellwood Cubberly, Merle Curti, and Lawrence A. Cremin are representative of this view. Both Cubberly (1934) and Curti (1959) have portrayed the Common School Era as a victory for democratic movements and the first step in opening U.S education to all. Furthermore, both historians, in varying degrees, portray the early school reformers such as Horace Mann and Henry Barnard as reformers dedicated to egalitarian principles (Curti is more critical than Cubberly).

Lawrence A. Cremin, in his three-volume history of U.S. education (1970, 1980, 1988) and in a study of the Progressive Era (1961) portrays the evolution of U.S. education in terms of two related processes: popularization and multitudinousness (Cremin, 1988). For Cremin, educational history in the United States involved both the expansion of opportunity and purpose. That is, as more students from diverse backgrounds went to school for longer periods of time, the goals of education became more diverse, with social goals often becoming as or more important than intellectual ones. Although Cremin does not deny the educational problems and conflicts, and he notes the discrepancies between opportunity and results—particularly for the economically disadvantaged—he never relinquished his vision that the genius of U.S. education lies with its commitment to popularization and multitudinousness. In his final book, *Popular Education and Its Discontents* (1990), Cremin summarized this democratic liberal perspective as follows: "That kind of organization [referring to U.S. higher education] is part of the genius of American education—it provides a place for everyone who wishes one, and in the end yields one of the most educated populations in the world" (p. 46).

Although democratic-liberals tend to interpret U.S. educational history optimistically, the evolution of the nation's schools has been a flawed, often conflictual march toward increased opportunities. Thus, historians such as Cremin do not see equity and excellence as inevitably irreconcilable, but rather see the tensions between the two as resulting in necessary compromises. The ideals of equality and excellence are just that: ideals. Democratic-liberals believe that the U.S. educational system must continue to move closer to each, without sacrificing one or the other too dramatically.

## The Radical-Revisionist School

Beginning in the 1960s, the optimistic vision of the democratic-liberal historians began to be challenged by radical historians, sociologists, and political economists of education. The radical-revisionist historians of education, as they have come to be called, revised the history of education in a more critical direction. These historians, including Michael Katz (1968), Joel Spring (1972), and Clarence Karier (1976), argue that the history of U.S. education is the story of expanded success for very different reasons and with very different results. Radical historians do not deny that the educational system has expanded; rather, they believe it expanded to meet the needs of the elites in society for the control of the working class and immigrants, and for economic efficiency and productivity. In addition, radicals suggest that expanded opportunity did not translate into more egalitarian results. Rather, they point out that each period of educational reform (the Common School Era, the Progressive Era, the Post-World War II) led to increasing stratification within the educational system, with working class, poor, and minority students getting the short end of the stick.

Let us examine the radical view on educational expansion and the question of whose interests it served. Michael Katz (1968) argued that it was the economic interests of nineteenth century capitalists that more fully explain the expansion of schooling and that educational reformers stressed the ability of schools to train factory workers, to socialize immigrants into U.S. values, and to create stability in the newly expanding urban environments. Likewise, historians Joel Spring (1972) and Clarence Karier (1976) both advanced the thesis that the expansion of the schools in the late nineteenth and early twentieth centuries was done more so in the interests of social control than in the interests of equity. Spring argued that this perspective

> advances the idea that schools were shaped as instruments of the corporate liberal state for mainstreaming social control.... The public schools were seen as an important instrument used by the government to aid in the rationalization and minimization of conflict by selecting and training students for their future positions in the economy and by imbuing the population with a sense of cooperation and national spirit. (1986, p. 154)

One of the problems with this view, pointed out by radicals who generally agree with this interpretation, is that it views the expansion of education as imposed on the poor and working class from above and often against their will. Other radical historians, including David Hogan (1978) and Julia Wrigley (1982), suggest that the working class and labor unions actively supported the expansion of public education for their own interests. Thus, the explanation of educational expansion is a more conflictual one rather than a simplistic tale of elite domination.

Despite these historiographical disagreements, radical historians agree that the results of educational expansion rarely met their putative democratic aspirations. They suggest that each new expansion increased stratification of working-class and disadvantaged students within the system, with these students less likely to succeed educationally. For example, political economists Samuel Bowles and Herbert Gintis (1976) noted that the expansion of the high school resulted in a comprehensive secondary system that tracked students into vocational and academic curriculums with placement, more often than not, determined by social class background and race. Furthermore, the expansion of higher education in the post-World War II period often resulted in the stratification between community colleges that stressed vocational education and four-year colleges and universities that stressed the liberal arts and sciences. Once again, radicals argue that placement in the higher education system is based on social class and race. Studies by Kevin Dougherty (1987) and Steven Brint and Jerome Karabel (1989) give ample evidence to support the view that the expansion of higher education has not resulted in equality of opportunity.

Thus, the radical interpretation of U.S. educational history is a more pessimistic one. While acknowledging educational expansion, they suggest that this process has benefited the elites more than the masses and has not produced either equality of opportunity or results. Further, they view the debates about equity and excellence as a chimera, with those who bemoan the decline of standards seeking to reimpose excellence with little regard for equality.

## Conservative Perspectives

In the 1980s, as we noted in Chapter 2, a rising tide of conservative criticism swept education circles. Although much of this criticism was political and, at times, ahistorical, it did have an implicit historical critique of the schools. Arguing that U.S. students knew very little and that U.S. schools were mediocre, the conservative critics such as William Bennett, Chester Finn, Jr., Diane Ravitch, E. D. Hirsch, Jr., and Allan Bloom all pointed to the failure of so-called progressive education to fulfill its lofty social goals without sacrificing academic quality. Although critics such as Ravitch and Hirsch supported the democratic-liberal goal of equality of opportunity and mobility through education, they believed that the historical pursuit of social and political objectives resulted in significant harm to the traditional academic goals of schooling.

Diane Ravitch (1977) provided a passionate critique of the radical-revisionist perspective and a defense of the democratic-liberal position. Yet, in the 1980s, Ravitch moved from this centrist position to a more conservative stance. In a series of essays and books, including *The Troubled Crusade* (1983), Ravitch argued that the preoccupation with using education to solve social problems has not solved these problems and, simultaneously, has led to the erosion of educational excellence. Although Ravitch remains faithful to the democratic-liberal belief that schools have expanded opportunities to countless numbers of the disadvantaged and immigrants, she has argued that the adjustment of the traditional curriculum to meet the needs of all of these groups has been a violation of the fundamental function of schooling, which is to develop the powers of intelligence (1985, p. 40). According to Ravitch, the progressive reforms of the twentieth century have denigrated the traditional role of schools in passing on a common culture and have produced a generation of students who know little, if anything, about their Western heritage. Although she believes the curriculum ought to be fair and nonracist, she has also argued that efforts at multiculturalism are often historically incorrect and neglect the fact that the heritage of our civilization, from a conservative vantage point, is Western.

Ravitch's conservatism is far more complex than that of other conservative critics such as Bennett, Bloom, Finn, and Hirsch. Where these authors, like Bloom in *The Closing of the American Mind* (1987) and Hirsch in *Cultural Literacy* (1987), never fully capture the complex relationship between educational reform and social and political milieu, Ravitch's *The Troubled Crusade* (1983) points to the putative decline of educational standards within the context of political movements to move us closer to a fair and just society. Ravitch understands the conflictual nature of U.S. educational history and simultaneously praises the schools for being a part of large-scale social improvement while damning them for losing their academic standards in the process. Bloom blames the universities for watering down their curriculums; Hirsch blames the public schools for valuing skills over content; and Bennett, in his role as Secretary of Education during the Reagan administration, called for a return to a traditional Western curriculum. None of these conservatives has analyzed as Ravitch has (perhaps because she is the only historian among them) the historical tensions between equity and excellence that are crucial to understanding the problem. Nonetheless, what they all have in common is the vision that the evolution of U.S. education has resulted in the dilution of academic excellence.

## CONCLUSION

As students of educational history, you may well be perplexed by the different interpretations of the history of U.S. education. How is it possible, you may ask, that given the same evidence, historians reach such vastly different conclusions? As we pointed out in Chapter 2, the interpretation of educational issues, including the interpretation of its history, depends to a large extent on one's perspective. Thus, each school of historical interpretation sees the events, data, and conflicts in different ways. We do not propose that there is one unified theory of the history of education, nor do we believe that the historical and sociological data support only one theory. Rather, we believe that there are patterns in the history of education and that the foundations perspective is a lens for looking at these patterns.

The history of U.S. education has involved a number of related patterns. First, it has been defined by the expansion of schooling to increasingly larger number of children for longer periods of time. Second, with this expansion has come the demand for equality of opportunity and ways to decrease inequality of results. Third is the conflict over goals, curriculum, and method, and the politization of these issues. Fourth is the conflict between education for a common culture, or a "distinctively American paideia, or self-conscious culture" (Cremin, 1990, p. 107) and education for the diversity of a pluralistic society. And fifth are the tensions between popularization and educational excellence. All of these processes speak to the fact that Americans have always asked a great deal, perhaps too much, from their schools, and that conflict and controversy are the definitive features of the evolution of the school.

The history of U.S. education is a complex story of conflict, compromise, and struggle. The disagreements over this history are summed up well by Diane Ravitch, defending the democratic-liberal tradition, and David Nassaw, arguing for a more radical interpretation. Ravitch (1977) stated:

> Education in a liberal society must sustain and balance ideals that exist in tension: equity and excellence. While different generations have emphasized one or the other, in response to the climate of the times, schools cannot make either ideal a reality, though they contribute to both. The schools are limited institutions which have certain general responsibilities and certain specific capacities; sometimes they have failed to meet realistic expectations, and at other times they have succeeded beyond realistic expectations in dispersing intelligence and opportunity throughout the community. In order to judge them by reasonable standards and in order to have any chance of improving their future performance, it is necessary to abandon the simplistic search for heros and devils, scapegoats and panaceas. (p. 173)

Nassaw (1979), in a very different vein, stated:

> The public schools emerge in the end compromised by reform and resistance. They do not belong to the corporations and the state, but neither do they belong to their communities. They remain "contested" institutions with several agendas and several purposes. The reformers have not in the past made them into efficient agencies for social channeling and control. Their opponents will not, on the other hand, turn them into truly egalitarian institutions without at the same time effecting radical changes in the state and society that support them. The public schools will, in short, continue to be the social arena where the tension is reflected and the contest played out between the promise of democracy and the rights of class division. (p. 243)

Thus, from their very different vantage points, Ravitch and Nassaw agree that schools are imperfect institutions with conflicting goals that have been the center of struggle throughout our history. There have been no easy answers to the complex questions we have examined. As teachers, you will become a part of this ongoing history, and we believe only through reflective consideration of the issues will you be able to understand the many conflicts of which you will be a part, let alone resolve these conflicts and make a difference.

In order to evaluate the issues raised in this chapter, one must look at empirical evidence, including, but not limited to, the historical record. That is, to analyze the extent to which schools have provided opportunity and mobility or the extent to which standards have fallen requires data. As you will see, the sociological approach to education has been central to this endeavor. In the next chapter, we will explore this sociological approach in depth.

The following articles illustrate some of the major historical periods, writers, and reforms discussed in this chapter. The first selection, "Broken Promises: School

Reform in Retrospect," written by radical political economists Samuel Bowles and Herbert Gintis, presents a radical critique of twentieth-century educational reform. Arguing that the liberal reforms of the twentieth century failed to produce equality of opportunity or results, Bowles and Gintis suggest that such reforms are doomed to failure in a capitalist society. This selection, excerpted from their important book *Schooling in Capitalist America* (1976), is an example of the radical-revisionist perspective on U.S. educational history.

The second selection, "Forgetting the Questions: The Problem of Educational Reform," written by historian of education Diane Ravitch, looks at educational reform from a very different vantage point. Arguing that twentieth-century reforms have centered on the sociological rather than the educational view, Ravitch, Assistant Secretary of Education for Research and Development in the Bush administration, criticizes the schools for ignoring their intellectual functions. Ravitch has been a severe critic of the revisionist historians, and this selection offers a very different view of U.S.educational history than that presented by Bowles and Gintis.

# Broken Promises: School Reform in Retrospect

SAMUEL BOWLES

HERBERT GINTIS

> We shall one day learn to supercede politics by education.—Ralph Waldo Emerson

Educational reform in the past decade has hardly marked a major innovation in social policy. Rather, it has seemed to most, including its most ardent supporters, a natural extension of over a century of progressive thought. Its apparent failure is not only disconcerting in its social consequences, but casts strong doubt on liberal educational theory as a whole, and invites a thorough reassessment of its basic concepts and their historical application.

In this [reading], we begin with a review of liberal educational views in the most cogent and sophisticated forms. We then proceed to assess their validity as revealed in both the historical record and contemporary statistical evidence. The discrepancy between theory and practice, we shall suggest, has been vast not only in recent years, but throughout the years for which evidence is available. The educational system has rarely behaved according to traditional precepts; rarely has it promoted either social equality or full human development. This conclusion bids us to offer a critique of traditional educational notions—one sufficiently detailed to motivate the alternative presented in later chapters in this book.

The use of education as a tool of social policy has a long and eminent history. For instance, the period from 1890–1920, marking the transition of the U.S. capitalist system from its earlier individualistic competitive structure to its contemporary corporate form, presented a picture of acute social dislocation much as our own.[1] Andrew Carnegie, a major protagonist of this drama, responded to the growing breakdown of "law and order" among working people with the National Guard, trainloads of strikebreakers, and the notorious Pinkerton men. But the survival of the new order over the long haul, all agreed, called for a bit more finesse. "Just see," Carnegie pointed out, "wherever we peer into the first tiny springs of the national life, how this true panacea for all the ills of the body politic bubbles forth—education, education, education."[1a] Carnegie proceeded, in the lull between battles, to found the Carnegie Foundation for the Advancement of Teaching. The Carnegie Foundation and its offshoots continue to this day to play a critical role in the evolution of U.S. education.

Carnegie's advocacy of schooling as the solution of the all-too-evident social ills of his day was echoed by other corporate leaders, by university presidents, trade union officials, and politicians; education quickly became the chosen instrument of social reformers.[2] Nor has enthusiasm waned with the passing years. Three-quarters of a century later, President Lyndon B. Johnson could proclaim that

"...the answer for all our national problems comes down to a single word: education." Why education for this critical role? The focal importance of schooling in U.S. social history and the attention devoted to it by current policy-makers and social critics can be understood only in terms of the way reformers have accommodated themselves to the seemingly inevitable realities of capitalist development.

Whatever the benefits of the capitalist economy, its modern critics and defenders alike have recognized that a system based on free markets in land and labor and the private ownership of the means of production, if left to itself, would produce a host of undesirable outcomes. Among these include the fragmentation of communities, the deterioration of the natural environment, alienated work and inhuman working conditions, insufficient supplies of necessary social services, and an unequal distribution of income.... The classical laissez-faire doctrine has been largely rejected in favor of what we call progressive liberalism. The basic strategy of progressive liberalism is to treat troublesome social problems originating in the economy as aberrations which may be alleviated by means of enlightened social programs. Among these correctives, two stand out: education and governmental intervention in economic life. Figuring prominently in the writings of liberals, both have become essential instruments of economic growth. Both, it is thought, can serve as powerful compensatory and ameliorative forces, rectifying social problems and limiting the human cost of capitalist expansion.

The importance of education and state intervention as complements to the normal operation of the economy cannot be denied. Yet these correctives have not resolved the problems to which they have been directed. Inequality, class stratification, racism, sexism, destruction of community and environment, alienating, bureaucratic, and fragmented jobs persist. Rising per capita income has, if anything, heightened dissatisfaction over them

to the point of unleashing a veritable crisis of values in the advanced capitalist societies in Europe and America.

The thrust of many modern critics of capitalism is not merely to berate the operation of its economic institutions per se, but to argue that education and state policy are relatively powerless to rectify social problems within the framework of a capitalist economy. The liberal position is, of course, that insofar as any reform is possible, it is possible within the present system, and can be achieved through enlightened social policy. The only constraints, it argues, are those dictated by technology and human nature in any materially productive society and, therefore, are common to any advanced economic system.

We take our stand with the critics. In this [reading], we shall focus our analysis on the educational system, maintaining that the range of effective educational policy in the United States is severely limited by the role of schooling in the production of an adequate labor force in a hierarchically controlled and class-stratified production system. Capitalism, not technology or human nature, is the limiting factor.

## DEMOCRACY AND TECHNOLOGY IN EDUCATIONAL THEORY

> The minds...of the great body of the people are in danger of really degenerating, while the other elements of civilization are advancing, unless care is taken, by means of the other instruments of education, to counteract those effects which the simplification of the manual processes has a tendency to produce.—James Mill, 1824

Scholars abhor the obvious. Perhaps for this reason it is often difficult to find a complete written statement of a viewpoint which is widely accepted. Such is the case with modern liberal educational theory. Discovering its conceptual underpinnings thus requires more than a little careful searching. What exactly is the theory underlying the notion of education as "panacea"? In reviewing the vast literature on this subject, we have isolated two intellectually coherent strands, one represented by John Dewey and his followers—the "democratic school"—and the other represented by functional sociology and neoclassical economics—the "technocratic-meritocratic school." These approaches are best understood by analyzing the way they deal with two major questions concerning the limits of educational policy. The first concerns the compatibility of various functions schools are supposed to perform. The second concerns the power of schooling to perform these functions. We shall treat each in turn.

In the eyes of most liberal reformers, the educational system must fulfill at least three functions. First and foremost, schools must help integrate youth into the various occupational, political, familial, and other adult roles required by an expanding economy and a stable polity. "Education," says John Dewey in *Democracy and Education,* probably the most important presentation of the liberal theory of education, "is the means of [the] social continuity of life." We refer to this process as the "integrative" function of education.

Second, while substantial inequality in economic privilege and social status are believed by most liberals to be inevitable, giving each individual a chance to compete openly for these privileges is both efficient and desirable. Dewey is representative in asserting the role of the school in this process:

> It is the office of the school environment...to see to it that each individual sets an opportunity to escape from the limitations of the social group in which he was born, and to come into living contact with a broader environment.[3]

Many liberal educational theorists—including Dewey—have gone beyond this rather limited objective to posit a role for schools in equalizing the vast extremes of wealth and poverty. Schooling, some have proposed, cannot only assure fair competition, but can also reduce the economic gap between the winners and the losers. We shall refer to this role of schooling in the pursuit of equality of opportunity, or of equality itself, as the "egalitarian" function of education.

Lastly, education is seen as a major instrument in promoting the psychic and moral development of the individual. Personal fulfillment depends, in large part, on the extent, direction, and vigor of development of our physical, cognitive, emotional, aesthetic, and other potentials. If the educational system has not spoken to these potentialities by taking individual development as an end in itself, it has failed utterly. Again quoting Dewey:

> The criterion of the value of school education is the extent in which it creates a desire for continued growth and supplies the means for making the desire effective in fact.... The educational process has no end beyond itself; it is its own end.[4]

We refer to this as the "developmental" function of education.

For Dewey, the compatibility of these three functions—the integrative, the egalitarian, and the developmental—derives from basic assumptions concerning the nature of social life. First, he assumed that occupational roles in capitalist society are best filled by individuals who have achieved the highest possible levels of personal development. For Dewey, personal development is economically productive. Second, Dewey assumed that a free and universal school system can render the opportunities for self-development independent of race, ethnic origins, class background, and sex. Hence the integrative, egalitarian, and developmental functions of schooling are not only compatible, they are mutually supportive.

But why may this be so? Dewey locates the compatibility of the three functions of education in the democratic nature of U.S. institutions.[5] For Dewey, the essence of self-development is the acquisition of control over personal and social relationships; and in this process, education plays a central role:

> ...Education is that...reorganization of experience which adds to the meaning of experience, and which increases ability to direct the course of subsequent experience.[6]

It follows in this framework that integration into adult life and self-development are compatible with equality of opportunity precisely in a democratic setting. In Dewey's own words:

> The intermingling in the school of youth of different races, differing religions, and unlike customs creates for all a new and broader environment. Common subject matter accustoms all to a unity of outlook upon a broader horizon than is visible to the members of any group while it is isolated.... A society which is mobile and full of channels for the distribution of a change occurring anywhere, must see to it that its members are educated to personal initiative and adaptability.[7]

Dewey argues the necessary association of the integrative, egalitarian, and developmental functions of education in a democracy. A more recent liberal perspective argues only their mutual compatibility. This alternative view is based on a conception of the economy as a technical system, where work performance is based on technical competence. Inequality of income, power, and status, according to this technocratic-meritocratic view, is basically a reflection of an unequal distribution of mental, physical and other skills. The more successful individuals, according to this view, are the more skillful and the more intelligent. Since cognitive and psychomotor development are vital and healthy components of individual psychic development and can be provided equally according to the "abilities" of the students upon their entering schools, the compatibility of these three functions of the educational system in capitalism is assured.

The popularity of the technocratic-meritocratic perspective can be gleaned from the policy-maker's reaction to the "rediscovery" of poverty and inequality in America during the decade of the 1960s. Unequal opportunity in acquiring skills was quickly isolated as the source of the problem.[8] Moreover, in assessing the efficacy of the educational system, both of preschool enrichment and of other school programs, measures of cognitive outcomes—scholastic achievement, for example—have provided the unique criteria of success.[9] Finally, the recent failure of educational policies significantly to improve the position of the poor and minority groups has, among a host of possible reappraisals of liberal theory, raised but one to preeminence: the nature-nurture controversy as to the determination of "intelligence."[10]

This technocratic-meritocratic view of schooling, economic success, and the requisites of job functioning supplies an elegant and logically coherent (if not empirically compelling) explanation of the rise of mass education in the course of industrial development. Because modern industry, according to this view, consists in the application of increasingly complex and intellectually demanding production technologies, the development of the economy requires increasing mental skills on the part of the labor force as a whole. Formal education, by extending to the masses what has been throughout human history the privilege of the few, opens the upper levels in the job hierarchy to all with the ability and willingness to attain such skills. Hence, the increasing economic importance of mental skills enhances the power of a fundamentally egalitarian school system to equalize economic opportunity.

This line of reasoning is hardly new. Well before the Civil War, educational reformers had developed the idea that the newly emerging industrial order would provide the opportunity for a more open society. In 1842, Horace Mann, then secretary of the Massachusetts State Board of Education and the most prominent educational reformer of the nineteenth century, put the case this way:

> The capitalist and his agents are looking for the greatest amount of labor or the largest income in money from their investments, and they do not promote a dunce to a station where he will destroy raw material or slaken industry because of his name or birth or family connections. The obscurest and humblest person has an open and fair field for competition.[11]

Unlike earlier economic systems in which incomes and social status were based on landed property which could easily be passed on from generation to generation, in the modern industrial era, Mann argued, one's station would be determined by one's own abilities and will to work:

> In great establishments, and among large bodies of laboring men, where all services are rated according to their pecuniary value... those who have been blessed with a good common school education rise to a higher and higher point in the kinds of labor performed, and also in the rate of wages paid, while the ignorant sink, like dregs, and are always found at the bottom.[12]

Thus, under the new capitalist order, an educational system which provides to all children the opportunity to develop one's talents can insure progress toward a more open class system and a greater equality of economic opportunity. Horace Mann was unambiguous in asserting that:

> ...Nothing but universal education can counter work this tendency to the domina-

tion of capital and the servility of labor. If one class possesses all of the wealth and the education, while the residue of society is ignorant and poor...the latter in fact and in truth, will be the servile dependents and subjects of the former.[13]

The modern technocratic-meritocratic perspective avoids Mann's class analysis but retains his basic assertions. According to the modern view, the egalitarianism of schooling is complemented by the meritocratic orientation of industrial society. Since in this view ability is fairly equally distributed across social class, and since actual achievement is the criterion for access to occupational roles, differences of birth tend toward economic irrelevance. Since whatever social-class based differences exist in an individual's "natural" aspirations to social status are minimized by the competitive orientation of schooling, expanding education represents a potent instrument toward the efficient and equitable distribution of jobs, income, and status. If inequalities remain at the end of this process, they must simply be attributed to inevitable human differences in intellectual capacities or patterns of free choice.

Thus as long as schooling is free and universal, the process of economic expansion will not only be consistent with the use of education as an instrument for personal development and social equality; economic expansion, by requiring educational expansion, will necessarily enhance the power of education to achieve these ends. So the argument goes.[14]

If we accept for the moment the compatibility of various functions of education, we are confronted with a second group of questions concerning the power of education to counteract opposing tendencies in the larger society. If the educational system is to be a central social corrective, the issue of its potential efficacy is crucial to the establishment of the liberal outlook. Dewey does not withdraw from this issue:

...The school environment...establishes a purified medium of action.... As society becomes more enlightened, it realizes that it is responsible not to transmit and conserve the whole of its existing achievements but only such which make for a better future society. The school is its chief agency for the accomplishment of this end.[15]

But such generalizations cannot substitute for direct confrontation with the thorny and somewhat disreputable facts of economic life. In the reality of industrial society, can the school environment promote either human development or social equality? Self-development may be compatible with ideal work roles, but can education change the seamy realities of the workaday world? Equality may be compatible with the other functions of education, but can the significant and pervasive system of racial, class, and sexual stratification be significantly modified by "equal schooling"?

Early liberals viewing the rising industrial capitalist system of the eighteenth and early nineteenth centuries did not ignore the dehumanizing conditions of work. Adam Smith, betraying his celebrated respect for the working person, notes:

> In the progress of the division of labor, the employment of the far greater part of those who live by labor...comes to be confined to a few very simple operations.... But the understandings of the greater part of men are necessarily formed by their ordinary employments.... [A man employed) generally becomes as stupid and ignorant as it is possible for a human creature to become.[16]

Yet he did believe that social policy could successfully counter the deleterious effects on the individual worker's development:

> His dexterity in his own particular trade seems...to be acquired at the expense of his intellectual, social and martial virtues. But in every improved and civilized society this is

the state into which the laboring poor...must necessarily fall, unless government takes some pains to prevent it.[17]

But modern liberal commentary has been less optimistic about the power of the educational environment to offset the dehumanizing conditions of work. Twentieth-century liberals have preferred to argue that proper education could improve the work environment directly by supplying experts with "well-balanced social interests." According to Dewey:

> ...The tendency to reduce such things as efficiency of activity and scientific management to purely technical externals is evidence of the one-sided stimulation of thought given to those in control of industry—those who supply its aims. Because of their lack of all-around and well-balanced social interests, there is not sufficient stimulus for attention to the human factors in relationships in industry.[18]

This balance would be supplemented by the natural "desire and ability to share in social control" on the part of educated workers:

> ...A right educational use of [science] would react upon intelligence and interest so as to modify, in connection with legislation and administration, the socially obnoxious features of the present industrial and commercial order.... It would give those who engage in industrial callings desire and ability to share in social control, and ability to become masters of their industrial fate.[19]

This approach became a fundamental tenet of educational reformers in the Progressive Era. Education, thought Dewey, could promote the natural movement of industrial society toward more fulfilling work, hence bringing its integrative and developmental functions increasingly into a harmonious union.

To complete our exposition of liberal theory, we must discuss the power of the educational system to promote social equality. For Dewey, of course, this power derives from the necessary association of personal growth and democracy—whose extension to all parts of the citizenry is a requisite of social development itself. In the technocratic version of liberal theory, however, the egalitarian power of the educational system is not automatically fulfilled. Were economic success dependent on race or sex, or upon deeply rooted differences in human character, the ability of schooling to increase social mobility would of course be minimal. But according to the modern liberal view, this is not the case. And where equal access is not sufficient, then enlightened policy may devise special programs for the education of the poor: job training, compensatory education, and the like.

Poverty and inequality, in this view, are the consequences of individual choice or personal inadequacies, not the normal outgrowths of our economic institutions. The problem, clearly, is to fix up the people, not to change the economic structures which regulate their lives. This, indeed, is the meaning of the "social power" of schools to promote equality.

Despite persistent setbacks in practice, the liberal faith in the equalizing power of schooling has dominated both intellectual and policy circles. Education has been considered not only a powerful tool for self-development and social integration; it has been seen, at least since Horace Mann coined the phrase well over a century ago, as the "great equalizer."

## EDUCATION AND INEQUALITY

Universal education is the power, which is destined to overthrow every species of hierarchy. It is destined to remove all artificial inequality and leave the natural inequalities to find their true level. With the artificial inequalities of caste, rank, title, blood, birth, race, color, sex, etc., will fall nearly all the

oppression, abuse, prejudice. enmity, and injustice, that humanity is now subject to.— Lester Frank Ward, *Education* c. 1872

A review of educational history hardly supports the optimistic pronouncements of liberal educational theory. The politics of education are better understood in terms of the need for social control in an unequal and rapidly changing economic order. The founders of the modern U.S. school system understood that the capitalist economy produces great extremes of wealth and poverty, of social elevation and degradation. Horace Mann and other school reformers of the antebellum period knew well the seamy side of the burgeoning industrial and urban centers. "Here," wrote Henry Barnard, the first state superintendent of education in both Connecticut and Rhode Island, and later to become the first U.S. Commissioner of Education, "the wealth, enterprise and professional talent of the state are concentrated...but here also are poverty, ignorance, profligacy and irreligion, and a classification of society as broad and deep as ever divided the plebeian and patrician of ancient Rome."[20] They lived in a world in which, to use de Tocqueville's words, "...small aristocratic societies...are formed by some manufacturers in the midst of the immense democracy of our age [in which]...some men are opulent and a multitude...are wretchedly poor."[21] The rapid rise of the factory system, particularly in New England, was celebrated by the early school reformers; yet, the alarming transition from a relatively simple rural society to a highly stratified industrial economy could not be ignored. They shared the fears that de Tocqueville had expressed following his visit to the United States in 1831:

When a work man is unceasingly and exclusively engaged in the fabrication of one thing, he ultimately does his work with singular dexterity; but at the same time he loses the general faculty of applying his mind to the direction of the work.... [While] the science of manufacture lowers the class of workmen, it raises the class of masters.... [If] ever a permanent inequality of conditions...again penetrates into the world, it may be predicted that this is the gate by which they will enter.[22]

While deeply committed to the emerging industrial order, the far-sighted school reformers of the mid-nineteenth century understood the explosive potential of the glaring inequalities of factory life. Deploring the widening of social divisions and fearing increasing unrest, Mann, Barnard, and others proposed educational expansion and reform. In his Fifth Report as Secretary of the Massachusetts Board of Education, Horace Mann wrote:

> Education, then beyond all other devices of human origin, is the great equalizer of the conditions of men—the balance wheel of the social machinery.... It does better than to disarm the poor of their hostility toward the rich; it prevents being poor.[23]

Mann and his followers appeared to be at least as interested in disarming the poor as in preventing poverty. They saw in the spread of universal and free education a means of alleviating social distress without redistributing wealth and power or altering the broad outlines of the economic system. Education, it seems, had almost magical powers.

> The main idea set forth in the creeds of some political reformers, or revolutionizers, is, that some people are poor because others are rich. This idea supposed a fixed amount of property in the community...and the problem presented for solution is, how to transfer a portion of this property from those who are supposed to have too much to those who feel and know that they have too little. At this point, both their theory and their expectation of reform stop. But the beneficent power of education would not be exhausted, even though it should peaceably abolish all the miseries that spring from the coexistence,

side by side of enormous wealth, and squalid want. It has a higher function. Beyond the power of diffusing old wealth, it has the prerogative of creating new.[24]

The early educators viewed the poor as the foreign element that they were. Mill hands were recruited throughout New England, often disrupting the small towns in which textile and other rapidly growing industries had located. Following the Irish potato famine of the 1840s, thousands of Irish workers settled in the cities and towns of the northeastern United States. Schooling was seen as a means of integrating this "uncouth and dangerous" element into the social fabric of American life. The inferiority of the foreigner was taken for granted. The editors of the influential *Massachusetts Teacher*, a leader in the educational reform movement, writing in 1851, saw "...the increasing influx of foreigners..." as a moral and social problem:

> Will it, like the muddy Missouri, as it pours its waters into the clear Mississippi and contaminates the whole united mass, spread ignorance and vice, crime and disease, through our native population?
>
> If...we can by any means purify this foreign people, enlighten their ignorance and bring them up to our level, we shall perform a work of true and perfect charity, blessing the giver and receiver in equal measure....
>
> With the old not much can be done; but with their children, the great remedy is *education*. The rising generation must be taught as our own children are taught. We say *must be* because in many cases this can only be accomplished by coercion.[25]

Since the mid-nineteenth century the dual objectives of educational reformers—equality of opportunity and social control—have been intermingled, the merger of these two threads sometimes so nearly complete that it becomes impossible to distinguish between the two. Schooling has been at once something done for the poor and to the poor.

The basic assumptions which underlay this comingling helps explain the educational reform movement's social legacy. First, educational reformers did not question the fundamental economic institutions of capitalism: Capitalist ownership and control of the means of production and dependent wage labor were taken for granted. In fact, education was to help preserve and extend the capitalist order. The function of the school system was to accommodate workers to its most rapid possible development. Second, it was assumed that people (often classes of people or "races") are differentially equipped by nature or social origins to occupy the varied economic and social levels in the class structure. By providing equal opportunity, the school system was to elevate the masses, guiding them sensibly and fairly to the manifold political, social, and economic roles of adult life.

Jefferson's educational thought strikingly illustrates this perspective. In 1779, he proposed a two-track educational system which would prepare individuals for adulthood in one of the two classes of society: the "laboring and the learned."[26] Even children of the laboring class would qualify for qualify for leadership. Scholarships would allow "...those persons whom nature hath endowed with genius and virtue..." to "...be rendered by liberal education worthy to receive and able to guard the sacred deposit of the rights and liberties of their fellow citizen."[27] Such a system, Jefferson asserted, would succeed in "...raking a few geniuses from the rubbish."[28] Jefferson's two-tiered educational plan presents in stark relief the outlines and motivation for the stratified structure of U.S. education which has endured up to the present. At the top, there is the highly selective aristocratic tradition, the elite university training future leaders. At the base is mass education for all, dedicated to uplift and control. The two traditions have always coexisted although their meeting point has drifted upward over the years, as mass education has spread upward from elementary school through high school, and now up to the post-high-school level.

Though schooling was consciously molded to reflect the class structure, education was seen as a means of enhancing wealth and morality which would work to the advantage of all. Horace Mann, in his 1842 report to the State Board of Education, reproduced this comment by a Massachusetts industrialist:

> The great majority always have been and probably always will be comparatively poor, while a few will possess the greatest share of the world's goods. And it is a wise provision of Providence which connects so intimately, and as I think so indissolubly, the greatest good of the many with the highest interest in the few.[29]

Much of the content of education over the past century and a half can only be construed as an unvarnished attempt to persuade the "many" to make the best of the inevitable.

The unequal contest between social control and social justice is evident in the total functioning of U.S. education. The system as it stands today provides eloquent testimony to the ability of the well-to-do to perpetuate in the name of equality of opportunity an arrangement which consistently yields to themselves disproportional advantages, while thwarting the aspirations and needs of the working people of the United States. However grating this judgment may sound to the ears of the undaunted optimist, it is by no means excessive in light of the massive statistical data on inequality in the United States. Let us look at the contemporary evidence.

We may begin with the basic issue of inequalities in years of schooling. As can be seen in Figure 1, the number of years of schooling attained by an individual is strongly associated with parental socioeconomic status. This figure presents the estimated distribution of years of schooling attained by individuals of varying socioeconomic backgrounds. If we define socioeconomic background by a weighted sum of income, occupation, and educational level of the parents, a child from the ninetieth percentile may expect, on the average, five more years of schooling than a child in the tenth percentile.[30]

A word about our use of statistics is in order. Most of the statistical calculations which we will present have been published with full documentation in academic journals. We provide some of the relevant technical information in our footnotes and Appen-

dix. However, those interested in gaining a more detailed understanding of our data and methods are urged to consult our more technical articles.

The data, most of which was collected by the U.S. Census Current Population Survey in 1962, refers to "non-Negro" males, aged 25–64 years, from "non-farm" background in the experienced labor force."[31] We have chosen a sample of white males because the most complete statistics are available for this group. Moreover, if inequality for white

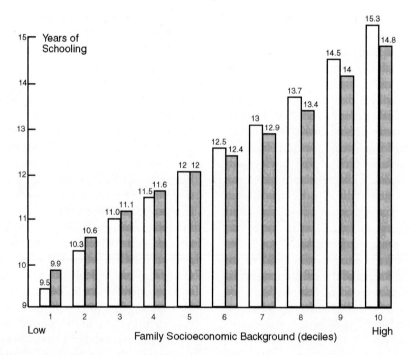

**FIGURE 1**
**Educational Attainments Are Strongly Dependent on Social Background Even for People of Similar Childhood IQs**

*Notes:* For each socioeconomic group, the left-hand bar indicates the estimated average number of years of schooling attained by all men from that group. The right-hand bar indicates the estimated average number of years of schooling attained by men with IQ scores equal to the average for the entire sample. The sample refers to "non-Negro" men of "nonfarm" backgrounds, aged 35–44 years in 1962.[36]

*Source:* Samuel Bowles and Valerie Nelson, "'The Inheritance of IQ,' and the Intergenerational Transmission of Economic Inequality," *The Review of Economics and Statistics,* Vol. LVI, No. 1. February 1974. Reprinted by permission.

males can be documented, the proposition is merely strengthened when sexual and racial differences are taken into account.

Additional census data dramatize one aspect of educational inequalities: the relationship between family income and college attendance. Even among those who had graduated from high school in the early 1960s, children of families earning less than $3,000 per year were over six times as likely *not* to attend college as were the children of families earning over $15,000.[32] Moreover, children from less well-off families are *both* less likely to have graduated from high school and more likely to attend inexpensive, two-year community colleges rather than a four-year B.A. program if they do make it to college.[33]

Not surprisingly, the results of schooling differ greatly for children of different social backgrounds. Most easily measured, but of limited importance, are differences in scholastic achievement. If we measure the output of schooling by scores on nationally standardized achievement tests, children whose parents were themselves highly educated outperform the children of parents with less education by a wide margin. Data collected for the U.S. Office of Education Survey of Educational Opportunity reveal, for example, that among white high school seniors, those whose parents were in the top education decile were, on the average, well over three grade levels in measured scholastic achievement ahead of those whose parents were in the bottom decile.[34]

Given these differences in scholastic achievement, inequalities in years of schooling among individuals of different social backgrounds are to be expected. Thus one might be tempted to argue that the close dependence of years of schooling attained on background displayed in the left-hand bars of Figure 1 is simply a reflection of unequal intellectual abilities, or that inequalities in college attendance are the consequences of differing levels of scholastic achievement in

high school and do not reflect any additional social class inequalities peculiar to the process of college admission.

This view, so comforting to the admissions personnel in our elite universities, is unsupported by the data, some of which is presented in Figure 1. The right-hand bars of Figure 1 indicate that even among children with identical IQ test scores at ages six and eight, those with rich, well-educated, high-status parents could expect a much higher level of schooling than those with less-favored origins. Indeed, the closeness of the left-hand and right-hand bars in Figure 1 shows that only a small portion of the observed social class differences in educational attainment is related to IQ differences across social classes.[35] The dependence of education attained on background is almost as strong for individuals with the same IQ as for all individuals. Thus, while Figure 1 indicates that an individual in the ninetieth percentile in social class background is likely to receive five more years of education than an individual in the tenth percentile; it also indicated that he is likely to receive 4.25 more years schooling than an individual from the tenth percentile with the same IQ. Similar results are obtained when we look specifically at access to college education for students with the same measured IQ. Project Talent data indicates that for "high ability" students (top 25 percent as measured by a composite of tests of "general aptitude"), those of high socioeconomic background (top 25 percent as measured by a composite of family income, parents' education, and occupation) are nearly twice as likely to attend college than students of low socioeconomic background (bottom 25 percent). For "low ability" students (bottom 25 percent), those of high social background are more than four times as likely to attend college as are their low social background counterparts.[37]

Inequality in years of schooling is, of course, only symptomatic of broader inequalities in the educational system. Not only do less well-off children go to school for fewer years, they are treated with less attention (or more precisely, less benevolent attention) when they are there. These broader inequalities are not easily measured. Some show up in statistics on the different levels of expenditure for the education of children of different socioeconomic backgrounds. Taking account of the inequality in financial resources for each year in school and the inequality in years of schooling obtained, Jencks estimated that a child whose parents were in the top fifth of the income distribution receives roughly twice the educational resources in dollar terms as does a child whose parents are in the bottom fifth.[38]

The social class inequalities in our school system, then, are too evident to be denied. Defenders of the educational system are forced back on the assertion that things are getting better; the inequalities of the past were far worse. And, indeed, there can be no doubt that some of the inequalities of the past have been mitigated. Yet new inequalities have apparently developed to take their place, for the available historical evidence lends little support to the idea that our schools are on the road to equality of educational opportunity. For example, data from a recent U.S. Census survey reported in Spady indicate that graduation from college has become no less dependent on one's social background. This is true despite the fact that high-school graduation is becoming increasingly equal across social classes.[39] Additional data confirm this impression. The statistical association (coefficient of correlation) between parents' social status and years of education attained by individuals who completed their schooling three or four decades ago is virtually identical to the same correlation for individuals who terminated their schooling in recent years.[40] On balance, the available data suggest that the number of years of school attained by a child depends upon family background as much in the recent period as it did fifty years ago.

Thus, we have empirical reasons for doubting the egalitarian impact of schooling. But what of those cases when education has been equalized? What has been the effect? We will investigate three cases: the historical decline in the inequality among individuals in years of school attained, the explicitly compensatory educational programs of the War on Poverty, and the narrowing of the black/white gap in average years of schooling attained.

Although family background has lost none of its influence on how far one gets up the educational ladder, the historical rise in the minimum legal school-leaving age has narrowed the distance between the top and bottom rungs. Inequality of educational attainments has fallen steadily and substantially over the past three decades.[41] And has this led to a parallel equalization of the distribution of income? Look at Figure 2. The reduction in the inequality of years of schooling has not been matched by an equalization of the U.S. income distribution.[42] In fact, a recent U.S. Labor Department study indicates that as far as labor earnings (wages and salaries) are concerned, the trend since World War II has been unmistakenly away from equality. And it is precisely inequality in labor earnings which is the target of the proponents of egalitarian school reforms.[43] But does the absence of an overall trend toward income equality mask in equalizing thrust of schooling that was offset by other disequalizing tendencies? Perhaps, but Jacob Mincer and Barry Chiswick of the National Bureau of Economic Research, in a study of the determinants of inequality in the United States, concluded that the significant reduction in schooling differences among white male adults would have had the effect—even if operating in isolation— of reducing income inequality by a negligible amount.[44]

Next, consider that group of explicitly egalitarian educational programs brought together in the War on Poverty. In a systematic economic survey of these programs, Thomas Ribich concludes that with very few excep-

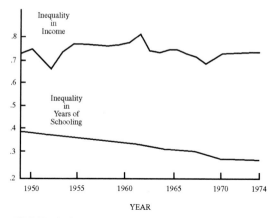

YEAR

**FIGURE 2**
**Equalization of Education Has Not Been Associated with Equalization of Income**

*Notes:* The upper line shows the trend over time in the degree of inequality of income, as measured by the standard deviation of the natural logarithm of annual income of males aged twenty-five or older. The lower line shows the trend over time in the degree of inequality of years of schooling, as measured by the coefficient of variation (the standard deviation divided by the mean) of the years of schooling attained by males aged twenty-five and older. Data for 1970 to 1974 are estimates based on U.S. Census data.

*Source:* Barry Chiswick and Jacob Mincer, "Time Series Changes in Personal Income Inequality in the U.S.," *Journal of Political Economy*, Vol. 80. No. 3. Part II (May-June 1972). © 1972 by the University of Chicago. Reprinted by permission of the publisher, University of Chicago Press.

tions, the economic payoff to compensatory education is low.[45] So low, in fact, that in a majority of cases studied, direct transfers of income to the poor would have accomplished considerably more equalization than the educational programs in question. The major RAND Corporation study by Averch came to the same conclusion.

Lastly, consider racial inequalities. In 1940, most black male workers (but a minority of whites) earned their livelihoods in the South, by far the poorest region; the education gap between nonwhites and whites was 3.3 years (38 percent of median white education).[46] By 1972, blacks had moved to more affluent parts of the country, and the educa-

tion gap was reduced to 18 percent (4 percent for young men aged 25–34 years).[47] Richard Freeman has shown that this narrowing of the education gap would have virtually achieved black/white income equality had blacks received the same benefits from education as whites.[48] Yet the income gap has not closed substantially: The income gap for young men is 30 percent, despite an education gap of only 4 percent.[49] Clearly as blacks have moved toward educational (and regional) parity with whites, other mechanisms—such as entrapment in center-city ghettos, the suburbanization of jobs, and perhaps increasing segmentation of labor markets—have intensified to maintain a more-or-less constant degree of racial income inequality. Blacks certainly suffer from educational inequality, but the root of their exploitation lies outside of education, in a system of economic power and privilege in which racial distinctions play an important role.

The same must be concluded of inequality of economic opportunity between men and women. Sexual inequality persists despite the fact that women achieve a level of schooling (measured in years) equivalent to men.

We conclude that U.S. education is highly unequal, the chances of attaining much or little schooling being substantially dependent on one's race and parents' economic level. Moreover, where there is a discernible trend toward a more equal educational system—as in the narrowing of the black education deficit, for example—the impact on the structure of economic opportunity is minimal at best. As we shall presently see, the record of the U.S. school system as a promoter of full human development is no more encouraging.

**EDUCATION AND PERSONAL DEVELOPMENT**

> The government of schools...should be *arbitrary*. By this mode of education we prepare our youth for the subordination of laws and

thereby qualify them for becoming good citizens of the republic. I am satisfied that the
most useful citizens have been formed from
those youth who have not known or felt their
own wills til they were one and twenty years
of age.—Benjamin Rush, 1786

School has never been much fun for children.
For parents as well, the school has often
seemed an alien world, hostile or indifferent
to the concerns of its charges. Indeed, the
annals of U.S. education exhibit what
amounts to an historical constant: the dreary
and rigid countenance of the school. With
the ground swell of muckraking journalism
in the decade of the 1890s, Joseph Mayer
Rice could rock the educational establishment with his "exposé" of the schools:

> The unkindly spirit of the teacher is strikingly
> apparent; the pupils, being completely subju-
> gated to her will, are silent and motionless,
> the spiritual atmosphere of the classroom is
> damp and chilly.[50]

Sensationalism? Hardly, at least to anyone
with firsthand knowledge of the schools of
the time. Yet sixty-eight years and a vigorous
reform movement later, Charles Silberman,
an editor of *Fortune* magazine and author of
a highly touted three-year Carnegie Foundation study of U.S. education, is pained to
find:

> ...The grim joyless places most American
> schools are, how oppressive and petty are the
> rules by which they are governed, how intel-
> lectually sterile and aesthetically barren the
> atmosphere, what an appalling lack of civility
> obtains on the part of the teachers and prin-
> cipals, what contempt they unconsciously
> display for children as children.[51]

Rice himself was particularly concerned
with the regimentation of students, with
teachers who "...blindly led their innocent
charges in singsong drill, rote repetition,
and, meaningless verbiage."[52] Relic of a pre-

vious age? Not quite. How unsettlingly similar is Silberman's description of typical classroom in the late 1960s. Singsong drill may
be out, but retained is the essence of regimentation:

> ...The slavish adherence to the time-table
> and lesson-plan, the obsession with routine
> *qua* routine, the absence of noise and move-
> ment, the joylessness and repression, the uni-
> versality of the formal lecture or teacher-
> dominated "discussion."[53]

Our argument in this section is simple
enough: Since its inception in the United
States, the public-school system has been
seen as a method of disciplining children in
the interest of producing a properly subordinate adult population. Sometimes conscious
and explicit, and at other times a natural
emanation from the conditions of dominance
and subordinacy prevalent in the economic
sphere, the theme of social control pervades
educational thought and policy. The forms
of school discipline, the position of the
teacher, and the moral conception of the
child have all changed over the years, but the
overriding objective has remained.

Unlike our modern educational critics, the
intellectual leaders of the New England Puritan communities thought little of children.
"You are all naturally in a miserable state and
condition," preached the cheery Jonathan
Edwards. "In a little while you will be in
eternity, some sooner and some later.... God
is angry with you every day. How dreadful to
have God angry with you.... Consider how it
will be when you come to die and are uncon-
verted." Children, it appeared, were ungod-
ly, altogether too playful, lacking in seriousness, and ill-disposed toward work. Worse
still, some parents appeared less than fully
committed to countering the natural tendencies of the young.

As early as 1647, the General Court (legislature) in Massachusetts invoked the power
of schooling to reinforce the moral training

of the family. The preamble of a law allowing local taxation for the support of public schools in that year outlined the evident need for such legislation:

> It being one chief project of that ould deluder, Satan, to keepe men from the knowledge of the Scriptures, as in former times by keeping them in an unknown tongue, so in these latter times by perswading from the uses of tongues, that so at lease the true sence and meaning of the originall might be clouded by false glosses of saint seeming deceivers....[54]

Not much came of the legislation, but the view that children needed some special disciplining to root out their susceptibility to error persisted. On the eve of the "Common School Revival" in 1834, Federalist Judge Joseph Story advised teachers to "...repress the inordinate love of innovation of the young, the ignorant, and the restless."[55]

That the school could supplement the beneficial effects of family upbringing, first voiced by the Puritan educators, became commonplace in the nineteenth century as the influx of immigrant workers threatened to "dilute" Yankee morality. Turn-of-the-century educational theorist Edward A. Ross stated the mission of schools succinctly, namely:

> ...to collect little plastic lumps of human dough from private households and shape them on the social kneadingboard.[56]

A statement signed by seventy-seven college presidents and city and state school superintendents and published by the U.S. government in 1874 put the case this way:

> In order to compensate for lack of family nurture, the school is obliged to lay more stress upon discipline and to make far more prominent the moral phase of education. It is obliged to train the pupil into habits of prompt obedience to his teachers and the practice of self control in its various forms.[57]

While the educational practice of regimentation of children has persisted, the fundamentalist conception of a child as immoral or savage has given way, through various stages, to a more appreciative view. To modern educators, the child appears as the primitive embodiment of the good and the natural—the noble savage, if you will. Children are spontaneous and joyful, unpredictable and trusting—traits to be cherished but sadly evanescent in the path toward maturity.[58]

At the same time, the educator's view of the family has changed. Once the trusted engine of moral training for youth, to which the school was considered a complement and ballast, the family increasingly appears in the writings of educators as the source of the child's inadequacy. Thus in the thought of the culture of poverty and cultural deprivation advocates, the school has been elevated to the status of family surrogate in the well-engineered Society.[59] The social roots of this transformed concept of the family-school relationship have little to do with any alteration in family structure, and less to do with any heightening of the public morality. The impetus stems rather from the professional educator's profound mistrust of, and even fear of, the families of black and poor children, and in an earlier period, of Irish and other immigrant families.[60] Nor is this mistrust alien to the logic of social control. For all its nobility, the noble savage remains savage, and integration into the world of adults requires regimentation.

The most striking testimonial to the hegemony of the social-control ideology is perhaps its clear primacy even among those who opposed such obvious manifestations of the authoritarian classroom as corporal punishment and teacher-centered discussion. The most progressive of progressive educators have shared the common commitment to maintaining ultimate top-down control over the child's activities. Indeed, much of the educational experimentation of the past century can be viewed as attempting to broaden the discretion and deepen the involvement of the child while maintaining hierarchical control over the ultimate processes and outcomes of the educational encounter. The goal has been to enhance student motivation while withholding effective participation in the setting of priorities.

Hence, like the view of the child, the concept of discipline has itself changed. Two aspects of this change are particularly important. First, the once highly personalized authority of the teacher has become a part of the bureaucratic structure of the modern school. Unlike the teachers in the chaotic early nineteenth-century district schools, modern teachers exercise less personal power and rely more heavily on regulations promulgated by higher authorities. Although frequently prey to arbitrary intervention by parents and other community members, the nineteenth-century teacher was the boss of the classroom. The modern teacher is in a more ambiguous position. The very rules and regulations which add a patina of social authority to his or her commands at the same time rigidly circumscribe the teacher's freedom of action.

Second, the aim of discipline is no longer mere compliance: The aim is now "behavior modification." Prompt and obedient response to bureaucratically sanctioned authority is, of course, a must. But sheer coercion is out of keeping with both the modern educator's view of the child and the larger social needs for a self-controlled—not just controlled—citizenry and work force. Discipline is still the theme, but the variations more often center on the "internalization of behavioral norms," on equipping the child with a built-in supervisor than on mere obedience to external authority and material sanctions.[61]

The repressive nature of the schooling process is nowhere more clearly revealed than in the system of grading, the most basic process of allocating rewards within the school. We will have gone some distance toward comprehending the school as it is—in going behind the educational rhetoric—if we can answer the question: Who gets what and why?

Teachers are likely to reward those who conform to and strengthen the social order of the school with higher grades and approval, and punish violators with lower grades and other forms of disapproval, independent of their respective academic and cognitive accomplishments. This fact allows us to investigate exactly what personality traits, attitudes, and behavioral attributes are facilitated by the educational encounter.

Outside of gross disobedience, one would suspect the student's exhibition of creativity and divergence of thought to be most inimical to the smooth functioning of the hierarchical classroom. For the essence of the modern educational encounter is, to use Paolo Freire's words, that teaching:

> ...becomes an act of depositing, in which the students are the depositories and the teacher is the depositor. Instead of communicating, the teacher issues communiques and makes deposits which the student patiently receive, memorize, and repeat. This is the "banking" concept of education.... The teacher teaches and the students are taught.... The teacher chooses and enforces his choice and the students comply.... The teacher acts and the students have the illusion of acting through the action of the teacher.[62]

Others refer to this conception as the "jug and mug" approach to teaching whereby the jug fills up the mugs.

Thus the hostility of the school system to student behavior even approaching critical consciousness should be evident in the daily lives of students. Getzels and Jackson[63] have shown that high school students perceive this to be the case. They subjected a group of 449 high school students to an IQ test and a battery of exams which purport to measure creativity.[64] They found no appreciable correlation between measured IQ and measured "creativity." The top 20 percent in IQ on the one hand, and in creativity on the other, were singled out and asked to rank certain personality traits (a) on the degree to which they would like to have these traits, and (b) on the degree to which they believed teachers would like the student to have. There was virtually complete agreement by the high IQ and the high creatives on which traits are preferred by teachers; in other words, these students view the demands made upon them in a similar way. However, the two groups disagreed on what traits they themselves would like to have: The correlation between the two groups' ratings of the personality traits "preferred for oneself" was quite low.[65] Most striking of all, however, was the finding that, while the high IQs' "preferred traits" correspond closely to their perception of the teachers' values, the high creatives' ranking of preferred traits was actually inversely related to the perceived teachers' ranking.[66] The high creatives do not fail to conform; rather they do not wish to conform.[67]

Getzel and Jackson's is but one of the many studies which link personality traits to school grades. We have undertaken a review of this literature, the results of which support the following interpretation.[68] Students are rewarded for exhibiting discipline, subordinacy, intellectually as opposed to emotionally oriented behavior, and hard work independent from intrinsic task motivation. Moreover, these traits are rewarded independently of any effect of "proper demeanor" on scholastic achievement.

Rather than plowing through this mass of data, we shall present the results of the most extensive of our sources. In the early 1960s, John L. Holland undertook a study of the determinants of high school success among a group of 639 National Merit Scholarship finalists—males for the most part in the top 10 percent of students in IQ and the top 15 percent in class rank.[69] Holland collected four objective measures of cognitive development from his subjects' College En-

trance Examination Board tests.[70] In addition, he collected some sixty-five measures of personality, attitude, self-concept, creativity, and home life through testing the students, their parents, and obtaining various ratings from their teachers.[71]

We have extensively analyzed this massive body of data.[72] Our first conclusion is that, while the group's high academic rank is doubtless related to their above-average IQs, differences in scholastic achievement among them were not significantly related to their grades, despite a good deal of variation in both achievement and grades within the group. More telling, however, is the fact that many of the personality variables were significantly and positively related to grades. Most important were the teachers' ratings of the students' *Citizenship* and the students' self-evaluation of *Drive to Achieve*.[73] Neither of these variables had any significant impact on actual achievement measures!

These results are not in themselves surprising. It is to be expected that students will be rewarded for their conformity to the social order of the school *(Citizenship)* as well as their personal motivation to succeed within the nexus of this social order *(Drive to Achieve)*. Only the most naive would expect school grades to depend on scholastic achievement alone.

But what do *Citizenship and Drive to Achieve* really reflect? In a liberated educational encounter, we would expect these traits to embody some combination of diligence, social popularity, creativity, and mental flexibility. Yet statistical analysis of the Holland data reveals a strikingly different pattern. Students who are ranked by their teachers as high on *Citizenship* and *Drive to Achieve* are indeed more likely to be diligent (e.g., they are high on such measures as *Deferred Gratification, Perseverance,* and *Control*) and socially popular (e.g., they are high on *Social Leadership* and *Popularity*). But they are, in fact, significantly below average on measures of creativity and mental flexibility (e.g., they are low on such measures as *Cognitive Flexibility, Complexity of Thought, Originality, Creativity,* and *Independence of Judgment*).[74] Moreover, further statistical analysis shows that these same traits of creativity and mental flexibility are directly penalized in terms of school grades, holding constant test scores, *Citizenship,* and *Drive to Achieve.*

The conclusions from this body of data seem inescapable. Conformity to the social order of the school involves submission to a set of authority relationships which are inimical to personal growth. Instead of promoting a healthy balance among the capacity for creative autonomy, diligence, and susceptibility to social regulation, the reward system of the school inhibits those manifestations of personal capacity which threaten hierarchical authority.

We have emphasized elements on the "hidden curriculum" faced in varying degrees by all students. But schools do different things to different children. Boys and girls, blacks and whites, rich and poor are treated differently. Affluent suburban schools, working-class schools, and ghetto schools all exhibit a distinctive pattern of sanctions and rewards. Moreover, most of the discussion here has focused on high-school students. In important ways, colleges are different; and community colleges exhibit social relations of education which differ sharply from those of elite four-year institutions. In short, U.S. education is not monolithic; our analysis will be expanded accordingly in future chapters.

Why do schools reward docility, passivity, and obedience? Why do they penalize creativity and spontaneity? Why the historical constancy of suppression and domination in an institution so central to the elevation of youth? Surely this is a glaring anomaly in terms of traditional liberal educational theory. The naive enthusiasm of the contemporary free-school movement suggests the implicit assumption that no one had ever tried to correct this situation—that the ideal of liber-

ated education is simply a new conception which has never been tried. Even sophisticated critics, such as Charles Silberman, tend to attribute the oppressiveness of schooling to simple oversight and irrationality:

> What is mostly wrong with public schools is not due to venality or indifference or stupidity but to mindlessness.... It simply never occurs to more than a handful, to ask why they are doing what they are doing to think seriously or deeply about the purposes or consequences of education.[75]

Yet, the history of the progressive-education movement attests to the intransigence of the educational system to "enlightened change" within the context of corporate capitalism.

Progressivism has been the keynote of modern educational theory embracing such pillars of intellect and influence as John Dewey, Charles W. Elliot, Alfred North Whitehead, William James, and G. Stanley Hall. The birth of the Association for the Advancement of Progressive Education in 1918 was merely the political codification of an already active social movement whose aim, in the words of its founder Stanwood Cobb, "...had little of modesty.... We aimed at nothing short of changing the entire school system of America."[76] Subscribing to Dewey's dictum that "...education is the fundamental method of social reform,..." the statement of principles of the Association for the Advancement of Progressive Education held its aim to be "...the freest and fullest development of the individual, based upon the scientific study of his mental, physical, spiritual, and social characteristics and needs."[77] However avant-garde today's liberal educationists feel themselves to be, they envision little more than did the Progressives in the dawning years of the century. Schooling was to provide the child with the freedom to develop "naturally" with a teacher as guide, not taskmaster. Intrinsic interest not external authority was to motivate all work. The leitmotif of the day was "taking the lid off kids," and the aim was to sublimate natural creative drives in fruitful directions rather than to repress them. Emotional and intellectual development were to hold equal importance, and activity was to be "real life" and "student-directed."

The mass media dramatically attest to the ideological victory of the Progressives: Professional journals, education textbooks, and even the various publications of the U.S. Office of Education mouthed the rhetoric of Progressivism. As Lawrence A. Cremin, a foremost historian of the Progressive Movement in education, notes:

> There is a "conventional wisdom"...in education...and by the end of World War II progressivism had come to be that conventional wisdom. Discussions of educational policy were liberally spiced with phrases like "recognized individual differences," "personality development," "the whole child," "the needs of learners," "intrinsic motivation," "persistent life situations," "bridging the gap between home and school," "Teaching children, not subjects," "adjusting the school to the child," "real-life experiences," "teacher pupil relationships," and "staff planning." Such phrases...signified that Dewey's forecast of the day when progressive education would eventually be accepted as good education had now finally come to pass.[78]

Yet the schools have changed little in substance.

Thus we must reject mindlessness along with venality, indifference, and stupidity as the source for oppressive education. A more compelling explanation of the failure to combat repression in U.S. schooling is simply that progressive education, though triumphant in educational theory, was never given a chance in practice. Indeed, this argument is often used by those adhering to the liberal perspective. Thus Raymond E. Callahan traces the failure of Progressivism to the growing preoccupation with order and efficiency in educational practice at the same time that progressive education was capturing hearts and minds in educational theory. Callahan argues that:

> ...Very much of what has happened in American education since 1900 can be explained on the basis of the extreme vulnerability of our schoolmen to public criticism and pressure and that this vulnerability is built into our pattern of local support and control.[79]

The direction the formal educational system took in this situation was dictated by the power of business interests and the triumphant ideology of "efficient management." Again Callahan:

> What was unexpected [in my investigation] was the extent not only of the power of the business-industrial groups, but of the strength of the business ideology.... I had expected more professional autonomy and I was completely unprepared for that extent and degree of capitulation by administrators to whatever demands were made upon them.[80]

This vulnerability had great implications for student, teacher, and administrator alike. "Business methods" in schools meant that administrator were to be recruited from the ranks of politicians and especially businessmen, rather than professional educators, and their orientation was toward cost-saving and control rather than quality of education. Business methods also meant that the teacher was to be reduced to the status of a simple worker, with little control over curriculum, activities, or discipline, and whose accountability to the administrator again involved classroom authority rather than the quality of classroom experience. Lastly, the student was reduced to an "object" of administration, "busy-work," and standardized tests coming to prevail over play and self-development.

In short, the history of twentieth-century education is the history not of Progressivism but of the imposition upon the schools of "business values" and social relationships reflecting the pyramid of authority and privilege in the burgeoning capitalist system. The evolution of U.S. education during this period was not guided by the sanguine statements of John Dewey and Jane Addams, who saw a reformed educational system eliminating the more brutal and alienating aspects of industrial labor. Rather, the time motion orientation of Frederick Taylor and "Scientific Management," with its attendant fragmentation of tasks, and imposition of bureaucratic forms and top-down control held sway.

Thus there are some grounds for the opinion that the modern liberal view of the self-development capacities of schooling has not been falsified by recent U.S. experience; rather, it has never been tried. A historian of Progressivism in U.S. education might well echo Gandhi's assessment of Western civilization: "It would be a good idea."

## A PREFACE TO THE CRITIQUE OF LIBERAL EDUCATIONAL REFORM

> Ignorance is the mother of industry as well as of superstition. Reflection and fancy are subject to err; but a habit of moving the hand or the foot is independent of either. Manufacture, accordingly, prospers most where the mind is least consulted, and where the workshop may...be considered an engine, the parts of which are men.—Adam Ferguson, *An Essay on the History of Civil Society*, 1767

Decades of broken promises cast strong doubt on modern liberal educational theory. But the anomalies which arise when theory and practice are juxtaposed cannot lay it finally to rest. As Thomas Kuhn has noted, even in the phsyical sciences, only a recognizably superior alternative seals the fate of faulty but generally accepted dogma.[81]

All the more true is this observation in the social sciences. In the case of liberal educational theory, the failures of educational reform we have presented are by no means decisive. The "necessary connection" among the integrative, egalitarian, and developmental functions of education may appear only in the long run. Capitalism may still be young, and does seem to promote a rhetoric of tolerance and egalitarianism, as well as a supreme emphasis on individualism and human development. That this rhetoric is consistently thwarted in practice may simply represent a perverse institutional inertia. While educational policy has failed in the past, maturity and increased expertise may render it vastly more potent in the future. No one ever claimed reform to be easy—only ultimately possible with proper dedication. Finally, there may be tangible limits—technologically determined—to the degree of social mobility, due to inherent differences in mental ability. The possibility has been asserted forcefully by such writers as Arthur Jensen and Richard Herrnstein.[82]

In short, decent respect for liberal theory demands it be critiqued on theoretical grounds as well as in terms of the social outcomes it predicts, and, preferably, with an alternative in mind. This will be our goal. While detailed presentation of our alternative will await future chapters, our argument may be summarized simply enough here: the failure of progressive educational reforms stems from the contradictory nature of the objectives of its integrative, egalitarian and developmental functions in a society whose economic life is governed by the institutions of corporate capitalism.

Both the democratic and technocratic versions of liberal education theory focus on the relationships into which individuals enter upon adulthood. In Dewey's democratic version, political life is singled out as central, while for the technocratic version, the technical aspects of production hold the honored position. Both have been blind to—or at least treated in quite unrealistic manner—the social relationships of capitalist production. Dewey's overall framework seems eminently correct. His error lies in characterizing the social system as democratic, whereas, in fact, the hierarchical division of labor in the capitalist enterprise is politically autocratic. Moreover, his central thesis as to the economic value of an educational system devoted to fostering personal growth is untrue in capitalist society. Dewey's view requires that work be a natural extension of intrinsically motivated activity. The alienated work of corporate life is inimical to instrinsic motivation.

In corporate capitalist society, the social relations of production conform, by and large, to the "hierarchical division of labor," characterized by power and control emanating from the top downward through a finely graduated bureaucratic order.[83] The social relationships of the typically bureaucratic corporate enterprise require special attention because they are neither democratic nor technical.

For Dewey, democracy is, in essence, "...a mode of conjoint communicative experience..." which "...repudiates the principle of external authority...in favor of voluntary disposition and interest." In this sense, the dominant forms of work for which the educational system prepares youth are profoundly antidemocratic. Under capitalism, work is characterized not by conjoint, but by hierarchical "communicative experience," and rigid patterns of dominance and subordinacy, where personal interaction is dictated primarily by rules of procedure set by employers: Dewey"s "voluntary disposition" of the worker extends only over the decision to work or starve.

Dewey is of course aware of the undemocratic control of production in capitalist society; indeed, he refers explicitly to "...those in control of industry—those who supply its aims." But he avoids the fatal consequence of this admission for his theory by de-emphasizing democratic process and focusing on outcomes: the quality of the decision made by industrial aristocrats. The dehumanized nature of work—in Dewey's time, exemplified by Taylorism and time-motion studies, and today, by the "human relations" school of organizational theory—is attributed to their "one-sided stimulations of thought," and hence responsive to liberal educational exposure. Here Dewey exhibits in raw form the liberal proclivity to locate the source of systemic failures in the shortcomings of individuals and to propose "expert" solutions which respect—even reinforce—the top-down control of social life under corporate capitalism.[84] Surely he could not have been unaware of the forces in a market-oriented economy forcing managerial decision continually toward profit maximization to which end secure hierachial authortiy and flexible control of the enterprise from the top are prime requisites.[85]

Similarly, the technocratic version of liberal educational theory suffers from an extremely partial characterization of the capitalist system. The major error in the technocratic school is its overemphasis on cognitive skills as the basic requirement of job adequacy. We shall show that cognitive requirements are by no means determinant, and indeed, can account for little of the association of education and economic success. Had the technocratic school looked at the social rather than the technical relations of production, it might have been more circumspect in asserting the compatibility of the integrative, egalitarian, and developmental functions of schooling. Indeed, it might have found that the way in which the school system performs its integrative function—through its production of stratified labor force for the capitalist enterprise—is inconsistent with its performance of either developmental or egalitarian functions. Focusing on cognitive variables, it cannot even entertain the idea that the correspondence between the social relations of prodution and the social relations of education—the essential mechanism of the integrative function of schooling—might preclude an egalitarian or truly humanistic education.

Thus the modern economy is a product of a social as well as a technical revolution. In the development of productive organization from precapitalist forms, through the relatively simple entrepreneur-worker relationship of the early factory system based on piecework, immediate supervision, and direct worker assessment to the modern complex, stratified, and bureaucratically ordered corporation or governmental organ, not simply the technical demands of work, but its social organization have changed drastically. Seen from the present, the Industrial Revolution may appear as a simple upgearing of the pace of technological change. From the point of view of those experiencing it, however, it constituted a thoroughgoing social upheaval involving not only radically new institutions in the governance of economic activity, but a radically different pattern of social interactions with demanding and pervasive requirements on the level of individual psychic functioning. Values, beliefs, modes of personal behavior, and patterns of social and economic loyalties were formed, transformed, and reproduced in the process of bringing the individual into line with the needs of capital accumulation and the extension of the wage-labor system.

## CONCLUSION

Of manufactures, of commerce, of both individual and national prosperity, nay even of science itself, the extended and abundant increase tends to complete the fatal circle: and, by decay, convulsion, anarchy, and misery, to produce a new and renovated order of things. In an advanced state of society, where the meridian is attained or passes, nothing can prevent or even protract the evil day, except the revivifying influence of education.—Thomas Bernard, "Extract from an Account of the Mendip Schools," *Report of the society for Bettering the Condition of the Poor,* 1799

The record of actual successes and failures of education as reform is not sufficient either to accept or to reject the liberal outlook. But it must be a point of departure in any serious inquiry into its potential contribution to social improvement. The record, as we have shown, is not encouraging. First, despite the concerted efforts of progressive educators of three generations, and despite the widespread assimilation of their vocabulary in the United States, schools, by and large, remain hostile to the individual's needs for personal development. Second, the history of U.S. education provides little support for the view that schools have been vehicles for the equalization of economic status or opportunity. Nor are they today. The proliferation of special programs for the equalization of educational opportunity had precious little impact on the structure of the U.S. education, and even less on the structure of income and opportunity in the U.S. economy. It is clear that education in the United States is simply too weak an influence on the distribution of economic status and opportunity to fulfill its promised mission as the Great Equalizer. Schooling remains a meager instrument in promoting full participation of racial minorities in the United States—indeed, even the expensive pilot projects in this direction seem to have failed rather spectacularly.

The educational system serves—through the correspondence of its social relations with those of economic life—to reproduce economic inequality and to distort personal development. Thus under corporate capitalism, the objectives of liberal educational reform are contradictory: It is precisely because of its role as producer of an alienated and stratified labor force that the educational system has developed its repressive and unequal structure. In the history of U.S. education, it is the intergrative function which has dominated the purpose of schooling, to the detriment of the other liberal objectives.

More fundamentally, the contradictory nature of liberal educational reform objectives may be directly traced to the dual role imposed on education in the interests of profitability and stability; namely, enhancing workers' productive capacities and perpetuating the social, political, and economic conditions for the transformation of the fruits of labor into capitalist profits. It is these overriding objectives of the capitalist class—not the ideals of liberal reformers—which have shaped the actuality of U.S. education and left little room for the school to facilitate the pursuit of equality or full human development. When education is viewed as an aspect of the reproduction of the capitalist division of labor, the history of school reforms in the United States appears less as a story of an enlightened but sadly unsuccessful corrective and more as an integral part of the process of capitalist growth itself.

We cannot rule out the possibility that a future dramatic and unprecedented shift toward equality of educational opportunity might act as a force for equality. Nor do we exclude the possibility that open classrooms and free schools might make a substantial contribution to a more liberating process of human development. Indeed, we strongly support reforms of this type is part of a general strategy of social and economic transformation. But to consider educational change in isolation from other social forces is altogether too hypothetical. The structure of U.S. education did not evolve in a vacuum; nor will it be changed, holding other things constant. Education has been historically a device for allocating individuals to economic positions, where inequality among the positions themselves is inherent in the hierachial division of labor, differences in the degree of monopoly power of various sectors of the economy, and the power of different occupational groups to limit the supply or increase the monetary returns to their services. Thus equalization of educational outcomes, rather than reducing inequality, would more likely simply shift the job of allocating individuals to economic positions to some other "institution." Similarly, a less repressive educational system will produce little more than the "job blues" unless it can make an impact upon the nature of work and the control over production.

This much, at least, we can say with some certainty: Repression, individual powerlessness, inequality of incomes, and inequality of opportunity did not originate historically in the educational system, nor do they derive from unequal and repressive schools today. The roots of repression and inequality lie in the structure and functioning of the capitalist economy. Indeed, we shall suggest in the next chapter that they characterize any modern economic system—including the socialist state—which denies people participatory control of economic life.

## ENDNOTES

1. John Tipple, *The Capitalist Revolution, 1800-1919* (New York: Pegasus, 1970); Robert H. Wiebe, *The Search for Order* (New York: Hill & Wang, 1967); G. Kolko, *The Triumph of Conservatism* (Chicago: Quadrangle Books, 1963); James Weinstein, *The Corporate Ideal in the Liberal State 1900–1918* (Boston: Beacon Press, 1968).
2. Henry J. Perkinson, *The Imperfect Panacea: American Faith in Education, 1865–1965* (New York: Random House, 1968).
3. John Dewey, *Democracy and Education* (New York: The Free Press, 1966), p. 20.
4. *Ibid.*, pp. 50–53.
5. *Ibid.*, p. 87.
6. *Ibid.*, p. 76.
7. *Ibid.*, pp. 2, 88.

8. Theodore W. Schultz, "Investment in Poor People," *Seminar on Manpower Policy and Programs,* Office of Manpower Policy Evaluation Research, Washington: Department of Labor, 1966.

9. Harvey Averch *et al.,* "How Effective Is Schooling: A Critical Review and Synthesis of Research Findings" (Santa Monica: The Rand Corporation, 1972).

10. Samuel Bowles and Herbert Gintis, "IQ in the U.S. Class Structure," in *Social Policy,* November-December 1972 and January-February 1973. (This controversy will be reviewed in Chapter 4.)

11. Horace Mann as quoted in Michael Katz (ed.), *School Reform: Past and Present* (Boston: Little Brown and Company, 1971), p. 141.

12. *Ibid.,* p. 142.

13. *Ibid.,* pp. 146–147.

14. Arthur A. Jensen, "How Much Can We Boost IQ and Scholastic Achievement?" *Harvard Educational Review,* Vol. 39, No. 1, 1969; Richard Herrnstein, "IQ," *Atlantic Monthly,* Vol. 228, No. 3, September 1971; Edward C. Banfield, *The Unheavenly City* (Boston: Little, Brown and Company, 1968); Daniel P. Moynihan and Nathan Glazer, *Beyond the Melting Pot* (Cambridge, Mass.: MIT Press, 1970).

15. Dewey (1966), *op. cit.,* p. 20.

16. Adam Smith, *The Wealth of Nations* (New York: Modern Library, 1937). p. 734.

17. *Ibid.,* p. 735.

18. Dewey (1966), *op. cit.,* p. 85.

19. *Ibid.,* p. 320.

20. Henry Barnard, *Papers for the Teacher: 2nd Series* (New York: F. C. Brownell, 1866), pp. 293-310.

21. Alexis de Tocqueville, as quoted in Jeremy Breecher, *Strike!* (San Francisco: Straight Arrow Books, 1972), pp. xi, xii.

22. *Ibid.,* p. 172.

23. Horace Mann as quoted in Michael Katz, ed., *School Reform Past and Present* (Boston: Little Brown and Company, 1971), p. 141.

24. *Ibid.,* p. 145.

25. *The Massachusetts Teacher* (October 1851), quoted in Katz (1971), *op. cit.,* pp. 169–170.

26. David, Tyack, *Turning Points in American Educational History* (Waltham, Mass.: Blaisdell, 1967), p. 89.

27. *Ibid.,* p. 109.

28. *Ibid.,* p. 89.

29. Mann, quoted in Katz ( 1971), *op. cit.,* p. 147.

30. This calculation is based on data reported in full in Samuel Bowles and Valerie Nelson, "The 'Inheritance of IQ' and the Intergenerational Transmission of Economic Inequality," *The Review of Economics and Statistics,* Vol. LVI, No. 1, February 1974. It refers to non-Negro males from non-farm backgrounds, aged 35–44 years. The zero-order correlation coefficient between socioeconomic background and years of schooling was estimated at 0.646. The estimated standard deviation of years of schooling was 3.02. The results for other age groups are similar.

31. See Appendix A, footnote 14, in Chapter 4 and the following sources: Bowles and Nelson (1974), *op. cit.;* Peter Blau and Otis D. Duncan, *The American Occupational Structure* (New York: John Wiley, 1967); Otis D. Duncan, D. C. Featherman, and Beverly Duncan, *Socioeconomic Background and Occupational Achievement, Final Report,* Project No. S-0074 (EO-191) (Washington, D.C.: Department of Health, Education and Welfare, Office of Education, 1968); Samuel Bowles, "Schooling and Inequality from Generation to Generation," *The Journal of Political Economy,* Vol. 80, No. 3, Part II, May–June 1972.

32. These figures refer to individuals who were high-school seniors in October, 1965, and who subsequently graduated from high school. College attendance refers to both two- and four-year institutions. Family income is for the twelve months preceding October 1965. Data is drawn from U.S. Bureau of the Census, *Current Population Reports,* Series P–60, No. 183, May 1969.

33. For further evidence, see U.S. Bureau of the Census (1969), *op. cit.;* and Jerome Karabel, "Community Colleges and Social Stratification," *Harvard Educational Review,* Vol. 424, No. 42, November 1972.

34. Calculation based on data in James S. Coleman *et al., Equality of Educational Opportunity* (Washington, D.C.: U.S. Government Printing Office, 1966), and Bowles and Gintis (1972), *op. cit.*

35. The data relating to IQ are from a 1966 survey of veterans by the National Opinion Research Center: and from N. Bayley and E. S. Schaefer, "Correlations of Maternal and Child Behaviors with the Development of Mental Ability: Data from the Berkeley Growth Study," *Monographs of Social Research in Child Development*, 29, 6 (1964).

36. This figure is based on data reported in full in our Appendix A and in Bowles and Nelson (1974), *op. cit.* The left-hand bars of each pair were calculated using the estimated correlation coefficient between socioeconomic background and education of 0.65. The results for other age groups were similar: 0.64 for ages 25–34 and 44–54, and 0.60 for ages 55–64 years. The right-hand bars were calculated from the normalized regression coefficient on socioeconomic background from an equation using backgound and early childhood IQ to predict years of schooling, which was estimated at 0.54. The results for other age groups were similar: 0.54 for ages 25–34 and 45–54, and 0.48 for ages 55–64. Socioeconomic background is defined as normalized sum of father's education, father's occupational status, and parents' income. The mean and standard deviation of years of schooling were estimated at 11.95 and 3.02, respectively.

37. Based on a large sample of U.S. high-school students as reported in: John C. Flannagan and William. W. Cooley, *Project Talent, One Year Follow-up Study*, Cooperative Research Project, No. 2333, University of Pittsburgh: School of Education, 1966.

38. Christopher Jencks *et al., Inequality: A Reassessment of the Effects of Family and Schooling in America* (New York: Basic Books, 1972), p. 48.

39. William L. Spady, "Educational Mobility and Access: Growth and Paradoxes," in *American Journal of Sociology*, Vol. 73, No. 3, November 1967; and Blau and Duncan, *op. cit.* (1967).

40. Blau and Duncan (1967), *op. cit.* See the reported correlations in Appendix A.

41. We estimate the coefficient of variation of years of schooling at about 4.3 in 1940 (relying on Barry Chiswick and Jacob Mincer, "Time Series Changes in Personal Income Inequality in the U.S." *Journal of Political Economy*, Vol. 80, No. 3, Part II [May–June 1972], Table 4 for the standard deviation of schooling and the Decennial Census for the mean), and at 2.95 in 1969 (relying on Chiswick and Mincer [1972] Table B10).

42. Calculated from Table B1 and Table B10 in Chiswick and Mincer (1972), *op. cit.*

43. Peter Henle, "Exploring the Distribution of Earned Income," *Monthly Labor. Review*, Vol. 95, No. 12, December 1972. Inequalities in income (profit, rent interest, and transfer payments plus labor earnings) may also have increased if the unmeasured income from capital gains and other tax shelters for the rich are taken into acount. See Jerry Cromwell, "Income Inequalities, Discrimination and Uneven Development," unpublished Ph.D. dissertation, Harvard University, May 1974.

44. Chiswick and Mincer (1972), op. *cit.*

45. Thomas I. Ribich, *Education and Poverty* (Washington, D.C.: Brookings Institution, 1968).

46. United States Bureau of the Census, *Current Population Reports*, Series P–60, October 1970, Table 75, p. 368.

47. United States Bureau of the Census, *Current Population Reports*, series P-60, November, 1972, Table 1, p. 14.

48. Michael Reich, *Racial Discrimination and the Distribution of Income, Ph.D.* dissertation, Harvard University, May 1973.

49. United States Bureau of the Census, *op. cit.* (December 1973), Table 47, p. 114.

50. Quoted in Tyack (1967), *op. cit.*, p. 315.

51. Charles Silberman, *Crisis in the Classroom* (New York: Vintage, 1971), p. 83.

52. Quoted in Lawrence Cremin, *The Transformation of the School* (New York: Alfred A. Knopf, 1961).

53. Silberman (1971), *op. cit.*, p. 10.

54. Tyack (1967), *op. cit.*, p. 3.

55. *Ibid.*, p. 15.

56. Ross, as quoted in Clarence Karier, Joel Spring, and Paul C. Violas, *Roots of Crisis* (Chicago: University of Illinois Press, 1973), p. 32.

57 Tyack (1967) *op. cit.*, p. 325.

58. Whence e e cummings' sharp lines: "...the children knew, but only a few/ and down they forgot as up they grew." e e cummings, *Poems, 1923-1954* (New York: Harcourt, Brace and World, 1954), p. 370.

59. Cf. Charles Valentine, *Culture and Poverty* (Chicago: University of Chicago Press, 1968). Early in the nineteenth century, Robert Dale Owen, the renowned utopian, had proposed that the interests of social equality dictated that the children of the poor be raised in public institutions.

60. Tyack (1967), *op. cit.;* Katz (1971), *op. cit.*

61. In Chapter 5 we will argue that both changes in the approach to discipline reflect the changing social relationships of production in the corporate capitalist economy.

62. Paulo Freire, *Pedagogy of the Oppressed* (New York: Herder and Herder, 1972), pp. 58–59.

63. J. W. Getzels and P. W. Jackson, "Occupational Choice and Cognitive Functioning," in *Journal of Abnormal and Social Psychology,* February 1960.

64. For a general discussion of the content and meaning of creativity tests, see Michael W. Wallach, *The Intelligence of Creativity Distinction* (New York: General Learning Corporation, 1971).

65. The exact correlation was r = 0.41.

66. The correlations between own and teacher's desired personality traits were r = 0.67 for the high IQs and r = 0.25 for the high creatives.

67. Both groups had similar scores on tests of achievement motivation—McClelland n-ach and Strodtbeck V-score.

68. Herbert Gintis, "Education, Technology, and the Characteristics of Worker Productivity, *American Economic Review,* May 1971.

69. John L. Holland, "Creative and Academic Performance Among Talented Adolescents, *Journal of Educational Psychology,* No. 52, 1961.

70. Verbal and Mathematical sections of the Scholastic Achievement Test, Humanities and Scientific Comprehension.

71. The interested reader should consult Holland (1961), *op. cit.* and Herbert Gintis, *Alienation and Power,* Ph.D. dissertation for Harvard University, May 1969.

72. Gintis (1969), *op. cit.* and (1971), *op. cit.*

73. Holland's personality measures will be presented in italics. Unless otherwise indicated, all are statistically significant at the 1 percent level.

74. In addition to the good citizenship-externally motivated student, a small portion of the high *Drive to Achieve* students exhibit a set of personality traits quite similar to those of the *Deviant Creatives* described in Getzel and Jackson's study, already presented. These students, high on *Artistic Performance and Creative Activities,* evidently reject the pressure to define their personal goals in terms compatible with high grades and teacher approbation, and their positive personality traits are uniformly penalized in terms of grades and teacher ratings for *Citizenship.*

75. Charles Silberman, (1971), *op. cit.*

76. As quoted in Lawrence Cremin (1964), *op. cit.*, p. 241.

77. *Ibid.,* pp. 240–241.

78. *Ibid.,* p. 328.

79. Raymond Callahan, *Education and the Cult of Efficiency* (Chicago: University of Chicago Press, 1962), preface.

80. *Ibid.*

81. Thomas S. Kuhn, *The Structure of Scientific Revolutions* (Chicago: The University of Chicago Press, 1962), p. 53.

82. Arthur A. Jensen, *Educability and Group Differences* (New York: Harper & Row, 1973); and Richard Herrnstein, *IQ in the Meritocracy* (Boston: Little, Brown and Company, 1973).

83. For a more complete discussion, see Richard C. Edwards, Michael Reich, and Thomas Weisskopf, *The Capitalist System* (Englewood Cliffs, N.J.: Prentice-Hall, 1972); André Gorz, "Technical Intelligence and the Capitalist Division of Labor," *Telos,* Summer 1972; and Chapter 3.

84. Clarence Karier, *Shaping the American Educational State: 1900 to the Present* (New York: The Free Press, 1975); and Clarence Karier, Joel Spring, and Paul C. Violas (1973), *op. cit.*

85. Indeed, it has been pointed out to us by Dr. F. Bohnsack in a personal communication that Dewey did begin to revise his views, especially after World War I:

> For this later time, at least, I would doubt whether we could say he characterized the social system as democratic. He saw and criticized the totalitarian features of existing society and the missing "...intrinsic growth orientation of education." As self-development and equality of opportunity, to him, were inconsistent with preparing workers for existing [alienated] jobs, he criticized such a preparation and wanted to change existing industrial education as well as industrial work.

See A. G. Wirth, *The Vocational-Liberal Studies Controversy between John Dewey and Others (1900–1917)* (Washington, D.C., 1970), and John Dewey, "Education vs. Trade-training," *The New Republic,* Vol. 3, No. 15, May 1915.

As Virginia Held has pointed out to us, Dewey, in his mature work, *Art as Experience* (New York: Minton, Balch and Company, 1934), went further to claim!

> The labor and employment problem of which we are so acutely aware cannot be solved by mere changes in wage, hours of work, and sanitary conditions. No permanent solution is possible save in a radical alteration, which affects the degree and kind of participation the worker has in the production and social disposition of the wares he produces. (p. 343)

# Forgetting the Questions:
# The Problem of Educational Reform

## DIANE RAVITCH

It would be difficult to find a sustained period of time in our history when Americans felt satisfied with the achievements of their schools. From the early nineteenth century on, it has been commonplace to find a fairly consistent recitation of complaints about the low state of learning, the poor training of teachers, the insufficient funding of education, the inadequacies of school buildings, and the apathy of the public. The temptation exists to attribute the concerns of the 1980s to this strain of despair about the historic gap between aspiration and reality, this sense that schools have always and will always fall short of their mission. But it would be wrong to do so, not only because it would encourage unwarranted complacency but because the educational problems of the present are fundamentally different from those of the past.

One important difference is that so much of the past agenda of educational reformers has been largely fulfilled. In one sense, the educational enterprise is the victim of its own successes, since new problems have arisen from the long-sought solutions to earlier problems. Idealistic reformers, eager to improve the schools and to extend their promise to all children, sought the appropriate lever of change. If only teachers had college degrees and pedagogical training; if only teachers would band together to form a powerful teachers' union; if only there were federal aid to schools; if only all children were admitted to school regardless of race or national origin; if only all students of high abil-

ity were admitted to college; if only colleges could accommodate everyone who wanted to attend; if only students had more choices and fewer requirements in their course work; if only schools were open to educational experimentation; if only there were a federal department of education...The "if only" list could be extended, but the point should be clear by now. All these "if onlies" have been put into effect, some entirely and others at least partially, and rarely have the results been equal to the hopes invested.

In reality, many present complaints are reactions to hard-won reforms of the past. Though the educational preparation of teachers is more extensive than ever, at least when measured by degrees and years of formal schooling, the education of teachers is still a subject of intense criticism. The realization has dawned in many quarters that a credential from a state university or a school of education is no guarantee that its bearer knows how to teach or what to teach, loves teaching or loves learning. Nor are today's critics delighted by the undeniable power of teachers' unions. True, the unions have used their political clout to improve teachers' salaries and to win vastly enlarged federal education expenditures, but unionization has not produced the educational changes that some of its advocates had anticipated. Similarly, the sense of achievement should have followed the removal of racial barriers to higher education quickly gave way to concerns about social stratification, vocationalization, and declining quality. The reforms of the 1960s were effective, though not in the way that reformers had hoped. Now everyone who wants to go to college can go to some college, though not necessarily that of his first choice. By 1980, at least one-third of all institutions of higher education admitted everyone who applied, more than one-half accepted most or all of those who met their qualifications, and less than 10 percent were "competitive," that is, accepted only a portion of qualified applicants. As college enrollments decline, the number of competitive colleges will grow fewer. Curricular reforms have broken down the coherence of the liberal arts curriculum, both in high school and college, so that students have a wide degree of choice and few requirements. And a federal department of education has at last been established, though with what benefits or burdens for schools and children it is too soon to say.

Yet having won so many victories, some of truly historic dimension, American education is still embattled, still struggling to win public support and approval, and, perhaps worse, still struggling to find its own clear sense of purpose. Paradoxically, the achievements of the recent past seem to have exhausted the usually ready stock of prescriptions for school reform and to have raised once again the most basic questions of educational purpose.

Like other major institutions in our society, the schools are continually judged by today's demands and today's performance, and no credit is extended by clients or critics for yesterday's victories. Which is as it should be. School criticism, as I noted earlier, is nothing new. Behind any criticism, however, are assumptions about what schools should and can do, and criticisms have shifted as assumptions about the goals and potentialities of schools have changed. Since the early nineteenth century, the tenor of school criticism has been essentially optimistic; no matter how despairing the critic, his working assumption has been that schools are valu-

able institutions, that they have within them the power to facilitate social, moral, and political regeneration, and that more money, or more public concern, or better teachers could extend the promise of schooling to everyone. If more people had more schooling, critics have contended, and if schools were amply financed and well staffed, there would be enormous benefit to the individual, the society, the economy, and the body politic. With relatively little dissent, Americans have believed in schooling—not because of a love of the hickory stick and the three Rs, or (as some latter-day critics would have it) because of the schools' ability to make children docile workers, but because Americans are deeply committed to self-improvement and the school is an institutionalized expression of that commitment.

Participation in formal schooling has grown sharply in recent decades. The proportion of seventeen-year-olds who graduated from high school grew from about 50 percent in 1940 to about 75 percent in the late 1960s. Similarly, the proportion of young people who entered college climbed from about 16 percent in 1940 to about 45 percent in 1968, at which time it leveled off. In no other country in the world does participation in formal schooling last as long, for so many people, as in the United States. To understand why this broad democratization of educational participation occurred, as well as why the 1980s began on a note of disillusionment, it is useful to consider some of the expectations we have attached to formal schooling.

Until well into the twentieth century, only a small minority of Americans attended college. College was not only expensive but exclusive. Many, perhaps most, colleges maintained quotas for some groups (like Jews and Catholics) and excluded others altogether (blacks). After World War II, more than 2 million veterans attended college, crowding and sometimes overwhelming America's campuses. The GI Bill launched the world's first experiment in universal access to higher education. While most veterans did not use their benefits to attend college, the experience of those who did benefited the individuals, the institutions, and the economy. In light of the success and popularity of the GI program, the conviction that college should be a right rather than a privilege gained broad support.

While demand for expanded access to higher education grew steadily in the states and nation, other political forces combined to advance the role of education as a weapon against poverty. The notion that knowledge is power was certainly not novel, nor was the very American belief that schooling is an antidote to crime, poverty, and vice. The school promoters of the early nineteenth century repeatedly argued that schooling would give people the means to improve themselves and thereby break the cycle of poverty. During the early 1960s, this traditional rhetoric was given new life by scholars and policymakers. Educational programs burgeoned as an integral part of the federal government's war on poverty. Jacob Riis had written in 1892, "the more kindergartens, the fewer prisons"; in 1965 Lyndon Johnson predicted that the lives of children in the Head Start summer program would be spent "productively and rewardingly rather than wasted in tax-supported institutions or in welfare-supported lethargy." The hope of eliminating poverty and inequality provided the major rationale not only for Operation Head Start but for general federal aid to education as well.

By the time the period of educational expansion reached a high tide in the middle 1960s, much was expected by a variety of publics. It was hoped that more education would:

- Reduce inequality among individuals and groups by eliminating illiteracy and cultural deprivation.
- Improve the economy and economic opportunity by raising the number of intelligent and skilled individuals.

- Spread the capacity for personal fulfillment by developing talents, skills, and creative energies.
- Prove to be an uplifting and civilizing influence in the nation's cultural life by broadly diffusing the fruits of liberal education.
- Reduce alienation and mistrust while building a new sense of community among people of similar education and similar values.
- Reduce prejudice and misunderstanding by fostering contact among diverse groups.
- Improve the quality of civic and political life.

These hopes and expectations were a heavy burden for the schools to bear. Perhaps predictably, they did not accomplish all that was asked of them. Most of the problems that were laid at the schools' doors remained just as problematic years later (and some critics would argue that the provision of more schooling had produced the opposite effect in every instance). Poverty and inequality did not disappear; their roots were elsewhere, and the schools were not able to cure deep-seated social and economic ills. While the disadvantaged received more schooling, so did the advantaged. Many poor youths entered the middle class by using educational opportunity, but others remained as poor as their parents. The value of a high school diploma declined not only because its possession became nearly universal but also, and most important, because high school graduates were not necessarily literate—mainly because of the well-intended effort to keep as many youths in school for as long as possible and to deny no one a diploma, regardless of his educational development. Society's investment in education probably did spur economic development, but it did not prevent the emergence of skepticism about the desirability of economic growth; in fact, it was precisely among the educated (and the advantaged) that economic growth became suspect because of its association with the bureaucratization, centralization, and depersonalization of modern economic life. It is impossible to gauge the effects of increased schooling on popular culture or high culture. Television, which invariably seeks the largest possible audience, undoubtedly has more power to shape popular culture than schools do (a mixed blessing, since television disperses both sitcom pap and major cultural events to mass audiences). Participation in popular culture and high culture has surely been broadened, yet it is arguable whether the quality of either has been elevated during recent decades. Nor is it possible to demonstrate that increased educational participation has eliminated distrust between groups or contributed to a new sense of community. On the contrary, educational institutions have become settings for expression of militant particularism along racial, religious, ethnic, sexual, cultural, and linguistic lines. Very likely the differences among groups have been accentuated in the past twenty years. But again, it would be difficult to hold the schools directly responsible for these trends. More likely, it appears, the schools are the stage on which such issues are acted out rather than the cause of their appearance. Nor can the schools claim to have improved the quality of political life, since political participation has waned along with public regard for political institutions. But once again, it was not the schools that were responsible for the apparent ebbing of civic commitment and the surge of political apathy, nor could they even serve as a counterforce against such attitudes. The same attitudes of distrust, skepticism, hostility, and apathy eroded the schools' own status in the social order. The same confusions that pervaded the social atmosphere also pervaded the schools. If they failed to teach citizenship, it was at least in part because teachers and parents were confused about what a good citizen was and

whether "citizenship" could be taught without imposing a partisan interpretation. In short, a society that is confused and contentious cannot look to its schools to straighten things out, for the schools will reflect the same confusion and contention.

In retrospect, it was folly to have expected the schools to transform society or to mold a new kind of person. The schools are by nature limited institutions, not total institutions. They do not have full power over their students' lives (even total institutions, like prisons, have discovered the difficulty of shaping or reshaping the lives and minds of those they fully control). Schools are not fully independent in their dealings with students; they are interrelated with, and dependent on, families, churches, the media, peer groups, and other agencies of influence. Nor can schools be considered as if they were machines, all operating in the same predictable manner. Teachers vary, administrators vary, students vary, communities vary, and therefore schools vary. The schools, being complex human institutions composed of actors with different goals, different interests, and different capacities, cannot be treated as if they were all interchangeable.

As it became clear that more schooling would not provide any magical solutions, the utopian hopes once focused on the schools dissipated. Having briefly been the repository of grand and even grandiose dreams of human betterment, the schools became a scapegoat for all the wide-ranging problems they had failed to solve. Having revealed that they were but fallible instruments of social change and that any change they promoted would only be incremental, the schools became the object of rage and scorn. They were portrayed as intractable, bureaucratic, even malevolent barriers to social change. But just as it was unrealistic to believe that the schools had the power to remake society by molding those who passed through their doors, it was equally unrealistic to assert that they were powerless, meaningless, superfluous institutions with no purpose other than the care and feeding of their own employees.

Nonetheless, when the dream of a school-led social revolution faded, school criticism shifted in tone. The voices of liberal critics—those who believed that men and women of goodwill might work together to improve schools by using this program or that curriculum—diminished to mere whispers. They were drowned out by critics who believed that only radical changes in teaching or in governing schools could "save" them; by those who believed that the public schools were beyond redemption and ought to be replaced by "free" schools; and by those who advocated the abolition of compulsory schooling and the "de-schooling" of society. For a time in the late 1960s and early 1970s, bookstore shelves fairly bulged with apocalyptic predictions about the imminent demise of schooling. One book, playing on the then current phrase "God is dead," was titled *School Is Dead*. While some of the writing of this period contained sharp and telling portraits of insensitive teachers and uncaring bureaucrats, others gave vent to undisguised anti-intellectualism in their attacks on academic standards, discipline, science, and rationality. In the larger culture—and, alas, especially in academic institutions—a great revival seemed to sweep the land, casting aside "old" doctrines of deferred gratification, structured learning, and professionalism while espousing mysticism, Eastern religions, the occult, astrology, and whatever else promised to touch the spontaneous, untrained inner spirit.

These trends had curricular and programmatic consequences. In colleges, students demanded, and usually won, the abolition of course requirements, the adoption of pass-fail grading, the de-emphasis of competition and testing, and extensive choice in selecting their own programs of study. As requirements for admission to college were relaxed,

high schools soon succumbed to many of the same pressures that had changed the colleges: Course requirements were eased, new courses proliferated, academic standards dropped, homework diminished, and adults generally relinquished their authority to direct student learning. At all levels, both in college and high school, educational administrators reduced, to the extent possible, the schools' role as *in loco parentis*. To some extent, this period of student assertiveness and adult retreat was the educational side of the movement against the war in Vietnam, which provoked youthful revolt against authority in many parts of the society and the culture. But even after the war ended, there remained a lingering hostility to science, technology, and reason—as though these were the root causes of the hated war.

As the 1980s opened, it appeared that this wave of anti-intellectualism had spent itself, for complaints about the schools suggested entirely different concerns. The well-publicized decline in Scholastic Aptitude Test (SAT) scores created a context for worrying about a national deterioration in the quality of education. Not that the SAT scores were important in themselves, but they provided a sense of a pattern in the carpet that had not previously been discernible. For several years college officials had reported a steady increase in the number of freshmen who read poorly and wrote atrociously; the phenomenon of remedial reading and remedial writing classes spread throughout higher education, even to elite institutions. The apparent explanation, at first, was that so many new students from poor families had begun to attend college, but analysis of the SAT drop showed that the score decline continued long after the socioeconomic profile of the college-going population had stabilized. Bits and pieces of evidence from other sources began to fit together. Other standardized measures of academic ability reported score declines paralleling the SATs. National newsmagazines discovered a writing crisis and a literacy crisis. Educational malpractice suits were filed by disgruntled parents because their children had received a high school diploma in spite of being "functionally illiterate." The Council for Basic Education, a lonely voice for liberal education since its founding in 1958, found itself back in the educational mainstream, while still a lonely voice for liberal education. Demands for minimum competency tests seemed to spring up spontaneously in almost every state, though no national organization existed to promote or coordinate the movement. As concern for educational standards spread in the middle 1970s, demands for testing grew—not only minimum competency tests for high school graduation but tests at critical checkpoints in the lower grades and tests for would-be teachers. Reaction against those demands was not long in coming. The assault upon standardized testing was led by consumer activist Ralph Nader and the National Education Association. Nader released a lengthy attack on the credibility of the SAT, the most widely used college admission test, and lobbied successfully in New York State and elsewhere for passage of a "truth-in-testing" law.

While it did generate controversy, the dispute over testing was superficial, for tests were neither a cause of nor a remedy for the underlying malaise in American education. Nearly all the educational controversies of the 1970s—whether over bilingualism or sex education or testing or open admissions or busing—dealt with some aspect of the educational process that was of great importance to some constituency, but none directly raised these questions: What does it mean to be an educated person? What knowledge is of most worth? Are the graduates of our schools educated people?

The very absence of such questioning suggests a failure in educational thinking. Educators and, most especially, educational policymakers have fallen into the habit of analyzing school issues almost entirely in so-ciological and economic terms. In recent years it has been customary to think of schooling as a quantifiable economic good to be distributed in accordance with principles of equity or in response to political demands. The sociological-economic perspective has come to dominate educational discussion and has informed public policy. Without doubt it has contributed to necessary changes in patterns of schooling, by redirecting resources in a fair manner and by opening up access to educational opportunities. But the functionalist perspective became dysfunctional when it crowded substantive educational concerns off the policymakers' agenda, when the desire to keep students in school was unaccompanied by interest in what they would learn while they stayed in school. What I am suggesting here is not a conflict between the functionalist perspective and the educational perspective, but the danger of analyzing the schools through only one of the two prisms. There has been a fairly persistent tendency, I would argue, to neglect the role of schools as educational institutions, to treat them as sociological cookie cutters without regard to the content of their educational program. When I consider why this is so, I conclude that there are several possible explanations.

First, the sociological perspective has become dominant because it relies on quantifiable data that are accessible. It is far easier to gain information about years of educational attainment and socioeconomic status than it is to ascertain the conditions of learning in any given school. Educators cannot agree on how to assess the educational climate or even on what should be learned. Thus it becomes irresistible to deal with, perhaps even become the captive of, data that are both available and measurable.

Second, the sociological perspective is a useful adjunct to the concept of the school as a tool of social reform. By measuring which groups are in school and how their social background relates to their choice of occupation, we can attempt to monitor how educational resources are allocated and whether schooling is contributing to social progress. While it is neither new nor unusual to regard the school as a lever of social reform, it is unusual and perhaps unwise to see the school *solely* as a tool of social reform and *solely* as a resource to be redistributed. One consequence is that the school's diploma is confused with the learning that it is supposed to represent. In recent years, policymakers have sought to equalize educational attainment (years-of-schooling) without regard to the quality of education. This is like putting people on a diet of 1,800 calories a day without caring whether they are consuming junk food or nutritious food. Years-of-schooling, or a diploma, has been treated as an end in itself. Thus we have seen courts require school districts to present a diploma to students who could not meet minimum state standards of literacy, as if it were the diploma itself they needed rather than the learning that the diploma is supposed to signify. When school reformers in the nineteenth century advocated universal education as a way of improving society, they meant a broad diffusion of knowledge and wisdom, not a broad diffusion of diplomas.

Third, educational analysts have relied on the sociological perspective because it is easier to raise the level of educational attainment than it is to raise the level of educational quality. Staying in school, not dropping out, and getting a diploma represents a clear, unambiguous goal that everyone can understand without quarrel. As soon as school officials begin to define what should be taught and learned during those years, disagreements arise, which are best settled by making the schools all things for all people.

For these reasons and others, educational policymakers have tended to view schooling as an instrument to achieve some other goal, only rarely as an end in itself. To the extent that they do so, they rob schooling of the very attributes that give it power. If a young man or woman has a high school diploma but can scarcely read or write, then the diploma is worthless. When a diploma, either at the high school or college level, represents a certificate of time served but not of the systematic development of intelligence and skill, then it is difficult to know why it should have any inherent value. And of course it does not.

An educational critique of schooling should have as its starting point, I believe, the idea that the essential purpose of schooling is to develop the powers of intelligence: thinking, knowing, reflecting, observing, imagining, appreciating, questioning, and judging. Beyond that, schooling has many additional purposes, both for the student and for society. Educational literature teems with lists of the many ways in which schools should meet individual and social needs. But the schools' first purpose is to encourage and guide each person in the cultivation of intelligence and the development of talents, interests, and abilities. Schools do many other things as well: They may provide food, social services, psychological services, medical care, and career guidance. But no matter how well or how poorly they fulfill these functions, the schools must be judged in the first instance by how well they do those things that only they can do. We expect the schools to teach children command of the fundamental skills that are needed to continue learning—in particular, the ability to read, write, compute, speak, and listen. Once they have command of these skills, they should progress through a curriculum designed to enlarge their powers. Such a curriculum would contain, for every student, history and social studies, language and literature, mathematics, science, and the arts. Students need to learn these skills and disciplines in school because, except for those are individuals who can educate themselves without a teacher, they are unlikely to have an another chance to do so.

The schools are responsible both for preserving a sense of the past and for providing the ability to think about, and function in, the present and the future. More than any other educational agency, they ought to have an intelligent understanding of the inexorable connection between past, present, and future. Certainly there is disagreement about the meaning of the past and how it relates to the present and the future, and awareness of such disagreement is often invoked to justify educational aimlessness. But much of what seems to be dissension is a chimera; democratic debate ought not to be confused with chaos, nor should pluralistic politics be confused with anarchy. Education proceeds from widely shared values, and we do, in fact, have widely shared values. We may not agree about how democracy is to be achieved and about whether we have too much or too little of it, but few would question the idea that each person has the right as a citizen to participate in the shaping of public issues. We believe in the idea of self-government and in the greatest possible involvement of citizens as voters, as volunteers in community organizations, as members of interest groups, and as spokesmen for different views. While we may differ over particular educational issues, there is general support for the idea that schooling is a necessary mechanism for achieving society's goals: to prepare the younger generation to be thoughtful citizens; to enable each person to appreciate and contribute to the culture; to sharpen the intellectual and aesthetic sensibilities for lifelong enjoyment; to develop readiness for the educational, occupational, and professional choices that each person will confront; to kindle a sense of responsibility for others and a sense of integrity; to teach children how to lead and how to follow; and to acquaint young people with the best models of achievement in every field while encouraging them to strive to realize their own potential.

If these are widely shared educational aims, and I believe they are, then none of them should be left to chance. The curriculum should be designed so that every student has the fullest opportunity to develop his

powers, intelligence, interests, talent, and understanding. Every student needs to know how to form and articulate his own opinions. To do so, he must learn how to read critically, how to evaluate arguments, how to weigh evidence, and how to reach judgments on his own. Every student, to understand the world in which he will be a participant, should be knowledgeable about history; should master some other language as well as his own; should discover the pleasures of literature, especially its power to reach across time and cultures and to awaken our sense of universality; should study science and technology, both as a citizen who will be asked to comprehend complex issues and as an individual who must live with constant change. Since we believe that everyone should be equally concerned about the problems of our society, then we must believe that everyone, every student, should be schooled in a way that meets his need to know history, science, mathematics, language, the arts, literature, and so on. And yet it is not simply on the grounds of utility, relevance, and political value that the case for liberal education rests. We do not *need* to know how to read Shakespeare; we can be good citizens without any knowledge of Athenian civilization, even though our concept of citizenship is based on the very period of which we are ignorant. We must concern ourselves with the survival of history, philosophy, literature, and those other humanistic disciplines that may lack immediate utility because without them ours would be an intellectually impoverished and spiritually illiterate civilization.

To some people, all this is so self-evident that it ought not be necessary to plead for the value of an education of substance and content. Yet it is necessary, because of the widespread disarray in high school and college curricula. In the face of changes that have occurred in the past decade or so, many educators seem unable to remember how to justify or defend or champion liberal education. The proposition that all students should be subject to curricular requirements that define the essentials of a good education has become controversial, rather than a starting point in defining the nature of a good curriculum.

Confronted with conflicting demands from those who want reduced requirements and those who want curricular substance, many schools have resolved the dilemma by reducing requirements while expanding electives. Thus student may take "history" courses to meet their minimal graduation requirement, but those so-called history courses may be little more than classes in current events or pop sociology. Or they may meet their English requirement by reading popular fiction, mystery stories, or science fiction. There is no harm in what is included; from the perspective of a liberal education, what is unfortunate is the wide body of knowledge that is excluded when course proliferation and lax requirements are joined together. Professors regularly encounter students who are ignorant of anything that happened before the Civil War as well as anything that happened, or was written, outside the United States. They may have *heard* of Plato and Aristotle in a survey course, but they have never read

anything written by either and have only a dim notion (usually wrong) of what they "stood for." Mention Dickens, Tolstoy, Conrad, or Melville, and perhaps they have heard of them too, but they "didn't take that course." Some professors who teach literature have been astonished to find students who know nothing of mythology or the Bible allusions to Job or Icarus must be explained to those who have no intellectual furniture in their minds, no stock of literary or historical knowledge on which to draw beyond their immediate experience. In the April 11, 1980, issue of *Commonweal,* J. M. Cameron soberly observed that if Freud attended school today, he might not be able to think up the Oedipus theory because he would not have enough mythology in his head to do so. We seem now to turn to television or the movies to teach the history and literature that were neglected in school. To permit knowledge to be fragmented, as we have, by serving it up cafeteria-style, with each person choosing whether to be minimally literate or to be a specialist, contributes to the diminution and degradation of the common culture.

## CHAPTER 3 REFERENCES

Andersen, J. (1988). *The education of blacks in the south, 1860–1935*. Chapel Hill: University of North Carolina Press.

Bailyn, B. (1960). *Education in the forming of American society*. Chapel Hill: University of North Carolina Press.

Bloom, A. (1987). *The closing of the American mind*. New York: Simon & Schuster.

Bowles, S., & Gintis, H. (1976). *Schooling in capitalist America: Educational reform and the contradictions of economic life*. New York: Basic Books.

Brint, S., & Karabel, J. (1989). *The diverted dream: Community colleges and the promise of educational opportunity in America, 1900–1985*. New York: Oxford University Press.

Button, W. H., & Provenzano, E. E. (1989). *History of education and culture in America*. Englewood Cliffs, NJ: Prentice Hall.

Coleman, J. S. (1966). *Equality of educational opportunity*. Washington DC: U.S. Government Printing Office.

Cremin, L. A. (1961). *The transformation of the school*. New York: Vintage Books.

Cremin, L. A. (1970). *American education: The colonial experience, 1607–1783*. New York: Harper and Row.

Cremin, L. A. (1980). *American education: The national experience, 1783–1876*. New York: Harper and Row.

Cremin, L. A. (1988). *American education: The metropolitan experience, 1876–1980*. New York: Harper and Row.

Cremin, L. A. (1990). *Popular education and its discontents*. New York: Harper and Row.

Cuban, L. (1984). *How teachers taught: Constancy and change in American classrooms, 1890–1980*. New York: Longman.

Cubberly, E. P. (1934). *Public education in the United States: A study and interpretation of American educational history*. Boston: Houghton Mifflin.

Curti, M. (1959). *Social ideas of American educators*. Patterson, NJ: Pageant Books.

Dewey, J. (1897). My pedagogic creed. In Martin S. Dworkin (Ed.), *Dewey on education* (pp. 19–32). New York: Teachers College Press.

Dewey, J. (1899). The school and society. In Martin S. Dworkin (Ed.), *Dewey on education* (pp. 33–90). New York: Teachers College Press.

Dewey, J. (1902). The child and the curriculum. In Martin S. Dworkin (Ed.) *Dewey on Education* (pp. 91–111). New York: Teachers College Press.

*Digest of Education Statistics*. (1989). Washington, DC: U.S. Department of Education.

Dougherty, K. (1987). The effects of community colleges: Aid or hindrance to socioeconomic attainment? *Sociology of Education, 60*(2): 86–103.

Dworkin, M. S., (Ed.). (1959). *Dewey on education*. New York: Teachers College Press.

Gutek, G. (1991). *An historical introduction to American education*. (2nd ed.). Prospect Heights, IL: Waveland Press.

Hirsch, E. D. (1987.) *Cultural literacy*. Boston: Houghton Mifflin.

Hofstadter, R. (1966). *Anti-intellectualism in American life*. New York: Rand.

Hogan, D. (1978, Fall). Education and the making of the Chicago working class, 1880–1930. *History of Education Quarterly, 18,* 227–270.

Karier, C. (Ed.). (1976). *Shaping the American educational state.* New York: Free Press.

Katz, M. B. (1968). *The irony of early school reform.* Cambridge, MA: Harvard University Press.

Kohl, H. (1967). *36 children.* New York: New American Library.

Kozol, J. (1967). *Death at an early age.* New York: Houghton Mifflin.

Lavin, D. E., Alba, R. D., & Silberstein, R. A. (1981). *Right versus privilege: The open admissions experiment at the City University of New York.* New York: Free Press.

Lee, G. (1961). *Crusade against ignorance: Thomas Jefferson on education.* New York: Teachers College Press.

Lukas, J. A. (1986). *Common ground.* New York: Vintage Books.

Malone, D., & Rauch, B. (1960). *Empire for liberty.* New York: Appelton-Century-Crofts.

Myrdal, G. (1944). *An American dilemma.* New York: Harper and Ruthers.

Nassaw, D. (1979). *Schooled to order.* New York: Oxford University Press.

National Commission on Excellence in Education. (1983). *A nation at risk.* Washington, DC: U.S. Government Printing Office.

Neill, A. S. (1960). *Summerhill.* New York: Holt.

Powell, A. G., Farrar, E., & Cohen, D. K. (1985). *The shopping mall high school.* Boston: Houghton Mifflin.

Ravitch, D. (1977). *The revisionists revised.* New York: Basic Books.

Ravitch, D. (1983). *The troubled crusade.* New York: Basic Books.

Sadovnik, A. R. (1993). *Equity and excellence in higher education.* New York: Peter Lang Publishers.

Silberman, C. S. (1970). *Crisis in the classroom.* New York: Random House.

Spring, J. (1972). *Education and the rise of the corporate state.* Boston: Beacon Press.

Spring, J. (1986). *The American school: 1642–1985.* New York: Longman.

Spring, J. (1989). *American education* (4th ed.). New York: Longman.

Westbrook, R. B. (1991). *John Dewey and American democracy.* Ithaca, NY: Cornell University Press.

Wright, L. B. (1957). *The cultural life of the American colonies.* New York: Harper & Brothers.

Wrigley, J. (1982). *Class, politics and public schools: Chicago, 1900–1950.* New Brunswick, NJ: Rutgers University Press.

## SUGGESTED READINGS

Albjerg, P. G. (1974). *Community and class in American education, 1865–1918.* New York: John Wiley.

Andersen, J. (1988). *The education of blacks in the south, 1860–1935.* Chapel Hill: University of North Carolina Press.

Antler, J. (1987). *Lucy Sprague Mitchell: The making of a modern woman.* New Haven, CT: Yale University Press.

Antler, J., & Biklen, S. K. (Eds.). (1990). *Changing education: Women as radicals and conservators.* Albany: State University of New York Press.

Aries, P. (1962). *Centuries of childhood: A social history of family life.* New York: Vintage Books.

Bailyn, B. (1960). *Education in the forming of American society.* Chapel Hill: University of North Carolina Press.

Bestor, A. (1953). *Educational wastelands.* Urbana, IL: University of Illinois Press.

Butts, R. F. (1978). *Public education in the United States: From revolution to reform.* New York: Holt, Rinehart and Winston.

Butts, R. F., & Cremin, L. A. (1953). *A history of education in American Culture.* New York: Holt.

Callahan, R. E. (1962). *Education and the cult of efficiency.* Chicago: University of Chicago Press.

Cavallo, D. (1981). *Muscles and morals: Organized playgrounds and urban reform, 1880–1920.* Philadelphia: University of Pennsylvania Press.

Counts, G. S. (1932). *Dare the schools build a new social order?* New York: John Day.

Cremin, L. A. (1961). *The transformation of the school.* New York: Vintage Books.

Cremin, L. A. (1972). *American education: The colonial experience, 1607–1783.* New York: Harper and Row.

Cremin, L. A. (1980). *American education: The national experience, 1783–1876.* New York: Harper and Row.

Cremin, L. A. (1988). *American education: The metropolitan experience, 1876–1980.* New York: Harper and Row.

Cremin, L. A. (1990). *Popular education and its discontents.* New York: Harper and Row.

Cuban, L. (1984). *How teachers taught: Constancy and change in American classrooms, 1890–1980.* New York: Longman.

Curti, M. (1971). *The social ideas of American educators.* Totowa, NJ: Littlefield, Adams & Company.

Cusick, P. A. (1983). *The egalitarian ideal and the American high school.* New York: Longman.

Finkelstein, B. (1989). *Governing the young: Teacher behavior in popular primary schools in 19th century United States.* London: Falmer Press.

Finklestein, B. (1992). Education historians as mythmakers. In G. Grant (Ed.), *Review of research education* (pp. 255–297). Washington, D.C.: American Educational Research Association.

Greer, C. (1973). *The great school legend.* New York: Viking Press.

Hofstadter, R. (1966). *Anti-intellectualism in American life.* New York: Rand.

Hogan, D. J. (1978). Education and the making of the Chicago working class, 1880–1930. *History of Education Quarterly, 18,* 227–270.

Hogan, D. J. (1985). *Class and reform: School and society in Chicago, 1880–1930.* Philadelphia: University of Pennsylvania Press.

Kaestle, C. F. (1973). *The evolution of an urban school system.* Cambridge, MA: Harvard University Press.

Kaestle, C. F. (1983). *Pillars of the republic: Common schools and American society, 1780–1860.* New York: Hill & Wang.

Kaestle, C. F. (1991). *Literacy in the United States: Readers and reading since 1800.* New Haven, CT: Yale University Press.

Kaestle, C. F., & Vinovskis, M. A. (1978). From apron strings to ABCs: Parents, children and schooling in nineteenth-century America. In J. Demos & S. S. Boocock (Eds.), *Turning points: historical and sociological essays on the family* (pp. 39–80). Chicago: University of Chicago Press.

Kaestle, C. F., & Vinovskis, M. A. (1980). *Education and social change in nineteenth-century Massachusetts.* New York: Basic Books.

Karier, C. (Ed.). (1976). *Shaping the American educational state.* New York: Free Press.

Karier, C., Violas, P., & Spring, J. (1973). *Roots of crisis: American education in the twentieth century.* New York: Rand McNally.

Katz, M. B. (1968). *The irony of Early school reform: Educational innovation in mid-nineteenth-century Massachusetts.* Cambridge, MA: Harvard University Press.

Katz, M. B. (1971). *Class, bureaucracy, and schools: The illusion of educational change in America.* New York: Praeger.

Katz, M. B. (1971). *School reform, past and present.* Boston: Little, Brown.

Katz, M. B. (1987). *Reconstructing American education.* Cambridge, MA: Harvard University Press.

Katznelson, I., & Weir, M. (1985). *Schooling for all.* New York: Basic Books.

Kluger, R. (1975). *Simple justice: The history of Brown v. Board of Education and black America's struggle for equality.* New York: Knopf.

Labaree, D. F. (1988). *The making of an American high school: The credentials market and the Central High School of Philadelphia, 1838–1939.* New Haven, CT: Yale University Press.

Lagemann, E. C. (1979). *A generation of women: Education in the lives of progressive reformers.* Cambridge, MA: Harvard University Press.

Lukas, J. A. (1986). *Common ground.* New York: Vintage Books.

Ravitch, D. (1974). *The great school wars, New York City, 1805–1973: A history of the public schools as battlefield of social change.* New York: Basic Books.

Ravitch, D. (1977). *The revisionists revised.* New York: Basic Books.

Ravitch, D. (1983). *The troubled crusade.* New York: Basic Books.

Reese, W. J. (1986). *Power and the promise of school reform: Grassroots movements during the progressive era.* Boston: Routledge & Kegan Paul.

Rury, J. L. (1991). *Education and women's work: Female schooling and the division of labor in urban America, 1870–1930.* Albany: State University of New York Press.

Spring, J. (1972). *Education and the rise of the corporate state.* Boston: Beacon Press.

Trow, M. (1961). The second transformation of American secondary education. *International Journal of Comparative Sociology, 2,* 144–166. Reprinted in Karabel, J., & Halsey, A. H. (Eds.), *Power and ideology in Education* (pp. 105–118.) New York: Oxford University Press, 1977.

Tyack, D. (1974). *The one best system.* Cambridge, MA: Harvard University Press.

Tyack, D. (1990). Restructuring in historical perspective: Tinkering toward utopia. *Teachers College Record, 92,* 170–191.

Tyack, D., & Hansot, E. (1982). *Managers of virtue: Public school leadership in America, 1820–1980.* New York: Basic Books.

Tyack, D., & Hansot, E. (1990). *Learning together: A history of coeducation in American public schools.* New Haven, CT: Yale University Press.

Westbrook, R. B. (1991.) *John Dewey and American democracy.* Ithaca, NY: Cornell University Press.

Wrigley, J. (1982). *Class, politics and public schools: Chicago, 1900–1950.* New Brunswick, NJ: Rutgers University Press.

# CHAPTER 4

# The Sociology of Education

Many years ago, the famous philosopher Alfred North Whitehead was asked, "Which is more important, facts or ideas?" He reflected for a while and said, "Ideas about facts." At its very core, sociological inquiry is about ideas and how they shape people's understandings of society. The desire to know and to transform society is not unique to sociologists; in fact, social curiosity has played a key role in humans' adaptive capacity. In one sense, sociology is simply a method for bringing social aspirations and fears into focus by forcing people to ask sharp and analytic questions about the societies and cultures in which they live. The tools of sociology can be thought of as empirical and conceptual. Sociology is empirical because most sociologists gather facts about society. Facts, however, do not speak for themselves; without arranging them into meaningful patterns, facts are virtually useless. Trying to uncover the underlying patterns that give facts to their larger meaning is the purpose of making social theories. Often, teachers think that social theories are of little use in teaching children. Nothing could be further from the truth.

Without some idea of how the major elements in society fit together, teachers are at a loss in understanding the relation between school and society, how their own profession has evolved, and why students behave the way they do in school and outside of school. An understanding of society is essential if teachers are to develop as reflective practitioners. In a society that is becoming increasingly multiethnic and multiracial, the need for a sociological perspective among educators is urgent. In this chapter, we will explore some of the main elements of the sociology of education; these elements include theories about the relation between school and society, whether or not schooling makes a significant difference in individual's lives, how schools influence social inequalities, and an examination of how school processes affect the lives of children, teachers, and other adults who are involved in the educational enterprise.

## THE USES OF SOCIOLOGY FOR TEACHERS

How can people create schools that are more effective environments for children to grow and learn? What is the relation between school and the larger society? Can schools produce more social and economic equality? These questions and many more have sparked the imaginations of generations of educators and those noneducators who have a deep interest in academic achievement, the welfare of children, and a more just, more open society. The kind of answers that are found to these questions will shape education and society for years. Without clear thinking, good information, and honest assessments, education as an institution is bound to move into the future like a ship without a rudder, floundering, directionless, and in danger of sinking. Before better educational programs can be disgned, educators must know what works and what does not. The empirical and conceptual tools of sociology are ideally suited to this task because they guide one toward systematic thinking and realism about what is actually possible. There are those who would argue sociology is not fully scientific, but compared to other ways of problem solving, sociology utilizes the principles and methods of science and, moreover, sociologists are self-critical. Because of the standards of the discipline, the work of sociologists must bare the scrutiny of other sociologists and the public at large.

Sociologists, then, are in a good position to view schools with a dispassionate eye and a critical awareness that simple solutions to complex educational problems are almost bound to fail and can be counterproductive. From these observations, it should be evident that teachers can learn a great deal from the sociology of education; for example, sociological research helps pinpoint the characteristics of schools that enable them to become effective learning environments. These characteristics include vigorous instructional leadership; a principal who makes clear, consistent, and fair decisions; an emphasis on discipline and a safe and orderly environment; instructional practices that focus on basic skills and academic achievement; collegiality among teachers who believe that students can and will learn; and frequent review of student progress.

To take another example, it is known that interactions in the classroom shape the learning experiences of the child. Sociologists have developed many techniques for understanding classroom interactions. One of the best known is Ned Flanders's Interaction Analysis Scale (Amidon & Flanders, 1971). This method involves the use of observers who watch classroom interactions and note these interactions on a standard scale. This process gives observers a thorough and objective measure of what really goes on in classrooms. Flanders hypothesized that student performance and learning is greatest when teacher influence is indirect; that is, when there were other classroom interactions besides "teacher talk." The hypothesis was upheld when observations showed that students in indirect teacher classrooms learned more and were more independent than students in classrooms where most, if not all, instructional activities were directed by the teacher.

As teachers, sociology provides you with a special analytic lens on education and school that, when you learn to use it, will give you greater insight and coherence in your approach to studying education. We hope that this clarity will help you improve your pedagogical practices and promote your professional growth. Part of becoming a professional is developing an intellectual and experiential frame of reference that is sufficiently sophisticated. It is our belief that this intellectual sophistication will help you integrate the world of education into its larger social context. This last observation leads to our first major issue in exploring how sociology can help us understand education in the "big picture." What is the relation between school and society?

## THE RELATION BETWEEN SCHOOL AND SOCIETY

Have you ever wondered why schools are the way they are? Why do teachers teach what they teach in the way they do? Can schools change society, or must society change if schools are to become different? Obviously, there are no simple answers to these questions; yet struggling to find answers, even for complex questions, is in itself a process of clarification. Sociologists of education often ask big questions about the relation between school and society because they believe that educators cannot really understand how schools operate, or why they operate as they do, without a working idea of how schools and society interact. To help them in this complex intellectual and empirical process, sociologists almost always have a theory about the organization of society and how it shapes the education of children. In particular, sociologists take an interest in how schools act as agents of cultural and social transmission.

Schools, as well as parents, churches and synagogues, and other groups, shape children's perceptions of the world by processes of *socialization*. That is, the values, beliefs, and norms of society are internalized within children so that they come to think and act like other members of society. In this sense, schools socially and culturally reproduce the existing society through the systematic socialization of its youngest members. Think of such a simple ritual as pledging allegiance to the flag. Through this culturally approved ritual, young children learn something about citizenship and patriotism.

Socialization processes can shape children's consciousness profoundly. Schools, for instance, wittingly or unwittingly, promote gender definitions and stereotypes when they segregate learning and extracurricular activities by gender, or when teachers allow boys to dominate class discussions and activities. Not only do schools shape students' perceptions and consciousness but they also act as important, perhaps the most important, sorters and selectors of students. Schools, through such practices as tracking, academically stratify students by curricular placement, which, in turn, influences the long-term social, economic, and cultural destinies of children. In effect, schools play a major role in determining who will get ahead in society and who will not.

How do schools select some students for educational mobility? Is it on the basis of merit or is it primarily on the basis of students' ascriptive characteristics, such as class, race, or gender? Or is it a combination of merit and social position that explains who gets into the educational "fast track" and who gets "cooled out"? The concept of equal educational opportunity is a key element in the belief system that maintains that the United States is a land of opportunity where hard work is rewarded. Is this belief based on real social facts or is it simply a myth that confuses people and leads them to believe that their relative social and economic failure is caused by personal inadequacies?

At an even deeper level, one might wonder why people study the subjects and materials they do. Who selects what people teach and learn, and why? Is knowledge value free or socially constructed? Can ideas ever be taken out of their contexts? For instance, history texts have traditionally overlooked the role of minorities and women in shaping U.S. society. How has this influenced people's perceptions of what is really historically significant and what is not?

## Theoretical Perspectives

From these remarks, it should be apparent to you that the sociology of education is a contentious field and that the questions sociologists ask about the relation between school and society are fundamental and complex. Because the scope of these questions are so large, sociologists usually begin their studies with an overall picture of how society looks in its most basic form. This is where theory comes in. A good definition of *theory* is "An integration of all known principles, laws, and information pertaining to a specific area of study. This structure allows investigators to offer explanations for relative phenomenon and to create solutions to unique problems" (Woolfolk, 1990, p. 585). Theory is like an x-ray machine; it allows one to see past the visible and obvious and examine the hidden structure. Unlike x-ray pictures, however, theoretical pictures of society are seldom crystal clear or easy to interpret. Why is this? Partly this is because people are members of society (i.e., people have been socialized by society) and it is very difficult to be objective or disinterested in the analysis of people. Theoretical pictures of society are created by human beings and interpreted by them. Thus, knowledge of the social world cannot be totally separated from one's personal and social situation. Still, should you let the fact that all knowledge is socially generated and interpreted discourage you from exploring those issues that shape your life? Obviously not. Without the struggle for objectivity and honesty, there is little hope that people can create a productive and just society.

Theory, then, as inadequate as it is, is one's best conceptual guide to understanding the relation between school and society because it gives one the intellectual scaffolding from which to hang empirical findings. Essentially, there are three major theories about the relation between school and society: functional, conflict, and interactional.

## Functional Theories

Functional sociologists begin with a picture of society that stresses the *interdependence* of the social system; these researchers are apt to often examine how well the parts are integrated with each other. Functionalists view society as a kind of machine, where one part articulates with another to produce the dynamic energy required to make society work. Perhaps the earliest sociologist to embrace a functional point of view about the relation of school and society was Emile Durkheim (1858–1917), who virtually invented the sociology of education in the late nineteenth and early twentieth centuries. His major works include *Moral Education* (1962), *The Evolution of Educational Thought* (1977), and *Education and Sociology* (1956). While Durkheim recognized that education had taken different forms at different times and places, he believed that education, in virtually all societies, was of critical importance in creating the moral unity necessary for social cohesion and harmony. For Durkheim, moral values were the foundation of society.

Durkheim's emphasis on values and cohesion set the tone for how present-day functionalists approach the study of education. Functionalists tend to assume that consensus is the normal state in society and that conflict represents a breakdown of shared values. In a highly integrated, well-functioning society, schools socialize students into the appropriate values and sort and select students according to their abilities. Educational reform, then, from a functional point of view, is supposed to create structures, programs, and curricula that are technically advanced, rational, and encourage social unity. It should be evident that most U.S. educators and educational reformers implicitly base their reform suggestions on functional theories of schooling. When, for example, *A Nation at Risk* was released in 1983, the argument was made by the authors of the report that schools were responsible for a whole host of social and economic problems. There was no suggestion that perhaps education might not have the power to overcome deep, social, and economic problems without changing other aspects of U.S. society.

## Conflict Theories

Not all sociologists of education believe that society is held together by shared values alone. Some sociologists argue that the social order is not based on some collective agreement, but on the ability of dominant groups to impose their will on subordinate groups through force, cooptation, and manipulation. In this view, the glue of society is economic, political, cultural, and military power. Ideologies or intellectual justifications created by the powerful are designed to enhance their position by legitimizing inequality and the unequal distribution of material and cultural goods as an inevitable outcome of biology, or history. Clearly, conflict sociologists do not see the relation between school and society as unproblematic or straightforward. Whereas functionalists emphasize cohesion in explaining social order, conflict sociologists emphasize struggle. From a conflict point of view, schools are similar to social battlefields, where students struggle against teachers, teachers against administrators, and so on. These antagonisms, however, are most often muted for two reasons: the authority and power of the school and the achievement ideology. In effect, the achievement ideology convinces students and teachers that schools promote learning and sort and select students according to their abilities and not according to their social status. In this view, the achievement ideology disguises the real power relations within the school, which, in turn, reflect and correspond to the power relations within the larger society (Bowles & Gintis, 1976).

Although Karl Marx (1818–1883) did not write a great deal about education specifically, he is the intellectual founder of the conflict school in the sociology of education. His analytic imagination and moral outrage were sparked by the social conditions found in Europe in the late nineteenth century. Industrialization and urbanization had produced a new class of workers—the proletariat—who lived in poverty, worked up to 18 hours a day, and had little, if any, hope of creating a better life for their children. Marx believed that the class system, which separated owners from workers and workers from the benefits of their own labor, made class struggle inevitable. He believed that, in the end, the proletariat would rise up and overthrow the capitalists, and, in doing so, establish a new society where men and women would no longer be alienated from their labor.

Marx's powerful and often compelling critique of early capitalism has provided the intellectual energy for subsequent generations of liberal and leftist thinkers who believe that the only way to a more just and productive society is the abolition or modification of capitalism and the introduction of socialism. Political economists Bowles and Gintis, in their book *Schooling in Capitalist America* (1976), used a Marxist perspective for examining the growth of the U.S. public school. To their minds, there is a direct correspondence between the organization of schools and the organization of society, and, until society is fundamentally changed, there is little hope of real school reform. It has been argued by other conflict sociologists of education, however, that traditional Marxism is too deterministic and overlooks the power of culture and human agency in promoting change.

An early conflict sociologist who took a slightly different theoretical orientation when viewing society was Max Weber (1864–1920). Like Marx, Weber was convinced that power relations between dominant and subordinate groups structured societies, but unlike Marx, Weber believed that class differences alone could not capture the complex ways human beings form hierarchies and belief systems that make these hierarchies seem just and inevitable. Thus, Weber examined status cultures as well as class position status as an important sociological concept, because it alerts one to the fact that people identify their group by what they consume and with whom they socialize.

Weber also recognized that political and military power could be exercised by the state, without direct reference to the wishes of the dominant classes. Moreover, Weber had an acute and critical awareness of how bureaucracy was becoming the dominant type of authority in the modern state and how bureaucratic ways of thinking were bound to shape educational reforms. Weber made the distinction between the "specialist" and the "cultivated" man. What should be the goal of education—training individuals for employment or for thinking? Or are these two goals compatible?

The Weberian approach to studying the relation between school and society has developed into a compelling and informative tradition of sociological research. Researchers in this tradition tend to analyze school organizations and processes from the point of view of status competition and organizational constraints. One of the first U.S. sociologists of education to use these concepts was Willard Waller. In *The Sociology of Teaching* (1965), Waller portrayed schools as autocracies in a state of "perilous equilibrium." Without continuous vigilance, schools would erupt into anarchy because students are essentially forced to go to school against their will. To

Waller's mind, rational models of school organization only disguise the inherent tension that pervades the schooling process. Waller's perspective is shared by many contemporary conflict theorists who see schools as oppressive and demeaning and portray student noncompliance with school rules as a form of resistance.

Another major research tradition that has emerged from the Weberian school of thought is represented by Randall Collins (1971, 1979), who has maintained that educational expansion is best explained by status group struggle. He argued that educational credentials, such as college diplomas, are primarily status symbols rather than indicators of actual achievement. The rise of credentialism does not indicate that society is becoming more expert, but that education is increasingly used by dominant groups to secure more advantageous places for themselves and their children within the occupation and social structure.

A recent variation of conflict theory that has captured the imagination of some U.S. sociologists began in France and England during 1960s. Unlike most Marxists who tend to emphasize the economic structure of society, cultural reproduction theorists, such as Bourdieu and Passeron (1977), examined how "cultural capital" is passed on by families and schools. The concept of "cultural capital" is important because it suggests that, in understanding the transmission of inequalities, one ought to recognize that the cultural characteristics of individuals and groups are significant indicators of status and class position.

There is a growing body of literature that suggest schools pass on to graduates specific social identities that either enhance or hinder their life chances. For example, a graduate from an elite prep school has educational and social advantages over many public school graduates in terms of college attendance and occupational mobility. This advantage has very little to do with what prep school students learn in school, and a great deal to do with the power of their schools' reputations for educating members of the upper class. The theories of Bourdieu and Passeron extend the work of other sociologists who have argued persuasively that human culture cannot be understood as a isolated and self-contained object of study but must be examined as part of a larger social and cultural structure. To understand the impact of culture on the lives of individuals and groups, one must understand the meanings that are attributed to cultural experiences by those who participate in them (Mannheim, 1952).

The conflict perspective, then, offers important insights about the relation between school and society. As you think about schools and education, we hope that you will utilize functional and conflict theoretical perspectives as a way of organizing your readings and perceptions. Before we turn from theory to more empirical issues about students and schools, there is a theoretical perspective that ought not to be overlooked.

## Interactional Theories

Interactional theories about the relation of school and society are primarily critiques and extensions of the functional and conflict perspectives. The critique arises from the observation that functional and conflict theories are very abstract and emphasize structure and process at a very general (macrosociological) level of analysis. Although this level of analysis helps in understanding education in the "big picture," macroso-ciological theories hardly provide an interpretable snapshot of what schools are like on an everyday level. What do students and teachers actually do in school? Interac-tional theories attempt to make the commonplace strange by turning on their heads everyday taken-for-granted behaviors and interactions between students and stu-dents, and between students and teachers. It is exactly what one does not question that is most problematic at a deep level. For example, the processes by which students are labeled gifted or learning disabled are, from an interactional point of view, important to analyze, because such processes carry with them many implicit assump-tions about learning and children. By examining the microsociological or the interac-tional aspects of school life, people are less likely to create theories that are logical and eloquent, but without meaningful content.

Some of the sociology of education's most brilliant theorists have attempted to synthesize the macro- and microsociological approaches. Basil Bernstein (1990), for instance, has argued that the structural aspects of the educational system and the interactional aspects of the system reflect each other and must be viewed wholistical-ly. He has examined how speech patterns reflect students' social class backgrounds and how students from working class backgrounds are at a disadvantage in the school setting because schools are essentially middle-class organizations. Bernstein has combined a class analysis with an interactional analysis, which links language with educational processes and outcomes.

In this section, we have tried to give you a sense of how theory can be used to explain the relation between school and society. These theories provide background metaphors and analytic focuses for the work of sociologists. We turn now to some specific areas of research that have interested sociologists of education for many years.

## EFFECTS OF SCHOOLING ON INDIVIDUALS

Do schools matter? This provocative question is one that most people feel they have already answered. It is safe to say that most Americans believe that schools have a significant impact on learning and on social and economic mobility. In this section, we examine some of the effects of schooling on individuals to see what the relative importance of schooling is in terms of what people learn, employment, job perfor-mance, income, and mobility.

### Knowledge and Attitudes

It may be surprising to you to learn that sociologists of education disagree strongly about the relative importance of schooling in terms of what knowledge and attitudes young people acquire in school. Nobody argues that schools have no impact on student development, but there are sharp divisions among researchers about how significant school effects are, when taking into account students' social class back-ground. Generally, it is found that the higher the social class background of the student, the higher his or her achievement level. According to such researchers as

Coleman and colleagues (1966) and Jencks and colleagues (1972), differences between schools account for very little of the differences in student achievement. Is this true? Does this finding make sense out of the world as we know it? Does it make no difference whether a student attends a school in a wealthy suburb or in underfinanced, overcrowded school in the inner city?

Actually, more recent research does indicate that differences between schools in terms of their academic programs and policies do make differences in student learning. One of the first researchers to show that differences in schools are directly related to differences in student outcomes was Ron Edmonds (1979), the pioneer of the effective schools movement. As mentioned earlier, the effective schools research demonstrates that academically oriented schools do produce higher rates of learning. More recent research, which compares public and private schools, also indicates that in schools where students are compelled to take academic subjects and where there is consistent discipline, student achievement levels go up. An important study by Heyns (1978) found that sixth- and seventh-grade students who went to summer school, used the library, and read a great deal in the summer made greater gains in knowledge than pupils who did not study in the summer. Moreover, it has been found that the actual amount of time students spend in school is directly related to how much students learn.

Other research has indicated that the more education individuals receive, the more likely they are to read newspapers, books, and magazines, and to take part in politics and public affairs. More highly educated people are also more likely to be liberal in their political and social attitudes. Education is also related to individuals' sense of well-being and self-esteem. Thus, it is clear that, even taking into account the importance of individual social class background when evaluating the impact of education, more years of schooling leads to greater knowledge and social participation.

## Employment

Most students believe that graduating from college will lead to greater employment opportunities, and they are right. In 1986, about 54 percent of the 8 million college graduates in the United States entered professional and technical jobs. Research has shown that large organizations, such as corporations, require high levels of education for white-collar, managerial, or administrative jobs (Collins, 1971). In fact, as we discussed earlier, credential inflation has led to the expectation among employers that their employees will have an ever-increasing amount of formal education. But do well-educated employees actually do a better job? Surprisingly, most research has shown that the amount of education is only weakly related to job performance. Berg (1970), for instance, studied factory workers, maintenance workers, department store clerks, technicians, secretaries, bank tellers, engineers, industrial research scientists, military personnel, and federal civil service employers and found that the level of education was essentially unrelated to job performance. From this evidence, it seems clear that schools act as gatekeepers in determining who will get employed in high-status occupations, but schools do not provide significant job skills for their graduates. People learn how to do their jobs by doing them, which is not so surprising.

The economic and social worth of an academic credential, however, cannot be fully measured by examining its effects on job performance. Perhaps because academic credentials help individuals to obtain higher-status jobs early in their careers, possession of a college degree is significantly related to higher income. In 1986, male high school graduates earned, on average, $23,759; colleges graduates, $37,538; and those with five or more years of postsecondary education, $46,286. Among women, the same pattern prevails except that, at all levels of education, women earn less than men. Women with professional degrees, on average, earn considerably less than men with college degrees. These differences are due to occupational segregation by sex and pay discrimination.

These general findings, however, mask a great deal of variation when examining the relation between educational level and income level. According to some research, young African-American males who are highly educated earn as much as their white male counterparts, but whether this remains true across the lifecourse remains to be seen. Many other factors besides education affect how much income people earn in their lifetimes; these include type of employer, age, union membership, and social class background. In fact, even the most thorough research cannot demonstrate that more than one-third of income is directly attributable to level of education. So, getting a college and professional degree is important for earning more money, but education alone does not fully explain differences in levels of income.

### Education and Mobility

The belief that occupational and social mobility begin at the schoolhouse door is a critical component of the American ethos. As part of what might be termed *civil religion,* there is an abiding faith among most Americans that education is the great equalizer in the "great status race." Of course, not everybody subscribes to this faith. In a fascinating study, McLeod (1987) found that working-class boys often reject the prevailing "attainment through education" ethos by emphasizing their relative lack of economic and social mobility through cultural values that glorify physical hardness, manual labor, and a certain sense of fatalism. In general, however, most Americans believe that more education leads to economic and social mobility; individuals rise and fall based on their merit. Turner (1960) called this *contest* mobility. He compared *contest* mobility in the United States to *sponsored* mobility in the United Kingdom, where students are selected at an early age for academic and university education and where social class background is very important in determining who will receive academic or vocational training.

In this regard, keep in mind another important distinction when thinking of education and mobility. Hopper (1971) has made the point that there is a difference between educational *amount* and educational *route*. That is, the number of years of education is one measure of educational attainment, but *where* people go to school also affects their mobility. Private and public school students may receive the same amount of education, but a private school diploma may act as a "mobility escalator" because it represents a more prestigious educational route (Cookson & Persell, 1985).

The debate as to whether the public school is really the great equalizer has not been resolved. For some groups, such as the middle class, increased education may be directly linked to upward occupational mobility; for the poor and rich, education may have little to do with mobility. An educational degree alone cannot lift many people out of poverty, and upper-class individuals do not lose their social class position if they fail to achieve a high-status educational degree. In general, the data do not support the belief that education alone provides individuals with great amounts of economic and social mobility.

Rosenbaum (1976) has offered one suggestion as to why this may be the case. He likened mobility to *tournament selection,* where winners are allowed to proceed to the next round of competition, and losers are dropped from the competition. Players (students) can be eliminated, but winners must still continue to compete. The problem with this tournament, however, is that the criteria for winning and losing include a great many variables that are related to students' social class, race, and gender characteristics, as well as merit variables, such as grade-point average and SAT scores. The complex interplay between merit and privilege creates a tournament where the rules are not entirely even-handed and not everyone has the opportunity to set the rules. Without a doubt, the relation between education and mobility will continue to be debated among scholars and policy makers. The popular belief that education opens the doors of opportunity, however, is likely to remain firmly embedded in the American ethos.

## INSIDE THE SCHOOLS

How can the sociology of education help one to understand schools in terms of their objectives, cultures, and how do they shape students perceptions and expectations? In other words, how do sociologists look at schools from an organizational point of view? How do such organizational characteristics as curricula, teacher behaviors, and student peer groups shape learning and social growth? Since most people are apt to think about learning and growth from a psychological perspective, it is illuminating to stand back and speculate how school structures can also influence student outcomes. Think of something as simple as school size. Larger schools can offer students more in the way of facilities, but large schools are also more bureaucratic and may restrain initiative. Smaller schools may allow more student and teacher freedom, but small schools often lack resources. In general, schools are getting larger, if for no other reason than they are cost effective. Whether schools are large or small, however, the content of what they teach is a topic of important study.

Curriculum expresses culture. The question is, Whose culture? For some time, sociologists of education have pointed out that curricula are not value free; they are expressions of certain groups' ideas, beliefs, and prejudices. Knowing something about the bias and viewpoints of those who write curricula awakens one to the relativity of knowledge and its social and cultural context.

As you know, not all students study the same curriculum. It is also a fact that curriculum placement within schools has a direct impact on the probabilities of students attending college. Approximately 36 percent of public high school students take what is called a college preparatory course of study, which includes such subjects as English, history, science, math, and foreign language; 20 percent take a vocational program; and approximately 44 percent are enrolled in a general program, which combines such courses as English with accounting and clerical courses. In private school, virtually all students are enrolled in an academic curriculum. Research has shown that curricular placement is the single biggest determinant of college attendance (Lee & Byrk, 1989). We will have a great deal to say about curriculum later in this book, but for now, it may be useful to underscore the importance of curriculum when studying schools from a sociological perspective, especially in terms of cultural transmission and the selective channelling of opportunity.

### Teacher Behavior

It may seem obvious, but teachers have a huge impact on student learning and behavior. Jackson (1968) found that teachers have as many as 1,000 interpersonal contacts each day with children in their classrooms. Teachers are extremely busy people; they must also wear many different occupational hats: instructor, disciplinarian, bureaucrat, employer, friend, confidant, educator, and so on. These various roles sometimes are compatible with each other, and sometimes they are not. This can lead to *role-strain,* where such conflicting demands are placed on teachers that they cannot feel totally comfortable in any role. Could this be a cause of teacher burnout?

Clearly, teachers are models for students and, as instructional leaders, teachers set standards for students and influence student self-esteem and sense of efficacy. In a fascinating study conducted by Rosenthal and Jacobsen (1968), teachers' expectations of students were found to directly influence student achievement. The researchers told some teachers in a California elementary school that children in their classes were likely to have a mental growth spurt that year. In reality, the intelligence test that the children had taken revealed nothing about their potential achievement level. The students had been placed in their classes randomly. At the end of the year, the researchers returned to school and gave another test to see which children had improved. Although all the children improved somewhat, those labeled "spurters" made significantly greater achievement gains than other children, especially in the first and second grades. Thus, the labels that teachers apply to children can influence actual performance. This form of *self-fulfilling prophecy* indicates that teachers' expectations play a major role in encouraging or discouraging students to work to their full potential.

Persell (1977) found that when teachers demanded more from their students and praised them more, students learned more and felt better about themselves. Research indicates that many teachers have lower expectations for minority and working-class students; this suggests that these students may be trapped within a vicious cycle of low expectation–low achievement–low expectation. In part, this cycle of failure may be responsible for high dropout rates and failure to achieve at grade level. Of course, teachers cannot be held responsible for all the failures of education; there are many nonpedagogic reasons why U.S schools are failing to educate so many children. Teachers should not be scapegoated for society's problems, but the findings on teacher expectations do indicate that the attitudes of teachers toward their students may have a significant influence on student achievement and perceptions of self. Also, it is important not to overlook the fact that there are many outstanding teachers who are dedicated and inspirational and who have helped motivate students to do their best.

## Student Peer Groups and Alienation

When you reflect on your high school and junior high experiences, you undoubtedly have strong memories of your fellow students and the various social groups that they created. Almost nobody wants to be labeled a "nerd," and in most schools, the student culture idealizes athletic ability, looks, and that detached style that indicates "coolness." In a sense, the adult culture of the teachers and administrators is in conflict with the student culture. This conflict can lead to alienation and even violence.

Stinchcombe (1964) found, for instance, that students in vocational programs and headed toward low-status jobs were the students most likely to join a rebellious subculture. In fact, student violence is increasing. Students are not only attacking each other in increasing numbers but they are also assaulting teachers. The number of beatings, rapes, and even murders that are perpetrated against teachers has become something of a national scandal, but compared to what students do to each other, the danger for teachers is minimal. Some argue that school violence is increasing because teachers are underpaid and classes are too large. This may explain some of the violence, but it certainly does not explain all of it. A hundred years ago, teachers taught for little money and had class sizes double or triple present-day standards and there was little school violence. In today's culture, violence is far more acceptable, even glorified in the popular media. Being "bad" is misconstrued as being tough and smart. School children are bombarded with imaginary and actual violence in their homes, in their schools, and on the streets. It has been estimated that by the time the average child is 12 years old, he or she has been exposed to 18,000 television murders.

Student subcultures continue to be important after high school. There are four major types of college students: careerists, intellectuals, strivers, and unconnected. Careerists generally came from middle- and upper middle-class backgrounds, won few academic honors, lost confidence during college, and were not intellectually motivated by their experience. Intellectuals usually came from highly educated families, studied in the humanities, were politically involved, and earned many academic honors. Strivers very often had a working-class background, came from ethnic or racial minorities, worked hard, often did not have a high grade-point average, but graduated with a real sense of accomplishment. The unconnected came from all backgrounds, participated in few extracurricular activities, and were the least satisfied among all the groups with their college experience.

It should be evident, then, that student cultures play an important role in shaping students' educational experiences. We also hope that it is evident to you that looking within school from a sociological perspective can be very illuminating. Schools are far more than mere collections of individuals; they develop cultures, traditions, and restraints that profoundly influence those who work and study within them. They socialize and sort and select students and, in doing so, reproduce society. In the next section, we examine an issue of critical importance: How do schools reproduce social, cultural, and economic inequalities?

## EDUCATION AND INEQUALITY

Suppose we asked you to draw a picture of American society. How would it look? Like a circle? A square? A shapeless blob? Let's rephrase this question a bit. In terms of the distribution of income, power, and property, would you say that the shape of American society is flat? Probably not. Most of us know that income, power, and property are unevenly distributed in society. There are the "haves" and the "have-nots." Thinking figuratively again, most of us would agree that the economic and social structure of the U.S. population resembles a triangle where most of the people can be found at the base.

In the United States, there are essentially five classes: the *upper class,* with 1 to 3 percent of the total U.S. population; the *upper middle class,* with 5 to 10 percent of the population; the *lower middle class,* with 30 to 35 percent of the population; the *working class,* with 40 to 45 percent of the population; and the *lower or underclass,* with 20 to 25 percent of the population. The distribution of income, power, and property among these classes is highly uneven. The top fifth of the U.S. population owns three-fourths of the nation's wealth, whereas the remaining four-fifths own only one-fourth of the of the wealth (Persell, 1990). The bottom fifth own less than 0.2 percent of the nation's wealth. In 1987, the top fifth of U.S. families earned 43.7 percent of all income, whereas the bottom fifth earned 4.6 percent of the income. Moreover, there is increasing evidence that income differences are getting wider and that the United States is increasingly becoming a bipolar society of great wealth, great poverty, and an ever-shrinking middle class.

Social class differences are not only reflected in differences in income but in other social characteristics such as education, family and child-rearing practices, occupation, place of residence, political involvement, health, consumer behavior, and religious belief. In short, if you know a family's or individual's class position, you have a good idea about their life-style and life chances. Moreover, class influences what people think, by shaping the way in which they think. Class position creates selective perception which, in turn, creates a world view that "explains" inequalities. Ideology, then, grows out of the class system and reinforces the class system through beliefs that justify or condemn the status quo. Those who are oppressed by the class system may resist and revolt and those who benefit usually cooperate with and defend the current form of *social stratification.*

People, however, are not just stratified by class; they are also stratified by race, ethnicity, age, and gender. In short, Americans live in a hierarchical society where mobility is blocked because of structural inequalities that have little or nothing to do with individuals' merits or abilities.

For some time, sociologists have speculated and argued about whether schools mitigate social inequalities by providing opportunities for those who would not normally have them. Can schools create a more open society? This is a topic of immense importance and complexity. In later chapters, we will examine this issue in depth; for now, however, it might be useful to review some of the major ways schools help transmit social and economic inequalities.

### Inadequate Schools

Perhaps the most obvious way that schools reproduce inequalities is through inadequate schools. We have already discussed the crisis in U.S. education and how numerous critics of contemporary schooling have pointed out that the way in which children are educated today will not prepare them for productive and fulfilling lives in the future. Urban education, in particular, has failed to educate minority and poor children. Moreover, differences between schools and school systems reinforce existing inequalities. Students who attend suburban schools and private schools get a better educational experience than other children (Coleman, Hoffer, & Kilgore, 1982). Students who attend the most elite private schools obtain substantial educational benefits, both in terms of their actual educational experience and the social value of their diplomas (Cookson & Persell, 1985).

### Tracking

There is compelling evidence that within-school tracking has a critical impact on student mobility (Oakes, 1985). In principle, *tracking* refers to the placement of students in curricular programs based on students' abilities and inclinations. In reality, it has been found in many thorough studies that tracking decisions are often based on other criteria, such as students' class or race. By and large, working-class students end up in vocational tracks and middle-class students in academic tracks. Studies have shown that students placed in "high-ability" tracks spend more time on actual teaching and learning activities; are able to use more interesting materials; and consistently receive better teachers, better laboratory facilities, and more extracurricular activities than do their lower-track peers (Oakes, 1985; Goodlad, 1984). Moreover, track placement directly affects cognitive development (Rosenbaum, 1976). Students in lower tracks experience more alienation and authoritarian teachers than high-track students.

### De Facto Segregation

Another important way schools reinforce (even create) inequalities, particularly racial and ethnic inequalities, is through *de facto* segregation. In the previous chapter, we discussed in some depth the effects of segregated schools on student achievement, not to mention the issue of basic rights and equities. Although this issue is far from resolved, most of the evidence indicates that racial mixed schools benefit minorities and do *not* suppress white achievement. One study found that African Americans from low-income communities who attended racially mixed schools were more likely to graduate from high school and college than similar African-American children who attended segregated schools. Moreover, African-American students who attended integrated schools were less likely to be arrested by the police, more likely to live in desegregated neighborhoods, and women were less likely to have a child before the age of 18. Thus, racial integration at the school level seems to be beneficial to minority students, and there is no conclusive evidence that majority students are harmed by integration.

The issue of segregation, or resegregation, will be with society for a long time, if for no other reason than most people live in racially segregated neighborhoods. Groups and individuals who believe that students should be allowed to choose the schools they wish to attend argue that school choice will break down the barriers to integration created by racial segregated neighborhoods. Whether school choice would really end segregation is still very debatable; certainly, the historical evidence from the South during the 1960s and 1970s is not reassuring. During this period, white families set up their own academies in order to avoid racially integrated public schools.

### Gender

Another way schools reproduce inequalities is through gender discrimination. Men and women do not share equally in U.S. society. Men are frequently paid more than women for the same work, and women, in general, have fewer occupational opportunities than men. Although this gender gap has been somewhat reduced for middle- and uppermiddle-class women in the last decade, inequalities persist, particularly for working-class and lower-class women. How do schools perpetuate this problem?

Although girls usually start school cognitively and socially ahead of boys, by the end of high school, girls have lower self-esteem and lower aspirations than do boys. Somewhere during the high school years, in particular, girls begin to show signs of not living up to their potentials. Is it the gender composition of the faculty and staff that influences girls to lower their aspirations? Most teachers are female, whereas most administrators are male; could this be sending a subliminal message to girls that they are somehow subordinate to men? Do teachers treat boys and girls differently by stereotyping them by behavior? Are girls supposed to be "nice" and "feminine" while boys are allowed to act out and gain the center of attention? Studies do show that boys get more teacher attention (good and bad) than girls.

Traditionally, textbooks have been biased against women by ignoring their accomplishments and social contributions. Until very recently, there was little discussion in textbooks of sexism or gender bias. Discrimination need not always be overt. Often, gender bias is subtle; for instance, women go to college at the same rate as men, but they often go to two-year colleges or to less academically prestigious institutions.

Thus, schools are active organizational agents in recreating gender inequalities. However, schools alone should be held accountable for gender discrimination. This form of social stratification is rooted in the values and organization of society; schools in some ways only reflect these societal problems. This is not to say that educators *intend* to reproduce class, ethnic, racial, and gender inequalities, but the *consequences* of certain school policies and processes may reproduce these inequalities. Moreover, there is some evidence that for middle-class students, schooling does provide a "channel of attainment." In the main, however, the best evidence indicates that schools, despite educators' best intentions, tend to reproduce social inequalities. A major aspect of any meaningful reform movement must address this issue if schools are really to open doors to equal opportunity.

## SOCIOLOGY AND THE CURRENT EDUCATIONAL CRISIS

To grasp the magnitude of the current crisis in U.S. education, it is essential to recognize that at least one-third of the nation's children are at risk at failing in school, even before they enter kindergarten. Demographer Harold Hodgkinson (1991) has described the condition of U.S. children in stark and poignant terms. Since 1987, one-fourth of all preschool children in the United States live in poverty. In 1990, approximately 350,000 children were born to mothers who were addicted to cocaine during pregnancy. Some 15 million children are being reared by single mothers whose family income averages about $11,400 a year. At least 2 million school-age children have no adult supervision after school, and every night between 50,000 and 200,000 children have no home. How can schools help children to become productive and happy adults when so many children begin life with such severe disadvantages?

The sociological imagination helps one understand what is and what can be when one tries to imagine schools and school systems that meet the challenges that are facing today's children and young adults. The current educational crisis is complex, and solutions to the pressing problems are difficult to find. But people should not despair; we need to begin the work of reconstructing U.S. education. Sociologists ask the tough questions about schools and they search for answers by collecting data. Sometimes the data support preconceived beliefs, sometimes they do not. In either case, sociologists are committed to finding out the truth about the relationship between school and society, and it is this truth-seeking activity that is most likely to lead to meeting the challenges facing education today.

The following selections illustrate the sociological imagination when applied to educational problems. Each article addresses an important issue on the relationship between school and society. The first article, "Functionalist and Conflict Theories of Educational Stratification," written by sociologist Randall Collins, outlines the functionalist and conflict theories of education. Collins presents a critique of functionalist theory and demonstrates why he believes conflict theory is a more suitable explanation of the role of education in American society.

The second selection, written by sociologist Ray C. Rist, "On Understanding the Processes of Schooling: The Contributions of Labeling Theory," provides an illustration of the interpretive or interactionist perspective. Rist demonstrates how labeling theory provides a useful tool for understanding what goes on inside schools. The interactionist perspective, as Rist suggests, is an alternative to the more structural approaches of functionalism and conflict theory.

The third selection, "Closing the Rift between Scholarship and Practice: The Need to Revitalize Educational Research," written by sociologist Peter W. Cookson,

Jr., presents a critique of the present state of education research. Cookson suggests that sociologists need to address more clearly the needs and concerns of teachers and students or risk becoming irrelevant to ongoing educational policy and reform.

# Functional and Conflict Theories of Educational Stratification

## RANDALL COLLINS

Education has become highly important in occupational attainment in modern America, and thus occupies a central place in the analysis of stratification and of social mobility. This paper attempts to assess the adequacy of two theories in accounting for available evidence on the link between education and stratification: a functional theory concerning trends in technical skill requirements in industrial societies; and a conflict theory derived from the approach of Max Weber, stating the determinants of various outcomes in the struggles among status groups. It will be argued that the evidence best supports the conflict theory, although technical requirements have important effects in particular contexts. It will be further argued that the construction of a general theory of the determinants of stratification in its varying forms is best advanced by incorporating elements of the functional analysis of technical requirements of specific jobs at appropriate points within the conflict model. The conclusion offers an interpretation of historical change in education and stratification in industrial America, and suggests where further evidence is required for more precise tests and for further development of a comprehensive explanatory theory.

## THE IMPORTANCE OF EDUCATION

A number of studies have shown that the number of years of education is a strong determinant of occupational achievement in America with social origins constant. They also show that social origins affect educational attainment, and also occupational attainment after the completion of education (Blau and Duncan, 1967:163–205; Eckland, 1965; Sewell et al., 1969; Duncan and Hodge, 1963; Lipset and Bendix, 1959: 189–192). There are differences in occupational attainment independent of social origins between the graduates of more prominent and less prominent secondary schools, colleges, graduate schools, and law schools (Smigel, 1964:39, 73–74, 117; Havemann and West, 1952:179–181; Ladinsky, 1967; Hargens and Hagstrom, 1967).

Educational requirements for employment have become increasingly widespread, not only in elite occupations but also at the bottom of the occupational hierarchy (see Table 1). In a 1967 survey of the San Francisco, Oakland, and San Jose areas (Collins, 1969), 17% of the employers surveyed required at least a high school diploma for employment in even unskilled positions;[1] a

*Source: American Sociological Review* 36 (1971): 1002–1019. Reprinted by permission of the American Sociological Association.

I am indebted to Joseph Ben-David, Bennett Berger, Reinhard Bendix, Margaret S. Gordon, Joseph R. Gusfield, Stanford M. Lyman, Martin A. Trow, and Harold L. Wilensky for advice and comment; and to Margaret S. Gordon for making available data collected by the Institute of Industrial Relations of the University of California at Berkeley, under grants from the U. S. Office of Education and the U. S. Department of Labor. Their endorsement of the views expressed here is not implied.

**TABLE 1**
**Percent of Employers Requiring Various Minimum Educational Levels of Employees, by Occupational Level.**

| | National Survey, 1937–38 | | | | | |
|---|---|---|---|---|---|---|
| | *Unskilled* | *Semi-Skilled* | *Skilled* | *Clerical* | *Managerial* | *Professional* |
| Less than high school | 99% | 97% | 89% | 33% | 32% | 9% |
| High school diploma | 1 | 3 | 11 | 63 | 54 | 16 |
| Some college | | | | 1 | 2 | 23 |
| College degree | | | | 3 | 12 | 52 |
| | 100% | 100% | 100% | 100% | 100% | 100% |
| | San Francisco Bay Area, 1967 | | | | | |
| Less than high school | 83% | 76% | 62% | 29% | 27% | 10% |
| High school diploma | 16 | 24 | 28 | 68 | 14 | 4 |
| Vocational training beyond high school | 1 | 1 | 10 | 2 | 2 | 4 |
| Some college | | | | 2 | 12 | 7 |
| College degree | | | | | 41 | 70 |
| Graduate degree | | | | | 3 | 5 |
| | 100% | 100% | 100% | 101% | 99% | 100% |
| | (244) | (237) | (245) | (306) | (288) | (240) |

*Sources:* H. M. Bell, *Matching Youth and Jobs* (Washington: American Council on Education, 1940), p. 264, as analyzed in Lawrence Thomas, *The Occupational Structure and Education* (Englewood Cliffs: Prentice-Hall, 1956), p. 346; and Randall Collins, "Education and Employment," unpublished Ph.D. dissertation, University of California at Berkeley, 1969, Table 111-1. Bell does not report the number of employers in the sample, but it was apparently large.

national survey (Bell, 1940) in 1937–1938 found a comparable figure of 1%. At the same time, educational requirements appear to have become more specialized, with 38% of the organizations in the 1967 survey which required college degrees of managers preferring business administration training, and an additional 15% preferring engineering training; such requirements appear to have been virtually unknown in the 1920s (Pierson, 1959:34–54). At the same time, the proportions of the American population attending schools through the completion of high school and advanced levels have risen sharply during the last century (Table 2). Careers are thus increasingly shaped within the educational system.

## THE TECHNICAL-FUNCTION THEORY OF EDUCATION

A common explanation of the importance of education in modem society may be termed the technical-function theory. Its basic propositions, found in a number of sources (see, for example, B. Clark, 1962; Kerr et al., 1960), may be stated as follows: (1) the skill requirements of jobs in industrial society constantly increase because of technological change. Two processes are involved: (a) the proportion of jobs requiring low skill decreases and the proportion requiring high skill increases; and (b) the same jobs are upgraded in skill requirements. (2) Formal education provides the training, either in specific

**TABLE 2**
Percentage Educational Attainment in the United States, 1869–1965.

| Period | High School Graduates Pop. 17 Yrs. Old | Resident College Students/ Pop. 18–21 | B.A.'s or 1st Prof. Degrees/ 1/10 of Pop. 15–24 | M.A.'s or 2nd Prof. Degrees/ 1/10 of Pop. 25–34 | Ph.,D.'s 1/10 of Pop. 25–34 |
|---|---|---|---|---|---|
| 1869–1870 | 2.0 | 1.7 | | | |
| 1879–1880 | 2.5 | 2.7 | | | |
| 1889–1890 | 3.3 | 3.0 | | | |
| 1899–1900 | 6.4 | 4.0 | 1.66 | 0.12 | 0.03 |
| 1909–1910 | 8.8 | 5.1 | 1.85 | 0.13 | 0.02 |
| 1919–1920 | 16.8 | 8.9 | 2.33 | 0.24 | 0.03 |
| 1929–1930 | 29.0 | 12.4 | 4.90 | 0.78 | 0.12 |
| 1939–1940 | 50.8 | 15.6 | 7.05 | 1.24 | 0.15 |
| 1949–1950 | 59.0 | 29.6 | 17.66 | 2.43 | 0.27 |
| 1959–1960 | 65.1 | 34.9 | 17.72 | 3.25 | 0.42 |
| 1963 | 76.3 | 38.0 | | | |
| 1965 | | | 19.71 | 5.02 | 0.73 |

*Sources:* Historical Statistics of the United Stares, Series A-28-29, H 327-338; Statistical Abstract of the United States 1966, Tables 3 and 194; Digest of Educational Statistics (U. S. Office of Education, 1967), Tables 66 and 88.

skills or general capacities, necessary for the more highly skilled jobs. (3) Therefore, educational requirements for employment constantly rise, and increasingly larger proportions of the population are required to spend longer and longer periods in school.

The technical-function theory of education may be seen as a particular application of a more general functional approach. The functional theory of stratification (Davis and Moore, 1945) rests on the premises (A) that occupational positions require particular kinds of skilled performance; and (B) that positions must be filled with persons who have either the native ability, or who have acquired the training, necessary for the performance of the given occupational role.[2] The technical-function theory of education may be viewed as a subtype of this form of analysis, since it shares the premises that the occupational structure creates demands for particular kinds of performance, and that training is one way of filling these demands. In addition, it includes the more restrictive premises (1 and 2 above) concerning the way in which skill requirements of jobs change with industrialization, and concerning the content of school experiences.

The technical-function theory of education may be tested by reviewing the evidence for each of its propositions (1a, 1b, and 2).[3] As will be seen, these propositions do not adequately account for the evidence. In order to generate a more complete explanation, it will be necessary to examine the evidence for the underlying functional propositions, (A) and (B). This analysis leads to a focus on the processes of stratification—notably group conflict—not expressed in the functional theory, and to the formalization of a conflict theory to account for the evidence.

Proposition (1a): *Educational requirements of jobs in industrial society increase because the proportion of jobs requiring low skill decreases and the proportion requiring high skill increases.* Available evidence suggests that this process accounts for only a minor part of educational upgrading, at least in a society that has passed the point of initial industrialization. Fifteen percent of the increase in education of the U.S. labor force during the twentieth century may be attributed to shifts in the occupational structure—a decrease in the proportion of jobs with low skill requirements and an increase in proportion of jobs with high skill requirements (Folger and Nam, 1964). The bulk of educational upgrading (85%) has occurred within job categories.

Proposition (1b): *Educational requirements of jobs in industrial society rise because the same jobs are upgraded in skill requirements.* The only available evidence on this point consists of data collected by the U.S. Department of Labor in 1950 and 1960, which indicate the amount of change in skill requirements of specific jobs. Under the most plausible assumptions as to the skills provided by various levels of education, it appears that the educational level of the U.S. labor force has changed in excess of that which is necessary to keep up with skill requirements of jobs (Berg, 1970:38–60). Over-education for available jobs is found particularly among males who have graduated from college and females with high school degrees or some college, and appears to have increased between 1950 and 1960.

Proposition (2): *Formal education provides required job skills.* This proposition may be tested in two ways: (a) Are better educated employees more productive than less educated employees? (b) Are vocational skills learned in schools, or elsewhere?

(a) *Are better educated employees more productive?* The evidence most often cited for the productive effects of education is indirect, consisting of relationships between *aggregate* levels of education in a society and its overall economic productivity. These are of three types:

(i) The national growth approach involves calculating the proportion of growth in the U.S. Gross National Product attributable to conventional inputs of capital and labor; these leave a large residual, which is attributed to improvements in skill of the labor force based on increased education (Schultz, 1961; Denison, 1965). This approach suffers from difficulty in clearly distinguishing among technological change affecting productive arrangements, changes in the abilities of workers acquired by experience at work with new technologies, and changes in skills due to formal education and motivational factors associated with a competitive or achievement-oriented society. The assignment of a large proportion of the residual category to education is arbitrary. Denison (1965) makes this attribution on the basis of the increased income to persons with higher levels of education interpreted as rewards for their contributions to productivity. Although it is a common assumption in economic argument that wage returns reflect output value, wage returns cannot be used to prove the productive contribution of education without circular reasoning.

(ii) Correlations of education and level of economic development for nations show that the higher the level of economic development of a country, the higher the proportion of its population in elementary, secondary, and higher education (Harbison and Myers, 1964). Such correlations beg the question of causality. There are considerable variations in school enrollments among countries at the same economic level, and many of these variations are explicable in terms of political demands for access to education (Ben-David, 1963–64). Also, the overproduction of educated personnel in countries whose level of economic development cannot absorb them suggests the demand for education need not come directly from the economy, and may run counter to economic needs (Hoselitz, 1965).

(iii) Time-tag correlations of education and economic development show that increases in the proportion of population in elementary school precede increases in economic development after a takeoff point at approximately 30–50% of the 7–14 years old age-group in school. Similar anticipations of economic development are suggested for increases in secondary and higher education enrollment, although the data do not clearly support this conclusion (Peaslee, 1969). A pattern of advances in secondary school enrollments preceding advances in economic development is found only in a small number of cases (12 of 37 examined in Peaslee, 1969). A pattern of growth of university enrollments and subsequent economic development is found in 21 of 37 cases, but the exceptions (including the United States, France, Sweden, Russia, and Japan) are of such importance as to throw serious doubt on any *necessary* contribution of higher education to economic development. The main contribution of education to economic productivity, then, appears to occur at the level of the transition to mass literacy, and not significantly beyond this level.

Direct evidence of the contribution of education to *individual* productivity is summarized by Berg (1970:85–104, 143–176). It indicates that the better educated employees are not generally more productive and in some cases are less productive, among samples of factory workers, maintenance men, department store clerks, technicians, secretaries, bank tellers, engineers, industrial research scientists, military personnel, and federal civil service employees.

(b) *Are vocational skills learned in school, or elsewhere?* Specifically vocational education

in the schools for manual positions is virtually independent of job fate, as graduates of vocational programs are not more likely to be employed than high school dropouts (Plunkett, 1960; Duncan, 1964). Most skilled manual workers acquire their skills on the job or casually (Clark and Sloan, 1966:73). Retraining for important technological changes in industry has been carried out largely informally on-the-job; in only a very small proportion of jobs affected by technological change is formal retraining in educational institutions used (Collins, 1969:147–158; Bright, 1958).

The relevance of education for nonmanual occupational skills is more difficult to evaluate. Training in specific professions, such as medicine, engineering, scientific or scholarly research, teaching, and law can plausibly be considered vocationally relevant, and possibly essential. Evidences comparing particular degrees of educational success with particular kinds of occupational performance or success are not available, except for a few occupations. For engineers, high college grades and degree levels generally predict high levels of technical responsibility and high participation in professional activities, but not necessarily high salary or supervisory responsibility (Perrucci and Perrucci, 1970). At the same time, a number of practicing engineers lack college degrees (about 40% of engineers in the early 1950s; see Soderberg, 1963:213), suggesting that even such highly technical skills may be acquired on the job. For academic research scientists, educational quality has little effect on subsequent productivity (Hagstrom and Hargens, 1968). For other professions, evidence is not available on the degree to which actual skills are learned in school rather than in practice. In professions such as medicine and law, where education is a legal requirement for admission to practice, a comparison group of noneducated practitioners is not available, at least in the modern era.

Outside of the traditional learned professions, the plausibility of the vocational importance of education is more questionable. Comparisons of the efforts of different occupations to achieve "professionalization" suggest that setting educational requirements and bolstering them through licensing laws is a common tactic in raising an occupation's prestige and autonomy (Wilensky, 1964). The result has been the proliferation of numerous pseudo-professions in modern society; nevertheless these fail to achieve strong professional organization through lack of a monopolizable (and hence teachable) skill base. Business administration schools represent such an effort. (See Pierson, 1959:9, 55–95, 140; Gordon and Howell, 1959:1–18, 40, 324–337). Descriptions of general, nonvocational education do not support the image of schools as places where skills are widely learned. Scattered studies suggest that the knowledge imparted in particular courses is retained only in small part through the next few years (Learned and Wood, 1938:28), and indicate a dominant student culture concerned with nonacademic interests or with achieving grades with a minimum of learning (Coleman, 1961; Becker et al., 1968).

The technical-function theory of education, then, does not give an adequate account of the evidence. Economic evidence indicates no clear contributions of education to economic development, beyond the provisions of mass literacy. Shifts in the proportions of more skilled and less skilled jobs do not account for the observed increase in education of the American labor force. Education is often irrelevant to on-the-job productivity and is sometimes counterproductive; specifically vocational training seems to be derived more from work experience than from formal school training. The quality of schools themselves, and the nature of dominant student cultures suggest that schooling is very inefficient as a means of training for work skills.

## FUNCTIONAL AND CONFLICT PERSPECTIVES

It may be suggested that the inadequacies of the technical-function theory of education derive from a more basic source: the functional approach to stratification. A fundamental assumption is that there is a generally fixed set of positions, whose various requirements the labor force must satisfy. The fixed demand for skills of various types, at any given time, is the basic determinant of who will be selected for what positions. Social change may then be explained by specifying how these functional demands change with the process of modernization. In keeping with the functional perspective in general, the needs of society are seen as determining the behavior and the rewards of the individuals within it.

However, this premise may be questioned as an adequate picture of the fundamental processes of social organization. It may be suggested that the "demands" of any occupational position are not fixed, but represent whatever behavior is settled upon in bargaining between the persons who fill the positions and those who attempt to control them. Individuals want jobs primarily for the rewards to themselves in material goods, power, and prestige. The amount of productive skill they must demonstrate to hold their positions depends on how much clients, customers, or employers can successfully demand of them, and this in turn depends on the balance of power between workers and their employers.

Employers tend to have quite imprecise conceptions of the skill requirements of most jobs, and operate on a strategy of "satisficing" rather than optimizing—that is, setting average levels of performance as satisfactory, and making changes in procedures or personnel only when performance falls noticeably below minimum standards (Dill et al., 1962; March and Simon, 1958:140–141). Efforts to predict work performance by objective tests have foundered due to difficulties in measuring performance (except on specific mechanical tasks) and the lack of control groups to validate the tests (Anastasi, 1967). Organizations do not force their employees to work at maximum efficiency; there is considerable insulation of workers at all levels from demands for full use of their skills and efforts. Informal controls over output are found not only among production workers in manufacturing but also among sales and clerical personnel (Roy, 1952; Blau, 1955; Lombard, 1955). The existence of informal organization at the managerial level, the widespread existence of bureaucratic pathologies such as evasion of responsibility, empire-building, and displacement of means by ends ("red tape"), and the fact that administrative work is only indirectly related to the output of the organization, suggest that managers, too, are insulated from strong technological pressures for use of technical skills. On all levels, wherever informal organization exists, it appears that standards of performance reflect the power of the groups involved.

In this light, it is possible to reinterpret the body of evidence that ascriptive factors continue to be important in occupational success even in advanced industrial society. The social mobility data summarized at the onset of this paper show that social origins have a direct effect on occupational success, even after the completion of education. Both case studies and cross-sectional samples amply document widespread discrimination against Negroes. Case studies show that the operation of ethnic and class standards in employment bases not merely on skin color but on name, accent, style of dress, manners, and conversational abilities (Noland and Bakke, 1949; Turner, 1952; Taeuber et al., 1966; Nosow, 1956). Cross-sectional studies, based on both biographical and survey data, show that approximately 60 to 70% of the American business elite come from upper-class and upper-middle-class families,

and fewer than 15% from working-class families (Taussia and Joselyn, 1932:97; Wamer and Abegglen, 1955:37–68; Newcomer, 1955: 53; Bendix, 1956:198–253; Mills, 1963: 110–139). These proportions are fairly constant from the early 1800's through the 1950's. The business elite is overwhelmingly Protestant, male, and completely white, although there are some indications of a mild trend toward declining social origins and an increase of Catholics and Jews. Ethnic and class background have been found crucial for career advancement in the professions as well (Ladinsky, 1963; Hall, 1946). Sexual stereotyping of jobs is extremely widespread (Collins, 1969:234–238).

In the traditional functionalist approach, these forms of ascription are treated as residual categories: carry-overs from a less advanced period, or marks of the imperfections of the functional mechanism of placement. Yet available trend data suggest that the link between social class origins and occupational attainment has remained constant during the twentieth century in America (Blau and Duncan, 1967:81–113); the proportion of women in higher occupational levels has changed little since the late nineteenth century (Epstein, 1970:7); and the few available comparisons between elite groups in traditional and modern societies suggest comparable levels of mobility (Marsh, 1963). Declines in racial and ethnic discrimination that appear to have occurred at periods in twentieth-century America may be plausibly explained as results of political mobilization of particular minority groups rather than by an increased economic need to select by achievement criteria.

Goode (1967) has offered a modified functional model to account for these disparities: that work groups always organize to protect their inept members from being judged by outsiders' standards of productivity, and that this self-protection is functional to the organizations, preventing a Hobbesian competitiveness and distrust of all against all. This argument re-establishes a functional explanation, but only at the cost of undermining the technological view of functional requirements. Further, Goode's conclusions can be put in other terms: it is to the advantage of groups of employees to organize so that they will not be judged by strict performance standards; and it is at least minimally to the advantage of the employer to let them do so, for if he presses them harder he creates dissension and alienation. Just how hard an employer *can* press his employees is not given in Goode's functional model. That is, his model has the disadvantage, common to functional analysis in its most general form, of covering too many alternative possibilities to provide testable explanations of specific outcomes. Functional analysis too easily operates as a justification for whatever particular pattern exists, asserting in effect that there is a proper reason for it to be so, but failing to state the conditions under which a particular pattern will hold rather than another. The technical version of job requirements has the advantage of specifying patterns, but it is this specific form of functional explanation that is jettisoned by a return to a more abstract functional analysis.

A second hypothesis may be suggested: the power of "ascribed" groups may be the *prime* basis of selection in all organizations, and technical skills are secondary consideration depending on the balance of power. Education may thus be regarded as a mark of membership in a particular group (possibly at times its defining characteristic), not a mark of technical skills or achievement. Educational requirements may thus reflect the interests of whichever groups have power to set them. Weber (1968:1000) interpreted educational requirements in bureaucracies, drawing especially on the history of public administration in Prussia, as the result of efforts by university graduates to monopolize positions, raise their corporate status, and thereby increase their own security and power vis-á-vis both higher authorities and clients. Gusfield (1958) has shown that educational require-

ments in the British Civil Service were set as the result of a power struggle between a victorious educated upper-middle-class and the traditional aristocracy.

To summarize the argument to this point: available evidence suggests that the technical-functional view of educational requirements for jobs leaves a large number of facts unexplained. Functional analysis on the more abstract level does not provide a testable explanation of which ascribed groups will be able to dominate which positions. To answer this question, one must leave the functional frame of reference and examine the conditions of relative power of each group.

## A CONFLICT THEORY OF STRATIFICATION

The conditions under which educational requirements will be set and changed may be stated more generally, on the basis of a conflict theory of stratification derived from Weber (1968:926–939; see also Collins, 1968), and from advances in modern organization theory fitting the spirit of this a approach.

A. *Status groups.* The basic units of society are associational groups sharing common cultures (or "subcultures"). The core of such groups is families and friends, but they may be extended to religious, educational, or ethnic communities. In general, they comprise all persons who share a sense of status equality based on participation in a common culture: styles of language, tastes in clothing and decor, manners and other ritual observances, conversational topics and styles, opinions and values, and preferences in sports, arts, and media. Participation in such cultural groups gives individuals their fundamental sense of identity, especially in contrast with members of other associational groups in whose everyday culture they cannot participate comfortably. Subjectively, status groups distinguish themselves from others in terms of categories of *moral evaluation* such as "honor," "taste," "breeding," "respectability," "propriety," "cultivation," " good fellows," "plain folks," etc. Thus the exclusion of persons who lack the ingroup culture is felt to be normatively legitimated.

There is no *a priori* determination of the number of status groups in a particular society, nor can the degree to which there is consensus on a rank order among them be stated in advance. These are not matters of definition, but empirical variations, the causes of which are subjects of other developments of the conflict theory of stratification. Status groups should be regarded as ideal types, without implication of *necessarily distinct* boundaries; the concepts remain useful even in the case where associational groupings and their status cultures are fluid and overlapping, as hypotheses about the conflicts among status groups may remain fruitful even under these circumstances.

Status groups may be derived from a number of sources. Weber outlines three: (a) differences in life style based on economic situation (i.e., class); (b) differences in life situation based on power position; (c) differences in life situation deriving directly from cultural conditions or institutions, such as geographical origin, ethnicity, religion, education, or intellectual or aesthetic cultures.

B. *Struggle for Advantage.* There is a continual struggle in society for various "goods"—wealth, power, or prestige. We need make no assumption that every individual is motivated to maximize his rewards; however, since power and prestige are inherently scarce commodities, and wealth is often contingent upon them, the ambition of even a small proportion of persons for more than equal shares of these goods sets up an implicit counter-struggle on the part of others to avoid subjection and disesteem. Individuals may struggle with each other, but since individual identity is derived primarily from membership in a status group, and because the cohesion of status groups is a key resource in the struggle against others, the primary focus of struggle is between status groups rather than within them.

The struggle for wealth, power, and prestige is carried out primarily through organizations. There have been struggles throughout history among organizations controlled by different status groups, for military conquest, business advantage, or cultural (e.g., religious) hegemony, and intricate sorts of interorganizational alliances are possible. In the more complex societies, struggle between status groups is carried on in large part *within* organizations, as the status groups controlling an organization coerce, hire, or culturally manipulate others to carry out their wishes (as in, respectively, a conscript army, a business, or a church). Organizational research shows that the success of organizational elites in controlling their subordinates is quite variable. Under particular conditions, lower or middle members have considerable *de facto* power to avoid compliance, and even to change the course of the organizations (see Etzioni, 1961).

This opposing power from below is strengthened when subordinate members constitute a cohesive status group of their own; it is weakened when subordinates acquiesce in the values of the organization elite. Coincidence of ethnic and class boundaries produces the sharpest cultural distinctions. Thus, Catholics of immigrant origins have been the bulwarks of informal norms restricting work output in American firms run by WASPS, whereas Protestants of native rural backgrounds are the main "rate-busters" (O. Collins et al., 1946). Selection and manipulation of members in terms of status groups is thus a key weapon in intraorganizational struggles. In general, the organization elite selects its new members and key assistants from its own status group and makes an effort to secure lower-level employees who are at least indoctrinated to respect the cultural superiority of their status culture.[4]

Once groups of employees of different status groups are formed at various positions (middle, lower, or laterally differentiated) in the organization, each of these groups may be expected to launch efforts to recruit more members of their own status group. This process is illustrated by conflicts among whites and blacks, Protestants and Catholics and Jews, Yankee, Irish and Italian, etc. found in American occupational life (Hughes, 1949; Dalton, 1951). These conflicts are based on ethnically or religiously founded status cultures; their intensity rises and falls with processes increasing or decreasing the cultural distinctiveness of these groups, and with the succession of advantages and disadvantages set by previous outcomes of these struggles which determine the organizational resources available for further struggle. Parallel processes of cultural conflict may be based on distinctive class as well as ethnic cultures.

C. *Education as Status Culture*. The main activity of schools is to teach particular status cultures, both in and outside the classroom. In this light, any failure of schools to impart technical knowledge (although it may also be successful in this) is not important; schools primarily teach vocabulary and inflection, styles of dress, aesthetic tastes, values and manners. The emphasis on sociability and athletics found in many schools is not extraneous but may be at the core of the status culture propagated by the schools. Where schools have a more academic or vocational emphasis, this emphasis may itself be the content of a particular status culture, providing sets of values, materials for conversation, and shared activities for an associational group making claims to a particular basis for status.

Insofar as a particular status group controls education, it may use to foster control within work organizations. Educational requirements for employment can serve both to select new members for elite positions who share the elite culture and, at a lower level of education, to hire lower and middle employees who have acquired a general respect for these elite values and styles.

## TESTS OF THE CONFLICT THEORY OF EDUCATIONAL STRATIFICATION

The conflict theory in its general form is supported by evidence (1) that there are distinctions among status group cultures—based both on class and on ethnicity—in modern societies (Kahl, 1957:127–156, 184–220); (2) that status groups tend to occupy different occupation positions within organizations (see data on ascription cited above); and (3) that occupants of different organizational positions struggle over power (Dalton, 1959; Crozier, 1964). The more specific tests called for here, however, are of the adequacy of conflict theory to explain the link between education and occupational stratification. Such tests may focus either on the proposed mechanism of occupational placement, or on the conditions for strong or weak links between education and occupation.

*Education as a Mechanism of Occupational Placement*. The mechanism proposed is that employers use education to select persons who have been socialized into the dominant status culture; for entrants to their own managerial ranks, into elite culture; for lower-level employees, into an attitude of respect for the dominant culture and the elite which carries it. This requires evidence that: (a) schools provide either training for the elite culture, or respect for it; and (b) employers use education as a means selection for cultural attributes.

(a) Historical and descriptive studies of schools support the generalization that they are places where particular status cultures are acquired, either from the teachers, from other students, or both. Schools are usually founded by powerful or autonomous status groups, either to provide an exclusive education for their own children, or to propagate respect for their cultural values. Until recently most schools were founded by religions, often in opposition to those founded by rival religions; throughout the 19th century, this rivalry was an important basis for the founding of large numbers of colleges in the U. S., and of the Catholic and Lutheran school systems. The public school system in the U. S. was founded mainly under the impetus of WASP elites with the purpose of teaching respect for Protestant and middle-class standards of cultural and religious propriety, especially in the face of Catholic, working-class immigration from Europe (Cremin, 1961; Curti, 1935). The content of public school education has consisted especially of middle-class, WASP culture (Waller, 1932:15–131; Becker, 1961; Hess and Torney, 1967).

At the elite level, private secondary schools for children of the WASP upper class were founded from the 1880s, when the mass indoctrination function of the growing public schools made them unsuitable as means of maintaining cohesion of the elite culture itself (Baltzell, 1958:327–372). These elite schools produce a distinctive personality type, characterized by adherence to a distinctive set of upper-class values and manners (McArthur, 1955). The cultural role of schools has been more closely studied in Britain (Bernstein, 1961; Weinberg, 1967), and in France (Bourdieu and Passeron, 1964), although Riesman and his colleagues (Riesman, 1958; Jencks and Riesman, 1968) have shown some of the cultural differences among prestige levels of colleges and universities in the United States.

(b) Evidence that education has been used as a means of cultural selection may be found in several sources. Hollingshead's (1949: 360–388) study of Elmtown school children, school dropouts, and community attitudes toward them suggests that employers use education as a means of selecting employees with middle-class attributes. A 1945–1946 survey of 240 employers in New Haven and Charlotte, N.C., indicated that they regarded education as a screening device for employees with desirable (middle-class) character and demeanor; white-collar positions particularly emphasized educational selection because these employees were considered most visible to outsiders (Noland and Bakke, 1949: 20–63).

A survey of employers in nationally prominent corporations indicated that they regarded college degrees as important in hiring potential managers, not because they were thought to ensure technical skills, but rather to indicate "motivation" and "social experience" (Gordon and Howell, 1959:121). Business school training is similarly regarded, less as evidence of necessary training (as employers have been widely skeptical of the utility of this curriculum for most positions) than as an indication that the college graduate is committed to business attitudes. Thus, employers are more likely to refuse to hire liberal arts graduates if they come from a college which has a business school than if their college is without a business school (Gordon and Howell, 1959:84–87; see also Pierson, 1959:90–99). In the latter case, the students could be said not to have had a choice; but when both business and liberal arts courses are offered and the student chooses liberal arts, employers appear to take this as a rejection of business values.

Finally, a 1967 survey of 309 California organizations (Collins, 1971) found that educational requirements for white-collar workers were highest in organizations which placed the strongest emphasis on normative control over their employees.[5] Normative control emphasis was indicated by (i) relative emphasis on the absence of police record for job applicants; (ii) relative emphasis on a record of job loyalty; (iii) Etzioni's (1961) classification of organizations into those with high normative control emphasis (financial, professional services, government, and other public services organizations) and those with remunerative control emphasis (manufacturing, construction; and trade). These three indicators are highly interrelated, thus mutually validating their conceptualization as indicators of normative control emphasis. The relationship between normative control emphasis and educational requirements holds for managerial requirements and white-collar requirements generally, both including and excluding professional and technical positions. Normative control emphasis does not affect blue-collar education requirements.

## VARIATIONS IN LINKAGE BETWEEN EDUCATION AND OCCUPATION

The conflict model may also be tested by examining the cases in which it predicts education will be relatively important or unimportant in occupational attainment. Education should be most important where two conditions hold simultaneously: (1) the type of education most closely reflects membership in a particular status group and (2) that group controls employment in particular organizational contexts. Thus, education will be most important where the fit is greatest between the culture of the status groups emerging from schools, and the status group doing the hiring; it will be least important where there is the greatest disparity between the culture of the school and of the employers.

This fit between school-group culture and employer culture may be conceptualized as a continuum. The importance of elite education is highest where it is involved in selection of new members of organizational elites, and should fade off where jobs are less elite (either lower level jobs in these organizations, or jobs in other organizations not controlled by the cultural elite). Similarly, schools which produce the most elite graduates will be most closely linked to elite occupations; schools whose products are less well socialized into elite culture are selected for jobs correspondingly less close to elite organizational levels.

In the United States, the schools which produce culturally elite groups, either by virtue of explicit training or by selection of students from elite backgrounds, or both, are the private prep schools at the secondary level; at the higher level, the elite colleges (the Ivy league, and to a lesser degree the major state universities); at the professional training level, those professional schools attached to the elite colleges and universities. At the secondary level, schools which produce respectably socialized, non-elite persons are the public high schools (especially those in middle-class residential areas); from the point of view of the culture of WASP employers, Catholic schools (and all-black schools) are less acceptable. At the level of higher education, Catholic and black colleges and professional schools are less elite, and commercial training schools are the least elite form of education.

In the United States, the organizations most clearly dominated by the WASP upper class are large, nationally organized business corporations, and the largest law firms (Domhoff, 1967:38–62). Those organizations more likely to be dominated by members of minority ethnic cultures are the smaller and local businesses in manufacturing, construction, and retail trade; in legal practice, solo rather than firm employment. In government employment, local governments appear to be more heavily dominated by ethnic groups, whereas particular branches of the national government (notably the State Department and the Treasury) are dominated by WASP elites (Domhoff, 1967: 84–114, 132–137).

Evidence on the fit between education and employment is available for only some of these organizations. In a broad sample of organizational types (Collins, 1971) educational requirements were higher in the bigger organizations, which also tended to be organized on a national scale, than in smaller and more localistic organizations.[6] The finding of

Perrucci and Perrucci (1970) that upper-class social origins were important in career success precisely within the group of engineers who graduated from the most prestigious engineering schools with the highest grades may also bear on this question; since the big national corporations are most likely to hire this academically elite group, the importance of social origins within this group tends to corroborate the interpretation of education as part of a process of elite cultural selection in those organizations.

Among lawyers, the predicted differences are clear: graduates of the law schools attached to elite colleges and universities are more likely to be employed in firms, whereas graduates of Catholic or commercial law schools are more likely to be found in solo practice (Ladinsky, 1967). The elite Wall Street law firms are most educationally selective in this regard, choosing not only from Ivy League law schools but from a group whose background includes attendance at elite prep schools and colleges (Smigel, 1964:39, 73–74, 117). There are also indications that graduates of ethnically dominated professional schools are most likely to practice within the ethnic community; this is clearly the case among black professionals. In general, the evidence that graduates of black colleges (Sharp, 1970:64–67) and of Catholic colleges (Jencks and Riesman, 1968: 357–366) have attained lower occupational positions in business than graduates of white Protestant schools (at least until recent years) also bolsters this interpretation.[7]

It is possible to interpret this evidence according to the technical-function theory of education, arguing that the elite schools provide the best technical training, and that the major national organizations require the greatest degree of technical talent. What is necessary is to test simultaneously for technical and status-conflict conditions. The most direct evidence on this point is the California employer study (Collins, 1971), which exam-

ined the effects of normative control emphasis and of organizational prominence, while holding constant the organization's technological modernity, as measured by the number of technological and organizational changes in the previous six years. Technological change was found to affect educational requirements at managerial and white-collar (but not blue-collar) levels, thus giving some support to the technical-function theory of education. The three variables—normative control emphasis, organizational prominence, and technological change—each independently affected educational requirements, in particular contexts. Technological change produced significantly higher educational requirements only in smaller, localistic organizations, and in organizational sectors not emphasizing normative control. Organizational prominence produced significantly higher educational requirements in organizations with low technological change, and in sectors de-emphasizing normative control. Normative control emphasis produced significantly higher educational requirements in organizations with low technological change, and in less prominent organizations. Thus, technical and normative status conditions all affect educational requirements; measures of association indicated that the latter conditions were stronger in this sample.

Other evidence bearing on this point concerns business executives only. A study of the top executives in nationally prominent businesses indicated that the most highly educated managers were not found in the most rapidly developing companies, but rather in the least economically vigorous ones, with highest education found in the traditionalistic financial and utility firms (Warner and Abegglen, 1955:141–143, 148). The business elite has always been highly educated in relation to the American populace, but education seems to be a correlate of their social origins rather than the determinant of their success (Mills, 1963:128; Taussig and Joslyn,

1932:200: Newcomer, 1955:76). Those members of the business elite who entered its ranks from lower social origins had less education than the businessmen of upper and upper-middle-class origins, and those businessmen who inherited their companies were much more likely to be college educated than those who achieved their positions by entrepreneurship (Bendix, 1956:230; Newcomer, 1955:80).

In general, the evidence indicates that educational requirements for employment reflect employers' concerns for acquiring respectable and well-socialized employees; their concern for the provision of technical skills through education enters to a lesser degree. The higher the normative control concerns of the employer, and the more elite the organization's status, the higher his educational requirements.

## HISTORICAL CHANGE

The rise in educational requirements for employment throughout the last century may be explained using the conflict theory, and incorporating elements of the technical functional theory into it at appropriate points. The principal dynamic has centered on changes in the supply of educated persons caused by the expansion of the school system, which was in turn shaped by three conditions:

(1) Education has been associated with high economic and status position from the colonial period on through the twentieth century. The result was a popular demand for education as mobility opportunity. This demand has not been for vocational education at a terminal or commercial level, short of full university certification; the demand has rather focused on education giving entry into the elite status culture, and usually only those technically-oriented schools have prospered which have most closely associated themselves with the sequence of education leading to (or from) the classical Bachelor's degree (Collins, 1969:68–70, 86–87, 89, 96–101).

(2) Political decentralization, separation of church and state, and competition among religious denominations have made founding schools and colleges in America relatively easy, and provided initial motivations of competition among communities and religious groups that moved them to do so. As a result, education at all levels expanded faster in America than anywhere else in the world. At the time of the Revolution, there were nine colleges in the colonies; in all of Europe, with a population forty times that of America, there were approximately sixty colleges. By 1880 there were 811 American colleges and universities; by 1966, there were 2,337. The United States not only began with the highest ratio of institutions of higher education to population in the world, but increased this lead steadily, for the number of European universities was not much greater by the twentieth century than in the eighteenth (Ben-David and Zloczower, 1962).

(3) Technical changes also entered into the expansion of American education. As the evidence summarized above indicates: (a) mass literacy is crucial for beginnings of full-scale industrialization, although demand for literacy could not have been important in the expansion of education beyond elementary levels. More importantly, (b) there is a mild trend toward the reduction in the proportion of unskilled jobs and an increase in the promotion of highly skilled (professional and technical) jobs as industrialism proceeds accounting for 15% of the shift in educational levels in the twentieth century (Folger and Nam, 1964). (c) Technological change also brings about some upgrading in skill requirements of some continuing job positions, although the available evidence (Berg, 1970:38–60) refers only to the decade 1950–1960. Nevertheless, as Wilensky (1964) points out, there is no "professionalization of everyone," as most jobs do not

require considerable technical knowledge on the order of that required of the engineer or the research scientist.

The existence of a relatively small group of experts in high-status positions, however, can have important effects on the structure of competition for mobility chances. In the United States, where democratic decentralization favors the use of schools (as well as government employment) as a kind of patronage for voter interests, the existence of even a small number of elite jobs fosters a demand for large-scale opportunities to acquire these positions. We thus have a "contest mobility" school system (Turner, 1960); it produced a widely educated populace because of the many dropouts who never achieve the elite level of schooling at which expert skills and/ or high cultural status are acquired. In the process, the status value of American education has become diluted. Standards of respectability are always relative to the existing range of cultural differences. Once higher levels of education become recognized as an objective mark of elite status, and a moderate level of education as a mark of respectable middle-level status, increases in the supply of educated persons at given levels result in yet higher levels becoming recognized as superior, and previously superior levels become only average.

Thus, before the end of the nineteenth century, an elementary school or home education was no longer satisfactory for a middle-class gentleman; by the 1930s, a college degree was displacing the high school degree as the minimal standard of respectability; in the late 1960s, graduate school or specialized professional degrees were becoming necessary for initial entry to many middle-class positions, and high school graduation was becoming a standard for entry to manual laboring positions. Education has thus gradually become part of the status culture of classes far below the level of the original business and professional elites.

The increasing supply of educated persons (Table 2) has made education a rising requirement of jobs (Table 1). Led by the biggest and most prestigious organizations, employers have raised their educational requirements to maintain both the relative prestige of their own managerial ranks and the relative respectability of middle ranks.[8] Education has become a legitimate standard in terms of which employers select employees, and employees compete with each other for promotion opportunities or for raised prestige in their continuing positions. With the attainment of a mass (now approaching universal) higher education system in modern America, the ideal or image of technical skill becomes the legitimating culture in terms of which the struggle for position goes on.

Higher educational requirements, and the higher level of educational credentials offered by individuals competing for position in organizations, have in turn increased the demand for education by the populace. The interaction between formal job requirements and informal status cultures has resulted in a spiral in which educational requirements and educational attainments become ever higher. As the struggle for mass educational opportunities enters new phases in the universities of today and perhaps in the graduate schools of the future, we may expect a further upgrading of educational requirements for employment. The mobilization of demands by minority groups for mobility opportunities through schooling can only contribute an extension of the prevailing pattern.

## CONCLUSION

It has been argued that conflict theory provides an explanation of the principal dynamics of rising educational requirements for employment in America. Changes in the technical requirements of jobs have caused more limited changes in particular jobs. The conditions of the interaction of these two determinants may be more closely studied.

Precise measures of changes in the actual technical skill requirements of jobs are as yet available only in rudimentary form. Few systematic studies show how much of particular job skills may be learned in practice, and how much must be acquired through school background. Close studies of what is actually learned in school, and how long it is retained, are rare. Organizational studies of how employers rate performance and decide upon promotions give a picture of relatively loose controls over the technical quality of employee performance, but this no doubt varies in particular types of jobs.

The most central line of analysis for assessing the joint effects of status group conflict and technical requirements are those which compare the relative importance of education in different contexts. One such approach may take organization as the unit of analysis, comparing the educational requirements of organizations both to organizational technologies and to the status (including educational) background of organizational elites. Such analysis may also be applied to surveys of individual mobility, comparing the effects of education on mobility in different employment contexts, where the status group (and educational) background of employers varies in its fit with the educational culture of prospective employees. Such analysis of "old school tie" networks may also simultaneously test for the independent effect of the technical requirements of different sorts of jobs on the importance of education. Inter-nation comparisons provide variations here in the fit between types of education and particular kinds of jobs which may not be available within any particular country.

The full elaboration of such analysis would give a more precise answer to the historical question of assigning weight to various factors in the changing place of education in the stratification of modern societies. At the same time, to state the conditions under which status groups vary in organizational power, including the power to emphasize or limit the importance of technical skills, would be to state the basic elements of a comprehensive explanatory theory of the forms of stratification.

## ENDNOTES

1. This survey covered 309 establishments with 100 or more employees, representing all major industry groups.
2. The concern here is with these basic premises rather than with the theory elaborated by Davis and Moore to account for the universality of stratification. This theory involves a few further propositions: (C) in any particular form of society certain occupational positions are functionally most central to the operation of the social system; (D) the ability to fill these positions, and/or the motivation to acquire the necessary training, is unequally distributed in the population; (E) inequalities of rewards in wealth and prestige evolve to ensure that the supply of persons with the necessary ability or training meshes with the structure of demands for skilled performance. This problems of stating functional centrality in empirical terms have been subjects of much debate.
3. Proposition 3 is supported by Tables 1 and 2. The issue here is whether this can be explained by the previous propositions and premises.
4. It might be argued that the ethnic cultures may differ in their functionality: that middle-class Protestant culture provides the self-discipline and other attributes necessary for higher organizational positions in modern society. This version of functional theory is specific enough to be subject to empirical test: are middle-class WASPs in fact better businessmen or government administrators than Italians, Irishmen, or Jews of patrimonial or working class cultural backgrounds?

Weber suggested that they were in the initial construction of the capitalist economy within the confines of traditional society; he also argued that once the new economic system was established, the original ethic was no longer necessary to run it (Weber, 1930:180–183). Moreover, the functional explanation also requires some feedback mechanism whereby organizations with more efficient managers are selected for survival. The oligopolistic situation in large-scale American business since the late 19th century does not seem to provide such a mechanism; nor does government employment. Schumpeter (1951), the leading expositor of the importance of managerial talent in business, confined his emphasis to the formative period of business expansion, and regarded the large, oligopolistic corporation an as arena where advancement came to be based on skills in organizational politics (1951: 122–124); these personalistic skills are arguably more characteristic of the patrimonial cultures than of WASP culture.

5. Sample consisted of approximately one-third of all organizations with 100 or more employees in the San Francisco, Oakland, and San Jose metropolitan areas. See Gordon and Thal-Larsen (1969) for a description of procedures and other findings.

6. Again, these relationships hold for managerial requirements and white-collar requirements generally, both including and excluding professional and technical positions, but not for blue-collar requirements. Noland and Bakke (1949:78) also report that larger organizations have higher educational requirements for administrative positions than smaller organizations.

7. Similar processes may be found in other societies, where the kinds of organizations linked to particular types of schools may differ. In England, the elite "public schools" are linked especially to the higher levels of the national civil service (Weinberg, 1967:139–143). In France, the elite Ecole Polytechnique is linked to both government and industrial administrative positions (Crozier, 1964: 238–244). In Germany, universities have been linked principally with government ad-

ministration, and business executives are drawn from elsewhere (Ben-David and Zloczower, 1962). Comparative analysis of the kinds of education of government officials, business executives, and other groups in contexts where the status group links of schools differ is a promising area for further tests of conflict and technical-functional explanations.

8. It appears that employers may have raised their wage costs in the process. Their behavior is nevertheless plausible, in view of these considerations: (a) the thrust of organizational research since Mayo and Barnard has indicated that questions of internal organizational power and control, of which cultural dominance is a main feature, take precedence over purely economic considerations; (b) the large American corporations, which have led in educational requirements, have held positions of oligopolistic advantage since the late 19th century, and this could afford a large internal "welfare" cost of maintaining a well-socialized work force; (c) there are inter-organizational wage differentials in local labor markets, corresponding to relative organizational prestige, and a "wage-escalator" process by which the wages of the leading organizations are gradually emulated by others according to their rank (Reynolds, 1951); a parallel structure of "educational status escalators" could plausibly be expected to operate.

## REFERENCES

Anastasi, Anne. 1967. "Psychology, psychologists, and psychological testing." American Psychologist 22 (April):297–306.

Baltzell, E. Digby. 1958. An American Business Aristocracy. New York: MacMillan.

Becker, Howard S. 1961. "Schools and systems of stratification." Pp. 93–104 in A. H. Halsey, Jean Floud, and C. Arnold Anderson (eds.), Education, Economy, and Society. New York: Free Press.

Becker, Howard S., Blanche Geer, and Everett C. Hughes. 1968. Making the Grade: The Academic Side of College Life. New York: Wiley.

Bell, H. M. 1940. Matching Youth and Jobs. Washington: American Council on Education.

Ben-David, Joseph. 1963–64. "Professions in the class systems of present-day Societies." Current Sociology 12:247–330.

Ben-David, Joseph and Awraham Zloczower. 1962. "Universities and academic systems in modern societies." European Journal of Sociology 31:45–85.

Bendix, Reinhard. 1956. Work and Authority in Industry. New York: Wiley.

Berg, Ivar. 1970. Education and Jobs. New York: Praeger.

Bernstein, Basil. 1961. "Social class and linguistic development." Pp. 288–314 in A. H. Halsey, Jean Floud, and C. Arnold Anderson (eds.), Education, Economy, and Society. New York: Free Press.

Blau, Peter M. 1955. The Dynamics of Bureaucracy. Chicago: University of Chicago Press.

Blau, Peter M. and Otis Dudley Duncan. 1967. The American Occupational Structure. New York: Wiley.

Bourdieu, Pierre and Jean-Claude Passeron. 1964. Las Heritiers: Les Etudiants et la Culture. Paris: Les Editions de Minuit.

Bright, James R. 1958. "Does automation raise skill requirements?" Harvard Business Review 36 (July-August):85-97.

Clark, Burton R. 1962. Educating the Expert Society. San Francisco: Chandler.

Clark, Harold F. and Harold S. Sloan. 1966. Classrooms on Main Street. New York: Teachers College Press.

Coleman, James S. 1961. The Adolescent Society. New York: Free Press.

Coleman, Orvis, Melville Dalton, and Donald Roy. 1946. "Restriction of output and social cleavage in industry." Applied Anthropology 5 (Summer):1–14.

Collins, Randall. 1968. "A comparative approach to political sociology." Pp. 42–67 in Reinhard Bendix et al. (eds.), State and Society. Boston: Little, Brown.

Collins, Randall. 1969. Education and Employment. Unpublished Ph.D. dissertation, University of California at Berkeley.

Collins, Randall. 1971. "Educational requirements for employment: A comparative organizational study." Unpublished manuscript.

Cremin, Lawrence A. 1961. The Transformation of the School. New York: Knopf.

Crozier, Michel. 1964. The Bureaucratic Phenomenon. Chicago: University of Chicago Press.

Curti, Merle. 1935. The Social Ideas of American Educators. New York: Scribners.

Dalton, Melville. 1951. "Informal factors in career achievement." American Journal of Sociology 56 (March):407–415.

Dalton, Melville. 1959. Men Who Manage. New York: Wiley.

Davis, Kingsley and Wilbert Moore. 1945. "Some principles of stratification." American Sociological Review 10:242–249.

Denison, Edward F. 1965. "Education and economic productivity." Pp. 328–340 in Seymour Harris (ed.), Education and Public Policy. Berkeley: McCutchen.

Dill, Willam R., Thomas L. Hilton, and Walter R. Reitman. 1962. The New Managers. Englewood Cliffs: Prentice-Hall.

Domhoff, G. William. 1967. Who Rules America? Englewood Cliffs, New Jersey: Prentice-Hall.

Duncan, Beverly. 1964. "Dropouts and the unemployed." Journal of Political Economy 73 (April): 121–134.

Duncan, Otis Dudley and Robert W. Hodge. 1963. "Education and occupational mobility: A regression analysis." American Journal of Sociology 68:629–644.

Eckland, Bruce K. 1965. "Academic ability, higher education, and occupational mobility." American Sociological Review 30:735–746.

Epstein, Cynthia Fuchs. 1970. Woman's Place: Options and Limits in Professional Careers. Berkeley: University of California Press.

Etzioni, Amitai. 1961. A Comparative Analysis of Complex Organizations. New York: Free Press.

Folger, John K. and Charles B. Nam. 1964. Trends in education in relation to the occupational structure." Sociology of Education 38:19–33.

Goode, William J. 1967. "The protection of the inept." American Sociological Review 32:5–19.

Gordon, Margaret S. and Margaret Thal-Larsen. 1969. Employer Policies in a Changing Labor Market: Berkeley Institute of Industrial Relations, University of California.

Gordon, Robert A. and James E. Howell. 1959. Higher Education for Business. New York: Columbia University Press.

Gusfield, Joseph R. 1958. "Equalitarianism and bureaucratic recruitment." Administrative Science Quarterly 2 (March):521–541.

Hagstrom, Warren O. and Lowell L. Hargens. 1968. "Mobility theory in the sociology of science." Paper delivered at Cornell Conference on Human Mobility, Ithaca, N.Y. (October 31).

Hall, Oswald. 1946. "The informal organization of the medical profession." Canadian journal of Economic and Political Science 12 (February): 30–44.

Harbison, Frederick and Charles A. Myers. 1964. Education, Manpower, and Economic Growth. New York: McGraw-Hill.

Hargens, Lowell and Warren O. Hagstrom. 1967. "Sponsored and contest mobility of American academic scientists." Sociology of Education 40:24–38.

Havemann, Ernest and Patricia Salter West. 1952. They Went to College. New York: Harcourt, Brace.

Hess, Robert D. and Judith V. Torney. 1967. The Development of Political Attitudes in Children. Chicago: Aldine.

Hollingshead, August B. 1949. Elmtown's Youth. New York: Wiley.

Hoselitz, Bert F. 1965. "Investment in education and its political impact." Pp. 541–565 in James S. Coleman (ed.), Education and Political Development. Princeton: Princeton University Press.

Hughes, Everett C. 1949. "Queries concerning industry and society growing out of the study of ethnic relations in industry." American Sociological Review 14:211–220.

Jencks, Christopher and David Riesman. 1968. The Academic Revolution. New York: Doubleday.

Kahl, Joseph A. 1957. The American Class Structure. New York: Rinehart.

Kerr, Clark, John T. Dunlop, Frederick H. Harbison, and Charles A. Myers. 1960. Industrialism and Industrial Man. Cambridge: Harvard University Press.

Ladinsky, Jack. 1963. "Careers of lawyers, law practice, and legal institutions." American Sociological Review 28 (February):47–54.

Ladinsky, Jack. 1967. "Higher education and work achievement among lawyers." Sociological Quarterly 8 (Spring):222–232.

Learned, W. S. and B. D. Wood. 1938. The Student and His Knowledge. New York: Carnegie Foundation for the Advancement of Teaching.

Lipset, Seymour Martin and Reinhard Bendix. 1959. Social Mobility in Industrial Society. Berkeley: University of California Press.

Lombard, George F. 1955. Behavior in a Selling Group. Cambridge: Harvard University Press.

March, James G. and Herbert A. Simon. 1958. Organizations. New York: Wiley.

Marsh, Robert M. 1963. "Values, demand, and social mobility." American Sociological Review 28 (August):567–575.

McArthur, C. 1955. "Personality differences between middle and upper classes." Journal of Abnormal and Social Psychology 50:247–254.

Mills, C. Weight. 1963. Power, Politics, and People. New York: Oxford University Press.

Newcomer, Mabel. 1955. The Big Business Executive. New York: Columbia University Press.

Noland, E. William and E. Wight Bakke. 1949. Workers Wanted. New York: Harper.

Nosow, Sigmund. 1956. "Labor distribution and the normative system." Social Forces 30: 25–33.

Peaslee, Alexander L. 1969. "Education's role in development." Economic Development and Cultural Change 17 (April):293–318.

Perrucci, Carolyn Cummings and Robert Perrucci. 1970, "Social origins, educational contexts, and career mobility." American Sociological Review 35 (June):451–463.

Pierson, Frank C. 1959. The Education of American Businessmen. New York: McGraw-Hill.

Plunkett, M. 1960. "School and early work experience of youth." Occupational Outlook Quarterly 4:22–27.

Reynolds, Lloyd. 1951. The Structure of Labor Markets. New York: Harper.

Riesman, David. 1958. Constraint and Variety in American Education. New York: Doubleday.

Roy, Donald. 1952. "Quota restriction and goldbricking in a machine shop." American Journal of Sociology 57 (March):427–442.

Schultz, Theodore W. 1961 "Investment in human capital." American Economic Review 51 (March): 1–16.

Schumpeter, Joseph. 1951. Imperialism and Social Classes. New York: Augustus M. Kelley.

Sewell, William H., Archibald O. Haller, and Alejandro Portes. 1969. "The educational and early occupational attainment process." American Sociological Review 34 (February): 82–92.

Sharp, Laure M. 1970. Education and Employment: The Early Careers of College Graduates. Baltimore: Johns Hopkins Press.

Smigel, Erwin O. 1964. The Wall Street Lawyer. New York: Free Press.

Soderberg, C. Richard. 1963. "The American engineer." Pp. 203–230 in Kenneth S. Lynn, The Professions in America. Boston: Beacon Press.

Taeuber, Alma F., Karl E. Taeuber, and Glen G. Cain. 1966. "Occupational assimilation and the competitive process: A reanalysis." American Journal of Sociology 72:278–285.

Taussig, Frank W. and C. S. Joslyn. 1932. American Business Leaders. New York: Macmillan.

Turner, Ralph H. 1952. "Foci of discrimination in the employment of nonwhites." American Journal of Sociology 58:247–256.

Turner, Ralph H. 1960. "Sponsored and contest mobility and the school system." American Sociological Review 25 (October):855–867.

Waller, Willard. 1932. The Sociology of Teaching. New York: Russell and Russell.

Warner, W. Lloyd and James C. Abegglen. 1955. Occupational Mobility in American Business and Industry, 1928–1952. Minneapolis: University of Minnesota Press.,

Weber, Max. 1930. The Protestant Ethic and the Spirit of Capitalism. New York: Scribners.

Weber, Max. 1968. Economy and Society. New York: Bedminster Press.

Weinberg, Ian. 1967. The English Public Schools: the Sociology of Elite Education. New York: Atherton Press.

Wilensky, Harold L. 1964. "The professionalization of everyone?" American Journal of Sociology 70 (September): 137–158.

# On Understanding the Processes of Schooling: The Contributions of Labeling Theory

## RAY C. RIST

There have been few debates within American education which have been argued with such passion and intensity as that of positing causal explanations of success or failure in schools.[1] One explanation which has had considerable support in the past few years, particularly since the publication of *Pygmalion in the Classroom* by Rosenthal and Jacobson (1968), has been that of the "self-fulfilling prophecy." Numerous studies have appeared seeking to explicate the mechanisms by which the teacher comes to hold certain expectations of the students and how these are then operationalized within the classroom so as to produce what the teacher had initially assumed. The origins of teacher expectations have been attributed to such diverse variables as social class, physical appearance, contrived test scores, sex, race language patterns, and school records. But the flurry of recent research endeavors, there has emerged a hiatus between this growing body of data and any larger theoretic framework. The concept of the self-fulfilling prophecy has remained simply that—a concept. The lack of a broader conceptual scheme has meant that research in this area has become theoretically stymied. Consequently, there has evolved instead a growing concern over the refinement of minute methodological nuances.

The thrust of this paper is to argue that there is a theoretical perspective developing in the social sciences which can break the conceptual and methodological logjam building up on the self-fulfilling prophecy.

Specifically, the emergence of *labeling theory* as an explanatory framework for the study of social deviance appears to be applicable to the study of education as well. Among the major contributions to the development of labeling theory are Becker, 1963, 1964; Broadhead, 1974; Lemert, 1951, 1972, 1974; Douglas, 1971, 1972; Kitsuse, 1964; Loffland, 1969; Matza, 1964, 1969; Scheff, 1966; Schur, 1971; Scott and Douglas, 1972; and Rubington and Weinberg, 1973.

If the labeling perspective can be shown to be a legitimate framework from which to analyze social processes influencing the educational experience and the contributions of such processes to success or failure in school, there would then be a viable *interactionist* perspective to counter both biological and cultural determinists' theories of educational outcomes. While the latter two positions both place ultimate causality for success or failure *outside* the school, the labeling approach allows for an examination of what, in fact, is happening *within* schools. Thus, labeling theory would call our attention for example, to the various evaluative mechanisms (both formal and informal) operant in schools, the ways in which schools nurture and support such mechanisms, how students react, what the outcomes are for interpersonal interaction based on how these mechanisms have evaluated individual students, and how, *over time,* the consequences of having a certain evaluative tag influence the options available to a student within a school. What follows first is a summary of a number of the

*Source:* From *Power and Ideology in Education* by Jerome Karabel and A. H. Halsey. Copyright © 1977 by Oxford University Press, Inc. Reprinted by permission.

key aspects of labeling theory as it has been most fully developed in the sociological literature; second is an attempt to integrate the research on the self-fulfilling prophecy with the conceptual framework of labeling theory. Finally, the implications of this synthesis are explored for both future research and theoretical development.

## I. BECOMING DEVIANT: THE LABELING PERSPECTIVE

Those who have used labeling theory have been concerned with the study of *why* people are labeled, and *who* it is that labels them as someone who has committed one form or another of deviant behavior. In sharp contrast to the predominant approaches for the study of deviance, there is little concern in labeling theory with the motivational and characterological nature of the person who committed the act.

Deviance is understood, not as a quality of the person or as created by his actions, but instead as created by group definitions and reactions. It is a social judgment imposed by a social audience. As Becker (1963:9) has argued:

> The central fact of deviance is that it is created by society. I do not mean this in the way it is ordinarily understood, in which the causes of deviance are located in the social situation of the deviant, or the social factors, which prompted his action. I mean, rather, that social groups create deviants by making the rules whose infraction constitute deviance, and by applying those rules to particular people and labeling them as outsiders. From this point of view, *deviance is not the quality of the act the person commits, but rather a consequence of the application by others of rules and sanctions to an "offender." This deviant is one to whom the label has been successfully applied. Deviant behavior is behavior that people so label.* (emphasis added)

The labeling approach is insistent on the need for a shift in attention from an exclusive concern with the deviant individual to a major concern with the *process* by which the deviant label is applied. Again citing Becker (1964:2):

> The labeling approach sees deviance always and everywhere as a process and interaction between at least two kinds of people: those who commit (or who are said to have committed) a deviant act, and the rest of the society, perhaps divided into several groups itself.... One consequence is that we become much more interested in the process by which deviants are defined by the rest of the society, than in the nature of the deviant act itself.

The important questions, then, for Becker and others, are not of the genre to include, for example: Why do some individuals come to act out norm-violating behavior? Rather, the questions are of the following sort: Who applied the deviant label to whom? Whose rules shall prevail and be enforced? Under what circumstances is the deviant label successfully and unsuccessfully applied? How does a community decide what forms of conduct should be singled out for this kind of attention? What forms of behavior do persons in the social system consider deviant, how do they interpret such behavior, and what are the consequences of these interpretations for their reactions to individuals who are seen as manifesting such behavior? (See Akers, 1973.)

The labeling perspective rejects any assumption that a clear consensus exists as to what constitutes a norm violation—or for that matter, what constitutes a norm—within a complex and highly heterogeneous society. What comes to be determined as deviance and who comes to be determined as a deviant is the result of a variety of social contingencies influenced by who has the power to enforce such determinations. Deviance is thus problematic and subjectively given. The case for making the societal reaction to rule-breaking a major independent variable in studies of deviant behavior has been succinctly stated by Kitsuse (1964: 101):

> A sociological theory of deviance must focus specifically upon the interactions which not only define behaviors as deviant, but also organize and activate the application of sanctions by individuals, groups, or agencies. For in modern society, the socially significant differentiation of deviants from the nondeviant population is increasingly contingent upon circumstances of situation, place social and personal biography, and the bureaucratically organized activities of agencies of social control.

Traditional notions of who is a deviant and what are the causes for such deviance are necessarily reworked. By emphasizing the processual nature of deviance, any particular deviant is seen to be a product of being caught, defined, segregated, labeled, and stigmatized. *This is one of the major thrusts of the labeling perspective–that forces of social control often produce the unintended consequence of making some persons defined as deviant even more confirmed as deviant because of the stigmatization of labeling. Thus, social reactions to deviance further deviant careers.* Erikson (1966) has even gone so far as to argue that a society will strive to maintain a certain level of deviance within itself as deviance is functional to clarifying group boundaries, providing scapegoats, creating outgroups who can be the source of furthering in-group solidarity, and the like.

The idea that social control may have the paradoxical effect of generating more of the very behavior it is designed to eradicate was first elaborated upon by Tannenbaum. He noted (1938:21):

> The first dramatization of the "evil" which separates the child out of his group...plays a

greater role in making the criminal than perhaps any other experience.... He now lives in a different world. He has been tagged.... The person becomes the thing he is described as being.

Likewise, Schur (1965:4) writes:

> The societal reaction to the deviant, then, is vital to an understanding of the deviance itself and a major element in—if not the cause of—the deviant behavior.

The focus on outcomes of social control mechanisms has led labeling theorists to devote considerable attention to the workings of organizations and agencies which function ostensibly to rehabilitate the violator or in other ways draw him back into conformity. Their critiques of prisons, mental hospitals, training schools, and other people-changing institutions suggest that the results of such institutions are frequently nearly the opposite of what they were theoretically designed to produce. These institutions are seen as mechanisms by which opportunities to withdraw from deviance are sealed off from the deviant, stigmatization occurs, and a new identity as a social "outsider" is generated. There thus emerges on the part of the person so labeled a new view of himself which is one of being irrevocably deviant.

This movement from one who has violated a norm to one who sees himself as a habitual norm violator is what Lemert (1972:62) terms the transition from a primary to a secondary deviant. A primary deviant is one who holds to socially accepted roles, views himself as a nondeviant, and believes himself to be an insider. A primary deviant does not deny that he has violated some norm, and claims only that it is not characteristic of him as a person. A secondary deviant, on the other hand, is one who has reorganized his social-psychological characteristics around the deviant role. Lemert (1972:62) writes:

Secondary deviation refers to a special class of socially defined responses which people make to problems created by the societal reaction to their deviance. These problems... become central facts of existence for those experiencing them.... Actions, which have these roles and self-attitudes as their referents make up secondary deviance. The secondary deviant...is a person whose life and identity are organized around the facts of deviance.

A person can commit repeated acts of primary deviation and never come to view himself or have others come to view him as a secondary deviant. Secondary deviation arises from the feedback whereby misconduct or deviation initiates social reaction to the behavior which then triggers further misconduct. Lemert (1951:77) first described this process as follows:

> The sequence of interaction leading to secondary deviation is roughly as follows: 1) primary deviation; 2) societal penalties; 3) further primary deviation; 4) stronger penalties and rejections; 5) further deviations, perhaps with hostilities and resentments beginning to focus upon those doing the penalizing; 6) crisis reached in the tolerance quotient, expressed in formal action by the community stigmatizing of the deviant; 7) strengthening of the deviant conduct as a reaction to the stigmatizing and penalties; and 8) ultimate acceptance of deviant social status and efforts at adjustment on the basis of the associated role.

Thus, when persons engage in deviant behavior they would not otherwise participate in and when they develop social roles they would not have developed save for the application of social control measures, the outcome is the emergence of secondary deviance. The fact of having been apprehended and labeled is the critical element in the subsequent construction of a deviant identity and pursuit of a deviant career.

## II. THE ORIGINS OF LABELING: TEACHER EXPECTATIONS

Labeling theory has significantly enhanced our understanding of the process of becoming deviant by shifting our attention from the deviant to the judges of deviance and the forces that affect their judgment. Such judgments are critical, for a recurrent decision made in all societies, and particularly frequent in advanced industrial societies, is that an individual has or has not mastered some body of information, or perhaps more basically, has or has not the capacity to master that information. These evaluations are made periodically as one moves through the institution of school and the consequences directly affect the opportunities to remain for an additional period. To be able to remain provides an option for mastering yet another body of information, and to be certified as having done so. As Ivan Illich (1971) has noted, it is in industrial societies that being perceived as a legitimate judge of such mastery has become restricted to those who carry the occupational role of "teacher." A major consequence of the professionalization of the role of teacher has been the ability to claim as a near exclusive decision whether mastery of material has occurred. Such exclusionary decision-making enhances those in the role of "teacher" as they alone come to possess the authority to provide certification for credentials (Edgar, 1974).

Labeling theorists report that in making judgments of deviance, persons may employ information drawn from a variety of sources. Further, even persons within the same profession (therapists, for example) may make divergent use of the same material in arriving at an evaluative decision on the behavior of an individual. Among the sources of information available to labelers, two appear primary: first-hand information obtained from face-to-face interaction with the person they may ultimately label, and second-hand information obtained from other than direct interaction.

The corollary here to the activities of teachers should be apparent. Oftentimes, the evaluation by teachers (which may lead to the label of "bright," "slow," etc.) is based on first-hand information gained through face-to-face interaction during the course of the time the teacher and student spent together in the classroom. But a goodly amount of information about the student which informs the teacher's evaluation is second-hand information. For instance, comments from other teachers, test scores, prior report cards, permanent records, meetings with the parents, or evaluations from welfare agencies and psychological clinics are all potential informational sources. In a variation of the division between first-hand and second-hand sources of information, Johnson (1973) has suggested that there are three key determinants of teacher evaluations: student's prior performance, social status characteristics, and present performance. Prior performance would include information from cumulative records (grades, test scores, notes from past teachers or counselors, and outside evaluators) while social status and performance would be inferred and observed in the on-going context of the classroom.

What has been particularly captivating about the work of Rosenthal and Jacobson (1968) in this regard is their attempt to provide empirical justification for a truism considered self-evident by many in education: School achievement is not simply a matter of a child's native ability, but involves directly and inextricably the teacher as well. Described succinctly, their research involved a situation where, at the end of a school year, more than 500 students in a single elementary school were administered the "Harvard Test of Inflected Acquisition." In actuality this test was a standardized, relatively nonverbal test of intelligence, Flanagan's (1960) Test of General Ability (TOGA). The teach-

ers were told that such a test would, with high predictive reliability, sort out those students who gave strong indication of being intellectual "spurters" or "bloomers" during the following academic year. Just before the beginning of school the following fall, the teachers were given lists with the names of between one and nine of their students. They were told that these students scored in the top twenty percent of the school on the test, though, of course, no factual basis for such determinations existed. A twenty percent subsample of the "special" students was selected for intensive analysis. Testing of the students at the end of the school year offered some evidence that these selected children did perform better than the nonselected. The ensuing debate as to the validity and implications of the findings from the study will be discussed in the next section.

The findings of Deutsch, Fishman, Kogan, North, and Whiteman (1964); Gibson (1965): Goslin and Glass (1967); McPherson (1966); and Pequignot (1966) all demonstrate the influence of standardized tests of intelligence and achievement on teacher's expectations. Goaldman (1971), in a review of the literature on the use of tests as a second-hand source of information for teachers, noted: "Although some of the research has been challenged, there is a basis for the belief that teachers at all levels are prejudiced by information they receive about a student's ability or character." Mehan (1971, 1974) has been concerned with the interaction between children who take tests and the teachers who administer them. He posits that testing is not the objective use of a measurement instrument, but the outcome of a set of interactional activities which are influenced by a variety of contingencies which ultimately manifest themselves in a reified "test score." Mehan suggests (1971):

Standardized test performances are taken as an unquestioned, non-problematic reflection of the child's underlying ability. The authority of the test to measure the child's real ability is accepted by both teachers and other school officials. Test results are accepted without doubt as the correct and valid document of the child's ability.

Characteristics of children such as sex and race are immediately apparent to teachers. Likewise, indications of status can be quickly inferred from grooming, style of dress, need for free lunches, information on enrollment cards, discussion of family activities by children, and visits to the school by parents. One intriguing study recently reported in this area is that by two sociologists, Clifford and Walster (1973:249). The substance of their study was described as follows:

> Our experiment was designed to determine what effect a student's physical attractiveness has on a teacher's expectations of the child's intellectual and social behavior. Our hypothesis was that a child's attractiveness strongly influences his teachers' judgments; the more attractive the child, the more biased in his favor we expect the teachers to be. The design required to test this hypothesis is a simple one: Teachers are given a standardized report card and an attached photograph. The report card includes an assessment of the child's academic performance as well as of his general social behavior. The attractiveness of the photos is experimentally varied. On the basis of this information, teachers are asked to state their expectations of the child's educational and social potential.

Based on the responses of 404 fifth grade teachers within the state of Missouri, Clifford and Walster concluded (1973:255):

> There is little question but that the physical appearance of a student affected the expectations of the teachers we studied. Regardless of whether the pupil is a boy or girl, the child's physical attractiveness has an equally strong association with his teacher's reactions to him.

The variables of race and ethnicity have been documented, by Brown (1968), Davidson and Lang (1960), Jackson and Cosca (1974), and Rubovits and Maehr (1973), among others, as powerful factors in generating the expectations teachers hold of children. It has also been documented that teachers expect less of lower-class children than they do of middle-class children (cf. Becker, 1952; Deutsch, 1963; Leacock, 1969; Rist, 1970, 1973; Stein, 1971; Warner, Havighurst, and Loeb, 1944; and Wilson, 1963). Douglas (1964), in a large scale study of the tracking system used in British schools, found that children who were clean and neatly dressed in nice clothing, and who came from what the teachers perceived as "better" homes, tended to be placed in higher tracks than their measured ability would predict. Further, when placed there they tended to stay and perform acceptably. Mackler (1969) studied schools in Harlem and found that children tended to stay in the tracks in which they were initially placed and that such placement was based on a variety of social considerations independent of measured ability. Doyle, Hancock, and Kifer (1971) and Palardy (1969) have shown teacher expectations for high performance in elementary grades to be stronger for girls than boys.

The on-going academic and interpersonal performance of the children may also serve as a potent source of expectations for teachers. Rowe (1969) found that teachers would wait longer for an answer from a student they believed to be a high achiever than for one from a student they believed to be a low achiever. Brophy and Good (1970) found that teachers were more likely to give perceived high achieving students a second chance to respond to an initial incorrect answer, and further, that high achievers were praised more frequently for success and criticized less for failure.

There is evidence that the expectations teachers hold for their students can be generated as early as the first few days of the school year and then remain stable over the months to follow (Rist, 1970, 1972, 1973; Willis, 1972). For example, I found during my three-year longitudinal and ethnographic study of a single, *de facto* segregated elementary school in the black community of St. Louis, that after only eight days of kindergarten, the teacher made permanent seating arrangements based on what she assumed were variations in academic capability. But no formal evaluation of the children had taken place. Instead, the assignments to the three tables were based on a number of socio-economic criteria as well as on early interaction patterns in the classroom. Thus, the placement of the children came to reflect the social class distinctions in the room—the poor children from public welfare families all sat at one table, the working class children sat at another and the middle class at the third. I demonstrated how the teacher operationalized her expectations of these different groups of children in terms of her differentials of teaching time, her use of praise and control, and the extent of autonomy within the classroom. By following the same children through first and second grade as well, I was able to show that the initial patterns established by the kindergarten teacher came to be perpetuated year after year. By second grade, labels given by another teacher clearly reflected the reality each of the three groups experienced in the school. The top group was called the "Tigers," the middle group the "Cardinals," and the lowest group, the "Clowns." What had begun as a subjective evaluation and labeling by the teacher took on objective dimensions as the school proceeded to process the children on the basis of the distinctions made when they first began.

Taken together, these studies strongly imply that the notion of "teacher expectations" is multi-faceted arid multi-dimensional. It appears that when teachers generate expectations about their students, they do so not only for reasons of academic or cognitive performance, but for their classroom interactional patterns as well. Furthermore, not only ascribed characteristics such as race, sex, class, or ethnicity are highly salient, interpersonal traits are also. Thus, the interrelatedness of the various attributes which ultimately blend together to generate the evaluation a teacher makes as to what can be expected from a particular student suggests the strength and tenacity of such subsequent labels as "bright" or "slow" or "trouble-maker" or "teacher's little helper." It is to the outcomes of the student's having one or another of these labels that we now turn.

## III. AN OUTCOME OF LABELING: THE SELF-FULFILLING PROPHECY

W. I. Thomas, many years ago, set forth what has become a basic dictum of the social sciences when he observed, "If men define situations as real, they are real in their consequences." This is at the core of the self-fulfilling prophecy. An expectation which defines a situation comes to influence the actual behavior within the situation so as to produce what was initially assumed to be there. Merton (1968:477) has elaborated on this concept and noted: "The self-fulfilling phase is, in the beginning, a *false* definition of the situation evoking a new behavior which makes the originally false conception come true." (emphasis in the original)

Here it is important to recall a basic tenet of labeling theory—that an individual does not become deviant simply by the commission of some act. As Becker (1963) stressed, deviance is not inherent in behavior *per se,* but in the application by others of rules and sanctions against one perceived as being an "offender." Thus, the only time one can accurately be termed a "deviant" is after the successful application of a label by a social audience. Thus, though many persons may commit norm violations, only select ones are subsequently labeled. The contingencies of race, class, sex, visibility of behavior, age, occupation, and who one's friends are all influence the outcome as to whether one is or is not labeled. Scheff (1966), for example, demonstrated the impact of these contingencies upon the diagnosis as to the severity of a patient's mental illness. The higher one's social status, the less the willingness to diagnose the same behavioral traits as indicative of serious illness in comparison to the diagnosis given to low status persons.

The crux of the labeling perspective lies not in whether one's norm violating behavior is known, but in whether others decide to do something about it. Further, if a label is applied to the individual, it is posited that this in fact causes the individual to become that which he is labeled as being. Due to the reaction of society, the change in the individual involves the development of a new socialized self-concept and social career centered around the deviant behavior. As Rubington and Weinberg (1973:7) have written:

> The person who has been typed, in turn, becomes aware of the new definition that has been placed upon him by members of his groups. He, too, takes this new understanding of himself into account when dealing with them.... When this happens, a social type has been ratified, and a person has been socially reconstructed.

As noted, Rosenthal and Jacobson's *Pygmalion in the Classroom* (1968) created wide interest in the notion of the self-fulfilling prophecy as a concept to explain differential performance by children in classrooms. Their findings suggested that the expectations teachers created about the children randomly selected as "intellectual bloomers" somehow caused the teachers to treat them differently, with the result that the children really did perform better by the end of the year. Though the critics of this particular research

(Snow, 1969; Taylor, 1970; Thorndike, 1968, 1969) and those who have been unsuccessful in replicating the findings (Claiborn, 1969) have leveled strong challenges to Rosenthal and Jacobson, the disagreements are typically related to methodology, procedure, and analysis rather than to the proposition that relations exist between expectations and behavior.

The current status of the debate and the evidence accumulated in relation to it imply that teacher expectations are *sometimes* self-fulfilling. The early and, I think, over-enthusiastic accounts of Rosenthal and Jacobson have obscured the issue. The gist of such accounts have left the impression, as Good and Brophy (1973:73) have noted, that the mere existence of an expectation will automatically guarantee its fulfillment. Rather, as they suggest:

> The fact that teachers' expectations can be self-fulfilling is simply a special case of the principle that any expectations can be self-fulfilling. This process is not confined to classrooms. Although it is not true that "wishing can make it so," our expectations do affect the way we behave in situations, and the way we behave affects how other people respond. In some instances, our expectations about people cause us to treat them in a way that makes them respond just as we expect they would.

Such a position would be borne out by social psychologists who have demonstrated that an individual's first impressions of another person do influence subsequent interactions (Dailey, 1952; Newcomb, 1947) and that one's self-expectations influence one's subsequent behavior (Aronson and Carlsmith, 1962; Brock and Edelman, 1965; and Zajonc and Brinkman, 1969).

The conditionality of expectations related to their fulfillment is strongly emphasized by labeling theorists as well. Their emphasis upon the influence of social contingencies on whether one is labeled, how strong the label, and if it can be made to stick at all, points to a recognition that there is a social process involved where individuals are negotiating, rejecting, accepting, modifying, and reinterpreting the attempts at labeling. Such interaction is apparent in the eight stages of the development of secondary deviance outlined above by Lemert. Likewise, Erikson (1964:17), in his comments on the act of labeling as a rite of passage from one side of the group boundary to the other, has noted:

> The common assumption that deviants are not often cured or reformed, then, may be based on a faulty premise, but this assumption is stated so frequently and with such conviction that it often creates the facts which later "prove" it to be correct. If the returning deviant has to face the community's apprehensions often enough, it is understandable that he, too, may begin to wonder whether he has graduated from the deviant role—and *so respond to the uncertainty by resuming deviant activity.* In some respects, this may be the only way for the individual and his community to agree as to what kind of person he really is, for it often happens that the community is only able to perceive his "true colors" when he lapses, momentarily, into some form of deviant performance. (emphasis added)

Explicit in Erikson's quote is the fact of the individual's being in interaction with the "community" to achieve some sort of agreement on what the person is "really" like. Though Erikson did not, in this instance, elaborate upon what he meant by "community," it can be inferred from elsewhere in its work that he sees "community" as manifesting itself in the institutions persons create in order to help organize and structure their lives. Such a perspective is clearly within the framework of labeling theory, where a major emphasis has been placed upon the role of institutions in sorting, labeling, tracking, and channeling persons along various routes de-

pending upon the assessment the institution has made of the individual.

One pertinent example of the manner in which labeling theory has been applied to the study of social institutions and their impact upon participants has been in an analysis of the relation of schooling to juvenile delinquency. There have been several works which suggest as a major line of argument that schools, through and because of the manner in which they label students, serve as a chief instrument in the creation of delinquency (Hirschi, 1969; Noblit and Polk, 1975; Polk 1969; Polk and Schafer, 1972; Schafer and Olexa, 1971). For example, Noblit and Polk (1975:3) have noted:

> In as much as the school is the primary institution in the adolescent experience—one that promises not only the future status available to the adolescent, but also that gives or denies status in adolescence itself—it can be expected that its definitions are of particular significance for the actions of youth. That is, the student who has been reported from success via the school has little reason to conform to the often arbitrary and paternalistic regulations and rules of the school. In a very real sense, this student has no "rational constraints" against deviance. It is through the sorting mechanisms of the school, which are demanded by institutions of higher education and the world of work, that youth are labeled and thus sorted into the situation where deviant behavior threatens little while providing some alternative forms of status.

It is well to reiterate the point—interaction implies behavior and choices being made by both parties. The person facing the prospect of receiving a new label imputing a systemic change in the definition of his selfhood may respond in any of a myriad number of ways to this situation. Likewise, the institutional definition of the person is neither finalized nor solidified until the end of the negotiation as to what precisely that label should be. But, in the context of a single student facing the authority and vested interests of a school administration and staff, the most likely outcome is that over time, the student will increasing move towards conformity with the label the institution seeks to establish. Good and Brophy 1973:75) have elaborated upon this process within the classroom as follows:

1. The teacher expects specific behavior and achievement from particular students.
2. Because of these different expectations, the teacher behaves differently toward the different students.
3. This teacher treatment tells each student what behavior and achievement the teacher expects from him and affects his self-concept, achievement motivation, and level of aspiration.
4. If this teacher treatment is consistent over time, and if the student does not actively resist or change it in some way, it will tend to shape his achievement and behavior. High-expectation students will be led to achieve at high levels, while the achievement of low-expectations students will decline.
5. With time, the student's achievement and behavior will conform more and more closely to that originally expected of him.

The fourth point in this sequence makes the crucial observation that teacher expectations are not automatically self-fulfilling. For the expectations of the teacher to become realized, both the teacher and the student must move towards a pattern of interaction where expectations are clearly communicated and the behavioral response is consonant with the expected patterns. But as Good and Brophy (1973:75) also note:

> This does not always happen. The teacher may not have clear-cut expectations about a particular student, or his expectations may continually change. Even when he has consistent expectations, he may not necessarily communicate them to the student through consistent behavior. In this case, the expec-

tation would not be self-fulfilling even if it turned out to be correct. Finally, the student himself might prevent expectations from becoming self-fulfilling by overcoming them or by resisting them in a way that makes the teacher change them.

Yet, the critique of American education offered by such scholars as Henry (1963), Katz (1971), Goodman (1964), or Reimer (1971), suggests the struggle is unequal between the teacher (and the institution a teacher represents) and the student. The vulnerability of children to the dictates of adults in positions of power over them leaves the negotiations as to what evaluative definition will be tagged on the children more often than not in the hands of the powerful. As Max Weber himself stated, to have power is to be able to achieve one's ends, even in the face of resistance from others. When that resistance is manifested in school by children and is defined by teachers and administrators as truancy, recalcitrance, unruliness, and hostility, or conversely defined as a lack of motivation, intellectual apathy, sullenness, passivity, or withdrawal, the process is ready to be repeated and the options to escape further teacher definitions are increasingly removed.

## POSTSCRIPT: BEYOND THE LOGJAM

This paper has argued that a fruitful convergence can be effected between the research being conducted on the self-fulfilling prophecy as a consequence of teacher expectations and the conceptual framework of labeling theory. The analysis of the outcomes of teacher expectations produces results highly similar to those found in the study of social deviance. Labels are applied to individuals which fundamentally shift their definitions of self and which further reinforce the behavior which had initially prompted the social reaction. The impact of the self-fulfilling prophecy in educational research is comparable to that found in the analysis of mental health clinics, asylums, prisons, juvenile homes, and other people-changing organizations. What the labeling perspective can provide to the study of educational outcomes as a result of the operationalization of teacher expectations is a model for the study of the *processes* by which the outcomes are produced. The detailing over time of the interactional patterns which lead to changes in self-definition and behavior within classrooms is sadly lacking in almost all of the expectation research to date. A most glaring example of this omission is the study by Rosenthal and Jacobson themselves. Their conclusions are based only on the analysis of a pre- and post-test. To posit that teacher expectations were the causal variable that produced changes in student performances was a leap from the data to speculation. They could offer only suggestions as to how the measured changes in the children's performance came about, since they were not in the classrooms to observe how assumed teacher attitudes were translated into subsequent actual student behavior.

To extend the research on the educational experiences of those students who are differentially labeled by teachers, what is needed is a theoretical framework which can clearly isolate the influences and effects of certain kinds of teacher reactions on certain types of students, producing, certain typical outcomes. The labeling perspective appears particularly well-suited for this expansion of both research and theoretical development on teacher expectations by offering the basis for analysis at either a specific or a more general level. With the former, for example, there are areas of investigation related to 1) types of students perceived by teachers as prone to success or failure; 2) the kinds of reactions, based on their expectations, teachers have to different students; and 3) the effects of specific teacher reactions on specific student outcomes. At a more general level, fruitful lines of inquiry might include 1) the outcomes in the post-school world of having received a negative vs. a positive label within the school; 2) the influences of factors such as social class and race on the categories of expectations teachers hold; 3) how and why labels do emerge in schools as well as the phenomenological and structural meanings that are attached to them; and 4) whether there are means by which to modify or minimize the effects of school labeling processes on students.

Labeling theory provides a conceptual framework by which to understand the processes of transforming attitudes into behavior and the outcomes of having done so. To be able to detail the dynamics and influences within schools by which some children come to see themselves as successful and act as though they were, and to detail how others come to see themselves as failures and act accordingly, provides in the final analysis an opportunity to intervene so as to expand the numbers of winners and diminish the numbers of losers. For that reason above all others, labeling theory merits our attention.

## ENDNOTE

1. The preparation of this paper has been aided by a grant (GS-41522) from the National Science Foundation–Sociology Program. The views expressed here are solely those of the author and no official endorsement by either the National Science Foundation or the National Institute of Education is to be inferred.

## REFERENCES

Akers, R. L. *Deviant Behavior: A Social Learning Approach.* Belmont, Cal.: Wadsworth, 1973.

Aronson, E., and Carlsmith, J. M. "Performance Expectancy as a Determinant of Actual Performance." *Journal of Abnormal and Social Psychology* 65 (1962): 179–182.

Becker, H. S. "Social Class Variations in the Teacher-Pupil Relationship." *Journal of Educational Sociology* 25 (1952):451–465.

Becker, H. S. *Outsiders.* New York: The Free Press, 1963.

Becker, H. S. *The Other Side.* New York: The Free Press, 1964.

Broadhead, R. S. "A Theoretical Critique of the Societal Reaction Approach to Deviance." *Pacific Sociological Review* 17 (1974): 287–312.

Brock, T. C., and Edelman, H. "Seven Studies of Performance Expectancy as a Determinant of Actual Performance." *Journal of Experimental Social Psychology* 1 (1965):295–310.

Brophy, J., and Good, T. "Teachers' Communications of Differential Expectations for Children's Classroom Performance: Some Behavioral Data." *Journal of Educational Psychology* 61 (1970):365–374.

Brown, B. *The Assessment of Self-Concept among Four Year Old Negro and White Children: A Comparative Study Using the Brown IDS Self-Concept Reference Test.* New York: Institute for Developmental Studies, 1968.

Claiborn, W. L. "Expectancy Effects in the Classroom: A Failure to Replicate." *Journal of Educational Psychology* 60 (1969):377–383.

Clifford, M. M., and Walster, E. "The Effect of Physical Attractiveness on Teacher Expectations." *Sociology of Education* 46 (1973): 248–258.

Dailey C. A. "The Effects of Premature Conclusion upon the Acquisition of Understanding of a Person." *Journal of Psychology* 33 (1952):133–152.

Davidson, H. H., and Lang, G. "Children's Perceptions of Teachers' Feelings toward Them." *Journal of Experimental Education* 29 (1960): 107–118.

Deutsch, M. "The Disadvantaged Child and the Learning Process," in *Education in Depressed Areas,* edited by H. Passow. New York: Teachers College Press, 1963.

Deutsch, M.; Fishman, J. A.; Kogan, L.; North, R.; and Whiteman, M. "Guidelines for Testing Minority Group Children." *Journal of Social Issues* 20 (1964):129–145.

Douglas, J. *The Home and the School.* London: MacGibbon and Kee, 1964.

Douglas, J. *The American Social Order.* New York: The Free Press, 1971.

Douglas, J. (ed.). *Deviance and Respectability.* New York: Basic Books, 1972.

Doyle, W.; Hancock, G.; and Kifer, E. "Teachers' Perceptions: Do They Make a Difference?" Paper presented at the meeting of the American Educational Research Association, 1971.

Edgar, D. E. *The Competent Teacher.* Sydney, Australia: Angus & Robertson, 1974.

Erikson, K. T. "Note on the Sociology of Deviance," in *The Other Side,* edited by H. S. Becker. New York: The Free Press, 1964.

Erikson, K. T. *Wayward Puritans.* New York: Wiley, 1966.

Flanagan, J. C. *Test of General Ability: Technical Report.* Chicago: Science Research Associates, 1960.

Gibson, G. "Aptitude Tests." *Science* 149 (1965): 583.

Goaldman, L. "Counseling Methods and Techniques: The Use of Tests," in *The Encyclopedia of Education,* edited by L. C. Deighton. New York: MacMillan, 1971.

Good, T., and Brophy, J. *Looking in Classrooms.* New York: Harper and Row, 1973.

Goodmam, P. *Compulsory Mis-Education* New York: Random House, 1964.

Goslin, D. A., and Glass, D. C. "The Social Effects of Standardized Testing on American Elementary Schools." *Sociology of Education* 40 (1967):115-131.

Henry, J. *Culture Against Man.* New York: Random House, 1963.

Hirschi, T. *Causes of Delinquency.* Berkeley: University of California Press, 1969.

Illich, I. *Deschooling Society.* New York: Harper & Row, 1971.

Jackson, G., and Cosca, C. "The Inequality of Educational Opportunity in the Southwest: An Observational Study of Ethnically Mixed Classrooms." *American Educational Research Journal* 11 (1974): 219–229.

Johnson, J. *On the Interface between Low income*

*Urban Black Children and Their Teachers during the Early School Years: A Position Paper.* San Francisco: Far West Laboratory for Educational Research and Development, 1973.

Katz, M. Class, *Bureaucracy and Schools.* New York: Praeger, 1971.

Kitsuse, J. "Societal Reaction to Deviant Behavior: Problems of Theory and Method," in *The Other Side,* edited by H. S. Becker. New York: The Free Press, 1964.

Leacock, E. *Teaching and Learning in City Schools.* New York: Basic Books, 1969.

Lemert, E. *Social Pathology.* New York: McGraw-Hill, 1951.

Lemert, E. *Human Deviance, Social Problems and Social Control.* Englewood Cliffs, N.J.: Prentice-Hall, 1972.

Lemert, E. "Beyond Mead: The Societal Reaction to Deviance." *Social Problems* 21 (1974): 457–468.

Lofland, J. *Deviance and Identity.* Englewood Cliffs, N.J.: Prentice-Hall, 1969.

Mackler, B. "Grouping in the Ghetto." *Education and Urban Society* 2 (1969): 80–95.

Matza, D. *Delinquency and Drift.* New York: Wiley, 1964.

Matza, D. *Becoming Deviant.* Englewood Cliffs, N.J.: Prentice-Hall, 1969.

McPherson, G. H. *The Role-set of the Elementary School Teacher: A case study.* Unpublished Ph.D. dissertation, Columbia University, New York, 1966.

Mehan, H. B. *Accomplishing Understanding in Educational Settings.* Unpublished Ph.D. dissertation, University of California, Santa Barbara, 1971.

Mehan, H. B. *Ethnomethodology and Education.* Paper presented to the Sociology of Education Association conference, Pacific Grove, California, 1974.

Merton, R. K. "Social Problems and Social Theory," in *Contemporary Social Problems,* edited by R. Merton and R. Nisbet. New York: Harcourt, Brace and World, 1968.

Newcomb, T. M. "Autistic Hostility and Social Reality." *Human Relations* 1 (1947):69–86.

Noblit, G. W., and Polk, K. *Institutional Constraints and Labeling.* Paper presented to the Southern Sociological Association meetings, Washington, D.C., 1975.

Palardy, J. M. "What Teachers Believe—What Children Achieve." *Elementary School Journal,* 1969, pp. 168–169 and 370–374.

Pequignot, H. "L'équation personnelle du juge." In *Semaine des Hopitaux* (Paris), 1966.

Polk, K. "Class, Strain, and Rebellion and Adolescents." *Social Problems* 17 (1969):214–224.

Polk, K., and Schafer, W. E. *Schools and Delinquency.* Englewood Cliffs, N.J.: Prentice-Hall, 1972.

Reimer, E. *School is Dead.* New York: Doubleday, 1971.

Rist, R. C. "Student Social Class and Teachers' Expectations: The Self-fulfilling Prophecy in Ghetto Education." *Harvard Educational Review* 40 (1970):411–450.

Rist, R. C. "Social Distance and Social Inequality in a Kindergarten Classroom: An Examination of the 'Cultural Gap' Hypothesis." *Urban Education* 7 (1972): 241–260.

Rist, R. C. *The Urban School: A Factory for Failure.* Cambridge, Mass.: The M. I. T. Press, 1973.

Rosenthal, R., and Jacobson, L. "Teachers' Expectancies: Determinants of Pupils' IQ Gains." *Psychology Reports* 19 (1966): 115–118.

Rosenthal, R., and Jacobson, L. *Pygmalion in the Classroom.* New York: Holt, Rinehart, and Winston, 1968.

Rowe, M. "Science, Silence and Sanctions." *Science and Children* 6 (1969):11–13.

Rubington, E., and Weinberg, M. S. *Deviance: The Interactionist Perspective.* New York: MacMillan, 1973.

Rubovits, P., and Maehr, M. L. "Pygmalion Black and white." *Journal of Personality and Social Psychology* 2 (1973): 210–218.

Schafer, W. E., and Olexa, C. *Tracking and Opportunity.* Scranton, Pa.: Chandler, 1971.

Scheff, T. *Being Mentally Ill.* Chicago; Aldine, 1966.

Schur, E. *Crimes without Victims.* Englewood Cliffs, N.J.: Prentice-Hall, 1965.

Schur, E. *Labeling Devient Behavior.* New York: Harper and Row, 1971.

Scott, R. A., and Douglas, J. C. (eds.). *Theoretical Perspectives on Deviance.* New York: Basic Books, 1972.

Snow, R. E. "Unfinished Pygimalion." *Contemporary Psychology* 14 (1969):197–199.

Stein, A. "Strategies for Failure." *Harvard Educational Review* 41 (1971):158–204.

Tannenbaum, F. *Crime and the Community.* New York: Columbia University Press, 1938.

Taylor, C. "The Expectations of Pygmalion's Creators." *Educational Leadership* 28 (1970): 161–164.

Thorndike, R. L. "*Review of Pygmalion in the Classroom.*" Educational Research Journal 5 (1968):708–711.

Thorndike. R. L. "But Do You Have to Know How to Tell Time?" *Educational Research Journal* 6 (1969):692.

Warner W. L.; Havighurst, R.; and Loeb, M.B. *Who Shall be Educated?* New York: Harper & Row, 1944.

Willis, S. *Formation of Teachers' Expectations of Student Academic Performance.* Unpublished Ph.D. dissertation, University of Texas, Austin, Texas, 1972.

Wilson, A. B. "Social Stratification and Academic Achievement," in *Education in Depressed Areas,* edited by H. Passow. New York: Teachers College Press, 1963.

Zajonc, R. B., and Brinkman, P. "Expectancy and Feedback as Independent Factors in Task Performance." *Journal of Personality and Social Psychology* 11 (1969):148–150.

# Closing the Rift between Scholarship and Practice: The Need to Revitalize Educational Research

PETER W. COOKSON, JR.

...

## "ABSTRACT EMPIRICISM" AND THE "NEW SCHOLASTICISM"

Like other sciences, sociology has its "architects and builders—its theorists and its experimentalists."[1] Discovering the proper relationship between theory and data, in fact, is a key intellectual process in the pursuit of sociological knowledge. Theory without data is empty, and data without theory is incomprehensible. There is more to research, however, than theory and data. The background assumptions that sociologists make, in fact, precede both theory and data. These assumptions determine not only what we study, but how and why.

Often these background assumptions are not expressed openly but are embedded in the vocabulary of a discipline. The claim, for instance, that sociologists can study education "scientifically"' is symptomatic of an underlying assumption that education, like natural phenomena has certain laws of development, which can be identified by a strict adherence to the scientific method. On the face of it such a claim seems to press us to the edge of credulity, but the legacy of logical positivism is so strong, that to openly question the scientific basis for studying education is close to heretical. Thus the linguistic tone and intellectual style of the studies published in the most prestigious journals is usually heavy, humorless, and sadly lacking in compassion.

Moreover, the prerequisites for publication include strict adherence to a specific form of presentation. Detachment, objectivity, and rigor are esteemed. Occasionally, however, the canons of the scientific style appear to constrict not only the way in which sociologists of education express themselves but the way in which they view their profession. By creating a narrow definition of acceptable research topics and demanding adherence to a specific style of presentation the research agenda of the sociology of education has been limited, perhaps driving out some sensitive and astute observers who cannot or will not conform to the prevailing style. Every discipline suffers from what the French call a "deformation professionelle"—a sort of self-inflicted intellectual wound that defines the world view of its practitioners. In the sociology of education, however, the "deformation professionelle" has cut so deep that it threatens to become terminal.

It may be that the rigid intellectual quality that characterizes so much work in the sociology of education is less a sign of strength than uncertainty and insecurity. Unlike natural scientists, sociologists can seldom carry out true experiments, and little chance exists to replicate studies. Thus there are few areas in the study of education where an accumulation of results leads to a general finding that can be believed with confidence. To fill the vacuum of uncertainty, some sociologists of education have been manufacturing huge amounts of numbers. With the help of the

*Source:* From *Educational Policy, 1* (3): 321–331. © 1987 Corwin Press. Reprinted by permission of Corwin Press, Inc.

computer, quantitative studies roll off the research assembly line with regularity and predictability. As early as 1963 Dodson warned that reliance on the computer was no substitute for independent thinking and craftsmanship.[2]

Numbers have the ring of authority, especially when they come in great quantities and are attached to "models." Researchers such as Karabel and Halsey have noted, however, that "abstract empiricism" has not fulfilled its promise as the one best method of studying education. By allowing methodology to determine research problems there is a real threat to the sociological imagination.

> In the face of a pervasive belief that it is impossible to examine admittedly important problems in a scientifically meaningful way, sociologists of education retreat into the study of "safe" if uninspired questions. Caution rather than curiosity is the order of the day, and expressions of intellectual initiative are dismissed as evidence of a lack of methodological realism.[3]

Moreover, empiricism has a logic of its own that may compound problems rather than simplify them. A recent example of this tendency is the study by James S. Coleman, Thomas Hoffer, and Sally Kilgore.[4] In a sense, their comparison between public, Catholic, and other private schools is misleading because the variance within each of these groups may be great as the variance between them. Catholic schools, for instance, are not a homogeneous group. Jesuit and Franciscan schools can vary a great deal in terms of discipline, curriculum, and student body composition. Within the public sector the range is even greater, so to compare public and Catholic schools as groups is somewhat misleading—a two-legged horse at best.

Because of its dominance, abstract empiricism could be thought of as a new form of scholasticism where the narrow adherence to traditional methods has elevated form over content. Much of today's empirical research has a logic of its own that seems only accidentally to touch on important educational problems. Of course, there are exceptions to this generalization, but in the main it seems fair to say that the pages of the discipline's journals do not bubble over with innovative research strategies or non-traditional subjects.

In fairness it should be said that a good number of sociologists of education are aware of the problems in their field. Certainly, one of the most influential and widely read statements about the sociology of the sociology of education and the discipline's future research agenda is Karabel and Halsey's introduction to their reader, *Power and Ideology in Education*.[5] They suggest that studies that integrate analysis of structure and process especially in regard to class reproduction offer sociologists a window of opportunity to break out of abstract empiricism. They cite the work of Basil Bernstein and Emile Durkheim as examples of how research can illuminate the relationship between the process of education and social structure. In particular, they suggest that Durkheim's "L'evolution Pédagogique en France" is a "model for future research in the sociology of education."[6] Given that Durkheim's book was based on lectures that he delivered in 1904–05, Karabel and Halsey's suggestion amounts to a kind of indictment of the field since then. They propose that Bernstein's work is in the Durkheimian tradition and therefore may be a "harbinger of a new synthesis." A question that comes to mind, however, is whether Karabel and Halsey's perspective is wide enough to encompass the many possibilities that the study of education offers scholars.

Certainly, the issue of class reproduction is of critical importance in assessing educational processes, but is it the only issue? In some ways, their proposed research agenda takes us even farther away from the schools than abstract empiricism. Symptomatic of this tendency is their suggestion that sociologists of education repair to the library in search of data. Their claim that the library contains "mountains of extraordinarily rich data" waiting to be mined may be true, but it is nonetheless rather inward looking.[7] The idea that education in all its complexity and richness can be studied in libraries rather than schools represents a kind of professional withdrawal of sociologists from their subject. Dodson's fear that the sociology of education would become an armchair discipline was not wholly unfounded. The view from afar has the advantage of breadth, but it lacks depth. Caught between abstract empiricism and theory, the sociological study of education stands the risk of becoming irrelevant to all but academic specialists.

It would seem obvious that a central task of sociology is the demystification of social processes. Ideal sociologists should be, in Alfred McClung Lee's words, "sensitive observers and literate recorders and interpreters of social behavior."[8] Unfortunately, sociologists have often been accused of being just the opposite. Armed, as it were, with the paraphernalia of research, the sociologist is sometimes perceived by the public-at-large as dressing up commonplace observations in confusing and pretentious language, commonly known as "sociologese." The sociology of education, perhaps in an effort to legitimize itself intellectually, has cultivated a highly refined form of sociologese. There exists the possibility that rather than reaching a wider audience, the work of sociologists of education will be read by a smaller and smaller group.

As the discipline enters its maturity, are its intellectual and creative horizons contracting or expanding? Are sociologists reaching a wider audience or drifting toward a kind of scholastic solipsism? Can sociologists of education afford to be "apart from the human condition they presumably seek to understand?"[9] Clearly, the audience for educational research ought to include at least some practitioners. Can the answer to the question—the sociology of education for whom?—really be, other sociologists?

## NEW DIRECTIONS IN EDUCATIONAL RESEARCH

Brian Salter and Ted Tapper in their study *Education, Politics and the State* make the comment that, "There is a severe danger that important educational change will take place in Britain unbeknown to many educational sociologists."[10] What could happen in Britain could also happen in the United States if the rift between scholarship and practice is not closed. Fortunately, some new research paradigms are developing that could put scholarship and practice into closer partnership. Three relatively new research strategies that might be productive are: action-research, collaborative research, and—for want of a better phrase—humanistic research.

The term "action research" was first used by Kurt Lewin to describe a type of research which is, "an activity engaged in by groups or communities with the aim of changing their circumstances in ways that are consistent with a shared conception of human values."[11] Moreover, action-research is a "reflexive social practice," in which there is no distinction drawn "between the practice being researched and the process of researching it."[12] John Elliott, who has directed several action-research projects and written extensively on the efficacy of action-research, suggests that this form of inquiry has developed into an international movement.[13]

Closely related to action-research is collaborative research as described by Jeannie Oakes, Sharon E. Hare, and Kenneth A. Sirotnik:

Collaborative efforts serve to inform theory as well as practice.... In collaborative research, analysis of what now exists and generation of directions for improvement are shaped and enriched by the exigencies of real life in schools.[14]

The authors go on to describe in detail the trials, tribulations, and possibilities of collaborative research by outlining the history of the Curriculum, Computers, and Collaboration project, which was started in 1983 through a joint effort of the University of California, Los Angeles, and two public school districts. According to the authors, cooperation between scholars and practitioners is not easily achieved. It is, however, possible and may be a necessity if the rift between research and practice is to be closed.

Closely related to Lewin's belief in reflexive social practices is the view expressed by Jerome S. Allender that research processes are fundamentally subjective. In a distinct break with logical positivism, Allender's humanistic approach to scholarship emphasizes that "educational research is fundamentally a personal and social process."[15] In Allender's estimation, we cannot divorce ourselves from what we study. The belief that there is an absolute truth that exists outside our own consciousness is a kind of scientific icon: an object of uncritical devotion that keeps us tied to a traditional conception of what constitutes meaningful scholarship. According to Allender, the acceptance, even appreciation, of relativism has "stimulated thinking and rethinking about how to set standards for quality research."[16] He takes issue with C. P. Snow's dichotomy between the scientific and humanistic cultures and argues, "The goal is to find knowledge that people can use to design and execute their actions in their daily relationships at all levels. The methods are focused on generating alternative possibilities."[17]

Objectivity in the positivistic sense ceases to exist in the subjective approach to research. One need not accept Allender's argument "in toto," however, to appreciate the contribution of humanistic scholarship in helping to close the gap that presently exists between scholarship and practice. If nothing else, the humanistic approach is like a breath of fresh intellectual air in that it invigorates our thinking and lightens the atmosphere that surrounds the somewhat stuffy conventions of orthodox research.

All three of the research approaches mentioned above share core characteristics which seem to point our thinking in a new and positive direction. To begin with, we ought to recognize that the distinction between scholarship and practice is essentially artificial and thus ought not to shape how we view the process of inquiry. Moreover, the fact that research is a personal quest as well as a scientific enterprise should not embarrass us but should become a source of pride. The world as we experience it is socially constructed, we are never solely observers. Whether we like it or not, we are participants.

To breathe life back into the study of education we ought to reformulate our purposes. Methodology and subject matter flow from background assumptions, and these assumptions are predicated on what we conceive of as our purpose. Purpose also implies responsibility. Should not social scientists assume at least some responsibility for the condition of education and design and execute studies, the purpose of which are to stimulate discussion and help to create policies that will make schools safer, happier, and more just environments? Researchers presumably bring not only special knowledge to the problems of education but special insights as well. A major task of researchers ought to be not only the collecting and analyzing of data but making their findings accessible to the broader educational community.

Each day millions of students attend schools that are little more than processing centers, and in the inner cities many schools resemble prisons. Don't those who study education have an obligation to students, teachers, administrators, and the larger society to help create schools that are less stultifying and more productive? Educational research without a sense of service stands the risk of losing its purpose and in doing so may forego an important opportunity to unite scholarship and practice. The consequence of this missed opportunity could be a widening of the rift between scholarship and practice to the disadvantage of researchers, schools, and society.

## ENDNOTES

1. Simon White, "Missing Mass, " *The Sciences* 25, no. 4 (July/August 1985): pp. 44–51, p. 44.
2. Dodson, p. 409.
3. Karabel and Halsey, p. 75.
4. James S. Coleman, Thomas Hoffer, and Sally Kilgore. *Public and Private Schools* (Chicago: National Opinion Research Center, 1981).
5. Karabel and Halsey, pp. 1–85.
6. Karabel and Halsey, p. 72.
7. Karabel and Halsey, p. 75.
8. Alfred McClung Lee, *Sociology For Whom?* (New York: Oxford University Press, 1978), p. 23.
9. Lee, p. 35.
10. Brian Salter and Ted Tapper, *Education. Politics and the State: Theory and Practice of Educational Change* (London: Grant McIntyre, 1981), p. 221.
11. John Elliott, "Educational Action Research," *In World Yearbook of Education 1985—Research Policy and Practice,* ed. John Nisbet and Stanley Nisbet (London: Kogan Page, 1985), pp. 231–250, p. 242.
12. Elliott, p. 242.
13. The Classroom Action-Research Network (CARN) based at the Cambridge Institute of Education in the United Kingdom was established in 1976 to disseminate ideas about the theory and practice of educational action-research and keep individuals and groups in touch with each other on a regular basis. Elliot, p. 231.
14. Jeannie Oakes, Sharon E. Hare, and Kenneth A. Sirotnik. "Collaborative Inquiry: A Congenial Paradigm In a Cantankerous World," *Teachers College Record* 87, no 4 (Summer 1986): pp. 545–561, p. 546.
15. Jerome S. Allender. "Educational Research: A Personal and Social Process," *Review of Educational Research* 56, no. 2 (Summer 1986): pp. 173–193, p. 174.
16. Allender, p. 174.
17. Allender, p. 181.

## CHAPTER 4 REFERENCES

Amidon, E. J., & Flanders, N. A. (1971). *The role of the teacher in the classroom.* Minneapolis: Paul S. Amidon and Associates, Inc.

Berg, I. (1970). *Education and jobs: The great training robbery.* New York: Praeger.

Bernstein, B. (1990). *The structuring of pedagogic discourse: Volume IV: Class, codes and control.* London: Routledge.

Bourdieu, P., & Passeron, J.-C. (1977). *Reproduction: In education, society, and culture.* Beverly Hills, CA: Sage.

Bowles, S., & Gintis, H. (1776). *Schooling in capitalist America.* New York: Basic Books.

Coleman, J. S., et al. (1966). *Equality of educational opportunity.* Washington, DC: U.S. Government Printing Office.

Coleman, J. S., Hoffer T., & Kilgore, S. (1982). *High school achievement.* New York: Basic Books.

Collins, R. (1971). Functional and conflict theories of educational opportunity. *Harvard Educational Review, 38,* 7–32.

Collins, R. (1979). *The credential society.* New York: Academic Press.

Cookson, P. W., Jr., & Persell, C. H. (1985). *Preparing for power: America's elite boarding schools.* New York: Basic Books.

Durkheim, E. (1956). *Education and sociology* (S. D. Fox, Trans.). New York: Free Press.

Durkheim, E. (1962). *Moral education: A study of the theory and application of the sociology of education.* New York: Free Press.

Durkheim, E. (1977). *The evolution of educational thought* (P. Collins, Trans.). Boston: Routledge & Kegan Paul.

Edmonds, R. R. (1979, March-April). Some schools work and more can. *Social Policy,* 28–32.

Goodlad, J. I. (1984). *A place called school.* New York: McGraw-Hill.

Heyns, B. (1978). *Summer learning and the effects of schooling.* New York: Academic Press.

Hodgkinson, H. (1991, September). Reform versus reality. *Phi Delta Kappan,* 9–16.

Hopper, E. (1971). Stratification, education and mobility in industrial societies. In E. Hopper (Ed.), *Readings in the theory of educational systems.* London: Hutchinson.

Jackson, P. (1968). *Life in the classroom.* New York: Holt, Rinehart and Winston.

Jencks, C., et al. (1972). *Inequality.* New York: Basic Books.

Lee, V., & Byrk, A. (1989). A multilevel model of the social distribution of high school achievement. *Sociology of Education, 62,* 172–192.

MacLeod, J. (1987). *Ain't no makin' it.* Boulder, CO: Westview.

Mannheim, K. (1952). *Essays on the sociology of knowledge.* New York: Oxford University Press.

Oakes, J. (1985). *Keeping track.* New Haven, CT: Yale University Press.

Persell, C. H. (1990). *Understanding society.* New York: HarperCollins.

Persell, C. H. (1977). *Education and inequality.* New York: Free Press.

Rosenbaum, J. E. (1976). *Making inequality: The hidden curriculum of high school tracking.* New York: Wiley.

Rosenthal, R., & Jacobsen, L. (1968). *Pygmalion in the classroom*. New York: Holt, Rinehart and Winston.

Stinchcombe, A. (1964). *Rebellion in a high school*. Chicago: Quadrangle Books.

Turner, R. H. (1960, October). Sponsored and contest mobility and the school system. *American sociological review, 25*, 855–867.

Waller, W. (1965). *The sociology of teaching*. New York: John Wiley & Sons.

Woolfolk, A. E. (1990). *Educational psychology* (4th ed.). Boston: Allyn and Bacon.

## SUGGESTED READINGS

Althusser, L. (1971). Ideology and ideological state apparatuses. In *Lenin and philosophy and other essays*. New York: Monthly Review Press.

Anyon, J. (1980). Social class and the hidden curriculum of work. *Journal of Education, 162*, 67–92.

Apple, M. (1982). *Education and power*. Boston: Routledge and Kegan Paul.

Archer, M. S. (1979). *Social origins of educational systems*. Beverly Hills: Sage.

Aronowitz, S. & Giroux, H. (1985). *Education under siege*. South Hadley, MA: Bergin and Garvey.

Becker, G. (1964). *Human capital*. New York: National Bureau of Economic Research.

Bernstein, B. (1973a). *Class, codes, and control* (Vol. 1). London: Paladin.

Bernstein, B. (1973b). *Class, codes, and control* (Vol. 2). London: Routledge and Kegan Paul.

Bernstein, B. (1977). *Class, codes, and control* (Vol. 3). London: Routledge and Kegan Paul.

Bernstein, B. (1990). *The structuring of pedagogic discourse: Volume IV: Class, codes and control*. London: Routledge.

Boli, J., Ramirez, F. O., & Meyer, J. W. (1985). Exploring the origins and expansion of mass education. *Comparative Education Review, 29*, 145–170.

Bourdieu, P. (1984). *Distinction: A social critique of the judgment of taste*. Cambridge, MA: Harvard University Press.

Bourdieu, P., & Passeron, J. -C. (1977). *Reproduction: In education, society, and culture*. Beverly Hills: Sage.

Bowles, S., & Gintis, H. (1776). *Schooling in capitalist America*. New York: Basic Books.

Carnoy, M. (1974). *Education as cultural imperialism*. New York: McKay.

Carnoy, M. (Ed.). (1975). *Schooling in a corporate society*. New York: McCay.

Carnoy, M., & Levin, H. (Eds.). (1976). *The limits of educational reform*. New York: Longman.

Carnoy, M., & Levin, H. (1985). *Schooling and work in the democratic state*. Stanford, CA: Stanford University Press.

Clark, B. (1962). *Educating the expert society*. San Francisco: Chandler.

Coleman, J. S., et al. (1966). *Equality of educational opportunity*. Washington, DC: U.S. Government Printing Office.

Coleman, J. S., Hoffer, T., & Kilgore, S. (1982). *High school achievement*. New York: Basic Books.

Collins, R. (1971). Functional and conflict theories of educational opportuntity. *Harvard Educational Review, 38,* 7–32.

Collins, R. (1979). *The credential society.* New York: Academic Press.

Cookson, P. W., Jr., & Persell, C. H. (1985). *Preparing for power: America's elite boarding schools.* New York: Basic Books.

DiMaggio, P. (1982, April). Cultural capital and school success: The impact of status culture participation on the grades of U.S. high school students. *American Sociological Review, 47,* 189–201.

Dreeben, R. (1968). *On what is learned in school.* Boston: Addison-Wesley.

Durkheim, E. (1956). *Education and sociology* (S. D. Fox, Trans.). New York: Free Press.

Durkheim, E. (1962). *Moral education: A study of the theory and application of the sociology of education.* New York: Free Press.

Durkheim, E. (1965). *The elementary forms of the religious life.* New York: Free Press.

Durkeim, E. (1977). *The evolution of educational thought* (P. Collins, Trans.) London: Routledge and Kegan Paul.

Giroux, H. (1983a). Theories of reproduction and resistance in the new sociology of education. *Harvard Educational Review, 53,* 257–293.

Goslin, D. (1965). *The school in contemporary society.* Atlanta: Scott, Foresman.

Karabel, J., & Halsey, A. H. (Eds.). (1977). *Power and ideology in education.* New York: Oxford University Press.

Lavin, D. E., Alba, R. D., & Silberstein, R. A. (1981). *Right versus privilege: The open admissions experiment at the City University of New York.* New York: Free Press.

Meyer, J. W. (1977, July). The effects of education as an institution. *American Journal of Sociology, 83,* 55–77.

Meyer, J. W., Tyack, D., Nagel, J., & Gordon A. (1979). Public education as nation-building in America. *American Journal of Sociology, 85,* 591–613.

Ramirez, F. O., & Boli, J. (1987). Global patterns of educational institutionalization. In G. M. Thomas et al. (Eds.), *Institutional structure: Constituting state, society, and the individual.* Newbury Park, CA: Sage.

Ramirez, F. O., & Boli, J. (1987, January). The political construction of mass schooling: European origins and worldwide institutionalization. *Sociology of Education, 60,* 15.

Waller, W. (1965). *The sociology of teaching.* New York: John Wiley & Sons.

Wexler, P. (1976). *The sociology of Education: Beyond equality.* Indianapolis, IN: Bobbs-Merrill.

Wexler, P. (1987). *Social analysis of education.* London: Routledge and Kegan Paul.

Whitty, G. (1985). *Sociology and school knowledge.* London: Metheun.

Willis, P. (1981). *Learning to labour.* New York: Columbia University Press.

CHAPTER **5**

# Philosophy of Education and Its Significance for Teachers

In Chapter 1, we argued that Americans place a great deal of faith in education, and particularly that Americans view schools as the great panacea for the multitude of problems that plague both individuals and society as a whole. In this chapter, we point out that the study of philosophy of education as an integral part of the foundations perspective will allow prospective teachers to reflect on educational issues from a particular perspective—the perspective of philosophy. This perspective encourages logical, systematic thinking. It stresses the importance of ideas and allows—indeed encourages—the act of reflection on every aspect of practice. Thus, philosophy acts as the building block for the reflective practitioner.

### THE PERSPECTIVE OF PHILOSOPHY OF EDUCATION

Practitioners often argue, as do students in schools of education, that although philosophy of education may add another dimension to the way in which they view schools, nevertheless, they haven't the time for a discipline that does not offer tangible results. Rather, they wish to learn *what* to do, not *why* to do it. For too many practitioners and students of education, the practice of teaching is reduced to action devoid of a rationale or justification.

We believe that the practice of teaching cannot be separated from a philosophical foundation. Philosophy, as applied to education, allows practitioners and prospective practitioners to apply systematic approaches to problem solving in schools and illuminates larger issues of the complex relationship of schools to the social order.

### What Is Philosophy of Education?

Philosophy of education differs from philosophy, as we have stated in Chapter 1. Philosophy of education is firmly rooted in practice, whereas philosophy, as a discipline, stands on its own with no specific end in mind. Given this difference, it is necessary to consider for a moment how a particular philosophy might affect practice.

All teachers, regardless of their action orientation, have a personal philosophy of life that colors the way in which they select knowledge; order their classrooms; interact with students, peers, parents, and administrators; and select values to emphasize within their classrooms. Engaging in philosophy helps teachers and prospective teachers to *clarify* what they do or intend to do and, as they act or propose to act, to *justify* or explain why they do what they do in a logical, systematic manner. Thus, the activity of doing philosophy aids teachers in understanding two very important notions: (1) who they are or intend to be and (2) why they do or propose to do what they do. Furthermore, through the action of clarification and justification of practice, teachers and prospective teachers think about practice and acquire specific information, which lends authority to their decision making.

### The Meaning of Philosophical Inquiry

Although people exist as individuals, they also exist within the greater context of their culture. Through interactions with the norms common to the culture, people form attitudes, beliefs, and values, which are then transmitted to others. As people go about this process of acquiring cultural norms, they may accept norms wholeheartedly, accept norms partially, or, in certain instances, totally reject them. Whatever people choose to embrace, if their choices are made in a logical, rational manner, they are engaged in the process of "doing philosophy."

To proceed in doing philosophy, certain key questions are posed that can be divided into three specific areas of philosophical inquiry. The first is called *metaphysics,* a branch of philosophy that concerns itself with questions about the nature of reality. The second is called *epistemology,* a branch of philosophy that concerns itself with questions about the nature of knowledge. Last is *axiology,* a branch of philosophy that concerns itself with the nature of values.

We believe that these distinctions in philosophy are important for prospective teachers to know, since ideas generated by philosophers about education usually fall under a particular branch of philosophy, such as epistemology. Furthermore, the ideas generated by philosophers interested in particular questions help people to clarify their own notions of existence, knowledge, and values—in sum, one's personal philosophy of life. Moreover, this philosophy of life, as one comes to understand it, becomes the foundation upon which people construct pedagogic practice.

## PARTICULAR PHILOSOPHIES OF EDUCATION

In the following pages, we will discuss several leading schools of philosophy that have influenced and continue to influence the way people view educational practice. We have included both classical philosophies and modern philosophies which, in our opinion, have made the most impact on the ways in which people think about schools. Many of the ideas overlap; many of the distinctions we make are artificial and, at times, arbitrary. Most important, we hope that readers will appreciate the fact that all successful practitioners borrow from many schools of thought.

### Idealism

We begin our discussion of particular schools of philosophy that have influenced educational thought with *idealism*, the first systematic philosophy in Western thought. Idealism is generally thought to be the creation of the Greek philosopher, Plato (427–347 B.C.), the pupil of Socrates, a famous Greek teacher and philosopher who lived in Athens (c. 469–399 B.C.). Socrates never wrote anything down; rather, he taught through establishing oral dialogues with his students or those he wished to engage in philosophical questions. Socrates saw himself, as Plato stated in *The Apology (The Defense)*, as "the gadfly of Athens." Through questioning, he forced his fellow Athenians to consider their life choices, and, in many instances, made them uncomfortable or often provoked them to anger. In 399 B.C., Socrates was executed for his beliefs. He was officially charged with corrupting the minds of the youth of Athens.

Plato wrote down Socrates' ideas and his method, which was the dialogue. While doing so, he probably added to Socrates' ideas, since he was only 28 years old when Socrates was executed, and he continued to write Socratic dialogue long after Socrates' death. Scholars concur with the idea that Plato augmented Socrates' beliefs, since it is generally held that Plato was far more sophisticated in his thinking than Socrates (Guthrie, 1969). Nevertheless, it is difficult for the uninitiated to distinguish between Socrates' and Plato's work. Thus, we will refer to this combination as *Platonic philosophy*.

*Generic Notions.*   Philosophers often pose difficult, abstract questions that are not easily answered. Plato helped to initiate this tradition through his concern for the search for *truth*.

Plato distrusted the world of matter; he believed that it was in a constant state of flux. Therefore, matter was an inaccurate measurement of truth since it was constantly changing. Plato also believed that the senses were not to be trusted, as they continually deceive us. Because truth for Plato was perfect and because truth is eternal, it was not to be found in the world of matter: "The unchanging realities we can apprehend by the mind only: the senses can show us only transient and imperfect copies of reality" (Kitto, 1951, p. 194).

The only constant for Plato was the field of mathematics, since $1 + 1 = 2$ will never change. In fact, it is eternal. The problem, however, with all of this is that mathematics is only one field of inquiry and so individuals must look to other modes of inquiry in the quest for truth. For Plato, this was the task of the philosopher.

Plato's method of doing philosophy was to engage another individual in a dialogue and, through the dialogue, question that individual's point of view. This questioning was done in a systematic, logical examination of both points of view. Ultimately, both parties would reach a synthesis of viewpoints that would be acceptable to both. This approach, called the *dialectic,* was used by Plato to move individuals from the world of matter to the world of ideas. Perhaps, as some philosophers suggest, Plato's philosophy should be called "ideaism" rather than idealism, since, for Plato, ideas were what mattered above all.

Plato thought education, in particular, was important as a means of moving individuals collectively toward achieving the *good.* He believed that the state should play an active role in education and that it should encourage the brighter students to follow a curriculum that was more abstract and more concerned with ideas rather than with concrete matter. Thus, he would have brighter students focusing on ideas and assign data collecting to the less able. Plato's "tracking system" was gender free; however, he proposed that those students who functioned on a more concrete level should assume roles necessary for maintaining the city-state, such as craftsmen, warriors, and farmers. Those who functioned on a more abstract level should rule. In fact, Plato put forth the idea of a philosopher-king: an individual who would lead the state to discover the ultimate *good.* Thus, Plato believed that rulers were individuals of thought, action, and obligation.

Since Plato's time, people have seen the state become a major force in determining the system of education. People have also witnessed how increasingly the school and tracking, in particular, determine the life chances of students. Additionally, people still cling to the importance Plato attached to education as the instrument that will enlighten rulers and aid them in achieving the highest *good.* Perhaps naively, people still believe that evil comes through ignorance, and that if only the rulers are educated, evil will be obliterated. Unfortunately, modern history has yet to validate this view.

*Modern Idealists.*    Since Plato, there has been a series of philosophers who have augmented Plato's original notions. For example, St. Augustine (354–430 A.D.) added religion to classical idealism; later philosophers, such as Rene Descartes (1596–1650), Immanuel Kant (1724–1804), and George Wilhelm Friedrich Hegel (1770–1831), added their particular visions to Platonic idealism.

*Goal of Education.*    Educators who subscribe to idealism are interested in the search for truth through ideas rather than through the examination of the false shadowy world of matter. Teachers encourage their students to search for truth as individuals. However, with the discovery of truth comes responsibility— responsibility of those who achieve realization of truth to enlighten others. Moreover, idealists subscribe to the notion that education is transformation: Ideas can change lives.

*Role of the Teacher.*    It is the teacher's responsibility to analyze and discuss ideas with students in order for students to move to new levels of awareness so that ultimately students can be transformed. Teachers should deal with abstract notions through the dialectic method but should aim to connect analysis with action as well.

In an idealist's classroom, the teacher plays an active role in discussion, posing questions, selecting materials, and establishing an environment, all of which ensure the teacher's desired outcome. An idealist teacher subscribes to the doctrine of *reminiscence,* described in the *Meno,* an important Platonic dialogue, which states that the role of the teacher is to bring out that which is already in the student's mind. Additionally, an idealist teacher supports moral education as a means of linking ideas to action. Last, the idealist teacher sees herself or himself as a role model in the classroom, to be emulated by students.

*Methods of Instruction.*    Idealist teachers take an active part in their students' learning. Although they lecture from time to time, perhaps to fill in background material not covered in the reading, they predominately use the dialectic approach described by Plato. Through questioning, students are encouraged to discuss, analyze, synthesize, and apply what they have read to contemporary society. Students are also encouraged to work in groups or individually on research projects, both oral and written.

*Curriculum.*    Idealists place great importance on the study of classics (i.e., great literature of past civilizations that illustrated contemporary concerns). For idealists, all contemporary problems have their roots in the past and can best be understood by examining how previous individuals dealt with them. A good example of an idealist curriculum would be the Great Books curriculum at Saint John's University, in Annapolis, Maryland. During their four years in college, students read, analyze, and apply the ideas of classical works to modern life. For elementary school-age children, there is a Great Books course promoted by individuals in the private sector and there exists as well a grass-roots movement to institute a core curriculum in elementary and junior high schools throughout the nation.

An interesting proposal that has not taken root is Mortimer Adler's *Paideia Proposal* (1982), which advocates great literature for children of all abilities. Adler proposed that elementary school children read great literature that would contain issues of relevance to all. Adler emphasized both content and process through the actual readings, much like the current whole language movement.

Many idealists also support a back-to-basics approach to education, which emphasizes the three Rs. Such an approach became popular among educational conservatives, such as President Reagan's Secretary of Education, William Bennett, in the 1980s.

## Realism

Realism is a philosophy that follows in the same historical tradition as idealism. Realism is associated with both Plato and Aristotle, although philosophers tend to view Aristotle as the leading proponent of realism. Aristotle (384–322 B.C.), a student of Plato's, was the son of a physician. He studied at Plato's Academy in Athens until Plato's death in 347 B.C. Aristotle also lived in Asia Minor and in Macedonia, where he was tutor to King Philip of Macedonia's son, Alexander. Aristotle's pupil later became Alexander the Great and a lover of all things Greek, thanks to Aristotle's influence.

In 355 B.C., Aristotle returned to Athens and started a school in the Lyceum, a public grove. Aristotle's career as a great teacher was cut short by the death of Alexander, his protector. The Athenians charged Aristotle with "impiety" and thus Aristotle was forced to leave Athens and settle in Euboea, where he remained until his death. Aristotle is particularly important because he was the first philosopher who developed a systematic theory of logic.

*Generic Notions.*   In our discussion of idealism, we noted that Plato argued for the centrality of ideas. Aristotle, however, believed that only through studying the material world was it possible for an individual to clarify or develop ideas. Thus, realists reject the Platonic notion that only ideas are real, and argue instead that the material world or matter is real. In fact, realists hold that matter exists, independent of ideas. Aristotle might have, in fact, argued that a triangle exists whether or not there is a thinking human being within range to perceive it.

If Plato were to study the nature of reality, he would begin with ideas, since he believed that the world of matter was shadowy and unreliable (see *The Allegory of the Cave*). Aristotle, however, in his quest for the nature of reality, would begin with the world of matter. It is important to note that both Plato and Aristotle subscribed to the importance of ideas but each philosopher dealt with them very differently.

Since the classical realism of Aristotle, many forms of realism have evolved. These range from the religious realism of Thomas Aquinas (1225–1274) to the modern realism of individuals such as Francis Bacon (1561–1626) and John Locke (1632–1704) to the contemporary realism of Alfred North Whitehead (1861–1947) and Bertrand Russell (1872–1970).

*Aristotle's Systematic Theory of Logic.*   Aristotle is particularly important because he was the first philosopher to develop a rational, systematic method for testing the logic of statements people make. Aristotle began his process with empirical research; then, he would speculate or use dialectic reasoning, that would culminate in a syllogism. A *syllogism* is a system of logic that consists of three parts: (1) a major premise, (2) a minor premise, and (3) a conclusion. A famous example of a syllogism, used by many philosophers is as follows:

> All men are mortal
> Socrates is a man
> therefore, Socrates is mortal. (Ozmon & Craver, 1990, p. 43)

For a syllogism to work, all of the parts must be correct. If one of the premises is incorrect, the conclusion will be fallacious. Basically, Aristotle used syllogisms to systematize thinking. The problem, however, with this method is that Aristotle never made it clear where the syllogism was to be placed in his schema or framework. Thus, subsequent philosophers may have misinterpreted Aristotelian logic, grossly misusing the syllogism.

As you may have concluded by now, philosophers have been posing questions concerned with "the good life" or "the importance of reason" from the Greeks through the present (and probably long before the Greeks, considering that recorded history began in 3500 B.C. in Sumer). Aristotle, as did his contemporaries, stressed the importance of moderation in all things—the importance of achieving balance in leading one's life. Reason, concluded Aristotle, was the instrument individuals could employ to achieve the proper balance or moderation in their lives. Education, therefore, became particularly important in achieving moderation since education would introduce individuals to the process of systematic, rigorous thought. Through education, individuals would learn to reason and thus become able to choose the path of moderation in their lives. Since Aristotle, there have been important subsequent developments in this school of philosophy.

*Neo-Thomism.*  Aristotle was never clear about the place of the syllogism in his schema, although classical scholars believe that the syllogism was to be the culmination of his system rather than the starting point (Bowder, 1982). Many medieval thinkers, however, used Aristotle's syllogism to begin their logical proofs and *deduced* from generalizations to specific conclusions.

Thomas Aquinas (1225–1274) was an important medieval authority on the works of Aristotle. A school of philosophy, Neo-Thomism, is derived from Aquinian thought based on Aristotle. Basically, Aquinas affected a synthesis of pagan ideas and Christian beliefs, employing reason as a means of ascertaining or understanding truth. Aquinas thought that God could be understood through reasoning but reasoning based on the *material world.* Thus, Aquinas and Aristotle both emphasized matter and ideas in their particular philosophical investigations.

Aquinas's philosophy became known as Neo-Thomism in the latter part of the nineteenth century when it was revived by the Vatican as a way of resolving the conflict between the natural sciences and the Catholic church. In particular, the church, through Neo-Thomism, could argue that there was no conflict between science and religion since scientific inquiry ultimately led to belief in God. Aquinas's influence on contemporary educational practice is especially profound in Catholic schools, that base their educational goals on balancing the world of faith with the world of reason.

*Modern Realism.*  Modern realism dates from the Renaissance, particularly with the work of Francis Bacon (1561–1626), who developed the inductive or scientific method of learning. Bacon was troubled by the reliance of classical realists on a prior or preconceived notion upon which thinkers deduced truths. Based on Aristotle's use of observable data, Bacon was able to develop a method starting with observations, that might culminate in a generalization, which then might be tested in specific instances for the purpose of verification.

John Locke (1632–1704), continuing in the scientific tradition established by Bacon, attempted to explain how people know things from the *empirical* point of view. He, too, chafed at the notion of *a priori ideas,* stating that the mind was a blank page, or *tabula rasa,* and what humans know is based on information gathered through the senses and through experience. Locke thought that the human mind ordered sense data and experience and then *reflected* on it.

*Contemporary Realists.*    Contemporary realists, or realists in modern times, have tended to focus on science and philosophy—in particular, on scientific issues that have philosophical dimensions. For example, Alfred North Whitehead came to philosophy through the discipline of mathematics and was concerned with the search for "universal patterns" (Ozmon & Craver, 1990, p. 50).

Bertrand Russell studied both mathematics and philosophy as a student at Trinity College and Cambridge University, and coauthored with Whitehead the important book, *Principia Mathematica.* Both men believed that the universe could be characterized through universal patterns; however, Russell proposed that these patterns could be verified and classified through mathematics. Both were interested in education. Whitehead confined his interests to writing about education—in particular, advocating (like Plato) the primacy of ideas. Nevertheless (like Aristotle), he recognized the necessity of grounding ideas within the context of the living world. Russell actually founded a school called Beacon Hill, in which he sought to put into practice some of his notions of education, particularly the idea of employing knowledge to social problems in order to create a better world.

*Goal of Education.*    Both Plato and Aristotle believed that important questions concerning such notions as the good life, truth, beauty, and so on could be answered through the study of ideas, using the dialectical method. They differed, however, in their studying points. Plato emphasized only the study of ideas to understand ideas. Aristotle believed that it was possible to understand ideas through studying the world of matter. For Plato, the real world was shadowy and deceptive; for Aristotle, the real world was the starting point in the quest for understanding philosophical concerns.

For contemporary realists, the goal of education is to help individuals understand and then apply the principles of science to help solve the problems plaguing the modern world. Again, the leading notion of realists is that through basic disciplines—and in particular, science—individuals will be able to fathom what philosophers have been debating since the beginning of their discipline: existence of the good life, but thanks to Aristotle, how it can be encouraged through science.

*Role of the Teacher.*    Teachers, according to contemporary realists, should be steeped in the basic academic disciplines in order to transmit to their students the knowledge necessary for the continuance of the human race. They should have a solid grounding in science, mathematics, and the humanities. Additionally, teachers must present ideas in a clear and consistent manner and demonstrate that there are definitive ways to judge works of art, music, poetry, and literature. From this point of view, it is the role of the teacher to enable students to learn objective methods of evaluating such works (Ozmon & Craver, 1990, p. 63).

*Methods of Instruction.*    Realists would support a number of methods—in particular, lecture and question and answer. Additionally, since realists believe in objective criteria for judging the value of artistic and literary works, they would support the lecture as a method of instruction in order to give students the knowledge necessary to make these evaluations. Finally, many realists support competency-based assessment as a way of ensuring that students learn what they are being taught (Osmon & Craver, 1990, p. 63). Remember that realists believe that the material world holds the key to the ideal world; therefore, realists would encourage questions that would help students in the classroom grasp the ideal through specific characteristics of particular manifestations.

*Curriculum.*   Curriculum for realists would consist of the basics: science and math, reading and writing, and the humanities. Realists believe that there is a body of knowledge that is essential for the student to master in order to be part of society. Indeed, as stated previously, this body of knowledge is viewed as being essential for the survival of society.

Recent debates have centered around various groups questioning whether, in fact, there is an essential core of knowledge and, if so, what might it consist of. In particular, the debate about cultural literacy, sparked by the work of E. D. Hirsch, and the championing of the primacy of history and geography in social studies curricula proposed by Diane Ravitch, Chester Finn, and Paul Gagnon (see the Bradley Commission, 1989, for a detailed discussion of these proposals) support the notion of specific knowledge that helps students to a better understanding of their culture. Those who might question just what "culture" consists of and support a curriculum that truly reflects the multiplicity of U.S. society are scholars of curriculum, such as James Banks (1988).

## Pragmatism

Pragmatism is generally viewed as an American philosophy that developed in the latter part of the nineteenth century. Generally speaking, the founders of this school of thought are George Sanders Pierce (1839–1914), William James (1842–1910), and John Dewey (1859–1952). However, there are European philosophers from earlier periods who might also be classified as pragmatists, such as Frances Bacon, John Locke, and Jean-Jacques Rousseau.

Pragmatism comes from the Greek word *pragma,* meaning work. Both George Sanders Pierce and William James are credited with having described pragmatism in part through the Biblical phrase, "By their fruits ye shall know them." James specifically makes such a reference in his book, *Varieties of Religious Experience* (James, 1978). That is, pragmatism is a philosophy that encourages people to find processes that work in order to achieve their desired ends. Although pragmatists do study the past, they generally are more interested in contemporary issues and in discovering solutions to problems in present-day terms. Pragmatists are action oriented, experientially grounded, and will generally pose questions such as, "What will work to achieve my desired end?" A pragmatic schema might look like this:

problem → speculative thought → action → results

Pragmatists might then ask, "Do the results achieved solve the problem?" If the question is answered in the affirmative, then the solution may be judged as valid.

Pragmatism's roots, as well as modern realism's roots, may be traced to the English philosopher and scientist, Francis Bacon (1561–1626), who we have previously discussed. Troubled with the Aristotelian legacy of deductive reasoning through the syllogism, Bacon sought a way of thinking in which people might be persuaded to abandon the traditions or "idols" of the past for a more experiential approach to the world. Because Bacon emphasized experience posited firmly within the world of daily existence, he can be thought of as a pioneer in the pragmatic school of philosophy. Furthermore, the method of reasoning he emphasized was *inductive,* which became the foundation of observational method in educational research.

Another modern realist, political philosopher John Locke (1632–1704), also followed in the pragmatic tradition. Locke was particularly interested in the ways in which people come to know things. He believed that the mind was a *tabula rasa,* a blank tablet, and that one acquires knowledge through one's senses (in opposition to Plato who, centuries earlier, had supported the notion of innate ideas). Locke believed that people can have ideas, that people can obtain these ideas through their senses but that they never verify them through the material or natural world. Locke's emphasis on the world of experience is particularly important for later developments in the philosophy of education.

Jean-Jacques Rousseau (1712–1778), a French philosopher, wrote mainly in France during the years preceding the French Revolution. Rousseau believed that individuals in their primitive state were naturally good and that society corrupted them. Society was harmful, for it led people away from pure existences. For Rousseau, the good life meant, simply stated, "back to nature." Thus, the Queen of France, Marie Antoinette, and her court at Versailles, influenced by Rousseau's ideas, attempted to return to nature by dressing as milk maids, shepherds, and shepherdesses.

Rousseau placed an important emphasis on *environment* and *experience,* which makes him important to subsequent pragmatic thinkers. He is mainly known to educators for his book *Emile,* which centers around a young boy who is removed from society to the country and learns experientially, through his environment, with the help of a tutor. Two points of interest are: (1) Emile does not read books until he reaches 12 years of age and (2) there is little regard for the education of women in Rousseau's scheme other than two chapters on Sophie, who eats sweets and cakes and plays with dolls, and whose *raison d'etre* is to be Emile's companion.

Rousseau is thought to be a romantic due to his preoccupation with individuals in their natural state. Nevertheless, his emphasis on experience and on the child in a state of nature, constantly growing and changing, paved the way for thinkers such as John Dewey.

John Dewey (1859–1952), intellectually, was heir to Charles Darwin, the British naturalist, whose theory of natural selection emphasized the constant interaction between the organism and its environment, thus challenging the Platonic and Aristotelian notions of fixed essences. Unlike the static, ordered world of the eighteenth-century philosophers, nineteenth-century pragmatists saw the world as dynamic and developing. Although Dewey acknowledged his intellectual debt to Hegel, an early nineteenth-century idealist, the idea of the dynamic quality of life was, to Dewey, of overriding importance. It could not have existed without the work of Charles Darwin.

Dewey, originally from Vermont, taught philosophy at the Universities of Minnesota, Michigan, Chicago, and Columbia. During this time, he formulated his own philosophy, introducing the terms *instrumentalism* and *experimentalism*. Instrumentalism refers to the pragmatic relationship between school and society; experimentalism refers to the application of ideas to educational practice on an experimental basis. While at the University of Chicago, he opened the Laboratory School (with his wife Alice Chapman Dewey), in which his ideas about education were applied.

Dewey's philosophy of education was the most important influence on what has been termed *progressive education*. Actually, progressive education from Dewey to the present has included a number of different approaches. Historically, the two most important have been child-centered progressivism, influenced by Dewey, and social reconstructionism, a radical interpretation of Dewey's work. Social reconstructionists, such as George Counts (1932) and Theodore Brameld (1956), viewed the schools as vehicles for improving and changing society. As we will suggest in Chapter 7, although social reconstructionists had some effect on curriculum, it has been Dewey's work that had the most profound intellectual and practical influence on U.S. progressive education. Our discussion of the progressive educational philosophy based on pragmatism therefore concentrates on Dewey's work.

*Dewey's Pragmatism: Generic Notions.*   Dewey's form of pragmatism—instrumentalism and experimentalism—was founded upon the new psychology, behaviorism, and the philosophy of pragmatism. Additionally, his ideas were influenced by the theory of evolution and by an eighteenth-century optimistic belief in progress. For Dewey, this meant the attainment of a better society through education. Thus, the school became an "embryonic community" where children could learn skills both experientially as well as from books, in addition to traditional information, which would enable them to work cooperatively in a democratic society.

Dewey's ideas about education, often referred to as *progressive*, proposed that educators start with the needs and interests of the child in the classroom, allow the child to participate in planning his or her course of study, employ project method or group learning, and depend heavily on experiential learning.

Dewey's progressive methodology rested on the notion that children were active, organic beings, growing and changing, and thus required a course of study that would reflect their particular stages of development. He advocated both freedom and responsibility for students, since those are vital components of democratic living. He believed that the school should reflect the community in order to enable graduating students to assume societal roles and to maintain the democratic way of life. Democracy was particularly important for Dewey. He believed that it could be more perfectly realized through education that would continually reconstruct and reorganize society.

*Goal of Education.*   Dewey's vision of schools was rooted in the social order; he did not see ideas as separate from social conditions. He fervently believed that philosophy had a responsibility to society and that ideas required laboratory testing; hence, he stressed the importance of the school as a place where ideas can be implemented, challenged, and restructured, with the goal of implementing students with the knowledge of how to improve the social order. Moreover, he believed that school should provide "conjoint, communicated experience"—that it should function as preparation for life in a democratic society.

In line with the progressive political atmosphere of the turn of the century, Dewey viewed the role of the school within the larger societal conditions of which it was a part. As such, Dewey's vision of schooling must be understood as part of the larger project of social progress and improvement. Although Dewey was certainly concerned with the social dimensions of schooling, he also was acutely aware of the school's effects on the individual. Thus, Dewey's philosophy of education made a conscious attempt to balance the social role of the school with its effects on the social, intellectual, and personal development of individuals. In other words, Dewey believed that the schools should balance the needs of society and community on the one hand and the needs of the individual on the other. This tension, or what the philosopher of education Maxine Greene (1988) termed the "dialectic of freedom," is central to understanding Dewey's work.

Dewey, like his contemporary, the French sociologist Emile Durkheim, saw the effects of modernization and urbanization on the social fabric of Western society. The rapid transformation in the nineteenth century from a traditional, agrarian world to a modern industrial one shattered the traditional bonds of solidarity and cohesion that held people together. Combined with the mass immigration to the United States in the late nineteenth century, the urban worlds of Chicago and New York City where Dewey spent his adult life were often fragmented and, in Durkheim's words, *anomic* (without norms). For both Durkheim and Dewey, the schools had to play a key role in creating a modern form of cohesion by socializing diverse groups into a cohesive democratic community.

The key to Dewey's vision is his view that the role of the school was to integrate children into not just any type of society, but a democratic one. Therefore, Dewey's view of integration is premised on the school as an embryonic democratic society where cooperation and community are desired ends. Dewey did not believe, however, that the school's role was to integrate children into a nondemocratic society. Rather, he believed that if schools instilled democratic and cooperative values in children, they would be prepared as adults to transform the social order into a more democratic one. Although he located this central function of schools, he never adequately provided a solution to the problem of integrating diverse groups into a community without sacrificing their unique characteristics. This is a problem still hotly debated.

For Dewey, the primary role of education was growth. In a famous section of *Democracy and Education,* Dewey stated that education had no other goals than growth—growth leading to more growth. As Lawrence Cremin (1990) noted,

> John Dewey liked to define the aim of education as growth, and when he was asked growth toward what, he liked to reply, growth leading to more growth. That was his way of saying that education is subordinate to no end beyond itself, that the aim of education is not merely to make parents, or citizens, or workers, or indeed to surpass the Russians or Japanese, but ultimately to make human beings who will live life to the fullest, who will continually add to the quality and

meaning of their experience and to their ability to direct that experience, and who will participate actively with their fellow human beings in the building of a good society. (p. 125)

Historian of education Diane Ravitch (1983, pp. 43–80) noted that Dewey's philosophies of education were often misunderstood and misapplied. As we discussed in Chapter 3, it was often misapplied as "life adjustment education" and learning through experience as vocational education; it was often misapplied with regard to freedom, with individual freedom often confused with license and becoming far more important than other processes; and it was often totally distorted by providing social class appropriate education (i.e., vocational education for the poor). Despite these distorted applications, Dewey's philosophy of education, often referred to as *progressive education,* was central to all subsequent educational theory. For Dewey, the role of the school was to be "a lever of social reform"; that is, to be the central institution for societal and personal improvement and to do so by balancing a complex set of processes.

*Role of the Teacher.*   In a progressive setting, the teacher is no longer the authoritarian figure from which all knowledge flows; rather, the teacher assumes the peripheral position of facilitator. The teacher encourages, offers suggestions, questions, and helps plan and implement courses of study. The teacher also writes curriculum and must have a command of several disciplines in order to create and implement curriculum.

*Methods of Instruction.*   Dewey proposed that children learn both individually and in groups. He believed that children should start their mode of inquiry by posing questions about what they want to know. Today, we refer to this method of instruction as the *problem-solving* or *inquiry method.* Books, often written by teachers and students together, were used; field trips and projects, that reconstructed some aspect of the child's course of study, were also an integral part of learning in Dewey's laboratory school. These methods in turn became the basis for other progressive schools founded in the Deweyan tradition.

Formal instruction was abandoned. Traditional blocks of time for specific discipline instruction were eliminated. Furniture, usually nailed to the floor, was discarded in favor of tables and chairs that could be grouped as needed. Children could converse quietly with one another, could stand up and stretch if warranted, and could pursue independent study or group work. What at first glance to the visitor used to formal pedagogy might appear as chaotic was a carefully orchestrated classroom with children going about learning in nontraditional yet natural ways. Lockstep, rote memorization of traditional schools was replaced with individualized study, problem solving, and the project method.

*Curriculum.*   Progressive schools generally follow Dewey's notion of a core curriculum, or an integrated curriculum. A particular subject matter under investigation by students, such as whales, would yield problems to be solved using math, science, history, reading, writing, music, art, wood or metal working, cooking, and sewing— all the academic and vocational disciplines in an integrated, interconnected way.

Progressive educators support starting with contemporary problems and working from the known to the unknown, or what is now called in social studies education, the curriculum of *expanding environments*. Progressive educators are not wedded to a fixed curriculum either; rather, curriculum changes as the social order changes and as children's interests and needs change.

There is some controversy over Dewey's ideas about traditional discipline-centered curriculum. Some contemporary scholars (Egan, 1992, pp. 402–404) has stated that Dewey's emphasis on the need for the curriculum to be related to the needs and interests of the child suggests he was against traditional subject matter and in favor of a child-centered curriculum based on imagination and intuition. Others, including Howard Gardner (1992, pp. 410–411), felt that Dewey proposed a balance between traditional disciplines and the needs and interests of the child. We concur with Gardner's reading of Dewey and believe that Dewey thought that an integrated curriculum provided the most effective means to this balance.

## Existentialism and Phenomenology

Like pragmatism, existentialism is a rather modern philosophy. Although its roots can be traced back to the Bible, as a philosophy that has relevance to education, one may date existentialism as beginning with the nineteenth-century European philosopher Soren Kierkegaard (1813–1855). More recent philosophers who work in this school include Martin Buber (1878–1965), Karl Jaspers (1883–1969), Jean Paul Sartre (1905–1986), and the contemporary philosopher Maxine Greene.

Phenomenology was primarily developed by Edmund Husserl (1859–1935), Martin Heidegger (1889–1976), and Maurice Merleau-Ponty (1908–1961). Since both existentialism and phenomenology have much in common, and since many phenomenologists are existentialists as well, we have chosen to combine our discussion of these two schools here.

*Generic Notions.*    Because existentialism is an individualistic philosophy, many of its adherents argue that it is not a particular school of philosophy at all. However, there are certain notions to which a majority of existentialists adhere. So, for our purposes, we will consider it as a particular philosophical movement that has important implications for education.

Unlike traditional philosophers, such as Plato and Aristotle, who were concerned with posing questions about epistemology, axiology, and metaphysics, existentialists pose questions as to how their concerns impact on the lives of individuals. Phenomenologists focus on the phenomena of consciousness, perception, and meaning, as they arise in a particular individual's experiences.

Basically, existentialists believe that individuals are placed on this earth alone and must make some sense out of the chaos they encounter. In particular, Sartre believed that "existence precedes essence"—that is, people must create themselves, and they must create their own meaning. This is done through the choices people make in their lives. Thus, individuals are in a state of constantly becoming, creating chaos and order, creating good and evil. The choice is up to the individual. The amount of freedom and responsibility people have is awesome, since they can, according to Sartre, make a difference in a seemingly absurd world. Although Sartre rejected the idea of the existence of God, other existentialists, especially its founder Soren Kierkergaard, were devout Christians who, while attacking contemporary Christianity, proposed "a great leap to faith" through which individuals might accept the existence of God. Whereas Kierkergaard was rallying against the scientific, objective approach to existence, Sartre was attempting to sort out meaning in a world that supported gross inhumane behavior—in particular, World War II and the Holocaust.

Phenomenologists are concerned with the way in which objects present themselves to people in their consciousness, and how people order those objects. Hermeneutics, an outgrowth of phenomenology, seeks to discover how people give objects meaning. Language is important here, since language is used to describe the various phenomena in life.

*Goal of Education.*   Existentialists believe that education should focus on the needs of individuals, both cognitively and affectively. They also believe that education should stress individuality; that it should include discussion of the nonrational as well as the rational world; and that the tensions of living in the world—in particular, anxiety generated through conflict—should be addressed. Existential phenomenologists go further; they emphasize the notion of *possibility,* since the individual changes in a constant state of becoming. They see education as an activity liberating the individual from a chaotic, absurd world.

*Role of the Teacher.*   Teachers should understand their own "lived worlds" as well as that of their students in order to help their students achieve the best "live worlds" they can. Teachers must take risks; expose themselves to resistant students; and work constantly to enable their students to become, in Greene's (1978) words, "wide awake." Introspection is useful in order to enable students to become in touch with their worlds and to empower them to choose and to act on their choices. Thus, the role of the teacher is an intensely personal one that carries with it a tremendous responsibility.

*Methods of Instruction.*   Existentialists and phenomenologists would abhor "methods" of instruction as they are currently taught in schools of education. They view learning as intensely personal. They believe that each child has a different learning style and it is up to the teacher to discover what works for each child. Martin Buber, an existentialist, wrote about an I-thou approach, whereby student and teacher learn cooperatively from each other in a nontraditional, nonthreatening, "friendship." The teacher constantly rediscovers knowledge, the student discovers knowledge, and together they come to an understanding of past, present, and future, particularly a future ripe with possibilities. Thus, the role of the teacher is to help students understand the world through posing questions, generating activities, and working together.

*Curriculum.*   Existentialists and phenomenologists would choose curriculum heavily biased toward the humanities. Literature especially has meaning for them since literature is able to evoke responses in readers that might move them to new levels of awareness, or, in Greene's (1978) words, "wide awakeness." Art, drama, and music also encourage personal interaction. Existentialists and phenomenologists believe in exposing students at early ages to problems as well as possibilities, and to the horrors as well as accomplishments humankind is capable of producing.

## Neo-Marxism

Neo-Marxist philosophies of education are those approaches that trace their intellectual roots and theoretical assumptions to the nineteenth-century economist and philosopher Karl Marx (1818–1883). Based on the radical critique of capitalism, these theories argue that the role of education in capitalist society is to reproduce the ideology of the dominant class and its unequal economic outcomes; and conversely, that the role of education ought to be to give students the insight to demystify this ideology and to become agents of radical educational and social change.

The neo-Marxist perspective is more an overall theory of society than a particular philosophy of education. That is, while its proponents suggest specific philosophical approaches to educational issues, they are a part of the longer critique of capitalist society and capitalist education. The neo-Marxist approach includes the political-economic analysis of education, such as the works of Samuel Bowles and Herbert Gintis (1976), the curriculum theories of Michael Apple (1978, 1979, 1982a, 1982b), the pedagogical work of Paulo Freire (1972), and the critical educational theory of Henry Giroux (1983). To understand the neo-Marxist philosophy of education, it is important to first understand some basic background issues.

*Generic Notions.*    The intellectual, theoretical, and methodological foundations of neo-Marxism are all found in the works of Karl Marx. Marx was an economist, sociologist (before the discipline of sociology was officially founded), and philosopher who left his native Germany in 1842, first for Paris and then to London, where he spent the remainder of his life. Marx is usually associated with the worldwide movement he inspired—communism—but his writings have been the foundation for a radical critique of capitalism throughout the twentieth century.

Although critics have pointed to problems with his theories (e.g., that socialism always proceeds out of the collapse of capitalism, which it has not; that capitalism is destined to collapse, which it has not), it is unfair to blame the problems and apparent failures of communist and socialist societies (e.g., in the former Soviet Union and Eastern Europe) on Marx himself, for he wrote very little on what socialism would look like. Rather, the bulk of his voluminous life's work concerned the understanding of capitalism.

Marx's works may be divided into two periods. The early philosophical works, including *The Economic and Philosophical Manuscripts* (1844), the *German Ideology* (1846), and *The Communist Manifesto* (1848) (the later two written with his lifetime friend and collaborator Frederick Engels), were concerned with philosophical and political issues such as alienation, freedom, ideology, and revolution. His later economic works, including the three volumes of *Das Capital* (1867–1894), are concerned with the economic laws of capitalism and the contradictions (a Marxian term meaning irreconcilable differences) that make its collapse inevitable.

Marx's theories are far too complex to do justice to in these brief pages. However, it is necessary to understand those parts of his theories that form the basis of neo-Marxist philosophies of education. Simply stated, Marx believed that the history of civilization was defined by class struggle—the struggle between the dominant economic group and subordinate economic groups. Although every society defined such groups according to its own economic system (e.g., under feudalism, the serfs and the nobility; under capitalism, the proletariat [workers] and the bourgeoisie [the capitalist owners]), it was the domination of subordinate economic groups by those who controlled the economy (or means of production) that marked each historical period and the revolution by subordinate groups that marked the collapse of an outmoded economic system and its replacement by a new and superior one.

For Marx, each new economic system moved civilization closer to his ideal: a society that would produce sufficient economic resources to allow all of its citizens to live productive and decent lives. Capitalism, for Marx, with its vast productive capacity, would have the potential to render economic scarcity and human misery obsolete. The problem, however, is that Marx believed that the laws of capitalist accumulation that give the bulk of its productive resources to those who own the means of production (capitalists) would make such a just society impossible. Therefore, Marx asserted that it was necessary for those who produced the resources (the workers) to recognize that it is in their collective interest to change the system to what he saw as the next logical stage in history: socialism, a society where the means of production are owned by the state in trust for the entire public. Marx believed that the laws of capitalism would lead to increasing economic crises (e.g., inflation, recession, depression), increasing poverty of the working class side by side with increasing wealth on the part of the small capitalist class. Thus, Marx believed that the working class would unite (class consciousness) and rebel (class struggle) to create a more just socialist society.

Numerous historical problems are evident with this theory. For instance, Marx did not foresee the rise of the welfare state to partially ameliorate such social problems, nor the success of labor unions in working within the system to gain significant economic rewards for workers. Theoretical problems also abound, such as the view of dominant and subordinate groups in narrow economic terms, rather than in broader social, political, and cultural terms. However, the general conflict theory of society (discussed more fully in Chapter 4) is central to understanding modern neo-Marxist philosophies of education.

The key component to this conflict theory is Marx's theory of social order and change. Although Marx indeed believed that economic laws are the foundation of any society, it is people, through conflict and struggle, who make history. Thus, the dominant group in any society must preserve order either through force and coercion, that is inherently unstable, or by convincing the subordinate groups that the system is fair and legitimate. For Marx, this is accomplished through *ideology*, or the ideas or belief system of the ruling class (Marx & Engels, 1846). Conversely, in order for change to take place, the subordinate group must see through this ideology and become conscious of its own interests (to change society). Thus, the subordinate groups must demystify the illusions of the dominant ideology and work toward change. It is education's role in transmitting this dominant ideology and its potential in allowing students to demystify it that is the main thrust of neo-Marxist philosophies of education.

*Goal of Education.* Modern neo-Marxist theories include what may be termed *reproduction theories* (Bowles & Gintis, 1976) and *resistance theories* (Freire, 1978; Giroux, 1981, 1983). Reproduction theories argue that the role of education in capitalist societies is to reproduce the economic, social, and political status quo. More specifically, the school through its ideology and curriculum (Apple, 1978, 1979, 1982a, 1982b) and pedagogic practices (McLaren, 1989) transmits the dominant beliefs to children and serves to legitimate the capitalist order. Resistance theories, while agreeing that schools often reproduce the dominant ideology, state they also have the potential to empower students to question it.

Therefore, resistance theories question the overly deterministic view of reproduction theories and state that such approaches deny what they call "human agency"— that is, the power of individuals to shape their own world and to change it. In this respect, resistance theories have a great deal in common with existentialists, as they believe that the process of education contains the tools to enable individuals both to understand the weaknesses in the dominant ideology and to construct alternative visions and possibilities. Further, what are termed *postmodernist* (Cherryholmes, 1988; Giroux, 1991) and *feminist* (Ellsworth, 1989; Laird, 1989; Lather, 1991; Martin, 1987) theories of education are closely related to this aspect of neo-Marxism, although not all postmodernists and feminists are neo-Marxists.

What all of these theorists have in common is the view that education should transform the dominant culture (for a complete discussion of postmodernism and feminism, see Giroux, 1991, and Sadovnik, 1993). Postmodernists and feminists disagree with neo-Marxists about who exactly comprises the dominant culture. Feminists argue that male domination is the problem; postmodernists are skeptical of any one theory that explains domination and therefore rejects the neo-Marxist emphasis on economic domination as too one dimensional (Lyotard, 1984).

*The Role of the Teacher.* The neo-Marxist philosophy of education concentrates on the teacher and student as part of a critical pedagogical process. The teacher, from this vantage point, must become a "transformative intellectual" (Giroux, 1988) whose role is to engage his or her students in a critical examination of the world. The student thus becomes part of an educational process that seeks to examine critically the society and its problems and to seek radical alternatives.

In some respects, this view of education is similar to the existential phenomenology of Greene (1977, 1988) in that it views the purpose of education as "wide awakeness." The difference is that Greene is less committed to an objective truth that constitutes such a state (that is, one reality that is true), whereas neo-Marxists believe that "wide awakeness" requires an objective truth that includes a critique of capitalism. Such a conclusion is open to considerable debate, even among those sympathetic to neo-Marxism. However, its idea that education ought to result in critical awareness of self and society is a view that goes well beyond neo-Marxist philosophy and is shared by many of the other philosophies discussed here, including pragmatism, existentialism, phenomenology, postmodernism, and feminism.

*Methods of Instruction.* Given their emphasis on education as transformation, neo-Marxists favor a dialectical approach to instruction, with the question-and-answer method designed to move the student to new levels of awareness and ultimately to change. Through rigorous analysis of the taken-for-granted aspects of the world, the goal of instruction is to reveal underlying assumptions of society and to help students see alternative possibilities.

*Curriculum.*    The neo-Marxist view of curriculum is that the curriculum is not objective or value free but is socially constructed (Apple, 1978, 1979, 1982a, 1982b; Young, 1971). This view suggests that the curriculum is the organized and codified representation of what those with the power to shape it want the children to know. Such a critical stance requires that teachers understand the ways in which curriculum represents a particular point of view and to become critical curriculum constructors—that is, individuals who can reshape the curriculum to represent a fairer view of the world (although for neo-Marxists, this fairer view of the world means a curriculum that is critical of capitalism).

As we will discuss in Chapter 7, this view of the curriculum is shared by feminist curriculum theorists (Macdonald & Macdonald, 1981; Miller, 1982; Mitrano, 1979) and postmodern theorists (Giroux, 1991). The difference, however, is that feminists and postmodernists often disagree about whose interests the curriculum represents. Feminists, for example, argue that it is patriarchal interests rather than capitalist interests that affect the curriculum. The view of curriculum shared by these theorists leads them to support more multicultural and feminist curricula, which emphasize those social groups who are not in power.

## CONCLUSION

In this chapter, we have presented some of the major philosophies of education. Through a discussion of how each school of philosophy views the goal of education, the role of the teacher, methods of instruction, and the curriculum, we have present- ed how philosophers of education view important educational issues. These schools of philosophy often overlap. As a teacher, you will, more often than not, make use of several approaches. It is important that you develop, clarify, and justify your own particular philosophical approach to teaching, as it will form the foundation of your practice. Moreover, as we suggest in Chapter 10, the successful school reforms at schools such as Central Park East in New York City are based on a sound philosoph- ical foundation. Thus, school improvement depends on both teachers and schools having a clear sense of purpose, and a philosophy of education provides the basis for such a purpose.

The following selections illustrate the philosophies of education discussed in this chapter. In the first selection, "My Pedagogic Creed," John Dewey presents the central aspects of the "new" or progressive education. Written in 1897, Dewey discusses his definition of education, the school, the curriculum, pedagogy, and the role of the school in social progress, and proposes a pragmatist philosophy of education.

In the second selection, "Wide-Awakeness and the Moral Life" philosopher of education Maxine Greene presents an existentialist philosophy of education. Greene passionately argues for teachers to become critically aware of the world around them and to help students better understand their own lives. This understanding, according to Greene, is a necessary condition for social improvement.

The third selection, "Reproduction and Resistance in Radical Theories of Schooling," by radical sociologist Stanley Aronowitz and radical educational theorist Henry Giroux outlines the radical neo-Marxist educational theory known as resistance theory. Aronowitz and Giroux suggest that teachers need a philosophy of education that enables them to help students demystify the false notions of reality offered by society. In addition, the authors view teachers as transformative intellectuals who must play a role in changing society.

# My Pedagogic Creed

## JOHN DEWEY

### ARTICLE I—WHAT EDUCATION IS

I believe that all education proceeds by the participation of the individual in the social consciousness of the race. This process begins unconsciously almost at birth, and is continually shaping the individual's powers, saturating his consciousness, forming his habits, training his ideas, and arousing his feelings and emotions. Through this unconscious education the individual gradually comes to share in the intellectual and moral resources which humanity has succeeded in getting together. He becomes an inheritor of the funded capital of civilization. The most formal and technical education in the world cannot safely depart from this general process. It can only organize it or differentiate it in some particular direction.

I believe that the only true education comes through the stimulation of the child's powers by the demands of the social situations in which he finds himself. Through these demands he is stimulated to act as a member of a unity, to emerge from his original narrowness of action and feeling, and to conceive of himself from the standpoint of the welfare of the group to which he belongs. Through the responses which others make to his own activities he comes to know what these mean in social terms. The value which they have is reflected back into them. For instance, through the response which is made to the child's instinctive babblings the child comes to know what those babblings mean; they are transformed into articulate language and thus the child is introduced into the consolidated wealth of ideas and emotions which are now summed up in language.

I believe that this educational process has two sides—one psychological and one sociological; and that neither can be subordinated to the other or neglected without evil results following. Of these two sides, the psychological is the basis. The child's own instincts and powers furnish the material and give the starting point for all education. Save as the efforts of the educator connect with some activity which the child is carrying on of his own initiative independent of the educator, education becomes reduced to a pressure from without. It may, indeed, give certain external results, but cannot truly be called educative. Without insight into the psychological structure and activities of the individual, the educative process will, therefore, be haphazard and arbitrary. If it chances to coincide with the child's activity it will get a leverage; if it does not, it will result in friction, or disintegration, or arrest of the child nature.

I believe that knowledge of social conditions, of the present state of civilization, is necessary in order properly to interpret the child's powers. The child has his own instincts and tendencies, but we do not know what these mean until we can translate them into their social equivalents. We must be able to carry them back into a social past and see them as the inheritance of previous race activities. We must also be able to project them into the future to see what their outcome and end will be. In the illustration just used, it is the ability to see in the child's babblings the

*Source:* "My Pedagogic Creed" by John Dewey. In Martin Dworkin (Ed.), *Dewey on Education.* Teachers College Press, 1959.
Number IX in a series under this title, in *The School Journal,* Vol. LIV, No. 3 (January 16, 1897), pp. 77–80.

promise and potency of a future social intercourse and conversation which enables one to deal in the proper way with that instinct.

I believe that the psychological and social sides are organically related and that education cannot be regarded as a compromise between the two, or a superimposition of one upon the other. We are told that the psychological definition of education is barren and formal—that it gives us only the idea of a development of all the mental powers without giving us any idea of the use to which these powers are put. On the other hand, it is urged that the social definition of education, as getting adjusted to civilization, makes of it a forced and external process, and results in subordinating the freedom of the individual to a preconceived social and political status.

I believe that each of these objections is true when urged against one side isolated from the other. In order to know what a power really is we must know what its end, use, or function is; and this we cannot know save as we conceive of the individual as active in social relationships. But, on the other hand, the only possible adjustment which we can give to the child under existing conditions, is that which arises through putting him in complete possession of all his powers. With the advent of democracy and modern industrial conditions, it is impossible to foretell definitely just what civilization will be twenty years from now. Hence it is impossible to prepare the child for any precise set of conditions. To prepare him for the future life means to give him command of himself; it means so to train him that he will have the full and ready use of all his capacities; that his eye and ear and hand may be tools ready to command, that his judgment may be capable of grasping the conditions under which it has to work, and the executive forces be trained to act economically and efficiently. It is impossible to reach this sort of adjustment save as constant regard is had to the individual's own powers, tastes, and interests—say, that

is, as education is continually converted into psychological terms.

In sum, I believe that the individual who is to be educated is a social individual and that society is an organic union of individuals. If we eliminate the social factor from the child we are left only with an abstraction; if we eliminate the individual factor from society, we are left only with an inert and lifeless mass. Education, therefore, must begin with a psychological insight into the child's capacities, interests, and habits. It must be controlled at every point by reference to these same considerations. These powers, interests, and habits must be continually interpreted—we must know what they mean. They must be translated into terms of their social equivalents—into terms of what they are capable of in the way of social service.

### ARTICLE II—WHAT THE SCHOOL IS

I believe that the school is primarily a social institution. Education being a social process, the school is simply that form of community life in which all those agencies are concentrated that will be most effective in bringing the child to share in the inherited resources of the race, and to use his own powers for social ends.

I believe that education, therefore, is a process of living and not a preparation for future living.

I believe that the school must represent present life—like as real and vital to the child as that which he carries on in the home, in the neighborhood, or on the playground.

I believe that education which does not occur through forms of life, or that are worth living for their own sake, is always a poor substitute for the genuine reality and tends to cramp and to deaden.

I believe that the school, as an institution, should simplify existing social life; should reduce it, as it were, to an embryonic form. Existing life is so complex that the child cannot be brought into contact with it without either confusion or distraction; he is either overwhelmed by the multiplicity of activities which are going on, so that he loses his own power of orderly reaction, or he is so stimulated by these various activities that his powers are prematurely called into play and he becomes either unduly specialized or else disintegrated.

I believe that as such simplified social life, the school life should grow gradually out of the home life; that it should take up and continue the activities with which the child is already familiar in the home.

I believe that it should exhibit these activities to the child, and reproduce them in such ways that the child will gradually learn the meaning of them, and be capable of playing his own part in relation to them.

I believe that this is a psychological necessity, because it is the only way of securing continuity in the child's growth, the only way of giving a back-ground of past experience to the new ideas given in school.

I believe that it is also a social necessity because the home is the form of social life in which the child has been nurtured and in connection with which he has had his moral training. It is the business of the school to deepen and extend his sense of the values bound up in his home life.

I believe that much of present education fails because it neglects this fundamental principle of the school as a form of community life. It conceives the school as a place where certain information is to be given, where certain lessons are to be learned, or where certain habits are to be formed. The value of these is conceived as lying largely in the remote future; the child must do these things for the sake of something else he is to do; they are mere preparation. As a result they do not become a part of the life experience of the child and so are not truly educative.

I believe that the moral education centers upon this conception of the school as a mode of social life, that the best and deepest moral training is precisely that which one gets through having to enter into proper relations with others in a unity of work and thought. The present educational system, so far as they destroy or neglect this unity, render it difficult or impossible to get any genuine, regular moral training.

I believe that the child should be stimulated and controlled in his work through the life of the community.

I believe that under existing conditions far too much of the stimulus and control proceeds from the teacher, because of neglect of the idea of the school as a form of social life.

I believe that the teacher's place and work in the school is to be interpreted from this same basis. The teacher is not in the school to impose certain ideas or to form certain habits in the child, but is there as a member of the community to select the influences which shall affect the child and to assist him in properly responding to these influences.

I believe that the discipline of the school should proceed from the life of the school as a whole and not directly from the teacher.

I believe that the teacher's business is simply to determine on the basis of larger experience and riper wisdom, how the discipline of life shall come to the child.

I believe that all questions of the grading of the child and his promotion should be determined by reference to the same standard. Examinations are of use only so far as they test the child's fitness for social life and reveal the place in which he can be of the most service and where he can receive the most help.

## ARTICLE III—THE SUBJECT-MATTER OF EDUCATION

I believe that the social life of the child is the basis of concentration, or correlation, in all his training or growth. The social life gives the unconscious unity and the background of all his efforts and of all his attainments.

I believe that the subject-matter of the school curriculum should mark a gradual differentiation out of the primitive unconscious unity of social life

I believe that we violate the child's nature and render difficult the best ethical results, by introducing the child too abruptly to a number of special studies of reading, writing, geography, etc., out of relation to this social life.

I believe, therefore, that the true center of correlation on the school subjects is not science, nor literature, nor history, nor geography, but the child's own social activities....

I believe that literature is the reflex expression and interpretation of social experience; that hence it must follow upon and not precede such experience. It, therefore, cannot be made the basis, although it may be made the summary of unification.

I believe once more that history is of educative value in so far as it presents phases of social life and growth. It must be controlled by reference to social life. When taken simply as history it is thrown into the distant past and becomes dead and inert. Taken as the record of man's social life and progress it becomes full of meaning. I believe, however, that it cannot be so taken excepting as the child is also introduced directly into social life.

I believe accordingly that the primary basis of education is in the child's powers at work along the same general constructive lines as those which have brought civilization into being.

I believe that the only way to make the child conscious of his social heritage is to enable him to perform those fundamental types of activity which make civilization what it is....

I believe that there is, therefore, no succession of studies in the ideal school curriculum. If education is life, all life has, from the outset, a scientific aspect, an aspect of art and culture, and an aspect of communication. It cannot, therefore, be true that the proper studies for one grade are mere reading and writing, and that at a later grade, reading, or literature, or science, may be introduced. The progress is not in the succession of studies but in the development of new attitudes towards, and new interests in, experience.

I believe finally, that education must be conceived as a continuing reconstruction of experience; that the process and the goal of education are one and the same thing.

I believe that to set up any end outside of education, as furnishing its goal and standard, is to deprive the educational process of much of its meaning and tends to make us rely upon false and external stimuli in dealing with the child....

# Wide-Awakeness and the Moral Life

## MAXINE GREENE

"Moral reform," wrote Henry David Thoreau, "is the effort to throw off sleep." He went on:

> Why is it that men give so poor an account of their day if they have not been slumbering? They are not such poor calculators. If they had not been overcome with drowsiness they would have performed something. The millions are awake enough for physical labor; but only one in a million is awake enough for effective intellectual exertion, only one in a hundred million to a poetic or divine life. To be awake is to be alive I have never yet met a man who was quite awake. How could I have looked him in the face? We must learn to reawaken and keep ourselves awake, not by mechanical aids, but by an infinite expectation of the dawn, which does not foresake us in our soundest sleep. I know of no more encouraging fact than the unquestionable ability of man to elevate his life by a conscious endeavor.[1]

It is of great interest to me to find out how this notion of wide-awakeness has affected contemporary thought, perhaps particularly the thought of those concerned about moral responsibility and commitment in this difficult modern age. The social philosopher Alfred Schutz has talked of wide-awakeness as an achievement, a type of awareness, "a plane of consciousness of highest tension originating in an attitude of full attention to life and its requirements."[2] This attentiveness, this *interest* in things, is the direct opposite of the attitude of bland conventionality and indifference so characteristic of our time.

We are all familiar with the number of individuals who live their lives immersed, as it were, in daily life, in the mechanical round of habitual activities. We are all aware how few people ask themselves what they have done with their own lives, whether or not they have used their freedom or simply acceded to the imposition of patterned behavior and the assignment of roles. Most people, in fact, are likely to go on in that fashion, unless—or until—"one day the 'why' arises," as Albert Camus put it, "and everything begins in that weariness tinged with amazement." Camus had wide-awakeness in mind as well; because the weariness of which he spoke comes "at the *end* of the acts of a mechanical life, but at the same time it inaugurates the impulse of consciousness."[3]

The "why" may take the form of anxiety, the strange and wordless anxiety that occurs when individuals feel they are not acting on their freedom, not realizing possibility, not (to return to Thoreau) elevating their lives. Or the "why" may accompany a sudden perception of the insufficiencies in ordinary life, of inequities and injustices in the world, of oppression and brutality and control. It may accompany, indeed it may be necessary, for an individual's moral life. The opposite of morality, it has often been said, is indifference—a lack of care, an absence of concern. Lacking wide-awakeness, I want to argue, individuals are likely to drift, to act on impulses of expediency. They are unlikely to identify situations as moral ones or to set themselves to assessing their demands. In

*Source:* Reprinted by permission of the publisher from Greene, Maxine, *Landscapes of Learning.* (New York: Teachers College Press, © 1978 by Teachers College, Columbia University. All rights reserved.) "Wide-Awakeness and the Moral Life" pp. 42–52.

such cases, it seems to me, it is meaningless to talk of obligation; it may be futile to speak of consequential choice.

This is an important problem today in many countries of the world. Everywhere, guidelines are deteriorating; fewer and fewer people feel themselves to be answerable to clearly defined norms. In many places, too, because of the proliferation of bureaucracies and corporate structures, individuals find it harder and harder to take initiative. They guide themselves by vaguely perceived expectations; they allow themselves to be programmed by organizations and official schedules or forms. They are like the hero of George Konrad's novel, *The Case Worker*. He is a social worker who works with maltreated children "in the name," as he puts it, "of legal principles and provisions." He does not like the system, but he serves it: "It's law, it works, it's rather like me, its tool. I know its ins and outs. I simplify and complicate it, I slow it down and speed it up. I adapt myself to its needs or adapt it to my needs, but this is as far as I will go."[4] Interestingly enough, he says (and this brings me back to wide-awakeness) that his highest aspiration is to "live with his eyes open" as far as possible; but the main point is that he, like so many other clerks and office workers and middle management men (for all their meaning well), is caught within the system and is not free to choose.

I am suggesting that, for too many individuals in modern society, there is a feeling of being dominated and that feelings of power-lessness are almost inescapable. I am also suggesting that such feelings can to a large degree be overcome through conscious endeavor on the part of individuals to keep themselves awake, to think about their condition in the world, to inquire into the forces that appear to dominate them, to interpret the experiences they are having day by day. Only as they learn to make sense of what is happening, can they feel themselves to be autonomous. Only then can they develop the sense of agency required for living a moral life.

I think it is clear that there always has to be a human consciousness, recognizing the moral issues potentially involved in a situation, if there is to be a moral life. As in such great moral presentations as *Antigone, Hamlet,* and *The Plague,* people in everyday life today have to define particular kinds of situations as moral and to identify the possible alternatives. In *Antigone,* Antigone defined the situation that existed after her uncle forbade her to bury her brother as one in which there were alternatives: she could indeed bury her brother, thus offending against the law of the state and being sentenced to death, or (like her sister Ismene) submit to the men in power. In *Hamlet,* the Danish prince defined the situation in Denmark as one in which there were alternatives others could not see: to expose the murderer of his father and take the throne as the true king or to accept the rule of Claudius and his mother and return as a student to Wittenberg. In *The Plague,* most of the citizens of Oran saw no alternative but to resign themselves to a pestilence for which there was no cure; but Dr. Rieux and Tarrou defined the same situation as one in which there were indeed alternatives: to submit—or to form sanitary squads and, by so doing, to refuse to acquiesce in the inhuman, the absurd.

When we look at the everyday reality of home and school and workplace, we can scarcely imagine ourselves taking moral positions like those taken by a Hamlet or a Dr. Rieux. One reason has to do with the overwhelming ordinariness of the lives we live. Another is our tendency to perceive our everyday reality as a given—objectively defined, impervious to change. Taking it for granted, we do not realize that that reality, like all others, is an interpreted one. It presents itself to us as it does because we have learned to understand it in standard ways.

In a public school, for instance, we scarcely notice that there is a hierarchy of authority; we are so accustomed to it, we forget that it is man-made. Classroom teachers, assigned a relatively low place in the hierarchy, share a way of seeing and of talking about it. They are used to watching schedules, curricula, and testing programs emanate from "the office." They take for granted the existence of a high place, a seat of power. If required unexpectedly to administer a set of tests, most teachers (fearful, perhaps, irritated or sceptical) will be likely to accede. Their acquiescence may have nothing at all to do with their convictions or with what they have previously read or learned. They simply see no alternatives. The reality they have constructed and take for granted allows for neither autonomy nor disagreement. They do not consider putting their objections to a test. The constructs they have inherited do not include a view of teachers as equal participants. "That," they are prone to say, "is the way it is."

Suppose, however, that a few teachers made a serious effort to understand the reasons for the new directive. Suppose they went out into the community to try to assess the degree of pressure on the part of parents. Suppose that they investigated the kinds of materials dispatched from the city or the state. Pursuing such efforts, they would be keeping themselves awake. They might become increasingly able to define their own values with regard to testing; they might conceivably see a moral issue involved. For some, testing might appear to be dehumanizing; it might lead to irrelevant categorizing; it might result in the branding of certain children. For others, testing might appear to be miseducative, unless it were used to identify disabilities and suggest appropriate remedies. For still others, testing might appear to be a kind of insurance against poor teaching, a necessary reminder of what was left undone. Discussing it from

several points of view and within an understood context, the teachers might find themselves in a position to act as moral agents. Like Dr. Rieux and Tarrou, they might see that there are indeed alternatives: to bring the school community into an open discussion, to consider the moral issues in the light of overarching commitments, or to talk about what is actually known and what is merely hypothesized. At the very least, there would be wide-awakeness. The members of the school community would be embarked on a moral life.

Where personal issues are concerned, the approach might be very much the same. Suppose that a young person's peer group is "into" drugs or alcohol or some type of sexual promiscuity. Young persons who are half asleep and who feel no sense of agency might well see no alternative to compliance with the group, when the group decides that certain new experiences should be tried. To such individuals, no moral situation exists. They are young; they are members; whether they want to particularly or not, they can only go along.

Other young persons, just as committed to the group, might be able to realize that there are indeed alternatives when, say, some of their comrades go out to find a supply of cocaine. They might be able to ponder those alternatives, to play them out in their imagination. They can accompany their friends on their search; they might even, if they are successful, get to sniff a little cocaine and have the pleasure such sniffs are supposed to provide. They can, on the other hand, take a moment to recall the feelings they had when they first smoked marijuana—the nervousness at losing touch with themselves, the dread about what might happen later. They can consider the fact that their friends are going to do something illegal, not playful, that they could be arrested, even jailed. They can confront their own reluctance to break the law (or even to break an ordinary rule), imagine what their parents would say, try to anticipate what they would think of themselves. At the same time, if they decide to back away, they know they might lose their friends. If they can remember that they are free, after all, and if they assess their situation as one in which they can indeed choose one course of action over another, they are on the way to becoming moral agents. The more considerations they take into account, the more they consider the welfare of those around, the closer they will come to making a defensible choice.

A crucial issue facing us is the need to find ways of educating young persons to such sensitivity and potency. As important, it seems to me, is the matter of wide-awakeness for their teachers. It is far too easy for teachers, like other people, to play their roles and do their jobs without serious consideration of the good and right. Ironically, it is even possible when they are using classroom manuals for moral education. This is partly due to the impact of a vaguely apprehended relativism, partly to a bland carelessness, a shrugging off (sometimes because of grave self-doubt) of responsibility, I am convinced that, if teachers today are to initiate young people into an ethical existence, they themselves must attend more fully than they normally have to their own lives and its requirements; they have to break with the mechanical life, to overcome their own submergence in the habitual, even in what they conceive to be the virtuous, and ask the "why" with which learning and moral reasoning begin.

"You do not," wrote Martin Buber, "need moral genius for educating character; you do need someone who is wholly alive and able to communicate himself directly to his fellow beings. His aliveness streams out to them and affects them most strongly and purely when he has no thought of affecting them...."[5] This strikes me as true; but I cannot imagine an aliveness streaming out from someone who is half-asleep and out of touch with

herself or himself. I am not proposing separate courses in moral education or value clarification to be taught by such a teacher. I am, rather, suggesting that attentiveness to the moral dimensions of existence ought to permeate many of the classes taught, that wide-awakeness ought to accompany every effort made to initiate persons into any form of life or academic discipline.

Therefore, I believe it important for teachers, no matter what their specialty, to be clear about how they ground their own values, their own conceptions of the good and of the possible. Do they find their sanctions in some supernatural reality? Are they revealed in holy books or in the utterances of some traditional authority? Do they, rather, depend upon their own private intuitions of what is good and right? Do they decide in each particular situation what will best resolve uncertainty, what works out for the best? Do they simply refer to conventional social morality, to prevailing codes, or to the law? Or do they refer beyond the law—to some domain of principle, of norm? To what extent are they in touch with the actualities of their own experiences, their own biographies, and the ways in which these affect the tone of their encounters with the young? Teachers need to be aware of how they personally confront the unnerving questions present in the lives of every teacher, every parent: What shall we teach them? How can we guide them? What hope can we offer them? How can we tell them what to do?

The risks are great, as are the uncertainties. We are no longer in a situation in which we can provide character-training with the assurance that it will make our children virtuous and just. We can no longer use systems of rewards and punishments and feel confident they will make youngsters comply. We recognize the futility of teaching rules or preaching pieties or presenting conceptions of the good. We can no longer set ourselves up as founts of wisdom, exemplars of righteousness, and expect to have positive effects. Children are active; children are different at the various stages of their growth. Engaged in transactions with an environment, each one must effect connections within his or her own experience. Using whatever capacities they have available, each one must himself or herself perceive the consequences of the acts he or she performs. Mustering their own resources, each one must embark—"through choice of action," as Dewey put it[6]—upon the formation of a self.

Moral education, it would seem, must be as specifically concerned with self-identification in a community as it is with the judgments persons are equipped to make at different ages. It has as much to do with interest and action in concrete situations as it does with the course of moral reasoning. It has as much to do with consciousness and imagination as it does with principle. Since it cannot take place outside the vital contexts of social life, troubling questions have to be constantly confronted. How can indifference be overcome? How can the influence of the media be contained? How can the young be guided to choose reflectively and compassionately, even as they are set free?

The problem, most will agree, is not to tell them what to do—but to help them attain some kind of clarity about how to choose, how to decide what to do. And this involves teachers directly, immediately—teachers as persons able to present themselves as critical thinkers willing to disclose their own principles and their own reasons as well as authentic persons living in the world, persons who are concerned—who care.

Many teachers, faced with demands like these, find themselves in difficult positions, especially if they are granted little autonomy, or their conceptions of their own projects are at odds with what their schools demand. Today they may be held accountable for teaching predefined competencies and skills or for achieving objectives that are often largely behavioral. At once, they may be expected to represent both the wider culture and the local community, or the international community and the particular community of the individual child. If teachers are not critically conscious, if they are not awake to their own values and commitments (and to the conditions working upon them), if they are not personally engaged with their subject matter and with the world around, I do not see how they can initiate the young into critical questioning or the moral life.

I am preoccupied, I suppose, with what Camus called "the plague"—that terrible distancing and indifference, so at odds with commitment and communion and love. I emphasize this because I want to stress the connection between, wide-awakeness, cognitive clarity, and existential concern. I want to highlight the fact that the roots of moral choosing lie at the core of a person's conception of herself or himself and the equally important fact that choosing involves action as well as thought. Moral action, of course, demands choosing between alternatives, usually between two goods, not between good and bad or right and wrong. The problem in teaching is to empower persons to internalize and incarnate the kinds of principles that will enable them to make such choices. Should I do what is thought to be my duty and volunteer for the army, or should I resist what I believe to be an unjust war. Should I steal the medicine to save my mother's life, or should I obey the law and risk letting her die?

These are choices of consequence for the self and others; and they are made, they can only be made in social situations where custom, tradition, official codes, and laws condition and play upon what people think and do. We might think of Huck Finn's decision not to return Jim to his owner or of Anna Karenina's decision to leave her husband. These are only morally significant in relation to a particular fabric of codes and customs and rules. Think of the Danish king's wartime decision to stand with Denmark's Jewish citizens, Daniel Ellsberg's decision to publish the Pentagon Papers, or Pablo Casals' refusal to conduct in fascist Spain. These decisions too were made in a matrix of principles, laws, and ideas of what is considered acceptable, absolutely, or conditionally good and right. To be moral involves taking a position towards that matrix, thinking critically about what is taken for granted. It involves taking a principled position of one's own (*choosing* certain principles by which to live) and speaking clearly about it, so as to set oneself on the right track.

It is equally important to affirm that it is always the individual, acting voluntarily in a particular situation at a particular moment, who does the deciding. I do not mean that individuals are isolated, answerable only to themselves. I do mean that individuals, viewed as participants, as inextricably involved with other people, must be enabled to take responsibility for their own choosing, must not merge themselves or hide themselves in what Soren Kierkegaard called "the crowd."[7] If individuals act automatically or conventionally, if they do only what is expected of them (or because they feel they have no right to speak for themselves), if they do only what they are told to do, they are not living moral lives.

Indeed, I rather doubt that individuals who are cowed or flattened out or depressed or afraid can learn, since learning inevitably involves a free decision to enter into a form of life, to proceed in a certain way, to do something because it is right. There are paradigms to be found in many kinds of teaching for those interested in moral education, since teaching is in part a process of moving people to proceed according to a specified set of norms. If individuals are wide-awake and make decisions consciously to interpret a poem properly, to try to understand a period in English history, or to participate in some type of social inquiry, they are choosing to abide by certain standards made available to them. In doing so, they are becoming acquainted with what it means to choose a set of norms. They are not only creating value for themselves, they are creating themselves; they are moving towards more significant, more understandable lives.

Consider, with norms and self-creation in mind, the case of Nora in Ibsen's *The Doll's House*. If she simply ran out of the house in tears at the end, she would not have been engaging in moral action. Granting the fact that she was defying prevailing codes, I would insist that she was making a decision in accord with an internalized norm. It might be called a principle of emancipation, having to do with the right to grow, to become, to be more than a doll in a doll's house. If asked, Nora might have been able to generalize and talk about the right of *all* human beings to develop in their own fashion, to be respected, to be granted integrity.

Principles or norms are general ideas of that kind, arising out of experience and used by individuals in the appraisal of situations they encounter as they live—to help them determine what they ought to do. They are not specific rules, like the rules against stealing and lying and adultery. They are general and comprehensive. They concern justice and equality, respect for the dignity of persons and regard for their points of view. They have much to do with the ways in which diverse individuals choose themselves; they are defined reflectively and imaginatively and against the backgrounds of biography. When they are incarnated in a person's life, they offer him or her the means for analyzing particular situations. They offer perspectives, points of view from which to consider particular acts. The Golden Rule is such a principle, but, as Dewey says, the Golden Rule does not finally decide matters just by enabling us to tell people to consider the good of others as they would their own. "It suggests," he writes, "the necessity of considering how our acts affect the interests of others as well as our own; it tends to prevent partiality of regard....In short, the Golden Rule does not issue special orders or commands; but it does clarify and illuminate the situations requiring intelligent deliberation."[8] So it was with the principle considered by Ibsen's Nora; so it is with the principle of justice and the principles of care and truth-telling. Our hope in teaching is that persons will appropriate such principles and learn to live by them.

Now it is clear that young people have to pass through the stages of heteronomy in their development towards the degree of autonomy they require for acting on principle in the way described. They must achieve the kind of wide-awakeness I have been talking about, the ability to think about what they are doing, to take responsibility. The teaching problem seems to me to be threefold. It involves equipping young people with the ability to identify alternatives, and to see possibilities in the situations confront. It involves the teaching of principles, possible perspectives by means of which those situations can be assessed and appraised, *as well as* the norms governing historical inquiry, ballet dancing, or cooperative living, norms that must be appropriated by persons desiring to join particular human communities. It also involves enabling students to make decisions of principle, to reflect, to articulate, and to take decisive actions in good faith.

Fundamental to the whole process may be the building up of a sense of moral directedness, of oughtness. An imaginativeness, an awareness, and a sense of possibility are required, along with the sense of autonomy and agency, of being present to the self. There must be attentiveness to others and to the circumstances of everyday life. There must be efforts made to discover ways of living together justly and pursuing common ends. As wide-awake teachers work, making principles available and eliciting moral judgments, they must orient themselves to the concrete, the relevant, and the questionable. They must commit themselves to each per-

son's potentiality for overcoming helplessness and submergence, for looking through his or her own eyes at the shared reality.

I believe this can only be done if teachers can identify themselves as moral beings, concerned with defining their own life purposes in a way that arouses others to do the same. I believe, you see, that the young are most likely to be stirred to learn when they are challenged by teachers who themselves are learning, who are breaking with what they have too easily taken for granted, who are creating their own moral lives. There are no guarantees, but wide-awakeness can play a part in the process of liberating and arousing, in helping people pose questions with regard to what is oppressive, mindless, and wrong. Surely, it can help people—all kinds of people—make the conscious endeavors needed to elevate their lives.

Camus, in an essay called "The Almond Trees," wrote some lines that seem to me to apply to teachers, especially those concerned in this way. He was talking about how endless are our tasks, how impossible it is to overcome the human condition—which, at least, we have come to know better than ever before:

> We must mend "what has been torn apart, make justice imaginable again—give happiness a meaning once more.... Naturally, it is a superhuman task. But superhuman is the term for tasks men take a long time to accomplish, that's all. Let us know our aims, then, holding fast to the mind.... The first thing is not to despair.[9]

## ENDNOTES

1. Henry David Thoreau, *Walden* (New York: Washington Square Press, 1963.), pp. 66–67.
2. Alfred Schutz, ed. Maurice Natanson, *The Problem of Social Reality,* Collected Papers I (The Hague: Martinus Nijhoff, 1967.), p. 213.

3. Albert Camus, *The Myth of Sisyphus* (New York: Alfred A. Knopf, 1955), p. 13.

4. George Konrad, *The Case Worker* (New York: Harcourt Brace Jovanovich, 1974), p. 168.

5. Martin Buber, *Between Man and Man* (Boston: Beacon Press, 1957), p. 105.

6. John Dewey, *Democracy and Education* (New York: Macmillan Company, 1916), p. 408.

7. Soren Kierkegaard, "The Individual," in *The Point of View for My Work as an Author* (New York: Harper & Row, 1962), pp. 102–136.

8. Dewey, *Theory of the Moral Life* (New York: Holt, Rinehart and Winston, 1960), p. 142.

9. Camus, "'The Almond Trees," in *Lyrical and Critical Essays* (New York: Alfred A. Knopf, 1968), p. 135.

# Reproduction and Resistance in Radical Theories of Schooling

## STANLEY ARONOWITZ
## HENRY GIROUX

In the last decade, Karl Marx's concept of reproduction has been one of the major organizing ideas informing socialist theories of schooling. Marx states that "every social process of production is, at the same time, a process of reproduction.... Capitalist production, therefore...produces not only commodities, not only surplus-value, but it also produces and reproduces the capitalist relation, on the one side the capitalist, on the other the wage-labourer."[1] Radical educators have given this concept a central place in developing a critique of liberal views of schooling. Moreover, they have used it as the theoretical foundation for developing a critical science of education.[2] Thus far, the task has been only partially successful.

Contrary to the claims of liberal theorists and historians that public education offers possibilities for individual development, social mobility, and political and economic power to the disadvantaged and dispossessed, radical educators have argued that the main functions of schools are the reproduction of the dominant ideology, its forms of knowledge, and the distribution of skills needed to reproduce the social division of labor. In the radical perspective, schools as institutions could only be understood through an analysis of their relationship to the state and the economy. In this view, the deep structure or underlying significance of schooling could only be revealed through analyzing how schools functioned as agencies of social and cultural reproduction—that is, how they legitimated capitalist rationality and sustained dominant social practices.

Instead of blaming students for educational failure, radical educators blamed the dominant society. Instead of abstracting schools from the dynamics of inequality and class-race-gender modes of discrimination, schools were considered central agencies in the politics and processes of domination. In contrast to the liberal view of education as the great equalizer, radical educators saw the objectives of schooling quite differently. As Paul Willis states, "Education was not about equality, but inequality.... Education's main purpose of the social integration of a class society could be achieved only by preparing most kids for an unequal future, and by insuring their personal underdevelopment. Far from productive roles in the economy simply waiting to be 'fairly' filled by the products of education, the 'Reproduction' perspective reversed this to suggest that capitalist production and its roles required certain educational outcomes."[3]

In our view, radical educators presented a serious challenge to the discourse and logic of liberal views of schooling, But they did more than that. They also tried to fashion a new discourse and set of understandings around the reproduction thesis. Schools were stripped of their political innocence and connected to the social and cultural matrix of capitalist rationality. In effect, schools were portrayed as reproductive in three senses. First, schools provided different classes and

*Source:* From Stanley Aronowitz and Henry Giroux, *Education Under Siege,* pp. 69–73, 104–109. South Hadley, MA: Bergin and Garvey, 1985, an imprint of Greenwood Publishing Group, Inc., Westport, CT. This selection was adapted from Henry Giroux, *Theory and Resistance in Education,* South Hadley, MA: Bergin and Garvey, 1983. Reprinted with permission.

social groups with the knowledge and skills they needed to occupy their respective places in a labor force stratified by class, race, and gender. Second, schools were seen as reproductive in the cultural sense, functioning in part to distribute and legitimate forms of knowledge, values, language, and modes of style that constitute the dominant culture and its interests. Third, schools were viewed as part of a state apparatus that produced and legitimated the economic and ideological imperatives that underlie the state's political power.

Radical reproduction theorists have used these forms of reproduction to fashion a number of specific concerns that have shaped the nature of their educational research and inquiry. These concerns have focused on analyses of the relationships between schooling and the workplace,[4] class-specific educational experiences and the job opportunities that emerge for different social groups,[5] the culture of the school and the class-defined cultures of the students who attend them,[6] and the relationship among the economic, ideological, and repressive functions of the state and how they affect school policies and practices.[7]

Reproduction theory and its various explanations of the role and function of education have been invaluable in contributing to a broader understanding of the political nature of schooling and its relation to the dominant society. But it must be stressed that the theory has not achieved its promise to provide a comprehensive critical science of schooling. Reproduction theorists have overemphasized the idea of domination in their analysis and have failed to provide any major insights into how teachers, students, and other human agents come together within specific historical and social contexts in order to both make and reproduce the conditions of their existence. More specifically, reproduction accounts of schooling have continually patterned themselves after structural-functionalist versions of Marxism which

stress that history is made "behind the backs" of the members of society. The idea that people do make history, including its constraints, has been neglected. Indeed, human subjects generally "disappear" amidst a theory that leaves no room for moments of self-creation, mediation, and resistance. These accounts often leave us with a view of schooling and domination that appears to have been pressed out of an Orwellian fantasy; schools are often viewed as factories or prisons, teachers and students alike act merely as pawns and role bearers constrained by the logic and social practices of the capitalist system.

By downplaying the importance of human agency and the notion of resistance, reproduction theories offer little hope for challenging and changing the repressive features of schooling. By ignoring the contradictions and struggles that exist in schools, these theories not only dissolve human agency, they unknowingly provide a rationale for *not* examining teachers and students in concrete school settings. Thus, they miss the opportunity to determine whether there is a substantial difference between the existence of various structural and ideological modes of domination and their actual unfolding and effects.

Recent research on schooling in the United States, Europe, and Australia has both challenged and attempted to move beyond reproduction theories. This research emphasizes the importance of human agency and experience as the theoretical cornerstones for analyzing the complex relationship between schools and the dominant society. Organized around what we loosely label as resistance theory, these analyses give central importance to the notions of conflict, struggle, and resistance.[8]

Combining ethnographic studies with more recent European cultural studies, resistance theorists have attempted to demonstrate that the mechanisms of social and cultural reproduction are never complete and always meet with partially realized elements of opposition.[9] In effect, resistance theorists have developed a theoretical framework and method of inquiry that restores the critical notion of agency. They point not only to the role that students play in challenging the most oppressive aspects of schools but also to the ways in which students actively participate through oppositional behavior in a logic that very often consigns them to a position of class subordination and political defeat.

One of the most important assumptions of resistance theory is that working-class students are not merely the by-product of capital, compliantly submitting to the dictates of authoritarian teachers and schools that prepare them for a life of deadening labor. Rather, as we pointed out in previous chapters, schools represent contested terrains marked not only by structural and ideological contradictions but also by collectively informed student resistance. In other words, schools are social sites characterized by overt and hidden curricula, tracking, dominant and subordinate cultures, and competing class ideologies. Of course, conflict and resistance take place within asymmetrical relations of power which always favor the dominant classes, but the essential point is that there are complex and creative fields of resistance through which class-, race- and gender-mediated practices often refuse, reject, and dismiss the central messages of the schools.

In resistance accounts, schools are relatively autonomous institutions that not only provide spaces for oppositional behavior and teaching but also represent a source of contradictions that sometimes make them dysfunctional to the material and ideological interests of the dominant society. Schools are not solely determined by the logic of the workplace or the dominant society; they are not merely economic institutions but are also political, cultural, and ideological sites that exist somewhat independently of the capitalist market economy. Of course, schools operate within limits set by society, but they function in part to influence and shape those limits, whether they be economic, ideological, or political. Moreover, instead of being homogeneous institutions operating under the direct control of business groups, schools are characterized by diverse forms of school knowledge, ideologies, organizational styles, and classroom social relations. Thus, schools often exist in a contradictory relation to the dominant society, alternately supporting and challenging its basic assumptions. For instance, schools sometimes support a notion of liberal education that is in sharp contradiction to the dominant society's demand for forms of education that are specialized, instrumental, and geared to the logic of the marketplace. In addition, schools still strongly define their role via their function as agencies for social mobility even though they currently turn out graduates at a faster pace than the economy's capacity to employ them.

Whereas reproduction theorists focus almost exclusively on power and how the dominant culture ensures the consent and defeat of subordinate classes and groups, theories of resistance restore a degree of agency and innovation to the cultures of these groups. Culture, in this case, is constituted as much by the group itself as by the dominant society. Subordinate cultures, whether working class or otherwise, partake of moments of self-production as well as reproduction; they are contradictory in nature and bear the marks of both resistance and reproduction. Such cultures are forged within constraints shaped by capital and its institutions, such as schools, but the conditions within which such constraints function vary from school to school and from neighborhood to neighborhood. Moreover, there are never any guarantees that capitalist values and ideologies will automatically succeed, regardless of how strongly they set the agenda. Put another way, "In the final analysis, human praxis is not determined by its preconditions; only the boundaries of possibility are given in advance."[10]

In this rather brief and abstract discussion, we have juxtaposed two models of educational analysis to suggest that theories of resistance represent a significant advance over the important but limited theoretical gains of reproduction models of schooling. But it is important to emphasize that, in spite of more complex modes of analysis, resistance theories are also marred by a number of theoretical flaws. In part, these flaws stem from a failure to recognize the degree to which resistance theories themselves are indebted to some of the more damaging features of reproduction theory. At the same time, however, resistance theories have too readily ignored the most valuable insights of reproduction theory and, in doing so, have failed to examine and appropriate those aspects of the reproduction model that are essential to developing a critical science of education. Furthermore, despite their concrete differences, resistance and reproduction approaches to education share the failure of recycling and reproducing the dualism between agency and structure, a failure that has plagued educational theory and practice for decades, while simultaneously representing its greatest challenge. Consequently, neither position provides the foundation for a theory of education that links structures and institutions to human agency and action in a dialectical manner.

The basis for overcoming this separation of human agency from structural determinants lies in the development of a theory of resistance that both questions its own assumptions and critically appropriates those aspects of schooling that are accurately presented and analyzed in the reproduction model. In other words, the task facing resistance theorists is twofold: first, they must structure their own assumptions to develop a more dialectical model of schooling and society; and secondly, they must reconstruct the major theories of reproduction in order to abstract from them their most radical and emancipatory insights....

## TOWARD A THEORY OF RESISTANCE

Resistance is a valuable theoretical and ideological construct that provides an important focus for analyzing the relationship between school and the wider society. More importantly, it provides a new means for understanding the complex ways in which subordinate groups experience educational failure, pointing to new ways of thinking about and restructuring modes of critical pedagogy. As we have noted, the current use of the concept of resistance by radical educators suggests a lack of intellectual rigor and an overdose of theoretical sloppiness. It is imperative that educators be more precise about what resistance actually is and what it is not, and be more specific about how the concept can be used to develop a critical pedagogy. It is also clear that a rationale for employing the concept needs to be considered more fully. We will now discuss these issues and briefly outline some basic theoretical concerns for developing a more intellectually rigorous and politically useful foundation for pursuing such a task.

In the most general sense, resistance must be grounded in a theoretical rationale that provides a new framework for examining schools as social sites which structure the experiences of subordinate groups. The concept of resistance, in other words, represents more than a new heuristic catchword in the language of radical pedagogy; it depicts a mode of discourse that rejects traditional explanations of school failure and oppositional behavior and shifts the analysis of oppositional behavior from the theoretical terrains of functionalism and mainstream educational psychology to those of political science and sociology. Resistance in this case redefines the causes and meaning of oppositional behavior by arguing that it has little to do with deviance and learned helplessness, but a great deal to do with moral and political indignation.

Aside from shifting the theoretical ground for analyzing oppositional behavior, the concept of resistance points to a number of assumptions and concerns about schooling that are generally neglected in both traditional views of schooling and radical theories of reproduction. First, it celebrates a dialectical notion of human agency that rightly portrays domination as a process that is neither static nor complete. Concomitantly, the oppressed are not seen as being simply passive in the face of domination. The notion of resistance points to the need to understand more thoroughly the complex ways in which people mediate and respond to the connection between their own experiences and structures of domination and constraint. Central categories that emerge in a theory of resistance are intentionality, consciousness, the meaning of common sense, and the nature and value of nondiscursive behavior. Second, resistance adds new depth to the notion that power is exercised on and by people within different contexts that structure interacting relations of dominance and autonomy. Thus, power is never unidimensional; it is exercised not only as a mode of domination, but also as an act of resistance. Last, inherent in a radical notion of resistance is an expressed hope for radical transformation, an element of transcendence that seems to be missing in radical theories of education which appear trapped in the theoretical cemetery of Orwellian pessimism.

In addition to developing a rationale for the notion of resistance, there is a need to formulate criteria against which the term can be defined as a central category of analysis in theories of schooling. In the most general sense, we think resistance must be situated in a perspective that takes the notion of emancipation as its guiding interest. That is, the nature and meaning of an act of resistance must be defined by the degree to which it contains possibilities to develop what Herbert Marcuse termed "a commitment to an emancipation of sensibility, imagination and reason in all spheres of subjectivity and objectivity."[11] Thus, the central element of analyzing any act of resistance must be a concern with uncovering the degree to which it highlights, implicitly or explicitly, the need to struggle against domination and submission. In other words, the concept of resistance must have a revealing function that contains a critique of domination and provides theoretical opportunities for self-reflection and struggle in the interest of social and self-emancipation. To the degree that oppositional behavior suppresses social contradictions while simultaneously merging with, rather than challenging, the logic of ideological domination, it does not fall under the category of resistance, but under its opposite—accommodation and conformism. The value of the concept of resistance lies in its critical function and in its potential to utilize both the radical possibilities embedded in its own logic and the interests contained in the object of its expression. In other words, the concept of resistance represents an element of difference, a counter-logic, that must be analyzed to reveal its underlying interest in freedom and its rejection of those forms of domination inherent in the social relations against which it reacts. Of course, this is a rather general set of standards upon which to ground the notion of resistance, but it does provide a notion of interest and a theoretical scaffold upon which to make a distinction between forms of oppositional behavior that can be used for either the amelioration of human life or for the destruction and denigration of basic human values.

Some acts of resistance reveal quite visibly their radical potential, while others are rather ambiguous; still others may reveal nothing more than an affinity for the logic of domination and destruction. It is the ambiguous area that we want to analyze briefly, since the other two areas are self-explanatory. Recently, we heard a "radical" educator argue that teachers who rush home early after school are, in fact, committing acts of resistance. She also claimed that teachers who do not adequately prepare for their classroom lessons are participating in a form of resistance as well. Of course, it is equally debatable that the teachers in question are simply lazy or care very little about teaching, and that what in fact is being displayed is not resistance but unprofessional and unethical behavior. In these cases, there is no logical, convincing response to either argument. The behaviors displayed do not speak for themselves. To call them resistance is to turn the concept into a term that has no analytical precision. In cases like these, one must either link the behavior under analysis with an interpretation provided by the subjects themselves, or dig deeply into the historical and relational conditions from which the behavior develops. Only then will the interest embedded in such behavior be open to interrogation.

It follows from our argument that the interests underlying a specific form of behavior may become clear once the nature of that behavior is interpreted by the person who exhibits it. But we do not mean to imply that such interests will automatically be revealed. Individuals may not be able to explain the reasons for their behavior, or the interpretation may be distorted. In this case, the interest underlying such behavior may be illuminated against the backdrop of social practices and values from which the behavior emerges. Such a referent may be found in the historical conditions that prompted the behavior, the collective values of a peer group, or the practices embedded in other social sites such as the family, the workplace, or the church. We want to stress that the concept of resistance must not be allowed to become a category indiscriminately hung over every expression of "oppositional behavior." On the contrary, it must become an analytical construct and mode of inquiry that is self-critical and sensitive to its own interests—radical consciousness raising and collective critical action.

Let us now return to the question of how we define resistance and view oppositional behavior, and to the implications for making such distinctions. On one level, it is important to be theoretically precise about which forms of oppositional behavior constitute resistance and which do not. On another level, it is equally important to argue that all forms of oppositional behavior represent a focal point for critical analysis and should be analyzed to see if they represent a form of resistance by uncovering their emancipatory interests. This is a matter of theoretical preciseness and definition. On the other hand, as a matter of radical strategy, *all* forms of oppositional behavior, whether actually resistance or not, must be examined for their possible use as a basis for critical analysis. Thus, oppositional behavior becomes the object of both theoretical clarification and the subject of pedagogical considerations.

On a more philosophical level, we want to stress that the theoretical construct of resistance rejects the positivist notion that the meaning of behavior is synonymous with a literal reading based on immediate action. Instead, resistance must be viewed from a theoretical starting point that links the display of behavior to the interest it embodies, going beyond the immediacy of behavior to the interest that underlies its often hidden logic, a logic that also must be interpreted through the historical and cultural mediations that shape it. Finally, we want to emphasize that the ultimate value of the notion of resistance must be measured not only by the degree to which it promotes critical thinking and reflective action but, more importantly, by the degree to which it contains the possibility of galvanizing collective political struggle among parents, teachers, and students around the issues of power and social determination.

We will now briefly discuss the value of a dialectical notion of resistance for a critical theory of schooling. The pedagogical value of resistance lies, in part, in the connections it makes between structure and human agency, on the one hand, and culture and the process of self formation on the other. Resistance theory rejects the idea that schools are simply instructional sites by not only politicizing the notion of culture, but also by analyzing school cultures within the shifting terrain of struggle and contestation. In effect, this represents a new theoretical framework for understanding the process of schooling which places educational knowledge, values, and social relations within the context of antagonistic relations and examines them within the interplay of dominant and subordinate school cultures. When a theory of resistance is incorporated into radical pedagogy, elements of oppositional behavior in schools become the focal point for analyzing different, and often antagonistic, social relations and experiences among students from dominant, and subordinate cultures. Within this mode of critical analysis, it becomes possible to illuminate how students draw on the limited resources at their disposal in order to reaffirm the positive dimensions of their own cultures and histories.

Resistance theory highlights the complexity of student responses to the logic of schooling. Thus, it highlights the need for radical educators to unravel how oppositional behavior often emerges within forms of contradictory consciousness that are never free from the reproductive rationality embedded in capitalist social relations. A radical pedagogy, then, must recognize that student resistance in all of its forms represents manifestations of struggle and solidarity that, in their incompleteness, both challenge and confirm capitalist hegemony. What is most important is the willingness of radical educators to search for the emancipatory interests that underlie such resistance and to make them visible to students and others so that they can become the object of debate and political analysis.

A theory of resistance is central to the development of a radical pedagogy for other reasons as well. It helps bring into focus those social practices in schools whose ultimate aim is the control of both the learning process and the capacity for critical thought and action. For example, it points to the ideology underlying the hegemonic curriculum, to its hierarchically organized bodies of knowledge, and particularly to the way in which this curriculum marginalizes or disqualifies working class knowledge as well as knowledge about women and minorities. Furthermore, resistance theory reveals the ideology underlying such a curriculum, with its emphasis on individual rather than collective appropriation of knowledge, and how this emphasis drives a wedge between students from different social classes. This is particularly evident in the different approaches to knowledge supported in many working class and middle class families. Knowledge in the working class culture is often constructed on the principles of solidarity and sharing, whereas within middle class culture, knowledge is forged in individual competition and is seen as a badge of separateness.

In short, resistance theory calls attention to the need for radical educators to unravel the ideological interests embedded in the various message systems of the school, particularly those embedded in its curriculum, systems of instruction, and modes of evaluation. What is most important is that resistance theory reinforces the need for radical educators to decipher how the forms of cultural production displayed by subordinate groups can be analyzed to reveal both their limitations and their possibilities for enabling critical thinking, analytical discourse, and learning through collective practice.

Finally, resistance theory suggests that radical educators must develop a critical rather than a pragmatic relationship with students. This means that any viable form of radical pedagogy must analyze how the relations of domination in schools originate, how they are sustained, and how students, in

particular, relate to them. This means looking beyond schools. It suggests taking seriously the counter-logic that pulls students
away from schools into the streets, the bars,
and the shopfloor culture. For many working
class students, these realms are "real time" as
opposed to the "dead time" they often experience in schools. The social spheres that
make up this counter-logic may represent the
few remaining terrains that provide the oppressed with the possibility of human agency
and autonomy. Yet, these terrains appear to
represent less a form of resistance than an
expression of solidarity and self-affirmation.

The pull of this counter-logic must be
critically engaged and built into the framework of a radical pedagogy. Yet, this is not to
suggest that it must be absorbed into a theory of schooling. On the contrary, it must be
supported by radical educators and others
from both inside and outside of schools. But
as an object of pedagogical analysis, this
counterlogic must be seen as an important
theoretical terrain in which one finds fleeting
images of freedom that point to fundamentally new structures in the public organization of experience.

Inherent in the oppositional public spheres
that constitute a counterlogic are the conditions around which the oppressed organize
important needs and relations. Thus, it represents an important terrain in the ideological
battle for the appropriation of meaning and
experience. For this reason, it provides educators with an opportunity to link the political
with the personal in order to understand how
power is mediated, resisted, and reproduced
in daily life. Furthermore, it situates the relationship between schools and the larger society within a theoretical framework informed
by a fundamentally political question. How
do we develop a radical pedagogy that makes
schools meaningful so as to make them critical, and how do we make them critical so as to
make them emancipatory?

But the basis for a radical pedagogy demands more than the development of a theo-

ry of resistance; it also needs to develop a
new discourse, one that appropriates the
most critical dimensions of Marxist theory
while simultaneously moving beyond it. In
other words, if the language of possibility is
to become a constitutive part of radical educational theory, it will have to ground itself in
a theoretical discourse that draws expansively
from a number of radical traditions. This the
issue we will deal with in the next chapter.

## ENDNOTES

1. Marx, *Capital,* I (Moscow: Progress Publishers, 1969), pp. 531, 532.
2. For a critical analysis of the significance of
   Marx's notion of reproduction in social theory; see Henri Lefebvre, *The Survival of Capi-
   talism,* trans. Frank Bryant (New York: St.
   Martin's Press, 1973). For a critical review of
   the literature on schooling that takes the notion of reproduction as its starting point see
   Michael Apple, *Ideology and Curriculum*
   (London: Routledge & Kegan Paul, 1979);
   Henry A. Giroux, *Ideology, Culture and the
   Process of Schooling* (Philadelphia: Temple
   Univ. Press, 1981); Geoff Whitty and Michael Young, ed., *Society, State, and Schooling*
   (Sussex, Eng.: Falmer Press, 1977); Len Bar-
   ton, Roland Meighan, and Stephen Walker,
   ed., Schooling, Ideology and Curriculum
   (Sussex, Eng.: Falmer Press, 1980); Samuel
   Bowles and Herbert Gintis, *Schooling in Capitalist America* (New York: Basic Books,
   1977).
3. Willis, "Cultural Production and Theories of
   Reproduction," in *Race, Class and Education,* ed. Len Barton and Stephen Walker
   (London: Croom Helm, 1983), p. 110.
5. Jean Anyon, "Social Class and the Hidden
   Curriculum of Work," *Journal of Education*
   162 (1980), pp. 67–92.
6. Pierre Bourdieu and Jean Claude Passeron,
   *Reproduction in Education, Society, and Cul-
   ture* (Beverly Hills, Calif.: Sage, 1977).
7. Nicos Poulantzas, *Classes in Contemporary
   Society* (London: Verso Books, 1978).
8. Representative examples include Michael Apple, *Education and Power* (London: Rout-

ledge & Kegan Paul, 1982); Richard Bates, "New Developments in the New Sociology of Education," *British Journal of Sociology of Education* 1 (1980), pp. 67–79; Robert W. Connell, Dean J. Ashenden, Sandra Kessler, and Gary W. Dowsett, *Making The Difference* (Sydney: Allen & Unwin, 1982); Geoff Whitty, *Ideology, Politics, and Curriculum* (London: Open Univ. Press, 1981); Henry A. Giroux, *Theory and Resistance in Education* (South Hadley, Mass.: Bergin and Garvey, 1983).

9. Paul Willis, *Learning to Labor* (New York: Columbia University Press, 1981); Women's Study Group, Centre for Contemporary Cultural Studies, ed., *Women Take Issue* (London: Hutchinson, 1978); David Robins and Philip Cohen, *Knuckle Sandwich: Growing Up in a Working Class City* (London: Pelican Books, 1978); Paul Corrigan, *Schooling and the Smash Street Kids* (London: Macmillan, 1979); Angela McRobbie and Trisha McCabe, *Feminism for Girls* (London: Routledge & Kegan Paul, 1981); Thomas Popkewitz, B. Robert Tabachnick, and Gary Wehlage, *The Myth of Educational Reform* (Madison, Wis.: Univ. of Wisconsin Press, 1982); Robert B. Everhart, "Classroom Management, Student Opposition, and the Labor Process" in *Ideology and Practice in Schooling,* ed. Michael Apple and Lois Weiss (Philadelphia: Temple Univ. Press, 1983); Paul Olson, "Inequality Remade: The Theory of Correspondence and the Context of French Immersion in Northern Ontario," *Journal of Education* 165 (1983), pp. 75–78.

10. Stanley Aronowitz, "Marx, Braverman, and the Logic of Capital," *The Insurgent Sociologist* 8 (1977), pp. 126–146.

11. Marcuse, *The Aesthetic Dimension* (Boston: Beacon Press, 1977).

## CHAPTER 5 REFERENCES

Adler, M. (1982). *The paideia proposal.* New York: Macmillan.

Apple, M. W. (1978). Ideology, reproduction, and educational reform. *Comparative Educational Review, 22* (3), 367–387.

Apple, M. W. (1979). *Ideology and curriculum.* Boston: Routledge and Kegan Paul.

Apple, M. W. (1982a). *Cultural and economic reproduction in education.* Boston: Routledge and Kegan Paul.

Apple, M. W. (1982b). *Education and power.* Boston: Routledge and Kegan Paul.

Banks, J. A. (1988). *Multiethnic education: Theory and practice.* Boston: Allyn and Bacon.

Bowder, D. (Ed.). (1982). *Who was who in the Greek world?* Oxford: Phaedon Press.

Bowles, S., & Gintis, H. (1976). *Schooling in capitalist America: Educational reform and the contradictions of economic life.* New York: Basic Books.

Bradley Commission. (1988). *Building a history curriculum.* Washington D.C.: Educational Excellence Network.

Bramald, T. (1956). *Toward a reconstructed philosophy of education.* New York: Holt, Rinehart and Winston.

Cherryholmes, C. (1988). *Power and criticism: Poststructural investigations in education.* New York: Teachers College Press.

Counts, G. (1932). *Dare the schools build a new social order?* New York: John Day.

Cremin, L. A. (1990). *Popular education and its discontents.* New York: Harper and Row.

Dewey, J. (1916). *Democracy and education: An introduction to the philosophy of education.* New York: Macmillan.

Egan, K. (1992). Review of *The unschooled mind: How children think and how schools should teach,* by Howard Gardner. *Teachers College Record, 94* (2), 397–406.

Ellsworth, E. (1989). Why doesn't this feel empowering? Working through the repressive myths of critical pedagogy. *Harvard Educational Review, 59* (3), 297–324.

Freire, P. (1972). *Pedagogy of the oppressed.* New York: Herder and Herder.

Freire, P. (1978). *Pedagogy in process.* New York: Seabury Press.

Gardner, H. (1991). *The unschooled mind: How children think and how schools should teach.* New York: Basic Books.

Gardner, H. (1992). A response. *Teachers College Record, 94* (2), 407–413.

Giroux, H. (1983). *Theory and resistance in education.* South Hadley, MA: Bergin and Garvey.

Giroux, H. (1988). *Teachers as intellectuals: Toward a critical pedagogy of learning.* South Hadley, MA: Bergin and Garvey.

Giroux, H. (1991). *Postmodernism, feminism, and cultural politics: Redrawing educational boundaries.* Albany, NY: SUNY Press.

Greene, M. (1978). *Landscapes of learning.* New York: Teachers College Press.

Greene, M. (1988). *The dialectic of freedom.* New York: Teachers College Press.

Guthrie, W. K. (1969). *A history of Greek philosophy, Volume 3, Part 2: Socrates.* Cambridge: Cambridge University Press.

James, W. (1978). *Varieties of religious experience.* New York: Norton.

Kitto, H. D. F. (1951). *The Greeks.* New York: Penguin.

Laird, S. (1989). Reforming "women's true profession": A case for "feminist pedagogy" in teacher education? *Harvard Educational Review, 58* (4), 449–463.

Lather, P. (1991). *Getting smart: Feminist research and pedagogy within the postmodern.* New York: Routledge.

Lyotard, J. F. (1984). *The postmodern condition.* (G. Bennington & B. Massumi, Trans.). Minneapolis: University of Minnesota Press.

Macdonald, J., & Macdonald, S. (1981). Gender values and curriculum. *Journal of Curriculum Theorizing, 3* (1), 299–304

Martin, J. R. (1987). Reforming teacher education, rethinking liberal education. *Teachers College Record, 88,* 406–409.

Marx, K. (1844/1964). *The economic and philosophical manuscripts of 1844.* New York: International Publishers.

Marx, K. (1867/1967). *Capital, Volume I.* New York: International Publishers.

Marx, K. (1893/1967). *Das Capital, Volume II.* New York: International Publishers.

Marx, K. (1894/1967). *Das Capital, Volume III.* New York: International Publishers.

Marx, K., & Engels, F. (1846/1947). *The German ideology.* New York: International Publishers. (Original work published 1846)

Marx, K., & Engles, F. (1848/1983). *The communist manifesto.* New York: International Publishers.

McLaren, P. (1989). *Life in schools.* New York: Longman.

Miller, J. (1982). Feminist pedagogy: The sound of silence breaking. *Journal of Curriculum Theorizing, 4,* 5–11.

Mitrano, B. (1979). Feminist theology and curriculum theory. *Journal of Curriculum Studies, 2,* 211–220.

Ozmon, H. A., & Craver, S.M. (1990). *Philosophical foundations of education.* Columbus, OH: Merrill.

Plato. (1971). *Meno.* New York: Macmillan.

Plato. (1986). *The dialogues of Plato.* New York: Bantam.

Ravitch, D. (1983). *The troubled crusade.* New York: Basic Books.

Rousseau, J. J. (1979). *Emile.* (A. Bloom, Trans.). New York: Basic Books.

Sadovnik, A. R. (1993). Postmodernism in the sociology of education: Closing the rift between theory, practice and research. In W. Pink & R. Noblit (Eds.), *Future directions in the sociology of education.* New Jersey: Hampton Press.

Young, M. F. D. (1971). *Knowledge and control: New directions for the sociology of education.* London: Collier-Macmillan.

## SUGGESTED READINGS

Adler, M. (1982). *The paideia proposal.* New York: Macmillan.

Aristotle. (1943). *Politics.* New York: Modern Library.

Bayles, E. (1966). *Pragmatism in education.* New York: Harper & Row.

Bramald, T. (1956). *Toward a reconstructed philosophy of education*. New York: Holt, Rinehart and Winston.

Cherryholmes, C. (1988). *Power and criticism: Poststructural investigations in education*. New York: Teachers College Press.

Childs, J. L. (1931). *Education and the philosophy of experimentalism*. New York: Century.

Counts, G. (1932). *Dare the schools build a new social order?* New York: John Day.

Cremin, L. A. (1990). *Popular education and its discontents*. New York: Harper and Row.

Dewey, J. (1897). *My pedagogic creed*. In M. S. Dworkin (Ed.), *Dewey on education* (pp. 19–32). New York: Teachers College Press.

Dewey, J. (1899). *The school and society*. In M. S. Dworkin (Ed.), *Dewey on education* (pp. 33–90). New York: Teachers College Press.

Dewey, J. (1902). *The child and the curriculum*. In M. S. Dworkin (Ed.), *Dewey on education* (pp. 91–111). New York: Teachers College Press.

Dewey, J. (1916). *Democracy and education: An introduction to the philosophy of education*. New York: Macmillan.

Dewey, J. (1938). *Experience and education*. New York: Macmillan.

Freire, P. (1972). *Pedagogy of the oppressed*. New York: Herder and Herder.

Freire, P. (1977). *Education for critical consciousness*. New York: Seabury Press.

Freire, P. (1978). *Pedagogy in process*. New York: Seabury Press.

Freire, P. (1985). *The politics of education*. South Hadley, MA: Bergin and Garvey.

Freire, P. (1987). *A pedagogy for liberation*. South Hadley, MA: Bergin and Garvey.

Gay, P. (Ed.). (1964). *John Locke on education*. New York: Teachers College Bureau of Publications.

Giroux, H. (1983). *Theory and resistance in education*. South Hadley, MA: Bergin and Garvey.

Giroux, H. (1988). *Teachers as intellectuals: Toward a critical pedagogy of learning*. South Hadley, MA: Bergin and Garvey.

Giroux, H. (1991). *Postmodernism, feminism, and cultural politics: redrawing educational boundaries*. Albany, NY: SUNY Press.

Greene, M. (1973). *Teacher as stranger: Educational philosophy for the modern age*. Belmont, CA: Wadsworth.

Greene, M. (1977). *Landscapes of learning*. New York: Teachers College Press.

Greene, M. (1988). *The dialectic of freedom*. New York: Teachers College Press.

Illich, I. (1970). *Deschooling Society*. New York: Harper and Row.

Marx, K. (1955). *The communist manifesto*. Chicago: H. Regney.

Morris, V. C. (1966). *Existentialism in education*. New York: Harper and Row.

Peters, R. S. (1965). *Ethics and education*. London: Allen and Unwin.

Peters, R. S. (Ed.). (1973). *The philosophy of education*. London: Oxford University Press.

Plato. (1945). *Republic*. New York: Oxford University Press.

Russell, B. (1926). *Education and the good life*. New York: Boni and Liverright.

Sartre, J. P. (1974). *Existentialism and human emotions*. New York: Philosophical Library.

Scheffler, I. (1960). *The language of education*. Springfield, IL: Charles Thomas.

Soltis, J. (Ed.). (1981). *Philosophy and education.* Eightieth Yearbook of the National Society for the Study of education, Part I. Chicago: National Society for the Study of Education.

Strain, J. P. (1975). Idealism: A clarification of an educational philosophy. *Educational Theory, 25,* 263–271.

*Teachers College Record.* (1979, Winter). Vol. *81,* (2), 127–248.

Vandenberg, D. (1971). *Being and education: An essay in existential phenomenology.* Englewood Cliffs, NJ: Prentice Hall.

Whitehead, A. N. (1957). *The aims of education and other essays.* New York: Free Press.

CHAPTER **6**

# Schools as Organizations and Teacher Professionalization

In this chapter, we explore the organizational characteristics of U.S. elementary and secondary education, school cultures, and the vocation of teaching. These topics are tied together by one underlying issue—the parameters and possibilities inherent in creating better schools. How can schools be distinguished organizationally, and why are some schools more effective learning environments than others? You undoubtedly have strong memories of the schools you attended, but have you ever wondered why these memories are so vivid? Why is it that schools create such powerful organizational cultures that deeply influence one's life and one's approach to learning? The schools that an individual attends shape not only his or her life chances but his or her perceptions, attitudes, and behaviors. Of course, schools operate in conjunction with families and society. No school is an island unto itself. Still, schools are powerful organizations that profoundly affect the lives of those children and adults who come in contact with them. It seems logical, therefore, that knowing more about schools' organizational characteristics is a first step in understanding their impact on students, teachers, and the society at large.

Education in the United States is a huge business. According to Verstegen and McGuire (1991, p. 388) in 1988, "elementary and secondary education was a $172 billion enterprise serving 40 million students in fifty states and the District of Columbia." Education is one of the nation's largest businesses. Understanding the complexity and enormity of the educational enterprise is a difficult task because it contains so many different elements. Just feeding all the youngsters who attend school every day is a substantial undertaking. The New York City Board of Education, for instance, serves more meals per day than Howard Johnsons Restaurants. Supplying schools with equipment, textbooks, and such consumable items as paper and pencils is in itself a big business. Obviously, one could go on in this vein, but the point should be clear. To understand education, one must look beyond the classroom itself and the interaction between teachers and pupils to the larger world where different interest groups compete with each other in terms of ideology, finances, and power.

Clearly, any one of the preceding topics would be worthy of a book itself. In this chapter, we provide an overview of some of the basic elements of the organization of U.S. education so that you will be able to make increasingly informed decisions about the nature of education and how you as a teacher can grow professionally. In that sense, the purpose of this chapter is to create a broad frame of reference that grounds the perceptions of education in their organizational and social realities. To this end, we have included a section of this chapter that deals with the structure of U.S. education and compares that structure briefly to the structure of education in Great Britain, France, the former Soviet Union, and Japan.

We then turn to what is often called *school processes;* that is, we examine the way in which school cultures are created and maintained. Accordingly, we discuss such elements of school culture as authority structures and the significance of bureaucracy. These observations naturally lead to questions concerning the nature of teaching and the need for greater teacher professionalization. Good teaching will always be at the core of learning. Creating the conditions where teachers can use and improve their craft should be a major objective of those who believe that education is a cornerstone for a better society.

## THE STRUCTURE OF U.S. EDUCATION

The organization of U.S. schools is complex on several levels. In this section, we examine the nation's elementary and secondary school system from the point of view of governance, size, degree of centralization, student composition, and its relative "openness." We also examine the duality of the U.S. school system; that is, in the United States, we have public and private educational systems that sometimes work in tandem and sometimes in opposition. The purpose of discussing the organization of schools should be clear—without a sense of structure one has little way of grasping it as a whole. If one was to paint a landscape of elementary and secondary education in the United States, it would require a picture of almost infinite complexity and subtlety. It is the product of ideology, pragmatism, and history. It is unlike virtually any other educational system because the U.S. system is so decentralized and so dedicated to the concept of equal educational opportunity. We turn now to the issue of who is legally responsible for education in the United States.

### Governance

When the Constitution of the United States was written, its authors indicated that those powers that were not mentioned explicitly as belonging to the federal government were retained by individual states. Because the federal government made no claims concerning its authority relative to education, the states retained their authority and responsibility for education. Thus, the United States has 50 separate state school systems. This picture is made even more complex by the fact that there is also a private school system within each state. There are few countries with this degree of decentralization. But this is just the beginning of the story, because most U.S. public schools are paid for by the revenue that is raised by local property taxes. As a consequence, tax payers within particular school districts have a substantial stake in the schools within their districts and they are able to make their voices heard through community school boards.

What this means, in effect, is that the U.S. public school system is, in large part, decentralized right down to the school district level. It is true that the state may mandate curriculum, qualifications for teaching, and safety codes, but the reality is that these mandates must be carried out not by agents of the state but by citizens of a particular school district. Is it any wonder that top-down reform in the United States is difficult to achieve?

Since the civil rights movement of the 1960s, the federal government has entered the educational policy field originally through the enforcement of students' civil rights. The role of the federal government in creating educational policy has increased since that time. This expansion of the federal role in education is perhaps best symbolized by the founding of the United States Department of Education in the late 1970s. During the era of Presidents Reagan and Bush, the U.S. Department of Education served primarily as a "bully-pulpit" for Secretaries of Education who helped to define the crisis in U.S. education and to provide blueprints for the resolutions of these crises. In actual fact, however, the Secretary of Education has relatively little authority when it comes to the governance of public schools.

## Size and Degree of Centralization

As indicated earlier, the elementary and secondary school system in the United States is extremely large. It is estimated that by the end of the century, more than 50 million youngsters will be enrolling in kindergarten through the twelvth grade and that the cost of educating these children will be over $230 billion annually. Interestingly enough, at the same time that the school system has been growing, it has been simultaneously becoming more centralized, presumably for reasons of efficiency. For instance, in the early 1930s, there were approximately 128,000 public school districts in the United States. By the late 1980s, this number had been reduced to slightly less than 16,000. Part of this consolidation process has been by virtue of elimination of single-teacher schools. In the early 1930s, there were approximately 143,000 such schools and by the late 1980s, there were only 777.

As a consequence of this consolidation, the average number of pupils per elementary public school rose from 91 in the early 1930s to 450 in the late 1980s. Public high schools expanded from 195 students per school in the early 1930s to 513 in the late 1980s (Witte, 1990, p. 15). At the same time schools are becoming larger, the number of pupils per teacher is decreasing. Today, the average public elementary school classroom averages 19 students, whereas 50 years ago, there were nearly 34 students per teacher. At the high school level, the average number of pupils per teacher is 16, wereas 50 years ago, it was 22.

What these statistics reveal is that there has been a considerable amount of consolidation and centralization in the last 50 years in U.S. public education. Although this trend may be cost effective, it may also have an negative impact on the diversity of schools that students may attend. Usually, large institutions are more bureaucratic than smaller ones and a high degree of centralization diminishes the amount of democratic participation. For example, because school districts have become larger, superintendents have become more powerful, and as a consequence teachers have had fewer opportunities to make fewer decisions regarding curriculum, conditions of employment, and school policy.

## Student Composition

In the 1980s, 71 percent of the students in primary and secondary schools were white. This percent, however, masks a great deal of variation in terms of racial composition between states and school districts. Of the 50 states and the District of Columbia, 9 have less than 50 percent of white students, and over a dozen states have almost no minority students. Some large states such as California, Texas, and New York are extremely mixed racially. Many urban school districts enroll mostly minority students. For instance, in New York City, 78 percent of the students are nonwhite; in Los Angeles, the figure is 82 percent; and in Detroit, 91 percent of the system's students are from minority backgrounds. In effect, what has happened is that nonminority families have moved out of the cities and into the suburbs, leading to a high degree of residential segregation. In some cities, less than 5 percent of the suburban population is minority.

What this means is that the student composition of U.S. schools is becoming more diverse at the same time that there has been a trend toward increasing residential segregation. Another way of expressing this is that *de jure* segregation has been replaced by *de facto* segregation. Student composition can also be viewed along other dimensions such as gender, class, ethnicity, and even ability. Later on, we will discuss how these characteristics of students can affect not only the student composition of schools but are related to educational and life outcomes. For example, we might wonder why it is that although approximately half the students in American education are female, so few of them are able to pursue technological or scientific careers. Schools are also segregated or stratified according to the wealth and income of their student bodies. Students who attend schools in wealthy school districts, for instance, are more likely to have more curriculum options, better teachers, and more extracurricular activities than are students who attend relatively poor school districts. We will have a great deal more to say about these issues in subsequent chapters.

## Degree of "Openness"

Public schools in the United States are organized as elementary, junior high or middle school, and high school. Elementary school usually encompasses kindergarten through grades 5 or 6; junior high, grades 7 through 9; middle school, grades 6 through 8; and high school, grades 9 through 12. Usually, children enter kindergarten at age 5 and graduate from high school at age 18. A key element to understanding the U.S. school system is that there are relatively few academic impediments placed before students if they choose to graduate from high school. Indeed, there may be many social and personal impediments that keep students from graduating from high school, but the school system is designed to give students many opportunities for advancement.

In this sense, the U.S. school system is quite open. All youngsters are entitled to enroll into public schools and to remain in school until they graduate. There is a powerful democratic ethos underlining the belief in the "common school." From a structural point of view, this means that there are multiple points of entry into the school system and there are few forced exits. When this openness is compared to other school systems, you will see that this is unusual, although most Americans would agree that schools should be as democratic as possible.

## Private Schools

There are approximately 28,000 elementary and secondary private schools in the United States, enrolling 5.6 million students. Private schools constitute 25 percent of all elementary and secondary schools and educate 12 percent of the student population (Cookson, 1989, p. 61). The mean student enrollment of private schools is 234; only 7 percent of private schools enroll more than 600 students. Unlike the public sector, which has been consolidating over the last 50 years, there has been a remarkable growth of private schools. In the early 1930s, for instance, there were less than 10,000 private elementary schools in the United States; 50 years later, there were nearly 17,000 such schools.

There is a tremendous amount of diversity in the private sector, although most private schools are affiliated with religious organizations. Private school researcher Donald Erickson (1986, p. 87) has noted 15 major categories of private schools: Roman Catholic, Lutheran, Jewish, Seventh Day Adventist, Independent, Episcopal, Greek Orthodox, Quaker, Mennonite, Calvinist, Evangelical, Assembly of God, Special Education, Alternative, and Military. It should also be mentioned that in the United States there is very little regulation of private education by state authorities. The separation of church and state ensures the relative autonomy of private schools as long as they do not violate safety regulations and the civil rights of students. Each state has slightly different regulations, but in the main, it is safe to say that the autonomy of private schools is protected by a series of decisions made by the United States Supreme Court.

Most private schools are located on the east and west coasts. Connecticut has the highest percent of private school students and Wyoming has the least. Even though the percent of students who attend private schools has remained relatively steady when compared to the public sector, there has been significant shift in the private sector in terms of enrollment patterns. Clearly, Roman Catholic schools are experiencing a decline in enrollment. In the period between 1965 and 1983, there was a 46 percent drop in the number of students who attended Roman Catholic schools. During the same period, virtually every other type of private school experienced a great growth in terms of students and number of schools. Other religious schools doubled and tripled in size. This trend has continued into the 1990s. Private schools tend to attract students from families that are relatively affluent and who have a commitment to education.

Throughout the 1980s, numerous studies seemed to indicate that private schools were more effective learning environments than were public schools. Various researchers claimed that private schools are communities and, because they compete for students, they are less bureaucratic than public schools, and as a consequence, they are more innovative. As you will see, there is a growing movement among some educational reformers to allow students to choose between public and private schools. It is difficult to know whether in fact this kind of school choice will lead to school improvement or whether allowing students to choose private schools will lead to increased educational and social stratification. Many of these issues will be discussed in future chapters.

## Conclusion

As this overview indicates, describing the U.S. elementary and secondary school system requires viewing the organization of schools from a variety of points of view. There is considerable diversity in the system despite the fact that there has been trend toward centralization in the public sector. The authority structure of the public school system is diffuse; ultimately, it is the people who are responsible for the schools. This fact should not be minimized. Individuals, families, and groups are able to influence education by voting, by attending school district board meetings, and by paying for schools through taxes. This democratization gives the American school system an unique egalitarian ethos. How does the U.S. system compare to other education systems? This is an important question to ask because it is through comparison that one can see the unique features of the U.S. school system and those features that the U.S. system shares with the other national systems. This broadening frame of reference gives one greater understanding about the relationship between educational structure, processes, and outcomes.

## INTERNATIONAL COMPARISONS

Countries vary considerably by how they organize their school systems. Few school systems are as complex as that in the United States; for instance, most countries have a National Ministry of Education or a Department of Education that is able to exert considerable influence over the entire educational system. Educational reforms can start from the top down with relative success because the state has the authority to enforce its decisions right down to the classroom level. Another dimension apparent in comparative analysis is the relative selectivity of systems. Education in the United States is fundamentally inclusive in its purposes; most other educational systems are not as inclusive. Individuals in other systems undergo a very rigorous academic rite of passage that is designed to separate the "academically talented" from the less gifted. The relative selectivity of a school system is an excellent indicator of its exclusiveness or inclusiveness.

What is the major purpose of the system? It is to train an academic elite or to provide a broad-based educational experience for a wide segment of the population? Clearly, the relative openness of an educational system is related to the culture from which it originates. In this sense, educational systems are the expression of the values of the larger society. Educational systems can be located relative to each other by examining their degree of openness and the amount of authority that is exercised over the educational system by the national government. For instance, as we will see, France is a highly centralized educational system compared to the system in the United States. Moreover, the educational system in France is designed to produce an academic elite compared to the system in the United States, where equality of educational opportunity for all children is a strong normative value.

## Great Britain

Before the nineteenth century, the education of children in Great Britain was considered to be a responsibility of parents. All schools were private. For the children of very wealthy families, parents often hired tutors. For poor children, there was no schooling. During the nineteenth century, there was the a system of charity schools for the poor. Most of these schools were operated by religious organizations. The establishment of a national educational system for all children in the early nineteenth century was opposed by the Church of England and Roman Catholics. The 1870 Education Act led to the beginnings of a national system, although the Church of England continued to maintain its own schools. This compromise between church and state led to the dual system of education that still exists in Great Britain, whereby state run schools are controlled by Local Education Authorities (LEAs), while the church schools continue to operate, often funded by the state through the LEAs.

Although there were many attempts to reform this system, it was not until the 1944 Education Act that a truly national system of education was established as part of an "integrated public service welfare state" (Walford, 1992). Free primary and secondary education was provided for all children. Despite the fact that the 1944 Education Act was designed to democratize Great Britain's school system, on the whole, the system recreated the class system by channeling students into different kinds of schools. Children from wealthy homes received academic training in grammar schools, and children from working-class homes received vocational training. In short, Great Britain had a decentralized educational system that was fundamentally elitist.

During the 1960s, there was an effort to democratize Great Britain's educational system. When Margaret Thatcher was elected prime minister in 1979, however, she promised to reform the educational system. Throughout the 1980s, the conservative government, led by Margaret Thatcher, attempted to reform the educational system by privatizing public education, by encouraging greater parental choice, and by reorganizing the administrative structure of the state educational system. There were a series of legislative changes, culminating in the 1988 Reform Act. This reform established a national curriculum and set national assessment goals. Governing bodies of all secondary schools and many primary schools were given control over their own budgets. Parental choice was encouraged and a pilot network of City Technology Colleges was established. Also, state schools were given the right to opt out of local educational authority control. Thus, the 1988 Educational Reform Act was a radical challenge to the educational system that had been established in 1944.

## France

The educational system in France is quite centralized compared to the United States and Great Britain. The central government in France controls the educational system right down to the classroom level. Traditionally, there have been two public school systems—one for ordinary people and one for the elite. Efforts to end this dual system have been only partially successful, although throughout the last two decades, there has been an attempt to create one comprehensive system. The French educational system is highly stratified. For the academically talented, who usually come from the upper classes, there is a system of elementary, secondary, and postsecondary schools that is highly selective, highly academic, and socially elite. At the top of the system, are the *grandes ecoles*, which are small specialized institutions that produce members of the country's governmental and intellectual elite.

According to a noted authority on French education, George Male (1992), the French educational system is "excessively verbal." That is, French students are taught to frame ideas almost as an end unto itself, even as a matter of aesthetics. This sense of using language aesthetically is closely related to the importance placed on intellectual attainment within the French system. At one level, the objective of the French system is to produce a small number of highly qualified intellectuals. To identify this small group, the government has instituted a set of examinations that effectively, and one might even say ruthlessly, sort out the academically talented from the less academically gifted. The French believe, by and large, that this system of examinations is meritocratic, even though it is common knowledge that the system stratifies students by social class background. The French educational system is frankly competitive.

Efforts to democratize the system have not succeeded. Despite a number of reforms associated with particular Ministers of Education, the French system continues to be centralized, competitive, and stratified. In 1984, the socialist government proposed to reduce state grants to private Catholic schools. The opposition to this proposal was so fierce that the plan was dropped, and since that time there have been few reform efforts, especially at the structural level.

## The Former Soviet Union

In 1991, the Soviet Union as a single geographical and national entity dramatically and abruptly ceased to exist. The importance of this event cannot be underestimated. Very little is known about how the end of the Soviet Union will affect the education of children in Russia and the other countries that have reemerged since the collapse of the Soviet system. It is interesting from a historical perspective how the Soviet educational system was organized, if for no other reason than as an example of how the best-planned educational policies will fail if they are unsupported by other cultural institutions.

The educational system that was established after the Bolshevik Revolution of 1917 was highly centralized, stratified, and deeply ideological. The purpose of the educational system was to create the "new Soviet man and woman." These new men and women were to become the leaders of the proletarian revolution that would transform the Soviet Union into a socialist paradise. Communist values were to be unquestioned and the educational system was conceived as being part of a planned economy that would produce a society where scarcity was virtually unknown. In reality, the Soviet system was quite stratified; that is, the children of high party members attended schools that taught foreign languages and prepared their students for university entrance, whereas the children of workers attended schools that were often underfunded and underequipped and produced graduates who took jobs in the Soviet factory system.

In the 1980s, it became increasingly clear to Soviet leaders and the Soviet people that the educational system was failing to educate Soviet students in the new skills that were required by technological change and international competition. Moreover, the system had become so rigid that it no longer provided significant opportunities for upward mobility. This situation led to a wave of educational reform in the Soviet Union. In the period between 1980 and 1985, there were a series of minor reforms that attempted to change the system by finetuning it. For example, the age at which children were to start the first grade went from 7 years to 6 years. Teachers were paid slightly more and there was more emphasis on technical training. After the assent to power of Mikhail Gorbachev, the Soviet educational system was transformed by a vision of education that allowed for decentralization, teacher initiative, and curriculum reform. As part of the policy of restructuring Soviet society (perestroika), education was to become more open, flexible, and responsive to the needs of students, parents, and communities. Naturally, such a huge change was difficult to implement. After all, teachers and administrators in the system had been trained under wholly different sets of values. The idea of creating an experimental school, more or less free of government control, is profoundly radical within the Soviet context.

Educational reform was made even more complex as the decade of the 1980s drew to a close and the 1990s began, because the Soviet Union's economy virtually collapsed and the very nature of the Soviet Union was in transition. Because the Soviet Union was composed of so many nationalities, there was little consensus between national groups, except that which has been imposed by the Soviet government. As the power of the Soviet government diminished, the demand for nationalistic autonomy increased. Social change exceeded the pace in which schools could be reformed. There is little doubt that education in the former Soviet Union is being dramatically changed. Former Soviet citizens are experimenting with new curricula, privatization, school choice, and new educational philosophies. Certainly, education in the former Soviet Union will be dramatically different at the end of the twentieth century than the education system that was established by the Bolshevik party in the beginning of the twentieth century.

**Japan**

In the 1980s, the educational system of Japan was thought by some experts as being exemplary when compared to the educational system in the United States (White, 1987). The Japanese educational system seemed to produce skilled workers and highly competent managers. In fact, Japan's economic rise in the 1980s represented a serious challenge to the international economic position of the United States. What is it about the Japanese system that makes it so distinctive?

The first national system of education in Japan was established in the 1880s under the central authority of the Ministry of Education, Science, and Culture. After World War II, the structure of schooling was changed when compulsory education was extended from six to nine years and democratic principles of equality of opportunity were suffused throughout the system. Parallel to the public system is a large and thriving private sector that plays an important role in providing educational opportunities at all levels of education. The Japanese system of education is highly competitive. To be admitted to a prestigious university, students are required to pass examinations that are extremely competitive. This emphasis on achievement and attainment is exemplified by the fact that Japanese students excel in every measured international standard up to the age of 17, both for the top students and for the 95 percent of students who graduate from high school.

What distinguishes the Japanese educational system from other educational systems in terms of its efficiency and effectiveness? Certainly, the educational system benefits by the work ethic that is so deeply entrenched in Japanese culture. Japanese parents have a high regard for the importance of education. The belief in education in Japan is so strong that it has led to the "double-schooling" phenomenon. In effect, many Japanese students are exposed to two educational systems. The first system is the traditional public schools and the second system are nonformal schools that act as a national system of tutorial opportunities for students. The largest nonformal school system in Japan is the "study institution" (Juku). It is estimated that there are over 10,000 Jukus in Japan.

This love of education has made Japan a nation of strivers, but not without its own drawbacks. The Japanese have always placed a high value on moral education. Ethical dimensions of a moral education are not always easily compatible with the values inherent in competition. Thus, the debate over education in Japan has more to do with national character than it does with structural reform. Reconciling the cultural values of achievement and competition with those of cooperation and mutuality will be the hallmark of Japanese educational reform in the coming years.

**Conclusion**

In sum, it is very apparent from the preceding four examples that educational systems and structures are in the process of change on an almost continuous basis. Educational systems are difficult to change because they are deeply embedded in their respective cultures. The values of a culture become institutionalized in an educational system. Every system is confronted with the same kinds of challenges. How many children shall be educated and what shall they learn? Every educational system attempts to select and sort students by their academic talent. The ethics and efficacy of any system is difficult to evaluate outside of its cultural context. Culture not only shapes structure, but it also shapes school processes. Knowing the organization of a school or school system is a bit like knowing the architectural plans for a house. From a set of plans, one knows a house's dimensions and its form, but one does not know what it feels like to live in that structure. In the next section, we examine some of the key elements that underlie school processes.

## SCHOOL PROCESSES AND SCHOOL CULTURES

When you think back over your educational experiences, you undoubtedly have strong memories of the schools that you attended. You may remember particular teachers (for better or for worse), you may recall the students in your classes, and perhaps particular incidences stand out in your mind. Certainly, you remember the cafeteria. If you have strong powers of recall, you may remember the schools you attended more globally in terms of atmosphere, culture, and even smells. When one walks into a school, it is obvious that one is in a very particular place. Schools are unlike other organizations and because of this, they remain etched in one's memories for a lifetime. Thus, when one speaks of school processes, what we really are identifying are the powerful cultural qualities of schools that make them so potent in terms of emotional recall, if not in terms of cognitive outcomes.

Explaining school cultures is not easy because culture, by definition, is exactly that which one takes most for granted. Roughly 60 years ago, a sociologist of education, Willard Waller, attempted to understand the culture of schools. He wrote, "The school is a unity of interacting personalities. The personalities of all who meet in the school are bound together in an organic relation. The life of the whole is in all its parts, yet the whole could not exist without any of its parts. The school is a social organism…" (p. 146). According to Waller (1965, p. 147), schools are separate social organizations because:

1. They have a definite population.
2. They have a clearly defined political structure, arising from the mode of social interaction characteristics of the school, and influenced by numerous minor processes of interaction.
3. They represent the nexus of a compact network of social relationships.
4. They are pervaded by a "we feeling."
5. They have a culture that is definitely their own.

Waller went on to describe schools as despotisms in a state of perilous equilibrium (1965, p. 150). What is meant by this is that schools have authority structures that are quite vulnerable and that a great deal of political energy is expended every day, thus keeping the school in a state of equilibrium. In other words, school cultures are extremely vulnerable to disruption and that continuity is often maintained by the use of authority. Curiously, without the compliance of students, the exercise of authority within schools would be virtually impossible. Metz (1978) examined the use of authority in public schools and discovered that there was chronic tension within schools, in part because of conflicting goals. The teachers often have pedagogic goals that are difficult to reconcile with the social goals of the students. Administrators often have organizational goals that are shared neither by the teachers nor the students. Communities can exert tremendous pressure on schools and thus aggravate tensions within schools.

It is ironic that organizations that are formally dedicated to the goals of learning should be riddled with so many tensions and competing interests. However, this is the social reality within which many real schools operate. Schools are political organizations in which there are numerous competing interests. Thus, the culture of any one particular school is the product of the political compromises that have been created in order for the school to be viable. As a student, you experience these political compromises from a particular point of view. Individually, students generally have little power, but collectively they have a great deal of power in terms of whether or not they will accept the school's authority. Very often, this authority is represented in terms of the principal. Studies show that it is the principal who establishes the goals for the school, the level of social and academic expectations, and the effectiveness of the discipline (Persell & Cookson, 1982; Semel, 1992).

Because schools are so deeply political, effecting change within them is very difficult. Groups and individuals have vested interests. For example, teachers, represented through their unions, have a great deal to say about the conditions of their employment. Local school board members often struggle with the teachers in terms of pay, productivity, and professional standards. Many of these conflicts are resolved through negotiation. This is possible because schools, especially public schools, are bureaucracies.

Sociologist Max Weber (1976) suggested that bureaucracies are an attempt to rationalize and organize human behavior in order to achieve certain goals. In theory, bureaucracies are characterized by explicit rules and regulations that promote predictability and regularity in decision making and minimize the significance of personal relationships. Rules of procedure are designed to enforce fairness. As one knows, however, bureaucracies can become so complex, so rule oriented, and so insensitive that they suppress individualism, spontaneity, and initiative. Bureaucratic rationality can often suppress the creativity required for learning. Is it reasonable to suppose that learning best takes place in 40- of 50-minute segments that are marked by the ringing of bells or the mechanical rasp of buzzers? Is it reasonable to suppose that learning best takes place when every student reads the same text book? Is it reasonable to suppose that learning is best measured by multiple-choice tests? In short, the demands of the bureaucracy can often be destructive to the very spontaneity and freedom that is required by teachers and students if they are to develop intellectually and personally.

Schools, as they are now organized, are shaped by a series of inherent contradictions that can develop cultures that are conflictual and even stagnant. Changing the cultures of schools requires patience, skill, and good will. Research on the effects of school-based management, for instance, indicate that it is not an easy task for teachers, administrators, parents, community members, and students to arrive at consensus.

An interesting example of how complex the restructuring of schools can be is the "Schools of Tomorrow...Today" project, run by the New York City Teachers Center Consortium of the United Federation of Teachers. The purpose of this project is to create schools that are "more centered on learner's needs for active, experiential, cooperative, and culturally-connected learning opportunities supportive of individual talents and learning styles" (Lieberman, Darling-Hammond, Zuckerman, 1991, p. ix). The aim of this project is to create schools that are "energized by collaborative inquiry, informed by authentic accountability, and guided by shared decision making." It was discovered that despite the best efforts of the restructuring participants within the schools, reform was difficult to achieve. Each of the 12 schools participating in the project had strikingly different approaches to change and experienced significantly different outcomes in terms of achieving the stated objectives.

The evaluators of this project identified four elements of change that applied to all the schools:

> Conflict is a necessary part of change. Efforts to democratize schools do not create conflicts, but they allow (and to be successful, *require*) previously hidden problems, issues, and disagreements to surface. Staff involvement in school restructuring must be prepared to elicit, manage, and resolve conflicts.

> New behaviors must be learned. Because change requires new relationships and behaviors, the change process must include building communication and trust, enabling leadership and initiative to emerge, and learning techniques of communication, collaboration, and conflict resolution.

> Team building must extend to the entire school. Shared decision making must consciously work out and give on-going attention to relationships within the rest of the school's staff. Otherwise, issues of exclusiveness and imagined elitism may surface, and perceived "resistance to change" will persist.

> Process and content are interrelated. The process a team uses in going about its work is as important as the content of educational changes it attempts. The substance of a project often depends upon the degree of trust and openness built up within the team and between the team and the school. At the same time, the usefulness and the visibility of the project will influence future commitments from and the relationships among the staff and others involved. (Lieberman, Darling-Hammond, Zuckerman, 1991, pp. ix–x)

As these quotes indicate, changing the culture of a school in order to make the school more learner centered requires time, effort, intelligence, and good will. Reflecting on the observations of Willard Waller, one can see that altering a particular school's culture is similar to diverting a river as it flows to the sea. Just as change is institutionalized, the institution itself changes. School processes are elusive and difficult to define, but all powerful nonetheless. This does not mean that planned change is not possible. It does mean that planned change requires new ways of thinking. It is our contention that teachers must be at the forefront of educational change and, therefore, the very definition of the profession must be redefined.

## TEACHERS, TEACHING, AND PROFESSIONALIZATION

In the prologue to his engaging and important book, *Horace's Compromise* (1984), Theodore Sizer describes Horace Smith, a 53-year-old, 28-year veteran of high school classrooms. Horace is an "old pro." He gets up at 5:45 A.M. in order to get to school before the first period of the day, which begins at 7:30 A.M. Horace puts in a long day, teaching English to high school juniors and seniors. In all, he will come in contact with 120 students. His days are long and demanding. Horace figures that by judiciously using his time, he is able to allot 5 minutes per week of attention on the written work of each student and an average of 10 minutes of planning for each 50-minute class. For this, he is paid $27,300. He earns another $8,000 a year working part time in a liquor store. Horace's daughter just graduated from law school and has her first job in a law firm. Her starting salary is $32,000 a year.

The story of Horace is by no means unusual. His loyalty, dedication, and hard work is repeated thousands of times by thousands of teachers every day. As this story indicates, there are numerous paradoxes related to the teaching profession. Teachers are expected to perform miracles with children but are seldom given the respect that professionals supposedly deserve. Teachers are asked to put in 60-hour weeks but are paid relatively small salaries. Teachers are expected to reform education, but are left out of the educational reform process. In short, teachers are the key players in education but their voices are seldom heard and their knowledge is terribly underutilized, and even devalued.

In this section we will briefly examine the nature of the teaching profession and the possibilities for further teacher professionalization. This topic is of utmost importance because we believe, as do John Goodlad and others, that teachers will be key players in educational reform in the future. After all, teachers are responsible for student learning. If they cannot assume responsibility for school improvement, how likely is it that schools will improve in terms of students learning?

### Who Become Teachers?

At the elementary level, female teachers outnumber males by a ratio of five to one. That is, 83.5 percent of elementary teachers are women. At the high school level, the ratio between men and women is roughly one to one. According to Walker, Kozma, and Green (1989, p. 16), most of today's teachers are entering middle age and are, on average, five years older than the typical U.S. worker. Only 1 percent of teachers are under age 25. Today's teachers are likely to be married, and nearly 9 out of 10 teachers are white. The average teacher is likely to have a master's degree, not be politically active, and remain within a single school district for a relatively long period of time. With the aging of the teaching force, there will be an increased demand for new teachers. It is projected that by the year 2000, more than 3 million teachers will be needed. This represents not only a real increase in the need for teachers relative to the number of individuals teaching today but it also indicates that more *new* teachers will need to be hired because of the large amount of retirements that will occur during the 1990s.

Recently, there has been a great deal of discussion about the qualifications of those entering the teaching profession. In 1982, for instance, the national average Scholastic Aptitude Test (SAT) score was 893; the average score among students intending to major in education was 813 (Walker, Kozma, & Green, 1989, p. 26). Although SAT scores may not be accurate predictors of professional development, they do indicate that, on average, students entering the teaching profession are relatively weak academically. When top high school seniors are asked to indicate their future professions, less than 10 percent indicate that they are interested in becoming teachers. What is perhaps even more alarming is that the best students who enter the teaching profession are the ones that are most likely to leave the profession at an early date. Another concern is that there are few minority teachers. The United States is becoming an increasingly multicultural society. One wonders about the educational effectiveness of an aging white teaching force in the context of increasing racial and ethnic diversity.

## The Nature of Teaching

Few professions are as demanding as teaching. Teachers must be skilled in so many areas of technical expertise and human relations. In their book, *The Complex Roles of the Teacher: An Ecological Perspective* (1984), Heck and Williams describe the many roles that teachers are expected to play in their professional lives. These roles include colleague, friend, nurturer of the learner, facilitator of learning, researcher, program developer, administrator, decision maker, professional leader and community activist. This is a daunting list and it leaves out the most important role of the teacher: the caring, empathetic, well-rounded person that can act as a role model to students, parents, and other professionals. Thus, on any single day, a teacher will be expected to wear many personal and professional "hats." This role switching is extremely demanding and may be one of the reasons for teacher burnout. It takes a great deal of emotional energy and imagination to maintain a sense of personal equilibrium in the face of meeting the needs of so many diverse groups.

Lieberman and Miller (1984), have explored what they call "the social realities of teaching." Through their research, they have been able to identify elements of the teaching experience that give it its unique flavor. According to Lieberman and Miller, the central contradiction of teaching is that "teachers have to deal with a group of students and teach them something and, at the same time, deal with each child as an individual. The teachers, then, have two missions: one universal and cognitive, and the other particular and affective" (p. 2). In order to reconcile this contradiction, teachers develop all kinds of classroom strategies that become highly personal and evolve into a teaching style that is more akin to an artistic expression than it is to a technocratic or scientific resolution. Teachers, according to Lieberman and Miller, are best viewed as craftspeople and most of the craft is learned on the job. Teaching is a somewhat messy and personal undertaking.

There are other social realities of teaching that are significant. For instance, rewards are derived from students. Very often, the greatest and perhaps the only positive feedback that teachers receive is from their students. Seymour Sarason has written that teaching is a lonely profession. By this, he means that teachers get few opportunities to have professional interactions with their peers, and administrators seldom take the time or make the effort to give the kind of positive feedback teachers need.

Another element that gives teaching its unique characteristics is that very little is known about the links between teaching and learning. Researchers have only a marginal knowledge of whether or not what is taught is what is learned and what the nature of learning is. This means that the knowledge base of teaching is relatively weak compared to the knowledge base of other professions. Few teachers are experts in learning theory and many are only minimally qualified in some of the content areas they teach. What is key in teaching is the exercise of control. Control precedes instruction. Without control, there are few opportunities for learning, and yet control can stifle learning. Walking the razor's edge between social claustrophobia in the classroom and chaos in the classroom requires a high degree of self-understanding and understanding of group behavior. This is made more difficult by the fact that the goals of teaching are not always clear. There is a great deal of talk about holding teachers accountable for student learning. But the fact is classrooms are communities, where many needs need to be met. To be an effective teacher requires a sensitivity to individual and group dynamics.

Lieberman and Miller (1984) devoted a great deal of time discussing the "dailiness of teaching." There is a rhythm to the teacher's day. Thinking back to Horace in *Horace's Compromise* (Sizer, 1984), one can see that his day is punctuated by a set of rules, interactions, and feelings that are played out on a day-to-day basis with a certain predictability. Each day has a rhythm, weeks have rhythms, months have rhythms, and seasons have rhythms. For instance, fall is a time of high hopes and promise. As the fall winds down, energy winds down. By Thanksgiving, there is a great need for a break from the routine. Between Thanksgiving and Christmas, there is a frantic round of activities that culminate with the Christmas break. January can be brief, but February can seem never to end. It is in February that most teachers begin to think of other professions. By March, spirits begin to rise. This is accelerated by the spring break and the last-minute rush to fulfill the promises made in September by the closing of school in June. And then one day in June, school ends: No more routines, no more rituals, just memories of the year past.

Few professions are as simultaneously routinized and creative as teaching. Good teachers are creators. They take the dailiness of teaching and turn each day into a special event. A great teacher can turn a mundane lesson into an exciting intellectual voyage, and a poor teacher can make students reject learning altogether. There are few rules about what it takes to be a good teacher. Certainly, most good teachers genuinely like their students, have a commitment to their subject matter, are reasonably orderly in terms of their classroom organization, and have at least a working sense of humor. But these qualities are not professional qualities per se. How can one ensure that the teaching force will be staffed by people who are academically sound and pedagogically artistic? Given the condition of education today, it is important, even critical, that teachers be trained in new ways and redefine the nature of their professionalism.

## Teacher Professionalization

Over 20 years ago, sociologist Dan Lortie (1975) pointed out that teaching, particularly elementary school teaching, is only partially professionalized. When he compared elementary school teachers to other professionals, he found that the prerequisites for professionalism among elementary school teachers were vaguely defined or absent altogether. For example, doctors have many clients, which means that they are not economically dependent on any single individual. This economic independence provides professional autonomy so that doctors need not always comply with the wishes of the client. Teachers are in a very different market situation. They receive their income from "one big client." There is little opportunity for teachers to teach independently of their school, and thus there is little opportunity for teachers to gain a reputation for excellence outside of their school or their school district. There is, in Lortie's words, "an incomplete subculture." Teacher socialization is very limited compared to other professions and there is little evidence that the socialization processes associated with becoming a teacher are highly professionalized or represent standards of behavior congruent with other professions. Lortie (1969, p. 213) concluded, "The general status of teaching, the teacher's role and the condition and transmission arrangements of its subculture point to a truncated rather than fully realized professionalization."

Educational researcher Linda M. McNeil (1988) has written about what she calls the contradictions of control. She pointed out that "in theory, the bureaucratic design of schools frees teachers to teach by assigning to administrators and business managers the duties of keeping the school 'under control'" (p. 433). But as McNeil indicated, when so much attention is placed upon keeping things under control, the educational purposes of the school can diminish in importance and teachers can begin to be part of a controlling process rather than an instructional one.

> As a result, teachers begin to take on the characteristics of the workers whose craft was splintered and recast when they became factory workers. When teachers see administrators emphasizing compliance with rules and procedures, rather than long term educational goals, teachers begin to structure their courses in ways that will elicit minimum participation from their students. When they see administrators run the schools according to impersonal procedures aimed at credentialing students, teachers begin to assert in their classrooms the authority they feel they are lacking in their schools as a whole. And when the complicated and often unpredictable task of educating a wide range of students is less valued than having quiet halls and finishing paperwork on time, teachers try to create in their own classrooms the same kind of efficiencies by which they are judged in the running of their schools. (McNeil, 1988, p. 433)

Clearly, Lortie and McNeil are pointing to a set of conditions within the teaching profession that makes genuine professional autonomy a difficult goal to attain. On the one hand, teachers are expected to be autonomous, thoughtful experts in education. On the other hand, the conditions of their employment leave little scope for autonomy, thoughtfulness, or expertise. Perhaps none of this would really matter if the compromise between the norms of professionalism and the norms of bureaucracy did not lead to a kind of intellectual and moral paralysis among many teachers. Trying to be a professional and a bureaucrat, while at the same time trying to fulfill the many roles of a teacher, is a task that cannot be reasonably fulfilled by most people. Thus, in the teaching profession there is a tendency toward malaise, a lack of self-worth, and even cynicism. A visit to a teachers' lounge can be bracing and challenging to the idealist because teachers' lounges are notorious sites for gossip and back-stabbing. This is not to say that teaching is an impossible profession. There are many incredible teachers who overcome these obstacles and are inspirational to their students and even to their colleagues.

It is difficult to think of ways of educating inspirational teachers. After all, teaching is so personal. For educators such as John Goodlad, however, the time has come when society must find ways of better educating teachers. In the mid-1980s, Goodlad and two colleagues created the Center for Educational Renewal at the University of Washington. Using the Center as a base, they conducted a number of studies about teacher education in the United States. Goodlad's (1991, p. 5) findings included the following: "(1) A debilitating lack of prestige in the teacher education enterprise, (2) Lack of program coherence, (3) Separation of theory and practice, and (4) A stifling regulated conformity." These findings underscore what many already know. There is a crisis in teacher education. Goodlad suggested that there is a need for a complete redesign of teacher education programs and that a share of this redesign be conducted by policy makers, state officials, university administrators, and faculty members in the arts and sciences as well as in the schools of education. He also suggested that the redesign of teacher education include input from parents, teachers in schools, and the community at large.

Goodlad believes that a teacher education program should include a clearly articulated relationship between education and the arts and sciences. He believes that students should stay together with teams of faculty members throughout their period of preparation and that universities commit enough resources to ensure first-rate teacher education programs. He is a strong believer that schools and universities should collaborate to operate joint educational projects as a way of preparing teachers for the real world of schools and as a way of revitalizing schools themselves. In short, Goodlad wants to raise the level of academic preparation for teachers, create a more cohesive curriculum, and professionalize teacher education by enlarging its clinical component.

Goodlad's ideas are far from radical. But if they were to be implemented, the way most teachers are prepared would be fundamentally altered. Clearly, there is a relationship between a higher level of preparation and professionalization. However, if teachers are to be truly professional, they must be able to share in the important decisions within the schools. School-based management, if it is to succeed, must empower teachers in terms of their decision-making capacities about curriculum, discipline, and other academic areas of importance. Whether or not school-based management will succeed as a reform will determine in no small degree the level of professionalization achieved by teachers. As one looks to the future, one can only hope that educational reformers will listen to teacher advocates such as John Goodlad who argue that without creating a new generation of teacher-leaders, there is little hope that schools will become more productive and just.

In this chapter we have discussed schools as organizations and teacher professionalization. Clearly, the many topics covered in this chapter deserve further discussion. The readings for this chapter touch on critical issues related to schools and teachers.

The first selection, written by sociologist Mary Haywood Metz, "Organizational Tensions and Authority in Public Schools," examines the organizational life of schools in terms of technology, structure, environment, and authority. In essence, Metz identifies those elements of school organization that create the "moral order" within schools. How does this moral order affect students' attitudes and behaviors and how does it influence the working conditions of teachers?

The second selection, "Contradictions of Reform," written by educational researcher Linda M. McNeil, discusses the conflicting goals of U.S. high schools. The bureaucratic structure of the high schools is designed to control large numbers of students, while at the same time nurturing each student as an individual. Teachers are at the very center of this contradiction. McNeil argues that "standardized generic education" limits teachers' abilities to be creative and risk taking. Without true collaboration between teachers, administrators, and students, there is little hope for genuine reform.

The third article, written by educator and lawyer Judith H. Cohen, "What Is a Teacher's Job?: An Examination of the Social and Legal Causes of Role Expansion and Its Consequences," outlines the legal constraints within which teachers must work as professionals. In a society that is becoming increasingly litigious, teachers must be aware of how laws governing students' rights and teachers' rights influence educational practices.

# Organizational Tensions and Authority in Public Schools

## MARY HAYWOOD METZ

Schools are formal organizations. So are ITT, the local laundromat, prisons, churches, and the Republican Party. One can learn a good deal by analyzing schools' characteristics and conflicts in terms sociologists have developed in the study of other kinds of organizations. These have been but scantily applied in the study of schools.[1]

This [reading] introduces the major elements of organizations which sociologists have found to be useful in explaining their form and their activities. It describes the distinctive character of these elements in schools. While I arrived at this formulation as a product of the study of Canton's schools, for the reader it provides an orientation at the outset. The analysis which follows in the rest of the book uses the theory of formal organizations as the dominant framework for explanation. This relatively focused theoretical approach is used in preference to the eclectic one which is more common in the sociological study of schools for the sake of analytical coherence.

## GOALS

Formal organizations exist for the accomplishment of formally stated goals. People enter an organization with an obligation to contribute to those goals; those who fail to do so may be disciplined. Outside groups which support an organization may punish it as an entity for failure to meet its announced goals. Thus production and profit for business, the glorification of God and fostering of Christian community for churches, and the winning of elections and responsible governing of the country for parties are the touchstone by which thousands of daily activities and decisions are—or are supposed to be—measured.

But many, if not most, organizations have goals which upon close inspection are varied or diffuse and difficult to measure. When this happens the different goals or different aspects of a diffuse goal will be in competition for scarce resources. They may contradict one another directly, or means which are most appropriate for reaching one may tend to subvert another.

In one sense there is remarkable clarity about the goals for which public schools are established. Each is created to educate the children of a given geographic area. But as soon as one asks what it means to educate the young, unanimity turns to debate. Educational goals are endless in their variety and subtle in their complexity. Most have a kind of halo which makes them hard to reject outright, even though any two of them may require conflicting attitudes and activities. For example, it is important to have children master a good deal of specific information and to teach children to follow instructions, but it is also important to stimulate their curiosity and teach them to follow out their own lines of questioning. In a given course or a given class these goals will frequently conflict. Consequently, in simply "educating" the children the public schools are usually seeking multiple and pragmatically contradictory ends.

Source: From *Classrooms and Corridors: The Crisis of Authority in Desegregated Secondary Schools* (pp. 15–32) by Mary Haywood Metz. Copyright © 1978 by the Regents of the University of California. Reprinted by permission.

Furthermore, every organization has to seek other goals besides the formal goals which provide its reason for being. If it is to remain an instrument capable of performing its formal goals, it has to insure its own healthy functioning and its own survival in the face of threats from without. It therefore has an array of instrumental goals which are as important as the formal goals to the accomplishment of its official task. These goals attract little notice when they are satisfactorily met, but when their attainment becomes difficult they can absorb more energy than the original purpose of the organization. Arrangements for meeting them can change or subvert the formal goals which an organization actually pursues. The overt or covert sacrifice of an organization's declared purposes for the sake of its survival or smooth functioning has been repeatedly documented in settings as diverse as government agencies, junior colleges, churches, prisons, and mental hospitals.[2]

For schools the most difficult instrumental goal is the maintenance of order among a student body which is only half socialized, comes and remains by legal compulsion, and frequently includes persons with radically different educational and social expectations.

Almost as difficult is the task of maintaining freedom from attack, let alone obtaining support or assistance, from the surrounding community. This community has a license to run the affairs of the schools with fairly close fiscal and policy supervision through local school taxes and elected local school boards. Yet parents and other interested members of the community may have a knowledge of the complexities of pedagogy and the practical necessities of running a school based primarily on memories of their childhood participation in schools. Their educational goals and social outlook may vary enormously as they bring their influence to bear on a single school or set of schools.

In Canton the schools' problem of conflicting goals was clearly visible. The teachers espoused a considerable variety of educational priorities, and many were passionate both in supporting their own and in criticizing others'. The problem of maintaining order among a diverse and skeptical set of students was preoccupying in one form or another for the staff at all the schools. And the community exerted unremitting pressures on the schools.

Schools in general, and in Canton dramatically so, are forced to make choices among their formal goals or to exist with managed or unmanaged conflict. And they must reconcile the requirements of these formal goals with the requirements of maintaining order among the students and support from the community, a task which…often requires sacrifices of the formal goals.

## TECHNOLOGY

The study of formal organizations more generally directs us to look for other conflicts in schools. It teaches that the character of the technology, the work process,[3] which an organization uses to accomplish its primary tasks tends to be a fundamental characteristic of the organization to which other characteristics must conform.[4] Whether or not there exists a technological process which reliably accomplishes one or another of the organization's goals affects the practical, if not the rhetorical, priorities among those goals.[5]

In the school, the question of technology is of central importance. The raw material of the school's work process, the students, is variable. Differences in cultural background, social position, and individual emotional and cognitive characteristics have an enormous impact on the educational process appropriate to a given child. Yet the process of learning in general, let alone in a given case, is poorly understood.[6]

A considerable range of technological approaches has been and is being used in schools without any incontrovertible demonstration that one is much superior to another, even with a given group of children.[7] It is rarely even claimed that a given approach is reliable appropriate with all students in the way that a chemical manufacturing process may be successful with all properly processed batches of ingredients.

Further, it is almost impossible to know when the school's technology has been successful and when it has not. Teachers have no way of checking on their students' memory of material even a year later, much less when they come to need it in the vicissitudes of adult life. Much learning is intended not as an end in itself but as a basis for developing broad capacities. It is expected that one develops a more logical mind from learning algebra or gains creativity from writing free-form poetry. But how can one assess such capacities reliably, let alone trace their origins? If education is supposed to impart strength of character or richness of personality, the problem of measurement defies description.

Technology, then, is a major problem for the public schools. They are faced with the task of creating changes in diverse raw material through processes which are poorly understood, in the absence of any universally effective means, and without any trustworthy way of measuring the success or failure of whatever methods they finally apply. These technological problems combine with the vague and conflicting goals of education to create a perfect setting for endless controversy. People can disagree forever about the accomplishment of vaguely stated purposes through inadequate means which create results that cannot be satisfactorily measured.[8]

The character of the school's technology thus compounds the tendency to conflict over diverse educational goals. It also makes it easy for a school to sacrifice elusive instructional goals to pressing ones for the maintenance of order. This is especially the case in those schools where students are hard to teach and given to resistance to adults and

interference with one another. Thus the weakness of the school's technology makes educational goals most vulnerable where they are most needed.[9]

In Canton disagreements about teaching goals were often intertwined with disagreements about technological effectiveness. Everyone wanted the children "to learn." But teachers' (and students') differing beliefs about the relative importance of different kinds of learning were inextricably mixed with their ideas about the nature and progression of the learning process.[10] And since it was very difficult to measure learning under different systems which were also different in their goals, the arguments had no solid external reference point. In such a situation, conflict cannot be objectively resolved and tensions can mount very high indeed, as they did at one of the schools.

## STRUCTURE

Technology shapes an organization not only in its interaction with multiple goals but in its impact on social structure. If the major technological processes of an organization are well understood and routine so that they can be broken into small standardized operations, the organization can be centralized and hierarchical with decisions made at the top and carried out by a large work force of persons with little skill. But when, as in the case of the school, the technology is not well understood and the variable character of the material prevents standardized operations, then the organization is most appropriately decentralized and "flat." The persons who perform the actual work of the organization need to be given relatively large and diffuse tasks with the right to make important decisions independently as they use their intuition to adjust their methods to the requirements of each specific instance.[11]

The spatial and temporal structure of the average American public secondary school is in many ways constructed for the pursuit of a non-routine technology. A single teacher works alone with a group of children for a whole school year. He works out of the sight and hearing of other adults and needs to co-ordinate his efforts with those of other teachers only in minimal ways. Each teacher has a comprehensive task in teaching the whole of a given subject to a constant group of children for a year and he is free to use his intuition and his personality as he goes about it.

In some school systems this isolation is accompanied by a larger autonomy. Teachers are given significant prerogatives in deciding both the content and the style of their teaching without fundamental questioning from colleagues or administrators. Such a situation can also alleviate strains arising from the school's multiple goals. Differences within a faculty need not be carried to the point of open debate leading to victory or defeat, but rather each teacher quietly follows his own ideas in his own classroom.

A model like this is followed—roughly at least—at the university level. But anyone familiar with a range of public schools knows that it is not typical. Teachers' autonomy is limited. In some districts, it is almost non-existent, as standardized curriculum guides prescribe not only the content but much of the method for each class. Two-way intercoms or directives to leave doors open may vitiate the physical isolation of the classroom, as they allow intrusions without warning. There may even be exact rules for teachers' treatment of a large range of classroom situations. These measures are extremes, but their existence underscores the fact that teachers' autonomy is a variable and not a constant factor in public schools. Constraints upon teachers' autonomy reflect fundamental organizational pressures which work upon school structure in direct contradiction to the pressures of the technological requirements of teaching.

## ENVIRONMENT

The most important of these pressures come from the students' attacks upon order and from the unfriendly intrusion of parents or community into the school's daily activities. Comparative studies of organizations have found that they cope most easily with environments likely to attack their practices if their structure is centralized and hierarchical and their technological procedures routinized and unambiguous.[12] This strategy is dramatically clear in the response of organizations with subordinates most prone to disorder: prisons.[13] Thus, the most pressing instrumental goals of the school, those of coping with a hostile environment of students or of parents (or other influential community members), suggest a social structure and a technological style diametrically opposed to that most suitable for furthering educational goals.

Typical public school structure reflects these contradictory pressures. The physical, temporal, and social separation of each class with the teacher is contradicted by the formal social structure of the school. Most are formally hierarchical bureaucracies, with the teachers directly responsible to a principal who is in turn responsible and accountable to superiors in the school district administration. The structure of the school is thus ambivalent.[14]

Districts vary in the way that practice shapes the actual operation of the organization. The teachers' independence with their classes may be both proclaimed and generally practiced, or the chain of command may be firmly emphasized. These variations will in each case be the result of a multitude of pressures coming from dominant conceptions of educational goals, from the technological requirements of teaching given kinds of students, and from pressures in the environment.[15] Still, each particular pattern constitutes a way of coping with a set of contradictory organizational imperatives, not a way of exorcising them. The potentiality for strain can be expected to remain, even though compromises blunt the effects of inherent tensions.

The severity of the conflict will vary considerably from district to district depending on the character of the students and community and the strategy of the school. Some student bodies offer only relatively mild problems of disorder, others severe ones. Parents vary in their interest in the schools and in their predisposition to be aggressive or cooperative in addressing what they perceive to be problems. School staffs vary in the diversity and the kind of educational goals which they seriously pursue. Some goals require more technological flexibility than others. Some student bodies respond to standardized techniques while others require the teachers to experiment and explore to the maximum as they go about the pedagogical process.

These differences in student body, community and staffs will appear in a plethora of particular constellations which will affect the daily life of the schools as total configurations. To say that it is necessary to look at the interplay of educational goals, technology, structure, and environmental pressures in order to understand events in the schools is thus to make only the barest beginning toward an analysis of any one school.

In Canton the contradictory pressures described here were especially severe. Both the lower class black children and the affluent white children resisted cooperation with the schools' routines. Order was chronically problematic. Furthermore, the black parents and the professional white parents watched the schools closely to maintain their children's rights and integrity in the face of school discipline. Both were ready to mount a vigorous attack on any practices they considered inappropriate. These pressures encouraged the schools to use protective measures and structures.

At the same time, both sets of parents insisted that the schools pursue effective academic education with their fullest energies. They monitored the schools' performance in this context as best they could. The character of the children at both ends of the academic scale was such as to present a technological challenge in accomplishing such education. To succeed the teachers often needed imaginative, unconventional, and flexible methods. These pressures encouraged the schools to allow teachers and students freedom to work out their methods together in a variety of ways. Flexible structures were required.

Canton's schools thus needed opposed methods and structures in pursuing instrumental and formal goals where both were especially difficult to achieve. They suffered from strain as a consequence.

At the level of formal policy, the school board and district administration stressed educational goals before all else. Following the expectations of the parents and the temper of the times, they encouraged varied and flexible technological approaches and established a decentralized structure which gave principals and classroom teachers a very large measure of autonomy in choosing their means and ends within the context of general policy. They therefore made a set of consistent choices for one set of goals and supporting organizational arrangements.

However, when problems of order or parental attacks did occur, the board and the district staff expected the staffs of the schools to be expeditious in dealing with them. The tensions arising from the contradictions the district faced thus were passed on to the individual schools. It was there that they were felt in strains upon daily activity and acted out in a variety of conflicts....

At both schools, district policy granting the teacher curricular flexibility and autonomy in the conduct of the class made the classroom a unit with significant independence from the wider school.... To understand the interaction of teachers and students as they went about defining their common purpose and procedures in the classroom, it is necessary to understand one more element of organizational life.

## AUTHORITY

In a formal organization authority provides the major means for carrying goals, technology, and structure from ideals into action. Especially in the classroom context, it is in closely studying relationships of authority that we will see the tensions of the school expressed in daily action. Principals and teachers fulfill their goals by directing others to participate in activities designed to accomplish them. Since principals and teachers have the formal responsibility for carrying out the school's goals and the right to see that others do their part, they possess authority.

Authority is distinguished from other relationships of command and obedience by the superordinate's *right* to command and the subordinate's *duty* to obey. This right and duty stem from the crucial fact that the interacting persons share a relationship which exists for the service of a *moral order to which both owe allegiance*. This moral order may be as diffuse as the way of life of a traditional society or as specific as the pragmatic goals of a manufacturing organization. But in any case, all participants have a duty to help realize the moral order through their actions. This duty may arise from emotional or moral attachment to the order itself, but may be as unsentimental as the manual worker's obligation to give a fair day's work in exchange for a fair day's pay.[16]

Authority exists to further the moral order. It exists because a person in a given position is more able than others to perceive the kinds of actions which will serve the interests of the moral order. On the basis of this capacity he has the right to issue commands which others have the duty to obey.

For the sake of generality it is helpful to call persons who give commands superordinates and those who receive them subordinates. The same individual may be simultaneously a superordinate and a subordinate as he acts out different aspects of a single role. Teachers are superordinates in interacting with students but subordinates in interacting with their principal.

Authority is a formal and continuing relationship, an institutionalized one. Strictly speaking it is a relationship of roles, not of persons. The superordinate's right to command rests both upon his occupancy of a role and his presumed ability to translate the needs of the moral order into specific activities which will support it. This ability may stem from several kinds of sources, ranging from the mystic endowments which let a Pope speak infallibly ex cathedra to the pragmatic knowledge of an executive who receives reports from several divisions of a company. The subordinate's duty to obey the superordinate rests upon the superordinate's claim to be acting for the moral order. If this claim is valid, then obedience to the superordinate is obedience to the needs of the moral order.

These characteristics of authority can be summarized in a formal definition. *Authority is the right of a person in a specified role to give commands to which a person in another specified role has a duty to render obedience. This right and duty rest upon the superordinate's recognized status as the legitimate representative of a moral order to which both superordinate and subordinate owe allegiance.*

Authority can thus be graphically represented by a triangle as in Figure 1. This model makes it clear that in every instance of authority one must consider not only the roles of superordinate and subordinate and their relationship but also the moral order and the relationship of both superordinate and subordinate to it. Any one of these elements or relationships affects the shape of every other.

Superordinate Role

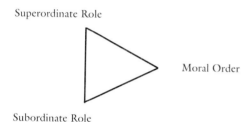

Moral Order

Subordinate Role

**FIGURE 1**
**THE ELEMENTS OF AUTHORITY**

Despite the crucial importance of the moral order as the basis of the relationship of superordinate and subordinate, they may not make reference to it in most of their transactions. Under ordinary circumstances, the subordinate *trusts* the superordinate's competence and good faith in the service of the moral order sufficiently to assume that the superordinate's specific commands further its requirements. The fact that the superordinate has given the command is sufficient guaranty of its validity. The act of obedience discharges the subordinate's obligation to the moral order.

In the give-and-take of daily contact, then, the position of the superordinate comes to be the immediate source of his right to command. And indeed the man in the street, even the semi-professional subordinate,[17] commonly comes to identify authority with the person of the superordinate. So long as events go along smoothly this model suffices. But when trouble arises, when the superordinate has to make unconventional or heavy demands, or when the subordinate grows restive, then both will tend to call upon the moral order directly to sustain—or object to—a command.

Social scientists have also concentrated upon the role of the superordinate in their investigations of variations in authority and the complexities which attend its practice. But also relevant are other questions asked less often by either social scientists or laymen. These revolve around the role of the subordinate, and around *his understanding* of his relationship with his superordinate and of his relationship with the moral order, and indeed around his understanding of the very nature of the moral order.[18]

These questions are less often addressed in considerations of authority, because the answers to them are frequently taken for granted. Much of the time authority works because subordinates never seriously analyze the character of their own role or its relationship to any of the other elements of authority. They accept the definitions of these matters supplied to them by superordinates. They usually do this because they are subordinates as a result of ascriptive positions which they have always held. They are of a race, social class, sex, or age which has traditionally held subordinate status and accepted commands from above in participating in the society's institutions. Alternatively, and often at the same time, they do not question these matters because they have no significant stake in most of them. In organizations, people who work at routine jobs are generally not very interested in their contribution to the organization's overall goals—so long as the company can meet its payroll.

Schools deal with the young, whose experience has traditionally been designed to re-enforce their assumption that they should trust all their elders by virtue of a difference in age. Children belong to an ascriptively subordinate group. However, the assumption of elders' wisdom and good will was radically undermined during the sixties for large numbers of upper middle class children. Poor black children, often already skeptical of these qualities in the school staff, became much more openly challenging. While many of the children of all the races attending Chauncey and Hamilton still accepted adults' trustworthiness, a large minority did not. They were therefore primed to ask pointed questions about justifications for commands given to them in relationships of authority.

One can in any case generally expect more close scrutiny of the moral order and its relationship to specific commands from subordinates in schools than in many other kinds of organizations. Diffuse goals and a non-routine technology require subordinates independently to understand and apply the principles inherent in a moral order. The more a school emphasizes these qualities in its goals and technology, the more subordinates will routinely make independent reference to the school's moral order.

Further, the distinctive, though not unique, place of students in schools encourages them to be independently attached to a moral order. First, students are themselves the material to be transformed. Even more than professional workers, they have every reason to feel intimately interested in both the overall character of the organization's product and the processes used to transform it.[19]

Secondly, students receive no pay for compliant participation. Other extrinsic rewards are meager. A high school diploma is valuable for almost anyone. But this is a distant and abstract reward for an eighth grader, and one he is likely to think will be his whether he is cooperative or not. Ambitious students for whom good grades and a good record will be useful in gaining access to higher education and other selective postsecondary options receive some extrinsic rewards for cooperation. But these too are relatively abstract. And if high grades are to have meaning for some students, others must receive low grades.[20] There will necessarily be a large number of students who do not expect much return for their work. Thus since students receive little extrinsic reward for their cooperation, the intrinsic rewards must be heightened proportionately if they are to have reason to be voluntarily cooperative with the school's program.

The school's task is infinitely complicated in this context by the existence of compulsory attendance. Students must go to school whether they want to or not, by compulsion of law. In most cases they must go to a particular school and even sit in the class of a particular teacher without any possibility of choice in the matter.

In such a context, students who reflect upon their situation are likely to move in one of two opposite directions. They may become intensely involved in the intrinsic character of their education taking it for its own reward and thus caring about its nature. Or they may become thoroughly alienated from a context which compels participation but offers neither extrinsic nor intrinsic rewards which are of value to them.[21]

In Canton a sizable group went to each extreme. The most able students from professional families were not under pressure to obtain outstanding grades because most would enter the highly respected state university rather than more selective private colleges. They looked to the intrinsic character of their education for reward. The least able or least conforming of the black students found the school to offer neither intrinsic rewards nor practical assistance. They withdrew from commitment to its moral order.

In this perspective, it is not surprising that the staffs of many schools try to prevent their students from reflecting upon their situation. They try instead to present them with a consistent pattern of expectations which is so widely taken for granted that students do not think to ask what rewards they are receiving. But in such schools the potential for the kinds of questioning of authority which occurred in Canton is still always present....

## ENDNOTES

1. In the mid-sixties an article on the school as an organization in a landmark compilation of theoretical and empirical knowledge about organizations emphasized the scanty body of knowledge to review. (See Charles Bidwell, "The School as a Formal Organization," p. 972.) A decade later, in a book summarizing our knowledge of "educational organiza-

tions," Ronald Corwin reviewed a significantly larger corpus of research but one still slim compared with that on a variety of other kinds of organizations. (See Ronald Corwin, *Education in Crisis,* especially Chapter 1.)

2. For examples in these categories see the following studies: Philip Selznick, *TVA and the Grassroots;* Burton R. Clark, *The Open Door College,* Donald L. Metz, *New Congregations;* Gresham Sykes, *The Society of Captives;* Charles Perrow, "Hospitals, Technology, Structure, and Goals."

3. The goals of an organization can be perceived as end states of a raw material which the organization exists to transform. This raw material need not be inanimate matter changed in physical or chemical ways; it may be a person or even a symbol. Technology is the process which transforms it. Technology in this sense need include no physical hardware. Salesmanship and non-directive psychotherapy are technologies. So is teaching.

4. Recent studies which treat the effect of technology upon organizational structure are: Joan Woodward, *Industrial Organization;* James Thompson, *Organizations in Action;* Charles Perrow, "A Framework for the Comparative Analysis of Organizations"; and Stanley Udy, *Organization of Work.* My treatment here follows Perrow most closely, but it also draws directly upon Udy.

5. For a cogent argument along these lines in the case of the mental hospital see Perrow, "Hospitals, Technology, Structure, and Goals."

6. In a review article, Boocock concludes that we do not know "what the effective teacher is or does." (See Sarane Boocock, "The School as a Social Environment for Learning," p. 44.) Jackson also makes this point in an empirically based discussion of teachers' strategies for inducing learning and for assessing their success in this effort. (See Philip Jackson, *Life in Classrooms,* pp. 159–63.)

7. There are of course many reports of dramatic improvements in given situations with a change of methods, but one has to remain skeptical, wondering about the probability of a "Hawthorne effect." Writers such as Herbert Kohl, Sylvia Ashton-Warner, and A. S. Neill, who report great improvements with

their methods, may create their effects less through their actual techniques than through their own belief in the efficacy of the method and their expectation that their children will learn though others expect them to fail. (See Herbert Kohl, *Thirty-Six Children;* Sylvia Ashton-Warner, *Teacher;* and A. S. Neill, *Summerhill.*) Indeed, one of the most effective tools at a teacher's disposal may be an expectation that his pupils will do well, regardless of the reason for his expectation. (See Robert Rosenthal and Lenore Jackson, *Pygmalion in the Classroom.*) Brophy and Good summarize the recent literature stimulated by the controversy over this study on the effects of teachers' expectations on pupils. (See Jere E. Brophy and Thomas L. Good, *Teacher-Student Relationships.*)

8. Or they may become ritualistic, asking no questions about the benefits of their daily efforts but mechanically following local practice and then disclaiming responsibility for the results. For a detailed description of the bases of this adjustment see Gertrude H. McPherson, *Small Town Teacher.*

9. Compulsory education, requiring all students to attend school and the public school to accept all comers, compounds the technological problems of the school by recruiting diverse and partially resistant raw material. At the same time—as Carlson points out—compulsory education ensures the public school at least minimal public support whether or not it is as effective or efficient as it could potentially be. (See Richard O. Carlson, "Environmental Constraints and Organizational Consequences.")

10. Lortie describes in detail the way that the technological conditions of teaching, along with the structure of the school and the reward system for teachers, interact with processes of recruitment and training of teachers to create prevalent occupational attitudes and behaviors. (See Dan C. Lortie, *Schoolteacher.*)

11. Stanley Udy, "The Comparative Analysis of Organizations," pp. 690–691.

12. Ibid.

13. For a discussion of relevant organizational processes and conflicts, see for example: Donald Cressey, "Prison Organizations"; Richard McCleery, *Policy Change in Prison*

*Management;* and Sykes, *Society of Captives.* Erving Goffman documents similar processes in a variety of "total institutions" which process large "batches" of people, prone to resist the desires of the organization. Such institutions vary from public mental hospitals to conscript armies. See his *Asylums,* especially Part I.

14. Most of the available analysis of schools which calls systematically upon the study of organizations deals with contradictions between schools' bureaucratic structures and teachers' need for autonomy in dealing with their technological problems. See James Anderson, *Bureaucracy in Education* for an extended discussion of these problems along with a review of the relevant educational and organizational literature. The book also reports a study of the effects of differential use of bureaucratic rules upon the staffs of ten junior high schools.

15. The expectations, or demands, of staff members for one kind of structure over another are an important element in this equation. Formally, personal preferences of particular staff members as whole persons—rather than as role players—are conceptualized as part of the organization's environment by students of organizations.

16. There is no acknowledgment of moral responsibility at all from subordinates in many organizations. Inmates in prisons are the most extreme examples. Many students in public schools also do not make such an acknowledgment of duty to educational ends. But it is my argument that failing such attachment, a genuine relationship of authority does not exist.

17. For example, Robert Peabody asked employees in a police department, a social work agency, and an elementary school for a definition of authority. At least one-fourth of each group responded by naming their superior. And a majority of those giving other defining qualities responded in some variation of the general phraseology, "authority is a person who..." However, supervisors were less likely than subordinates to define authority in personal terms. (See Robert Peabody, *Organizational Authority,* pp. 87–90.)

18. The analysis of authority I am using here combines the approaches of Max Weber and Chester I. Barnard. Weber's classic analysis and his three types of authority—charismatic, traditional, and rational legal—stress the moral order, the role of the superordinate, and the relationship between these two. Weber gives relatively minor attention to the role of the subordinate and its relationship to the other elements of authority. (See Max Weber, *From Max Weber,* pp. 96–252.) Barnard, on the other hand, defines authority as the acceptance of a command by the subordinate. He argues that a subordinate gives such acceptance if the command is in accordance with the needs of a shared moral order as *the subordinate understands* those needs. (See Chester I. Barnard, The *Functions of the Executive,* pp. 163–74.) In the context of the school, where compliance depends heavily on students' intrinsic rewards, Barnard's insights are especially relevant. For a fuller discussion of the derivation and details of the model of authority used here see Mary Haywood Metz, "Authority in the Junior High School," Chapter One.

19. Indeed the best analogy for students in schools is in many respects not that of other organizational subordinates but that of clients interacting with free professionals. However, this relationship is altered by the necessity to regulate their activities for the sake of organizational routine as well as education. For an exploration in detail of the differences between professional–client relations and those of students and schools see Charles Bidwell, "Students and Schools."

20. Dreeben analyzes the process by which teachers in the elementary grades teach children to value grades as inherent rewards. (See Robert Dreeben, *On What is Learned in School,* pp. 37–39.)

21. For a somewhat different perspective on the same set of problems see William Spady, "The Authority System of the School and Student Unrest."

# REFERENCES

Anderson, J. G. *Bureaucracy in Education.* Baltimore: Johns Hopkins Univ. Press, 1968.

Ashton-Warner, Sylvia. *Teacher.* New York: Bantam Books, 1964.

Barnard, C. I. *The Functions of the Executive.* Cambridge, MA: Harvard Univ. Press, 1962.

Bidwell, C. "The School as a Formal Organization." In *Handbook of Organizations,* J. March, ed. pp. 972–1022. Chicago: Rand McNally, 1965.

____."Students and Schools." In *Organizations and Clients,* W. R. Rosengren and M. Lefton, ed., pp. 37–70. Columbus, OH: Merrill, 1970.

Boocock, S. S. "The School as a Social Environment for Learning." *Sociology of Education* 46 (1973): 15–50.

Brophy, J. E., and Good, T. L. *Teacher-Student Relationships.* New York: Holt, Rinehart & Winston, 1974.

Carlson, Richard O. "Environmental Constraints and Organizational Consequences." In *Behavioral Science and Educational Administration Yearbook, Part II,* Daniel Griffiths, ed., pp. 262–76 Chicago: Univ. of Chicago Press, 1964.

Clark, Burton R. *The Open Door College.* New York: McGraw-Hill, 1960.

Corwin, Ronald G. *Education in Crisis.* New York: Wiley, 1974.

Cressey, Donald. "Prison Organizations," In *Handbook of Organizations, J.* March, ed., pp. 1023–70. Chicago: Rand McNally, 1965.

Dreeben, Robert. *On What Is Learned in School.* Reading, MA: Addison-Wesley, 1968.

Goffman, Erving. *Asylums.* Garden City, NY: Anchor Books, 1961.

Jackson, Philip. *Life in Classrooms.* New York; Holt, Rinehart & Winston, 1968.

Kohl, Herbert. *36 Children.* New York: The New American Library, 1967.

Lortie, Dan C. *Schoolteacher.* Chicago: Univ. of Chicago Press, 1975.

McCleery, Richard. *Policy Change in Prison Management.* East Lansing: Governmental Research Bureau, Michigan State Univ., 1957.

McPherson, G. *Small Town Teacher.* Cambridge, MA: Harvard Univ. Press, 1972.

Metz, Donald L. *New Congregations.* Philadelphia: Westminster Press, 1967.

Metz, Mary Haywood. "Authority in the Junior High School." Unpublished doctoral dissertation, University of California, Berkeley, 1971.

Neill, A. S. *Summerhill.* New York: Hart Publishing Co., 1960.

Peabody, Robert. *Organizational Authority.* New York: Atherton Press, 1964.

Perrow, C. "Hospitals, Technology, Structure, and Goals." In *Handbook of Organizations, J.* March, ed., pp. 910-71. Chicago: Rand McNally, 1965.

___. "A Framework for the Comparative Analysis of Organizations." *American Sociological Review* 32 (April 1967): 194–208.

Rosenthal, R., and Jacobson, L. *Pygmalion in the Classroom.* New York: Holt, Rinehart & Winston, 1968.

Selznick, P. *TVA and the Grassroots.* Berkeley: University of California Press, 1949.

Svkes, Gresham. *The Society of Captives.* Princeton: Princeton University Press, 1958.

Thompson, James. *Organizations in Action.* New York: McGraw-Hill, 1967.

Udy, S. H., Jr. "The Comparative Analysis of Organizations." In *Handbook of Organizations,* J. March, ed., pp. 678-709. Chicago: Rand McNally, 1965.

___. *Organization of Work.* New Haven: Human Relations Area Files Press, 1959.

Weber, M. *From Max Weber: Essays in Sociology.* Trans., edit, and intro. by H. H. Gerth and C. W. Mills. New York-. Oxford Univ. Press, 1958.

Woodward, Joan. *Industrial Organization.* New York: Oxford University Press, 1965.

# Contradictions of Reform

## LINDA M. McNEIL

If you can't teach at this school, you can't teach—Magnet high school teacher (spring 1984)

We're not teachers any more. We're workers now.—Magnet high school teacher (spring 1986)

Ms. Watts is an extraordinary science teacher. She is one of the teachers who come to my mind when I think of Patricia Graham's recommendation that we recruit into the profession people who have a "passion for teaching," a passionate love of their subject and a deep commitment to bringing it to their students.

Ms. Watts' academic background includes degrees in science and engineering; she represents the level of professional knowledge and training for which schools are accustomed to being outbid by industry. She has taught in a predominately Hispanic high school, and she now teaches in an integrated magnet school in which black students are the majority.

Ms. Watts begins her physics course with the reading of a play about the ethics of physics. Right from the start, her students learn that science is full of emotions, moral dilemmas, and personal involvement. She tries to organize all her courses around the concepts and processes that help students see science in the world around them. Ms. Watts is the kind of teacher who is both willing and expertly able to expend the time to build her lessons in ways that will involve her students in the scientific questions and procedures she finds so exciting.

Although she was very reluctant to leave her previous teaching position, Ms. Watts welcomed the chance to teach in a magnet program whose official purpose is to engage students in active learning. Within such a program, she knew she would not only be allowed but required to create distinctive curricula in physics and physical science that would draw on her own "best" knowledge in these fields. In the company of other teachers developing active, engaging courses, she would be able to work on ways to structure classroom activities to link her students to the concepts and processes of the physical sciences.[1]

During Ms. Watts' first year of teaching, the district had pilot-tested a system of proficiency exams that, over a two-year period, would take both the choices of curriculum-building and the of testing students away from teachers like Ms. Watts and place them in the hands of consultants who design standardized tests. The content of Ms. Watts' courses would be divided into closely sequenced, numbered sections of factual content—"proficiencies." All of her lesson plans would need to be coded by number to show which element of the curriculum students were becoming "proficient" in during each lesson. The district office would supply her with a computer-gradable, multiple-choice final examination composed of the proficiencies recast as questions.

From her first year in the district, then, Ms. Watts' physical science course was proficiency-based. She was convinced that this format

*Source:* "The Contradictions of Control, Part 3: Contradictions of Reform" by Linda M. McNeil, *Phi Delta Kappan,* March 1988. Reprinted by permission.

did a disservice to her students and an even greater disservice to science. "You have to spend a month on [the physics of] machines," she says. "You get to the end of it and the students hate it, and you hate it for what it does to them. They may be able to figure out the right answer on the proficiency test, but they don't know anything about machines."

The curriculum mandated by the district is heavily computational and assumes background in algebra that many students do not have (and are not required to have) when they enroll in the course. The curriculum (like the tests from which it derives) is not about machines and how they work; it is about calculation, about using formulas to describe the mechanics of machines. "The students aren't going to remember those formulas—never. They are only going to remember that it was a pain," Ms. Watts says. "And this will add to the general population of people out there who say, 'Science is hard. I don't want to do science.' This is not a conceptual course, an introductory course. It's a calculation and manipulation course. I'm not allowed and don't have time to give them a conceptual basis—to say, 'You can make a better machine.'" In her physics class, Ms. Watts has tried to preserve the links between student and content, links that she has seen the proficiencies severing in the freshman physical science course. "If the district makes a proficiency test for physics," she says, "I will quit. That's it, period. I will not do it."

If Ms. Watts bases her physical science course on the district's numbered proficiencies and if 70% of her students make scores of 70% or better on the proficiency exams handed down from the district office, the district's reforms will be said to have worked. Ms. Watts' students will have "covered" the same chapter each week and will have worked the same computational problems as other high school freshmen in the district. They will have attained a minimum standard of knowledge in physical science.

In the process, according to Ms. Watts, they will have learned very little about what science is, about how to "do" science, about how science can be a part of their thinking. Her professional knowledge of science and her students' personal curiosities about the way the world works will have been set aside, while she and they meet in an exchange of "school science" that neither finds very meaningful. The institutional requirements will have been met, but Ms. Watts is fairly sure that any chance to learn real science will have been lost for her students.

The first two articles in this series suggested that behind the overt symptoms of poor quality in our schools lie very complicated organizational dynamics. The quality of the curriculum, the range of teaching styles, and the level of student commitment may not be what is "wrong" with schools. Each of these is an indication of the health (or lack of health) of the fundamental structure of the school. But an attempt to reform any one "problem" without giving attention to the underlying structural flaws may, as in the proficiencies imposed on Ms. Watts' courses, inadvertently make matters worse.

In Part 1 of this series, "Administrators and Teachers," I suggested that the American high school today embodies conflicting goals: educating individual students and at the same time processing large groups of students through to their credentials. The structure of the high school reflects this contradiction: school administration has evolved bureaucratic procedures to organize and control large numbers of students to insure that they are in the appropriate physical "place" and in the appropriate "place" on the path to a diploma. At the same time, the public expectation is that teachers will carry on the legacy of educating and caring for individual students—teaching course content and promoting learning.

As the most vulnerable of school employees, teachers stand at the point of conflict and must resolve the tension between these two contradictory purposes. The extensive classroom observations discussed in *Contradictions of Control: School Structure and School Knowledge* demonstrated that, when teachers feel that the administration and the school's reward structure subordinate educational goals to procedural controls, they will begin to treat their students in a similarly controlling manner. Feeling little sense of efficacy in the school as a whole, teachers will create their own efficiencies and establish their own authority in their classrooms by tightly controlling course content.

In Part 2, "Teachers, Students, and Curriculum," I described teachers who taught *defensively*, deliberately presenting simplified, fragmented bits of information to their students in the hope that students would comply with minimum requirements and leave the teacher in charge of the pacing of the course. These teachers often taught their most important content in the form of easily tested lists, they mystified complex topics, and they frequently omitted controversial or current material that might generate student discussion and thus disrupt the efficient "coverage" of the material.

Interviews with both students and teachers revealed that the "school knowledge" they dealt with in class bore little resemblance to the much more complex and sophisticated personal knowledge of the teachers. Students (and many school reformers) misread the dullness of lectures as a lack of teacher knowledge, and teachers mistook students' disappointment with this diluted content for apathy and a lack of curiosity. Although the students in the schools I studied did comply with course requirements in most cases, ironically they came to devalue what they learned at school. It seemed too divorced from the "real world" they knew from home and jobs and television. Indeed, "school knowledge" held little credibility for them.[2]

In my study of teachers' treatment of course content in a variety of school settings,

one school demonstrated that, when the procedures, resources, and structures of the school are organized in support of academics (rather than in conflict with them), teachers feel supported to bring their best knowledge to their students.[3] In Chapter 6 of *Contradictions of Control* I describe Nelson High School's educational priorities, which helped encourage teachers to bring their best professional knowledge into their classrooms. Finding that one school, where knowledge did not seem artificial, where teachers allowed their students to see them learning and asking questions (rather than tightly controlling all discussion), where scarce resources went first to instruction in a variety of imaginative ways, caused me to wonder what other structural arrangements might support the educational purposes of schools and overcome the organizational tendencies that reinforce defensive teaching.

## MAGNET SCHOOLS: STRUCTURED FOR EXCELLENCE

Nelson High School was an exception to the pervasive pattern of defensive teaching, student disengagement, and administrative attention to minimal compliance. This one school's building-level support for teaching and learning raised the issue of the difference that district level support might make in promoting the quality of education. More resources and policies originate at the district level than at the building level. If at the district level the tension between educating students and controlling them could be resolved in favor of the educational purposes of schooling, perhaps teachers would be even freer to bring their knowledge into the classroom.

A large urban district's system of magnet schools provided an opportunity to investigate this possibility. The district touts its magnet schools as "the best schools money can't buy." Organized as the district's response to court-ordered desegregation, the system of magnet schools promotes racial diversity by offering specialized curricula and excellent instruction. The district established specialized schools for such programs as engineering, fine arts, the health professions, gifted and talented students, law enforcement, aviation, computer science, and business. Teachers were hired according to their willingness and ability to create new courses and to work with colleagues to design distinctive programs. They were expected to teach so well that students all over the city would be willing to ride buses for an hour or more each day in order to attend these special schools.[4]

The federal court required reports on the programs and on student enrollments. District-level support for the magnet school program began with the efforts of the research and evaluation office in documenting enrollment statistics by race, but it also included the efforts of staff members in newly created administrative offices who worked with program development and provided support services in such areas as pupil transfers, transportation, and student recruitment. Although these supports centered first on equity, building-level magnet school coordinators were added as quasi-administrative staff to play leading roles in program development and daily oversight. In addition, some schools found added resources through corporate and foundation donations, state vocational funds for equipment purchases, and in participation from volunteers and school/community partnerships.

Months of daily classroom observations and interviews with teachers and students showed conclusively that teaching is very different in settings in which teachers do not have to choose between meeting minimum bureaucratic standards and teaching their students. When teachers do not have to teach in conflict with administrative policies, they are more likely to demand the best of their

students, to learn along with their students, and to place few barriers between their professional knowledge and their classroom treatment of their subject.

Watching excellent, engaging teaching thrive in the supportive structures of these magnet schools and seeing the resulting engagement of students of widely ranging abilities affirmed the possibility that school organization need not stand in the way of "real teaching." These very positive observations and their implications for non-magnet schools were to have been the sole subject of my research.

However, my study took an unexpected turn when these teachers, who had been hired to specialize; came under the influence of centralized policies of "reform" that aimed to standardized teaching and the content of lessons. The contrast between their work as professionals in magnet schools and the new directives that required conformity to a centralized model of practice provides a dramatic story of the dangers of centralized school reforms and their power to create the very mediocrity that they are intended to eliminate.

Before the reforms, these magnet school teachers exhibited a high degree of professionalism in their work with colleagues and students. Several mentioned that they had chosen to work in the magnet schools not only because they cared about school integration but because the specialization of the magnet schools would permit them to function as curriculum developers in a state otherwise known for its statewide adoption of textbooks.

Teachers in the few magnet schools that required high entrance standards said that they felt ambivalent about teaching in "elite" public schools. They chose to remain because of their belief that "all students should be taught this way"—though in their district it was impossible to have the freedom to design courses anywhere except in a magnet school.

"Teaching this way" meant first having the opportunity to collaborate with other teachers in developing the overall plan for the school. In a district in which faculty governance, even in the form of lively discussion in faculty meetings, is generally absent, magnet schools offer teachers a voice in shaping the program and a sense that a coherent educational program exists. Teachers in the magnet schools tended to develop a strong faculty culture, built around their commitment to desegregation, their participation in a specialized program, and their roles as professionals in schools aimed at excellence.

The magnet schools were not luxurious places in which to teach. In one school, teachers worked under asbestos-laden ceilings. Even at the science-specialty magnet school, science teachers rarely had adequate equipment for simple laboratory experiments. School libraries across the district were sparse, and they were no less so in most of the magnet schools. Some magnet schools had been placed as school-within-a-school programs in inner-city buildings whose declining enrollments needed a boost. Many of the school grounds were treeless, asphalt deserts that had long histories of neglect.

While more cheerful, better-equipped buildings and libraries would have made their teaching easier (and strained their personal pocketbooks less), these teachers found that the organizational support present in their magnet schools was a resource critical to their teaching. They managed to develop interesting courses and engaging teaching styles; they upheld a standard of excellence in a district historically known for the excellence of only a few schools in wealthier neighborhoods. They brought minority students into programs that would give them an opportunity to prepare for college, and they made science and engineering attractive fields for minority students and for girls. Their students spent hours riding buses and more hours reading literature, composing poetry, entering engineering design contests, discovering public and university libraries, and even asking questions in class.

The teaching in these magnet schools differed from school to school and from teacher to teacher. The common element seemed to be the teacher's ability to bring their "passion for teaching" into the classroom and to make classroom knowledge credible to students by making students participants in shaping it.

The teachers I reported on in *Contradictions of Control* had trivialized content by using it as a means of controlling students and by teaching defensively in order to gain at least minimal compliance from students and avoid unnecessary inefficiencies. The teachers in the magnet schools, on the other hand, did not feel that they were teaching in opposition to student apathy or administrative passion for efficiency. Their treatment of course content was almost exactly the opposite of defensive teaching.[5]

The midwestern teachers who taught defensively presented their most important course content in the form of lists of facts and fragments of information. They covered much material quickly, and their students knew what would be tested. The unintended consequence of their actions was the lack of credibility that such oversimplified, decontextualized information had for the students.

By contrast, teachers in the magnet schools tended to integrate rather than to fragment course content. They made—and allowed students to make—connections between lectures, readings, personal experience, current events, information from mentors in the community, and independent projects. Unlike the defensive presentation of the history of labor as a list of labor leaders and the dates of strikes, one teacher in a magnet school had her students stage a trial of robber barons. Through careful research and role-playing each student became a resource for the rest of the class on such matters as the competing interests of laborers, the survivors of workplace accidents, and the politicians, industrialists, journalists, and legal experts of the period. Her students debated "their" positions with fervor and were able to refer to issues and events they had studied long after the names and dates in a list-based lecture would have been forgotten.

The defensive practice of mystifying complex information rather than explaining it would itself have mystified most of these magnet school teachers. Rather than keep their lecture moving quickly by avoiding complex or controversial material, many of these teachers felt a direct commitment to demystify the world for their students. Exit polling after a federal election sent racially integrated teams of students into black, working-class white, and upper-class white neighborhoods to poll voters. Such terms as *interest group* and *social class* were no longer just vocabulary words in the government text.

A biology teacher knew that city children rarely think of being surrounded by nature. He required each student to build a collection of insects or leaves over the course of the semester, so that they could begin to appreciate the hundreds species around them and the purposes of scientific classification. The students also began to think about environments and habitats and to see themselves as gathers of information.

Mystification teaches children to "trust the experts" not to bother learning difficult things. Demystification begins to make the world theirs. When school knowledge incorporates personal dimensions, tools of inquiry—whether specialized vocabulary, steps in measurement in the laboratory, or ways of thinking—becomes useful to students for their own ends, rather that disconnected parts of "skill" units that teachers are compelled to teach.

The defensive teaching strategy that most offended the students I talked with in the *Contradictions of Control* study was the tendency of teachers to omit topics that were extremely current or controversial. Whether in sciences or in the humanities, limiting classroom knowledge to things about which experts had reached consensus maintained the teacher's authority over content and kept the students in the role of passive recipients.

The teachers in the magnet schools were much more likely to bring current issues and their own current reading and learning into their courses. A biology teacher attended summer institutes to learn more about biology and studied microbiology with a professor at a medical college. As a result, her courses were enriched, and she contributed to the district wide curriculum in those areas. More important, her excitement for learning was never hidden from her students. The week a scientific journal carried dramatically new information about DNA, this teacher brought the journal—and her own genuine excitement—to her biology students.

When the time came for students to choose a subject and a teacher/advisor for their independent projects, many selected this teacher and a biological topic. Some even found mentors in the medical and industrial research communities as an additional resource. These students were willing to be fumbling amateurs in the company of experts because they had seen their teacher take similar risks and achieve good results. "School science" and the continually developing field of biology were not separate in the minds of these students. Similarly, two teachers developed active assignments for bringing students into the study of the stock market, and a history teacher skirted no controversies when she allowed a Hispanic student to talk to the class about proposed immigration laws in light of his own parents' status as undocumented aliens.

These magnet school teachers and others like them offered no apologies for the work they demanded of students; few settled for minimal, passive compliance. High school teachers whose courses were related to the health professions felt a special imperative to keep their courses up to date by dealing with the personal, scientific, and ethical demands that the students would face in their rotations through the labs and practice areas of local hospitals. In doing so, they demonstrated what both Fred Newmann and Theodore Sizer have termed *authentic* evaluation: the assessment of students' performance for a purpose beyond generating grades for the grade book.[6] To have made the work easy merely to avoid student complaints and potential resistance would have been to lay the groundwork for serious incompetence once these students reached the hospital. Instead, the students wore their lab coats and their new skills with great pride, as participants in their own learning, participants whose knowledge mattered.

These magnet school teachers rarely had the physical materials that they needed for their teaching. Many subsidized classroom resources out of their own pockets and taught in inelegant city schools, when they would have been in great demand in more comfortable suburban settings. They chose the magnets because in them they could work as professionals, empowered by the structure of the school to place their students and their subjects at the center of their teaching. They had avoided school settings in which they would be de-skilled by state-adopted lists of textbooks and prescribed curricula. The results of their choice showed in teaching that kept school knowledge integrated with their personal knowledge, with their professional knowledge of their subjects, with the growing information and changing events around them, and with their students' capacities to become engaged in learning.

## MEANWHILE DOWNTOWN...

My study of magnet schools was to have ended with the documentation of the kinds of teaching and the resulting course content

and levels of student involvement that characterized schools in which the tension between administrative controls and educational purposes was clearly resolved in favor of the latter. Many of the teachers in the magnet schools would be prime candidates for certification by the Carnegie Forum's National Board or for positions as "lead teachers." The magnet schools in which they taught would have demonstrated within a traditional school structure excellent models of variations that empowered teachers.

However, when the school district and the state moved to enact "school reforms," these strong teachers were not distinguished from their weaker colleagues. They fell under the jurisdictions of two levels of reform, both of which aimed to improve teaching through tighter management of teachers. Both the state and the district aimed to bring up the lowest levels of educational quality, and both aimed to standardize teaching. *Both levels of reform significantly shifted the structural conditions of teaching and placed these engaging teachers squarely in conflict with new administrative controls over teaching and curriculum.* The district-level reforms removed the design of curriculum and of student assessments from the teachers' control. The state-level reforms dictated the teachers' role in the classroom and redefined teaching style as "teacher behaviors."

## Proficiency-Based Curricula

The district-level reforms took the form of a proficiency system. Partly in response to the superintendent's anticipation that the state would soon impose a set of standardized tests on the schools and partly from genuine concern over such factors as the uneven quality of education, grade inflation in weak schools, and wide variations in teacher competence, the district staff sought a means for raising the quality of education in the schools most severely at risk.

Such an effort might have taken a very different direction had it arisen as a curriculum issue, an issue of oversight of principals, or even a staff development matter. In this district, however, the problem arose in the research and evaluation office, and the solution was thought to lie in better *testing*.

The research staff borrowed a test model previously used for assessing minimum levels of mastery of basic skills in an at-risk school. For reasons of cost and ready availability, the minimum competency test, rather than a "yardstick" of academic excellence from, for example, the district's stronger schools, became the model for the assessment of teaching.

Under this reform plan, the quality of teaching was to be assessed through the testing of students. Curriculum was to be reformed to achieve not academic quality but ease of testing. Staff members recall that curriculum was criticized as lacking "clarity," in the words of the testing office, the goals and purposes needed to be made "measurable." Up-to-dateness, comprehensibility for various groups of students, rigor of thought, use of high-quality resources, coherence of information, and variety of instructional activities were subordinated to measurability.

Curriculum committees (and this process remains mystified for the teachers) consisting of central office staff members, local graduate students, some teachers, and apparently some clerical assistants selected aspects of each course on which students were to become "proficient." The curriculum components were taken apart, sequenced, numbered, and sub-numbered in a manner reminiscent of the transformation of factories by "efficiency experts" early in the century.[7]

For each semester's work, a private testing firm designed tests of student outcomes that were multiple-choice and computer-gradable. A teacher who followed the prescribed curriculum in sequence, keeping pace with the district's guide, would "cover" the material in time for the test. All lesson plans were to be numbered to match appropriate proficiencies, and some principals required that the day's proficiencies be posted for students to see. Teacher merit pay, building principals' bonuses, and newspaper comparisons of school scores were all linked to student performance on the proficiencies.

A subject such as English, with an enormous range of content, was limited to proficiencies in the form of reading comprehension selections and grammar. Other subjects, such as social studies and science, were transformed into fragments of fact and bits of jargon, similar to the lectures typical of the defensive teaching I found in my earlier study. Although central office curriculum staff members were concerned about critical thinking and conceptual content, the reductionist format of the proficiency tests and related curriculum material reinforced convergent, consensus-based thanking, with the student in the role of recipient and rote learner rather than active participant. The teacher's role was reduced to that of monitor.

To blunt the effects of the proficiency-based curricula—which official district policy claimed to be the minimum standard, not the entire curriculum, but which in fact overwhelmed class time—the magnet school teachers began to deliver "double-entry" lessons. The biology teacher who was working with medical college researchers refused to dumb down her lessons to match the proficiencies: one day she wrote a simplified formula for photosynthesis on the board, telling students to write it in their notebooks and learn it for the proficiency test. For the remaining two weeks' lessons, the teacher provided another, more complex version of the formula that the students helped derive through lab activities.

Frequently, the magnet school teachers would have to put their "real" lessons on hold for a few days in order to lecture on the proficiencies, or they would have to continually point out proficiencies during each lesson, so that students could keep them separate from the "real" information. The students were not unaware that often the "official" content contradicted the complicated interpretations and reflected only partial information and oversimplified processes.

It was ironic that the teachers in these magnet schools, whose teaching embodied an integration of their personal knowledge, their professional knowledge, their students' developing knowledge, and the knowledge they arrived at jointly in the classroom, were being required to cordon off their knowledge of their students and of their subject from the official "school knowledge."

Rather than call on these "best" teachers as models and resources the district reformers placed measurability ahead of substance. Like the administrators described in Part 1 of this series, they subordinated the educational purposes of the institution to the procedural ones. Unlike the defensive teachers, however, the magnet school teachers generally refused lo be de-skilled by the proficiencies. Either they went to great lengths to overcome the inadequacies of the new system and took time out to "cover" proficiency material at the expense of other course activities (rather than transform the whole course into fragments and facts), or they helped students keep parallel sets of notes.

When proficiency scores began to be tied to teacher assessment and merit pay, these teachers began to talk of leaving the profession or at least the school district. When Ms. Watts said that she would refuse to teach physics under the proficiency system, she was speaking for many of her colleagues. When ways to work around the proficiencies and the administrative controls with which they were aligned became too confining, the magnet school teachers would not acquiesce in the de-skilling that these approaches represented.

## Teacher Assessment

The state mechanism for assessing the classroom practice of teachers paralleled the district prescriptions for curriculum and student testing. Measurability was paramount, and the wisdom of teachers was discounted. Again, in the name of reform and in an effort to even out the quality of teaching across the state, an instrument was developed to standardize practice and hold teachers accountable to central management.

The assessment instrument, modeled perhaps unwittingly on the activity-analysis efficiency procedure for pacing assembly lines, transforms the tasks of the teacher into a set of *generic behaviors*. Derived from the language of classroom management and the narrowest applications of cognitive psychology, the list of 45 behaviors (55 in the first year it was used) enumerates such teacher actions as varying activities and waiting for student responses to questions. Providing "closure" at the end of class and using praise words are also among the behaviors that assessors look for.

The behaviors are meant to be scientifically derived from "research" on effective teachers (such studies are listed in a bibliography at the end of the teacher's guide to the assessment process). These "objective" measures include just three evaluation levels for the observer: "satisfactory," "needs improvement," and "exceptional quality"—the last a very subjective term for which little guidance is given either to the teachers or to the administrator/assessors.

The teacher assessment instrument is directly tied to teachers' progress through the career ladder and in fact was the cost teachers paid politically to have the state legislature approve a career ladder system of salary advancement The assessment system leaves little to chance regarding its implementation: the frequency of the observations, the number of hours of training for assessors, the scores needed to advance on the career ladder are all carefully specified.

However, the educational aspects of teacher practice are not specified. The latest edition of the assessment form does have a place for the teacher's signature, but it still does not have a place for a teacher to explain *why* certain classroom activities were undertaken or how the teacher's role in the class that day related to his or her knowledge of the students' needs or to the purposes of the lesson.

Administrator/assessors are not required to have subject-matter expertise in the courses they observe. (After all, these behaviors are supposed to be generic.) Worst of all, the assessment instrument reinforces the extreme of teacher centered classroom practice. Many of the teachers described in Part 2 of this series as teaching defensively could have earned high scores on the assessment instrument, even though their students found teacher controlled knowledge boring and trivial.

Decades of research on child development and the entire movement toward enhancing teachers' knowledge are ignored by this mandatory, statewide assessment system. Most teachers feel that to do the items listed on the form (enough of them to produce a high score) during one 50-minute class period would be to perform more as a marionette than as a teacher.

The teachers who want to hold onto a more personalized, professional teaching style must work around the assessment instrument, just as they must work around the proficiencies. Their students figure out quickly that class will be different on assessment days. A teacher who has developed writing workshops and is known for creative ways to relate writing assignments to literature says that when the assessor is due, she teaches a very traditional grammar lesson. "They would never understand our literature lesson," she asserts.

A 25-year veteran second-grade teacher reports that she has never felt politically motivated by a school policy before. But now "they have taken away my ability to do what I know my students need." A teacher of Advanced Placement courses reported using praise words during the class his assessor observed; later, the students who were accustomed to the teacher's probing questions and impatience with glibness, asked, "What were you *doing* in there today? Are you feeling all right?"

Teachers' views of administrative inability to link their best practice with the assessment instrument are not overstated. In a workshop devoted to placing students in the role of active workers in the classroom, a teacher asked how this could be reconciled with the teacher centered system of assessment. A principal stood up and said, "That's easy to figure out. When I go to assess a teacher and see the kids are working on projects or group activities, I just leave and come another day. It's like being there when the projector is running—you just come back some other time."

That principal and the designers and implementers of the assessment system have mistaken technique for teaching, classroom management for pedagogy. They are supported by a body of reductionist research and by political pressure for placing quality controls on public expenditures for education. It is little wonder that the magnet school teachers, who had chosen schools in which they could integrate their teaching style and course content and could continue developing their courses and their expertise, now feel like workers on assembly lines.

## THE CONTRADICTION

The contradictions of control evident in these two reforms, the proficiencies and the generic assessment system, are even more serious than those I discussed in Parts 1 and 2 of this series. First, by leaping from symptoms (some weak teaching, some low achievement scores) to remedies, these top-down reforms not only ignore many of the dynamics that produce low-quality instruction, but they actually reinforce them. By applying across-the-board generic remedies, they are dumbing down the best teaching even as they try to raise the bottom. Disclaimers that these efforts establish "minimums" have little credibility when the best teachers are the ones who feel most alienated and who are talking of leaving the profession (several have done so since this research began).

Good teaching can't be engineered into existence. But an engineering approach to schooling can crowd out good teaching. Instead of holding up a variety of models for practice and learning from their strengths, these reforms continue our historically flawed search for "one best way" to run our schools. These reforms take a cynical view of teachers' ability to contribute constructively to schooling; they choose to make the content, the assessment of students, and the decisions about pedagogy all teacher-proof, so that a standardized model will become the norm.

Such reforms render teaching and the curriculum inauthentic. If we are to engage students in learning, we must reverse this process. When school knowledge is not credible to students, they opt out and decide to wait until "later" to learn "what you really need to know." Mechanical teaching processes knowledge in a way that guarantees it will be something other than credible. Centralized curricula, centralized tests of outcomes, and standardized teacher behaviors can only frustrate those teachers whose "passion for teaching" has shown students (and the rest of us) what education should be about.

The teachers in the magnet schools I studied now have a superintendent who thinks that teachers should participate in curriculum development. That superintendent is working with the school board to dismantle the proficiency system, perhaps in favor of a system of diagnostic tests (that will help teachers

learn more about their students rather than control the curriculum) and in favor of new curricula produced by groups of teachers.

Meanwhile, the state assessment system has been ratcheted into place in exchange for increased teacher pay. The resources for pay increments along the career ladder have dissolved with the state's economic problems, but the system remains in place nevertheless. The state school chief has deflected criticism by suggesting that critics who oppose the system may not understand school reform; he has also implied that only the weakest teachers would oppose it.

Despite a national effort to professionalize and board-certify teachers and to increase their latitude for leadership within schools, outcomes testing is now on the national agenda, in the form of congressional approval for extending the reach of the National Assessment of Educational Progress. Before the federal government increases its role in outcomes testing and before a centralized curriculum inevitably evolves, this experience in this state should serve as an example that, educationally speaking, the emperor of standardized, generic education wears no clothes. The effects of such standardized reforms contradict the rhetoric of their purpose and leave us more educationally impoverished than when we began. Genuine reform will have to address the structural tensions within schools and seek, not minimum standards, but models of excellence. Reforms that make schools educational will require not adversarial relations between administrators and teachers, but the best collaborative efforts of all who work in and for our schools.

## ENDNOTES

1. Ms. Watts is a fictitious name, but the teacher I am describing is a very real, dedicated teacher who consented to be interviewed and quoted for my study of magnet schools.

2. See "Contradictions of Control, Part 1: Administrators and Teachers." *Phi Delta Kappan,* January 1988, pp. 333–39; and "Contradictions of Control, Part 2: Teachers, Students, and Curriculum," *Phi Delta Kappan,* February 1988. pp. 432–38.

3. See Linda M. McNeil, *Contradictions of Control: School Structure and School Knowledge* (New York: Methuen/Routledge & Kegan Paul, 1986), Ch. 6.

4. This ethnographic study of magnet high schools was funded by a grant from the National Institute of Education. See Linda M. McNeil, *Structuring Excellence and Barriers to Excellence* (Washington. DC.:, National Institute of Education/Office of Educational Research and Improvement, 1987).

5. See *Contradictions of Control,* Ch. 7.

6. Fred Newmann's project on alternative, "authentic" assessments has been profiled in a fall 1987 *Newsletter* of the National Center for Effective Secondary Schools, University of Wisconsin-Madison. Theodore Sizer's Coalition of Essential Schools aims for "exhibitions" of students' work, as advocated in his book, *Horace's Compromise* (New York: Houghton Mifflin, 1984).

7. See Raymond Callahan, *Education and the Cult Of Efficiency* (Chicago: University of Chicago Press, 1962), which reminds us that school reforms are always born of good intentions and always have unintended consequences.

# What Is a Teacher's Job?: An Examination of the Social and Legal Causes of Role Expansion and Its Consequences

## JUDITH H. COHEN

## I. INTRODUCTION

As the needs of society have changed, so too has the role of the school. Schools now provide services to children that traditionally were not within their responsibility. From day care centers to school breakfast programs, from school-based health clinics to after-school "latchkey kid" care, school services have taken on expanded dimensions to provide for children when either the family or the community has failed to do so. Reforms and expansions have transformed our schools into "a vast social service agency."[1] One commentator has stated that we demand not just education from our schools, we also expect schools to "cure society's ills."[2]

As the functions of the school systems have undergone transformation, so too has the role of the teacher in today's schools. While the primary role of the teacher has been that of educating children, societal needs and other external mandates for change have significantly altered the work of teachers. In the past, the family and other professionals assumed primary responsibility for the well-being of children. Today, however, much of this work falls within the purview of teachers in a new "catch-all" role.

Recently, a group of teachers enrolled in a graduate course was asked this question: "Are there roles that you have undertaken as a teacher that you did not expect when you began your career?" There were many nods of acknowledgment and when asked to describe some of these unexpected roles, these were among the responses:

> As a special education teacher (elementary) I have found myself counseling parents almost as much as I teach their children. I also feel that I work on children's self esteem and confidence as much (or more than) I teach academics.
>
> I meet a girl every [morning] at 7:30 to supervise the locker room door and locker room while she showers. Her parents own a store and have her out of the house to help work by 6:00 A.M.
>
> Last year I found myself playing the role of a psychologist. I had a child with severe emotional and behavioral problems. He took up a lot of time which was precious time taken away from my main role as teacher.
>
> Playground babysitter, mother role, cleaner, fixer, counselor.[3]

When questioned further about their personal reactions to assuming these "non-traditional" teaching roles, the teachers' replies revealed lack of preparation to take on some of the new roles, confusion about role priorities, and feelings of often being overburdened. Most significantly, the replies demonstrated the teachers' genuine concern

*Source:* Judith H. Cohen (1991). *Harvard Journal of Law & Public Policy 14,* (2), pp. 427–455. Reprinted with permission of the *Harvard Journal of Law & Public Policy.*

about being expected to help children in ways that go beyond their traditional instructional role:

> [Counseling parents] is a big responsibility and one that I do not feel I am qualified for. I do it, however, despite possible ramifications, because I feel that the parents really need this and it makes a difference.
>
> I was never trained to have to aid children in personal hygiene. Luckily, my principal got permission from the superintendent and parents to allow this [showering] to happen. This child could not continue to come to school in the condition she had been in and someone had to do something.
>
> It's a good feeling to see the smiles. It saddens me to see them cry. (Being a mother-counselor] is very tiring and draining, but also an awakening and enlightening experience.
>
> I don't want *all* the responsibility *all* the time.... [It] causes problems, because it interferes with teaching.[4]

This Article examines the social and legal causes of the expansion of the role of teachers in our schools and in our society, and describes several of the consequences. The analysis indicates that if teachers are going to be called upon to take on responsibilities that previously had been within the realm of other professionals, their roles need clarification. The Article also provides suggestions for modifying the preparation of teachers for today's schools and for creating the support systems that teachers need to be both effective and secure in their new roles.

## II. THE EXPANSION OF THE TEACHER'S ROLE

### A. Societal Pressures

For many children today, the teacher may be the only stable and continuing adult presence in their lives. It is therefore not surprising that the teaching role has had to take on many new dimensions. Those dimensions are determined by the varying needs of the children in a teacher's class. But who are the "typical" children in our schools, and what needs do they present?

From the time of "The Great War on Poverty" of the 1960s to the present day, there has been a "chronicle of growing concentrations of students with less of what is required to benefit fully from public schooling."[5] These students suffer from poverty, family instability, drug and alcohol abuse, and neglect. They often are of minority membership, have handicapping conditions, or are immigrants who have just arrived in this country. Additionally, the children frequently are not well-motivated, have poor literacy skills, and show little respect for authority.[6]

Many of the special needs of today's children are a function of the fact that children are often the victims of severe poverty.[7] This problem is particularly acute with regard to minority children. While the national statistics are alarming, those that pertain to children of the inner city and extreme rural areas, and to children of minority populations are shocking. Forty-five percent of black children and thirty-nine percent of Hispanic children were poor in 1987, compared with fifteen percent of whites.[8]

Children who are born in poverty make special demands on our school system because they have the most health problems but the least access to care.[9] Recent reports on child health in America have concluded that "[a]ll is not well with America's children."[10] T. Berry Brazelton, a prominent pediatrician, in a recent *New York Times Magazine* cover story asked the poignant question, "Why Is America Failing Its Children?" He succinctly put the problem in these terms:

> As a pediatrician with 40 years' experience with 25,000 children, mostly middle class, I have begun to regard the growing neglect and poverty of the young as the biggest

threat to the nation's future. I also see evidence that we could start preventing this terrible waste, with remedies available right now—but we seem to have lost the will even to think about it.[12]

Additional burdens have been placed on our schools by the huge movements of immigrants, often bringing to our country impoverished children from Southeast Asia and Central and South America. These children often speak foreign languages, come from vastly different cultures, and also suffer from poverty. While acculturating members of minority groups into the mainstream of American life has always been a role of schools, the other social needs of these children, and the inability of the family and social service professionals to provide care, accentuate this role in today's schools. "Public schools have been given the task of socializing these students, often a task that must precede educating them."[13]

Even the children of the "typical storybook" American family of the 1950s today have very serious needs. From the years 1960 to 1972, the annual number of divorces increased by eighty percent to over 800,000 per year,[14] with the result that "by 1980 12 million school-age children or one-fifth of the school population were living with one parent."[15] Living in a one-parent family has been found to be a significant factor in decreased cognitive development and decreased success in adult life, caused by a lack of educational achievement, bleak occupational and economic attainment, dependence on welfare, and poor self-esteem.[16] These children are more likely than those who have two parents to fail their classes, pose discipline problems, abuse controlled substances, and drop out or be absent from school.[17]

Teachers are also encountering problems created by the increasing frequency with which children leave for school in the morning hours without parental supervision and then return to their homes after school hours,

again without any supervision. A 1982 study found that 5.2 million school aged children under thirteen are "latchkey" children.[18] The lack of parental supervision has been linked to behavior problems and delinquency.[19]

Possibly the neediest children, and the ones who make the most demands of our schools, are those whose lives are confounded by drug abuse. As the large population of children born to drug-addicted mothers reaches the schools,[20] teachers are more frequently finding problems with low-range intelligence, neuro-behavioral deficits, growth disorders, and the whole range of problems associated with premature birth.[21] Children from drug-abusive families often come to school poorly fed, improperly clothed, and tired. Additionally, they suffer from a host of behavioral and emotional problems that make them less able to succeed in the classroom. These children lack the stability and support necessary to develop positive self-esteem.

All of these statistics and observations means but one thing: The "typical" child in today's classroom is more likely to suffer from poverty, abuse, and neglect than ever before. This reality has forced teachers—often the only stable, adult presence in the lives of these children—to take on the responsibilities of social-service providers and to care for children in ways never before expected. Consequently, the role of our teachers has been transformed from one primarily concerned with educating children to one that focuses first on meeting the basic needs of children that must be provided before they can be successfully educated.

### B. Legal Pressures

The social plight of today's children has not been the only factor contributing to the transformation of the role of teachers in today's schools. Equally dramatic pressures for change have originated from the courts. The environment of the school has been significantly changed by judicial decisions. A well-respected sociologist of education has written that "the most potent source for change [in education] has come not from within the school system, or from state and federal policy makers, but from the courts."[22]

Judicial decisions that affect teachers and their jobs have involved such broad areas as educational equity, professional malpractice, and students' rights.[23] It has been observed that "the collective impact of these decisions has been to inhibit teacher discretion."[24] Schools and teachers have had no choice but to assimilate and accommodate these dramatic changes.[25]

Probably the most significant of these changes resulted from the 1954 desegregation decision, *Brown v. Board of Education of Topeka*,[26] which has been described as a major revolution in American education.[27] This and other decisions[28] forever changed the composition of students in the American classroom. By bringing students from a range of backgrounds together into one classroom, these decisions forced teachers to raise their awareness of a myriad of social and legal issues that they previously had largely ignored.[29]

With the passage by Congress of the Education for All Handicapped Children Act (EAHCA),[30] another major revolution in American education occurred.[31] This legislation significantly increased the number of children with handicapping conditions placed in mainstream classrooms. Teachers are accordingly required to serve a much broader range of students who, as a result of their handicapping conditions, have diverse educational and psychological needs. The EAHCA also imposes due process requirements on teachers and school systems, thereby impacting teachers' day-today functions.[32]

The courts have visited a further impact on our schools through the relatively recent students' rights cases. These cases have created a heightened awareness of the protection of civil liberties and constitutional rights in the school environment.[33] Such issues as student dress codes, free speech, discipline and suspension, sensitive curriculum topics, and book choices are being approached with increased sensitivity. While teachers vehemently support the need to uphold individual rights and to respect the rights of students, this support is not without reservation. As one commentator has noted:

> In schools beset by chronic student misconduct, according students their due process rights and completing the paperwork required by various regulations may tax personnel, retarding their ability to maintain a reasonable degree of order. When dismissed students who have behaved in a blatantly disrespectful or dangerous way are reinstated because of procedural technicalities, teachers fear reprisals and worry about classroom control. Teachers also are concerned that overemphasis on student rights may undermine respect for authority and encourage students to challenge any teacher action.[34]

More and more, teachers are also becoming aware of the potential legal ramifications of their everyday actions. Is it "legal" to celebrate religious holidays? Can a teacher restrict student-run publications? Does a teacher have free choice in assigning books to be read or choosing a textbook? These are issues about which teachers traditionally were never concerned. Today, while they long for past levels of academic freedom, teachers work in the fear of litigation.[35]

These social and legal pressures, which have transformed the nature of our schools, have thrust teachers today into a position of being much more than just educators. Teachers have assumed responsibilities as surrogate parents, health providers, psychologists, counselors, nutritionists, care-givers, and social workers. As public school funding is cut and resources scaled back, already underpaid and over-extended teachers will surely find themselves filling even more roles.

A good example of the pressures teachers face at work is the present climate within the New York City schools. When the school year began in September 1990, a newspaper headline read: "New York Schools Open, Facing Test: Do More With Less."[36] The accompanying story noted that, at the same time that New York City students are acknowledged to be "poorer and…perhaps more troubled than ever before, the schools are required to meet their needs with less money than they had the previous year."[37]

The calls to raise the quality of education and simultaneously reduce educational funding, along with the other social and legal pressures discussed above, place an unfair burden on our teachers.[38] Unfortunately, few have acknowledged either the expansion of teachers' roles or their exemplary performance in fulfilling the nontraditional roles they have assumed.[39]

## III. CONSEQUENCES OF EXPANDING THE TEACHER'S ROLE

As teachers' roles have expanded, adverse consequences have arisen. All too often, teachers are finding themselves poorly trained for their new roles and confused about role priorities. "[T]he job of teaching has undergone a complex series of changes, changes leading to increased task ambiguity and insecurity."[40] As teachers take on more and different responsibilities, concern has grown that teachers may become unsure of what their primary purpose is, or even what may be done "legally" as part of a teacher's job.

Furthermore, many teachers complain that as the schools and their roles have undergone expansion and transformation, the "paperwork" dilemma and chain of command have become all the more intrusive and burdensome. School bureaucracies, with

their expanding regulatory tendencies, threaten the autonomy of teachers. As two commentators have observed, loss of autonomy causes a "serious threat to teachers' sense of efficacy,"[41] where efficacy is defined as "teachers' situation-specific expectation that they can help students learn."[42]

Whenever teachers do not believe that they can positively affect student learning, their personal sense of competence is diminished, and their behavior changes. This in turn adversely affects student behavior and learning.[43] Much has been written about job "burnout" and job-related stress in all occupations. Nevertheless, teacher dissatisfaction, problems with recruitment, and exit from the profession show that the problem is particularly acute within the educational community.[44]

Seven major causes of job burnout have been documented in the literature: lack of control over one's destiny; lack of occupational feedback and communication; work overload or underload, contact; overload; role conflict or ambiguity; individual factors; and training deficiencies.[45] Many, if not all, of these causes stem from the increasingly common situation in which a teacher is ill-prepared for the multi-dimensional tasks entailed in today's teaching job. Such a teacher often is confused and overwhelmed by the role ambiguity and ultimately sees few positive or long-term results. One commentator has observed: No individual can be all things to all people, especially today. Because of societal demands, increased technology, changes in the family, and a lack of trust in institutions, the typical job in today's industrial society has become more complicated, technical, political, and tenuous than ever before."[46]

Their multiple roles often force teachers to attempt to please varying and sometimes opposing constituencies, including school administrators, fellow teachers, parents, children, and their own family members. If teachers cannot resolve their conflicting role priorities, tension invariably results.

The increase in school-related litigation in recent years further evidences the consequences of teachers' role expansion and the resulting uncertainty. Litigation involving teachers has increased substantially in the past two decades.[47] The issues over which teachers litigate as plaintiffs have also changed. Job security has replaced teacher certification and teacher conduct as the principal issue in litigation involving teachers.[48] Whether role expansion and the resulting role ambiguity have created the impetus for this increased level of litigation has yet to be determined, but the pattern that consistently appears in school litigation is clear. Although power in the schools still resides with the school board, today's teachers are more likely than ever to seek legal redress when they perceive that their interests have been adversely affected.[49] Such litigation thus may represent a new form of teacher empowerment.[50]

As the responsibilities of teachers have expanded, so too have their needs for information and support to assist them in executing those responsibilities. Today, when teachers assume additional responsibilities within the school environment, or when they teach subjects that are particularly controversial, they are often required to operate without guidelines. Because schools do not provide teachers with role definitions, and teachers are not given sufficient guidelines, it is not surprising that teachers sometimes unintentionally overstep unknown boundaries.

The lack of sufficient guidelines in combination with the expansion of teachers' roles bring to light an even more fundamental issue: defining the mission of schooling. Without a clear definition of the school's mission, how can teachers know what their job entails? The debate continues to rage about the primary purposes of public education. Amazingly, the answer to the question "What are schools for?" has been given little attention both within schools and within institutions that prepare teachers.[51] It is not surprising, therefore, that some of the most dramatic changes in schools have been the unintended consequences of social pressures and not the outcome of a well-articulated philosophy of education or well-delineated role definition for teachers.[52]

Although the mission of American education is ambiguous, new demands for excellence in American education abound. A superintendent of schools commented that "the nation's schools are searching for concrete goals so that they may get on with the work of attaining them; but they cannot develop their own mission by themselves. Schools will need guidance from the rest of society."[53] If schools are to be the "cornerstone of American democracy,"[54] a realistic and attainable mission must be formulated.

What should be taught in the schools is an important aspect of the definition of education's mission. School curricula today consist of a variety of topics that are often the result of which fad is "hot" and which lobbying group has the greatest influence, rather than being the product of thoughtful choices and weighing of priorities. The inclusion of controversial, politically charged topics within the school's curriculum raises further the issue of what should be taught in schools and what is appropriately taught at home and through religion. Some believe that the teacher should share responsibility for training youth by teaching such moral precepts as respect, generosity, and intellectual honesty.[55] Others believe that the schools should teach more about religion in order to ensure that students receive a complete understanding of how history, literature, and the arts have been influenced by faith.[56] It is unlikely, however, that a heterogeneous community would ever agree that teaching about morality and religion are public school teachers' responsibilities.

## IV. LEGAL PROBLEMS CREATED BY ROLE EXPANSION AND ROLE AMBIGUITY

As teachers are asked to assume responsibilities that go beyond their traditional roles, especially when the responsibilities involve controversial matters, teachers must be educated about the associated legal ramifications. If we expect teachers to be effective, we must provide them with policies and procedures to accompany their new roles.

A recent incident involving two teachers who worked as advisers to a high school yearbook vividly illustrates both the changing nature of the role of today's teachers and the need for better guidelines. The publication of the yearbook that these two teachers advised created national attention when it was found to contain obscenities, anti-Semetic remarks, and racial slurs.[57] As a result of the Supreme Court's 1988 decision in *Hazelwood School District v. Kuhlmeier*,[58] schools have an increased responsibility for the content of student publications. Perhaps unaware of this precedent, the teachers mentioned above may not have understood their potential power—and obligation—to abridge the students' free speech rights if the speech threatened to disrupt materially school work or to violate the rights of others.[59] The controversial language, therefore, was left in the yearbook. Even though the teachers may not have been informed of the extent of their editorial prerogative, the superintendent of the school district placed responsibility for the problem on the two advisers and called for their termination.

The advisers agreed to accept a ten-day suspension and to issue public apologies. While it is most regrettable that any student was demeaned by the contents of the yearbook, it is also troubling that only after this incident did the school "district consider[] a set of standards for student publications."[60] Teachers should not be held solely responsible for an error when the school district permitted them to operate without appropriate procedures.

A recent incident in a Long Island school sparked further debate over the proper role of today's teacher. In spring 1988, Janet Morgan, a tenured, middle-school social studies teacher, gave her class an essay assignment in which the students were asked to react to a statement made by Jimmy (the Greek) Snyder about the role of blacks in sports that resulted in his firing by a television network. As part of the assignment, Ms. Morgan, who is black, gave the students copies of an editorial cartoon and letters to the editor published in a daily newspaper. One of the published letters was written by Ms. Morgan herself.[61]

When parents complained that Ms. Morgan should not have expressed her opinion to the students, the superintendent asked that she retract the assignment. Ms. Morgan refused to do this and also refused to turn over her lesson plan and grading sheet as requested. The refusal led to Ms. Morgan's suspension and a very bitter controversy that ultimately has been reviewed by the New York State Commissioner of Education.[62]

The incident resulted in a lively debate over academic freedom and the teacher's role in the classroom. The community in which Ms. Morgan taught is racially divided, with a large number of poor, black families living on one side of a major avenue, and more affluent, non-minority families living on the other side. The community contains all the elements of tension that could easily divide families and educators along racial lines, irrespective of the teaching issue under debate.

Ms. Morgan has claimed that her choice of teaching procedures is an aspect of academic freedom. The school district disagreed and claimed that Ms. Morgan has refused to acknowledge their rightful authority to supervise her actions. New York State Commissioner of Education Sobol ruled that Ms.

Morgan was guilty of insubordination by not submitting the grade book as requested, but more importantly, he rejected the school district's request that Ms. Morgan be dismissed. Dr. Sobol's remarks on academic freedom clearly reflect his interpretation of the teacher's role in today's classroom:

> School administrators play an important role in overseeing curriculum, but teachers must be given latitude to enable them to teach the curriculum in the most effective manner. Within the broad parameters of curriculum, a teacher must be free to engage in classroom discussion and debate in order to stimulate the exchange of ideas and critical thinking. Teachers are not neutral conduits of information from some external source to pupils' minds; they are active participants in the process of inquiry, raising questions, stimulating thought, and modeling commitment by expressing their own views.[63]

Unfortunately, the controversy has not yet come to an end. The school district has filed an appeal to the New York State Supreme Court. The district contends that Commissioner Sobol did not follow previous case law in rendering his opinion, and, moreover, if the decision is upheld on the basis of academic freedom, school administrators will be unable to influence either the content of classroom teaching or the methodologies that teachers employ.[64]

Another example of the problems created when teachers are expected to perform without clear guidelines is the debate regarding how to teach the mandated "hot potatoes" of the new school curriculum: sex education and AIDS.[65] Here, the debate has focused on whether the purpose of teaching these subjects is to instruct students that "certain behaviors are simply wrong and must be avoided or whether children should be educated to make their own informed decisions.[66]

As this debate continues, teachers are understandably uncomfortable with their role in teaching these subjects. A private conver-

sation with an official of the United Federation of Teachers (UFT) confirmed that the UFT is very aware of teachers' insecurity in their role as instructors of family life and sex education.[67] Teacher complaints to the UFT have focused on inadequate preparation to teach these topics and the lack of textual materials. Teachers obviously need training, support, and role clarity when they are asked to assume responsibility for teaching these and other controversial subjects.

The State of New York has started the process of providing its teachers guidelines in some of these nettlesome areas by universally defining teachers' responsibilities to report child abuse.[68] The legislature has also enacted legislation that requires school districts to provide specific training for teachers in this area.[69] Accordingly, each school district in New York is now required to educate teachers about the signs and symptoms of child abuse and to establish procedures for reporting child abuse. These procedures are intended to ensure confidentiality for the reporting teacher and to protect the child.

These guidelines, however, are just the first step. Comparable guidelines need to be developed in all states to address the full range of legal and social issues with which today's teachers are faced. Only with such guidelines will teachers know and understand their rights, their responsibilities, and, even more significantly, their roles.

## V. SUMMARY AND CONCLUSIONS

Current research on educational reform has led some to claim that teaching is a profession in jeopardy. Two experts have concluded that "our research indicates that the psychosocial conditions in the schools—the isolation of teachers, their uncertainty, their lack of support and recognition, and their sense of powerlessness and alienation—make it difficult for teachers to maintain a high sense of efficacy." [70]

The transformation of the role of our teachers and the uncertainties that have resulted are undoubtedly primary reasons for why the teaching profession has been so jeopardized. Today's teachers are as much providers of social services as they are educators. Their roles today are very different from the "traditional" teacher of past generations, yet their training remains largely the same. Teachers are often unaware of and still ill-prepared for the legal and social ramifications of their new responsibilities.

But while the expansion of the role of our teachers has undoubtedly had many adverse consequences, there are some positive aspects to the expansion. The multiplicity of psycho-social needs of children are better addressed by many segments of the education establishment. Support services for children, not only academic but psychological and medical services as well, are being built into school programs.[71]

In addition, new programs are being created in which schools are truly working in partnership with other community institutions and are involving parents as part of the school team, thereby building trust relationships among parents, teachers, and school administrators.[72] Such concepts as "school-based management" and joint decision making are being incorporated into the operation and management of schools, giving teachers more ownership in the programs in which they work. The concept of "teaching as a profession" has been used to elevate the stature of the work that teachers do and thus to attract and keep well-qualified teachers. Teacher preparation has been expanded to include new dimensions to equip teachers with the skills and knowledge that they will need to be effective professionals in today's environment.[73] Teaching internships, which provide more "on the job" training, have been reemphasized. It appears that teachers also are less compliant in passively accepting regulations or conditions that make their jobs untenable, more active in their professional unions, and more willing to become litigants against school districts if they feel their rights are being usurped.

In spite of these positive developments, more needs to be done, including the following:

1. Strengthen pre-service and in-service teacher education programs to inform teachers about the roles they will be expected to fulfill and to equip them with the necessary skills to perform effectively in those roles.
2. Create support systems in the school so that teachers have both referral networks and access to assistance when they discover students with unmet needs and when they themselves require assistance to address the problems of very needy children.
3. Improve the job security, monetary compensation, and status of teachers, and work to elevate public opinion regarding the value and expertise of teachers' roles in the lives of children.
4. Clarify teacher roles in the school system and provide guidelines for teaching controversial subject areas. Teachers should be included in the development of district guidelines and procedures, and new teachers should become well acquainted with this information.

While these specific suggestions should be implemented, more broad-based concerns should be addressed as well.[74] Many recognize that teachers' jobs have changed dramatically to meet the needs of our nation's youth, but there has been no general public acknowledgment of the complex work that teachers do.

The priorities of education must be made clear. How can this nation strive for excellence in the world marketplace and produce well-educated and technologically sophisticated citizens when so many children are lacking the basics of a decent life? If social service systems cannot address the needs of today's youths, and if the schools are to continue to be providers of more than education alone, educational priorities and the work of teachers need to be reconceptualized by public policy makers.

School personnel should be trained to become "resource locators and coordinators, constantly scanning school and community in order to match needs in a mutually productive manner."[75] The job of teaching must also be made exciting, rewarding, and enjoyable. Teachers must be chosen based upon criteria that will distinguish them as professionals; they must be trained as professionals; and they should be acknowledged and compensated as professionals. Schools should be reorganized both to meet the needs of children and to remove the bureaucratic constraints that presently demean teachers.

For the good of our youth, it must be acknowledged that teachers are composed of a group of dedicated individuals who are ready, willing, and able to tackle the demands of the classroom and the needs of the children in their charge. Until it is fully acknowledged, however, that the role of teaching has been dramatically changed by the dynamics of societal needs and legal dictates, and until systems are created to educate and support teachers for these new responsibilities, many teachers will remain frustrated, confused, overburdened, and ultimately less able to educate our children.

## ENDNOTES

1. M. Kirst, *Who Controls Our Schools?* 49 (1984).
2. D. Ravitch, *The Troubled Crusade, American Education, 1945–1980,* at xii (1983).
3. These are written comments from students enrolled in one of my graduate education courses at Adelphi University, Fall 1990.
4. *See supra* note 3.
5. D. Duke, *Teaching: The Imperiled Profession* 45 (1984).

6. *See id.*
7. *See* Brazelton, *Why Is America Failing Its Children?,* N.Y. Times, Sept. 9, 1990, 6 (Magazine), at 40, 42:

   Children are the poorest group in society, with more than one in five living in a household whose income is below the poverty level. $12,700 for a family of four. Despite medical advances, the United States infant mortality rate is worse than in some third world countries, and every *day* more than 100 American babies die before their first birthday. About one million teen-agers become pregnant each year, and as many as 18 percent of newborns in some city hospitals are born exposed to alcohol, crack and other hard drugs.

8. *See id. See also* Henry, *Child Poverty Up: Blacks Hit Hardest,* Youth Law News, July-Aug. 1985, at 12:

   The 1980's have not been a good time for children in the United States, particularly those who are black. Poverty among all children now exists at the highest rate in 20 years, since before the "War on Poverty." And black children are three times as likely to be poor as are white children.

9. *See* Brazelton, *supra* note 7, at 42.
10. G. Silver, *Child Health, America's Future* 61 (1978).
11. Brazelton, *supra* note 7.
12. *Id.* at 42. The statistics relating to child abuse and neglect are as startling as are those regarding poverty. In 1976, slightly more than one-half million cases of child abuse and neglect were reported. In 1988, that number jumped to almost 2.5 million. *See* Barden. *Foster Care System Reeling, Despite Law Meant to Help.* N.Y. Times, Sept. 21, 1990, at A18, col. 5. In 1986, more than half the children in foster care were placed there to protect them from their own parents or guardians. *See id.*
13. D. Duke, *supra* note 5, at 46.
14. *See id* at 47.
15. *Id.*
16. *See* I. Garfinkel & S. McLanahan, *Single Mothers and Their Children: A New American Dilemma I,* 11–14 (1986).
17. *See id.*
18. *See* D. Duke, *supra* note 5, at 47.

19. *See id.* The startling statistics of juvenile delinquency clearly illustrate the magnitude of these behavioral problems. In 1987, more than 53,305 children were confined in publicly-run detention facilities, the highest number since such data were first collected in 1971. *See* Marcotte, *Criminal Kids,* A.B.A. J., Apr. 1990, at 61. Although the data reveal that the number of youths being held for murder, manslaughter, robbery, and aggravated assault have declined, the number being held for alcohol or drug offenses, truancy and neglect and abuse have increased by 50 percent since 1985. *See id.* at 63.

20. A legal commentator brings problem into focus by saying that "[i]f cocaine use during pregnancy were considered a disease, its impact on children would be considered a national health care crisis." Fink, *Effects of Crack and Cocaine Upon Infants: A Brief Review of the Literature,* L. Guardian Rep., 1990, No. 2, at 1, 1 (published by the Appellate Divisions of the Supreme Court of the State of New York) (quoting Revkin, *Crack in the Cradle, Discover,* Sept. 1989, at 63).

21. *See id* at 5, 6.

22. S. Sarason, *The Culture of the School and the Problem of Change 9* (1982). *See also* L. Fischer, D. Schimmel & C. Kelly, *Teachers and the Law xxv* (1987):

    Today's schools exist and function in the midst of a complex legal environment, and it is difficult not to be aware of a wide range of legal issues that influence the lives of teachers, students, parents and administrators. It is increasingly clear that educators ignore the law at their own peril.

23. *See* D. Duke, *supra* note 5, at 61.

24. *Id.*

25. *See* S. Sarason, *supra* note 22, at 9.

26. 347 U.S. 483 (1954).

27. *See* S. Sarason, *supra* note 22, at 6. The recent national debates on equity, equal opportunity, and educational funding have increased awareness that court decisions alone have not created educational equity by race or ethnic group. The disparate impact of educational funding is readily observable by a comparison of inner-city and suburban school systems. "White flight" has left minority students disproportionately represented in inner-city

public schools, which cannot compete for highly qualified teachers with the resources, working conditions, and salaries offered by affluent suburban schools.

28. *See, e.g.,* Bolling v. Sharpe, 347 U.S. 497 (1954).

29. While population of students continues to become more racially and ethnically diverse, the population of their teachers (outside urban and poverty areas) has remained predominantly white despite efforts to recruit and keep more minority teachers. *See* Lochr, *The "Urgent Need" for Minority Teachers,* Educ. Week, Oct. 5, 1988, at 32, col. 1. Minority students outside urban and poverty areas most often do not have role models of minority teachers and do not see a teaching faculty representative of our pluralistic society.

30. Pub. L. No. 94–142, 89 Stat. 773 (1975) (codified as amended at 20 U.S.C. 1400–1485 (1988)).

31. *See* S. Sarason, *supra* note 22, at 6.

32. *See id.* (citing 20 U.S.C. 1415).

33. *See, e.g.,* Tinker v, Des Moines School Dist., 393 U.S. 503 (1969).

34. D. Duke, *supra* note 5, at 62.

35. *See* Stelzer & Banthin, *Teachers Do Have Rights, Update on Law-Related Educ.,* Spring 1982, at 41. The most recent report of the Carnegie Foundation found that only 55 percent of the teachers surveyed were satisfied with the degree of control over their jobs, as compared to 75 percent in 1987. *See Poll Finds Drop in Teacher Satisfaction With Degree of Control Over their Jobs,* Educ. Week, Sept. 5, 1990, at 9, col. 1.

36. N.Y. Times, Sept. 10, 1990, at Al, col. 2.

37. *Id.*

38. Much of the blame for the declining quality of education today, has been focused on the competence of those who teach. To increase that level of competence, many are advocating changes in what had been an automatic process of teacher certification. The certification process now often includes testing for pre-service teachers and variations in a teacher's course of study. A particularly troubling consequence of testing for teacher certification is the adverse impact on minority candidates. Teachers have brought legal challenges against such tests in many states, on the bases

that the tests produce invalid results and violate due process rights. *See Cohen, Legal Challenges to Testing for Teacher Certification: History, Impact and Future Trends,* 18 J.L. & EDUC. 229, 230 (1989).

39. *See* D. Duke, *supra* note 5. at 122 ("Without teachers, it would be difficult to locate a group of comparable size which is so disposed to work for the benefit of the young.").

40. *Id.* at 119.

41. P. Aston & R. Webb, *Making a Difference—Teachers' Sense of Efficacy and Student Achievements* 23 (1986).

42. *Id* at 3,

43. *See id* at 145–46.

44. The *Carnegie* Foundation has documented this problem using data collected from a recent survey of 21,000 elementary and secondary public school teachers. The survey concluded that "teachers are increasingly unhappy with their lack of authority, with their conditions and with the movement for better schools itself ....", *Broad Teacher Dissatisfaction is Pointed Up in National Poll,* N.Y. Times, Sept. 2, 1990, ‡ 1, at 24, col. 5

45. *See* A. Cedoline, *Job Burnout in Public Education 40* (1982).

46. *Id. at 50*

47. *See* Hooker, *Commentary—Teachers and the Courts, 1965—1986,* 48 Educ. L. Rep. P. 7, 7 (1989) (analyzing litigation involving teachers in public schools during the years 1965 to 1986).

48. *See id.* at 10.

49. *See id.*

50. Unfortunately, the education community has not been able to redress many of the significant problems without the expense and delay, of litigation.

51. *See* S. Sarason, *supra* note 22, at 261.

52. *See* id at 186.

53. Hess, *The Dynamics of Change in American Society: Implications for School Teachers,* Gov't Union Rev., Fall 1986, at 11, 11.

54. *Id.*

55. *See* Delattre, *Teaching Integrity: The Boundaries of Moral Education,* Educ. Week, Sept. 5, 1990, at 56, col. 1 (calling for an increase in the teaching of morality as part of the school's mission).

56. *See* N.Y. Times, Aug. 5, 1990, ‡ 4A, at 25, col. 1.

57. *See Yearbook Incidents Spark Debate on Advisers' Role,* Educ. Week, June 13, 1990. at (6, col. 1.

58. 484 U.S. 260 (1988).

59. *See* Kuhlmeier v. Hazelwood School Dist., 795 F.2d 1368 (8th Cir. 1986).

60. *Update,* Educ. Week, Sept. 12, 1990, at 3, col. 2.

61. *See Sobol Malverne Erred,* Newsday, Apr. 21, 1990, at 3, col. *1. See also* Address by Terence O'Neil, Annual School Law Conference, Suffolk and Nassau Academies of Law (Dec. 5, 1990).

62. *See Sobol: Malverne Erred, supra* note 61; Address by Terence O'Neil, *supra* note 61.

63. Board of Educ. of the Malverne Union Free School Dist. v. Janet Morgan, No. 12320, slip op. at 4 (Comm'r, Educ. Dep't of State of N.Y. Apr. 17, 1990).

64. *See* Address by Terence O'Neil, *supra note* 61.

65. *See* Suro, *Family Feuds,* N.Y. Times, Aug. 5, 1990, § 4A, at 26, col. 1.

66. *Id.*

67. Telephone interview with official of the United Federation of Teachers, New York City (Aug. 1990).

68. *See* N.Y, Soc. Serv. Law § 413 (McKinney 1990).

69. *See* N.Y. Educ. Law § 3004 (McKinney 1990).

70. P. Ashton & R. Webb, *supra* note 41, at 150.

71. *See* Schwartz, *Making the Grade,* New York Mag, June 11, 1990, at 36, 39.

72. *See* Brazelton, *supra* note 7, at 90. As a Law Guardian for children in Nassau County Family Court, I have had the opportunity to participate in multi-disciplinary team meetings held by school districts to monitor and ensure the well-being of students in their districts. One such team with which I work is composed of teachers, school administrators, school psychologists, school district social workers, hospital-based child-study team members, community counseling personnel, grandparents, and the law guardian. This unique partnership helps to coordinate efforts and provide for the multiple needs of a preschool, developmentally-delayed child

born prematurely to addictive parents, and to the child's two school-aged siblings who are also in special education programs.

73. *See, e.g.,* N.Y. Comp. Codes R. & Regs. tit. 8, § 80.14 (amendment proposed Apr. 6, 1990):

An approved teacher education program is one which prepares the teacher to create a developmentally appropriate learning environment; to work effectively with children from minority cultures, children from homes where English is not spoken, children with handicapping conditions, and gifted and talented children; to provide appropriate opportunities for children to engage individually and cooperatively in self-initiated, group-initiated, and teacher initiated activities that will enable them to construct their own understandings of social relationships, relationships in the physical environment, and the use of linguistic, numerical, and artistic symbols and tools for increasing understanding and communicating; to record and assess children's progress; to collaborate effectively with co-workers; to communicate, plan, and work effectively with children's families; and to use community resources, programs, and services appropriately....

74. *See, e.g.,* D. Duke. *supra* note 5, at 134–49.

75. S. Sarason, *supra* note 22, at 276.

## CHAPTER 6 REFERENCES

Cookson, P. W., Jr. (1989). United States of America: Contours of continuity and controversy in private schools. In G. Walford, (Ed.), *Private schools in ten countries: Policy and practice.* London: Routledge.

Erickson, D. (1986). Choice and private schools: Dynamics of supply and demand. In D. C. Levy (Ed.), *Private education: Studies in choice and public policy* (pp. 82–109). New York: Oxford University Press.

Goodlad, J. I. (1991, November). Why we need a complete redesign of teacher education. *Educational Leadership,* 49, 7–10.

Heck, S. F., & Williams, C. R. (1984). *The complex roles of the teacher: An ecological perspective.* New York: Teachers College Press.

Lieberman, A., Darling-Hammond, L., & Zuckerman, D. (1991, August). *Early lessons in restructuring schools.* New York: National Center for Restructuring Education, schools, and Teaching.

Lieberman, A., & Miller, L. (1984). The social realities of teaching. In A. Lieberman and L. Miller (Eds.), *Teachers, their world, and their work.* Alexandria, VA: Association for Supervision and Curriculum Development.

Lortie, D. (1975). *School-teacher.* Chicago: University of Chicago Press.

Male, G. A. (1992). Educational reform in France. In P. W. Cookson, Jr., A. Sadovnik & S. Semel, (Eds.), *International handbook of educational reform.* Westport, CT: Greenwood Press.

McNeil, L. M. (1988, Feburary). Contradictions of control, Part 2: Teachers, students, and curriculum. *Phi Delta Kappan,* 69 (6), 432–438.

Metz, M. H. (1978) Organizational tensions and authority in public schools. In M. H. Metz, (Ed.), *Classrooms and corridors.* Berkeley: University of California.

Percell, C. H., & Cookson, P. W., Jr. (1982). *The effective principal in action.* Reston, VA: National Association of Secondary Principals.

Semel, S. F. (1992). *The Dalton School: The transformation of a progressive school.* New York: Peter Lang Publishers.

Sizer, T. R. (1984). *Horace's compromise: The dilemma of the American high school.* Boston: Houghton Mifflin.

Verstegen, D., & McGuire, C. K. (1991). The dialectic of reform. *Educational Policy,* 5, 386–411.

Walford, G. (1992). Educational Reform in Great Britain. In P. W. Cookson, Jr., A. Sadovnik, & S. Semel (Eds.), *International handbook of educational reform.* Westport, CT: Greenwood Press.

Walker, J. H., Kozma, E. J., & Green, R. P., Jr. (1989). *American education: Foundations and policy.* St. Paul, MN: West.

Waller, W. (1965). *The sociology of teaching.* New York: Wiley.

Weber, M. (1976). Types of authority. In L. A. Coser & B. Rosenberg (Eds.), *Sociological theory: A Book of readings.* New York: Macmillan.

White, M. (1987). *Japanese educational challenge.* New York: Free Press.

Witte, J. F. (1990). Choice and control: An analytical overview. In W. H. Clune & J. F. Witte (Eds.), *Choice and control in American Education, Volume 1: The theory of choice and control in American education.* New York: Falmer.

## SUGGESTED READINGS

Arons, S. (1986). *Compelling belief: The culture of American schooling*. Amherst, MA: University of Massachusetts Press.

Barr, R., & Dreeben, R. (1983). *How schools work*. Chicago: University of Chicago Press.

Bidwell, C. (1965). The school as a formal organization. In J. G. March (Ed.), *Handbook of organizations* (pp. 994–1003). Chicago: Rand McNally.

Boyer, E. (1983). *High school*. New York: Harper and Row.

Bronfennbrenner, U. (1970). *Two worlds of childhood: U.S. and U.S.S.R.* New York: Russell Sage.

Coleman, J. S. (1961). *The adolescent society*. Glencoe, IL: The Free Press.

Coleman, J. S. (1965). *Adolescents and the schools*. New York: Basic Books.

Cookson, P. W., Jr., (1989). United States of America: Contours of continuity and controversy in private schools. In G. Walford (Ed.), *Private schools in ten countries: Policy and practice*. London: Routledge.

Cookson, P. W., Jr., & Persell, C. H. (1985). *Preparing for power*. New York: Basic Books.

Cookson, P. W., Sadovnik, A. R., & Semel, S. F. (Eds.). (1992). *International handbook of educational reform*. Westport, CT: Greenwood Press.

Corwin, R. (1970). *Militant professionalism: A study of organizational conflict in high schools.* New York: Appleton-Century-Crofts.

Darling-Hammond, L. (1984). *Beyond the commission reports: The coming crisis in teaching.* Santa Monica, CA: Rand.

Dworkin, A. G. (1987). *Teacher burnout in the public schools: Structural causes and consequences for children*. Albany, NY: State University of New York Press.

Gardner, H. (1989). *To open minds: Chinese clues to the dilemma of contemporary education.* New York: Basic Books.

Goodlad, J. I. (1979). *What schools Are for*. Bloomington, IN: Phi Delta Kappa

Goodlad, J. I. (1984). *A place called school: Prospects for the future*. New York: McGraw Hill.

Grant, G. (1988). *The world we created at Hamilton High*. Cambridge, MA: Harvard University Press.

Jackson, P. W. (1968). *Life in classrooms*. New York: Holt, Rinehart and Winston.

Johnson, S. M.. 1990. *Teachers at work: Achieving success in our schools*. New York: Basic Books.

Kraushaar, O. F. (1972). *American nonpublic schools: Patterns of diversity*. Baltimore, MD: Johns Hopkins University Press.

Lieberman, A., & Miller, L. (1984). *The social realities of teaching*. In A. Lieberman & L. Miller (Eds.), *Teachers, their world, and their work*. Alexandria, VA: Association for Supervision and Curriculum Development.

Lightfoot, S. L. (1983). *The good high school*. New York: Basic Books.

Lortie, D. (1975). *School teacher: A sociological study*. Chicago: University of Chicago Press.

McNeil, L. M. (1986). *Contradictions of control: School structure and school knowledge*. New York: Routledge.

McNeil, L. M. (1988a). Contradictions of control, Part I: Administrators and teachers. *Phi Delta Kappan, 69* (5), 333–339.

McNeil, L. M. (1988b). Contradictions of control, Part II: Teachers, students and curriculum. *Phi Delta Kappan, 69* (6), 432–438.

McNeil, L. M. (1988c). Contradictions of control, Part III: Contradictions of reform. *Phi Delta Kappan, 69* (7), 478–485.

Metz, M. H. (1978). *Classrooms and corridors: The crisis of authority in desegregated secondary schools.* Berkeley, CA: University of California Press.

Metz, M. H. (1986). *Different by design: The context and character of three magnet schools.* New York: Routledge and Kegan Paul.

Meyer, J. W. (1977, July). The effects of education as an institution. *American Journal of Sociology, 83,* 55–77.

Parsons, T. (1959). The school class as a social system. *Harvard Educational Review, 29,* 297–308.

Passow, A. H., et al. (1976). *The national case study: An empirical comparative study of education in twenty-one countries.* New York: Wiley.

Sizer, T. R. (1984). *Horace's compromise: The dilemma of the American high school.* Boston: Houghton Mifflin.

Sizer, T. R. (1992). *Horace's school: Redesigning the American high school.* Boston: Houghton Mifflin.

Swidler, A. (1979). *Organizations without authority: Dilemmas of social control in free schools.* Cambridge, MA: Harvard University Press.

Waller, W. (1965). *The sociology of teaching.* New York: Wiley.

White, M. (1987). *The Japanese educational challenge: A commitment to children.* New York: The Free Press.

Wirt, F., & Kirst, M. (1982). *Schools in conflict.* San Francisco: McCutchan.

Zajda, J. I. (1980). *Education in the U.S.S.R.* New York: Pergamon.

C H A P T E R 7

# Curriculum, Pedagogy, and the Transmission of Knowledge

In Chapter 6, we looked at the organization and structure of U.S. schools. In this chapter, we will examine what goes on inside of the schools by focusing on curriculum and teaching practices. As we argued in Chapter 4, sociologists of education suggest that schools produce important cognitive and noncognitive results and affect students' lives in significant ways. The important question, however, is how do the schools do this? The answer, in part, lies in what the schools teach and how they teach it. This chapter explores these issues in detail.

## WHAT DO THE SCHOOLS TEACH?

Teachers and students in teacher education programs too often think about what the schools teach in very simplistic terms. Their answer to the question is that the schools teach a specific curriculum, one that is mandated by the state education department and implemented in an organized manner within the schools. This view defines the curriculum as an objective and organized body of knowledge to be transmitted to students. Unfortunately, such a view simplifies the complexity of the curriculum and ignores the social and political dimensions of what is taught in schools.

Traditional approaches to the curriculum have been concerned with the science of the curriculum. These approaches view the curriculum as objective bodies of knowledge and examine the ways in which this knowledge may be designed, taught, and evaluated. Using a technical-rational model, traditional curriculum theorists and curriculum planners are not concerned with why the curriculum looks as it does, but rather with how it can be effectively designed and transmitted to students. Students in teacher education programs, from this perspective, are taught to design curriculum using goals and objectives and to evaluate it in terms of the effectiveness of student learning. Although there may be some practical merit for prospective teachers to understand how to develop curriculum strategies, these traditional approaches eschew important political, sociological, historical, and philosophical questions about what is taught in schools. The effects of such teacher education practices is that teachers look at the curriculum from this "objectivist" perspective and therefore seldom question critically the central component of what they do on a daily basis: transmit knowledge and values to students.

Beginning in the 1960s and 1970s, sociologists of education and curriculum began to challenge the traditional theories of curriculum. Rather than viewing curriculum as an objective body of knowledge, they suggested that the curriculum is an organized body of knowledge that represents political, social, and ideological interests. The "new sociology of education" ushered in by the works of Michael F. D. Young (1971) and Basil Bernstein (1973, 1977) in Britain looked critically at the curriculum as a reflection of the dominant interests in society and suggested that what is taught in schools is a critical component of the effects of schooling.

Drawing on the insights of the sociology of knowledge (Berger & Luckmann, 1967; Durkheim, 1947, 1954; Mannheim, 1936; Marx & Engels, 1947), the new sociology did not view the curriculum as value neutral, but rather as the subject for critical and ideological analysis. Although the new sociology certainly had a radical flavor to it and inspired what has been labeled "critical curriculum theory" (Apple 1978, 1982a, 1982b; Giroux 1981, 1983a, 1983b), the insights of the sociology of curriculum do not always have a radical perspective. What is important about the sociological approach to the curriculum is that it rejects the view that the curriculum is objective and instead insists that the curriculum be viewed as subjectively reflecting particular interests within a society. What these interests are and how the curriculum reflects them is a question of ideological debate as well as for empirical investigation.

We will return to sociological studies of the curriculum later in this chapter. First, we will examine the historical and philosophical dimensions of the curriculum. Whereas the sociology of curriculum analyzes what is taught in schools, the history of the curriculum examines what was taught, the politics of the curriculum examines the battles and conflicts over what is and should be taught, and the philosophy of the curriculum examines what ought to be taught and why.

## THE HISTORY AND PHILOSOPHY OF THE CURRICULUM

The history of the curriculum helps explain why the curriculum looks as it does today. Kliebard (1986), in his book *The Struggle for the American Curriculum: 1893–1958,* outlines four different types of curriculum in the twentieth century: humanist, social efficiency, developmental, and social meliorist, each of which had a different view of the goals of schooling.

The *humanist curriculum* reflects the idealist philosophy that knowledge of the traditional liberal arts is the cornerstone of an educated citizenry and that the purpose of education is to present to students the best of what has been thought and written. Traditionally, this curriculum focused on the Western heritage as the basis for intellectual development, although some who support this type of curriculum argue that the liberal arts need not focus exclusively on the Western tradition. This curriculum model dominated nineteenth-century and early twentieth-century U.S. education and was codified in the National Education Association's Committee of Ten report issued in 1893, "which recommended that all secondary students, regardless of whether they intended to go to college, should be liberally educated and should study English, foreign languages, mathematics, history, and science" (Ravitch, 1983, p. 47).

Although the view that a Western liberal arts curriculum for all secondary students did not remain the dominant model of secondary schooling in the twentieth century, recent conservative critics have called for a return to the humanist curriculum. As we noted earlier, critics such as Bennett (1988), Hirsch (1987), and Ravitch and Finn (1987) have argued that U.S. students do not know enough about their cultural heritage because the school curriculum has not emphasized it for all students. They have proposed that the schools should return to a traditional liberal arts curriculum for all students and that this curriculum should focus, although not necessarily exclusively, on the Western tradition. Bennett (1988), as Secretary of Education during the Reagan administration, took an activist posture in promoting such curriculum reform. In his proposals for a model elementary and secondary curriculum, he emphasized the need for a traditional core of subjects and readings that would teach all students a common set of worthwhile knowledge and an array of intellectual skills.

From a functionalist perspective, the conservative curriculum reformers of the 1980s and 1990s believe that the purpose of schooling is to transmit a common body of knowledge in order to reproduce a common cultural heritage. As we noted earlier, the problem with this view, from a conflict perspective, is that it assumes a common culture, which may not exist. It is this disagreement about the role of schools in transmitting a common culture that has been at the heart of disagreements over curriculum in the twentieth century.

The *social efficiency curriculum* was a philosophically pragmatist approach developed in the early twentieth century as a putatively democratic response to the development of mass public secondary education. As we suggested in Chapter 3, the introduction of the comprehensive high school was marked by the processes of differentiated curriculum, scientific management of the schools and the curriculum, and standardized testing of students for placement into ability groups and/or curriculum tracks (Oakes, 1985, Chapter 2; Powell, Cohen, & Ferrar, 1985, Chapter 5). Rather than viewing the need for a common academic curriculum for all students, as with the humanist tradition, the social efficiency curriculum was rooted in the belief that different groups of students, with different sets of needs and aspirations, should receive different types of schooling. Although this perspective emerged from the progressive visions of Dewey about the need for individualized and flexible curriculum, many critics (Cremin, 1961; Hofstadter, 1966; Sadovnik, 1991; Tyack, 1974) believe that the social efficiency curriculum was a distortion of his progressive vision.

The publication of the *Cardinal Principles of Secondary Education* in 1918 by the National Education Association's Commission on the Reorganization of Secondary Schools represented a direct contrast to the humanist tradition of the Committee of Ten. This report ushered in what Ravitch (1983, p. 48) has termed *pedagogical progressivism* and stressed the relationship between schooling and the activities of adults within society. Given the stratified nature of adult roles, the school curriculum was tailored to prepare students for these diverse places in society. The result, as we argued in Chapter 3, was that students often received very different curricula, based on their race, class, and gender. In criticizing the distortion of early progressivism, Ravitch (1983, p. 48) wrote, "The social efficiency element of the *Cardinal Principles,* which inverted Dewey's notion of the school as a lever of social reform into the school as a mechanism to adjust the individual to society, became the cornerstone of the new progressivism." It is important to note the distinction made between this new progressivism and its social efficiency bent and the principles of Dewey, that we believe were profoundly distorted by this view of curriculum.

The development of the social efficiency curriculum in the twentieth century was related to the scientific management of the schools. Based on the writings of Frederick Taylor about the management of the factory system, the administration of schools began to mirror this form of social organization, with its emphasis on efficiency, time on task, and a social division of labor (see Callahan, 1962; Tyack, 1974; Tyack & Hansot, 1982). The scientific management of the curriculum involved both the division of knowledge into strictly defined areas and its transmission into scientifically defined goals and objectives, as well as the division of students into different aspects of the curriculum, based on ability. Beginning in the early twentieth century, the definition of ability became increasingly based on performance on standardized tests.

The development of standardized testing was inextricably related to the differentiation of the curriculum. At the elementary school level, intelligence tests and reading tests were used to assign students to ability groups and ability-grouped classes. At the secondary level, standardized tests, as well as previous school achievement (and other factors not related to ability), were used to place students into different curriculum tracks: academic, for college bound students; vocational, to prepare students directly for the postsecondary world of work; and general, which usually was an academic curriculum taught at a lower level. These practices, which will be discussed later in this chapter, have become a defining characteristic of U.S. education. The important point, however, is that the development of standardized testing became the process by which students were placed in different curriculum tracks, putatively in a fair and meritocratic manner. The extent to which such placement has been meritocratic (i.e., based on ability) has been a controversial and hotly debated issue. It will be discussed in Chapter 9.

Putting the fairness of curriculum placement aside for the moment, the basic assumption of the social efficiency curriculum that different groups of students should receive different curricula has come increasingly under criticism from both conservatives and radicals. Conservatives argue that the separation of the curriculum into different tracks has led to the denigration of the traditional purpose of schooling—to pass on a common culture to all citizens. Radicals argue that the placement into curriculum tracks has been based on race, class, and gender and thus has limited the life chances of minority, working class, and female students, who, because they are often more likely to elect or wind up in general or vocational tracks, are less likely to go on to college. These are empirical questions that will be discussed in Chapter 9.

The important point is that the curriculum tracking associated with the social efficiency curriculum is a subject of considerable research and debate. Moreover, many critics question the moral basis of providing different students with such radically different school experiences. This issue returns us to the very nature and purpose of schooling in a complex and diverse society: Should it be the same for everyone or should it be variable and flexible, given the diverse nature of the social division of labor?

The *developmentalist curriculum* is related to the needs and interests of the student rather than the needs of society. This curriculum emanated from the aspects of Dewey's writings related to the relationship between the child and the curriculum (Dewey, 1956), as well as developmental psychologists such as Piaget, and it emphasized the process of teaching as well as its content. This philosophically progressive approach to teaching was student centered and was concerned with relating the curriculum to the needs and interests of each child at particular developmental stages. Thus, it stressed flexibility in both what was taught and how it was taught, with the emphasis on the development of each student's individual capacities. Moreover, the developmental curriculum stressed the importance of relating schooling to the life experiences of each child in a way that would make education come alive in a meaningful manner. The teacher, from this perspective, was not a transmitter of knowledge but rather a facilitator of student growth.

Although school and curriculum historians (Kliebard, 1986; Spring, 1989) pointed out that the developmental curriculum model was not very influential in the U.S. public schools, they also noted that it has been profoundly influential in teacher education programs, as well as an important model in independent and alternative schools. It was in the private, independent sector that this view of curriculum and pedagogy first became dominant, with Dewey's progressive principles implemented in a number of independent progressive schools, such as Bank Street (Antler, 1987), City and Country (Pratt, 1924), Dalton (Semel, 1992), Putney (Lloyd, 1987), and Shady Hill (Yeomans, 1979).

Furthermore, in the 1960s and 1970s, the reemergence of what Ravitch (1983, pp. 239–256) has called *romantic progressivism* occurred, placing its philosophical allegiance squarely within this form of curriculum and pedagogy. Among its most radical proponents was the British psychoanalyst and educator A. S. Neill, whose boarding school Summerhill had no required curriculum and became a prototype of the "open" and "free" schools of the period.

Although the influence of the developmental curriculum has been marginal in the public schools (Cuban, 1984) and its advocacy waned in the conservative era of the 1980s and 1990s, there are still remnants of it in both the public and private sectors. In the private sector, many of the early progressive schools still exist and in varying degrees still reflect their early progressive character. Some, such as Bank Street and City and Country, remain faithful to their founders' visions; others, such as Dalton, have been transformed considerably into a more traditional humanist model (Semel, 1992). In the public sector, the whole-language movement for teaching reading and writing is developmental in its approach. Rather than teaching reading and writing through traditional basal readers, it relates literacy instruction to the experiences and developmental stages of children (Bennett & LaCompte, 1990, p. 186).

The *social meliorist curriculum,* that was philosophically social reconstructionist (the radical wing of progressive education), developed in the 1930s, both out of the writings of Dewey, who was concerned with the role of the schools in reforming society (Dewey, 1956), as well as a response to the growing dominance of the social efficiency curriculum. Two of the most influential of the social meliorists were two Teachers College (Columbia University) professors, George Counts and Harold Rugg, who radicalized Dewey's philosophy into an explicit theory that the schools should change society, or, at the least, help solve its fundamental problems. In books such as Counts's *Dare the Schools Build a New Social Order?* (1932) and Rugg's writings on curriculum, these critics proposed that the school curriculum should teach students to think and to help solve societal problems, if not to change the society itself.

Although this view of curriculum never challenged the dominance of the social efficiency model, it has continued to influence curriculum theory in the United States and elsewhere. The social meliorist tradition is the precursor to what is called *contemporary critical curriculum theory,* with Apple and Giroux's work the most important examples. Additionally, philosophers such as Maxine Greene and Paulo Freire, discussed in Chapter 5, adopt a consciously social meliorist view of curriculum, which stresses the role of the curriculum in moving students to become aware of societal problems and to become active in changing the world. Although these writings are sometimes presented to prospective teachers in teacher education programs, the effects of the social meliorist model in public schools is minimal. For the most part, it has been the social efficiency curriculum, much more than the other three models, that is responsible for what is taught in U.S. schools.

The social efficiency curriculum resulted in the organization of the curriculum into distinct tracks. Although we will discuss the stratification of the curriculum later in this chapter, it is important to note that the degree of overlap between various segments of the curriculum varied according to the type of school and its philosophy of curriculum. Bernstein (1977) argued that curriculum may be either strongly classified (i.e., where there is a strong distinction between academic subjects such as mathematics, science, history, literature, music, art, etc.) or weakly classified (i.e., where there is integration and overlap between academic subjects (such as mathematics and science, social studies, humanities—including history, literature, art, music, etc.). Additionally, in the social efficiency curriculum there may be strong classification between academic and vocational curricula, with students taking the majority of their courses in one area or the other, or weak classification, with students taking courses in both areas. There have been both philosophical and sociological factors in the organization of the curriculum.

From a philosophical vantage point, traditionalists (conservatives) supported the humanist curriculum model and the strong classification between academic subjects. This was necessary, they argued, to properly transmit the traditional cultural knowledge. Progressives tended to support a more integrative curriculum, discouraging the separation of subjects. In many of the early progressive schools, such as the Lincoln School in New York City, an integrative core curriculum revolving around common themes rather than subjects was favored. This approach is now reappearing in the contemporary whole-language movement and in the thematic core curriculum at New York City's Central Park East School, a public progressive school.

From a sociological vantage point, the organization of the curriculum has been stratified according to the social class composition of the school. Elite private schools, for example, have always had a humanist curriculum with strong classification between academic subjects. Public high schools have had a social efficiency curriculum with strong classification between academic and vocational subjects. Within the public system, the degree to which the academic track has mirrored the humanist curriculum has varied, often in relation to the social class composition of the students. Progressive private and public schools have had a weakly classified academic curriculum, that reflected their particular philosophy of education, but as Bernstein (1977) suggested, this philosophy reflected their particular middle- and upper middle-class preferences. Thus, the organization of the curriculum has not been and is not now a simple matter. It relates to philosophical, sociological, and political factors. We now turn to the sociological and political dimensions.

## THE POLITICS OF THE CURRICULUM

The politics of curriculum analyzes the struggles over different conceptions of what should be taught. As we have noted, the history of the U.S. curriculum may be understood in terms of different models of school knowledge. Throughout the twentieth century, various groups, both inside and outside the schools, have fought to shape and control the schools' curriculum. Who these groups are and how much control they have is a subject of debate. For example, functionalists, subscribing to a pluralist democratic model of schooling, believe that the curriculum represents a democratic consensus about what should be taught. Neo-Marxist conflict theorists believe that the dominant capitalist class controls what is taught in school. Non-Marxist conflict theorists believe that many groups struggle over the curriculum, with different groups winning and losing at different historical periods.

Ravitch (1983) has documented the long and conflictual struggles that have marked U.S. educational history. Her history of education in the twentieth century reveals a pattern of conflict between various groups about the purpose and goals of the schools. Within this context, the curriculum became contested terrain—the subject of heated controversy and disagreements. Earlier in this chapter, we presented the four curriculum models that have predominated in the twentieth century; in this section, we will discuss the politics of curriculum and how various groups attempt to shape the curriculum to reflect their own interests and ideologies.

The central question in the politics of the curriculum is: *Who shapes the curriculum?* As the new sociology of education suggests, the curriculum is not a value-neutral, objective set of information to be transmitted to students; rather, it represents what a culture wants its students to know. From this perspective, curriculum represents culturally valued knowledge. The question remains, however: Whose values are represented and how do groups manage to translate their values into the subjects that are taught in school?

These questions are first and foremost related to power. The ability to shape the curriculum requires that groups have the power to affect the selection of instructional materials and textbooks. There are two models of political power used by political scientists. The first, the pluralist model (Dahl, 1961), argues that the political system in the United States is not controlled by any one group; rather, the decisions are made through the input of many groups, each attempting to exercise influence and control. The second, the political elite model (Domhoff, 1967, 1983; Mills, 1956), argues that a small number of powerful groups (i.e., those with wealth and political influence) dominate the political landscape and have disproportionate control over political decision making.

Although the controversy over which of the two views is correct has not been settled, we believe that the reality, as in most controversies, lies somewhere in the middle. The U.S. political system allows for participation from many groups, but it also requires a great deal of money and power to successfully affect political decisions. On this level, the political elite model finds considerable support. Nonetheless, the evidence does not support the view that less powerful groups cannot win some of the time or that a ruling elite manages to control the political arena. For example, the ability of a coalition of community groups in New York City to defeat the proposed Westway Project (to rebuild the collapsed West Side Highway), which was supported by the most powerful and wealthy interests in the city, is an example of the ability of the less powerful to sometimes emerge victorious. Thus, political decision making is a complex, conflictual process in which many groups vie for advantage, with those with more wealth and power having distinct advantages but not total domination. In the educational arena, these conflicts are certainly apparent.

Conflicts over curriculum are more likely to occur in the public schools than in the private ones. The reason for this is fairly clear. Parents who send their children to private or parochial schools do so, in part, because they support the particular school's philosophy. Where there are conflicts in the private sector, it is usually about disagreements within a particular philosophical or religious tradition, as opposed to between two or more different philosophies. In the public sector, however, there is rarely agreement about educational matters and thus the curriculum, like other aspects of the educational system, is the focus of considerable debate. In a society with diverse cultural groups, it is inevitable that what the schools teach will not be the product of consensus. The questions are: How do all of the groups affect what is taught in classrooms, and which groups are successful in accomplishing this task?

Kirst (1984, p. 114) has outlined the different levels of influence on the school curriculum in Table 7–1. As the table indicates, there are multiple factors that influence curriculum policy making at the national, state, and local levels. Curriculum decisions occur through a number of different channels, including the legislative and executive branches of government; the levels of the school system; and other interests, including professional associations, bureaucratic interests, and private interests (such as business and parent groups). As we discussed in Chapter 6, unlike many countries where there is governmental control of education and thus a national curriculum, education in the United States is controlled at the state and local levels. Therefore, curriculum policy making is, for the most part, a state and local matter, although in the last decade the federal government has taken an increasingly activist role in education. Nonetheless, the federal government, through its Department of Education or through the president himself (e.g., President Bush's proposals for educational reform in 1991), is one part of the process, not the determining factor.

Although each of these political actors listed above has input into the curriculum, it is evident that all do not have equal input. If there is any one group with more influence than the others, it is the education profession itself, consisting of state-level educational bureaucrats, administrators at the district and school levels, and teachers. The traditional humanist curriculum and the social efficiency curriculum, which have dominated U.S. education to a large degree, reflect the values and interests of professional educators. Moreover, as Ravitch (1983) and Kliebard (1986) noted, the struggle over the U.S. curriculum has involved primarily educators and has revolved around different philosophies of education.

Although there is no denying that there have been influences from outside the educational establishment—including students, parents, and politicians—their influence has not been nearly as significant. The U.S. curriculum has reflected the

**TABLE 7–1**
**Influences on Curriculum Policy Making**

|  | National | State | Local |
|---|---|---|---|
| General Legislative | Congress | State Legislature | City Council (usually has no influence) |
| Educational Legislative | U.S. House Committee on Education & Labor | State School Board | Local School Board |
| Executive | President | Governor | Mayor (usually has no influence) |
| Administrative School | U.S. Department of Education | State Department of Education | Superintendent |
| Bureaucratic | National Science Foundation (Division of Curriculum Improvement) | State Department of Education (Division of Instruction) | Department Chairmen, Teachers |
| Professional Association | National Testing Agencies such as Educational Testing Service (ETS) | Accrediting Associations; State Subject Matter Affiliates, National Education Association | County Association of Superintendents |
| Private Interests | Foundations & Business Corporations, Political & Service Organizations | | |

*Source:* From Federick M. Wirt and Michael W. Kirst, *Political and Social Foundations of Education,* copyright 1972 by McCutchan Publishing Corporation, Berkeley, CA 94702. Permission granted by the publisher.

professional values of educators. Additionally, it has mirrored the increased power of expertise in the twentieth century. As Collins (1977) argued, the rise of professions has led to the use of professional expertise as a means of influence. In the case of the curriculum, professional educators have made valuable use of their expertise as a means to legitimate their control over the curriculum.

Despite the dominance of professional educators in determining the curriculum, other groups have sought control with varying degrees of success. More often than not, conflicts over the curriculum have symbolized significant political and cultural conflicts. For example, in 1925, amidst the fundamentalist religious movements of the period, the Scopes Trial reflected the tensions between schooling and particular groups opposed to the official curriculum. More importantly, the trial represented the role of the school in reflecting the values of a modern society and the opposition of those still faithful to traditional societal values.

This trial involved the prosecution of a Tennessee biology teacher, John Scopes, who violated the state law prohibiting the teaching of evolution and requiring the teaching of creationism. In the decades following the publication of Darwin's *On the Origin of the Species* (1859), conflict between secular theories of evolution and religious theories of creationism raged on. Backed by the American Civil Liberties Union, Scopes used a biology textbook that taught evolution and was arrested. The trial, which literally became a circus and a symbol of the conflict between the old and the new, involved two important individuals in U.S. political and legal history: William Jennings Bryan, the populist leader and fundamentalist crusader who assisted the prosecution, and Clarence Darrow, the liberal legal crusader, who represented the defendant. In Tennessee, where fundamentalism was widely accepted, and with a judge who was clearly biased against Scopes (Garraty, 1985, p. 430), the defendant was found guilty and fined $100.

This case represented the battle between the values of the secular modern world and the values of the traditional religious world. Despite the belief of the majority of educators that evolution was the correct scientific interpretation, the power of a conservative state legislature to shape the curriculum won out, at least temporarily. Over the years, however, the professional expertise of scientists has been dominant. Today, fundamentalists are still trying to eliminate the teaching of evolution or to include creationism as a viable alternative theory.

In the 1940s and 1950s, controversies over curriculum were widespread. As part of the intellectual attack on progressive education, a number of educational and cultural critics argued that progressivism had watered down the traditional curriculum and replaced it with a social efficiency curriculum. Critics such as Arthur Bestor (1953) called for a return to the classical humanist curriculum and to an emphasis on the intellectual functions of schooling.

Whereas many of these critiques were based on academic and intellectual grounds, some of the conflicts revolved around blatantly political issues. With the rise of anticommunism during the McCarthy Era (where alleged Communists were brought before the House on Un-American Activities Committee and a Senate Investigative Committee chaired by Senator Joseph McCarthy of Wisconsin), the school curriculum became the subject of political turmoil. Anti-Communist groups pressured school districts to eliminate textbooks and instructional materials that they believed to be Communist. Moreover, progressive education, as a whole, was seen as part of a Communist conspiracy and labeled REDucation (Ravitch, 1983, p. 105). During this period, books by noted progressive educators such as Harold Rugg were banned in many districts, teachers at both the K–12 and university levels were required to take loyalty oaths, and many teachers and professors were dismissed as Communists or Communist sympathizers. This was a period in which conservatives actively sought to control what was taught in school, both by controlling the curriculum and the faculty.

One of the best examples of the politics of schooling during this period occurred in Pasadena, California. In 1948, Willard Goslin, a celebrated progressive educator, was hired as superintendent. As Cremin (1990, pp. 87–88) noted, for the next two years, a strongly organized group of conservatives attacked the superintendent's policies, the school curriculum, and its teaching methods. In 1950, under considerable pressure and amidst continual conflict, Superintendent Goslin was forced to resign. Cremin has suggested that this case is a prime example of the historical tendency for Americans to use politics as a means for controlling education, with political disagreements often a key aspect of the fight for control.

Although this period was a shameful era in U.S. history, Ravitch (1983) pointed out that the incidents of book banning were by no means the rule. Many districts successfully battled the book-banning activists. Moreover, by the 1950s, the tide began to turn, with both the legislative and judicial branches reacting against McCarthyism. However, during this time, conscious efforts were made to control what was taught in schools, and the wounds inflicted did not easily heal.

During the past 10 years, new controversies surrounding the curriculum have emerged. In the 1970s and 1980s, conservative groups argued that many books— including Ken Kesey's (1977) *One Flew Over the Cuckoo's Nest,* Richard Wright's (1969) *Native Son,* and Joseph Heller's (1985) *Catch 22*—were unsuitable for use in public schools. In some districts, books were banned and taken off reading lists and library shelves.

Although the cases of book banning are the most sensational examples of the attempt to control curriculum, the struggle over what is conveyed to students occurs in more routine ways, such as in the selection of textbooks. Kirst (1984, pp. 118–122) provided an illuminating discussion of the factors affecting textbook adoptions. He suggested that a number of forces—including the economics of publishing, the dominance of those states such as Texas and California with statewide adoption policies, the clout of political pressure groups, the guidelines of professional associations, and the input of educators—all combine to create a complex and politically charged process. The attempt to meet the demands of such a complex and often contradictory set of pressure groups leads to what many critics suggest are textbooks with little controversy and less life (Sewall, 1991). According to Kirst, although textbook publishers are constantly concerned with which group they will offend and thus risk losing market share, they are unfortunately less concerned with such significant issues as content and presentation.

The difficulties in textbook publishing are part of a larger curricular issue—that is: What is the appropriate content of the curriculum? In the 1980s, the question of what should be taught became a difficult and controversial subject. Beginning with the conservative claim that U.S. students know very little because the schools have abandoned their traditional role in transmitting the nation's cultural heritage, questions about the definition of the cultural heritage became central to curriculum debates. While conservatives such as Finn and Hirsch argued that the school curriculum should consist largely of the Western tradition, liberals and radicals countered that this tradition unfairly ignored the important traditions of non-Western groups, people of color, women, and other minority groups.

This controversy affected both the K–12 level and the postsecondary level. At the K–12 level in New York state, a commission was appointed in 1990 by Commissioner of Education Thomas Sobel to revise the social studies curriculum in light of the demands of some groups for a more multicultural curriculum and the counterclaims by other groups that such demands were both racist and encouraged historical inaccuracies. On the one hand, supporters of multicultural curriculum charged that the traditional curriculum was ethnocentric and reinforced the low self-esteem of minority groups because they rarely were presented with historical role models. On the other hand, conservative critics responded that in order to give equal time to all groups, the teaching of history would be revised in a distorted and inaccurate manner (Ravitch, 1989).

The conflict between parental values and the curriculum was clearly illustrated in New York City in 1992 when District 24 in Queens objected to the New York City Board of Education's new multicultural curriculum. This curriculum was titled "Children of the Rainbow" and it called for the teaching of tolerance for homosexual families to elementary school children. Outraged parents and community leaders, first in District 24 and then throughout New York City, challenged the curriculum, arguing that schools do not have the right to teach "immoral" values to children. Proponents of the curriculum argued that the intent behind the curriculum was to foster tolerance and respect for all groups and that the schools were the appropriate place for such an education.

Some of the curriculum's optional teaching materials, including "Heather Has Two Mommies" and "Daddy has a Roommate," became the focus of heated conflict between New York City Chancellor Joseph Fernandez and a number of local school boards. The Chancellor suspended the District 24 Community School Board for refusing to comply with the curriculum or to offer a suitable alternative; the Board of Education reinstated the community school board and called on all parties to reach a compromise that would maintain the integrity of the multicultural curriculum. Although the conflict has yet to be resolved fully, the issue has revealed strong feelings about homosexuality and the fact that significant numbers of parents are strongly opposed to schools teaching what parents consider values to their children. It also underscores the political dimension of the curriculum and how the often moral aspects of such political conflict become educational issues. In the aftermath of this conflict, the New York City Board of Education did not renew Fernandez's contract.

At the postsecondary level, debates about the need for a core curriculum for all students and what that core should be have raged from campus to campus. At Stanford University, for example, the requirement that all undergraduates take a core curriculum stressing Western civilization was abolished after considerable controversy and was replaced with requirements stressing multiculturalism. At the University of Chicago and Columbia University, where undergraduates have for decades taken a core curriculum stressing Western civilization, these curricula have been retained despite vigorous criticism.

By the early 1990s, the term *politically correct* became part of the popular culture. It referred to definitions of what is construed as acceptable language, curriculum, and ideas. It was initially coined by campus conservatives who argued that universities were dominated by radicals who have conspired to alter the traditional curriculum and who "censor" all ideas that they deem offensive (e.g., see D'Souza, 1991; Kimball, 1990). Critics responded that the university has always reflected the dominant interests of society and that the curriculum is in dire need of revision in a more democratic and representative manner.

Although there have been serious debates on many campuses on the important philosophical issues underlying these disagreements—such as the purpose of higher education and the nature of a literary canon, or whether one exists—to a large degree, the media has simplified the issue of political correctness in such a way that it has become a symbol not for the critical questions it raises but for the putative silliness of university life. More importantly, the conflicts over curriculum correctness and free speech (that is, do individuals have the right to say offensive things, and who decides what is and what is not offensive?) have raised the specter of McCarthyism and all the ugliness that it represented.

What is clear from these examples is that curriculum debates are hotly contested because they represent fundamental questions about the purposes of schooling. The transmission of knowledge, as we have suggested, is never objective or value neutral. Rather, it represents what particular interest groups believe students should know. Because there is little agreement about this, it is no surprise that there is significant conflict over the content of the curriculum. We have also suggested that the shaping of the curriculum is a complex process with many groups having input; but if there is one dominant group in this process, it is professional educators, whose expertise enables them to justify their claims. However, professional educators are not a cohesive interest group, so many of the most heated curriculum debates involve disagreements within this group about the nature and purpose of the curriculum.

## THE SOCIOLOGY OF THE CURRICULUM

Sociologists of curriculum have focused on not only what is taught but why it is taught. As we have mentioned, sociologists of curriculum reject the objectivist notion that curriculum is value neutral; rather, they view it as a reflection of particular interests within a society. Additionally, sociologists believe that the school curriculum includes both what is formally included as the subject matter to be learned—the formal curriculum—as well as the informal or hidden curriculum. The hidden curriculum includes what is taught to students through implicit rules and messages, as well as through what is left out of the formal curriculum. For example, very few of our undergraduate or graduate students can list more than one nineteenth-century American feminist. In fact, many do not know that there was a feminist movement in the nineteenth century (for a complete discussion, see Leach, 1980). Why is this the case? We believe it is because the history of women has never been a part of the school curriculum. Certain ideas, people, and events are not part of the curriculum because those who formulate it do not deem them important enough. From the standpoint of the formal curriculum, this is a political and social statement; in terms of the hidden curriculum, students receive a message that these things are just not important, which ultimately is a powerful force in shaping human consciousness. The sociology of curriculum, as the following discussion will illuminate, is concerned with both the formal and informal curriculum.

The sociology of the curriculum concentrates on the function of what is taught in schools and its relationship to the role of schools within society. As we stated in Chapter 4, functionalist and conflict theories of school and society differ about the roles of schools in U.S. society. Functionalists believe the role of the schools is to integrate children into the existing social order—a social order that is based on consensus and agreement. Conflict theorists believe that the role of schools is to reproduce the existing social order—a social order that represents the dominant groups in society. Based on these differences, the two theories have different perspectives on the school curriculum.

Functionalists argue that the school curriculum represents the codification of the knowledge that students need to become competent members of society. From this perspective, the curriculum transmits to students the cultural heritage required for a cohesive social system. Thus, the role of the curriculum is to give students the knowledge, language, and values to ensure social stability, for without a shared common culture social order is not possible.

The general functionalist theory, derived by the work of Emile Durkheim (1961, 1977) in the late nineteenth and early twentieth centuries, was concerned with the role of schools in combating the social and moral breakdown initiated by modernization. As the processes of industrialization, secularization, and urbanization weakened the bonds between people and the rituals that traditionally gave people a sense of community, Durkheim argued that the schools had to teach students to fit into the less cohesive modern world.

Modern functionalist theory, developed in the United States, through the works of Talcott Parsons (1959) and Robert Dreeben (1968), stressed the role of the schools in preparing students for the increasingly complex roles required in a modern society. This society, according to functionalists, is a democratic, meritocratic, and expert society (Hurn, 1993, pp. 44–47) and the school curriculum is designed to enable students to function within this type of society. According to Hurn (pp. 193–194), functionalists believe that in the twentieth century, the curriculum had to change to meet the new requirements of the modern world. In this respect, the schools began to move away from the teaching of isolated facts through memorization to the general task of teaching students how to learn. Thus, for functionalists, the specific content of the curriculum, such as history or literature, is less important than the role of the schools in teaching students how to learn—a skill vital in an increasingly technocratic society.

In addition to teaching general cognitive skills, functionalists believe that the schools teach the general values and norms essential to a modern society. According to Parsons (1959) and Dreeben (1968), the modern society is one where individuals are rewarded based on achievement and competence. This meritocratic system is reflected in the way schools operate, with the norm of universalism (that people are treated according to universal principles of evaluation) rather than particularism (that people are treated according to individual characteristics, such as family background, personality, etc.) the basis for evaluation.

Finally, functionalists believe that schools teach students the values that are essential to a modern society. According to this theory, modern society is a more cosmopolitan and tolerant one than traditional society, and schools teach students to respect others, to respect differences, and to base their opinions on knowledge rather than tradition. Such attitudes are necessary in a society where innovation and change are the foundation of technological development, and schools teach students these vitally important things. In summary, the functionalist theory is a positive view of the role of the schools and suggests that what schools teach are the general norms, values, and knowledge required for the maintenance and development of modern society.

According to conflict theorists, who provide a far more radical view of the roles of schools in society, the functionalist perspective of what is taught in schools is more a reflection of ideology than empirical reality. Conflict theorists do not believe that the schools teach liberal values and attitudes such as tolerance and respect. Rather, they believe that the schools' hidden curriculum teaches the attitudes and behaviors required in the workplace and that the formal curriculum represents the dominant cultural interests in society.

As we pointed out in Chapter 4, neo-Marxists, such as Bowles and Gintis (1976), believe that the hidden curriculum of the school teaches the character traits, behaviors, and attitudes needed in the capitalist economy. According to their correspondence theory, school organization and processes reflect the social needs of the economic division of labor, with the schools preparing students to fit into the economic order. From this perspective, the hidden curriculum differentially prepares students from different social class backgrounds with the type of personality traits required in the workplace. For example, working-class children attend working-class schools where the values of conformity, punctuality, and obedience to authority are relayed through the hidden curriculum; middle-class children attend middle-class schools where the hidden curriculum is more likely to teach the values of initiative and individual autonomy; upper-class children attend elite private schools where the hidden curriculum rewards independence, creativity, and leadership. Thus, working-class students are prepared for working-class jobs, middle-class students are prepared for middle-class jobs, and upper-class students are prepared for leadership positions in the corporate and political arenas. Although, as we will argue later in this chapter, this view of schooling is far too neat and rational, there are significant social class-related differences between schools. We will also show that there are significant curriculum and pedagogical differences *within* schools and that these differences may be as important as the ones *between* different schools.

Whereas neo-Marxists such as Bowles and Gintis emphasize the importance of the hidden curriculum in the shaping of values, other conflict theorists stress the effects of the formal and hidden curriculum on the reproduction of consciousness (Hurn, 1993, p. 197). According to these social reproduction theorists, such as Apple and Bourdieu, the role of the curriculum is to shape the way people think and in doing so to reproduce the dominant interests of society. Thus, for Apple (1978, 1979a, 1979b, 1982a, 1982b) the school curriculum represents the dominant class, cultural, and gender interests within society, and students internalize these interests as they go through schools. Bourdieu (1973) and Bourdieu and Passeron (1977) argued that the school curriculum represents a form of cultural capital, which separates different groups within the system of social stratification. This cultural capital symbolizes the "high culture" of the dominant groups within society as opposed to the popular culture of the masses.

Since the school system, according to conflict theorists, is highly stratified according to social class, and because students from different social class backgrounds learn different things in school, the cultural capital required for membership in the dominant groups is not universally learned but is acquired by children whose families already possess such knowledge. The system is not completely closed, however, as the system of curriculum tracking teaches at least some students in all secondary schools this high-status knowledge. The important point is that through the cultural capital transmitted through the school curriculum, the class differences in society are reflected not merely in terms of economic wealth and income but through cultural differences. Thus, through a subtle yet complex process, the schools transmit both a common body of knowledge to all students, usually at the elementary school level, and a stratified body of knowledge to students, usually at the secondary level. According to conflict theorists, this process allows for societal reproduction on the one hand and for class and cultural stratification on the other hand.

Hurn (1993, pp. 197–198) suggested that these forms of radical conflict theory are far more ideological than they are empirical. Although they point to a number of important functions of the curriculum, they do not provide sufficient evidence about the nature of the curriculum or curriculum change to support their assertions. Additionally, in arguing that school curriculum both reproduces the overall interests of the dominant groups in society by reflecting their interests and separates groups based on differential access to such a curriculum, the theory never fully explains how this is possible. If the school curriculum functions both as a means of societal reproduction and cultural separation, specifically how does it accomplish this herculean task? Moreover, the theory needs to document empirically the ways in which the curriculum reproduces social stratification between dominant and subordinate groups by looking at the curriculum and teaching practices in different schools serving different groups. To date, this has not been accomplished sufficiently.

A different variety of conflict theory, that we discussed in Chapter 4, is the neo-Weberian conflict theory of Randall Collins. For Collins, both functionalist and neo-Marxist conflict theory are far too rational. These theories, according to Collins (1979), posit too cohesive a link between the economy, the workplace, and the schools. If the role of the curriculum is truly to give students the knowledge and skills needed in the workplace, then how does one explain the relatively weak relationship between schooling and work-related skills? Collins has argued that most work skills are learned on the job, not in schools. Further, he has suggested that schools transmit a cultural currency (Hurn, 1993, pp. 198–199) to students through a credentialing process, and that the actual content of what is learned in schools is less relevant than the credential. Thus, it is not that the specific content of the curriculum is functionally related to the workplace, but it is that the credential given by schools reflects the ability of some groups to attain it and the failure of other groups to do so.

For Collins, the link between the school curriculum and the skills required in the workplace is very weak. Moreover, he has stated that the curriculum reflects the interests of various groups rather than one dominant group. If anything, the traditional school curriculum, with its emphasis on the liberal arts and sciences, reflects the cultural beliefs of those who shape the curriculum—the middle-class professional educators who have primary input into curricular matters. It is their cultural values that are represented in schools as much as the values of the upper class.

Finally, this view demonstrates that what is taught in schools must be understood as part of the larger process of cultural conflict and stratification, with school knowledge important not so much for its functional value but for its value in attaining access to specific occupations. It is this belief that the credential is related to occupational performance rather than the fact that it actually is that makes it so important. To the contrary, Collins has suggested that the actual knowledge and skills learned in acquiring a credential do not correlate highly with the actual requirements of most occupations. Therefore, Collins has provided a more cynical and skeptical view of what is taught in schools and has suggested that a more multidimensional view of conflict is required to understand the complexities of the curriculum.

## PEDAGOGIC PRACTICES: HOW THE CURRICULUM IS TAUGHT

Thus far in this chapter, we have focused on what is taught in schools and why it is taught. As students, you are aware that how something is taught is as important as, and at times more important than, the content. On the most simplistic level, how something is taught is important to you because it can make the difference between learning the material or not learning it. Moreover, we have all sat in classes with teachers who certainly knew their subject matter but did not have the ability or teaching skills to convey it to the class. Conversely, the ability to teach something without the requisite knowledge of the subject matter is equally problematic. Thus, the relationship between curriculum, the content of education, and pedagogy (the process of teaching) is an interdependent one, with each being a necessary but insufficient part of the act of teaching.

On a more complex level, the process of teaching, like the curriculum, is not an objective skill agreed on by all practitioners; rather, it is also the subject of disagreements over what constitutes appropriate teaching practices. Additionally, sociologists of education (Bernstein, 1990; Sadovnik, 1991) suggest that different pedagogic practices, like different curricula, are differentially offered to different groups of students, often based on class, racial, ethnic, and gender differences.

## THE PHILOSOPHY OF TEACHING: DIFFERING VIEWS ON PEDAGOGIC PRACTICES

Philip Jackson, in his insightful book, *The Practice of Teaching* (1986), provided a thoughtful discussion of the philosophical dimensions of teaching. He suggested that there have been different views about teaching—some see it as an art or craft while others see it as a scientific enterprise with distinct and testable methodological principles. Although the scope of this chapter does not permit us to go into this in detail, this section will outline some of the salient features of the major philosophical viewpoints on teaching practices.

Jackson (1986, pp. 115–145) distinguishes between the two dominant traditions of teaching: the mimetic and the transformative. In Chapters 2, 3, and 5, we referred to progressive and traditional (conservative) models in U.S. education. Using these terms, the mimetic tradition loosely coincides with the traditional (conservative) model and the transformative with the progressive model.

The *mimetic* tradition is based on the viewpoint that the purpose of education is to transmit specific knowledge to students. Thus, the best method of doing this is through what is termed the *didactic method,* a method that commonly relies on the lecture or presentation as the main form of communication. At the heart of this tradition is the assumption that the educational process involves the relationship between the knower (the teacher) and the learner (the student), and that education is a process of transferring information from one to the other. Based on the belief that the student does not possess what the teacher has, the mimetic model stresses the importance of rational sequencing in the teaching process and assessment of the learning process (i.e., a clear statement of learning goals and a clear means to assess whether or not students have acquired them.) The emphasis on measurable goals and objectives has become a central component of many teacher education programs, with the attempt to create a science of teaching often viewed as the key to improving educational achievement.

The *transformative* tradition rests on a different set of assumptions about the teaching and learning process. Although learning information makes the student different than he or she was before, this model defines the function of education more broadly and, according to some, more ambiguously. Simply put, proponents of this tradition believe that the purpose of education is to change the student in some meaningful way, including intellectually, creatively, spiritually, and emotionally. In contrast to the mimetic tradition, transformative educators do not see the transmission of knowledge as the only component of education and thus they provide a more multidimensional theory of teaching. Additionally, they reject the authoritarian relationship between teacher and student and argue instead that teaching and learning are inextricably linked.

Thus, the process of teaching involves not just the didactic transfer of information but the conversation between teacher and student in such a way that the student becomes an integral part of the learning process. Although the lecture may be used in this tradition, the dialectical method, that involves the use of questioning, is at the core of its methodology. Derived from the teaching methods of Socrates, as presented in the dialogues of Plato, and given philosophical grounding in the works of John Dewey, transformative educators believe that all teaching begins with the active participation of the student and results in some form of growth. Exactly what type of growth is desired varies with the specific goals of the classroom, but given the broader spectrum of goals outlined by transformative educators, it is more difficult to assess and measure educational outcomes. Moreover, the transformative tradition tends to reject the scientific model of teaching and instead views teaching as an artistic endeavor.

Dewey was somewhat ambiguous about what he believed to be the goals of education, saying that the goal of education was simply growth leading to more growth (Cremin, 1990, p. 125). In recent years, however, the transformative tradition has often defined growth within a radical critique of the status quo. Critical theorists such as Freire (1972, 1977, 1978) and Giroux (1981, 1983a, 1983b, 1988, 1991), existential phenomenologists such as Greene (1978, 1988), and feminist theorists such as Belenky (1986), Laird (1989), and Martin (1987) believe that the purpose of education is to change human consciousness and in doing so begin to change society. These perspectives view teaching as a political activity; its goal is to transform students' minds as the first step in radical social transformation.

For example, feminist theorists (Macdonald & Macdonald, 1981; Miller, 1982; Mitrano, 1979) believe that traditional curriculum and pedagogy reproduce the dominant patriarchal relations of society and reinforce male domination. They teach competition and sexism, rather than cooperation and gender equality. Therefore, feminists suggest that a curriculum and pedagogy that teach caring and that are explicitly antisexist is required.

Critical theorists, who are political radicals, argue that traditional curriculum and pedagogy reproduce the consciousness required in a competitive, capitalist society. They suggest that a critical pedagogy is required—one that enables students to critique the dominant ideologies of society and that is explicitly concerned with democratic and egalitarian principles. Thus, for the radical wing of the transformative tradition, growth leading to more growth is unacceptable, as the definition of growth is left at the level of the individual student. What is necessary, they argue, is individual growth that leads to social change. It should be noted also that these contemporary educational theories are examples of the social meliorist tradition outlined earlier in this chapter.

A major difference between the mimetic (traditional) and transformative (progressive) models of teaching relates to the question of authority relations in the classroom. Given the fact that the traditional model views the teacher as the knowledgeable authority in the classroom, traditional classrooms usually have explicit authority relations, with teachers in charge and students in a subservient position. The lesson is usually teacher directed, with students speaking when spoken to and in response to direct questions. The progressive model usually has less authoritarian authority relations in the classroom, with authority internalized within the student rather than in direct response to the teachers' higher authority. Although there are differences in authority, they are often less explicitly structured. Additionally, students usually have more input in their education and the classroom is often more child centered than teacher directed.

It is important to point out that these two models of teaching are ideal types, and that most classrooms are neither totally one nor totally the other. Most teachers combine different methods of teaching and most classrooms are neither totally authoritarian nor totally unstructured. Nonetheless, most classrooms, schools, and teachers lean in one direction or the other, based on philosophical and sociological factors. On a philosophical level, the belief in one model over the other is an essential determinant of classroom practice; on a sociological level, the use of different models appears to correlate with class differences.

For example, Bernstein's (1990) work on pedagogic practices has indicated that the looser authority relations of what he calls invisible pedagogy (usually found in progressive education) are found in schools with middle- and upper middle-class populations; the more authoritarian relations of what he calls visible pedagogy (usually found in traditional education) are found in schools with poor and working-class populations as well as in schools with upper-class populations. Although the poor and the working class seem to receive the same form of pedagogic practices, they receive a very different form of curriculum from the upper class, with the upper class receiving a classical humanist curriculum and the poor and working class receiving a social efficiency curriculum (that often is vocationally based). Bernstein argued that these class differences in pedagogic practices are the result of the different functions of schooling for different groups.

The important point here is that different teaching practices are not the result of philosophical preferences only, nor are they randomly distributed between schools in a nonrational manner. They are also related to sociological factors and may be important in understanding differences in academic achievement between groups. We will explore this in more detail in our discussion of the stratification of the curriculum and again in Chapter 9, when we discuss explanations of unequal educational achievement among different groups.

## THE STRATIFICATION OF THE CURRICULUM

As we have noted, the social efficiency curriculum has been the dominant model in U.S. public education since the 1920s. From this period onward, U.S. schools offered a stratified curriculum to students, with some students receiving an academic curriculum and others receiving a vocational or general curriculum. Curriculum stratification (i.e., the division of the curriculum), usually at the secondary school level, is not the only form of differentiation in U.S. schools. Ability grouping, or the separation of students into groups based on putative ability (usually based on standardized tests), is another important form of stratification. Ability grouping begins at the elementary school level with reading and mathematics groups within the same classroom, and is often extended in the upper elementary and middle school levels with separate classes with the same curriculum but different ability levels. These ability groups are often directly related to high school curriculum tracks (different curricula and different abilities) or ability groups (similar curricula and different abilities).

It is important to note that ability grouping and curriculum tracking are related aspects of the curriculum stratification system. Students, from elementary school through college, may be separated according to ability, curriculum, or both. For example, there are a number of different ways that schools organize the curriculum. First, some schools require all students to learn the same curriculum and group students without regard to ability (heterogeneous grouping). Second, other schools require all students to learn the same curriculum and group students based on ability (homogeneous grouping). Third, other schools stratify students based on both ability and the curriculum, with high-ability students at the secondary level enrolled in an academic curriculum and low-ability students enrolled in a vocational or general curriculum. Finally, although these differences are found within schools, there are also important differences between schools, both public and private, in terms of their curriculum and pedagogy.

These differences between schools are often based on the social class differences of the students who attend them. They are found at all levels of education through the university, where the U.S. system provides different types of postsecondary education based on both curriculum and ability (e.g., from vocational education and liberal arts education at the community colleges, to liberal arts education at selective elite private colleges and universities, to variations of both at other public and private colleges and universities).

The factors affecting ability group and/or curricula track placement, as well as the outcomes of such placement, have been the subject of considerable debate in the sociology of education. For example, the degree to which track placement is based on meritocratic criteria and actually reflect ability—or the degree to which it is based on nonmeritocratic criteria such as race, class, and gender—are important empirical questions. Additionally, the effects of such placement on the life chances and educational careers of groups of students are likewise crucial to understanding the relationship between schooling and inequalities. These issues will be explored in detail in Chapter 9, which discusses explanations of educational inequality. At this point it is important to understand that the U.S. schools are stratified by curriculum and ability, and these differences are reflected both between schools at all levels (e.g., differences between public and private schools at all levels and differences between public schools at all levels) and within schools through tracking and ability grouping. Further, it is important to understand why such practices exist.

The rationales for curriculum tracking and ability grouping are complex, as they speak to some of the most fundamental questions concerning teaching and learning. First, should all students learn the same things or should different groups of students learn different things, depending on their needs, interests, and future plans? Second, is there a common body of knowledge that all students, regardless of their future plans, should learn? Third, if all students should learn the same things, at least for a part of their education, should they learn them in heterogeneous groups or homogeneous ability groups? That is, given individual differences in ability, can students of different abilities learn the same material at the same pace, without some students falling behind or others being held back? Or is it more effective to teach students of different abilities at different paces in order to ensure that they all eventually learn the same material?

Debates about these questions have been central to U.S. education since the 1920s. In terms of the curriculum, the dominant social efficiency model has accepted the view that all students should not be required to take the same curriculum and that the secondary school curriculum should meet the different aspirations of different groups of students. In terms of ability grouping, the separation of students into homogeneous ability groups, beginning at the elementary level, has been a salient feature of U.S. education from about the same time (e.g., see Oakes, 1985). Moreover, there is often a strong relationship between elementary school ability grouping and secondary school track placement (Hurn, 1993; Oakes, 1985).

According to Oakes (1985), ability grouping and tracking have been based on four rationales. The first is that students learn more effectively in homogeneous groups and that students with different abilities require different and separate schooling. The second is that "slower" students develop a more positive self-image if they do not have to compete with "brighter" students. The third is that placement procedures accurately reflect students' academic abilities and prior accomplishments. The last rationale is that homogeneous groups are easier to manage and teach. Oakes argued that each of these are myths that cannot be supported by empirical evidence and that ability grouping and curriculum tracking have unfairly limited the lives of students from lower socioeconomic backgrounds who are far more likely to be placed in lower tracks. In Chapter 9, we will review the evidence on the effects of these processes; for now, it is important to understand that they have been significant organizational processes in the stratification of curriculum and pedagogy.

## THE EFFECTS OF THE CURRICULUM: WHAT IS LEARNED IN SCHOOLS?

Thus far in this chapter, we have discussed the organization of the curriculum and its effect on what is taught in schools. It is important to note, however, that what is taught in schools is not necessarily equivalent to what is learned in schools. Much of the discussion about curriculum assumes that the curriculum is important precisely because it affects student consciousness, values, and so on. This is true only to the extent that the school curriculum is actually internalized by students; if it is not (i.e., if the students do not actually learn what is taught or what is in the curriculum), then the claim that schooling transmits important knowledge to students and that it has important social functions may be more ideological than real.

Hurn (1993, pp. 199–201) pointed out that there are a number of methodological problems in studying school effects, in general, and what students learn cognitively and noncognitively, in particular. First, it is difficult to separate school effects from more general processes of childhood and adolescent development. To what extent the increased knowledge of children as they get older is due to schooling and to what extent it is due to developmental patterns and maturation is difficult to ascertain. Second, it is difficult to separate the effects of schooling from other variables, including social class and cultural factors. For example, one may be able to ascertain that students with more education have more academic knowledge than those with lower levels of education or that they may have more liberal political values. However, it is not easy to demonstrate that these differences have been caused by the independent effects of schooling rather than the effects of social class or cultural differences external to the processes of schooling.

Despite these difficulties, some things are known about the effects of schooling that suggest that schools have some important effects on students. First, the evidence indicates that students who have higher levels of educational attainment do know more about school subjects than those with lower levels of attainment. Research on school effects (Hurn, 1993, pp. 201–204) suggests that schooling does increase knowledge; that there is a strong correlation between formal schooling and tests of cognitive skills, such as reasoning, mathematics, and so on; and that evidence from the United States and other societies (Hurn, 1993, pp. 206–216) shows that schools have powerful effects on cognitive development. This evidence suggests that the cynical view of conflict theorists such as Collins (that little is really learned in school and that schooling is mostly a credentialing process) is not fully supported by empirical evidence. This does not refute Collin's claim that school knowledge is not necessary for the workplace (this is a different question), but it does demonstrate that schools do teach things to students (whether it is valuable or not is as much an ideological as it is an empirical question).

A second issue related to the effects of schooling regards the effects of different schools and different tracks within schools. This is a very controversial question, with proponents of the effective school movement arguing that there are specific school characteristics that correlate highly with learning. At the same time, however, there is evidence (Hurn, 1993) to suggest that school characteristics, independent of other factors such as the social class background of students, make little difference in student learning.

Although we will review these disagreements more fully in Chapter 9 in our discussion of education and inequality, it is important to note here that some research on curriculum tracking does provide an important piece of the puzzle. If students in different curriculum tracks within the same school—or more importantly, within different ability groups with similar curricula within the same school—have substantially different educational experiences and this results in vastly different educational learning outcomes, then one may conclude that schooling does have important effects. Oakes's (1985) research on tracking and ability grouping suggested such a process. Although we will suggest in Chapter 9 that these findings are not universally accepted (as it is difficult to rule out the independent effects of outside factors such as family), they do provide some support for the argument that schools affect different groups of students in significantly different ways.

Another important aspect of what students learn in school concerns the non-cognitive effects of schooling. Since both functionalists (Dreeben, 1968) and conflict theorists (Bowles & Gintis, 1976) believe that schools teach important societal values and beliefs to students (albeit they disagree about whose values and what they are), it is important to empirically document the actual effects in this area. The empirical evidence is incomplete and inconclusive, but there are some conclusions that may be drawn. First, there is some evidence (Hurn, 1993, p. 205) that increased levels of education lead to greater tolerance, greater openness, and less authoritarianism. Further, the evidence does not support the radical view that schools in capitalist societies teach conformity, docility, and obedience to authority as the only values; the effects of schooling are more complicated. Finally, given the multiple influences on values, including the role of the family and the media, it is difficult to isolate the independent role of schooling. Hurn (1993, p. 218) has suggested, "Students in contemporary society are exposed to a wide variety of *competing values and ideals* both within and in the wider environment, and many of these implicit and explicit messages cancel each other out. Thus although *particular* and *unusual* schools may have quite powerful effects on some students, schooling in *general* cannot be said to have enduring or important effects on one set of attitudes and values rather than another."

Although we agree that the effects of schooling on values and attitudes has been exaggerated by both functionalists and Neo-Marxists, the fact that some schools do have powerful effects on student attitudes, that students in different curriculum tracks are often taught and learn different attitudes, and that students with more education have different attitudes and values does suggest that schools do have some effects on students. That it is difficult, as Hurn points out, to disentangle these effects from other societal institutions demonstrates the complex relationship between schooling and other educating institutions; it does not suggest that schooling is unimportant.

## CONCLUSION

This chapter has discussed the content and process of schooling: curriculum and pedagogy. We have suggested that curriculum and pedagogy are not objective phenomena, but rather must be understood within the context of their sociological, philosophical, political, and historical roots. The curriculum represents what particular groups think is important and, by omission, what they believe is not important. What is included and excluded is often the subject of debate and controversy. Teachers too often are excluded from such decisions, but as we argued in Chapter 1, you, as teachers, must be part of these debates. Only through an understanding of the complex issues involved can you become active and critical curriculum makers rather than passive reproducers of a curriculum into which you have no input.

Most importantly, we have pointed out that what is taught and how it is taught are complex matters with profound consequences, both for individuals and society. Although there are differences of opinion concerning the effects of curriculum organization and pedagogic practices, it is evident that differences in these areas are not random; they affect different groups of students in different ways. In the next chapters (8 and 9), we will explore the broader question of schooling and inequality and examine how both factors within the schools, such as curriculum and pedagogy, as well as outside the school, such as family, neighborhood, economics, and other variables, are related to unequal educational attainment and achievement.

The following articles examine issues relating to curriculum and pedagogy. The first article, "The Text and Culture Politics," written by curriculum theorist Michael W. Apple, provides a radical examination of the politics of the curriculum. Through an examination of the content of textbooks, Apple argues that the curriculum represents the interests of the dominant groups in society. Therefore, Apple suggests that curriculum decisions are always political and conflictual.

The second article, "The Mimetic and the Transformative: Alternative Outlooks on Teaching," written by educational theorist and researcher Philip Jackson, compares two different models of teaching: the mimetic and the transformative. Through an examination of their basic premises and methods, Jackson demonstrates how each model has been a significant part of the way teachers teach.

The third article, "Taking Women Students Seriously," written by feminist writer Adrienne Rich, poignantly describes the ways in which colleges and universities treat female students. Based on her experiences in college and graduate school, Rich indicates that female students are not treated as the intellectual equals of male students and that sexism limits the intellectual and emotional development of women. Although written over 15 years ago, feminist educational research suggests that her analysis is as relevant today as it was then.

# The Text and Cultural Politics

## MICHAEL W. APPLE

Reality doesn't stalk around with a label. What something is, what it does, one's evaluation of it, all this is not naturally preordained. It is socially constructed. This is the case even when we talk about the institutions that organize a good deal of our lives. Take schools, for example. For some groups of people, schooling is seen as a vast engine of democracy—opening horizons, ensuring mobility, and so on. For others, the reality of schooling is strikingly different. It is seen as a form of social control or, perhaps, as the embodiment of cultural dangers, institutions whose curricula and teaching practices threaten the moral universe of the students who attend them.

While not all of us may agree with the latter diagnosis of what schools do, this position contains a very important insight. It recognizes that behind Spencer's famous question about "What knowledge is of most worth?" there lies another, even more contentious question, "*Whose* knowledge is of most worth?"

During the past 2 decades, a good deal of progress has been made on answering the question of whose knowledge becomes socially legitimate in schools (see, e.g., Apple, in press; Apple & Weis, 1983). While much still remains to be understood, we are now much closer to having an adequate understanding of the relationship between school knowledge and the larger society than before. Yet little attention has actually been paid to that one artifact that plays such a major role in defining whose culture is taught—the textbook. Of course, there have been literally thousands of studies of textbooks over the years.[1] But by and large, until relatively recently, most of these remained unconcerned with the politics of culture. All too many researchers could still be characterized by the phrase coined years ago by C. Wright Mills, "abstract empiricists." These "hunters and gatherers of social numbers" remain unconnected to the relations of inequality that surround them (Inglis, 1988, p. 9).

This is a distinct problem since texts are not simply "delivery systems" of "facts." They are the simultaneous results of political, economic, and cultural activities, battles, and compromises. They are conceived, designed, and authored by real people with real interests. They are published within the political and economic constraints of markets, resources, and power (Luke, 1988, pp. 27–29). And what texts mean and how they are used are fought over by communities with distinctly different commitments and by teachers and students as well.

In this article, I shall discuss ways of approaching textbooks that illuminate these power relations. In the process, I shall caution us against employing overly reductive kinds of perspectives and shall point to the importance of newer forms of textual analysis that stress the politics of how students actually create meanings around texts. Finally, I shall point to some of the implications of this for our discussions of curriculum policy.

*Source:* Michael Apple, "The Text and Cultural Politics," *Educational Researcher, 21*(7): 4–11, 19. Copyright 1992 by the American Educational Research Association. Reprinted by permission of the publisher.

# THE POLITICS OF OFFICIAL KNOWLEDGE

As I have argued in a series of volumes, it is naive to think of the school curriculum as neutral knowledge (Apple, 1985, 1988b, 1990). Rather, what counts as legitimate knowledge is the result of complex power relations and struggles among identifiable class, race, gender, and religious groups. Thus, education and power are terms of an indissoluble couplet. It is during times of social upheaval that this relationship between education and power becomes most visible. Such a relationship was and continues to be made manifest in the struggles by women, people of color, and others to have their history and knowledge included in the curriculum. Driven by an economic crisis and a crisis in ideology and authority relations, this relationship has become even more visible in the past decade or so in the resurgent conservative attacks on schooling. "Authoritarian populism" is in the air, and the New Right has been more than a little successful in bringing its own power to bear on the goals, content, and process of schooling (Apple, 1988a).

The movement to the right has not stopped outside the schoolroom door. Current plans for centralization of authority over teaching and curriculum, often cleverly disguised as "democratic" reforms, are hardly off the drawing board before new management proposals or privatization initiatives are introduced. In the United States, evidence for such offensives abounds with the introduction of mandatory competency testing for students and teachers, the calls for a return to a (romanticized) common curriculum, the reduction of educational goals to the goals of primarily business and industry, the proposals for voucher or "choice" plans, the pressure to legislate morality and values from the right, and the introduction of state-mandated content on "free enterprise" and the like. Similar tendencies are more than a little evident in Britain and in some cases are even more advanced.

All of this has brought about countervailing movements in the schools. The slower but still interesting growth of more democratically run schools, of practices and policies that give community groups and teachers considerably more authority in text selection and curriculum determination, in teaching strategy, in the use of funds, in administration, and in developing more flexible and less authoritarian evaluation schemes is providing some cause for optimism in the midst of the conservative restoration (Bastian, Fruchter, Gittell, Greer, & Haskins, 1986).

Even with these positive signs, however, it is clear that the New Right has been able to rearticulate traditional political and cultural themes. In so doing, it has often effectively mobilized a mass base of adherents. Among its most powerful causes and effects has been the growing feeling of disaffection about public schooling among conservative groups. Large numbers of parents and other people no longer trust either the institutions or the teachers and administrators in them to make "correct" decisions about what should be taught and how to teach it. The rapid growth of evangelical schooling, of censorship, of textbook controversies, and the emerging tendency of many parents to teach their children at home rather than send them to state-supported schools are clear indications of this loss of legitimacy (see, e.g., Rose, 1988).

The ideology that stands behind this is often very complex. It combines a commitment to both the "traditional family" and clear gender roles with the commitment to "traditional values" and literal religiosity. Also often packed into this is a defense of capitalist economics, patriotism, the "western tradition," anticommunism, and a deep mistrust of the "welfare state" (Hunter, 1988). When this ideology is applied to schooling, the result can be as simple as dissatisfaction with an occasional book or assignment. On the other hand, the result can be a major conflict that threatens to go well beyond the boundaries of our usual debates about schooling.

Few places in the United States are more well known in this latter context than Kanawha County, West Virginia. In the mid-seventies, it became the scene of one of the most explosive controversies over what schools should teach, who should decide, and what beliefs should guide our educational programs. What began as a protest by a small group of conservative parents, religious leaders, and business people over the content and design of the textbooks that had been approved for use in local schools soon spread to include school boycotts, violence, and a wrenching split within the community that in many ways has yet to heal (Moffett, 1988).

Though perhaps less violent, many similar situations have occurred since then in a number of districts throughout the country. For instance, the recent experiences in Yucaipa, California—where the school system and largely conservative and fundamentalist protesters have been locked in what at times seemed to be nearly an explosive situation—documents the continuing conflict over what schools are for and whose values should be embodied in them. Here, too, parents and community members have raised serious challenges over texts and over cultural authority, including attacks on the material for witchcraft and occultism, a lack of patriotism, and the destruction of sacred knowledge and authority.

It is important to realize, then, that controversies over "official knowledge" that usually center around what is included and excluded in textbooks really signify more profound political, economic, and cultural relations and histories. Conflicts over texts are often proxies for wider questions of power relations. They involve what people hold most dear. And, as in the case of Kanawha County and Yucaipa, they can quickly escalate into conflicts over these deeper issues.

Yet textbooks are surely important in and of themselves. They signify—through their content *and* form—particular constructions of reality, particular ways of selecting and organizing that vast universe of possible knowledge. They embody what Raymond Williams called the *selective tradition*—someone's selection, someone's vision of legitimate knowledge and culture, one that in the process of enfranchising one group's cultural capital disenfranchises another's (Williams, 1961; see also Apple, 1990).

Texts are really messages to and about the future. As part of a curriculum, they participate in no less than the organized knowledge system of society. They participate in creating what a society has recognized as legitimate and truthful. They help set the canons of truthfulness and, in that way, also help recreate a major reference point for what knowledge, culture, belief, and morality really are (Inglis, 1985, pp. 22–23).

Yet such a statement—even with its recognition that texts participate in constructing ideologies and ontologies—is basically misleading in many important ways. For it is not a "society" that has created such texts, but specific groups of people. "We" haven't built such curriculum artifacts in the simple sense that there is universal agreement among all of us and this is what gets to be official knowledge. In fact, the very use of the pronoun "we" simplifies matters all too much.

As Fred Inglis (1985) so cogently argues, the pronoun *we*:

> smoothes over the deep corrugations and ruptures caused precisely by struggle over how that authoritative and editorial "we" is going to be used. The [text], it is not melodramatic to declare, really is the battleground for an intellectual civil war, and the battle for cultural authority is a wayward, intermittingly fierce, always protracted and fervent one. (p. 23)

Let me give one example. In the 1930s, conservative groups in the United States mounted a campaign against one of the more progressive textbook series in use in schools. *Man and His Changing World* by Harold Rugg (Rugg, 1938) and his colleagues became the subject of a concerted attack by the National Association of Manufacturers, the American Legion, The Advertising Federation of America, and other "neutral" groups. They charged that Rugg's books were socialist, anti-American, anti-business, and so forth. The conservative campaign was more than a little successful in forcing school districts to withdraw Rugg's series from classrooms and libraries. So successful were they that sales fell from nearly 300, 000 copies in 1938 to only approximately 20,000 in 1944 (Schipper, 1983).

We, of course, may have reservations about such texts today, not least of which would be the sexist title. But one thing that the Rugg case makes clear is that the politics of the textbook is not something new by any means. Current issues surrounding texts—their ideology, their very status as central definers of what we should teach, even their very effectiveness and their design—echo the past moments of these concerns that have had such a long history in so many countries.

Few aspects of schooling are currently subject to more intense scrutiny and criticism than the text. Perhaps one of the most graphic descriptions is provided by A. Graham Down of the Council for Basic Education:

> Textbooks, for better or worse, dominate what students learn. They set the curriculum, and often the facts learned, in most subjects. For many students, textbooks are their first and sometimes only early exposure to books and to reading. The public regards textbooks as authoritative, accurate, and necessary. And teachers rely on them to organize lessons and structure subject matter. But the current system of textbook adoption has filled our schools with Trojan horses—glossily covered blocks of paper whose words emerge to deaden the minds of our nation's youth, and

make them enemies of learning. (A. Graham Down in Tyson-Bernstein, p. viii)

This statement is made just as powerfully by the author of a recent study of what she has called "America's textbook fiasco."

> Imagine a public policy system that is perfectly designed to produce textbooks that confuse, mislead, and profoundly bore students, while at the same time making all of the adults involved in the process look good, not only in their own eyes, but in the eyes of others. Although there are some good textbooks on the market, publishers and editors are virtually compelled by public policies and practices to create textbooks that confuse students with non sequiturs, that mislead them with misinformation, and that profoundly bore them with pointlessly arid writing. (Tyson-Bernstein, 1988, p. 3)

## REGULATION OR LIBERATION AND THE TEXT

In order to understand these criticisms and to understand both some of the reasons why texts look the way they do and why they contain some groups' perspectives and not others', we also need to realize that the world of the book has not been cut off from the world of commerce. Books are not only cultural artifacts, they are economic commodities as well. Even though texts may be vehicles of ideas, they still have to be "peddled on a market" (Darnton, 1982, p. 199). This is a market, however, that—especially in the national and international world of textbook publishing—is politically volatile, as the Kanawha County experience so clearly documented.

Texts are caught up in a complicated set of political and economic dynamics. Text publishing often is highly competitive. In the United States, where text production is a commercial enterprise situated within the vicissitudes of a capitalist market, decisions about the "bottom line" determine what books are published and for how long. Yet this situation is not just controlled by the "invisible hand" of the market. It is also largely determined by the highly visible "political hand" of state textbook-adoption policies.[2]

Nearly half of the states—most of them in the southern tier and the "sun belt"—have state textbook-adoption committees that by and large choose what texts will be purchased by the schools in that state. The economics of profit and loss of this situation make it imperative that publishers devote nearly all of their efforts to guaranteeing a place on these lists of approved texts. Because of this, the texts made available to the entire nation, and the knowledge considered legitimate in them, are determined by what will sell in Texas, California, Florida, and other large textbook-adoption states. There can be no doubt that the political and ideological controversies over content in these states, controversies that were often very similar to those that surfaced in Kanawha County and Yucaipa, have had a very real impact on what and whose knowledge is made available. It is also clear that Kanawha County and Yucaipa were affected by and had an impact on these larger battles over legitimate knowledge.

Economic and political realities structure text publishing not only internally, however. On an international level, the major text-publishing conglomerates control the market of much of the material not only in the capitalist centers but in many other nations as well. Cultural domination is a fact of life for millions of students throughout the world, in part because of the economic control of communication and publishing by multinational firms, in part because of the ideologies and systems of political and cultural control of new elites within former colonial countries.[3] All of this, too, has led to complicated relations and struggles over official knowledge and the text between "center" and "periphery" and within these areas as well.

I want to stress that all of this is not simply—as in the case of newly emerging nations, Kanawha County, or the Rugg textbooks—of historical interest. As I noted, the controversies over the form and content of the textbook have not diminished. In fact, they have become even more heated, in the United States in particular. The changing ideological climate has had a major impact on debates over what should be taught in schools and on how it should be taught and evaluated. There is considerable pressure to raise the standards of texts, make them more "difficult," standardize their content, make certain that they place more stress on "American" themes of patriotism, free enterprise, and the "western tradition," and link their content to statewide and national tests of educational achievement.

These kinds of pressures are felt not only in the United States. The text has become the center of ideological and educational conflict in a number of other countries as well. In Japan, for instance, the government approval of a right-wing history textbook that retold the story of the brutal Japanese invasion and occupation of China and Korea in a more positive light has stimulated widespread international antagonism and has led to considerable controversy in Japan as well.

Along these same lines, at the very time that the text has become a source of contention for conservative movements, it has stood at the center of controversy for not being progressive enough. Class, gender, and race bias has been widespread in the materials. All too often, "legitimate" knowledge does not include the historical experiences and cultural expressions of labor, women, people of color, and others who have been less powerful.[4]

All of these controversies are not "simply" about the content of the books students find—or don't find—in their schools, though obviously they are about that as well.

The issues also involve profoundly different definitions of the common good (Raskin, 1986), about our society and where it should be heading, about cultural visions, and about our children's future. To quote from Inglis again, the entire curriculum, in which the text plays so large a part, is "both the text and context in which production and values intersect; it is the twistpoint of imagination and power (Inglis, 1985, p. 142). In the context of the politics of the textbook, it is the issue of power that should concern us the most.

The concept of power merely connotes the capacity to act and to do so effectively. However, in the ways we use the idea of power in our daily discourse, "the word comes on strongly and menacingly, and its presence is duly fearful" (Inglis, 1988, p. 4). This "dark side" of power is, of course, complemented by a more positive vision. Here, power is seen as connected to a people acting democratically and collectively, in the open, for the best ideals.[5] It is this dual concept of power that concerns us here, at the level of both theory (how we think about the relationship between legitimate knowledge and power) and practice (how texts actually embody this relationship). Both the positive and the negative senses of power are essential for us to understand these relationships. Taken together, they signify that arguments about textbooks are really a form of cultural politics. They involve the very nature of the connections between cultural visions and differential power.

This, of course, is not new to anyone who has been interested in the history of the relationship among books, literacy, and popular movements. Books—and one's ability to read them—have themselves been inherently caught up in cultural politics. Take the case of Voltaire, that leader of the Enlightenment who so wanted to become a member of the nobility. For him, the Enlightenment should begin with the "grands." Only when it had captured the hearts and minds of society's commanding heights, only then could it concern itself with the masses below. But for Voltaire and many of his followers, one caution should be taken very seriously. One should take care to prevent the masses from learning to read (Darnton, 1982, p. 13).

For others, teaching "the masses" to read could have a more "beneficial" effect. It enables a "civilizing" process, in which dominated groups would be made more moral, more obedient, more influenced by "real culture" (Batsleer, Davies, O'Rourke, & Weedon, 1985). And for still others, such literacy could bring social transformation in its wake. It could lead to a "critical literacy," one that would be part of larger movements for a more democratic culture, economy, and polity (Lankshear with Lawler, 1987). The dual sense of the power of the text emerges clearly here.

Thus, activities that we now ask students to engage in every day, activities as "simple" and basic as reading and writing, can be at one and the same time forms of regulation and exploitation *and* potential modes of resistance, celebration and solidarity. Here, I am reminded of Caliban's cry, "You taught me language; and my profit on't is, I know how to curse" (quoted in Batsleer et al., 1985, p. 5).

This contradictory sense of the politics of the book is made clearer if we go into the classrooms of the past. For example, texts have often been related to forms of bureaucratic regulation of both teachers' lives and those of students. Thus, one teacher in Boston in 1899 relates a story of what happened in her first year of teaching during an observation by the school principal. As the teacher rather proudly watched one of her children read aloud an assigned lesson from the text, the principal was less than pleased with the performance of the teacher or her pupil. In the words of the teacher:

> The proper way to read in the public school in 1899 was to say, "page 35, chapter 4" and holding the book in the right hand, with the

toes pointing at an angle of forty-five degrees, the head held straight and high, the eyes looking directly ahead, the pupil would lift up his voice and struggle in loud, unnatural tones. Now, I had attended to the position of the toes, the right arm, and the nose, but had failed to enforce the mentioning of page and chapter. (Fraser, 1989, p. 128)

Here, the text participates in both bodily and ideological regulation. The textbook in this instance is part of a system of enforcing a sense of duty, morality, and cultural correctness. Yet, historically, the standardized text was struggled *for* as well as against by many teachers. Faced with large classes, difficult working conditions, insufficient training, and, even more importantly, little time to prepare lessons for the vast array of subjects and students they were responsible for, teachers often looked upon texts not necessarily as impositions but as essential tools. For young women elementary school teachers, the text helped prevent exploitation (Apple, 1988b). It solved a multitude of practical problems. It led not only to deskilling, but to time to become more skilled as a teacher as well.[6] Thus, there were demands for standardized texts by teachers even in the face of what happened to that teacher in Boston and to so many others.

This struggle over texts was linked to broader concerns about who should control the curriculum in schools. Teachers, especially those most politically active, constantly sought to have a say in what they taught. This was seen as part of a larger fight for democratic rights. Margaret Haley, for instance, one of the leaders of the first teachers' union in the United States, saw a great need for teachers to work against the tendency toward making the teacher "a mere factory hand, whose duty it is to carry out mechanically and unquestioningly the ideas and orders of those clothed with authority of position" (Margaret Haley, quoted in Fraser, 1989, p. 128). Teachers had to fight against the deskilling or, as she called it, "factoryiz-

ing" methods of control being sponsored by administrative and industrial leaders. One of the reasons she was so strongly in favor of teachers' councils as mechanisms of control of schools was that this would considerably reduce the immense power over teaching and texts that administrators then possessed. Quoting John Dewey approvingly, Haley wrote:

> If there is a single public-school system in the United States where there is official and constitutional provision made for submitting questions of methods, of discipline and teaching, and the questions of curriculum, textbooks, etc. to the discussion of those actually engaged in the work of teaching, that fact has escaped my notice. (Margaret Haley quoted in Fraser, 1989, p. 138)

In this instance, teacher control over the choice of textbooks and how they were to be used was part of a more extensive movement to enhance the democratic rights of teachers on the job. Without such teacher control, teachers would be the equivalent of factory workers whose every move was determined by management.

These points about the contradictory relationships teachers have had with texts and the way such books depower and empower at different moments (and perhaps at the same time) document something of importance. It is too easy to see a cultural practice or a book as totally carrying its politics around with it, "as if written on its brow for ever and a day." Rather, its political functioning "depends on the network of social and ideological relations" it participates in (Bennett, 1986a, p. xvi). Text writing, reading, and use can be retrogressive or progressive (and sometimes some combination of both) depending on the social context. Textbooks can be fought against because they are part of a system of moral regulation. They can be fought for both as providing essential assistance in the labor of teaching and as part of a larger strategy of democratization.

What textbooks do, the social roles they play for different groups, is then very complicated. This has important implications not only for the politics of how and by whom textbooks are used, but for the politics of the internal qualities, the content and organization, of the text. Just as crucially, it also has an immense bearing on how people actually read and interpret the text. It is to these issues that I now want to turn.

## THE POLITICS OF CULTURAL INCORPORATION

We cannot assume that because so much of education has been linked to processes of class, gender, and race stratification,[7] all of the knowledge chosen to be included in texts simply represents relations of, say, cultural domination or includes only the knowledge of dominant groups. This point requires that I speak theoretically and politically in this section of my argument, for all too many critical analyses of school knowledge—of what is included and excluded in the overt and hidden curricula of the school—take the easy way out. Reductive analysis comes cheap. Reality, however, is complex. Let us look at this in more detail.

It has been argued in considerable detail elsewhere that the selection and organization of knowledge for schools is an ideological process, one that serves the interests of particular classes and social groups (see Apple, 1990, and Apple & Christian-Smith, 1991). However, as I just noted, this does not mean that the entire corpus of school knowledge is "a mirror reflection of ruling class ideas, imposed in an unmediated and coercive manner." Instead, "the processes of cultural incorporation are dynamic, reflecting both continuities and contradictions of that dominant culture and the continual remaking and relegitimation of that culture's plausibility system" (Luke, 1988, p. 24). Curricula aren't imposed in countries like the United

States. Rather, they are the products of often intense conflicts, negotiations, and attempts at rebuilding hegemonic control by actually incorporating the knowledge and perspectives of the less powerful under the umbrella of the discourse of dominant groups.

This is clear in the case of the textbook. As disenfranchised groups have fought to have their knowledge take center stage in the debates over cultural legitimacy, one trend has dominated in text production. In essence, little is usually dropped from textbooks. Major ideological frameworks do not get markedly changed. Textbook publishers are under considerable and constant pressure to include *more* in their books. Progressive *items* are perhaps mentioned, then, but not developed in depth (Tyson-Bernstein, 1988, p. 18). Dominance is partly maintained here through compromise and the process of "mentioning." Here, limited and isolated elements of the culture and history of less powerful groups are included in texts. Thus, for example, a small and often separate section is included on "the contributions of women" and "minority groups," but without any substantive elaboration of the view of the world as seen from their perspective.

Tony Bennett's discussion of the process by which dominant cultures actually become dominant is worth quoting at length here:

> Dominant culture gains a purchase not in being imposed, as an alien external force, on to the cultures of subordinate groups, but by reaching into these cultures, reshaping them, hooking them and, with them, the people whose consciousness and experience is defined in their terms, into an association with the values and ideologies of the ruling groups in society. Such processes neither erase the cultures of subordinate groups, nor do they rob "the people" of their "true culture": what they do is shuffle those cultures on to an ideological and cultural terrain in which they can be disconnected from whatever radical impulses which may (but need not) have fuelled them and be connected to

more conservative or, often, downright reactionary cultural and ideological tendencies. (T. Bennett, 1986b, p. 19)

In some cases, "mentioning" may operate in exactly this way, integrating selective elements into the dominant tradition by bringing them into close association with the values of powerful groups. There will be times, however, when such a strategy will not be successful. Oppositional cultures may at times use elements of the dominant culture against such groups. Bennett goes on, describing how oppositional cultures operate, as well:

> Similarly, resistance to the dominant culture does not take the form of launching against it a ready-formed, constantly simmering oppositional culture—always there, but in need of being turned up from time to time. Oppositional cultural values are formed and take shape only in the context of their struggle with the dominant culture, a struggle which may borrow some of its resources from that culture and which must concede some ground to it if it is to be able to connect with it—and thereby with those whose consciousness and experience is partly shaped by it—in order, by turning it back upon itself, to peel it away, to create a space within and against it in which contradictory values can echo, reverberate and be heard. (T. Bennett, 1986b, p. 19)

Some texts may, in fact, have such progressive "echoes" within them. There are victories in the politics of official knowledge, not only defeats.

Sometimes, of course, not only are people successful in creating some space where such contradictory values can indeed "echo, reverberate and be heard," but they transform the entire social space. They create entirely new kinds of governments, new possibilities for democratic political, economic, and cultural arrangements. In these situations, the role of education takes on even more importance, since new knowledge, new ethics, and a new reality seek to replace the old. This is one of the reasons that those of us committed to more participatory and democratic cultures inside and outside of schools must give serious attention to changes in official knowledge in those nations that have sought to overthrow their colonial or elitist heritage. Here, the politics of the text takes on special importance, since the textbook often represents an overt attempt to help create a new cultural reality. The case of the creation of more democratic textbooks and other educational materials based on the expressed needs of less powerful groups in Grenada during the years of the New Jewel Movement provides a cogent example here (see Jules, 1991).

New social contexts, new processes of text creation, a new cultural politics, the transformation of authority relations, and new ways of reading texts, all of these can evolve and help usher in a positive rather than a negative, sense of the power of the text. Less regulatory and more emancipatory relations of texts to real people can begin to evolve, a possibility made real in many of the programs of critical literacy that have had such a positive impact in nations throughout the world. Here people help create their own "texts," ones that signify their emerging power in the control of their own destinies.

However, we should not be overly romantic here. Such transformations of cultural authority and mechanisms of control and incorporation will not be easy.

For example, certainly the ideas and values of a people are not directly prescribed by the conceptions of the world of dominant groups and just as certainly there will be many instances where people have been successful in creating realistic and workable alternatives to the culture and texts in dominance. Yet we do need to acknowledge that the social distribution of what is considered legitimate knowledge *is* skewed in many nations. The social institutions directly concerned with the "transmission" of this knowledge, such as schools and the media, *are* grounded in and structured by the class, gender, and race inequalities that organize the society in which we live. The area of symbolic production is not divorced from the unequal relations of power that structure other spheres (see Hall, 1988, p. 44).

Speaking only of class relations—although much the same could be said about race and gender—Stuart Hall, one of the most insightful analysts of cultural politics, puts it this way:

> Ruling or dominant conceptions of the world do not directly prescribe the mental content of the illusions that supposedly fill the heads of dominated classes. But the circle of dominant ideas *does* accumulate the symbolic power to map or classify the world for others; its classifications do acquire not only the constraining power of dominance over other modes of thought but also the initial authority of habit and instinct. It becomes the horizon of the taken-for-granted: what the world is and how it works, for all practical purposes. Ruling ideas may dominate other conceptions of the social world by setting the limit on what will appear as rational, reasonable, credible, indeed sayable or thinkable within the given vocabularies of motive and action available to us. Their dominance lies precisely in the power they have to contain within their limits, to frame within their circumference of thought, the reasoning and calculation of other social groups. (Hall, 1988, p. 44)

In the United States, there has been a movement of exactly this kind. Dominant groups—really a coalition of economic modernizers, what has been called the old humanists, and neoconservative intellectuals—have attempted to create an ideological consensus around the return to traditional knowledge. The "great books" and "great ideas" of the "western tradition" will preserve democracy. By returning to the common culture that has made this nation great, schools will increase student achievement and discipline, increase our international competitiveness, and ultimately reduce unemployment and poverty.

Mirrored in the problematic educational and cultural visions of volumes such as Bloom's *The Closing of the American Mind* (1987) and Hirsch's *Cultural Literacy* (1986), this position is probably best represented in quotes from former Secretary of Education William Bennett. In his view, we are finally emerging out of a crisis in which "we neglected and denied much of the best in American education." For a period, "we simply stopped doing the right things [and] allowed an assault on intellectual and moral standards." This assault on the current state of education has led schools to fall away from "the principles of our tradition" (W. Bennett, 1988, p. 9).

Yet, for Bennett, "the people" have now risen up. "The 1980's gave birth to a grass roots movement for educational reform that has generated a renewed commitment to excellence, character, and fundamentals." Because of this, "we have reason for optimism" (W. Bennett, 1988, p. 10). Why? Because:

> The national debate on education is now focused on truly important matters: mastering the basics;…insisting on high standards and expectations; ensuring discipline in the classroom; conveying a grasp of our moral and political principles; and nurturing the character of our young. (W. Bennett, 1988, p. 10)

Notice the use of "we," "the people," here. Notice as well the assumed consensus on "basics" and "fundamentals" and the romanticization of the past of both schools and the larger society. The use of these terms, the attempt to bring people in under the ideological umbrella of the conservative restoration, is very clever rhetorically. As many people in the United States, Britain, and elsewhere—where rightist governments have been very active in transforming what education is about—have begun to realize, however, this ideological incorporation is having no small measure of success at the level of policy and at the level of whose knowledge and values are to be taught (Apple, 1988a).

If this movement has its way, the texts made available and the knowledge included in them will surely represent a major loss for many of the groups who have had successes in bringing their knowledge and culture more directly into the body of legitimate content in schools. Just as surely, the ideologies that will dominate the official knowledge will represent a considerably more elitist orientation than what we have now.

Yet, perhaps *surely* is not the correct word here. The situation is actually more complex than that, something we have learned from many of the newer methods of interpreting how social messages are actually "found" in texts.

Allan Luke has dealt with such issues very persuasively. It would be best to quote him at length here:

> A major pitfall of research in the sociology of curriculum has been its willingness to accept text form as a mere adjunct means for the delivery of ideological content: the former described in terms of dominant metaphors, images, or key ideas; the latter described in terms of the sum total of values, beliefs, and ideas which might be seen to constitute a false consciousness. For much content analysis presumes that text mirrors or reflects a particular ideological position, which in turn can be connected to specific class interests.... It is predicated on the possibility of a one-to-one identification of school knowledge with textually represented ideas of the dominant classes. Even those critics who have recognized that the ideology encoded in curricular texts may reflect the internally contradictory character of a dominant culture have tended to neglect the need for a more complex model of text analysis, one that does not suppose that texts are simply readable, literal representations of "someone else's" version of social reality, objective knowledge and human relations. For texts do not always mean or com-

municate what they say. (Luke, 1988, pp. 29–30)

These are important points, for they imply that we need more sophisticated and nuanced models of textual analysis. While we should certainly not be at all sanguine about the effects of the conservative restoration on texts and the curriculum, if texts don't simply represent dominant beliefs in some straightforward way and if dominant cultures contain contradictions, fissures, and even elements of the culture of popular groups, then our readings of what knowledge is "in" texts cannot be done by the application of a simple formula.

We can claim, for instance, that the meaning of a text is not necessarily intrinsic to it. As poststructuralist theories would have it, meaning is "the product of a system of differences into which the text is articulated." Thus, there is not "one text," but many. Any text is open to multiple readings. This puts into doubt any claim that one can determine the meanings and politics of a text "by a straightforward encounter with the text itself." It also raises serious questions about whether one can fully understand the text by mechanically applying any interpretive procedure. Meanings, then, can be and are multiple and contradictory, and we must always be willing to "read" our own readings of a text, to interpret our own interpretations of what it means (Grossberg & Nelson, 1988). Answering the question of "whose knowledge" is in a text is not at all simple, it seems, though clearly the right would very much like to reduce the range of meanings one might find.

This is true of our own interpretations of what is in textbooks. But it is also just as true for the students who sit in schools and at home and read (or in many cases don't read) their texts. I want to stress this point, not only at the level of theory and politics as I have been doing here, but at the level of practice.

We cannot assume that what is "in" the text is actually taught. Nor can we assume that what is taught is actually learned. Teachers have a long history of mediating and transforming text material when they employ it in classrooms. Students bring their own classed, raced, and gendered biographies with them as well. They, too, accept, reinterpret, and reject what counts as legitimate knowledge selectively. As critical ethnographies of schools have shown, students (and teachers) are not empty vessels into which knowledge is poured. Rather than what Freire (1973) has called "banking" education going on, students are active constructors of the meanings of the education they encounter.[8]

We can talk about three ways in which people can potentially respond to a text: dominated, negotiated, and oppositional. In the dominated reading of a text, one accepts the messages at face value. In a negotiated response, the reader may dispute a particular claim, but accept the overall tendencies or interpretations of a text. Finally, an oppositional response rejects these dominant tendencies and interpretations. The reader "repositions" herself or himself in relation to the text and takes on the position of the oppressed (Modleski, 1986, p. xi). These are, of course, no more than ideal types and many responses will be a contradictory combination of all three. But the point is that not only do texts themselves have contradictory elements; audiences construct their own responses to texts. They do not passively receive texts, but actually read them based on their own class, race, gender, and religious experiences.

An immense amount of work needs to be done on student acceptance, interpretation, reinterpretation, or partial and/or total rejection of texts. While there is a tradition of such research, much of it quite good, most of this work in education is done in an overly psychologized manner. It is more concerned with questions of learning and achievement than it is with the equally important and prior issues of whose knowledge it is that students are learning, negotiating, or opposing and what the sociocultural roots and effects are of such processes. Yet we simply cannot fully understand the power of the text, what it does ideologically and politically (or educationally, for that matter) unless we take very seriously the way students actually read them—not only as individuals but as members of social groups with their own particular cultures and histories (see Ellsworth, 1988). For every textbook, then, there are multiple texts—contradictions within it, multiple readings of it, and different uses to which it will be put. Texts—be they the standardized, grade-level-specific books so beloved by school systems or the novels, trade books, and alternative materials that teachers use either to supplement these books or simply to replace them—are part of a complex story of cultural politics. They can signify authority (not always legitimate) or freedom.

To recognize this, then, is also to recognize that our task as critically and democratically minded educators is itself a political one. We must acknowledge and understand the tremendous capacity of dominant institutions to regenerate themselves "not only in their material foundations and structures but in the hearts and minds of people." Yet, at the very same time, we need to never lose sight of the power of popular organizations, of real people, to struggle, resist, and transform them (Batsleer et al., 1985, p. 5). Cultural authority, what counts as legitimate knowledge, what norms and values are represented in the officially sponsored curriculum of the school, all of these serve as important arenas in which the positive and negative relations of power surrounding the text will work themselves out. And all of them involve the hopes and dreams of real people in real institutions, in real relations of inequality.

From all that I have said here, it should be clear that I oppose the idea that there can be one textual authority, one definitive set of "facts" that is divorced from its context of power relations. A "common culture" can never be an extension to everyone of what a minority mean and believe. Rather, and crucially, it requires not the stipulation and incorporation within textbooks of lists and concepts that make us all "culturally literate," *but the creation of the conditions necessary for all people to participate in the creation and re-creation of meanings and values.* It requires a democratic process in which all people—not simply those who see themselves as the intellectual guardians of the "western tradition"—can be involved in the deliberation of what is important.[9] It should go without saying that this necessitates the removal of the very real material obstacles—unequal power, wealth, time for reflection—that stand in the way of such participation (Williams, 1989, pp. 37–38).

The very idea that there is one set of values that must guide the "selective tradition" can be a great danger, especially in contexts of differential power. Take, as one example, a famous line that was printed on an equally famous public building. It read: "There is one road to freedom. Its milestones are obedience, diligence, honesty, order, cleanliness, temperance, truth, sacrifice, and love of country." Many people may perhaps agree with much of the sentiment represented by these words. It may be of some interest that the building in which they appeared was in the administration block of the concentration camp at Dachau (Horne, 1986, p. 76).

We must ask, then, are we in the business of creating dead texts and dead minds? If we accept the title of educator—with all of the ethical and political commitments this entails—I think we already know what our answer should be.

## ENDNOTES

1. For a current representative sample of the varied kinds of studies being done on the textbook, see Woodward, Elliot, and Carter Nagel, 1988. We need to make a distinction between the generic use of *texts* (all meaningful materials created by human activity) and textbooks. My focus in this essay will be mostly on the latter, though many schools and many teachers use considerably more than standardized textbook material. For a discussion about and analysis of this wider range of material, see Apple and Christian-Smith, 1991.

2. For a history of the social roots of such adoption policies, see Apple, 1989.

3. The issue surrounding cultural imperialism and colonialism are nicely laid out in Altbach and Kelly, 1984. For an excellent discussion of international relations over texts and knowledge, see Altbach, 1988.

4. For some of the most elegant discussions of how we need to think about these "cultural silences," see Apple and Christian-Smith, 1991, and Roman and Christian-Smith with Ellsworth, 1988.

5. Inglis, 1988, p. 4, I placed "dark side" in inverted commas in the previous sentence because of the dominant tendency to unfortunately equate darkness with negativity. This is just one of the ways popular culture expresses racism. See Omi and Winant, 1986.

6. For further discussion of deskilling and reskilling, see Apple, 1985, 1988b.

7. The literature here is voluminous. For a more extended treatment see Apple, 1985, and McCarthy and Apple, 1989.

8. See, for example, Will, 1981; McRobbie, 1978; Everhart, 1983; Weis, 1990; and Trudell, in press. The list could be continued.

9. This is discussed in more detail in the preface to Apple, 1990.

## REFERENCES

Altbach, P. (1988). *The knowledge context*. Albany: State University of New York Press.

Altbach, P., & Kelly, G. (Eds.). (1984). *Education and the colonial experience*. New York: Transaction Books.

Apple, M. W. (1985). *Education and power*. New York: Routledge.

Apple, M. W. (1988a). Redefining equality: Authoritarian populism and the conservative restoration. *Teachers College Record, 90,* 167–184.

Apple, M. W. (1988b). *Teachers and texts: A political economy of class and gender relations in education.* New York: Routledge.

Apple, M. W. (1989). Regulating the text: The socio-historical roots of state control. *Educational Policy, 3,* 107–123.

Apple, M. W. (1990). *Ideology and curriculum* (2nd ed.). New York: Routledge.

Apple, M. W. (in press). *The politics of official knowledge.* New York: Routledge.

Apple, M. W., & Christian-Smith, D. (Ed.). (1991). *The politics of the textbook.* New York: Routledge.

Apple, M. W., & Weis, L. (Eds.). (1983). *Ideology and practice in schooling.* Philadelphia: Temple University Press.

Bastian, A., Fruchter, N., Gittell, M., Greer, C., & Haskins, K. (1986). *Choosing equality: The case for democratic schools.* Philadelphia: Temple University Press.

Batsleer, J., Davis, T., O'Rourke, R., & Weedon, C. (1985). *Rewriting English: Cultural politics of gender and class.* New York: Methuen.

Bennett, T. (1986a). Introduction: Popular culture and the turn to Gramsci. In T. Bennett, C. Mercer, & J. Woollacott (Eds.), *Popular culture and social relations* (pp. xi–xix). Philadelphia: The Open University Press.

Bennett, T. (1986b). The politics of the "popular" and popular culture. In T. Bennett, C. Mercer, & J. Woollcott (Eds.), *Popular culture and social relations* (pp. 6-21). Philadelphia: The Open University Press.

Bennett, W. (1988). *Our children and our country.* New York: Simon & Schuster.

Bloom, A. (1987). *The Closing of the American mind.* New York: Simon & Schuster.

Christian-Smith, L. (1991). *Becoming a woman through romance.* New York: Routledge.

Darnton, R. (1982). *The literary underground of the old regime.* Cambridge, MA: Harvard University Press.

Ellsworth, E. (1988). *Illicit pleasures:* Feminist spectators and *Personal Best.* In L. Roman, L. Christian-Smith, with E. Ellsworth (Eds.), *Becoming feminine: The politics of popular culture* (pp. 102–119). Philadelphia: Falmer.

Ellsworth, L. (1989). Why doesn't this feel empowering? *Harvard Educational Review, 59,* 297–324.

Everhart, R. (1983). *Reading, writing and resistance.* Boston: Routledge.

Fraser, J. W. (1989). Agents of democracy: Urban elementary school teachers and the conditions of teaching. In D. Warren (Ed.), *American teachers: Histories of a profession at work* (pp. 118–156). New York: Macmillan.

Freire, Paulo. (1973). *Pedagogy of the oppressed.* New York: Herder & Herder.

Grossberg, L., & Nelson, C. (1988). Introduction: The territory of Marxism. In C. Nelson & L. Grossberg (Eds.), *Marxism and the interpretation of culture* (pp. 1–13). Urbana, IL: University of Illinois Press.

Hall, S. (1988). The toad in the garden: Thatcherism among the theorists. In C. Nelson & L. Grossberg (Eds.), *Marxism and the interpretation of culture* (pp. 35–57). Urbana, IL: University of Illinois Press.

Hirsch, E. D., Jr. (1986). *Cultural literacy.* New York: Houghton-Mifflin.

Horne, D. (1986). *The public culture.* Dover, NH: Pluto Press.

Hunter, A. (1988). *Children in the service of conservatism.* Madison, WI: University of Wisconsin Institute for Legal Studies.

Inglis, F. *(1985). The management of ignorance: A political theory of curriculum.* New York: Basil Blackwell.

Inglis, F. (1988) *Popular culture and political power.* New York: St. Martin's.

Jules, D. (1991). Building democracy: Content and ideology in Granadian educational texts, 1979–1983. In M. W. Apple & L. Christian-Smith (Eds.), *The politics of the textbook* (pp. 259–288). New York: Routledge.

Lankshear, C., with Lawler, M. (1987). *Literacy, schooling and revolution.* Philadelphia: Falmer.

Luke, A. (1988). *Literacy, textbooks and ideology.* Philadelphia: Falmer.

McCarthy, C., & Apple, M. W. (1989). Race, class and gender in American educational research. In L. Weis (Ed.), *Class, race and gender in American education* (pp. 9-39). Albany: State University of New York Press.

McRobbie, A. (1978). Working class girls and the culture of femininity. In Women's Studies Group (Ed.), *Women take issue* (pp. 96–108). London: Hutchinson.

Modleski, T. (1986). Introduction. In T. Modleski (Ed.), *Studies in entertainment* (pp. ix–xix). Bloomington: Indiana University Press.

Moffett, J. (1988). *Storm in the mountains.* Carbondale, IL: Southern Illinois University Press.

Omi, M., & Winant, H. (1986). *Racial formation in the United States.* New York: Routledge.

Raskin, M. (1986). *The common good.* New York: Routledge.

Roman, L., & Christian-Smith, L., with Ellsworth, E. (Eds.). (1988). *Becoming feminine: The politics of popular culture.* Philadelphia: Falmer.

Rose, S. *(1988). Keeping them out of the hands of Satan.* New York: Routledge.

Rugg, H. *Man and his changing world.* New York: Ginn.

Schipper, M. (1983). Textbook controversy: Past and present. *New York University Education Quarterly, 14,* 31–36.

Trudell, B. (in press). *Doing sex education.* New York: Routledge.

Tyson-Bernstein, H. *A conspiracy of good intentions: America's textbook fiasco.* Washington, DC: The Council on Basic Education.

Weis, L. (1990). *Working class without work.* New York: Routledge.

Williams, R. (1961). *The long revolution.* London: Chatto & Windus.

Williams, R. (1989). *Resources of hope.* New York: Verso Books.

Willis, P. *(1981). Learning to labor.* New York: Columbia University Press.

Woodward, A., Elliot, D., & Carter Nagel, K. (Eds.). (1988). *Textbooks in school and society.* New York: Garland.

# The Mimetic and the Transformative: Alternative Outlooks on Teaching

## PHILIP W. JACKSON

The Greek sophist Protagoras allegedly claimed that on every subject two opposite statements could be made, each as defensible as the other. Whether or not he was right in a universal sense is something for logicians and rhetoricians to decide. However, insofar as the affairs of everyday life are concerned, he seems to have hit upon a fundamental truth, for we encounter daily all manner of "opposite statements," each with its share of supporters and critics.

As might be expected, education as a field of study is no exception to the rule. There too, differing outlooks, poles apart at first glance, are as common as elsewhere. Who, for example, is unfamiliar with the many verbal exchanges that have taken place over the years between "'traditional" educators on the one side and their "progressive" opponents on the other, debates in which the merits of "child-centered" practices are pitted against those considered more "subject-centered"?

This [reading] introduces a dichotomy that encompasses the differences just named as well as others less familiar, though it is not usually talked about in the terms I will employ here. Indeed, the names of the two outlooks to be discussed have been purposely chosen so as to be *un*familiar to most followers of today's educational discussions and debates. My reason for this is not to introduce novelty for its own sake, much less to add glitter by using a pair of fancy terms. Instead, it is to avoid becoming prematurely embroiled in the well-known controversies associated with phrases like "child-centered" and "subject-centered," controversies that too often degenerate into mud-slinging contests which reduce the terms themselves to little more than slogans and epithets. A similar fate may well await the pair of terms to be introduced here. But for the time being the fact that they are rather new, or at least newly employed within an educational context, should prevent that.

In brief, I contend in this chapter that two distinguishably different ways of thinking about education and of translating that thought into practice undergird most of the differences of opinion that have circulated within educational circles over the past two or three centuries. Framed within an argument, which is how they are usually encountered, each of these two outlooks seeks to legitimate its own vision of how education should be conducted. It does so by promoting certain goals and practices, making them seem proper and just, while ignoring others or calling them into question.

These dichotomous orientations are not the exact opposites of which Protagoras spoke, though they are often presented that way by people propounding one or the other. How they *are* related to each other is a question I will consider in some detail in the second half of this chapter. For now, however, it will suffice to call their relationship enigmatic. Most of the time their challengers and defenders are depicted at swords' points, but there is a perspective from which the two outlooks appear complementary and interde-

*Source:* Reprinted by permission of the publisher from Jackson, Philip, *The Practice of Teaching.* (New York: Teachers College Press, © 1986 by Teachers College, Columbia University. All rights reserved.), pp. 115–129.

pendent. Indeed, there are angles of vision from which what originally seemed to be two diametrically opposed orientations suddenly appear to be one.

What shall we name these two points of view? As the chapter title already reveals, I recommend they be called the "mimetic" and the "transformative." I also propose we think of them not simply as two viewpoints on educational matters but as two traditions within the domain of educational thought and practice. Why *traditions*? Because each has a long and respectable history going back at least several hundred years and possibly beyond. Also, each is more than an intellectual argument. Each provokes feelings of partisanship and loyalty toward a particular point of view; each also entails commitment to a set of related practices. In short, each comprises what might be called (following Wittgenstein[1]) a "form of life," a relatively coherent and unified way of thinking, feeling, and acting within a particular domain—in this instance, the sphere of education. The term "traditions" stands for that complexity. Its use reminds us that each outlook stretches back in time, and that each has a "lived" dimension that makes it something much more than a polemical argument.

## THE MIMETIC TRADITION

We turn to the "mimetic" tradition first not because it is any older or any more important than the one called "transformative," but principally because it is the easier of the two to describe. In addition, it is closer to what most people today seem to think education is all about. Thus, presenting it first has the advantage of beginning with the more familiar and moving to the less familiar. Third, it is more harmonious with all that is thought of as "scientific" and "rigorous" within education than is its competitor. To all who rank that pair of adjectives highly, as I reservedly

do myself, therein lies an additional reason for putting it first.

This tradition is named "mimetic" (the root term is the Greek word *mimesis,* from which we get "mime" and "mimic") because it gives a central place to the transmission of factual and procedural knowledge from one person to another, through an essentially *imitative* process. If I had to substitute another equally unfamiliar word in its place, with which to engage in educational debate, I would choose "epistemic"—yet another derived from the Greek, this from *episteme,* meaning knowledge. The first term stresses the *process* by which knowledge is commonly transmitted, the second puts its emphasis on the *content* of the transaction. Thus we have the "mimetic" or the "epistemic" tradition; I prefer the former if for no other reason than that it places the emphasis where I believe it belongs, on the importance of *method* within this tradition.

The conception of knowledge at the heart of the mimetic tradition is familiar to most of us, though its properties may not always be fully understood even by teachers committed to this outlook on teaching. For this reason it seems essential to say something about its properties.

First of all, knowledge of a "mimetic" variety, whose transmission entails mimetic procedures, is by definition identifiable in advance of its transmission. This makes it secondhand knowledge, so to speak, not in the pejorative sense of that term, but simply in that it has to have belonged to someone first before it can belong to anyone else. In short, it is knowledge "presented" to a learner, rather than "discovered" by him or her.[2]

Such knowledge can be "passed" from one person to another or from a text to a person; we can thus see it as "detachable" from persons *per se,* in two ways. It is detachable in the first place in that it can be preserved in books and films and the like, so that it can "outlive" all who originally possessed it. It is detachable, secondly, in the sense that it can be forgotten by those who once knew it. Though it can be "possessed," it can also be "dispossessed" through memory loss. Moreover, it can be "unpossessed" in the sense of never having been "possessed" in the first place. A correlate of its detachability is that it can be "shown" or displayed by its possessor, a condition that partially accounts for our occasional reference to it as "objective" knowledge.

A crucial property of mimetic knowledge is its reproducibility. It is this property that allows us to say it is "transmitted" from teacher to student or from text to student. Yet when we speak of it that way we usually have in mind a very special kind of process. It does not entail handing over a bundle of some sort as in an actual "exchange" or "giving." Rather, it is more like the transmission of a spoken message from one person to another or the spread of bacteria from a cold-sufferer to a new victim. In all such instances both parties wind up possessing what was formerly possessed by only one of them. What has been transmitted has actually been "mirrored" or "reproduced" without its ever having been relinquished in the process.

The knowledge involved in all transmissions within the mimetic tradition has an additional property worth noting: It can be judged right or wrong, accurate or inaccurate, correct or incorrect on the basis of a comparison with the teacher's own knowledge or with some other model as found in a textbook or other instructional materials. Not only do judgments of this sort yield a measure of the success of teaching within this tradition, they also are the chief criterion by which learning is measured.

My final remark about knowledge as conceived within the mimetic tradition may already be obvious from what has been said. It is that mimetic knowledge is by no means limited to "bookish" learning, knowledge expressible in words alone. Though much of

it takes that form, it also includes the acquisition of physical and motor skills, knowledge to be *performed* in one way or another, usually without any verbal accompaniment whatsoever. "Knowing that" and "knowing how" is the way the distinction is sometimes expressed.[3]

Here then are the central epistemological assumptions associated with the mimetic tradition. The key idea is that some kind of knowledge or skill can be doubly possessed, first by the teacher alone (or the writer of the textbook or the computer program), then by his or her student. In more epigrammatic terms, the slogan for this tradition might well be: "What the teacher (or textbook or computer) knows, that shall the student come to know."

How might the goal of this tradition be achieved? In essence, the procedure for transmitting mimetic knowledge consists of five steps, the fourth of which divides in two alternate routes, "a" or "b," dependent on the presence or absence of student error. The series is as follows:

Step One: *Test.* Some form of inquiry, either formal or informal, is initiated to discover whether the student(s) in question already knows the material or can perform the skill in question. This step is properly omitted if the student's lack of knowledge or skill can be safely assumed.

Step Two: *Present.* Finding the student ignorant of what is to be learned, or assuming him or her to be so, the teacher "presents" the material, either discursively—with or without the support of visual aids—or by modeling or demonstrating a skillful performance or some aspect thereof.

Step Three: *Perform/Evaluate.* The student, who presumably has been attentive during the presentation, is invited or required to repeat what he or she has just witnessed, read, or heard. The teacher (or some surrogate device, such as a test scoring machine) monitors the student's performance, making a judgment and sometimes generating a numerical tally of its accuracy or correctness.

Step Four (A): (Correct performance) *Reward/Fix.* Discovering the performance to be reasonably accurate (within limits usually set in advance), the teacher (or surrogate device) comments favorably on what the student has done and, when deemed necessary, prescribes one or more repetitions in order to habituate or "fix" the material in the student's repertoire of things known or skills mastered.

Step Four (B): (Incorrect performance) *Enter Remedial Loop.* Discovering the student's performance to be wrong (again within limits usually established in advance), the teacher (or surrogate) initiates a remedial procedure designed to correct the error in question. Commonly this procedure begins with a diagnosis of the student's difficulty followed by the selection of an appropriate corrective strategy.

Step Five: *Advance.* After the unit of knowledge or skill has been "fixed" (all appropriate corrections having been made and drills undertaken), the teacher and student advance to the next unit of "fresh" instruction, returning to Step One, if deemed necessary by the teacher, and repeating the moves in sequential order. The sequence of steps is repeated until the student has mastered all the prescribed knowledge or until all efforts to attain a prescribed level of mastery have been exhausted.

In skeletal form, this is the way instruction proceeds within the mimetic tradition. Readers familiar with cybernetic models will readily recognize the five steps outlined as an instance of what is commonly referred to as a "feedback loop" mechanism, an algorithmic device equipped with "internal guidance circuitry."[4]

Which teachers teach this way? Almost all do so on occasion, yet not all spend an equal amount of time at it. Some teachers work within the mimetic tradition only on weekends, figuratively speaking, about as often as a "do-it-yourself-er" might wield a hammer or turn a wrench. Others employ the same techniques routinely on a day-to-day basis, as might a professional carpenter or mechanic.

Which do which? That question will be treated at some length later in this chapter, where I will take up the relationship between the two traditions. For now it will suffice to observe in passing what is perhaps obvious, that teachers intent upon the transmission of factual information, plus those seeking to teach specific psychomotor skills, would more likely use mimetic procedures than would those whose conception of teaching involved educational goals less clearly epistemic in nature.

What might the latter category of goals include? To answer that question we must turn to the second of the two dominant outlooks within educational thought and practice, which I have chosen to call:

## THE TRANSFORMATIVE TRADITION

The adjective "transformative" describes what this tradition deems successful teaching to be capable of accomplishing: a transformation of one kind or another in the person being taught—a qualitative change often of dramatic proportion, a metamorphosis, so to speak. Such changes would include all those traits of character and of personality most highly prized by the society at large (aside from those having to do solely with the possession of knowledge *per se*). They also would include the eradication or remediation of a corresponding set of undesirable traits. In either case, the transformations aimed for within this tradition are typically conceived of as being more deeply integrated and ingrained within the psychological make-up of the student—and therefore as perhaps more enduring—than are those sought within the mimetic or epistemic outlook, whose dominant metaphor is one of "adding on" to what already exists (new knowledge, new skills, etc.) rather than modifying the would-be learner in some more fundamental way.

What traits and qualities have teachers working within the transformative tradition sought to modify? Our answer depends on when and where we look. Several centuries ago, for example, when the mission of schools was primarily religious, what was being sought was nothing other than students' salvation through preparing them for Bible reading and other religiously oriented activities. Such remains the goal of much religious instruction today, though the form of its expression may have changed somewhat.

Over the years, as schooling became more widespread and more secular in orientation, educators began to abandon the goal of piety *per se,* and focused instead upon effecting "transformation" of character, morals, and virtue. Many continue to speak that way today, though it is more common to name "attitudes," "values," and "interests" as the psychological traits many of today's teachers seek to modify.

However one describes the changes sought within the transformative tradition, it is interesting that this undertaking is usually treated as more exalted or noble than the more mimetic type of teaching. Why this should be so is not readily apparent, but the different degrees of seriousness attached to the two traditions are apparent in the metaphors associated with each of them.

As I have already said, within the mimetic tradition knowledge is conceived of as something akin to material goods. Like a person materially wealthy, the possessor of knowledge may be considered "richer" than his ignorant neighbor. Yet, like the materially rich and poor, the two remain fundamentally equal as human beings. This metaphor of knowledge as coins in one's purse is consonant with the concomitant belief that it is

"detachable" from its owner, capable of being "shown," "lost," and so forth. A related metaphor, one often used to lampoon the mimetic tradition, depicts the learner as a kind of vessel into which knowledge is "poured" or "stored." What is important about all such metaphors is that the vessel in question remains essentially unchanged, with or without its "contents."

The root image within the transformative tradition is entirely different. It is much closer to that of a potter working with clay than it is to someone using the potter's handiwork as a container for whatever contents such a vessel might hold. The potter, as we know, not only leaves her imprint on the vessel itself in the form of a signature of some kind, she actually molds and shapes the object as she creates it. All who later work with the finished product have a different relationship to it entirely. They may fill it or empty it to their hearts' content. They may even break it if they wish. But all such actions accept the object in question as a "given," something whose essence is fundamentally sacrosanct.

The metaphor of teacher-as-artist or teacher-as-creator gives the transformative tradition an air of profundity and drama, perhaps even spirituality, that is largely lacking within the mimetic tradition, whose root metaphor of mere addition of knowledge or skill is much more prosaic. But metaphors, as we know, are mere figures of speech. No matter how flattering they might be, they don't tell us whether such flattery is deserved. They leave us to ask whether teachers working within the transformative tradition actually succeed in doing what they and others sometimes boast they can do. And that's not all they leave unanswered. Beyond the question of whether transformative changes due to pedagogical interventions really occur at all there awaits the more practical question of *how* they happen. What do teachers do to bring them about? As we might guess, it is easier to answer the former question than the latter.

Fictional accounts of teachers who have had enduring effects on their students of the kind celebrated within the transformative tradition are familiar enough to be the stock in trade of the pedagogical novel. *Goodbye, Mr. Chips* and *The Prime of Miss Jean Brodie*[5] are but two of such works that come to mind most readily. Each exemplifies a teacher who has a profoundly transformative influence on his or her students. But what of real life? Do teachers *there* make a difference of the same magnitude as do the fictional Chipses and Brodies?

An answer to that question which I find quite convincing is contained in a study undertaken by Anne Kuehnle, a student of mine a few years back. In preparation for her term paper in a course on the analysis of teaching, work which later became the basis of her master's thesis, Kuehnle distributed questionnaires to 150 friends and neighbors in her hometown of Elmhurst, Illinois; she asked them to write a paragraph or two about the teachers they remembered most vividly. The results were striking. Not only did most respondents comply enthusiastically with the request, their descriptions yielded literally scores of vignettes showing the transformative tradition in action. Here are but three of them, chosen almost at random.

> He moved the learning process from himself to us and equipped us to study independently. We were able to see such mundane concepts as money supply, price mechanism, supply and demand, all around us. We became interested. We actually talked economics after class! In Eckstein's class I became aware that I was there to evaluate, not ingest, concepts. I began to discriminate...

> She was, to me, a glimpse of the world beyond school and my little town of 800 people. She was beautiful, vivacious, witty, and had a truly brilliant mind. Her energy knew no limit—she took on all the high school English classes, class plays, yearbook, began interpretive reading and declamatory con-

tests, started a library in the town, and on and on. *She* was our town's cultural center.

> His dedication rubbed off on nearly all of us. I was once required to write him a 12-page report, and I handed in an 84-page research project. I always felt he deserved more than the minimum.[6]

These three examples are quite representative of the protocols quoted throughout Kuehnle's report. So if we can trust what so many of her respondents told us—and I am inclined to do so, for had I been asked I would have responded much as they did—there seems no shortage of testimonial evidence to support the conclusion that at least some teachers do indeed modify character, instill values, shape attitudes, generate new interests, and succeed in "transforming," profoundly and enduringly, at least some of the students in their charge. The question now becomes: How do they do it? How are such beneficial outcomes accomplished?

As most teachers will readily testify, the answer to that question will disappoint all who seek overnight to become like the teachers described in Kuehnle's report. It seems there *are* no formulas for accomplishing these most impressive if not miraculous feats of pedagogical skill. There are neither simple instructions for the neophyte nor complicated ones for the seasoned teacher. There is not even an epigram or two to keep in mind as guides for how to proceed, nothing analogous to the ancient "advice" that tells us to feed a cold and starve a fever.

And yet that last point is not quite as accurate as were the two that came before it. For if we look carefully at what such teachers do and listen to what others say about their influence, we begin to see that they *do* have some characteristic ways of working after all, "modes of operation" that, even if they can't be reduced to recipes and formulas, are worth noting all the same. The three of these modes most readily identifiable seem to me to be:

**1.** *Personal modeling.* Of the many attributes associated with transformative teaching, the most crucial ones seem to concern the teacher as a person. For it is essential to success within that tradition that teachers who are trying to bring about transformative changes personify the very qualities they seek to engender in their students. To the best of their ability they must be living exemplars of certain virtues or values or attitudes. The fulfillment of that requirement achieves its apex in great historical figures, like Socrates and Christ, who epitomize such a personal model; but most teachers already know that no attitude, interest, or value can be taught except by the teacher who himself or herself believes in, cares for, or cherishes whatever it is that he or she holds out for emulation.

**2.** *"Soft" suasion.* Among teachers working toward transformative ends, the "showing" and "telling" so central to the mimetic tradition (actions contained in Step Two: *Present* of the methodological paradigm outlined above) are replaced by less emphatic assertions and by an altogether milder form of pedagogical authority. The teaching style is rather more forensic and rhetorical than it is one of proof and demonstration. Often the authority of the teacher is so diminished by the introduction of a questioning mode within this tradition that there occurs a kind of role reversal, almost as though the student were teaching the teacher. This shift makes the transformative teacher look humbler than his or her mimetic counterpart, but it is by no means clear that such an appearance is a trustworthy indicator of the teacher's true temperament.

**3.** *Use of narrative.* Within the transformative tradition "stories" of one kind or another, which would include parables, myths, and other forms of narrative, play a large role. Why this should be so is not immediately clear, but it becomes so as we consider what is common to the transformations that the schools seek to effect. The common element, it turns out, is their moral nature. Virtues, character traits, interests, attitudes, values— as educational goals all of them fall within the moral realm of the "right" or "proper" or "just." Now when we ask about the function or purpose of narrative, one answer (some might say the only one) is: to moralize.[7] Narratives present us with stories about how to live (or how not to live) our lives. Again, Socrates and Christ come readily to mind as exemplars of the teacher-as-storyteller as well as the teacher about whom stories are told.

The examples of Socrates and Christ as both transformative models and as storytellers help us to realize that differences in the conception of teaching within the two traditions go far beyond the question of what shall be taught and how it shall be done. They extend to the psychological and epistemological relationship between the teacher and his or her students.

Within the mimetic tradition the teacher occupies the role of expert in two distinct ways. He or she supposedly is in command of a specifiable body of knowledge or set of skills whose properties we have already commented upon. Such knowledge constitutes what we might call *substantive* expertise. At the same time the teacher is thought to possess the know-how whereby a significant portion of his or her substantive knowledge may be "transmitted" to students. The latter body of knowledge, whose paradigmatic contours have also been sketched, constitutes what we might call the teacher's *methodological* expertise. The students, by way of contrast, might be described as doubly ignorant. They neither know what the teacher knows, substantively speaking, nor do they know how to teach it in methodological terms. This dual condition of ignorance places them below the teacher epistemologically no matter where they stand regarding other social attributes and statuses.

Within the transformative tradition, the superiority of the teacher's knowledge, whether substantive or methodological, is not nearly so clear-cut. Nor is the teacher's status in general vis-à-vis his or her students. Instead, the overall relationship between the two is often vexingly ambiguous if not downright upsetting to some students; it can even become so at times to teachers themselves. Nowhere are many of these ambiguities portrayed more dramatically than in the early Socratic dialogues of Plato.[8] In the person of Socrates we witness perhaps the most famous of all transformative teachers in action. He is also a teacher whose actions are often as puzzling as they are edifying.

Does Socrates know more than his students? Well of course he does, says commonsense, why else would so many seek him out for advice and confront him with the most profound of questions? Yet, as we know, Socrates rarely if ever answers the questions he is asked, often professing to know less about the answer than does the questioner himself. Is he feigning ignorance when he behaves that way? It is not always easy to tell, as we can gather from the frequent expressions of puzzlement on the part of those conversing with him. And what about his method? How canny is he as a teacher? Does he really know what he is doing every step of the way or is he more or less bumbling along much of the time, never quite sure of where he is going or of how to get there? Again, it is hard to say for sure. There are times when he seems completely in control of the situation, but other times when he seems utterly confused about what to say or do next; he even goes so far as to say so. Finally, what shall we make of the social relationship between Socrates and his fellow Athenians? Where do they stand in relation to each other? That too is a difficult question to answer definitively. Certainly he was greatly revered by many of his followers—Plato, of course, chief among them. But he was just as obviously envied by some and actively disliked by others.

A fuller treatment of the complexities and ambiguities of the Socratic method is beyond the scope of this work.[9] However, the little I have already said should make the point that ambiguities like those in the Socratic dialogues are common to the transformative tradition within teaching wherever it may be found. They are so because all such teachers are engaged in what is fundamentally *a moral undertaking* much like that of Socrates, whether they acknowledge it or not. Moreover, it is also a *philosophic* undertaking. That too is not always recognized by those actually engaged in such an enterprise.

What does it mean to speak of transformative teaching in these terms? In what sense is it either a moral or a philosophic undertaking? It is moral in that it seeks moral ends. Teachers working within the transformative tradition are actually trying to bring about changes in their students (and possibly in themselves as well) that make them better persons, not simply more knowledgeable or more skillful, but better in the sense of being closer to what humans are capable of becoming—more virtuous, fuller participants in an evolving moral order.

It is philosophic in that it employs philosophical means. No matter how else they might describe their actions, teachers working within the transformative tradition seek to change their students (and possibly themselves as well) by means neither didactic nor dogmatic. Instead, they use discussion, demonstration, argumentation. Armed only with the tools of reason, the transformative teacher seeks to accomplish what can be attained in no other way. Here is how one student of the process describes its operation within philosophy proper.

> We have discovered philosophy to be the sum total of those universal rational truths that become clear only through reflection. To philosophize, then, is simply to isolate these rational truths with our intellect and to express them in general judgments....
>
> The teacher who seriously wishes to impart philosophical insight can aim only at teaching the art of philosophising. He can do no more than show his students how to un-

dertake, each for himself, the laborious regress that alone affords insight into basic principles. If there is such a thing at all as instruction in philosophy, it can only be instruction in doing one's own thinking; more precisely, in the independent practice of the art of abstraction.[10]

Another commentator on the same subject sums up the difference by referring to himself as "a philosopher, not an expert" "The latter," he goes on to explain, "knows what he knows and what he does not know: the former does not. One concludes, the other questions—two very different language games."[11]

But talk of teachers being engaged in a moral and philosophic enterprise has its difficulties. For one thing, it sounds rather pretentious, especially when we consider some of the more mundane aspects of the average teacher's work—the routines of giving assignments, grading papers, taking attendance, keeping order in the classroom, and so on. Little of such activity deserves to be called either moral or philosophical. Moreover, teachers themselves do not seem to talk that way about what they do. Least of all do those who do it best, like Socrates.

The way out of these difficulties is to deny neither the moral and philosophical dimensions of teaching nor the prosaic nature of much that teachers actually do. Rather it requires that we acknowledge the compatibility of both viewpoints, seeing them as complementary rather than mutually exclusive. In short, nothing save a kind of conceptual narrow-mindedness keeps us from a vision of teaching as both a noble and a prosaic undertaking. Erasmus approached that insight several centuries ago when he remarked that "In the opinion of fools [teaching] is a humble task, but in fact it is the noblest of occupations."[12] Had he been a trifle more charitable he might have added that the fools were not totally wrong. Their trouble was that they were only half right.

Teachers themselves often overlook the moral dimensions of their work, but that failing must be treated as a problem to be solved, rather than as evidence of the amorality of teaching itself. There is no doubt that one can teach without giving thought to the transformative significance of what he or she is doing. But whether it should be so performed is another question entirely. Moreover, though the teacher may pay no attention whatsoever to such matters, we must ask if they are thereby eliminated as a class of outcomes. The well-known phenomenon of *unintended consequences,* sometimes referred to as "incidental learnings" when they take place within the context of a classroom, leads us to suspect that the delivery of moral messages and actions of transformative significance may often take place whether the teacher intends them to or not. Indeed, it is far more interesting to ask whether such outcomes are inevitable, which is equivalent to asking whether all teachers are ultimately working within the transformative tradition whether they realize it or not.

## ENDNOTES

1. Ludwig Wittgenstein, *Philosophical Investigations* (Oxford: Basil Blackwell, 1968) p. 9e.
2. Aristotle once remarked that "All instruction given or received by way of argument proceeds from pre-existent knowledge." *(Posterior Analytic, Book* I, 71a) By this he meant that we must begin with major and minor premises whose truth is beyond dispute before we can move to a novel conclusion. This is not quite the same as claiming that all knowledge is secondhand, but it does call attention to how much of the "known" is properly described as having been "transmitted" or "passed along" to students from teachers or teacher surrogates, such as textbooks or computers.
3. For a well-known discussion of that distinction, see Gilbert Ryle, The *Concept of Mind* (New York: Barnes and Noble, 1949).

4. See, for example, G. A. Miller, E. Galanter, and K. H. Pribham, *Plans and the Structure of Behavior* (New York: Holt, 1960).

5. James Hilton, *Goodbye Mr. Chips* (Boston: Little, Brown and Co., 1934) and Muriel Spark, *The Prime of Miss Jean Brodie* (Philadelphia: Lippincott, 1961).

6. Anne Kuehnle, "Teachers remembered," unpublished master's thesis, University of Chicago, June 1984.

7. See Hayden White, "The value of narrativity in the representation of reality," in W. J. T. Mitchell (ed.), *On Narrative* (Chicago: University of Chicago Press, 1981), 1–24. Also, John Gardner, *On Moral Fiction* (New York: Basic Books, 1978). Gardner points out that "the effect of great fiction is to temper real experience, modify prejudice, humanize." (p. 114)

8. See Edith Hamilton and Huntington Cairns (eds.), *The Collected Dialogues of Plato* (Princeton, New Jersey: Princeton University Press, 1961). See especially the *Charmides, Laches, Euthydemus, Protagoras, Gorgias, and Meno.*

9. For a fuller treatment of these and other ambiguities having to do with Socrates' teaching style see Gregory Vlastos, "Introduction: The paradox of Socrates," in Gregory Vlastos (ed.), *The Philosophy of Socrates* (Notre Dame, Indiana: University of Notre Dame Press, 1980), 1–21. Several other essays in that volume treat specialized aspects of the subject, such as Socrates' use of the technique of *elenchus.* See also, W. K. C. Guthrie, *Socrates* (Cambridge: Cambridge University Press, 1971), especially "The ignorance of Socrates," pp. 122–129. Also, Gerasimos Xenophon Santas, *Socrates* (Boston: Routledge & Kegan Paul, 1979). An unusually enlightening essay on the Socratic method is contained in Leonard Nelson, *Socratic Method and Critical Philosophy* (New York: Dover Publications, 1965), 1–40.

10. Nelson, *Socratic Method*, 10–11.

11. Jean-Francois Lvotard, *The Postmodern Condition: A Report on Knowledge* (Minneapolis: University of Minnesota Press, 1984), xxv.

12. Claude M. Fuess and Emory S. Basford (eds.), *Unseen Harvests: A Treasury of Teaching* (New York: Macmillan, 1947): v.

# Taking Women Students Seriously

## ADRIENNE RICH

I see my function here today as one of trying to create a context, delineate a background, against which we might talk about women as students and students as women. I would like to speak for awhile about this background, and then I hope that we can have, not so much a question period, as a raising of concerns, a sharing of questions for which we as yet may have no answers, an opening of conversations which will go on and on.

When I went to teach at Douglass, a women's college, it was with a particular background which I would like briefly to describe to you. I had graduated from an all-girls' school in the 1940s, where the head and the majority of the faculty were independent, unmarried women. One or two held doctorates, but had been forced by the Depression (and by the fact that they were women) to take secondary school teaching jobs. These women cared a great deal about the life of the mind, and they gave a great deal of time and energy—beyond any limit of teaching hours—to those of us who showed special intellectual interest or ability. We were taken to libraries, art museums, lectures at neighboring colleges, set to work on extra research projects, given extra French or Latin reading. Although we sometimes felt "pushed" by them, we held those women in a kind of respect which even then we dimly perceived was not generally accorded to women in the world at large. They were vital individuals, defined not by their relationships but by their personalities; and although under the pressure of the culture we were all certain we

wanted to get married, their lives did not appear empty or dreary to us. In a kind of cognitive dissonance, we knew they were "old maids" and therefore supposed to be bitter and lonely; yet we saw them vigorously involved with life. But despite their existence as alternate models of women, the *content* of the education they gave us in no way prepared us to survive as women in a world organized by and for men.

From that school, I went on to Radcliffe, congratulating myself that now I would have great men as my teachers. From 1947 to 1951, when I graduated, I never saw a single woman on a lecture platform, or in front of a class, except when a woman graduate student gave a paper on a special topic. The "great men" talked of other "great men," of the nature of Man, the history of Mankind, the future of Man; and never again was I to experience, from a teacher, the kind of prodding, the insistence that my best could be even better, that I had known in high school. Women students were simply not taken very seriously. Harvard's message to women was an elite mystification: we were, of course, part of Mankind: we were special, achieving women, or we would not have been there; but of course our real goal was to marry—if possible, a Harvard graduate.

In the late sixties, I began teaching at the City College of New York—a crowded, public, urban, multiracial institution as far removed from Harvard as possible. I went there to teach writing in the SEEK Program, which predated Open Admissions and which

*Source:* "Taking Women Students Seriously" is reprinted from *On Lies, Secrets, and Silence, Selected Prose 1966–1978,* by Adrienne Rich, by permission of W. W. Norton & Company, Inc. Copyright © 1979 by W. W. Norton & Company Inc.

The talk that follows was addressed to teachers of women. It was given for the New Jersey College and University Coalition on Women's Education, May 9, 1978.

was then a kind of model for programs designed to open up higher education to poor, black, and Third World students. Although during the next few years we were to see the original concept of SEEK diluted, then violently attacked and betrayed, it was for a short time an extraordinary and intense teaching and learning environment. The characteristics of this environment were a deep commitment on the part of teachers to the minds of their students; a constant, active effort to create or discover the conditions for learning, and to educate ourselves to meet the needs of the new college population; a philosophical attitude based on open discussion of racism, oppression, and the politics of literature and language; and a belief that learning in the classroom could not be isolated from the student's experience as a member of an urban minority group in white America. Here are some of the kinds of questions we, as teachers of writing, found ourselves asking:

1. What has been the student's experience of education in the inadequate, often abusively, racist, public school system, which rewards passivity and treats a questioning attitude or independent mind as a behavior problem? What has been her or his experience in a society that consistently undermines the selfhood of the poor and the nonwhite? How can such a student gain that sense of self which is necessary for active participation in education? What does all this mean for us as teachers?

2. How do we go about teaching a canon of literature which has consistently excluded or depreciated nonwhite experience?

3. How can we connect the process of learning to write well with the student's own reality, and not simply teach her/him how to write acceptable lies in standard English?

When I went to teach at Douglass College in 1976, and in teaching women's writing workshops elsewhere, I came to perceive stunning parallels to the questions I had first encountered in teaching the so-called disadvantaged students at City. But in this instance, and against the specific background of the women's movement, the questions framed themselves like this:

1. What has been the student's experience of education in schools which reward female passivity, indoctrinate girls and boys in stereotypic sex roles, and do not take the female mind seriously? How does a woman gain a sense of her *self* in a system—in this case, patriarchal capitalism—which devalues work done by women, denies the importance and uniqueness of female experience, and is physically violent toward women? What does this mean for a woman teacher?

2. How do we, as women, teach women students a canon of literature which has consistently excluded or depreciated female experience, and which often expresses hostility to women and validates violence against us?

3. How can we teach women to move beyond the desire for male approval and getting "good grades" and seek and write their own truths that the culture has distorted or made taboo? (For women, of course, language itself is exclusive: I want to say more about this further on.)

In teaching women, we have two choices: to lend our weight to the forces that indoctrinate women to passivity, self-depreciation, and a sense of powerlessness, in which case the issue of "taking women students seriously" is a moot one; or to consider what we have to work against, as well as with, in ourselves, in our students, in the content of the curriculum, in the structure of the institution, in the society at large. And this means, first of all, taking ourselves seriously: Recognizing that central responsibility of a woman to herself, without which we remain always the Other, the defined, the object, the victim; believing that there is a unique quality of validation, affirmation, challenge, support, that one woman can offer another. Believing in the value and significance of women's experience, traditions, perceptions. Thinking of ourselves seriously not as one of the boys, not as neuters, or androgynes, but *as women*.

Suppose we were to ask ourselves, simply: What does a woman need to know? Does she not, as a self-conscious, self-defining human being, need a knowledge of her own history, her much-politicized biology, an awareness of the creative work of women of the past, the skills and crafts and techniques and powers exercised by women in different times and cultures, a knowledge of women's rebellions and organized movements against our oppression and how they have been routed or diminished? Without such knowledge women live and have lived without context, vulnerable to the projections of male fantasy, male prescriptions for us, estranged from our own experience because our education has not reflected or echoed it. I would suggest that not biology, but ignorance of our selves, has been the key to our powerlessness.

But the university curriculum, the high-school curriculum, do not provide this kind of knowledge for women, the knowledge of Womankind, whose experience has been so profoundly different from that of Mankind. Only in the precariously budgeted, much condescended-to area of women's studies is such knowledge available to women students. Only there can they learn about the lives and work of women other than the few select women who are included in the "mainstream" texts, usually misrepresented even when they do appear. Some students, at some institutions, manage to take a majority of courses in women's studies, but the mes-

sage from on high is that this is self-indulgence, soft-core education: the "real" learning is the study of Mankind.

If there is any misleading concept, it is that of "coeducation": that because women and men are sitting in the same classrooms, hearing the same lectures, reading the same books, performing the same laboratory, experiments, they are receiving an equal education. They are not, first because the content of education itself validates men even as it invalidates women. Its very message is that men have been the shapers and thinkers of the world, and that this is only natural. The bias of higher education, including the so-called sciences, is white and male, racist and sexist; and this bias is expressed in both subtle and blatant ways. I have mentioned already the exclusiveness of grammar itself: "The student should test himself on the above questions"; "The poet is representative. He stands among partial men for the complete man". Despite a few half-hearted departures from custom, what the linguist Wendy Martyna has named "He-Man" grammar prevails throughout the culture. The efforts of feminists to reveal the profound ontological implications of sexist grammar are routinely ridiculed by academicians and journalists, including the professedly liberal *Times* columnist, Tom Wicker, and the professed humanist, Jacques Barzun. Sexist grammar burns into the brains of little girls and young women a message that the male is the norm, the standard, the central figure beside which we are the deviants, the marginal, the dependent variables. It lays the foundation for androcentric thinking, and leaves men safe in their solipsistic tunnel-vision.

Women and men do not receive an equal education because outside the classroom women are perceived not as sovereign beings but as prey. The growing incidence of rape on and off the campus may or may not be fed by the proliferation of pornographic magazines and X-rated films available to young males in fraternities and student unions; but it is certainly occurring in a context of widespread images of sexual violence against women, on billboards and in so-called high art. More subtle, more daily than rape is the verbal abuse experienced by the woman student on many campuses—Rutgers for example—where, traversing a street lined with fraternity houses, she must run a gauntlet of male commentary and verbal assault. The undermining of self, of a woman's sense of her right to occupy space and walk freely in the world, is deeply relevant to education. The capacity to think independently, to take intellectual risks, to assert ourselves mentally, is inseparable from our physical way of being in the world, our feelings of personal integrity. If it is dangerous for me to walk home late of an evening from the library, *because I am a woman and can be raped,* how self-possessed, how exuberant can I feel as I sit working in that library? How much of my working energy is drained by the subliminal knowledge that, as a woman, I test my physical right to exist each time I go out alone? Of this knowledge, Susan Griffin has written:

> ...more than rape itself, the fear of rape permeates our lives. And what does one do from day to day, with *this* experience, which says, without words and directly to the heart, *your existence, your experience, may end at any moment.* Your experience may end, and the best defense against this is not to be, to deny being in the body, as a self, to... avert your gaze, make yourself as a presence in the world, less felt.[1]

Finally, rape of the mind. Women students are more and more often now reporting sexual overtures by male professors—one part of our overall growing consciousness of sexual harassment in the workplace. At Yale a legal suit has been brought against the university by a group of women demanding an explicit policy against sexual advances toward female students by male professors. Most young women experience a profound mixture of humiliation and intellectual self-doubt over seductive gestures by men who have the power to award grades, open doors to grants and graduate school, or extend special knowledge and training. Even if turned aside, such gestures constitute mental rape, destructive to a woman's ego. They are acts of domination, as despicable as the molestation of the daughter by the father.

But long before entering college the woman student has experienced her alien identity in a world which misnames her, turns her to its own uses, denying her the resources she needs to become self-affirming, self-defined. The nuclear family teaches her that relationships are more important than selfhood or work; that "whether the phone rings for you, and how often," having the right clothes, doing the dishes, take precedence over study or solitude; that too much intelligence or intensity may make her unmarriageable; that marriage and children—service to others—are, finally, the points on which her life will be judged a success or a failure. In high school, the polarization between feminine attractiveness and independent intelligence comes to an absolute. Meanwhile, the culture resounds with messages. During Solar Energy Week in New York I saw young women wearing "ecology" T-shirts with the legend: CLEAN, CHEAP AND AVAILABLE; a reminder of the 1960s antiwar button which read: CHICKS SAY YES TO MEN WHO SAY NO. Department store windows feature female mannequins in chains, pinned to the wall with legs spread, smiling in positions of torture. Feminists are depicted in the media as "shrill," "strident," "puritanical," or "humorless," and the lesbian choice—the choice of the woman-identified woman—as pathological or sinister. The young woman sitting in the philosophy classroom, the political science lecture, is already gripped by tensions between her nascent sense of self-worth, and the battering force of messages like these.

Look at a classroom: look at the many kinds of women's faces, postures, expressions. Listen to the women's voices. Listen to the silences, the unasked questions, the blanks. Listen to the small, soft voices, often courageously trying to speak up, voices of women taught early that tones of confidence, challenge, anger, or assertiveness, are strident and unfeminine. Listen to the voices of the women and the voices of the men; observe the space men allow themselves, physically and verbally, the male assumption that people will listen, even when the majority of the group is female. Look at the faces of the silent, and of those who speak. Listen to a woman groping for language in which to express what is on her mind, sensing that the terms of academic discourse are not her language, trying to cut down her thought to the dimensions of a discourse not intended for her *(for it is not fitting that a woman speak in public);* or reading her paper aloud at breakneck speed, throwing her words away, deprecating her own work by a reflex prejudgement: *I do not deserve to take up time and space.*

As women teachers, we can either deny the importance of this context in which women students think, write, read, study, project their own futures; or try to work with it. We can either teach passively, accepting these conditions, or actively, helping our students identify and resist them.

One important thing we can do is *discuss* the context. And this need not happen only in a women's studies course; it can happen anywhere. We can refuse to accept passive, obedient learning and insist upon critical thinking. We can become harder on our women students, giving them the kinds of "cultural prodding" that men receive, but on different terms and in a different style. Most young women need to have their intellectual lives, their work, legitimized against the claims of family, relationships, the old message that a woman is always available for service to others. We need to keep our standards

very high, not to accept a woman's preconceived sense of her limitations; we need to be hard to please, while supportive of risk-taking, because self-respect often comes only when exacting standards have been met. At a time when adult literacy is generally low, we need to demand more, not less, of women, both for the sake of their futures as thinking beings, and because historically women have always had to be better than men to do half as well. A romantic sloppiness, an inspired lack of rigor, a self-indulgent incoherence, are symptoms of female self-depreciation. We should help our women students to look very critically at such symptoms, and to understand where they are rooted.

Nor does this mean we should be training women students to "think like men." Men in general think badly: in disjuncture from their personal lives, claiming objectivity where the most irrational passions seethe, losing, as Virginia Woolf observed, their senses in the pursuit of professionalism. It is not easy to think like a woman in a man's world, in the world of the professions; yet the capacity to do that is a strength which we can try to help our students develop. To think like a woman in a man's world means thinking critically, refusing to accept the givens, making connections between facts and ideas which men have left unconnected. It means remembering that every mind resides in a body; remaining accountable to the female bodies in which we live; constantly retesting given hypotheses against lived experience. It means a constant critique of language, for as Wittgenstein (no feminist) observed, "The limits of my language are the limits of my world." And it means that most difficult thing of all: listening and watching in art and literature, in the social sciences, in all the descriptions we are given of the world, for the silences, the absences, the nameless, the unspoken, the encoded—for there we will find the true knowledge of women. And in breaking those silences, naming our selves, uncovering the hidden, making ourselves present, we begin to define a reality which resonates to *us,* which affirms *our* being, which allows the woman teacher and the woman student alike to take ourselves, and each other, seriously: meaning, to begin taking charge of our lives.

## ENDNOTE

1. Quoted from the manuscript of her forthcoming book, *Rape: The Power of Consciousness;* to be published in 1979 by Harper & Row.

## CHAPTER 7 REFERENCES

Antler, J. (1987). *Lucy Sprague Mitchell: The making of a modern woman*. New Haven, CT: Yale University Press.

Apple, M. W. (1978). Ideology, reproduction, and educational reform. *Comparative Education Review, 22* (3), 367–387.

Apple, M. W. (1979a). *Ideology and curriculum*. Boston: Routledge & Kegan Paul.

Apple, M. W. (1979b). The other side of the hidden curriculum: Correspondence theories and the labor process. *Journal of Education, 162,* 7–66.

Apple, M. W. (1982a). *Cultural and economic reproduction in education*. Boston: Routledge & Kegan Paul.

Apple, M. W. (1982b). *Education and power*. Boston: Routledge & Kegan Paul.

Belenky, M. F., Clinchy, B. M., Goldberger, N. R., & Tarule, J. M. (1986). *Women's ways of knowing: The development of self, voice, and mind*. New York: Basic Books.

Bennett, K. P., & LeCompte, M. D. (1990). *How schools work*. New York: Longman.

Bennett, W. (1988). *James Madison High School*. Washington, DC: U.S. Office of Education.

Berger, P. L., & Luckmann, T. (1967). *The social construction of reality: A treatise in the sociology of knowledge*. New York: Anchor Books.

Bernstein, B. (1973). *Class, codes and control, Vol. I*. London: Paladin.

Bernstein, B. (1977). *Class, codes and control, Vol. III*. London: Routledge & Kegan Paul.

Bernstein, B. (1990). *The structuring of pedagogic discourse: Vol. 4 of Class, codes and control*. London: Routledge.

Bestor, A. (1953). *Educational wastelands*. Urbana, IL: University of Illinois Press.

Bourdieu, P. (1973). Cultural reproduction and social reproduction. In R. Brown (Ed.), *Knowledge, education, and cultural change* (pp. 71–112). London: Tavistock Publications.

Bourdieu, P., & Passeron, J. C. (1977). *Reproduction in education, society, and culture*. London: Sage.

Bowles, S., & Gintis, H. (1976). *Schooling in capitalist America: Educational reform and the contradictions of economic life*. New York: Basic Books.

Callahan, R. (1962). *Education and the cult of efficiency*. Chicago: University of Chicago Press.

Collins, R. (1979). *The credential society*. New York: Academic Press.

Collins, R. (1977). Functional and conflict theories of educational stratification. In J. Karabel & A. H. Halsey (Eds.), *Power and Ideology in education* (pp. 118–36). Cambridge: Oxford University Press.

Counts, G. (1932). *Dare the schools build a new social order?* New York: John Day.

Cremin, L. A. (1961). *The transformation of the school*. New York: Vintage Books.

Cremin, L. A. (1990). *Popular education and its discontents*. New York: Harper and Row.

Cuban, L. (1984). *How teachers taught: Constancy and change in American classrooms, 1890–1980*. New York: Longman.

Dahl, R. A. (1961). *Who governs?* New Haven, CT: Yale University Press.

Darwin, C. (1982). *On the origin of the species.* New York: Penguin. (Original work published 1859)

D'Souza, D. (1991). *Illiberal education: The politics of race and sex on campus.* New York: The Free Press.

Dewey, J. (1956). *The child and the curriculum and the school and society.* Chicago: University of Chicago Press. (Original work published 1899)

Domhoff, G. W. (1967). *Who rules America?* Englewood Cliffs, NJ: Prentice-Hall.

Domhoff, G. W. (1983). *Who rules America now?* Englewood Cliffs, NJ: Prentice-Hall.

Dreeben, R. (1968). *On what is learned in school.* Reading, MA: Addison-Wesley.

Durkheim, E. (1947). *The division of labor in society.* Glencoe, IL: The Free Press. (Original work published 1893)

Durkheim, E. (1954). *The elementary forms of religious life.* Glencoe, IL: The Free Press. (Original work published 1915)

Durkheim, E. (1961). *Moral education: A study in the theory and application of the sociology of education.* (E. K. Wilson & H. Schnurer, Trans.). E. K. Wilson (Ed.). Glencoe, IL: The Free Press.

Durkheim, E. (1977). *The evolution of educational thought.* London: Routledge and Kegan Paul. (Originally published as *L'evolution pédagogique en France* in 1938)

Freire, P. (1972). *Pedagogy of the oppressed.* New York: Herder and Herder.

Freire, P. (1977). *Education for critical consciousness.* New York: Seabury Press.

Freire, P. (1978). *Pedagogy in process.* New York: Seabury Press.

Garraty, J. A. (1985). *A short history of the American nation, Vol. B—Since 1865.* New York: Harper and Row.

Giroux, H. A. (1981). *Ideology, culture and the process of schooling.* Philadelphia: Temple University Press.

Giroux, H. A. (1983a). Theories of reproduction and resistance in the new sociology of education. *Harvard Educational Review, 53,* 257–293.

Giroux, H. A. (1983b). *Theory and resistance in education: A pedagogy for the opposition.* Hadley, MA: Bergin and Garvey.

Giroux, H. A. (1988). *Teachers as intellectuals.* Granby, MA: Bergin and Garvey.

Giroux, H. A. (1991). *Postmodernism, femininsm, and cultural theory.* Albany, NY: SUNY Press.

Greene, M. (1978). Wide awakeness and the moral life. In M. Greene (Ed.), *Landscapes of learning,* (pp. 42–52). New York: Teachers College Press.

Greene, M. (1988). *The dialectic of freedom.* New York: Teachers College Press.

Heller, J. (1985). *Catch 22.* New York: Dell.

Hirsch, E. D. (1987). *Cultural literacy.* Boston: Houghton Mifflin.

Hofstadter, R. (1966). *Anti-intellectualism in American life.* New York: Random.

Hurn, C. J. (1993). *The limits and possibilities of schooling* (3rd ed.). Boston: Allyn and Bacon.

Jackson, P. (1986). *The practice of teaching.* New York: Teachers College Press.

Kesey, K. (1977). *One flew over the cuckoo's nest.* New York: Penguin.

Kimball, R. (1990). *Tenured radicals: How politics has corrupted higher education.* New York: Harper and Row.

Kirst, M. W. (1984). *Who controls our schools?* New York: W. H. Freeman.

Kliebard, H. M. (1986). *The struggle for the American curriculum 1893–1958.* Boston: Routledge & Kegan Paul.

Laird, S. (1989). Reforming "Women's true profession": A case for "Feminist pedagogy" in teacher education? *Harvard Educational Review, 58* (4), 449–463.

Leach, W. (1980). *True love and perfect union: The feminist reform of sex and society.* New York: Basic Books.

Lloyd, S. M. (1987). *The Putney school: A progressive experiment.* New Haven, CT: Yale University Press.

Macdonald, J., & Macdonald, S. (1981). Gender values and curriculum. *Journal of Curriculum Theorizing, 3* (1), 299–304.

Mannheim, K. (1936). *Ideology and Utopia: An introduction to the sociology of knowledge.* New York: Harcourt, Brace & World.

Martin, J. R. (1987). Reforming teacher education, rethinking liberal education. *Teachers College Record, 88,* 406–409.

Marx, K., & Engels, E. (1947). *The German ideology.* New York: International Publishers. (Original work published 1846)

Miller, J. (1982). Feminist pedagogy: The sound of silence breaking. *Journal of Curriculum Theorizing, 4,* 5–11.

Mills, C. W. (1956). *The power elite.* New York: Oxford University Press.

Mitrano, B. (1979). Feminist theology and curriculum theory. *Journal of Curriculum Studies, 2,* 211–220.

Oakes, J. (1985). *Keeping track: How schools structure inequality.* New Haven, CT: Yale University Press.

Parsons, T. (1959). The school class as a social system. *Harvard Educational Review, 29,* 297–308.

Powell, A., Cohen, D., & Ferrar, E. (1985). *The shopping mall high school.* Boston: Houghton Mifflin.

Pratt, C. (1924). *Experimental practice in the city and country school.* New York: E. P. Dutton.

Ravitch, D. (1983). *The troubled crusade: American education, 1945–1980.* New York: Basic Books.

Ravitch, D. (1989). *Multiculturalism in the curriculum.* Presentation to the Manhattan Institute.

Ravitch, D., & Finn, C. E., Jr. (1987). *What do our seventeen year olds know?* New York: Basic Books.

Sadovnik, A. R. (1991). Basil Bernstein's theory of pedagogic practice: A structuralist approach. *Sociology of Education, 64* (1), 48–63.

Semel, S. F. (1992). *The Dalton school: The transformation of a progressive school.* New York: Peter Lang Publishers.

Sewall, G. (1991). Common culture and multiculture. *Social Studies Review, 7.*

Spring, J. H. (1989). *American education* (4th ed.). New York: Longman.

Tyack, D. (1974). *The one best system.* Cambridge, MA: Harvard University Press.

Tyack, D., & Hansot, E. (1982). *Managers of virtue.* New York: Basic Books.

Wright, R. (1969). *Native son.* New York: Harper and Row.

Yeomans, E. (1979). *The Shady Hill School: The first fifty years.* Cambridge, MA: Windflower Press.

Young, M. F. D. (1971.) *Knowledge and control: New directions for the sociology of education.* London: Collier-Macmillan.

## SUGGESTED READINGS

Altbach, P. G. et al. (Eds.). (1991). *Textbooks in American society: Politics, policy, and pedagogy.* Albany, NY: State University of New York Press.

Anyon, J. (1983). Workers, labor and economic history, and textbook content. In M. W. Apple & L. Weis (Eds.), *Ideology and practice in schooling* (pp. 37–60). Philadelphia: Temple University Press.

Apple, M. W. (1979a). *Ideology and curriculum.* Boston: Routledge & Kegan Paul.

Apple, M. W. (1982). *Education and power.* Boston: Routledge and Kegan Paul.

Apple, M. W. (1986). *Teachers and texts: A political economy of class and gender relations in education.* New York: Metheun.

Apple, M. W. (1987). *Teachers and texts.* Boston: Routledge and Kegan Paul.

Apple, M. W. (1993). *Official knowledge: Democratic education in a conservative age.* New York: Routledge.

Apple, M. W., & Christian-Smith, L. K. (Eds.). (1991). *The politics of the textbook.* London: Routledge.

Banks, J. A. (1988). *Multiethnic education: theory and practice* (2nd ed.). Boston: Allyn and Bacon.

Belenky, M. F., Clinchy, B. M., Goldberger, N. R., & Tarule, J. M. (1986). *Women's ways of knowing: The development of self, voice, and mind.* New York: Basic Books.

Bennett, E. W. (1988). *James Madison High School.* Washington, DC: U.S. Office of Education.

Bernstein, B. (1977). *Class, codes and control. Vol. III.* London: Routledge & Kegan Paul.

Bernstein, B. (1990). *The structuring of pedagogic discourse: Vol. 4 of Class, codes and control.* London: Routledge.

Cuban, L. (1984). *How teachers taught: Constancy and change in American classrooms, 1890–1980.* New York: Longman.

DelFattore, J. (1992). *What Johnny shouldn't read: Textbook censorship in America.* New Haven, CT: Yale University Press.

Dewey, J. (1956). *The child and the curriculum and the school and society.* Chicago: University of Chicago Press. (Original work published 1899)

Dreeben, R. (1968). *On what is learned in school.* Reading, MA: Addison-Wesley.

FitzGerald, F. (1979). *America revised: History schoolbooks in the twentieth century.* Boston: Little, Brown.

Freire, P. (1972). *Pedagogy of the oppressed.* New York: Herder and Herder.

Freire, P. (1977). *Education for critical consciousness.* New York: Seabury Press.

Freire, P. (1978). *Pedagogy in process.* New York: Seabury Press.

Gardner, H. (1991). *The unschooled mind: How children think and how schools should teach.* New York: Basic Books.

Giroux, H. (1988). *Teachers as intellectuals.* Granby, MA: Bergin and Garvey.

Giroux, H. (1991). *Postmodernism, femininsm, and cultural theory.* Albany, NY: SUNY Press.

Greene, M. (1978). Wide awakeness and the moral life. In M. Greene (Ed.), *Landscapes of Learning* (pp. 42–52). New York: Teachers College Press.

Greene, M. (1988). *The dialectic of freedom.* New York: Teachers College Press.

Greene, M. (1993). The passions of pluralism: Multiculturalism and the expanding community. *Educational Researcher, 22* (1), 13–18.

Hirsch, E. D., Jr. (1988). *Cultural literacy: What every American needs to know.* New York: Random House.

Keddie, N. (1971). Classroom knowledge. In M. F. D. Young (Ed.), *Knowledge and control.* London: Collier.

Kirst, M. W. (1984). *Who controls our schools?* New York: W. H. Freeman.

Kliebard, H. M. (1986). *The struggle for the American curriculum 1893–1958.* Boston: Routledge and Kegan Paul.

Lagemann, E. C. (1989). *The politics of knowledge: The Carnegie Corporation, philanthropy, and public policy.* Hanover, NH: University Press of New England.

Laird, S. (1989). Reforming "Women's true profession": A case for "Feminist pedagogy" in teacher education? *Harvard Educational Review, 58* (4), 449–463.

Page, A. L., & Clelland, D. A. (1978, September). The Kanawha County textbook controversy. *Social Forces, 57,* 265–281.

Peshkin, A. (1986). *God's choice: The total world of a fundamentalist Christian school.* Chicago: University of Chicago Press.

Powell, A., Cohen, D., & Ferrar, E. (1985). *The shopping mall high school.* Boston: Houghton Mifflin.

Sadovnik, A. R. (1991). Basil Bernstein's theory of pedagogic practice: A structuralist approach. *Sociology of Education, 64* (1), 48–63.

Semel, S. F. (1992). *The Dalton School: The transformation of a progressive school.* New York: Peter Lang Publishers.

Weiler, K. (1988). *Women teaching for change.* South Hadley, MA: Bergin and Garvey.

Whitty, G. (1985). *Sociology and school knowledge: Curriculum theory, research and politics.* London: Metheun.

Young, M. F. D. (1971). *Knowledge and control: New directions for the sociology of education.* London: Collier-Macmillan.

CHAPTER **8**

# Equality of Opportunity
# and Educational Outcomes

The evolution of the U.S. education system is a story that is profoundly moving because it is a narrative of struggle. From the founding of the Republic, there has been a deep belief on the part of the American people in equality of opportunity. Echoing throughout the Declaration of Independence and the Constitution of the United States are the voices of people who demand to be treated with respect, dignity, and equality. From its inception, public education has been conceived of as a social vehicle for minimizing the importance of class and wealth as a determinant of who shall get ahead. Before the word *meritocracy* was invented, Americans believed that hard work, thrift, and a little bit of luck should determine who receives the economic and social benefits that the society has to offer. To some degree, education has helped to make this dream come true. Yet, there is an underside to this story. The United States has only been partially successful in developing an educational system that is truly meritocratic and just.

In this chapter, we examine this belief in equal opportunity in the context of the social realities of life in the United States. We ask very fundamental questions. To what degree do schools mitigate the significance of such ascriptive characteristics as class, race, and gender in determining who shall receive the benefits of education? Do differences between schools make a difference in who gets ahead? What is the relationship between education and economic outcomes? And last, is it reasonable to characterize the U.S. educational system as meritocratic or does the educational system simply reproduce existing social and economic inequalities?

In 1842, Horace Mann said, "Education, then, beyond all other devices of human origin, is the great equalizer of the conditions of men—the balance wheel of the social machinery" (Walker, Kozma, & Green, 1989, p. 133). From the viewpoint of the early 1990s, can one say with certainty that Horace Mann's dream has become a reality? The answer to this question requires empirical investigation. To determine the relationship between education and equality is a complex intellectual task. Interpreting these facts is also complex. Perhaps you remember from Chapter 2 our discussion of the three fundamental points of view: conservative, liberal, and radical. Nowhere are the differences between these three groups more clearly drawn than in their rivaling interpretations of the empirical facts concerning the degree of equality in the United States. There is, so to speak, a set of calculations that could be called life arithmetic. But there is also a set of interpretations that accompany this arithmetic that are shaded by the shadow of ideology. We do not, nor could we, definitively resolve these debates. However, based on the data that are available, we would be less than candid if we did not admit that, to our way of thinking, U.S. society is deeply stratified by class, race, and gender. These forms of stratification negatively impact on the mobility of certain individuals and groups. Throughout the 1980s, the emphasis on educational reform focused on competition and excellence. In a society that is increasingly multicultural, we believe that reform must also focus on cooperation and equity.

## CALCULATING EDUCATIONAL AND LIFE OUTCOMES

Most people are aware that society is stratified— there are rich people, poor people, and people in between. People are discriminated against on the basis of gender and race. Curiously, the significance of these issues are often muted by public perceptions that in the United States, individuals, through their own efforts, can overcome the effects of stratification. That is, educational and social mobility are matters of individual life experiences. Although it is true that certain individuals do become upwardly mobile because of their success in business or because they possess an unusual talent, the stark fact is that the overwhelming number of individuals will remain in the social class into which they were born. Social stratification is a structural characteristic of societies. Human differences do not cause social stratification; social stratification causes human differences.

Sociologist Daniel Rossides (1976, p. 15) defined *social stratification* as follows: "Social stratification is a hierarchical configuration of families (and in industrial societies in recent decades, unrelated individuals) who have differential access to whatever is of value in the society at a given point and over time, primarily because of social, not biopsychological, variables." He went on to point out that "a full system of social stratification emerges only when parents can see to it that their children inherit or acquire a social level equal or superior to their own regardless of innate ability" (p. 16). In other words, parents attempt to roll the dice of life chances in favor of their children so that they may be successful in terms of material comfort, security, personal fulfillment, and occupation.

Rossides (1976) described three basic forms of social stratification. *Caste stratification* occurs in agrarian societies where social level is defined in terms of some strict ascriptive criteria such as race and/or religious worth. *Estate stratification* occurs in agrarian societies where social level is defined in terms of the hierarchy of family worth. *Class stratification* occurs in industrial societies that define social level in term of a hierarchy of differential achievement by individuals, especially in economic pursuits. Within each one of these major forms of stratification there can be other hierarchies (i.e., patriarchal distinctions between men and women) and the three major forms of stratification can overlap within any given society. For example, in the United States, individuals can experience caste stratification because of their race, while simultaneously experiencing class stratification because of their occupation and lack of property.

With this discussion as a prelude, one can begin to look at the United States in terms of social stratification. There can be little doubt that the population of the United States is stratified by class. Very briefly, approximately 1 to 2 percent of Americans are members of the upper class, approximately 15 percent of Americans are upper middle class, another 25 percent belong to the lower middle class, 40 percent are working class, and 20 percent belong to what has been called the under class. Each of these classes have a somewhat different relationship to the economy. The upper class derives most of its wealth through the possession of property; the upper middle class is essentially a professional and managerial class; the lower middle class are likely to be semi-professionals such as school teachers and small business owners; the working class derive their income directly from their labor and are often paid an hourly wage; and the under class are marginal to the economy and are often extremely poor.

In the last 10 years, the upper and upper middle class in the United States have become increasingly wealthy while the other classes have experienced a relative decline in terms of their economic security and income. In fact, the United States is the most unequal industrial country in terms of the distribution of income. According to Phillips (1990, p. 11), "America's top 420,000 households alone accounted for 26.9 percent of U.S. family net worth—in essence, 26.9 percent of the nations' wealth. The top ten percent of households, meanwhile, controlled approximately 68 percent." In 1988, approximately 1.3 million Americans were millionaires, which is double the number of millionaires in 1980. In 1953, there were only 27,000 millionaires in the United States. It was not since the latter part of the nineteenth century that the United States has experienced such an upsurge of wealth into the upper classes.

Again, according to Phillips (1990), the "downside of the American dream" is that individuals in the lower middle class, the working class, and the under class have suffered a decline in terms of their incomes when income is adjusted for inflation. To cite one example, in 1972, weekly per worker income was $366.00. In 1987, the weekly per worker income was $312.00, when adjusted for inflation. These data indicate that when calculating the effects of class in determining an individual's or group's life arithmetic, one must not fail to take into account the increasing significance of class.

Clearly, connecting the linkages between class and other forms of stratification and educational outcomes is extremely complex. In her book, *Education and Inequality* (1977), Persell provided a model for analyzing the relationship of what she calls "the societal structure of dominance" and educational outcomes. By examining

Figure 8–1, you can see that there is a set of interrelated social and school variables that create the context for the production of educational outcomes. In brief, economic and political resources directly influence the selectivity of schools and the authority structures within schools, which, in turn, influence the climate of expectations and patterns of interactions within schools.

To illustrate these relationships, imagine a public school located in a wealthy white suburb and a public school located in an urban neighborhood. The suburban school will differ significantly from the urban school in terms of its resources, its ability to monitor students' progress, its discipline, its climate of expectations, and its culture. In effect, the suburban school is similar to a private school in that it can provide better educational opportunities for its students than the urban school, which has very few resources and educates students who come to school with few advantages.

Sociologists of education have studied the relationship between education and mobility in great detail. Sometimes the study of mobility is referred to as the *status-attainment process*. Summarizing this literature is virtually impossible since there is no consensus about how much education influences attainment. Clearly, the number of years of education an individual possesses is directly linked to occupation and income. For example, individuals who attain managerial and professional statuses are very likely to have a bachelor's degree from college and to have attended some

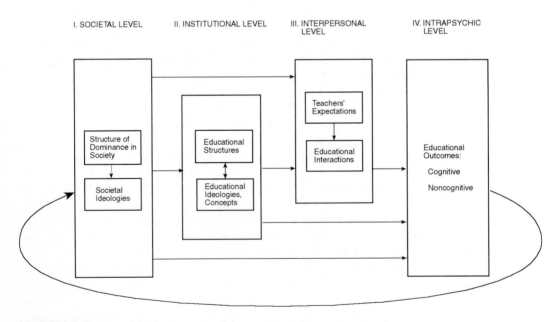

**FIGURE 8–1**
**Theoretical Model of Relevant Variables and Their Interrelationships**
*Source:* Reprinted with the permission of The Free Press, a Division of Macmillan, Inc. from *Education and Inequality: A Theoretical Empirical Synthesis* by Caroline Hodges Persell. Copyright © 1977 by The Free Press.

graduate school. Laborers and individuals in the service fields are, on average, likely to have a high school diploma. In terms of wages, individuals with a high school diploma are paid, on average, $7.00 per hour for their work, whereas individuals who possess advanced degrees are paid approximately $11.00 per hour for their labor.

To complicate matters further, other forms of stratification also influence income. In 1987, a man with five years or more of college earned nearly $42,000 a year on average, whereas a woman with the same educational qualifications earned $30,000 a year. If minorities and nonminorities are compared in terms of how much they earn, one discovers that, as in the case of gender, nonminority individuals earn considerably more money than do minority individuals.

Shortly, we will discuss the effects of race and gender on educational attainment, but for now, the central point to be made is that there is a relationship between education and attainment, although it is certainly not an open contest, as was alleged by Turner (1960) over 30 years ago. You may recall from Chapter 4 that we discussed the work of Rosenbaum (1976), who suggested that educational mobility was similar to what he called "tournament selection." In this form of competition, winners are allowed to proceed to the next round and losers are dropped. Some students are eliminated, but "winning" students must still continue to compete. Unfortunately, from the point of view of equality of opportunity, this tournament is not played on a truly level field. Privilege can tilt the field to the advantage of whites, males, and the wealthy. The empirical results of this tilting are discussed next.

**Class**

Students in different social classes have different kinds of educational experiences. There are several factors that can influence these class-based experiences. For instance, education is extremely expensive. The longer a student stays in school, the more likely he or she needs parental financial support. Obviously, this situation favors wealthier families. Families from the upper class and the middle class are also more likely to expect their children to finish school, whereas working-class and under-class families often have lower levels of expectation for their children. From a cultural point of view, schools represent the values of the middle and upper classes.

Studies show that the number of books in a family's home is related to the academic achievement of its children. Middle and upper middle-class children are more likely to speak "standard" English. Clearly, the ability to use this standard English is an educational asset. Teachers have been found to think more highly of middle-class and upper middle-class children than they are of working-class and under-class children because working-class and under-class children do not speak middle-class English. This phenomenon leads to labeling children, ostensibly according to their abilities, but covertly according to their social class backgrounds. Also, data show that peer groups have a significant influence on students' attitudes toward learning. In a school that enrolls many middle-class students, there is a high likelihood that more emphasis is placed on high academic achievement than in a school where there are few middle-class children.

It is little wonder, then, that class is directly related to achievement and to educational attainment; there is a direct correlation between parental income and children's performance on achievement tests, as well as placement in ability groups and curriculum track in high school. Study after study shows that class is related to achievement on reading tests and basic skills tests. Children from working-class and under-class families are more likely to underachieve, drop out, and resist the curriculum of the school. In terms of going on to college, there is little doubt that the higher an individual's social class, the more likely he or she is to enroll in college and to receive a degree. The more elite the college, the more likely the college is to enroll upper-class and upper middle-class students. In sum, social class and level of educational attainment are highly correlated. This finding represents a challenge to those who believe in equality of opportunity.

### Race

Despite the Civil Rights legislation of the 1960s, U.S. society is still highly stratified by race. An individual's race has a direct impact on how much education he or she is likely to achieve. Among 18-year-olds, for instance, roughly 12 percent of white students drop out of school, whereas 15 percent of African-American students and 27 percent of Hispanic students are likely to drop out of school. Among 17-year-olds, 89 percent of white students will be able to read at the intermediate level, which includes the ability to search for specific information, interrelate ideas, and make generalizations about literature, science, and social studies materials. However, 66 percent of African-American students have reached that level of reading proficiency and 70 percent of Hispanic students are reading at the intermediate level. It is not surprising, therefore, that these lower levels of proficiency are reflected by the fact that minorities have, on average, lower SAT scores than white students. As you know, there is a direct link between SAT scores and admission to college. There is also a link between SAT scores and being awarded scholarships for study in postsecondary institutions.

That race is related to educational outcomes is undeniable, although, given the nature of U.S. society, it is extremely difficult to separate race from class. In a society as segregated as that in the United States, it is not surprising that minority students receive fewer and inferior educational opportunities than white students. Explanations as to why minorities underachieve compared to whites vary. But, at one level, the answer is not terribly complex. Minorities do not receive the same educational opportunities as whites, and their rewards for educational attainment are significantly less.

### Gender

Historically, an individual's gender was directly related to his or her educational attainment. Even though women are often rated as being better students than men, in the past they were less likely to attain the same level of education. Today, females are less likely to drop out of school than males and are more likely to have a higher level of reading proficiency than males. The same is true for writing. The one area that males outperform females is in mathematics proficiency. There are numerous explanations as to why males do better than females in mathematics, the most convincing of which is related to the behavior of classroom teachers who tend to assume that females will not do as well as males in mathematics. Overall, males are more likely to score higher on the SATs than females. It should be added that more women are now attending postsecondary institutions than men, although it is true that many of the postsecondary institutions that women attend are less academically and socially prestigious than those postsecondary institutions attended by men (Persell, Catsambis, & Cookson, 1992).

In the last 20 years, gender differences between men and women, in terms of educational attainment, appear to have been reduced. There are still significant advantages for men when competing for the most prestigious academic prizes, however. Whether men receive preferential treatment within schools is an issue that will be discussed in the next chapter. There is little doubt that society discriminates against women occupationally and socially. Given this, one might wonder about the relationship between educational attainment and occupational attainment for women. Are these two forms of attainment highly correlated or, in fact, is there only a weak relationship between educational attainment and occupational attainment for women?

## Conclusion

In this section, we have examined the relationship between social stratification and educational outcomes. We have made a strong case that the ideal of equal opportunity is somewhat tarnished by the reality that an individual's origin has a significant impact on his or her destination. Education is related to mobility, but this relationship is made complex by the fact that education cannot erase the effects of inequality. Class and race, in particular, continue to haunt the egalitarian ideal that all children should be treated equally. Thinking in terms of life arithmetic, one might say that in the equation of educational outcomes, who you are is almost as significant a factor as what you know. Critics of this position might argue that effective schools can make a difference in terms of providing equality of opportunity. In the next section, we examine the issue of whether school differences have a significant impact on educational outcomes.

## SCHOOL DIFFERENCES AND EDUCATIONAL OUTCOMES

There is now a great controversy as to whether differences between schools lead to significant differences in terms of student outcomes. This may surprise you. After all, it seems only common sense that the better the school, the greater its positive impact on students. A deep faith in the power of education to overcome ignorance and inequality virtually requires one to believe that there is a close and powerful relationship between the characteristics of schools and their effects on students. Untangling this issue is a complex intellectual challenge.

The essential problem can be stated as follows: To what degree can student outcomes, whether they be cognitive or affective, be attributed directly to the organizational characteristics of schools? How can family influences, maturation, and peer influences be separated from the organizational influences of schools on students? Obviously, this is not an either/or proposition—hence, the complexity of the problem. This problem is compounded by the fact that schools have direct and indirect effects on students' lives. For example, one direct effect is the amount of cognitive growth that can be attributed to years of schooling. Indirect effects are more difficult to measure but, nonetheless, are very significant because they relate to the social consequences of having attended certain types of schools. Thus, the graduate of a socially elite private school may have gone to school the same number of years as the graduate of an inner-city public school, but the social marketability of their degrees are quite different. The higher the social status of a school, the more likely the school will be able to increase the social statuses of its graduates. Considering what is known about the class system, this should not be totally surprising, even though it may be somewhat repugnant. This issue was raised briefly in Chapter 4, when we discussed the difference between educational amount and educational route.

There are two major rivaling hypotheses concerning the relationship between school characteristics and student outcomes. The first hypothesis states that there is a strong, positive correlation between school quality and student achievement. Curiously, conservatives, liberals, and radicals all seem to subscribe to this hypothesis. Conservatives and liberals see this positive correlation as an expression of meritocracy, whereas radicals see this correlation as an expression of oppression. The second hypothesis is not popular in the educational community or with the public at large. This hypothesis states that there is a very weak relationship between school characteristics and student outcomes. That is, the organizational characteristics of schools are not strong enough to undo the cognitive and social consequences of class background. In other words, degrees simply credentialize students; the actual content of what they have learned is not terribly significant (Meyer, 1977; Collins, 1975). Testing these rivaling hypotheses is a demanding empirical task.

In this section, we examine the issues raised by the preceding rivaling hypotheses. Not all of the evidence is in; therefore, hard and fast conclusions cannot be drawn. But the debate is significant because in the balance lies significant policy decisions.

## The Coleman Study (1966)

If you were to pick up almost any textbook on education, you would most likely read that differences among schools account for a variety of student outcomes. Almost everybody in education and in the public at large are committed to the civil religion that education is meritocratic and transformative. Almost every educational reform movement rests on this assumption. To say that differences among schools do not really matter that much in terms of student cognitive outcomes is close to civil heresy. Up until the 1960s, no one really challenged the assumption that school characteristics were extremely important in determining student outcomes. It seemed common sense that the more books a school had and the more degrees the teachers had, the more the students would learn.

With the advent of computers, large-scale survey analysis became possible by the mid-1960s. Researchers could collect huge amounts of national data and analyze the data relatively rapidly. On the forefront of this type of research was the sociologist James Coleman. During this period, Coleman received an extremely large grant to study the relationship between the organizational characteristics of schools and student achievement. The motivation behind this grant was to demonstrate that African-American students and white students had fundamentally different schooling experiences. It was hoped by policy makers that Coleman's study would provide the rationale for federally funding those schools that were primarily attended by minority students.

The results of Coleman's study were shocking because what he found, in essence, was that the organizational differences between schools were not particularly important in determining student outcomes when compared to the differences in student-body compositions between schools. On average, students who attended schools that were predominantly middle class were more likely to do better on tests of achievement than students who attended school where middle-class students were not a majority. Peer group association could be more important than the number of books in the library. It should not surprise you at this point that Coleman's findings caused a tremendous controversy. After all, if differences among schools are only weakly related to student outcomes, what did this say about the power of education to overcome inequalities?

**Responses to Coleman: Round One.**   There were two major responses to Coleman's findings. On the one hand, other sociologists examined and reexamined Coleman's data. On the other hand, a group of minority scholars, led by Ron Edmonds of Harvard University, set about the task of defining those characteristics of schools that made them effective. Edmonds argued strongly that all students could learn and that differences between schools had a significant impact on student learning. We will discuss in some depth the "effective school" movement in Chapters 9 and 10.

Within the sociological community, the debate concerning Coleman's findings produced a number of studies that, when all the dust settled, more or less substantiated what Coleman and his colleagues had found. Despite the nation's best intentions, differences among schools are not powerful predictors of differences in student outcomes. After an extensive review of the literature, McDill (1978, p. 2) concluded:

> In the past twelve years a body of empirical knowledge has accumulated, beginning with the *Equality of Educational Opportunity* survey (Coleman et al., 1966), and based on both cross-sectional and longitudinal studies, which unequivocally indicates that, overall, between school differences in any measurable attribute of institutions are only modestly related to a variety of outcome variables.

In other words, where an individual goes to school has little effect on his or her cognitive growth or educational mobility. This seems to be a case where the data and common sense separate. Can it be true that the characteristics of an academically elite school are relatively insignificant in terms of student outcomes? Clearly, the implications of these findings would lead one to believe that the road to equality of opportunity does not go through the schoolhouse door. The political nature of these findings were explosive. After all, if student body composition has such a major effect on student learning, then the policy implication is clearly that poor students should go to school with middle-class students in order to equalize their educational opportunities. This assumption was the foundation that justifies busing students between schools and between school districts.

During the 1970s, this debate continued and some researchers began to examine the effects of magnet schools on student learning, arguing that schools that were innovative, learner centered, and mission driven could make a difference in what students learned and how they learned it. These studies were intriguing and provided a ray of research hope for those optimists who still believed in the efficacy of education to provide equal opportunities for all children. Still, from a research point of view, these findings were not terribly convincing. At this point, James Coleman and his colleagues at the University of Chicago reentered the debate.

**The Coleman Study (1982)**

In 1982, James Coleman, Thomas Hoffer, and Sally Kilgore published *High School Achievement: Public, Catholic and Private Schools Compared.* Like the first Coleman report, this book set off a firestorm of controversy. Coleman and his associates found that when they compared the average test scores of public school and private school sophomores, there was not one subject in which public school students scored higher than private school students. In reading, vocabulary, mathematics, science, civics, and writing tests, private school students outperformed public school students sometimes by a wide margin. Coleman and his associates (1982, p. 177) concluded:

> In the examination of effects on achievement, statistical controls on family background are introduced, in order to control on those background characteristics that are most related to achievement. The achievement differences between the private sectors and the public sector are reduced (more for other private schools than for Catholic schools) but differences remain.

In other words, differences among schools do make a difference. The Coleman findings of 1966 were challenged by the Coleman findings of 1982. Coleman and his colleagues argued that private schools were more effective learning environments than public schools because they place more emphasis on academic activities and because private schools enforce discipline in a way that is consistent with student achievement. In short, private schools demand more from their students than do public schools. As in 1966, the more recent Coleman findings were challenged by a number of sociologists and other scholars. And, as in 1966, Coleman's findings essentially withstood the criticisms leveled at them. However, the interpretations of these findings are still a matter of debate.

**Responses to Coleman: Round Two.**    The debate over the *High School and Beyond* findings has centered on the interpretations attached to the magnitude of the findings. What Coleman and his associates saw as significant, others saw as nearly insignificant. For example, Jencks (1985) used Coleman's findings to compute the estimated yearly average achievement gain by public and Catholic school students. He estimated that the annual increment attributable to Catholic schooling was tiny. To put it simply, the differences that do exist between public and Catholic schools are statistically significant, but in terms of significant differences in learning, the results are negligible. The interpretation was echoed by Alexander and Pallas (1983, p. 122):

> What then of Coleman, Hoffer, Kilgore's claim that Catholic schools are educa-tionally superior to public schools? If trivial advantage is what they mean by such a claim, then we suppose we would have to agree. But judged against reasonable benchmarks, there is little basis for this conclusion.

Subsequent studies that have compared public and private schools have also found that private schools seem to "do it better" (Chubb & Moe, 1990; Bryk, Lee, & Holland, 1993). The same criticisms that have been directed at Coleman and his colleagues, however, can be directed at Chubb and Moe. Yes, private schools seem to have certain organizational characteristics that are related to student outcomes, but are these relationships as significant as some researchers claim? This debate is not resolved, and one can expect, throughout the 1990s, that more research and more controversy will surface.

## Conclusion

Do school differences make a difference in terms of student outcomes? At this point, probably the best answer to this question is a highly qualified and realistic yes. Schools that are less bureaucratic and more academically oriented are better learning environ-ments for students. But, and this is a big *but,* these findings should not be interpreted to mean that private schools are substantially superior to public schools and therefore the public system should be privatized. On a related note, if people think of school organizations and student outcomes within the class structure, it is quite likely that differences among schools matter for middle-class children because they are the beneficiaries of the meritocratic scramble for educational advantage. For very wealthy students, the schools they attend bear almost no relationship to the money they will inherit, and for very poor students, their economic and social disadvantages are so profound that schools have little hope of altering their life chances.

## EDUCATIONAL ATTAINMENT AND ECONOMIC ACHIEVEMENT

As we saw earlier, college graduates are likely to earn higher salaries than high school graduates, and it should be noted here that high school graduates are likely to be paid more per hour than people who have not graduated from high school. Jencks (1979, p. 230) has written, "The best readily observable predictor of a young man's eventual status or earnings is the amount of schooling he has had. This could be because schooling is an arbitrary rationing devise for allocating scarce jobs; or because schooling imparts skills, knowledge, or attitudes that employers value; or because schooling alters men's aspirations."

That education is related to employment and economic achievement is undeniable. In 1987, for instance, a man 25 years or older, with three to five years of high school, was likely to earn roughly $22,000 a year. From then on, each increment in educational attainment (four years of high school, one to three years of college, four years of college, and five years or more of college) is associated with higher income. In 1987, for example, a man with five years or more of college was likely to earn $45,000 a year. The same pattern holds true for women, only for each level of educational attainment, they earn roughly $10,000 less a year than men. Looking at the relationship between educational attainment and economic achievement in another light, one can see is a strong inverse relationship between unemployment and educational attainment. That is, the more highly educated an individual is, the more unlikely it is that he or she will be unemployed.

From our previous discussion, you are aware of the fact that educational attainment alone does not explain economic achievement. Class background is a powerful predictor of economic achievement. The higher an individual's class background, the more likely he or she is to earn more money than individuals from other classes. Moreover, the higher the prestige of the occupation, the more likely it is to be filled with people with relatively high academic credentials. In surveys of occupational prestige, the professions are consistently rated to be more prestigious than other occupations, and to become a professional usually requires a great deal of education.

Not withstanding this discussion, it is not clear what it is about eduction that makes it so economically valuable. Jencks (1979) posed three possible explanations for the close relationship between educational attainment and economic achievement. It could be that education is simply a sorting device. That is, educational credentials signal to employers the market value of a prospective employee, with little reference to what the employee actually knows. Another possible explanation for why education is related to economic achievement is that educated people actually know something that is valuable to employers. The employer hires the individual with more education because he or she is more expert. The third explanation that Jencks offered concerning the relationship between education and economic achievement is that there is an interaction between years of schooling and aspirations. That is, motivated people stay in school and staying in school motivates people to achieve. There is, among some people, a hunger for education that far exceeds the rational need for a marketplace credential. After all, most college professors make relatively small amounts of money when compared to their years of education. Some people simply enjoy learning.

Sociologists have tested these rivaling explanations. Collins (1971), for instance, asked employers why they hired college graduates for managerial jobs. Did employers actually inquire into what prospective employees knew? Was there a test of potential employees' expertise? Or was it simply the credential that seemed to matter in the decision-making process? You may remember our discussion of the differences between functional and conflict theorists in Chapter 2. Collins was testing the relative efficacy of these two theories. If employers made employment decisions based on what prospective employees knew, this would substantiate the functionalist perspective because it would support the argument that the amount of schooling was a reliable index for expertise. On the other hand, if employers made employment decisions simply on the basis of a prospective employees' paper credentials, then this would be an argument for the conflict perspective. In effect, employers would be hiring individuals based on the social status of possessing a credential, rather than on the individuals' knowledge and expertise.

Collins found that, on balance, the conflict perspective was supported. Employers seldom even knew what prospective employees had studied in school, nor did they consider such knowledge to be particularly relevant in making their employment decisions. A businessman who saw education primarily as an initial screening devise said:

> Industry places a high value on the college degree, not because it is convinced that four years of schooling insure that individuals acquire maturity and technical competence, but rather because it provides an initial point of division between those more trained and those less trained; those better motivated and those less motivated; those with more social experience and those with less. (cited in Persell, 1977, p. 159)

In his book *Education and Jobs: The Great Training Robbery* (1970), Ivar Berg found that years of schooling are generally related (and sometimes negatively related) to job performance ratings. That is, his findings were very similar to those of Collins: Education counts but mostly as a social credential and not as an academic indicator of presumed expertise. Berg (1970, p. 185) wrote:

> Educational credentials have become the new property in America. Our nation, which has attempted to make the transmission of real and personal property difficult, has contrived to replace it with an inheritable set of values concerning degrees and diplomas which will most certainly reinforce the formidable class barriers that remain, even without the right within families to pass benefits from parents to their children.

It seems that from the available evidence, one can conclude that although educational attainment is directly related to economic achievement, the reason for this relationship has very little to do with technical competence but a great deal to do with social acceptability. These findings may surprise you—even shock you. Nobody maintains that the intrinsic value of an education is of no economic or social value. What is being said is that in a class system, educational credentials are valuable assets in the great status race, above and beyond their intrinsic intellectual value.

## EDUCATION AND INEQUALITY: MOBILITY OR REPRODUCTION?

In this chapter, we have put to the test the American belief in equality of educational opportunity and found that this belief is based partly on reality and partly on blind faith. The amount of education an individual receives is directly related to his or her life chances. But life chances are also directly related to where an individual is located in the class structure. Life chances are also directly related to race and, to a somewhat lesser degree, gender. Organizational characteristics of schools do have a slight impact on student outcomes such as achievement, but these differences are quite small. The larger truth is that differences between the organizational characteristics of schools only marginally affect the life chances of students, especially if social class is held constant. Although educational credentials are good predictors of economic achievement, the reason for this relationship has less to do with the amount of learning that has taken place than it has to do with the power of credentials to send social signals of respectability.

From this account, it should be clear that although education provides a method of economic and social mobility, in the main, education reproduces the existing class structure. Marxist scholars, such Bowles and Gintis (1976), have argued that there is a direct correspondence between the class system and the educational system. Although we do not subscribe to a deterministic or mechanical view of the relationship between school and society, it does appear that educational opportunities are closely related to one's social class position and that for the overwhelming majority of people, there is little likelihood that their educational credentials will lift them out of their social class of origin.

The issues that have been raised in this chapter are so fundamental and so related to the concept of democracy that they will continue to shape U.S. educational policy for the foreseeable future. The passionate belief of Americans that education can resolve economic and social problems will be put to the test in the years ahead. Although our hearts want to believe that through education we can achieve equality of opportunity, our heads must remain skeptical. The empirical evidence indicates that the United States is a long way away from achieving equal educational opportunity.

In this chapter, we have touched on many important issues regarding the relationship between education, occupation, and the reproduction of social inequalities. We include four articles that highlight some of the issues that have been discussed in this chapter. The first article, written by political scientist John F. Witte, is "Inferences from Studies of Public/Private School Differenceses." Witte addresses the fundamental problems of drawing policy decisions based on research. To what degree can one feel comfortable with the argument that private schools are more effective learning environments than public schools? Should the public subsidize private schools based on the kinds of research findings that Witte presents?

The second article, "A Black Student's Reflection on Public and Private Schools," written by Imani Perry, provides a poignant analysis of an African-American student's struggle with issues of race and schooling. Written when she was a high school student, Perry discusses the differences between her education at both public and private schools and the miseducation of African Americans in U.S. society.

Next, "Chartering and Bartering: Elite Education and Social Reproduction," written by sociologists Caroline Hodges Persell and Peter W. Cookson, Jr., illuminates the relationship between college counselors in elite U.S. boarding schools and U.S. colleges and universities that are academically selective. This article documents the process by which informal personal relationships bind institutions together. These relationships have little or nothing to do with the maintenance of a meritocracy but have a great deal to do with the transmission of privilege.

The fourth selection, "The Effects of Community Colleges: Aid or Hinderance to Socioeconomic Attainment?," written by sociologist Kevin Dougherty, is about the effects of community colleges on students' educational mobility. Some 36 percent of all students in higher education enroll in community colleges. Many people believe that the community college provides students with an opportunity to maximize their educational potentials. It has also been argued, however, that community colleges "cool out" students in the sense that aspirations become deflected and potentials are left undeveloped. We have not discussed the relationship between equal opportunity and higher education thus far. This article provides us with the opportunity to examine this critical issue.

# Inferences from Studies
# of Public/Private School Differences

JOHN F. WITTE

## FUNDAMENTAL INFERENTIAL PROBLEMS

The debate over what is likely to result under choice programs is often based on inferential evidence drawn from studies of differences in organization and outcomes between existing public and private schools. Given the hybrid system that would undoubtedly develop with a widespread choice system, it is unclear if such information is very useful in making policy decisions. Under most proposed systems, including the amalgamated system proposed by Chubb and Moe, both types of schools would be operating in very different environments. If, however, the evidence was overwhelming that either current public or private schools produce far superior educational results, we might at least recommend what shape that hybrid system should take. The evidence, however, is not overwhelming.

An additional problem is that the information that has framed the debate in the 1980s is derived almost exclusively from the High School and Beyond (HSB) study, a 1980–1984 study of 1,000 public and private high schools. The inferential problems are obvious. High schools enroll 40% of public school pupils but only 25% of private school students. High schools are very different from elementary or middle schools: They differ in size, attendance rates, organization, curriculum complexity, tracking, disciplinary problems, and the amount of learning per year that students acquired.

In addition, if Catholic schools are the model private school comparison, which they are in HSB, Catholic high schools differ substantially from Catholic elementary schools. The latter are almost all run by parishes with very simple organizations that give primary responsibility to the parish priest, the principal, and a school board. The students are mostly Catholic, and religious training is a major element of instruction. Catholic high schools, on the other hand, are run either as independent schools (40% often associated with religious orders), diocesan schools (40%), or parish schools (20%). The governing structures vary considerably, as do the student populations. Religious instruction is much less emphasized in most Catholic high schools.

To build the case for choice on research conducted almost exclusively at the high school level raises major questions both in terms of the comparison between public and private schools and in terms of generalizing within each sector.[1]

## BASIC RESEARCH DESIGNS

Because HSB was a panel study that tracked sophomores from 1980 into their senior year, the primary research analyzed 2-year changes in student scores on a battery of standardized tests. Several studies have also been done of the characteristics of those students who dropped out between their sophomore and

*Source:* John F. Witte, "Public Subsidies for Private Schools: What We Know and How to Proceed." *Educational Policy,* 6 (2), June 1992. Copyright © 1992, Corwin Press. Reprinted by permission of Corwin Press, Inc.

senior years. For test scores, the research task was to try to explain the variation in achievement changes from 1980 to 1982 for the sophomore cohort (36 sophomores in each school). The primary method was to use multivariate regression models that estimated achievement gains based on a large number of independent variables. Table 1 lists these variables and the level of the data.

Student family background characteristics and educational experiences were based primarily on student self-reports. Statistical controls were included for family background differences (family structure, income, parent education, and so on), student characteristics (prior achievement and academic records, race, and education expectations), courses taken by the student, and whether the student was in an academic track. School variables were also included as explanatory variables. In studies using the full set of schools, school variables were limited to size, student composition (percentage poor and percentage minority), school location (city, suburbs, and rural), and school resources. Several studies employing a subsample of approximately 400 schools also included extensive data on school organization and practices collected through follow-up surveys in 1984 with administrators and teachers (the Administrator and Teachers Survey). The 1984 data

were applied backward in time to the change scores between 1980 and 1982.

Studies focusing on the differences between public and private schools (rather than, for example, simply trying to determine what predicts achievement gains in public schools) analyzed these differences in one of two ways. The first, used by Coleman, Hoffer, and Greeley (Coleman & Hoffer, 1987; Hoffer, Greeley, & Coleman, 1985), estimated separate multivariate models for students in public and private schools and then compared the different effects of independent variables and estimated achievement gains in each sector. Other researchers included all students together and then employed a simple binary variable (0 if public, 1 if private) to estimate the independent effect of school sector. This approach was recommended by most of the econometricians analyzing these data. The sector variable estimates the differences in achievement gains (or the probability of dropping out), controlling for the variance explained by the other variables. Both the statistical significance and the size of these estimated effects are important in answering the question of private school superiority. Because of sampling response problems, most researchers included only public and Catholic high schools, excluding other private and elite private schools from their analyses.[2]

## TABLE 1
### Summary of Hypothesized Variables Affecting High School Achievement

Individual student variables
  Prior achievement and educational experience (achievement tests, remedial courses, educational expectation, and disciplinary record)
  Family background characteristics (socioeconomic status, race, parent expectations, and family education resources)
School/district-level variables
  School/district resources (dollars spent, salaries, buildings, and educational resources)
  School context (size and aggregate student characteristerics: percentage poor, percentage minority)
  School policies (tracking, course taking, discipline, homework, and truancy)
  School governance (principal leadership, teacher influence, teamwork, and morale)
  External authorities (influence of school boards, district administrators, and state agencies and parental involvement and influence)

## MEASURING ACHIEVEMENT

One of the problems with basing policy recommendations on HSB research is that student achievement has been almost exclusively boiled down to a set of six multiple-choice achievement tests given to 72 students in each school. Many education experts argue that such tests are a very poor measure of overall learning and achievement. Currently, test experts not only challenge standardized tests as the sole indicator of achievement but single out this form of single-step, single-referent test item as particularly bad (Cohen, 1991; National Council of Teachers of Mathematics, 1989).

In addition to these general issues, the HSB tests themselves present specific problems. Reliability of tests is measured in two ways. The first measures the relationship of each item to the overall subject being measured. This is done by computing and aggregating the correlations between items. For all the subject tests except the civics tests, the HSB tests were in this sense reliable by normal standards. However, a second measure of reliability is to use a test-retest methodology to determine if the same subjects have similar results on two or more trials of the same test. If not, the tests contain an inordinate degree of measurement error. Meyer's (1988) article questioned the reliability of the HSB tests on this ground. He found that the reliability of the tests were math = .30 (which means that it has a predicted measurement error of .7, or 70%), reading = .20, vocabulary = .16, writing = .35, science = .05, and civics = .16. There are ways to correct for this error statistically, but to date, Meyer is the only one who has employed the correct statistical model to do so (see his Table A–1).

## HOW MUCH IS LEARNED IN HIGH SCHOOL?

One of the findings from HSB that seems to trouble researchers less than it might trouble policy makers is that very little learning oc-curs between the sophomore and senior years. The HSB test battery used in most analyses includes 115 items: 38 in math, 19 in reading, 21 in vocabulary, 17 in writing, and 20 in science. *Excluding dropouts,* the sophomores, on average, answered 61.3 items correctly and the seniors (repeating the same tests) 67.5. That is a gain of approximately 11 % of the items they could have mastered (6.4/[115–61.3]). In statistical terms, they improved approximately .2 standard deviations. Although researchers have argued that these modest gains may be expected given that the last 2 years of high school are the accumulation of 12 years of school, another interpretation is that a considerable amount remains that could have been learned but was not. A more cynical observer would question whether or not high school matters much at all in terms of educational achievement.

This learning rate is even more problematic when compared to elementary schools. The learning rate in the first seven grades on standardized tests not unlike HSB tests is, on average, 1 standard deviation per year (Glass, McGraw, & Smith, 1981). The high school rate based on HSB is approximately .1 standard deviation per year. This not only reinforces the inferential problems discussed earlier but suggests two conclusions. First, if we want to understand why students learn, we should focus on when they are learning, and that means studying elementary and not high schools. Second, with so little learning taking place, it is difficult to produce effects that really seem to make a difference, except in relative terms. For example, it raises an issue (discussed shortly) as to whether it makes sense to consider overturning our existing education system in order to gain one or two more correct answers on a 115-item standardized achievement test. Because those are the sizes of effects that emerge for some of the variables linked to achievement gains, including school organization variables and whether the student is in a public or private school, the issue is extremely relevant.

## WHAT EXPLAINS HIGHER ACHIEVEMENT GAINS?

Research based on HSB data covers 10 years and includes dozens of studies. The details involved in these research projects are complex; samples, variables, statistical techniques, and conclusions vary (see Witte, 1990, for a tedious summary). There is general agreement, however, on one set of variables. Everyone agrees that the following have consistent, systematic, and policy-relevant effects on educational achievement; they are also not surprising:

- *Prior achievement,* as measured by sophomore tests and prior academic and behavioral records, always has a significant and strong effect on senior achievement.
- *Family and student background characteristics* (e.g., family socioeconomic status, parent education and expectations, and race) are statistically significant and are consistently among the largest effects relative to other variables in predicting student achievement gains.
- Students in an *academic track,* students taking more *academic courses,* and students enrolled in *advanced or honors courses* consistently learn more, but the estimates vary depending on modeling specifications.

Other variables predict achievement gains in some studies but not in others that use different statistical models or techniques:

- For some studies, *school composition* (percentage low SES, percentage minority, and ethnic diversity), and the *percentage of students in an academic track* have significant effects. In other studies, when a student's academic track and course taking are controlled, school-level composition variables are no longer relevant. The substantive importance of these effects is also uncertain because they arc measured as relative school effects.

- Several studies indicate that *school environment* (staff morale and attitudes toward education, personnel practices, strong leadership, high expectations, and so on) is related to improved achievement. The results are hard to interpret in substantive terms that apply to individual student learning. In addition, the effects appear to be marginal in terms of the amount of gain that one can expect from significant changes in relative organizational effectiveness.

## WHAT IS THE EFFECT OF PRIVATE SCHOOLS ON STUDENT ACHIEVEMENT?

The simple answer is very little. In absolute terms, Catholic high school students do much better than public high school students both on the sophomore test and in how much more they master between the sophomore and senior years. The simple means are depicted in Table 2. For simplicity, reading, vocabulary, and writing tests were combined into a verbal composite score and general and advanced math and science into a math/science composite score. Catholic school students do better on all grounds—sophomore, senior, and gain scores in both subject areas. They do relatively better, however, on the verbal composite. Overall, they end up answering 10.4 more questions correctly (out of 115) than do public school students. The real question is why, and is it a function of being in a private school?

To determine whether these differences are due to the private nature of these schools, difference in the student bodies, the courses that students take, tracking practices, and other variables must be taken into account. If those are the relevant variables that equalize students and practices, choice and private school status would be meaningless. Statistically, multivariate analyses can provide these types of controls. The relevant result is the remaining effect of being in a private school

TABLE 2
**Mean Achievement Scores of Public and Catholic School Students, 1980 to 1982**

|  | Public | | | Catholic | | |
|---|---|---|---|---|---|---|
|  | *Sophomore* | *Senior* | *Gain* | *Sophomore* | *Senior* | *Gain* |
| Verbal composite   (57 items) | 30.6 | 34.6 | 4.0 | 35.6 | 40.3 | 4.7 |
| Math/science composite   (58 items) | 30.1 | 32.2 | 2.1 | 33.7 | 36.9 | 3.2 |

*Source:* Computations are derived from Willms (1985, Table 1).
*Note.* Drop-out students are not included.

once one controls for other variables.... This effect is measured by a sector variable that indicates if a student is in a public school (coded 0) or a private school (coded 1).

Controlling for differences in relevant variables, the private school or sector variable remains statistically significant in most studies estimating achievement on standardized tests.[3] However, from a policy perspective, *the size of the effect* is even more important than statistical significance. There are two reasons for this. First, with the very large samples used in these studies, it was much easier to attain a statistically significant result than in studies based on small samples that have much higher sampling error.[4] Second, the size of the effect indicates the size of the resulting gain in achievement that would be predicted if the independent variables could be changed.

The modest size of the effect of private schools on achievement was adequately summarized in sociologist Christopher Jencks's (1985) important article. Using estimates by those who claim Catholic school superiority (Hoffer et al., 1985), Jencks computed the estimated year average achievement gain by public and Catholic students measured in standard deviations of the sophomore test and found the following:

> Public school students scores on the HS&B tests rise by an average of .15 standard deviations per year. Catholic-school students' scores rise by an average of .18 standard deviations per year if they start at the Catholic-school mean and by .19 standard deviation per year if they start at the public-school mean. The annual increment attributable to

Catholic schooling thus averages .03 or .04 standard deviation per year. By conventional standards this is a tiny effect, hardly worth study. But conventional standards may be misleading in this case. (p. 133)

He then went on to explain the modest gains in 11th and 12th grade compared with prior learning. This argument could lead to the conclusion that relative to the small gain for everyone, the Catholic difference is significant. He ended, however, by translating the effect into an average yearly increment in the 9.5 years of Catholic school that Catholic students average. The conclusion from Jencks's analysis put a final nail in the coffin: "Each additional year of Catholic schooling raises the typical Catholic-school students achievement by .11/9.5 = .01 standard deviations per year, and each year of public schooling depresses the typical public-school students achievement by .02 standard deviations" (p. 134).

In reexamining the work of Greeley, Hoffer, and Coleman, Alexander and Pallas (1985) put the magnitude of the Catholic school effect in substantive terms. They estimated that differences are so trivial that even if public schools could be changed to look like Catholic schools on relevant factors, it would shift the public schools from the 50th to only the 53rd percentile ranking on standardized tests. They conclude:

> What then of Coleman, Hoffer, and Kilgore's claim that Catholic schools are educationally superior to public schools? If trivial advantage is what they mean by such a claim, then

we suppose we would have to agree. But judged against reasonable benchmarks, there is little basis for this conclusion. (p. 122)

## ENDNOTES

1. A recently published study (Witte & Walsh, 1990) focusing on the importance of parental involvement and effective schools characteristics on achievement in city and suburban public schools demonstrated that these factors have different effects, and quite different estimation models are applicable at the elementary, middle, and high school levels.

2. The response rate for Catholic high schools was 79% (68 of 86) and for other private schools only 50% (14 of 28 eligible). Substitutions had to be used for the schools that refused (Coleman, Hoffer, & Kilgore, 1982, Table 1–1, p. 12). The elite private schools, because of their cost and selectivity, were anomalies from the beginning. Based on the bias implied in the non-Catholic sample, nearly all researchers heeded the early advice of Goldberger and Cain (1982) to drop those schools. Exceptions are Coleman, Hoffer, and Greeley who included them but performed separate analyses with notes of caution. Only Chubb and Moe lumped them together with Catholic schools. They repeated their analysis in an appendix using only public schools.

3. Exceptions are Willms (1985) and Lee and Bryk (1989).

4. Sampling error is the error that exists when generalizing from a study sample (HSB students) to the targeted population (all U.S. high school students). This depends primarily on sample size and should not be confused with measurement error of individual variables, such as the tests described earlier, or the error in relying on students providing family background data.

## REFERENCES

Alexander, K. L., & Pallas, A. M. (1985). School sector and cognitive performance: When is a little a little? *Sociology of Education, 58,* 115–128.

Cohen, D. K. (1991). Governance and instruction: The promise of decentralization and choice. In W. H. Clune & J. F. Witte (Eds.), *Choice and control in American education: Vol. 1. The theory of choice and control in education* (pp. 337–86). New York: Falmer.

Coleman, J. S., & Hoffer, T. (1987). *Public and private high schools.* New York: Basic Books.

Coleman, J. S., Hoffer, T., & Kilgore, S. (1982). *High school achievement.* New York: Basic Books.

Glass, G. V., McGraw, B., & Smith, M. L. (1981). *Meta-analysis in social research.* Beverly Hills, CA: Sage.

Goldberger, A., & Cain, G. (1982). The causal analysis of cognitive outcomes in the Coleman, Hoffer and Kilgore report. *Sociology of Education, 55,* 103–122.

Hoffer, T., Greely, A. M., & Coleman, J. S. (1985). Achievement growth in public and Catholic high schools. *Sociology of Education, 58,* 74–97.

Jencks, C. (1985). How much do high school students learn? *Sociology of Education, 58,* 128–135.

Lee, V. E., & Bryk, A. S. (1989). A multilevel model of the social distribution of high school achievement. *Sociology of Education, 62,* 172–192.

Meyer, R. H. (1988). *Applied versus traditional mathematics: New economic models of the contribution of high school courses to mathematics proficiency.* Washington, DC: National Assessment of Vocational Education.

National Council of Teachers of Mathematics. (1989). *Curriculum standards for school mathematics.* Reston, VA: Author.

Willms, J. D. (1985). Catholic school effects on academic achievement: New evidence from the High School and Beyond follow-up study. *Sociology of Education, 58,* 98–114.

Witte, J. F. (1990, August). *Understanding high school education: After a decade of research, do we have any confident policy recommendations?* Paper presented at the annual meeting of the American Political Science Association, San Francisco.

Witte, J. F., & Walsh, D. (1990). A systematic test of the effective schools model. *Educational Evaluation and Policy Analysis, 12,* 188–212.

# A Black Student's Reflection on Public and Private Schools

IMANI PERRY

My name is Imani Perry. I am a fifteen-year-old Black female who has experienced both private and public education. These experiences have led me to believe there are significant differences between the two types of education that deserve to be acknowledged and resolved by society as a whole.

After ten years in private schools I made the decision to attend a public school. I left because I felt isolated as a person of color. I yearned to have a large, strong Black community be a part of my development. I believed that I would find such a community in the public high school of my city, which is a fairly urban school with approximately 2,600 students, 20 percent of whom are Black.

Despite the fact that I had never been in a traditional public school environment, when I decided to go to one I had certain expectations about the teaching. I assumed that the teaching philosophy would be similar to that of the private schools I had attended. I expected that any teaching differences that did exist would be limited to less sophisticated reading, or a less intense work load. As I quickly learned, the differences were more substantial.

I believe the differences I found in the teaching between the private and public schools that I attended would best be illustrated by several examples of what I encountered. My initial realization of this difference began with an argument I had with a math teacher over a point value on a test. I felt that he should give partial credit for

problems with computational errors rather than procedural errors or conceptual misunderstanding. I presented this point to the math teacher, who responded by saying math is computation and the theories and concepts of math are only used to compute. I was astonished by this statement. Coming from a school where the teachers' stated goal for freshman math was to begin to teach you how to become a "theoretical mathematician," my entire perception of math was different. Perhaps that emphasis of theoretical math was also extreme; nevertheless, I believe that a good math teacher believes that computation in math should be used to assist in the organization of theories. Computation is a necessary but not sufficient step toward math knowledge. I felt this teacher was probably the product of schooling that did not emphasize the artistic qualities of math. While I could sympathize with his position, I felt that all I loved about math—new ideas, discussing unproved theorems, and developing personal procedures—was being ignored. I withdrew from this course only to find the ideological differences emerged again in my advanced English class at the public school, particularly in essay writing.

In this class, once we wrote a paper—mind you, with no assistance from the teacher—the process ended. We did not discuss papers, receive constructive criticism, or improve them through rewriting. Despite the fact that there was no proofreading assistance offered, 10 percent of the grade was taken off for

*Source:* Perry, Imani, "A Black Student's Reflection on Public and Private Schools," *Harvard Educational Review,* 58:3, pp. 332–336. Copyright © 1988 by the President and Fellows of Harvard College. All rights reserved.

sentence errors. It seemed as if the teacher assumed we no longer needed to continue developing our writing skills.

In my last school, which had an abundance of excellent essayists, my English teacher would have a detailed description of what he felt about each paper. At points where he felt one deserved praise or criticism, he would make comments in the margin. He would not neglect to correct punctuation errors—such as commas instead of semicolons—but these errors were not the sole criteria for our grades, especially if the writing was good. The emphasis was upon improving intellectual and organizational skills to raise the quality of the writing.

These examples illustrate my belief that my learning environment had changed from a place where thought and theory were emphasized to a place where form and precision were emphasized. The teaching system at the public school appears to assume that at some point in our education, learning and thinking are no longer important. Schooling in this situation becomes devoted to making things look correct. This is in sharp contrast to my private schools, where proper form was something I learned was necessary, but secondary in importance to the content and organization of what is produced.

Because of this difference in the concept of teaching and learning, there is also a difference in what and who teachers consider intelligence. The teaching at the public school has less to do with thinking and processing ideas, and more to do with precision and detail in appearance. Therefore, students who are considered intelligent by the public school faculty possess different skills than those at the private schools I have attended. In the public school a student is considered intelligent if he or she is well-behaved and hard working. The ability to grasp a subject in its entirety—from theory to practice—is not valued.

For example, in the fall of 1987 there was an academic contest, where my school was competing against other public schools. All the teachers I encountered were very enthusiastic about it. The students who were selected to participate were raised on a pedestal. These students, most of whom were clean-cut and apparently straight-laced, were to serve as our models of very intelligent students. They were drilled in formulas, book plots, and other information for several days a week. It seemed as if the teachers were not concerned with whether the students digested the depth of these subjects and resources as long as the students completed all the reading, memorized the facts, and could repeat the information. The contest was more a demonstration of a memory function than anything else. In my opinion there is nothing wrong with such a contest, but it should be recognized for what it is and is not. One thing it is not is a true measure of knowledge and ability. This was never recognized by the school.

Another example of how a different view of intelligence is manifested in this public school is the school's view of two students whom I know. I will identify them as Student A and Student B. Student B is an intellectual. She reads, is analytical in her discussions and is knowledgeable. Student A is very precise with his homework, answers the patronizing questions the teachers ask ('What color was the horse?" "Black with a white spot!" "Correct!"), and is very "all-American" in behavior and appearance. Student A is considered more intelligent at this public school because he displays skills that are considered signs of intelligence at this school. The intelligence criteria at this school are more related to superficial qualities such as appearance, knowing facts, etc., rather than the intellectual qualities that student B possesses. Student B displays an ability to learn and write in creative and analytical formats. I left a school where the criterion for intelligence was the student's thought process resulting from the information, for a school where the information was the measure of intelligence.

In reflecting on schooling it is important to realize that all people, including teachers, have biases based on the physical appearances of other people. On the train most people are more likely to see next to the clean-shaven Harvard freshman than next to the Mohawked, multiple-earringed punk-rocker. In teachers, however, these biases should diminish as they begin to know a student. Unfortunately, in the public school there is an absence of teacher-student contact. Because of this lack of contact there are no criteria by which intelligence can be determined, besides grades, appearance, and behavior. As I mentioned before, the grading system at this school often reflects one's ability to memorize and not one's thinking and analytical abilities. Moreover, since people are biased in their acceptance of different appearances, students who look different are judged differently. The only way they can make up for this difference is to be "well behaved," and, as I will mention later, the definition of well-behaved is arbitrary.

All these issues I have discussed have very negative effects for students from minority groups, more specifically the Black and Hispanic youths who make up a large percentage of most urban schools. It is those Black and Hispanic students who retain strong cultural characteristics in their personalities who are most negatively acted by teachers' emphasis on behavior, appearance, and respect for authority.

Public schools' emphasis on the teaching of form merely trains students for low-powered or menial jobs that do not require analytical thought. It is evident when most students are discussing what they intend to be that their goals are most often focused toward areas and professions about which they have some idea or knowledge. If in class you've never spoken about how language and colloquialisms are reflections of the society you are studying, you definitely will not be thinking of being a linguist. And if you are only asked to type a paper summarizing the book, rather than writing an analysis of it, the primary skill shown is typing. This should not be the main skill which is emphasized.

The neglect of intellectual development also occurs in higher-level classes, but at least the resources, books, etc., available to students are not altogether lacking in intellectual value. Occasionally these resources will have depth and content, be philosophical, or insightful. But in lower-level classes, where minority students are most often found and where bad textbooks are used without outside resources, the reading has less content, and the point of reading is to perfect reading skills, not to broaden thinking skills or gain knowledge of how the subject is currently affecting us. It is often not possible to broaden your thinking skills or knowledge with the books used in lower-level classes, which are more often stripped of any content. In an upper-level class, if you have a parent who wants you to know the subject in depth, and to think about it, it is possible to do that detached from the school environment, because the subject matter may have content, or have some meaning beyond the words. My high-level sophomore English class read *Moby Dick* as an outside reading. We didn't discuss the symbolism or religious qualities of it, but I am aware of them because I read critical essays and discussed them with my mother. If one is reading a book which has been stripped of meaningful content, it is not helpful to do outside research, because it is lacking in meaning.

Many students from minority groups are being trained only in form and not in creative ways of thinking. This I believe causes disenchantment among students. Upper-class students are not as affected, because of their social class, and their "social responsibility" to be achievers. This is especially true of upper-class students in a public school whose social-class peers are in private schools. But instead of striving to be true learners, they quickly learn how to be good students by being well-behaved. What well-behaved means is always taking the teacher's word as absolute truth and never questioning the teacher's authority. This definition of well-behaved is of course culturally based and can be in opposition to cultures of Black and Hispanic students.

In Black and Hispanic cultures, respect and obedience come and develop with the relationship. Rather than being automatic, respect must be earned. For example, one will occasionally hear a Black child say to a stranger, "You can't tell me what to do, you're not my mother." But at the same time, often one will see Black kids following the orders and rules of an adult friend of the family, whom they would under no circumstances disrespect. In addition, in Black and Hispanic cultures it appears that adult and child cultures are more integrated than those of other ethnic groups. For example, parties in the Hispanic community will often have an age range from toddler to elderly. Children are often present in the conversation and socializing of adults and are not treated as separate, as they may be in other cultures.

When this relationship is not made between teacher and student, it is not an acceptable educational situation, because the Black and Hispanic students are now expected to respect someone in a different manner than their culture has socialized them to. Often students are not aware of the fact that the demands being placed on them by the relationship conflict with those of their culture. They then show signs of what a teacher views as a lack of the respect that he/she deserves. The student might feel it is just a sign that they do not know the teacher and have no obligation to him or her. Many times I have seen a dumbstruck student of color sent to detention; when asked what he or she did, the student will seriously say that he or she has no idea; perhaps that he or she sucked his or her teeth in dismay, or something of that sort.

Black and Hispanic students have less of a chance at building strong relationships with any teachers because their appearance and behavior may be considered offensive to the middle-class White teaches. These students show signs of what White teachers, and some teachers of color, consider disrespect, and they do not get the nurturing relationships that develop respect and dedication. They are considered less intelligent, as can be seen in the proportion of Blacks and Hispanics in lower-level as opposed to upper-level classes. There is less of a teacher-student contact with "underachievers," because they are guided into peer tutoring programs. Perhaps this is understandable, because the teachers have less of a vested interest in the achievement of students that are not of their community, or have less of an idea of how to educate them. Public school teachers are no longer part of the same community as the majority of their students. The sad part of the situation is that many students believe that this type of teaching is what academic learning is all about. They have not had the opportunity to experience alternative ways of teaching and learning. From my experience in public school, it appears that many minority students will never be recognized as capable of analytical and critical thinking.

In the beginning of this article I spoke about my decision to leave my private school because of feeling isolated. After three months at a large urban public school I found myself equally isolated—intellectually as well as racially. My thinking process has gradually affected my opinions and character. I am in upper-level classes in which there are barely any kids of color, except Asians. Black and Hispanic students have been filtered down into lower-level classes. Most of the students I meet are kind, interesting people whom I like and respect. However, because the environment of the school is one in which ideas are not valued or fostered, I find it difficult to discuss issues with them, because my thoughtfulness has flourished, while others have been denied an opportunity to explore their intellectual development. I am now at a point of deciding which isolation is worse, cultural/racial or intellectual-opinion-based and slightly racial. This is a decision many Black students who have attended private schools at some time are wrestling to make, a decision that will affect their development, knowledge, and viewpoint of education, and their relationships to educators—those supposed possessors of greater knowledge than themselves.

## AFTERWORD

Since the writing of this article I have returned to a private school with the feeling that one's educational development is too much to sacrifice. I now attend a private high school with a strong unified Black community, as well as academic merit. Even though I did not remain at the urban public school, I valued my experience there, mostly because through it I learned one of the most blatant forms of oppression and inequity for lower-class students in American society, and I appreciate the opportunities with which I have been blessed.

# Chartering and Bartering:
# Elite Education and Social Reproduction

CAROLINE HODGES PERSELL
PETER W. COOKSON, JR.

The continuation of power and privilege has been the subject of intense sociological debate. One recurring question is whether the system of mobility is open or whether relationships of power and privilege are reproduced from one generation to the next. If reproduction occurs, is it the reproduction of certain powerful and privileged families or groups (cf. Robinson, 1984)? Or, does it involve the reproduction of a structure of power and privilege which allows for replacement of some members with new recruits while preserving the structure?

The role of education in these processes has been the subject of much dispute. Researchers in the status attainment tradition stress the importance for mobility of the knowledge and skills acquired through education thereby emphasizing the meritocratic and open basis for mobility (e.g., Alexander and Eckland, 1975; Alexander et al., 1975; Blau and Duncan, 1967; Haller and Portes, 1973; Otto and Haller, 1979; Kerckhoff, 1984; Sewell et al., 1969, 1970; Wilson and Portes, 1975). On the other hand, theorists such as Bowles and Gintis (1976) suggest education inculcates certain non-cognitive personality traits which serve to reproduce the social relations within a class structure; thus they put more emphasis on non-meritocratic features in the educational process.

Collins (1979) also deals with non-meritocratic aspects when he suggests that educational institutions develop and fortify status groups, and that differently valued educational credentials protect desired market positions such as those of the professions. In a related vein, Meyer (1977) notes that certain organizational "charters" serve as "selection criteria" in an educational or occupational marketplace. Meyer defines "charter" as "the social definition of the products of [an] organization" (Meyer 1970:577). Charters do not need to be recognized formally or legally to operate in social life. If they exist, they would create structural limitations within a presumably open market by making some people eligible for certain sets of rights that are denied to other people.

Social observers have long noted that one particular set of schools is central to the reproduction and solidarity of a national upper class, specifically elite secondary boarding schools (Baltzell, 1958, 1964; Domhoff, 1967, 1970, 1983; Mills, 1956). As well as preparing their students for socially desirable colleges and universities, traditionally, such schools have been thought to build social networks among upper class scions from various regions, leading to adult business deals and marriages. Although less than one percent of the American population attends such schools, that one percent represents a strategic segment of American life that is seldom directly studied. Recently, Useem and Karabel (1984) reported that graduates of 14 elite boarding schools were much more likely than non-graduates to become part of the "inner

*Source:* Copyright © 1985 by the Society for the Study of Social Problems. Reprinted from *Social Problems, 33,* (2), December, 1985, pp. 114–129, by permission.

circle" of Fortune 500 business leaders. This evidence suggests that elite schools may play a role in class reproduction.

Few researchers have gained direct access to these schools to study social processes bearing on social reproduction. The research reported here represents the first systematic study of elite secondary boarding schools and their social relations with another important institution, namely colleges and universities.

The results of this research illustrate Collins' view that stratification involves networks of "persons making bargains and threats... [and that] the key resource of powerful individuals is their ability to impress and manipulate a network of social contacts" (1979: 26). If such were the case, we would expect to find that upper class institutions actively develop social networks for the purpose of advancing the interests of their constituencies.

By focusing on the processes of social reproduction rather than individual attributes or the results of intergenerational mobility, our research differs from the approaches taken in both the status attainment and status allocation literature. Status attainment models focus on individual attributes and achievements, and allocation models examine structural supports or barriers to social mobility; yet neither approach explores the underlying processes. Status attainment models assume the existence of a relatively open contest system, while reproduction and allocation models stress that selection criteria and structural barriers create inequalities, limiting opportunities for one group while favoring another (Kerckhoff, 1976, 1984). Neither attainment nor allocation models show how class reproduction, selection criteria, or structural opportunities and impediments operate in practice.

Considerable evidence supports the view that structural limitations operate in the labor market (e.g., Beck et al., 1978; Bibb and Form, 1977; Stolzenberg, 1975) but, with the exception of tracking, little evidence has been found that similar structural limitations

exist in education. Tracking systems create structural impediments in an open model of educational attainment (Oakes, 1985; Persell, 1977; Rosenbaum, 1976, 1980), although not all research supports this conclusion (e.g., Alexander et al., 1978; Heyns, 1974).

In this paper we suggest that there is an additional structural limitation in the key transition from high school to college. We explore the possibility that special organizational "charters" exist for certain secondary schools and that a process of "bartering" occurs between representatives of selected secondary schools and some college admissions officers. These processes have not been clearly identified by prior research on education and stratification, although there has been some previous research which leads in this direction.

## EMPIRICAL LITERATURE

Researchers of various orientations concur that differences between schools seem to have little bearing on student attainment (Averch et al., 1972; Jencks et al., 1972; Meyer, 1970, 1977). Indeed, Meyer (1977) suggests the most puzzling paradox in the sociology of American education is that while schools differ in structure and resources, they vary little in their effects because all secondary schools are assumed to have similar "charters." Meyer believes that no American high school is specially chartered by selective colleges in the way, for instance, that certain British Public Schools have been chartered by Oxford and Cambridge Universities. Instead, he suggests that "all American high schools have similar status rights, (and therefore) variations in their effects should be small" (Meyer, 1977: 60).

Kamens (1977: 217–218), on the other hand, argues that "schools symbolically redefine people and make them eligible for membership in societal categories to which specific sets of rights are assigned." The work of Alexander and Eckland (1977) is consistent with this view. These researchers found that students who attended high schools where the social status of the student body was high also attended selective colleges at a greater rate than did students at other high schools, even when individual student academic ability and family background were held constant (Alexander and Eckland, 1977). Their research and other work finding a relationship between curricular track placement and college attendance (Alexander et al., 1978; Alexander and McDill, 1976; Jaffe and Adams, 1970; Rosenbaum, 1976, 1980) suggest that differences between schools may affect stratification outcomes.

Research has shown that graduation from a private school is related to attending a four-year (rather than a two-year) college (Falsey and Heyns, 1984), attending a highly selective college (Hammack and Cookson, 1980), and earning higher income in adult life (Lewis and Wanner, 1979). Moreover, Cookson (1981) found that graduates of private boarding schools attended more selective colleges than did their public school counterparts, even when family background and Scholastic Aptitude Test (SAT) scores were held constant. Furthermore, some private colleges acknowledge the distinctive nature of certain secondary schools. Klitgaard (1985: Table 2.2) reports that students from private secondary schools generally had an advantage for admission to Harvard over public school graduates, even when their academic ratings were comparable. Karen (1985) notes that applications to Harvard from certain private boarding schools were placed in special colored dockets, or folders, to set them apart from other applications. Thus, they were considered as a distinct group. Not only did Harvard acknowledge the special status of certain schools by color-coding their applicants' folders, attendance at one of those schools provided an advantage for acceptance, even when parental back-

ground, grades, SATS, and other characteristics were controlled (Karen, 1985).

## NETWORKS AND THE TRANSMISSION OF PRIVILEGE

For these reasons we believe it is worth investigating whether certain secondary schools have special organizational charters, at least in relation to certain colleges. If they do, the question arises, how do organizational charters operate? Network analysts suggest that "the pattern of ties in a network provides significant opportunities and constraints because it affects the relative access of people and institutions to such resources as information, wealth and power" (Wellman, 1981: 3). Furthermore, "because of their structural location, members of a social system differ greatly in their access to these resources" (Wellman, 1981: 30). Moreover, network analysts have suggested that class-structured networks work to preserve upper class ideology, consciousness, and life style (see for example Laumann, 1966: 132–36).

We expect that colleges and secondary schools have much closer ties than has previously been documented. Close networks of personal relationships between officials at certain private schools and some elite colleges transform what is for many students a relatively standardized, bureaucratic procedure into a process of negotiation. As a result, they are able to communicate more vital information about their respective needs, giving selected secondary school students an inside track to gaining acceptance to desired colleges. We call this process "bartering."

## SAMPLE AND DATA

Baltzell (1958, 1964) noted the importance of elite secondary boarding schools for upper class solidarity. However, he was careful to distinguish between those boarding schools that were truly socially elite and those that had historically served somewhat less affluent and less powerful families. He indicates that there is a core group of eastern Protestant schools that "set the pace and bore the brunt of criticism received by private schools for their so-called 'snobbish,' 'undemocratic' and even 'un-American' values" (Baltzell, 1958: 307–308). These 16 schools are: Phillips (Andover) Academy (MA), Phillips Exeter Academy (NH), St. Paul's School (NH), St. Mark's School (MA), Groton School (MA), St. George's School (RI), Kent School (CT), The Taft School (CT), The Hotchkiss School (CT), Choate Rosemary Hall (CT), Middlesex School (MA), Deerfield Academy (MA), The Lawrenceville School (NJ), The Hill School (PA), The Episcopal High School (VA), and Woodberry Forest School (VA). We refer to the schools on Baltzell's list as the "select 16."[1]

In 1982 and 1983, we visited a representative sample of 12 of the select 16 schools. These 12 schools reflect the geographic distribution of the select 16 schools. In this time period we also visited 30 other "leading" secondary boarding schools drawn from the 1981 *Handbook of Private Schools'* list of 289 "leading" secondary boarding schools. This sample is representative of leading secondary boarding schools nationally in location, religious affiliation, size, and the sex composition of the student body. These schools are organizationally similar to the select 16 schools in offering only a college preparatory curriculum, in being incorporated as non-profit organizations, in their faculty/student ratios, and in the percent of boarders who receive financial aid. They differ somewhat with respect to sex composition, average size, the sex of their heads, and number of advanced placement courses (see Table 1). However, the key difference between the select 16 schools and the other "leading" schools is that the former are more socially elite than the latter. For instance, in one of the select 16 boarding schools in 1982, 40 percent of the current students' parents were listed *in Social Register.*[2]

All 42 schools were visited by one or both of the authors. Visits lasted between one and five days and included interviews with administrators, teachers and students. Most relevant to this study were the lengthy interviews with

**TABLE 1**
**Comparison of Population and Two Samples of Boarding Schools**

|  | Total Population (N = 289) | Other Boarding School Sample (N = 30) | Select 16 Sample (N = 12) |
|---|---|---|---|
| Percent with college preparatory curriculum | 100 | 100 | 100 |
| Percent with no religious affiliation | 65 | 70 | 67 |
| Percent incorporated, not-for-profit | 83 | 90 | 83 |
| Average faculty/student ratio | 0.17 | 0.15 | 0.15 |
| Average percent of boarders aided | 15 | 16 | 18 |
| Percent of schools which are all-boys | 28 | 17 | 33 |
| Percent of schools which are all-girls | 17 | 28 | 0 |
| Percent coeducational schools | 55 | 55 | 67 |
| Percent with male heads | 92 | 73 | 100 |
| Average number of advanced courses | 3.5 | 4.8 | 6.7 |
| Average size | 311 | 322 | 612 |

*Note:* Computed from data published in the *Handbook of Private Schools* (1981).

the schools' college advisors. These interviews explored all aspects of the college counseling process, including the nature and content of the advisors' relationships with admissions officers at various colleges. At a representative sample of six of the select 16 schools and a representative sample of 13 of the other "leading" schools a questionnaire was administered to seniors during our visits.[3] The questionnaire contained more than 50 items and included questions on parental education, occupation, income, number of books in the home, family travel, educational legacies as well as many questions on boarding school life and how students felt about their experiences in school. Overall, student survey and school record data were collected on 687 seniors from the six select 16 schools and 658 seniors from other leading schools. Although not every piece of data was available for every student, we did obtain 578 complete cases from six select 16 schools and 457 cases from ten leading schools.[4] School record data included student grade point averages, Scholastic Aptitude Test (SAT) scores, class rank, names of colleges to which students applied, names of colleges to which students were accepted, and names of colleges students will attend. This material was supplied by the schools after the seniors graduated, in the summer or fall of 1982 and 1983. With this population actual enrollment matches school reports with high reliability. The record data have been linked with questionnaire data from the seniors and with various characteristics of the college. The colleges students planned to attend, were coded as to academic selectivity, Ivy League, and other characteristics not analyzed here.[5]

## CHARTERING

Historical evidence shows that the select 16 schools have had special charters in relation to Ivy League colleges in general, and Harvard, Yale, and Princeton in particular. In the

1930s and 1940s, two-thirds of all graduates of 12 of the select 16 boarding schools attended Harvard, Yale, or Princeton (Karabel, 1984). But, by 1973, this share had slipped noticeably to an average of 21 percent, although the rate of acceptance between schools ranged from 51 percent to 8 percent (Cookson and Persell 1978: Table 4). In the last half century, then, the proportion of select 16 school graduates who attended Harvard, Yale or Princeton dropped substantially.

This decrease was paralleled by an increase in the competition for admission to Ivy League colleges. According to several college advisors at select 16 boarding schools, 90 percent of all applicants to Harvard in the 1940s were accepted as were about half of those in the early 1950s. In 1982, the national acceptance rate for the eight Ivy League schools was 26 percent, although it was 20 percent or less at Harvard, Yale and Princeton *(National College Data Bank,* 1984).

The pattern of Ivy League college admissions has changed during this time. Ivy League colleges have begun to admit more public school graduates. Before World War II at Princeton, for example, about 80 percent of the entering freshmen came from private secondary schools (Blumberg and Paul, 1975: 70). In 1982, 34 percent of the freshman class at Harvard, 40 percent of Yale freshmen, and 40 percent of Princeton freshmen were from nonpublic high schools *(National College Data Bank, 1984).*

This shift in college admissions policy, combined with increased financial aid and an inflationary trend in higher education that puts increased emphasis on which college one attends, contributes to the large number of applications to certain colleges nationally. Thus, while in the past decade the number of college age students has declined, the number of students applying to Ivy League colleges has increased (Mackay-Smith, 1985; Maeroff, 1984; Winerip, 1984).

In view of these historical changes, is there any evidence that the select 16 schools still retain special charters in relation to college admissions? When four pools of applications to the Ivy League colleges are compared, the acceptance rate is highest at select 16 schools, followed by a highly selective public high school, other leading boarding schools, and finally the entire national pool of applications (Table 2).[6]

While we do not have comparable background data on all the applicants from these various pools, we do know that the students in the highly selective public high school have among the highest academic qualifications in the country.[7] Their combined SAT scores, for example, average at least 150 points higher than those of students at the

**TABLE 2**
**Percent of Applications That Were Accepted at Ivy League Colleges from Four Pools of Applications**

| College name | Select 16 Boarding Schools[a] (1982–83) | Other Leading Boarding Schools[b] (1982–83) | Selective Public High School[c] (1984) | National Group of Applicants[d] (1982) |
|---|---|---|---|---|
| Brown University | | | | |
| Percent accepted | 35 | 20 | 28 | 22 |
| Number of applications | 95 | 45 | 114 | 11,854 |
| Columbia University | | | | |
| Percent accepted | 66 | 29 | 32 | 41 |
| Number of applications | 35 | 7 | 170 | 3,650 |
| Cornell University | | | | |
| Percent accepted | 57 | 36 | 55 | 31 |
| Number of applications | 65 | 25 | 112 | 17,927 |
| Dartmouth | | | | |
| Percent accepted | 41 | 21 | 41 | 22 |
| Number of applications | 79 | 33 | 37 | 8,313 |
| Harvard University | | | | |
| Percent accepted | 38 | 28 | 20 | 17 |
| Number of applications | 104 | 29 | 127 | 13,341 |
| Princeton University | | | | |
| Percent accepted | 40 | 28 | 18 | 18 |
| Number of applications | 103 | 40 | 109 | 11,804 |
| University of Pennsylvania | | | | |
| Percent accepted | 45 | 32 | 33 | 36 |
| Number of applications | 40 | 19 | 167 | 11,000 |
| Yale University | | | | |
| Percent accepted | 40 | 32 | 15 | 20 |
| Number of applications | 92 | 25 | 124 | 11,023 |
| Overall percent accepted | 42 | 27 | 30 | 26 |
| Total number of applications | 613 | 223 | 960 | 88,912 |

*Notes:*
a.  Based on school record data on applications of 578 seniors.
b.  Based on school record data on the applications of 457 seniors.
c.  Based on data published in the school newspaper.
d.  Based on data published in the *National College Data Bank* (1984).

leading boarding schools. On that basis they might be expected to do considerably better than applicants from boarding schools: which they do at some colleges but not at Harvard, Yale or Princeton.

The most revealing insights into the operation of special charters, however, are provided by a comparison between select 16 boarding schools and other leading boarding schools—the most similar schools and the ones on which we have the most detailed data.

Students from select 16 schools apply to somewhat different colleges than do students from other leading boarding schools. Select 16 school students were much more likely to apply to one or more of the eight Ivy League and at least one of the other highly selective colleges than were students from other leading boarding schools (Table 3). Among those who applied, select 16 students were more likely to be accepted than were students from other boarding schools, and, if accepted, they were slightly more likely to attend.

Before we can conclude that these differences are due to a school charter, we need to control for parental SES[8] and student SAT scores.[9] This analysis is shown in Table 4.

One striking finding here is the high rate of success enjoyed by boarding school students in general. At least one-third and as many as 92 percent of the students in each cell of Table 4 are accepted. Given that the average freshman combined SAT score is more than 1175 at these colleges and universities, it is particularly notable that such a large proportion of those with combined SAT scores of 1050 or less are accepted.

In general, high SAT scores increase chances of acceptance, but the relationship is somewhat attenuated under certain conditions. Students with low SAT scores are more likely to be accepted at highly selective colleges if they have higher SES backgrounds, especially if they attend a select 16 school. These students seem to have relatively high "floors" placed under them, since two thirds of those from select 16 schools and more than half of those from other schools were accepted by one of the most selective colleges.[10]

The most successful ones of all are relatively low SES students with the highest SATs attending select 16 schools—92 percent of whom were accepted. Students from relatively modest backgrounds appear to receive a "knighting effect" by attending a

TABLE 3
**Boarding School Students' College Application, Chances of Acceptance, and Plans to Attend**

|  | Ivy League Colleges % (N) | Highly Selective Colleges % (N) |
|---|---|---|
| A. Percent of boarding school samples who applied | | |
| Select 16 boarding schools | 61 (353) | 87 (502) |
| Other leading boarding schools | 28 (129) | 61 (279) |
| B. Percent of applicants who were accepted | | |
| Select 16 boarding schools | 54 (191) | 84 (420) |
| Other leading boarding schools | 36 (47) | 64 (178) |
| C. Percent of acceptees who plan to attend | | |
| Select 16 boarding schools | 79 (151) | 81 (340) |
| Other leading boarding schools | 53 (25) | 77 (137) |

select 16 school. Thus, select 16 schools provide mobility for some individuals from relatively less privileged backgrounds. To a considerable degree all students with high SATS, regardless of their SES, appear to be "turbocharged" by attending a select 16 school compared to their counterparts at other leading schools.

At every level of SATs and SES, students' chances of acceptance increase if they attend a select 16 school. Such a finding is consistent with the argument that a chartering effect continues to operate among elite educational institutions. The historical shifts toward admitting more public school students on the part of Ivy League colleges and the increased competition for entry, described above, have meant that more effort has been required on the part of select 16 schools to retain an advantage for their students. We believe that certain private boarding schools have buttressed their charters by an increasingly active bartering operation.

## BARTERING

Normally, we do not think of the college admissions process as an arena for bartering. It is assumed that colleges simply choose students according to their own criteria and

needs. Few students and no high schools are thought to have any special "leverage" in admissions decisions. Our research revealed, however, that select 16 boarding schools—perhaps because of their perennial supply of academically able and affluent students—can negotiate admissions cases with colleges. The colleges are aware that select 16 schools attract excellent college prospects and devote considerable attention to maintaining close relationships with these schools, especially through the college admissions officers. Secondary school college advisors actively "market" their students within a context of tremendous parental pressure and increasing competition for admission to elite colleges.

## SELECT 16 COLLEGE ADVISORS AND IVY LEAGUE ADMISSIONS DIRECTORS: THE OLD SCHOOL TIE

Of the 11 select 16 school college advisors on whom data were available, 10 were graduates of Harvard, Yale, or Princeton. Of the 23 other leading boarding school college advisors on whom data were available, only three were Ivy League graduates, and none of them was from Harvard, Yale, or Prince-

**TABLE 4**
**Percent of Students Who Applied to the Most Highly Selective Colleges Who Were Accepted, with SAT Scores SES, and School Type Held Constant**

| | Student Combined SAT Scores | | | | | |
|---|---|---|---|---|---|---|
| | *High (1580–1220)* | | *Medium (1216–1060)* | | *Low (1050–540)* | |
| Student Socioeconomic Status | Select 16 Schools % (N) | Other Leading Boarding Schools % (N) | Select 16 Schools % (N) | Other Leading Boarding Schools % (N) | Select 16 Schools % (N) | Other Leading Boarding Schools % (N) |
| High | 87 (93) | 70 (33) | 80 (73) | 64 (36) | 65 (34) | 53 (30) |
| Medium | 89 (100) | 71 (28) | 85 (66) | 76 (46) | 44 (18) | 35 (51) |
| Low | 92 (72) | 72 (25) | 78 (51) | 69 (32) | 55 (33) | 33 (49) |

*Note:* Based on student questionnaires and school record data on 1035 seniors for whom complete data were available.

ton. College advisors are overwhelmingly white men. At the select 16 schools only one (an acting director) was a woman, and at other schools five were women. Some college advisors have previously worked as college admissions officers. Their educational and social similarity to college admissions officers may facilitate the creation of social ties and the sharing of useful information. Research shows that the exchange of ideas most frequently occurs between people who share certain social attributes (Rogers and Kincaid, 1981).

College advisors at select 16 schools tend to have long tenures—15 or more years is not unusual. On the other hand, college advisors at other schools are more likely to have assumed the job recently. A college advisor at one select 16 school stressed the "importance of continuity on both sides of the relationship." Thus, it is not surprising that select 16 schools hold on to their college advisors.

Select 16 college advisors have close social relationships with each other and with elite college admissions officers that are cemented through numerous face-to-face meetings each year. All of the select 16 schools are on the east coast, whereas only 70 percent of the other leading boarding schools are in that region. However, even those leading boarding schools on the east coast lack the close relationships with colleges that characterize the select 16 schools. Thus, geography alone does not explain these relationships.

The college advisors at most of the boarding schools we studied have personally visited a number of colleges around the country. Boarding schools often provide college advisors with summer support for systematic visits, and a number of geographically removed colleges offer attractive incentives, or fully paid trips to their region (e.g., Southern California). These trips often take place during bitter New England winters, and include elegant food and lodging as well as a chance to see colleges and meet admissions officers.

However, the college advisors at select 16 schools are likely to have visited far more schools (several mentioned that they had personally visited 60 or 70 schools) than college advisors at other schools (some of whom had not visited any). They are also much more likely to visit regularly the most selective and prestigious colleges.[11]

Numerous college admissions officers also travel to these boarding schools to interview students and meet the college advisors. The select 16 schools have more college admissions officers visit than do other schools: more than 100 in any given academic year is not unusual. College advisors have drinks and dinner with selected admissions officers, who often stay overnight on campus. As one college advisor noted, "We get to establish a personal relationship with each other." Moreover, Ivy League colleges bring students from select 16 schools to their campus to visit for weekends.

By knowing each other personally, college advisors and admissions officers "develop a relationship of trust," so that they can evaluate the source as well as the content of phone calls and letters. We observed phone calls between college advisors and admissions officers when we were in their offices. Several college advisors mentioned, "It helps to know personally the individual you are speaking or writing to," and one college advisor at a select 16 school said, "I have built up a track record with the private colleges over the years."

Virtually all of the select 16 school college advisors indicated that in the spring—before colleges have finished making their admissions decisions—they take their application files and drive to elite colleges to discuss "their list." They often sit in on the admissions deliberations while they are there. In contrast, the other schools' college advisors generally did not make such trips. Such actions suggest the existence of strong social networks between select 16 school college advisors and elite college admissions officers.

## HOW THE SYSTEM WORKS: "FINE TUNING" THE ADMISSIONS PROCESS

Bartering implies a reciprocal relationship, and select 16 schools and elite colleges have a well-developed system of information exchange. Both sides have learned to cooperate to their mutual benefit. College advisors try to provide admissions officers with as much information about their students as possible to help justify the acceptance of a particular applicant. Select 16 schools have institutionalized this process more than other schools. The most professional operation we found was in a select 16 school where about half the graduating class goes to Harvard, Yale or Princeton. There, the college advisor interviews the entire faculty on each member of the senior class. He tape records all their comments and has them transcribed. This produces a "huge confidential dossier which gives a very good sense of where each student is." In addition, housemasters and coaches write reports. Then the college advisor interviews each senior, dictating notes after each interview. After assimilating all of these comments on each student, the college advisor writes his letter of recommendation, which he is able to pack with corroborative details illustrating a candidate's strengths. The thoroughness, thought, and care that goes into this process insures that anything and everything positive that could be said about a student is included, thereby maximizing his or her chances for a favorable reception at a college.[12]

Information also flows from colleges to the secondary schools. By sitting in on the admissions process at colleges like Harvard, Princeton, and Yale, select 16 school college advisors say they "see the wealth and breadth of the applicant pool." They get a first-hand view of the competition their students face. They also obtain a sense of how a college "puts its class together," which helps them to learn strategies for putting forward their own applicants.

By observing and participating in the admissions process, select 16 school college advisors gain an insider's view of a college's selection process. This insider's knowledge is reflected in the specific figures select 16 advisors mentioned in our conversations with them. One select 16 school college advisor said that a student has "two and one half times as good a chance for admission to Harvard if his father went there than if he did not." Another said, "while 22 percent in general are admitted to Ivy League colleges, 45 percent of legacies are admitted to Ivy League colleges." In both cases, they mentioned a specific, quantified statement about how being a legacy affected their students' admissions probabilities.[13] Similarly, several select 16 school college advisors mentioned the percentages of the freshman class at Harvard and Yale that were from public and private schools, and one even mentioned how those percentages have changed since 1957. College advisors at other schools do not lace their conversations with as many specific figures nor do they belong to the special organization that some of the select 16 schools have formed to share information and strategies.

The special interest group these schools have formed is able to negotiate with the colleges to their students' advantage. For instance, the college advisors explained that select 16 school students face greater competition than the average high school student and carry a more rigorous course load.[14] Therefore, this group persuaded the colleges that their students should not receive an absolute class rank, but simply an indication of where the students stand by decile or quintile. Colleges may then put such students in a "not ranked" category or report the decile or quintile rank. No entering student from such a secondary school is clearly labeled as the bottom person in the class. To our knowledge, only select 16 schools have made this arrangement.

Armed with an insider's knowledge of a college's desires, select 16 school college advisors seek to present colleges with the most appropriate candidates. As one select 16 school college advisor said, "I try to shape up different applicant pools for different colleges," a process that has several components. First, college advisors try to screen out hopeless prospects, or as one tactfully phrased it, "I try to discourage unproductive leads." This is not always easy because, as one said, "Certain dreams die hard." College advisors in other schools were more likely to say that they never told students where they should or should not apply.

One select 16 school requires students to write a "trial college essay" that helps the college advisor ascertain "what kind of a student this is." From the essay he can tell how well students write, determine whether they follow through and do what they need to do on time, and learn something about their personal and family background. With faculty and student comments in hand, college advisors can begin to assemble their applicant pools. One thing they always want to learn is which college is a student's first choice, and why. This is useful information when bartering with colleges.

Some college advisors are quite frank when bartering, for example, the select 16 college advisor who stressed, "I am candid about a student to the colleges, something that is not true at a lot of schools where they take an advocacy position in relation to their students.... We don't sell damaged goods to the colleges." College advisors at other schools did not define their role as one of weeding out candidates prior to presenting them to colleges, although they may do this as well. It would seem then that part of the gate-keeping process of admission to college is occurring in select 16 secondary schools. College advisors, particularly those with long tenures at select 16 schools, seem quite aware of the importance of maintaining long-term credibility with colleges, since credibility influences how effectively they can work for their school in the future.

While the children of certain big donors (so-called "development cases") may be counseled with special care, in general the college advisors have organizational concerns that are more important than the fate of a particular student. Several select 16 school college advisors spoke with scorn about parents who see a rejection as the "first step in the negotiation." Such parents threaten to disrupt a delicate network of social relationships that link elite institutions over a considerable time span.

At the same time, college advisors try to do everything they can to help their students jump the admissions hurdle. One select 16 school college advisor said:

> I don't see our students as having an advantage (in college admissions). We have to make the situation unequal. We do this by writing full summary reports on the students, by reviewing the applicants with the colleges several times during the year, and by traveling to the top six colleges in the spring.... [Those visits] are an advocacy proceeding on the side of the students. The colleges make their best decisions on our students and those from [another select 16 school] because they have the most information on these students.

Another select 16 college advisor said. "We want to be sure they are reading the applications of our students fairly, and we lobby for our students." A third select 16 college advisor made a similar statement, "When I drive to the [Ivy League] colleges, I give them a reading on our applicants. I let them know if I think they are making a mistake. There is a lobbying component here."

Select 16 college advisors do not stop with simply asking elite college admissions officers to reconsider a decision, however. They try to barter, and the colleges show they are open to this possibility when the college admissions officer says, "Let's talk about your group." One select 16 college advisor said he stresses to colleges that if his school recommends someone and he or she is accepted, that student will come. While not all colleges heed this warranty, some do.

One select 16 college advisor said, "It is getting harder than it used to be to say to an admissions officer, 'take a chance on this one,' especially at Harvard which now has so many more applications." But it is significant that he did not say that it was impossible. If all else fails in a negotiation, a select 16 college advisor said, "we lobby for the college to make him their absolute first choice on the waiting list." Such a compromise represents a chance for both parties to save face.

Most public high school counselors are at a distinct disadvantage in the bartering process because they are not part of the interpersonal network, do not have strategic information, and are thus unable to lobby effectively for their students. One select 16 advisor told us about a counselor from the Midwest who came to an Ivy League college to sit in on the admissions committee decision for his truly outstanding candidate—SATs in the 700s, top in his class, class president, and star athlete. The select 16 college advisor was also there, lobbying on behalf of his candidate—a nice undistinguished fellow (in the words of his advisor, "A good kid,") with SATs in the 500s, middle of his class, average athlete, and no strong signs of leadership. After hearing both the counselors, the Ivy League college chose the candidate from the select 16 school. The outraged public school counselor walked out in disgust. Afterwards, the Ivy League college admissions officer said to the select 16 college advisor, "We may not be able to have these open meetings anymore." Even in the unusual case where a public school counselor did everything that a select 16 boarding school college advisor did, it was not enough to secure the applicant's admission. Despite the competitive environment that currently surrounds admission to elite colleges, the admissions officers apparently listen more closely to advisors from select 16 boarding schools than to public school counselors.

## CONCLUSIONS AND IMPLICATIONS

The graduates of certain private schools are at a distinct advantage when it comes to admission to highly selective colleges because of the special charters and highly developed social networks these schools possess. Of course, other factors are operating as well. Parental wealth (which is not fully tapped by a measure of SES based on education, occupation, and income), preference for the children of alumni, Advanced Placement (AP) coursework, sports ability especially in such scarce areas as ice hockey, crew or squash, and many other factors also influence the process of college admission. Elite boarding schools are part of a larger process whereby more privileged members of society transmit their advantages to their children. Attendance at a select 16 boarding school signals admissions committees that an applicant may have certain valuable educational and social characteristics.

Significantly, neither the families nor the secondary schools leave the college admissions process to chance or to formal bureaucratic procedures. Instead, they use personal connections to smooth the process, and there is reason to believe that those efforts affect the outcomes. The "knighting effect" of select 16 schools helps a few low SES, high SAT students gain admission to highly selective colleges, evidence of sponsored mobility for a few worthy youngsters of relatively humble origins. Our findings are consistent with Kamens' (1974) suggestion that certain schools make their students eligible for special social rights. Furthermore, the interaction between social background, SATs, and select 16 school attendance suggests that both individual ability and socially structured advantages operate in the school-college transition.

These results illustrate Collins' (1979) view that stratified systems are maintained through the manipulation of social contacts. They show one way that networks and stratification processes are interconnected. College access is only one aspect of the larger phenomenon of elite maintenance and reproduction. Elite boarding schools no doubt contribute as well to the social contacts and marriage markets of their graduates. What this instance shows is that reproduction is not a simple process. It involves family and group reproduction as well as some structural replacement with carefully screened new members. There is active personal intervention in what is publicly represented as a meritocratic and open competition. The internal processes and external networks described here operate to construct class privileges as well as to transmit class advantages, thereby helping to reproduce structured stratification within society.

If this example is generalizable, we would expect that economically and culturally advantaged groups might regularly find or create specially chartered organizations and brokers with well-developed networks to help them successfully traverse critical junctures in their social histories. Such key switching points include the transition from secondary school to college, admission to an elite graduate or professional school, obtaining the right job, finding a mentor, gaining a medical residency at a choice hospital (Hall, 1947, 1948, 1949) getting a book manuscript published (Coser et al., 1982), having one's paintings exhibited at an art gallery or museum, obtaining a theatrical agent, having one's business considered for venture capital or bank support (Rogers and Larsen, 1984), being offered membership in an exclusive social club, or being asked to serve on a corporate or other board of directors (Useem, 1984).

In all of these instances, many qualified individuals seek desired, but scarce, social and/or economic opportunities. Truly open competition for highly desired outcomes leaves privileged groups vulnerable. Because the socially desired positions are finite at any given moment, processes that give an advantage to the members of certain groups work to limit the opportunities of individuals from other groups.[15] In these ways, dominant groups enhance their chances, at the same time that a few worthy newcomers are advanced, a process which serves to reproduce and legitimate a structure of social inequality.

## ENDNOTES

We wish to thank E. Digby Baltzell, Steven Brint, Kevin Dougherty, Eliot Freidson, Kathleen Gerson, David Greenberg, Wolf Heydebrand, Herbert Menzel, John Meyer, Karen Miller, Richard R. Peterson, Edwin Schur, Susan Shapiro, Beth Stevens, and a number of anonymous reviewers for their thoughtful reactions to this paper.

1. Others besides Baltzell have developed lists of elite private schools, including Baird (1977), Domhoff (1967, 1970, 1983), and McLachlan (1970).

2. We were not able to compute the percent of students in *Social Register* for every school because most schools do not publish the names of their students. Hence, we were not able to look their families up in *Social Register*. We do know that less than .000265 percent of American families are listed in *Social Register*. See Levine (1980) for an historical discussion of the social backgrounds of students at several of the select 16 schools.

3. We asked to give the student questionnaires at nine of the 12 select 16 schools and six of those nine schools agreed. At the other leading schools, we asked to give the questionnaires at 15 and 13 schools agreed.

4. Three leading schools did not supply the college data.

5. Following Astin et al. (1981: 7), we measured selectivity. with the average SAT scores of the entering freshmen.

6. The entire national applicant pool includes the relatively more successful subgroups within it. If they were excluded, the national acceptance rate would be even lower.

7. Students admitted to this selective public high school must be recommended by their junior high school to take a competitive entrance exam, where they must score very well. The school was among the top five in the nation with respect to the number of National Merit Scholarships won by its students, and

each year a number of students in the school win Westinghouse science prizes. This school was selected for purposes of comparison here because academically it is considered to be among the very top public schools in the nation. However, it does not have the social prestige of the select 16 boarding schools.

8. SES was measured by combining father's education, father's occupation, and family income into a composite SES score. These SES scores were then standardized for this population, and each student received a single standardized SES score.

9. The combined verbal and mathematics scores were used.

10. We performed separate analyses for boys and girls to see if sex was related to admission to a highly selective college when type of boarding school, SATs. and SES were held constant, and generally it was not. Girls who attend either select 16 or other leading boarding schools do as well: or better in their admission to college as do their male counterparts, with the single exception of girls at select 16 schools in the top third on their SATs and SES. In that particular group, 92 percent of the boys but only 77 percent of the girls were accepted at the most highly selective colleges. Since that is the only exception, boys and girls are discussed together in the text of the paper.

11. Our field visits and interviews with college advisors at two highly selective public high schools and three open admissions public high schools show that college advisors at even the most selective public high schools generally do not personally know the admissions officers at colleges, particularly at the most selective and Ivy League colleges, nor do they talk with them over the phone or in person prior to their admissions decisions.

12. Such a procedure requires considerable financial and personnel resources. Select 16 schools have more capital intensive and professional office services supporting their college admissions endeavor than other schools. Most of them have word processors, considerable professional staff, and ample secretarial and clerical help.

13. We did not ask students what colleges their parents attended so we could not control for college legacy in our analysis. Future research on the admissions process should do so.

14. One way select 16 schools establish their reputations as rigorous schools is through the numbers of their students who succeed on the Advanced Placement (AP) Exams given by the College Entrance Examination Board. Compared to other secondary schools, select 16 schools offer larger numbers of advanced courses (Table 1), encourage more students to take them, coach students very effectively on how to take the test, and maintain contacts with the people who design and read AP exams so that they know what is expected and can guide students accordingly. (See Cookson and Persell, 1985, for more discussion of these processes.) Other schools are much less likely than select 16 ones to have teachers who have graded AP exams or to know people who have helped to write the tests.

15. See Parkin (1979) for a discussion of social closure as exclusion and usurpation.

## REFERENCES

Alexander, Karl L., Martha Cook and Edward L. McDill 1978 "Curriculum tracking and educational stratification: some further evidence." American Sociological Review 43:47–66.

Alexander, Karl L. and Bruce K. Eckland 1975 "Contextual effects in the high school attainment process." American Sociological Review 40:402–16.

———— 1977 "High school context and college selectivity: institutional constraints in educational stratification." Social Forces 56:166–88.

Alexander, Karl L., Bruce K. Eckland and Larry J. Griffin 1975 "The Wisconsin model of socioeconomic achievement: a replication." American Journal of Sociology 81:324–42.

Alexander, Karl L. and Edward L. McDill 1976 "Selection and allocation within schools: some causes and consequences of curriculum placement." American Sociological Review 41:963–80.

Astin, Alexander W., Margo R. King, and Gerald T. Richardson 1981 The American Freshman: National Norms for Fall 1981. Los Angeles:

Laboratory for Research in Higher Education, University of California.

Averch, Harvey A., Steven J. Carroll, Theodore S. Donaldson, Herbert J. Kiesling, and John Pincus 1972 How Effective is Schooling? A Critical Review and Synthesis of Research Findings. Santa Monica, CA: The Rand Corporation.

Baird, Leonard L. 1977 The Elite Schools. Lexington, MA: Lexington Books.

Baltzell, E. Digby 1958 Philadelphia Gentlemen. New York: Free Press.

_____ 1964 The Protestant Establishment. New York: Random House.

Beck, E. M., Patrick M. Horan, and Charles M. Tolbert II 1978 "Stratification in a dual economy." American Sociological Review 43: 704–20.

Bibb, Robert C. and William Form 1977 "The effects of industrial, occupational and sex stratification on wages in blue-collar markets." Social Forces 55:974–96.

Blau, Peter and Otis D. Duncan 1967 The American Occupational Structure. New York: Wiley.

Blumberg, Paul M. and P. W. Paul 1975 "Continuities and discontinuities in upper-class marriages." Journal of Marriage and the Family 37:63–77.

Bowles, Samuel and Herbert Gintis 1976 Schooling in Capitalist America. New York: Basic Books.

Collins, Randall 1979 The Credential Society. New York: Academic Press.

Cookson, Peter Willis, Jr. 1981 "Private secondary boarding school and public suburban high school graduation: an analysis of college attendance plans." Unpublished Ph.D. dissertation, New York University.

Cookson, Peter W., Jr. and Caroline Hodges Persell 1978 "Social structure and educational programs: a comparison of elite boarding schools and public education in the United States," Paper presented at the annual meeting of the American Sociological Association, San Francisco.

_____ 1985 Preparing for Power: America's Elite Boarding Schools. New York: Basic Books.

Coser, Lewis A., Charles Kadushin, and Walter W. Powell 1982 Books: The Culture & Commerce of Publishing. New York: Basic Books

Domhoff, G. William 1967 Who Rules America? Englewood Cliffs: Prentice-Hall.

_____ 1970 The Higher Circles. New York: Vintage.

_____ 1983 Who Rules America Now? Englewood Cliffs: Prentice-Hall.

Falsey, Barbara and Barbara Heyns 1984 "The college channel: private and public schools reconsidered." Sociology of Education 57: 111–22

Hall, Oswald 1946 "The informal organization of the medical profession." Canadian Journal of Economics and Political Science 12:30–41.

_____ 1948 "The stages of a medical career." American Journal Sociology 53:327–36.

_____ 1949 "Types of medical career" American Journal of Sociology 55:243–53.

Haller, Arclibald O. and Alejandro Portes 1973 "Status attainment processes." Sociology of Education 46:51–91.

Hammack, Floyd M. and Peter W. Cookson, Jr 1980 "Colleges attended by graduates of elite secondary schools." The Educational Forum 44:483–90.

Handbook of Private Schools 1981 Boston: Porter Sargent Publishers, Inc.

Heyns, Barbara 1974 "Social selection and stratification within schools." American Journal of Sociology 79:1434–51.

Jaffe, Abraham and Walter Adams 1970 "Academic and socio-economic factors related to entrance and retention at two- and four-year colleges in the late 1960s." New York: Bureau of Applied Social Research, Columbia University.

Jencks, Christopher, Marshall Smith, Henry Acland, Mary Jo Bane, David Cohen, Herbert Gintis, Barbara Heyns, and Stephan Michelson 1972 Inequality. New York: Basic Books.

Kamens, David 1974 "Colleges and elite formation: the case of prestigious American colleges." Sociology of Education 47:354–78.

_____ 1977 "Legitimating myths and educational organization: the relationship between organizational ideology and formal structure." American Sociological Review 42:208–19.

Karabel, Jerome 1984 "Status-group struggle, organizational interests, and the limits of institutional autonomy: the trasnsformation of Harvard, Yale, and Princeton 1918–1940." Theory and Society 13:1–40.

Karen, David 1985 "Who gets into Harvard? Selection and exclusion." Unpublished Ph.D. dissertation. Department of Sociology, Harvard University.

Kerckhoff, Alan C. 1976 "The status attainment process: socialization or allocation?" Social Forces 55:368–81.

_____ 1984 "The current state or social mobility research." Sociology Quarterly 25:139–53.

Klitgaard, Robert 1985 Choosing Elites. New York: Basic Books.

Laumann, Edward O. 1966 Prestige and Associatation in an Urban Community: An Analysis of an Urban Stratification System. Indianapolis: Bobbs-Merrill.

Levine, Steven B. 1980 "The rise of American boarding schools and the development of a national upper class." Social Problems 28:63–94.

Lewis, Lionel S, and Richard A. Wanner l979 "Private schooling and the status attainment process." Sociology of Education 52:99–112.

Mackay-Smith, Anne 1985 "Admissions crunch: top colleges remain awash in applicants despite a smaller pool." Wall Street Journal (April 2):1,14.

Maeroff, Gene I. 1984 "Top Eastern colleges report unusual rise in applications." New York Times (February 21):A1,C10.

McLachlan, James 1970 American Boarding Schools: A Historical Study, New York: Charles Scribner's Sons.

Meyer, John 1970 "The charter: Conditions of diffuse socialization in school." Pp. 564–78 in W. Richard Scott (ed.), Social Processes and Social Structure. New York: Holt, Rinehart.

_____ 1977 "Education as an institution." American Journal of Sociology 83:55–77.

Mills, C. Wright 1956 The Power Elite. London: Oxford University Press.

National College Data Bank 1984 Princeton: Peterson's Guides, Inc.

Oakes, Jeannie 1985 Keeping Track: How Schools Structure Inequality. New Haven: Yale University Press.

Otto, Luther B. and Archibald O. Haller 1979 "Evidence for a social psychological view of the status attainment process: four studies compared." Social Forces 57:887–914.

Parkin, Frank 1979 Marxism Class Theory: A Bourgeois Critique. New York: Columbia University Press.

Persell, Caroline Hodges 1977 Education and Inequality. New York: The Free Press.

Robinson, Robert V. 1984 "Reproducing class relations in industrial capitalism." American Sociological Review 49: 182–96.

Rogers, Everett M. and D. Lawrence Kincaid 1981 Communications Networks: Toward a New Paradigm for Research. New York: The Free Press.

Rogers, Everett M. and Judith K. Larsen 1984 Silicon Valley Fever: The Growth of High-Tech Culture. New York: Basic Books.

Rosenbaum, James E. 1976 Making Inequality: The Hidden Curriculum of High School Tracking. New York: Wiley.

_____ 1980 "Track misperceptions and frustrated college plans: an analysis of the effects of tracks and track perceptions in the national longitudinal survey." Sociology of Education 53:74–88.

Sewell, William H., Archibald O. Haller, and Alejandro Portes 1969 "The educational and early occupational attainment process." American Sociological Review 34:82–91.

Sewell, William H., Archibald O. Haller, and George W. Ohlendorf 1970 "The educational and early occupational status achievement process: Replication and revision." American Sociological Review 35:1014–27.

Social Register 1984 New York: Social Register Association.

Stolzenberg, Ross M. 1975 "Occupations labor markets and the process of wage attainment." American Sociological Review 40:645–65.

Useem, Michael 1984 The Inner Circle: Large Corporations and the Rise of Business Political Activity in the U.S. and U.K. New York: Oxford University Press.

Wellman, Barry 1981 "Network analysis from method and metaphor to theory and substance." Working Paper Series 1B, Structural Analysis Programme, University of Toronto.

Wilson, Kenneth L. and Alejandro Portes 1975 "The Educational attainment process: Results from a national sample." American Journal of Sociology 81:343–63.

Winerip, Michael 1984 "Hot colleges and how they get that way." New York Times Magazine. (November 18):68ff.

# The Effects of Community Colleges: Aid or Hindrance to Socioeconomic Attainment?

## KEVIN DOUGHERTY

In this century, the community college has emerged as one of the central elements of the U.S. higher education system.[1] Totally absent until 1900, community colleges now number nearly one thousand and enroll 36 percent of all students in higher education (National Center for Education Statistics [NCES] 1985, p. 14). Moreover, community colleges have become a central artery into higher education for working-class and minority students. Students in public two-year colleges are considerably more likely than students in four-year colleges to be nonwhite and to have parents who hold working-class jobs, make less than the median family income, and have not gone to college. For example, 41.4 percent of students in public two-year colleges have family incomes of less than $20,000, and 20.8 percent are nonwhite. The comparable percentages for students in four-year colleges are 31.0 percent and 16.6 percent, respectively (U.S. Bureau of the Census 1985, pp. 58–59, NCES 1984, p. 65).

Community-college supporters and activists have argued that these colleges serve society by providing social mobility and teaching the technical skills needed by a complex industrial economy (Cohen and Brawer 1982, p. 1; Eells 1931, p. 93; Medsker 1960, p. 4; Monroe 1972, pp. 32–37). Medsker articulates this group's functionalist view of the community college:

[The two-year college] is perhaps the most effective democratizing agent in higher education. It decentralizes post-high school opportunities by placing them within reach of a large number of students. It makes higher education available at low cost to the student and at moderate cost to society.... Furthermore, the American technological economy requires many persons trained at an intermediate level—not full-fledged engineers or scientists but high-level technicians or semiprofessionals. (1960, p. 4)

In the last fifteen years, however, the community college has come under intense criticism from several scholars who constitute what I call the class-reproduction school of community-college scholarship. This school argues that community colleges reproduce the class structure of our capitalist society by producing graduates trained and socialized for work in capitalist enterprises and by insuring that children inherit their parents' social-class positions (Bowles and Gintis 1976, pp. 208, 212; Karabel 1972, pp. 523–24; Nasaw 1979, p. 235; Pincus 1974, p. 18; Zwerling 1976, p. xix). Karabel states,

Hailed as the "democratizers of higher education," community colleges are, in reality, a vital component of the class-based tracking system. The modal junior college student, though aspiring to a four-year diploma upon entrance, receives neither an associate nor a

*Source: Sociology of Education* (April 1987): 86–103. Reprinted by permission of American Sociological Association. I thank Steven Brint, Jerome Karabel, David Lavin, Frances Rust, Beth Stevens, and several anonymous reviewers for their comments on this paper. I also thank Carolle Thomas for her diligent research assistance. An earlier version of this paper was presented at the 1986 meetings of the American Educational Research Association, San Francisco.

**411**

bachelor's degree. The likelihood of his persisting in higher education is *negatively* influenced by attending a community college. (1972, p. 555)

This clash of perspectives has produced a vigorous, even vitriolic, debate over the merits of the community college (Vaughan 1980; Zwerling 1976). But despite its vigor, the debate has not yet been settled. There is still no agreement on the effects of community colleges, and there is very little discussion of how those effects are produced. One reason, discussed below, is that the contending parties use very different measurements of the community college's effectiveness. Moreover, most of the debaters have relied on weak, often anecdotal data to make their cases.

This paper advances the debate over the effects of community colleges in two ways. First, it critically reviews the results of several different studies of the relative impact of community colleges, four-year colleges, and other postsecondary schools on the educational and economic attainment of their entrants. This critical review leads to the conclusion that community-college entrance definitely hinders both the educational and economic attainment of students who aspire to a baccalaureate but probably aides the educational attainment of students who aspire to a vocational degree. However, we cannot determine the effects of community-college entrance on the economic success of vocationally oriented students. Second, the paper synthesizes a wide variety of research to explain why entrance into a community college hinders the educational attainment of students who aspire to a baccalaureate.[2]

## RESEARCH DESIGN

The first objective—to measure the relative impact of community colleges on the educational and economic attainment of their entrants—is by no means easy. Community-college commentators have advanced quite different standards to judge the effectiveness of community colleges. The class-reproduction school gauges the success of the community college primarily by comparing the proportions of community-college entrants and four-year-college entrants who eventually secure bachelor's degrees.[3] Their focus on baccalaureate attainment stems from their belief that about three fourths of community-college students aspire to a bachelor's degree (Karabel 1972, pp. 530–36; Pincus 1974, p. 21; Zwerling 1976, p. 81). The functionalist school, on the other hand, rejects the use of baccalaureate attainment as the main standard of community-college effectiveness. Instead, they measure the community college's contribution to occupational and income attainment and the degree to which it broadens access to higher education (Cohen and Brawer 1982, pp. 356–57). Their competing standard is grounded in the belief that most community-college students do not wish a baccalaureate. Cohen and Brawer (1982, p. 46), for example, argue that only 15 to 33 percent of all community-college entrants aspire to a bachelor's degree.

Neither the class-reproduction nor the functionalist school is correct in its assessment of community-college entrants' aspirations and in the standards it consequently proposes. The real number of baccalaureate aspirants lies between their two estimates. I estimate that 30 to 40 percent of all community-college entrants aspire to a baccalaureate. Another 30 to 40 percent want an associate's degree but not a baccalaureate. The remaining 20 to 30 percent seek adult or community education courses (for purposes of recreation, personal development, or remedial education). The class-reproduction school's estimate that two thirds of community-college entrants aspire to a baccalaureate is too high; as Cohen and Brawer (1982, p. 46) note, it comes from the American Council of Education-Cooperative Institutional Research Program (ACE-CIRP) freshman national norms, which ignore part-time entrants, who are numerous and have lower aspirations than full-time entrants (Sheldon 1982). On the other hand, the functionalist school's figure of 15 to 33 percent, which is based on flawed data, is too low.[4]

This paper addresses the following questions:[5]

1. How do students entering community colleges compare with students entering four-year colleges and other kinds of colleges in baccalaureates attained? How do these three kinds of entrants compare in years of education attained? The first question pertains to the one third of community-college entrants who aspire to a baccalaureate; the second pertains to all community-college entrants.

2. How do community-college entrants compare with other college entrants in the prestige and income of the jobs they enter? How do they compare in rates of unemployment? These questions are particularly pertinent to students who do not aspire to a baccalaureate.

3. What particular aspects of the community college's organization and relationship to other higher educational institutions explain the lower educational attainment of community-college entrants, particularly those aspiring to a baccalaureate?

The first two sets of questions will be answered by examining several different quantitative studies of student outcomes. These studies analyze a variety of surveys, including the National Longitudinal Survey of the High School Class of 1972 (NLS–72), the National Longitudinal Survey of Labor Market Experience (NLSLME), the ACE-CIRP annual survey of college freshmen, and several more specialized surveys. These studies were chosen because they are the most recent and the most methodologically rigorous studies available. In particular, they allow us to compare the attainments of community-college entrants and other college entrants and to control for key differences in prematriculation characteristics, most notably, family background, high school academic record, and educational and occupational aspirations. In addition, these studies use longer follow-up periods than other broadly based studies of student outcomes. One follows up its respondents ten years after college entrance, another nine years, and two others seven years.

To answer the third question, I sort the obstacles that community-college entrance puts to educational attainment into three main processes that fit together in a funnel-like structure: attrition within the community college, difficulty transferring to four-year colleges, and attrition after transfer. I then marshall findings from a wide variety of quantitative and qualitative studies to illuminate how these three processes operate. These studies range from the nationwide surveys used to answer the first two questions to quantitative studies of state community-college systems and ethnographic studies of individual community colleges.

## THE EVIDENCE ON COMMUNITY-COLLEGE EFFECTS

### Educational Attainment

There are several careful quantitative studies describing the impact on educational attainment of entering a community college rather than a four-year college or postsecondary vocational school. Despite differences in sampling, follow-up periods, and analytic methods, these studies arrive at the same findings. Baccalaureate aspirants who enter community colleges attain significantly fewer bachelor's degrees and years of education than similar students who enter four-year colleges. However, vocational aspirants seem to do better if they enter a community college rather than a four-year college or post-secondary vocational school (see Table 1).

TABLE 1

**Educational Attainment of Entrants to Two-Year Colleges, Four-Year Colleges, and Postsecondary Vocational Schools**

| | Study | | | | | |
|---|---|---|---|---|---|---|
| | *Velez (1985)* | *Anderson (1984)* | *Breneman and Nelson (1981)* | *Alba and Lavin (1981)* | *Astin (1982)* | *Somers et al. (1971)* |
| Study characteristics | | | | | | |
| Data set used | NLS-72 | NLS-72 | NLS-72 | CUNY | ACE | Own |
| Year students entered college | 1972 | 1972 | 1972 | 1970 | 1971 | |
| Year students left college | | | | | | 1966 |
| Year students followed up | 1979 | 1976 | 1976 | 1975 | 1980 | 1969 |
| College program studied | Academic | Academic | Academic, Vocational | Academic, Vocational | Academic, Vocational | Vocational |
| Findings | | | | | | |
| Percentage attaining a baccalaureate | | | | | | |
| Four-year entrants | | | | | | |
| Public and private | 79.0 | | 44.2 | | n.a. | |
| Public only | | | | 31.2 | | |
| State college only | | n. a. | | | | |
| Two-year entrants | | | | | | |
| Public and private | 31.0 | | | | | |
| Public only | | n.a. | 10.8 | 12.8 | n.a. | |
| Difference in percentage attaining baccalaureate | | | | | | |
| No controls | 48.0 | n.a. | 33.4 | 18.4 | n.a. | |
| With controls | 18.7* | 13.4* | 11.3* | 11.2* | n.a.[a] | |
| Years of education attained | | | | | | |
| Four-year entrants | | | | | | |
| Public and private | | | 15.1 | | | |
| State college only | | n. a. | | | | |
| Two-year entrants (public only) | | n.a. | 14.0 | | | |
| Difference in years attained | | | | | | |
| No controls | | n. a. | 1.1 | | | |
| With controls | | 0.25* | 0.3* | | | |
| Percentage pursuing more education | | | | | | |
| Community college | | | | | | 69.2 |
| Postsecondary vocational school | | | | | | 10.1 |
| Difference in percentage pursuing more education | | | | | | |
| No controls | | | | | | 59.1 |
| With controls | | | | | | 59.0* |
| Control variables | | | | | | |
| Social background | | | | | | |
| Sex | x | x | x[b] | x | x | x |
| Race | x | x | x | x | x | x |
| SES | x | x | x[b] | | x | x |

**TABLE 1**  *(continued)*
**Educational Attainment of Entrants to Two-Year Colleges, Four-Year Colleges, and Postsecondary Vocational Schools**

| | Study | | | | | |
|---|---|---|---|---|---|---|
| | Velez (1985) | Anderson (1984) | Breneman and Nelson (1981) | Alba and Lavin (1981) | Astin (1982) | Somers et al. (1971) |
| Age | | | | | X | X |
| Language spoken at home | | | X[b] | | | |
| Religion | X | X | | | | |
| Marital status | | | X | | | X |
| Location of home | | | | | | X |
| Aspirations | | | | | | |
|   Students educational aspirations | X | X | X | X | X | |
|   Student's occupational aspirations | | X | | | X | |
|   Parents' educational aspirations | X | X | X | | | |
|   Peers' post-h.s. plans | | | X[b] | | | |
|   College decision date | | | X | | | |
|   Student's perception of college ability | | X | X[b] | | | |
| High school experiences | | | | | | |
|   Test scores | X | X | | | X | |
|   Grades or class rank | X | X | X | X | X | |
|   Curriculum | X | X | X | X | X | |
|   Hours spent on homework | | | X[b] | | | |
|   Change in high schools | | | X | | | |
|   Location of high school | | | X | | | |
|   Hours spent at job | | | X | | | |
|   Racial composition of high school | | | | | X | |
| College experiences | | | | | | |
|   Living arrangements | X | | X | | | |
|   Hours spent at job | | | X | | | |
|   Work on campus | X | | | | | |
|   Enrollment status (FT/PT) | | | X | | | |
|   College program | X[c] | X[c] | X | | | X |
|   Time in academic program | | | X | | | |
|   Job relatedness of program | | | | | | X |
|   College grades | X | | X | | | |
|   Children at follow-up | | | X | | | |

[a]Reports *partial correlations* between college and attainment of a baccalaureate for five racial-ethnic groups. The correlations for community-college entrants range from −0.20 to 0.01. The correlations for four-year-college entrants range from −0.01 to 0.08. See discussion in the text.
[b]Variable was used in baccalaureate attainment equation but not in years attained equation.
[c]The sample included only those students in the academic program.
*Significant at the .05 level.

Using the NLS-72,[6] Velez (1985) examined students who entered the *academic* programs of community colleges and four-year colleges in fall 1972 and who were followed up in fall 1979.[7] He found that seven years after college entrance 79 percent of the students who had entered an academic program in a four-year college, but only 31 percent of the students who had entered an academic program in a two-year college, received a bachelor's degree—a difference of 48 percent (p. 197).[8] And the *net* difference (i.e., that remaining after controlling for the prematriculation differences in student composition) is still large—18.7 percent (p. 199). (See Table 1 for a list of the prematriculation characteristics Velez controlled.) Using the same sample, follow-up period, and controls, Anderson (1984) found that students who entered community colleges lagged behind students who entered state four-year colleges by 13.4 percent in bachelor's degrees attained (pp. 33–34).[9]

The finding that community-colleges entrants are considerably less likely to receive a bachelor's degree than similar four-year-college entrants is not restricted to studies using the NLS-72. Alba and Lavin (1981) also found a significant net difference among 1970 baccalaureate aspirants entering the community colleges and four-year colleges of the City University of New York who were followed up in 1975. Although the CUNY community colleges promote the pursuit of a baccalaureate more than most, Alba and Lavin still found that the senior-college entrants received 11.2 percent more bachelor's degrees than the community-college entrants, even net of differences in prematriculation characteristics. Astin (1982, pp. 98–100) examined a nationwide sample of 1971 full-time college entrants aspiring to at least a bachelor's degree and found that by 1980, the community-college entrants were uniformly less likely to have baccalaureates than the four-year-college entrants, even net of entering student characteristics. For example, for whites, the partial correlation be-

tween the percentage attaining a bachelor's degree and community-college entrance was –0.14; but the partial correlation between the percentage attaining a bachelor's degree and entrance to different types of four-year colleges was between –0.04 and 0.15. The pattern was similar for blacks, Chicanos, and Indians but not for Puerto Ricans.

Anderson (1984) examined years of education attained and found that students who entered academic programs in community colleges attained 0.25 year less schooling than similar students who entered academic programs in four-year state colleges (pp. 33–34). Breneman and Nelson (1981) report a similar difference in a study not restricted to baccalaureate aspirants. They found that four years after college entrance, community-college entrants had attained 0.3 year less schooling than four-year college entrants (and 11.3 percent fewer baccalaureates), net of differences in pre-enrollment characteristics (pp. 82–83).

Baccalaureate aspirants clearly fare better if they enter a four-year college, but this may not be true of college entrants with lower aspirations. Breneman and Nelson (p. 90) estimate that 44 percent of community-college entrants (and 20 percent of four-year-college entrants) attain more education if they enter a community college rather than a four-year college. These students are more likely to be nonacademically oriented, nonwhite, and of low socioeconomic status than students who benefit more from entering a four-year college.[10] This finding is reinforced by another analysis of the NLS-72, which shows that fall 1972 college entrants who aspired to *less* than a bachelor's degree were less likely to have dropped out of higher education by fall 1974 if they had entered a two-year college rather than a four-year college (NCES 1977*b*, pp. 71, 74).

Somers, Sharpe, and Myint (1971) reached a similar conclusion when they compared the impact on vocational students of entering a community college with the impact of entering a postsecondary vocational-technical school. In a nationwide 1969 follow-up of 1966 graduates of vocational programs, they found that community-college vocational graduates were more likely to pursue education after graduation than postsecondary vocational-school graduates, even after controlling for pre-enrollment differences (Somers et al. 1971, pp. 168–75).

In sum, baccalaureate aspirants who enter community colleges attain fewer bachelor's degrees and less years of education than students who enter four-year colleges. However, students who aspire to a vocational degree seem to do better (though the evidence is weak) if they enter a community college rather than a four-year college or postsecondary vocational school.

## Economic Attainment

Several different kinds of studies allow us to measure the relative economic benefit of entering a community college: studies comparing the economic attainments of community-college entrants and four-year-college entrants, studies comparing community-college vocational students and students entering post secondary vocational-technical schools, and studies comparing graduates and dropouts of community-college vocational-education programs. The results of these studies arc summarized in Table 2. They lead to the conclusion that among students who aspire to a baccalaureate, those entering community colleges fare less well economically than those entering four-year colleges. However, we do not know if this finding holds for students who do not aspire to a baccalaureate, particularly older students. Moreover, we cannot determine whether community-college education is superior to post-secondary vocational-technical education or to no post-secondary education at all.

Anderson (1984), Monk-Turner (1983), and Breneman and Nelson (1981) exemplify the first type of study. They compared community-college entrants with four-year-college entrants and found statistically significant differences in occupational attainment but no clear difference in earnings, net of differences in pre-enrollment characteristics. (The pre-enrollment characteristics controlled in each study are listed in Table 2.) This finding clearly holds for baccalaureate aspirants; Anderson's sample was restricted to academic-program entrants, most of whom were baccalaureate aspirants, and her findings were replicated by Breneman and Nelson and by Monk-Turner.

Anderson found that among NLS-72 fall 1972 entrants to two-year and four-year *academic programs* followed up in 1979, those who had entered community colleges secured jobs that were 2.4 points lower on the Duncan index but that paid 5 cents more an hour than the jobs secured by those who had entered four-year colleges (p. 36).[11] Monk-Turner, however, found a net difference of 3.5 points on the Duncan index in favor of four-year-college entrants among NLSLME respondents who were working full time ten years after high school graduation (pp. 395, 401).[12] Finally, Breneman and Nelson found that among NLS-72 men employed full time in October 1976, those who had entered community colleges secured jobs that were significantly lower in status, but essentially the same in income, than the jobs secured by those who had entered four-year colleges. However, they argue that this parity in income is likely to break down in the long run because of the significant advantage four-year-college entrants have in occupational attainment, which is strongly correlated with income.

The second group of studies—comparisons between community-college vocational students and similar students in postsecondary vocational technical schools—partially address the limitations of the studies above. They examine vocationally oriented students, they are not restricted to recent high school graduates, and they look at post secondary vocational-technical schools as well as community colleges, although they ignore four-

TABLE 2

**Economic Attainment of Entrants to Two-Year Colleges, Four-Year Colleges, and Postsecondary Vocational Schools**

| | Study | | | | |
|---|---|---|---|---|---|
| | *Monk-Turner (1984)* | *Anderson (1981)* | *Breneman and Nelson (1981)* | *Wilms (1980)* | *Somers et al. (1971)* |
| Study characteristics | | | | | |
| Data set used | NLSLME | NLS-72 | NLS-72 | Own | Own |
| Year students entered college | 1966,1968 | 1972 | 1972 | 1973 | |
| Year students graduated | | | | | 1966 |
| Year students followed up | 1976,1977 | 1979 | 1976 | 1976 | 1969 |
| College program studied | Academic, Vocational | Academic | Academic, Vocational | Vocational | Vocational |
| Occupational scale used | Duncan (1–96) | Duncan (1–96) | Duncan (1–999) | | NORC (1–90) |
| Findings | | | | | |
| Mean status of current occupation | | | | | |
| Four-year entrants | | | | | |
| Public and private | 61.1 | | 486 | | |
| State college only | | n.a. | | | |
| Two-year entrants (public only) | 49.3 | n.a. | 424 | | 49.0 |
| Postsecondary vocational school entrants | | | | | 42.9 |
| Difference in status | | | | | |
| No controls | 11.8 | n.a. | 62.0 | | 6.1 |
| With controls | 3.5* | 2.4* | n.a.* | | n.a. |
| Mean earnings in current job | | | | | |
| Four-year entrants | | | | | |
| Public and private | | | $142[a] | | |
| State college only | | n.a. | | | |
| Two-year entrants (public only) | | n.a. | $159[a] | n.a.[b] | $3.20[c] |
| Post secondary vocational school entrants | | | | n.a.[b] | $2.70[c] |
| Difference in earnings | | | | | |
| No controls | | n.a. | −$17[a] | n.a. | $0.50[c] |
| With controls | | −$0.05 | n.a. | n.a.* | $0.29* |
| Unemployment rate | | | | | |
| Four-year entrants (all) | | | 8.8%[d] | | |
| Two-year entrants (public only) | | | 7.7%[d] | | 3.3%[e] |
| Postsecondary vocational school entrants | | | | | 7.7%[e] |
| Difference in unemployment rate | | | | | |
| No controls | | | 1.1%[d] | | −4.4%[e] |
| With controls | | | 0.5%[d] | | n.a. |
| Control variables | | | | | |
| Social background | | | | | |
| Sex | x | x | | x | x |
| Race | x | x | x | | x |
| SES | x | x | x[f,g] | x | x |
| Age | | | | x | x |
| Language spoken at home | | | x | | |

**TABLE 2** (*continued*)
**Economic Attainment of Entrants to Two-Year Colleges, Four-Year Colleges, and Postsecondary Vocational Schools**

| | Study | | | | |
|---|---|---|---|---|---|
| | Monk-Turner (1983) | Anderson (1984) | Breneman and Nelson (1981) | Wilms (1980) | Somers et al. (1971) |
| Religion | | x | | | |
| Location of home | x | | | | x |
| Size of hometown | x | | x[h] | | x |
| Marital status | x | | x | | x |
| Number of children | | | x[g] | | |
| Living arrangements | | | x[f,g] | | |
| Aspirations | | | | | |
|   Student's educational aspirations | x | x | x | | |
|   Student's occupational aspirations | | x | | | |
|   Parents' educational aspirations | | x | | | |
|   Student's perception of college ability | | x | | | |
| High school experiences | | | | | |
|   Test scores | x | x | | | |
|   Grades or class rank | | x | x | | |
|   Curriculum | | x | x[f,g] | | |
|   Change in high schools | | | x[h] | | |
|   Location of high school | | | x | | |
|   Hours spent at job | | | x | | |
| Early college experiences | | | | | |
|   Enrollment status (FT/PT) | | | x[f,g] | | |
|   College program | | x | x[f,g] | | x |
| Educational attainment | x | | x[g] | x | x |
| Job relatedness of education | | | | | x |
| Occupational characteristics | | | | | |
|   Years since enrolled full time | | | x | | |
|   Years at current job | x | | x[g] | x | |
|   Occupational status | | | x[g] | | |
|   Hours worked per week | x | | x[g] | x | |
|   Number of employees in firm | | | x[f,g] | | |
|   Number of employees in office | | | x[f,g] | | |
|   Number of employees respondent supervises | | | x[f,g] | | |
|   Attitude toward work | | | x[h] | | |

[a]Weekly wages.
[b]Figures are for first job. Current job figures are not reported.
[c]Hourly wages.
[d]Percentage of last year that respondent was unemployed.
[e]Whether unemployed last year.
[f]Variable was not used in current occupational status equation.
[g]Variable was used in mean earnings equation.
[h]Variable was used in unemployment equation.
*Significant at the .05 level.

year colleges. In February 1976, Wilms (1980) followed up several thousand students who had entered 21 community colleges and 29 proprietary vocational schools in four major cities in fall 1973. He found that the proprietary-school attenders had significantly higher beginning weekly salaries than the community-college attenders, even when he controlled for various pre- and post-matriculation differences (pp. 117–118). However, Somers et al. (1971), in a 1969 nationwide survey of 1966 graduates of vocational-education programs in community colleges and postsecondary vocational-technical schools, found that graduates of community-college vocational-education programs secured more prestigious and remunerative jobs and suffered less unemployment than graduates of postsecondary vocational-technical schools, net of differences in various student characteristics. Unfortunately, the contradiction between the two studies cannot be resolved, since neither study has a clear edge in methodological rigor. Though Wilms did not control for occupation prepared for, he did follow up nongraduates as well as graduates of vocational programs; Somers et al. did not.

Pincus (1980) exemplifies the last kind of study—comparisons between graduates and dropouts of community-college vocational-education programs. After reviewing reports by community-college agencies in several different states, he concluded that the vocational graduates were more often employed than the nongraduates, but they fared no better and perhaps worse in income (pp. 350–53). The ultimate meaning of this finding is in question, however. As Pincus noted, it would have been preferable to control for differences in background and academic performance between graduates and nongraduates, but the data that would have allowed this were unavailable.

In sum, among students who aspire to a baccalaureate, students who enter community colleges fare less well economically than comparable students who enter four-year colleges. However, we do not know if this finding holds for students who do not aspire to a baccalaureate, particularly older students. Also, because the evidence is contradictory or of poor quality, we also do not know whether community-college education is superior to postsecondary vocational-technical education or to no postsecondary education in economic benefits for students who do not aspire to a baccalaureate.

## Summary

The evidence on the effectiveness of community colleges provides support for both supporters and critics of the community college. But on balance, the evidence lies more on the side of the critics.

The evidence supports the class-reproduction theory that community colleges are inferior to four-year colleges in facilitating both the educational and the economic attainment of students who aspire to a baccalaureate.

But the functionalist supporters of the community college are partially vindicated: Community colleges do seem to be more effective than both four-year colleges and postsecondary vocational technical schools in facilitating the educational attainment of students who do not aspire to a baccalaureate. However, the evidence on the relative effectiveness of community colleges in promoting the economic success of these students is contradictory and quite sparse.

## CAUSES OF COMMUNITY-COLLEGE EFFECTS

In this section, I develop a model to explain why community-college entrance interferes with baccalaureate aspirants' educational attainment. I focus on educational attainment because it is an important outcome in its own right and because it constitutes the principal medium through which community colleges affect their entrants' economic success. Breneman and Nelson (1981, pp. 84–85) found that when years of education attained are controlled, the direct effect of community-college entrance on occupational status falls to insignificance and the direct effect of community-college entrance on income drops sharply.

Many different factors explain why community-college entrance hinders the educational attainment of students. The interrelationships among these factors constitute three main processes:

**1.** In the first two years of college, institutional factors produce a higher dropout rate among community-college entrants than among comparable four-year-college entrants. The key institutional factors underlying this process are community colleges' low academic selectivity and lack of dormitories.

**2.** Among students who survive the first two years of college, community-college entrants encounter greater institutional obstacles to continuation into the upper division of four-year colleges than comparable four-year-college entrants. The key factors here are community colleges' strong vocational orientation, the distaste of four-year colleges for community-college transfers, the scarcity of financial aid for community-college transfers, and the simple fact that movement to the upper division requires movement to a new and unfamiliar school.

**3.** Among students who do enter the upper division of four-year colleges, community-college entrants encounter greater institutional hindrances to continuation in the upper division of four-year colleges than comparable four-year college entrants. These factors include frequent loss of credits, difficulty securing financial aid, difficulty becoming socially integrated into the four-year college, and poorer preparation for upper-division work and consequent difficulty becoming academically integrated into the four-year college.

These three processes are articulated in a funnel-like structure that operates like the tournament mobility system conceived by Rosenbaum (1976). In such a system, which is a variant of the contest mobility system described by Turner (1960), students go through a series of tests. If they survive one test, they pass on to the next; if they fail at any point, they drop out of the contest.

## Attrition in the Freshman and Sophomore Years

Of the students in the NLS-72 who entered college in fall 1972, 39.3 percent of those who entered two-year colleges dropped out of higher education by fall 1974. The dropout rate for students who entered four-year colleges was 23.5 percent. By fall 1974, then, 15.8 percent more two-year-college entrants that four-year-college entrants had dropped out of higher education (NCES 1977*b*, pp. 135–36).[13]

Unfortunately, the NCES did not estimate the net difference in dropout rates—controlling for differences in pre-enrollment characteristics—between two-year-college and four-year-college entrants. However, Astin (1972), using a national sample of 1966 college entrants, estimated equations to predict separately the dropout rates by 1970 of two-year-college and four-year-college entrants. He found that when the two-year-college equation was applied to four-year-college entrants, it *overestimated* the dropout rate at 151 of 194 four-year colleges. Conversely, the four-year-college equation *underestimated* the dropout rate at 14 of 23 two-year colleges (pp. 10, 47–48).[14]

But how do community colleges contribute to their entrants' higher dropout rate? Research on this question is still rather primitive; almost all research on dropouts has focused on four-year-college dropouts (Tinto 1975; Pantages and Creedon 1978). But two factors stand out: the community colleges' lack of residential facilities and their lower academic selectivity and prestige.

A number of scholars have pointed to community colleges' lack of residential facilities as an important *institutional* cause of higher dropout rates (Anderson 1981, p. 12; Astin 1977a, pp. 109, 217, 1977b, pp. 91–92, 165–68; Karabel 1972, pp. 533n; Velez 1985, pp. 196–97). Community colleges virtually never maintain dormitories: most four-year colleges do.[15] On-campus residence powerfully contributes to student persistence. It promotes student success in college by fostering contact with faculty and other students, participation in extracurricular activities, and satisfaction with campus life. At the same time, on-campus residence weakens the influences of the home and neighborhood, which create obligations and allegiances that divert time and energy from school work (Astin 1977a; Tinto 1975, pp. 107, 109–10; Velez 1985, pp. 198–99).

Community colleges also adversely affect their entrants' persistence rates by being less selective academically and less prestigious. Several studies have found that academic selectivity has a significant positive impact on persistence, independent of other college characteristics and student characteristics (Anderson 1984, pp. 33, 36; Astin 1982, pp. 101–102; Tinto 1975, pp. 114–15). The community college's low academic selectivity impinges on its students' academic achievement, and thus dropout rates, in two ways.

Because community colleges are less selective, community-college entrants more often find themselves surrounded by peers who are not interested in or good at academic work and who discourage those who are. This anti-academic student culture is rooted in the fundamental ambivalence of working-class and minority students toward education. Most of these students want to do well, but they are also afraid of failing. Furthermore, they believe academic success requires them to take on the culture of an alien group and to repudiate (and be repudiated by) their

family and peers. Hence, working-class and minority students develop powerful norms against academic success (London 1978, chaps. 3–4; Neumann and Riesman 1980, p. 58; Weis 1985, pp. 102, 122, 134–37, 153–54).[16]

At the same time, community-college entrants seem to receive less academic support from their teachers than four-year-college entrants (London 1978, chaps. 2, 5; Neumann and Riesman 1980, p. 61; Weis 1985, pp. 84, 89–90, 93). On the whole, community-college teachers seem to have lower expectations of their students. They perceive their students as less academically able and motivated, so they concentrate on reaching a few and largely ignore the rest. This process sets up a vicious circle; students and faculty each find that their prejudices toward the other are powerfully confirmed. Community-college teachers' diminished expectations of their students reflect the difficulty of teaching students who arrive at college bereft of many of the skills that colleges traditionally expect and that make teaching go smoothly. They also reflect the unhappiness of community-college teachers, particularly those in the liberal arts, who find themselves in low-status colleges teaching nontraditional students. Moreover, many community-college teachers often differ greatly in background from their working-class and minority students; thus they find it hard to appreciate their students' world views, motivations, and real strengths.

## Problems in Transferring to Four-Year Colleges

Even when community-college entrants do persist in college, they move on to the upper division of four-year colleges at a lower rate than four-year-college entrants.[17] For example, 24.4 percent of students who entered two-year colleges in fall 1972 transferred to four-year colleges by fall 1974.[18] Meanwhile,

76.4 percent of students who entered four-year colleges were still enrolled in four-year colleges in fall 1974 (NCES 1977*a*, 6–9, 72–74, 1977*b*, pp. 22–26, 191–92). These differences stand up even when pre-existing student characteristics and differential attrition are controlled. For example, NLS-72 data indicate that 49.3 percent of two-year-college entrants who aspired to a baccalaureate *and* who survived the first two years of college transferred to a four-year college by their third year. Meanwhile, 96.2 percent of similar four-year-college entrants were still in four-year schools in their third year (NCES 1977*a*, pp. 8–13. 1977*b*, pp. 50–51, 135–36).[19]

Attending a community college hinders students' transfer to four-year schools in two ways. Many students lose their desire to transfer. And students who still wish to transfer find it difficult to do so.

Students lose their desire to transfer for various reasons. Transfer involves a difficult readjustment. Community-college entrants have to move to a new school, perhaps in a different community, where they might stay only two or three years. Four-year-college entrants find no such chasm lying between their sophomore and junior years. Hence, they need less encouragement from their college teachers and counselors to continue into the junior year.

Moreover, community colleges fail to provide adequate support for transfer. Community colleges are less interested today in their transfer programs than in their vocational programs. This vocational orientation has created lower transfer rates. The California state community college board found that vocationally oriented community colleges have significantly lower transfer rates to the University of California than more transfer-oriented community colleges, even net of differences between community colleges in student-body composition (race and grades) and proximity to the university (California Community Colleges 1984, pp. 17–19).

Similarly, Anderson (1984, pp. 33–34) found—that net of differences in student-body characteristics, academic selectivity, etc.—NLS-72 college entrants were significantly less likely to receive a bachelor's degree if they entered vocationally oriented two-year or four-year colleges.

Community-college vocational-education programs weaken their students' desire to transfer because their goal is to move their students directly into the labor market. The teachers in these programs are often recruited from the trades for which they train students and have relatively little interest in and knowledge about how students can be aided in transferring to four-year colleges.

Of course, many community-college entrants enroll in vocational programs because this is their original desire. But many become vocational students because the community college shunts them in this direction. Community colleges exert a vocationalizing influence through several channels. They spread before students a vast array of attractively packaged vocational programs. They give vocational-education programs new and attractive facilities and blur the distinction between academic and vocational-education programs. They proclaim that vocational-education graduates do as well as baccalaureates. Finally, community colleges develop elaborate counseling programs to reconcile their supply of and students' demand for vocational education (Dougherty 1986*b*, Brint and Karabel forthcoming; Clark 1960).

But even if community-college entrants retain a desire to transfer, they encounter problems in being admitted to four-year colleges and in securing financial aid. Community colleges do not control an upper division to which they can pass on students they wish. Rather, they depend on four-year colleges to accept students. And there is evidence that four-year colleges are less willing to take in community-college transfers than to pass on their own native students. Willingham and Findikyan (1969, pp. 5–6) found that among a varied sample of 146 four-year colleges, 27 percent of all students wishing to transfer from two-year colleges and 62 percent of vocational students were rejected. Many of these transfer applicants are rejected because of academic deficiencies. Still, there is evidence that four-year colleges have a definite distaste for community-college transfer applicants, particularly those from vocational programs. Willingham and Findikyan (1969, p. 25) found that among the 146 four-year colleges they surveyed, only 26 percent encouraged transfers in their publications, only 17 percent prepared special material for transfers, and only 27 percent visited junior colleges (Willingham and Findikyan 1969, pp. 5–6).[20]

Community colleges also have little control over whether transfer applicants will receive financial aid, and many applicants do not. The NLS-72 found that students who transferred from two-year colleges received fewer scholarships and other grants than students who initially entered four-year colleges (19.3 percent versus 38.9 percent), although they received as many loans (22.1 percent versus 23.8 percent).[21] A study of accepted transfer applicants to the University of California who did not matriculate (19 percent of those accepted) found that a major reason was finances (Baratta and Apodaca 1984, p. 6).

## Attrition After Transfer

Even after transferring to four-year colleges, community-college entrants are still at greater risk of dropping out because of factors that are tied to the community college. Community-college transfers to four-year colleges are significantly more likely than comparable four-year-college natives to drop out of four-year college. As Table 3 indicates, several studies—some national and some state-specific—have found that three to five years after transferring, about a third of all transfers have dropped out. After a few more years, even

more are felled. By comparison, four-year-college natives in California and New York who are also entering the junior year have a considerably lower dropout rate.

How much of this difference in dropout rates is due to institutional factors rooted in the awkward coupling of four-year and two-year colleges and how much is due to the lower ability and lack of motivation of two-year-college transfers? (NCES 1977a, pp. 32, 75). Unfortunately, there are no studies comparing the educational attainments of community-college transfers and four-year-college natives net of differences in their pre-college characteristics and experiences.

In any case, there is evidence that four institutional factors do contribute significantly to transfer students' greater dropout rate: credit loss, difficulty getting financial aid, lack of social integration into the four-year college, and sharp drops in grades. First, a fair number of transfer students lose credits in transit to four-year colleges. This credit loss harms transfer students' educational attainment by slowing them down and making them vulnerable to competing demands and attractions. A study of transfers from Maryland community colleges found that 6 percent lost 13 or more credit hours, i.e., at least one semester (Maryland State Board for Community Colleges 1983, p. 12). Several national studies conducted during the 1960s discovered that 10 to 12 percent of two-year-college transfers lost at least a semester's worth of credits (Godfrey and Holmstrom 1970, p. 167; Knoell and Medsker 1965, p. 61; Willingham and Findikyan 1969, p. 30). Several factors cause credit loss. Most four-year colleges refuse to give more than two years' credit. They also routinely disallow credit for community-college courses that have no equivalent in their own curriculum or that are upper-division courses in their eyes. And four-year colleges often give no credit or only partial credit for community-college courses in which the student received a D, although four-year-college natives usually receive credit for D's (Kintzer and Wat-

**TABLE 3**
**Educational Outcomes for Two-Year Transfers and Four-Year Natives**

| | Study | | | | | |
|---|---|---|---|---|---|---|
| | *California Community Colleges (1984)* | *Florida State Education Department (1983)* | *Holmstrom and Bisconti (1974)* | *Trent and Medsker (1968)* | *Folger et al. (1970)* | *Knoell and Medsker (1965)* |
| Study characteristics | | | | | | |
| Coverage | California | Florida | U.S. | U.S. | U.S. | U.S. |
| Data set used[a] | CSU | FSED | ACE | CSHE | Talent | CSHE |
| Year students entered college | n.a. | n.a. | 1968 | 1959 | 1960 | 1958 |
| Year students transferred | 1975 | 1976 | n.a. | n.a. | n.a. | 1960 |
| Year students followed up | 1980 | 1978 | 1972 | 1963 | 1965 | 1963 |
| Findings | | | | | | |
| Percentage dropping out[b] | | | | | | |
| Within two years | | | | | | |
|   Two-year transfers | | 32.0 | 14.3 | 21.0 | | |
|   Four-year natives | | 19.8 | | | | |
| Within three years | | | | | | |
|   Two-year transfers | | | | | 32.0 | 29.0 |
| Within five years | | | | | | |
|   Two-year transfers | 35.6 | | | | | |
|   Four-year natives | 23.9 | | | | | |
| Percentage attaining a baccalaureate[b] | | | | | | |
| Within two years | | | | | | |
|   Two-year transfers | | | 40.8 | 33.0 | | |
|   Four-year natives | | | 57.2 | 37.0 | | |
| Within three years | | | | | | |
|   Two-year transfers | | | | | 40.0 | 62.0 |
| Within five years | | | | | | |
|   Two-year transfers | 61.1 | | | | | |
|   Four-year natives | 67.8 | | | | | |
| Percentage still in college[b] | | | | | | |
| After two years | | | | | | |
|   Two-year transfers | | | 44.9 | 46.0 | | |
| After three years | | | | | | |
|   Two-year transfers | | | | | 28.0 | 9.0 |
| After five years | | | | | | |
|   Two-year transfers | 3.3 | | | | | |
|   Four-year natives | 8.3 | | | | | |

[a]The California data pertain to fall 1975 transfers to the California State University system (CSU) who came in as juniors and to CSU natives who became juniors the same year. The CSU enrolls about 60 percent of all California community-college transfers to public and private four-year colleges (California Community-Colleges 1984). The Florida data are for fall 1976 transfers to three state universities (University of Florida, University of South Florida, and Florida Technological University) who came in as juniors and for university natives who became juniors the same year (Florida State Education Department 1983). The ACE data are from the American Council of Education's annual survey of entering *full-time* freshmen. The CSHE surveys were conducted by the Center for the Study of Higher Education at the University of California at Berkeley. Talent is the Project Talent's national survey of high school graduates.

[b]Holmstrom and Bisconti, Trent and Medsker, and Folger et al. did not report the time elapsed between the year transfer students entered four-year colleges and the year they were followed up. But since the majority of students transfer between the sophomore and junior years, the follow-up probably came after two years at the four-year college in Holmstrom and Bisconti's and Trent and Medsker's studies and after three years in Folger et al.'s study.

tenbarger 1985, chap. 2; Knoell and Medsker 1965, p. 61; Maryland State Board for Community Colleges 1983, p. 12; Winandy and McGrath 1970, pp. 189–90).

Transfer students also have difficulty getting financial aid. As noted above, they receive financial aid less often than four-year natives. This lack of financial aid increases the chances that transfer students will withdraw or flunk out. Transfer students who drop out of college usually give lack of money as their main reason (Knoell and Medsker 1965, p. 71). Lack of financial aid causes students to drop out because it forces them to take jobs, which interfere with their social and academic integration into the four-year institution.

Third, transfer students find it difficult to become socially integrated into the four-year institutions they have entered; thus, their grades, commitment to college, and ultimately, persistence suffer (Astin 1977*b*, pp. 154, 168; Knoell and Medsker 1965, p. 68). For example, among Los Angeles community-college transfers to UCLA, those who dropped out were significantly more likely to have most of their friends outside UCLA (Kissler, Lara, and Cardinal 1981, pp. 9–10). Among the reasons that transfers find it harder than natives to integrate themselves socially are their greater need to work to support themselves, the greater pressure they are under to get good grades so that they can validate their admission, the lack of orientation programs directed specifically to transfer students, and the fact that clubs and other extracurricular activities at four-year colleges usually focus their recruitment of new members on freshmen.

Finally, transfer students find it hard to perform well academically at four-year colleges. Studies repeatedly find that they tend to suffer rather sharp drops in their grades in the first year after transfer (Cohen and Brawer 1982, pp. 349–50; Hills 1965, Kintzer and Wattenbarger 1985; Knoell and Medsker 1965; pp. 27–28). For example, the median GPA of fall 1982 community-college trans-

fers to the University of California and California State University systems dropped one-half point at UC and one-third point at CSU on a five-point scale (California Community Colleges 1984, pp. 26, 30, F-2). Similarly, fall 1979 Illinois community-college transfers to Illinois public and private universities suffered an average drop of about one-third grade point between their community-college GPA and their first-year university GPA (Illinois Community College Board 1984, p. 11).[22] In turn, bad grades are significantly associated with greater attrition. Among Los Angeles community-college transfers to UCLA, those who dropped out had significantly lower grades at UCLA than those who continued (Kissler et al. 1981, pp. 9–10). Transfer students' grade drop leads to attrition quite directly when students are simply dismissed or put on academic probation. Additionally, poor grades lead many to voluntarily withdraw.

Clearly, a good part of the grade shock that community-college students encounter stems from the disparity between their abilities and the tougher standards of the four-year colleges. But it also stems from institutional factors, particularly, less access to financial aid and poorer academic preparation in the community college.

As discussed in the previous section, transfer students are less likely to receive financial aid than four-year-college natives. And this disability significantly and independently depresses their upper-division grades and persistence rates. A study of fall 1977 transfers from Los Angeles community colleges to UCLA found that the students' grades at UCLA were significantly and negatively associated with their amount of unmet financial need, even when their community-college GPAs and quality of preparation were controlled (Kissler et al. 1981, pp. 6–8). Moreover, community-college transfers get poorer grades than four-year-college natives because their lower-division preparation, on the average, is inferior (Aulston 1974, pp. 116–118;

Kissler et al. 1981, pp. 6–8; Knoell and Medsker 1965, pp. 60, 98). For example, the fall 1977 transfers to UCLA received much less writing instruction in the lower division than the UCLA natives. Two thirds of the transfers said that at UCLA, they frequently had to write papers integrating ideas from various parts of a course, but only one third said they had done this frequently at the community college. The transfers' lack of writing experience had a significant and independent effect on their upper-division grades and persistence rates, even when their demographic characteristics, community-college grades, community college courses, and study habits were controlled (Lara 1981, pp. 2, 8–9).

## SUMMARY AND CONCLUSIONS

This paper has a two-fold task: to determine the effects of community colleges on educational and economic attainment and to determine how the community college produces those effects. The first section of this paper critically reviews the findings of a wide range of studies that compare the impacts of community colleges and other kinds of postsecondary institutions on their entrants' educational attainment and economic success. It concludes that the critics from the class-reproduction school somewhat more accurately characterize the community colleges' effects than do the supporters of the functionalist school.[23] Community colleges are significantly less able than four-year colleges to facilitate the educational and economic attainment of the approximately 30 to 40 percent of community-college entrants seeking bachelor's degrees. Generally, baccalaureate aspirants entering community colleges secure significantly fewer bachelor's degrees, fewer years of education, less prestigious jobs, and in the long run, poorer paying jobs than comparable students entering four-year colleges. On the other hand, community colleges may be superior—but here the data are much weaker—to four-year colleges for the 30 to 40 percent of community-college entrants who seek a subbaccalaureate degree. Vocational-education aspirants seem to attain more years of education if they enter a community college rather than a four-year college or postsecondary vocational school. However, the data are too sparse and contradictory to be conclusive on which type of institution best promotes the *economic* success of students who do not aspire to a baccalaureate.

The second section of the paper develops a model to explain why entrance into a community college hinders the educational attainment of baccalaureate aspirants. This model states that the factors hindering community-college entrants' educational attainment constitute three main processes that are linked in a funnel-like structure: attrition in the community college, difficulty transferring to four-year colleges, and attrition after transfer. Within each process, several mechanisms are at work. The greater attrition in the community college is significantly and independently associated with the community colleges' low academic selectivity and prestige and lack of dormitories. Second, community-college entrants find it difficult to transfer because their desire to transfer is weakened by the community college's vocational emphasis and the need to enter a new college. Moreover, even if their desire to transfer remains strong, they are less able to secure acceptance and financial aid from four-year colleges. Finally, attrition after transfer is precipitated by the sharp drop in grades that many students suffer, lack of financial aid, difficulty becoming socially integrated into the new school, and frequent loss of credits.

My conclusions are based on the convergence of a wide variety of studies. Still, there is a considerable need for further research on the extent and nature of the effects of community colleges. Such research is urgently needed because of the central role community colleges play in our higher education system and therefore in our system of social stratification.

We particularly need research oriented to three main tasks. The first task is to refine our estimates of the magnitude of community-college effects in several different areas. To begin, it would be useful to determine the transfer rates of community-college entrants and the continuation rates of four-year-college entrants net of differences in family background, educational aspirations, academic ability, and several other variables. In such a study, it would be illuminating to determine the number of community-college students, particularly vocational majors, who initially plan to transfer to a four-year school but either fail to apply or apply but fail to go on.

Another area in which refined estimates are needed involves attrition in the upper division. We need a systematic comparison of the upper-division attrition rates of four-year-college natives, community-college transfers, and transfers from other types of institutions net of precollege and lower-division characteristics.

Third, we need to move beyond the two-way comparison of community colleges with four-year colleges and examine the effects of community colleges relative to both four-year colleges and public and private postsecondary vocational-technical schools. It would be especially illuminating to compare the effects of community colleges with the effects of other types of colleges that share varying combinations of the characteristics typical of community colleges: low tuition, accessibility, unselectiveness, and vocational emphasis. Through such a study, we can more precisely determine the relative impact of the community college and the particular characteristics—which may not be peculiar to the community college—that contribute to that impact.

The second main task is to contextualize these effects by examining how they interact with variations in student characteristics. We need to carefully explore how community-college effects shift in magnitude and direction as students vary in social class, sex, race, educational aspirations, type of program, and age. As we have seen, there is intriguing, although somewhat weak, evidence that community-college effects differ greatly by students' aspirations. Two interactions of community-college effects with age are particularly worth exploring. One concerns the effect of community colleges on students entering college many years after high school. All the major studies on community-college effects focus on college students who are just out of high school. But this is problematic in the case of community colleges; only about half of community-college students enter within a year or two of high school graduation (U.S. Bureau of the Census 1985, P. 54).[24] The second interaction involving age concerns time elapsed since leaving college. We need to examine whether follow-up periods longer than the seven to ten years that now dominate in studies of community-college effects yield different results.[25]

The third task is to test the relative importance of the various components of the model of community-college effects developed in the second section of this paper. That model was constructed by piecing together findings from various narrow-gauged studies. This procedure, which was dictated by the current state of research, does not allow us to determine what mechanisms are particularly lethal to the academic and economic life chances of community-college entrants. Hence, we need studies that examine the simultaneous impact of many, if not all, of the factors identified above.

## ENDNOTES

1. The term *community college* is used here to denote public two-year institutions that offer both academic and vocational education.

Community colleges make up the bulk of two-year colleges in both number and enrollment.

2. The purposes and causes (i.e., the motives and actors) behind the expansion of the community college are addressed in Dougherty (1986*a*, 1986*b*).

3. However, members of the class-reproduction school have recently begun to consider the economic returns to a community-college education. See Pincus (1980, 1986) and Karabel (1986).

4. There are no national figures on the distribution of aspirations among community-college entrants. The figures presented here are estimated from studies of the aspirations of community-college entrants in California, Maryland, and Virginia (Adams and Roesler 1977, p. 15; Beaver and Kruckenburg 1985, pp. 66–70; McConochie 1983, p. 10; Sheldon 1982, pp. 1–34). My estimate is higher than Cohen and Brawer's (1982) principally because they mistakenly based their estimate in part on a Washington study that measures the aspirations of community-college students enrolled at all levels, rather that the aspirations of community-college *entrants* alone (Meier 1979).

5. Because of the lack of current data, I was unable to consider two additional standards. One was the effect of relative availability of various types of college on college-entrance rates for different localities and kinds of students. Unfortunately, the studies on this subject are few and, given the enormous growth of community colleges in the last twenty years, out of date (Medsker and Trent 1964; Tinto 1973, 1974). The other standard that could not be applied was success in adult and community education. The issue of how one defines success in this area has been given little attention, and in any case, the main surveys of student outcomes ignore adult students.

6. The NLS-72 questioned over 20,000 spring 1972 high school seniors nationwide and followed them up in fall 1973, 1974, 1976, and 1979.

7. Velez (1985) and Anderson (1984) sampled only community-college entrants who enrolled in academic programs and excluded those who enrolled in vocational and other programs. In essence, they concentrated on the community-college and four-year-college students most likely to pursue a baccalaureate.

8. Velez's data are from two-year colleges generally rather than just community colleges. That is, he included data from private junior colleges and two-year branches of state universities. However, community colleges enroll the vast majority of two-year-college students, so the data should apply with little distortion to community colleges in particular.

9. Unfortunately, Anderson compared community-college entrants with entrants to six different kinds of institutions: public and private two-year colleges, four-year colleges, and universities. I compare community colleges to state four-year colleges because public four-year nondoctoral-level colleges enroll 22.5 percent of all students in higher education, more than public universities (19.3 percent) and all private institutions (22.3 percent) (NCES 1985, p. 8).

10. Breneman and Nelson obtained this figure by estimating separate regression equations for the educational attainment of four-year-college entrants and the attainment of public two-year-college entrants. They then applied the coefficients from each regression equation to the values for each student and determined which students would benefit more from the application of the regression weights for the community-college equation than from the application of the weights for the four-year-college equation.

11. Anderson's figures might underestimate the real success of four-year-college entrants, however. She included in her sample respondents still in school, as long as they had some job. Since four-year-college entrants are more often still in school and working part-time seven years after first entering college, her analysis tends to deflate their occupational prestige and income.

12. Monk-Turner undoubtedly underestimated the real impact of college type on occupational attainment because she controlled for educational attainment and type of college entered at the same time. Breneman and Nel-

son (1981, pp. 84–85) found that much of the effect of college type on economic attainment is mediated by years of education attained.

13. Not surprisingly, community-college attrition rates are higher for the socioeconomically and academically disadvantaged. Nonwhite students of low socioeconomic status with poor high school records have higher community-college attrition rates than students with the obverse characteristics (Astin 1972; NCES 1977*b*, pp.22, 135–36, 150).

14. For two-year-college and four-year-college entrants separately, Astin (1972, pp. 10, 47–48) regressed students' continuation into the second year of college on a host of characteristics, including sex, race, socioeconomic status, high school test scores and grades, and respondents' and parents' educational aspirations at the beginning of college.

15. Anderson (1981, p. 14) found that 59 percent of the four-year-college entrants in the NLS-72 lived on campus.

16. For generalizations of this point to education as a whole, see Apple (1982), Giroux (1981), and Willis (1977).

17. The transfer rates reported above are on a two-year follow-up of students who entered college directly out of high school. Unfortunately, transfer rates based on the NLS-72 seven-year (1979) follow-up have not been reported. And other data on transfer rates are much poorer. Cohen, Brawer, and Bensimon (1985, p. 3) estimated, with no clear evidence, that 13 to 15 percent of all community-college entrants eventually go on to four-year schools. Very few states publish data on the proportion of an entering cohort that eventually transfers. Those studies that do report such data report quite different transfer rates: e.g., 9.5 percent in California in a three-year follow-up of all entrants and 24.3 percent in Maryland in a four-year follow-up of degree-credit entrants (Sheldon 1982, McConochie 1983, pp. 18–19).

18. As with attrition rates, transfer rates for community-college entrants vary systematically by the major demographic variables. White male community-college entrants of high socioeconomic status with good high school records have higher transfer rates than stu-

dents with the obverse characteristics (Holmstrom and Bisconti 1974, pp. 71–86; NCES 1977*a*, pp. 28, 32, 70–73; Van Alstyne et al., 1973, pp. 1–5).

19. Even if the 38.3 percent of two-year-college entrants who aspired to a baccalaureate and who were still enrolled in two-year colleges in fall 1974 did eventually transfer—which is quite unlikely—the community-college transfer rate would total only 87.6 percent, well below the 96.2 percent continuation rate for four-year-college entrants who aspired to a baccalaureate and who survived the first two years of college (NCES 1977*b*, pp. 191–92).

20. During the 1970s, four-year colleges' distaste for community-college transfers seemingly weakened as higher education enrollments hit a plateau and state governments moved to ease transfer from community colleges to state universities (Kintzer and Wattenbarger 1985, pp. 36–38). However, we have no firm data on the extent of this reorientation of sentiment.

21. The gap is probably smaller today, since transfer students are more numerous and colleges compete vigorously for students. Yet, there is still no federal program specifically for transfer students, and many states have taken little initiative in this area. Again, more research is needed.

22. It is often claimed that transfers' upper-division grades soon recover from "transfer shock." However, this claim is based on a comparison of the mean GPA of students who are two or three years past transfer with the GPA of students who transferred within the previous year. This cross-sectional approximation of a longitudinal analysis does not correct for the fact that the older transfer students no longer include the many transfer students who did badly the first year and dropped out.

23. This does not mean that the class reproductionists' assessment of the *motives* behind this effect is also correct. The desire to hinder students' mobility played a very small role in the rise of the community college (Dougherty 1986*a*, 1986*b*).

24. This restriction of survey data to younger entrants may not greatly bias the estimates for baccalaureate aspirants, since older com-

munity-college entrants are largely uninterested in pursuing a baccalaureate (Sheldon 1982). On the other hand, the restriction in age may affect the estimates for economic attainment to a significant, but unknown, degree.

**25.** In fact, studies with different follow-up periods may well find different effects, but they will probably be in the same direction as those found so far. For example, for CUNY, Lavin et al. (1986) found that fourteen years after college entrance, 62.4 percent of four-year-college entrants, but only 27.6 percent of community-college entrants, had attained bachelor's degrees. Thus, the gap at CUNY increased from 18 percent after five years to 25 percent after fourteen years. Similarly, studies using longer follow-up periods may find even greater differences in economic attainment because they will not have to exclude, as shorter-range studies do, large numbers of four-year-college entrants who are still in college, attending professional and graduate schools.

# REFERENCES

Adams, June J., and Elmo Roesler. 1977. *A Profile of First-Time Students at Virginia Community Colleges, 1975–76*. Richmond: Virginia Community College System. (ERIC No. ED 153 694)

Alba, Richard, and David Lavin. 1981. "Community Colleges and Tracking in Higher Education." *Sociology of Education* 54:223–47.

Anderson, Kristine. 1981. "Post-High School Experiences and College Attrition." *Sociology of Education* 54:1–15.

___. 1984. *Institutional Differences in College Effects*. Boca Raton: Florida Atlantic University. (ERIC No. ED 256 204)

Apple, Michael. 1982. *Education and Power*. New York: Routledge and Kegan Paul.

Astin, Alexander. 1972. *College Dropouts: A National Study*. Report No. 7(1). Washington, DC: American Council on Education.

___. 1977a. *Four Critical Years*. San Francisco: Jossey-Bass.

___. 1977b. *Preventing Students from Dropping Out*. San Francisco: Jossey-Bass.

___. 1982 *Minorities in American Higher Education*. San Francisco: Jossey-Bass.

Aulston, M. D. 1974. "Black Transfer Students in White Colleges." *NASPA Journal* 12:116–23.

Baratta, Frank, and Ed Apodaca. 1984. *A Profile of California Community College Transfer Students at the University of California*. Berkeley: University of California. (ERIC No. ED 260 754)

Beaver, Evelyn, and Joanne Kruchenburg. 1985. *Annual Report of Enrollment, Fall 1985*. Sacramento: California Community Colleges. (ERIC No. ED 261 740)

Bowles, Samuel, and Herbert Gintis. 1976. *Schooling in Capitalist America*. New York: Basic Books.

Breneman, David, and Susan Nelson. 1981. *Financing Community Colleges*. Washington, DC: Brookings Institution.

Brint, Steven, and Jerome Karabel. Forthcoming. *The Transformation of the Two-Year College*.

California Community Colleges. 1984. *Transfer Education*. Sacramento: Office of the Chancellor. (ERIC No. ED 250 025)

Clark, Burton. 1960. *The Open Door College*. New York: McGraw-Hill.

Cohen, Arthur M., and Florence B. Brawer. 1982. *The American Community College*. San Francisco: Jossey-Bass.

Cohen, Arthur M., Florence B. Brawer, and Estela Bensimon. 1985. *Transfer Education in American Community Colleges*. Los Angeles: UCLA, Center for the Study of Community Colleges. (ERIC No. ED 255 250)

Dougherty, Kevin. 1986a. "The Politics of Community College Expansion: Beyond the Functionalist and Class Reproduction Theories." Unpublished paper, Department of Sociology, Manhattanville College.

___. 1986b. "The Vocationalization of the Community College." Unpublished paper, Department of Sociology, Manhattanville College.

Eells, Walter C. 1931. *The Junior College*. Boston: Houghton-Mifflin.

Florida State Education Department. 1983. *A Longitudinal Study Comparing University Native and Community College Transfer Students in the State University System of Florida*. Tallahassee: Florida State Education Department. (ERIC No. ED 256 405)

Folger, John, Helen Astin, and Alan Bayer. 1970. *Human Resources and Higher Education*. New York: Russell Sage.

Giroux, Henry. 1981. *Ideology, Culture, and the Process of Schooling*. Philadelphia: Temple University Press.

Godfrey, Eleanor P., and Engin L. Holmstrom. 1970. *Study of Community Colleges and Vocational Technical Centers*. Washington, DC: Bureau of Social Science Research. (ERIC No. ED 053 718)

Hills, J. R. 1965. "Transfer Shock: The Academic Performance of the Junior College Transfer." *Journal of Experimental Education* 33: 201–15.

Holmstrom, Engin, and Ann S. Bisconti. 1974. *Transfers from Junior Colleges to Senior Colleges*. Washington, DC.: American Council on Education.

Illinois Community College Board. 1984. *Fall 1979 Transfer Study, Report 4: Third and Fourth Year Persistence and Achievement*. Springfield: Illinois Community College Board. (ERIC No. ED 254 275)

Karabel, Jerome. 1972. "Community Colleges and Social Stratification." *Harvard Educational Review* 42:521–62.

———. 1986. "Community Colleges and Social Stratification in the 1980s." Pp. 13–30 in *The Community College and its Critics*, edited by L. Steven Zwerling. New Directions in Community Colleges No. 54. San Francisco: Jossey-Bass.

Kintzer, Frederick, and James L. Wattenbarger. 1985. *The Articulation/Transfer Phenomenon*. Washington, DC: American Association of Community and Junior Colleges. (ERIC No. ED 257 539)

Kissler, Gerald, Juan Lara, and Judith Cardinal. 1981. *Factors Contributing to the Academic Difficulties Encountered by Students who Transfer from Community Colleges to Four-Year Institutions*. Los Angeles: UCLA. (ERIC No. ED 203 920)

Knoell, Dorothy, and Leland L. Medsker. 1965. *From Junior College to Senior College*. Washington, DC: American Council on Education.

Lara, Juan. 1981. *Differences in Quality of Academic Effort between Successful and Unsuccessful Community College Transfer Students*. Los Angeles: UCLA. (ERIC No. ED 201 359)

Lavin, David, James Murtha, Barry Kaufman, and David Hyllegard. 1986. "Long-Term Educational Attainment in an Open-Access University System: Effects of Ethnicity, Economic Status, and College Type." Paper presented at the annual meetings of the American Educational Research Association, San Francisco.

London, Howard. 1978. *The Culture of a Community College*. New York: Praeger.

Maryland State Board for Community Colleges. 1983. *The Role of Community Colleges in Preparing Students for Transfer to Four-Year Colleges and Universities*. Annapolis: Maryland State Board for Community Colleges. (ERIC No. ED 230 255)

McConochie, Daniel. 1983. *Four Years. Later: Follow-up of 1978 Entrants. Maryland Community Colleges*. Annapolis: Maryland State Board for Community Colleges (ERIC No. ED 234 850)

Medsker, Leland L. 1960. *The Junior College*. New York: McGraw-Hill.

Medsker, Leland L., and James Trent. 1964. *The Influence of Different Types of Public Higher Education Institutions on College Attendance from Varying Socioeconomic and Ability Levels*. Berkeley: University of California. Center for the Study of Higher Education. (ERIC No. ED 002 875)

Meier, Terre. 1979. *Washington Community College Factbook. Addendum A: Student Enrollments Academic Year 1978–79*. Olympia: State Board for Community College Education. (ERIC No. ED 184 616)

Monk-Turner, Elizabeth. 1983. "Sex, Educational Differentiation, and Occupational Status." *Sociological Quarterly* 24:393–404.

Monroe, Charles R. 1972. *A Profile of the Community College*. San Francisco: Jossey-Bass.

Nasaw, David. 1979. *Schooled to Order.* New York: Oxford University Press.

National Center for Education Statistics. 1977*a. Transfer Students in Institutions of Higher Education.* Washington. DC: U.S. Government Printing Office.

___. 1977*b. Withdrawal from Institutions of Higher Education.* Washington, DC: U.S. Government Printing Office.

___. 1984. *Fall Enrollment in Colleges and Universities,* 1982. Washington, DC: U.S. Government Printing Office.

___. 1985. *Fall Enrollment in Colleges and Universities.* 1983. Washington, DC: U.S. Government Printing Office.

Neumann, William, and David Riesman. 1980. "The Community College Elite." Pp. 53–71 in *Questioning the Community College Role,* edited by George Vaughan. New Directions in Community Colleges No. 32. San Francisco: Jossey-Bass.

Pantages, T. J., and C. F. Creedon. 1978. "Studies of College Attrition: 1950–1975." *Review of Education Research* 48:49–101.

Pincus, Fred L. 1974. "Tracking in Community Colleges." *Insurgent Sociologist* 4:17–35.

___. 1980. "The False Promises of Community Colleges: Class Conflict and Vocational Education." *Harvard Educational Review* 50:332–61.

___. 1986. "Vocational Education: More False Promises." Pp. 41–52 in *The Community College and its Critics,* edited by L. Steven Zwerling. New Directions in Community Colleges No. 54. San Francisco: Jossey-Bass.

Rosenbaum, James. 1976. *Making Inequality.* New York: Wiley.

Sheldon, Stephen. 1982. *Statewide Longitudinal Study : Report on Academic Year 1978–1981. Part 5, Final Report.* Los Angeles: Pierce College. (ERIC No. ED 217 917)

Somers, Gerald, Laure Sharpe, and Thelma Myint. 1971. *The Effectiveness of Vocational and Technical Programs.* Madison: University of Wisconsin, Center for Studies in Vocational and Technical Education. (ERIC No. ED 055 190)

Tinto, Vincent. 1973. "College Proximity and Rates of College Attendance." *American Educational Research Journal* 10:273–93.

___. 1974. "Public Junior Colleges and the Substitution Effect in Higher Education." Paper presented at the annual meetings of the American Educational Research Association. (ERIC No. ED 089 808)

___. 1975. "Dropout from Higher Education: A Theoretical Synthesis of Recent Research." *Review of Educational Research* 45:89–125.

Trent, James, and Leland L. Medsker. 1968. *Beyond High School.* San Francisco: Jossey-Bass.

Turner, Ralph. 1960. "Modes of Social Ascent Through Education." *American Sociological Review* 25:855–67.

U.S. Bureau of the Census. 1985. "School Enrollment—Social and Economic Characteristics of Students: October 1981 and 1980." *Current Population Reports,* ser. P-20, no. 400. Washington, DC: U.S. Government Printing Office.

Van Alstyne, Carol, Cathy Henderson, Charles Fletcher, and Yi Sien. 1973. *Comparison of the Characteristics of Transfer and Nontransfer College Students.* Washington. DC: American Council on Education (ERIC No. ED 085 028)

Vaughan, George, ed. 1980. *Questioning the Community College Role.* New Directions in Community Colleges No. 32. San Francisco: Jossey-Bass.

Velez, William. 1985. "Finishing College: The Effects of College Type." *Sociology of Education* 58:191–200.

Weis, Lois. 1985. *Between Two Worlds: Black Students in an Urban Community College.* Boston: Routledge and Kegan Paul.

Willingham, Warren, and Nurhan Findikyan. 1969. *Patterns of Admission for Transfer Students.* New York: College Entrance Examination Board.

Willis, Paul. 1977. *Learning to Labour.* New York: Schocken.

Wilms, Wellford. 1980. *Vocational Education and Social Mobility.* Los Angeles; UCLA. (ERIC No. ED 183 966)

Winandy, Donald, and Robert McGrath. 1970. "A Study of Admissions Policies and Practices for Transfer Students in Illinois." *College and University* 45:186–92.

Zwerling, L. Steven. 1976. *Second Best: The Crisis of the Junior College*. New York: McGraw-Hill.

## CHAPTER 8 REFERENCES

Alexander, K., & Pallas, A. M. (1983). Private schools and public policy: New evidence on cognitive achievement in public and private schools. *Sociology of Education, 56,* 170–182.

Berg, I. (1970). *Education and jobs: The great training robbery.* New York: Praeger.

Bowles, S., & Gintis, H. (1776). *Schooling in capitalist America.* New York: Basic Books.

Bryk, A. S., Lee, V. E., & Holland, P. B. (1993). *Catholic schools and the common good.* Cambridge, MA: Harvard University Press.

Chubb, J. E., & Moe, T. M. (1990). *Politics, markets, and America's schools.* Washington, DC: Brookings Institution.

Coleman, J. S., Hoffer, T., & Kilgore, S. (1982). *High school achievement: Public, Catholic and private schools compared.* New York: Basic Books.

Coleman, J. S., Campbell, E. Q., Hobson, C. J., McPartland, J., Mood, A. M., Weinfield, F. D., & York, R. L. (1966). *Equality of educational opportunity.* Washington, DC: Government Printing Office.

Collins, R. (1971). Functional and conflict theories of educational opportunity. *Harvard Educational Review, 38,* 7–32.

Collins, R. (1975). *Conflict sociology: Toward an explanatory science.* New York: Academic Press.

Jencks, C. (1979). *Who gets ahead? Determinants of economic success in America.* New York: Basic Books.

Jencks, C. (1985). How much do high school students learn. *Sociology of Education, 58,* 128–35.

McDill, E. (1978). *An updated answer to the question: Do schools make a difference?* Paper presented at the National Institute of Education: International Conference on School Organization and Effect, San Diego, CA.

Meyer, J. (1977, July). Education as an institution. *American Journal of Sociology, 83,* 55–77.

Persell, C. H. (1977). *Education and inequality.* New York: The Free Press.

Persell, C. H., Catsambis, S., & Cookson, P. W., Jr. (1992, July). Differential asset conversion: Class and gendered pathways to selective colleges. *Sociology of Education, 65.*

Phillips, K. (1990). *The politics of rich and poor.* New York: Random House.

Rosenbaum, J. E. (1976). *Making inequality: The hidden curriculum of high school tracking.* New York: Wiley.

Rossides, D. W. (1976). *The American class system: An introduction to social stratification.* New York: Houghton Mifflin.

Turner, R. H. (1960, October). Sponsored and contest mobility and the school system. *American Sociological Review, 25,* 855–867.

Walker, J. H., Kozma, E. J., & Green, R. P., Jr. (1989). *American education: Foundations and policy.* St. Paul, MN: West.

## SUGGESTED READINGS

Becker, G. (1964). *Human capital.* New York: National Bureau of Economic Research.

Berg, I. (1970). *Education and jobs: The great training robbery.* New York: Praeger.

Blau, P., & Duncan. O. D. (1967). *The American occupational structure*. New York: Wiley.

Boudon, R. (1974). *Education, opportunity, and social inequality: Changing prospects in Western society*. New York: Wiley.

Bowles, S., & Gintis, H. (1776). *Schooling in capitalist America*. New York: Basic Books.

Brint, S., & Karabel, J. (1989). *The dreamed deferred: American community colleges, 1945–1980*. New York: Oxford University Press.

Bryk, A. S., Lee, V. E., & Holland, P. B. (1993). *Catholic schools and the common good*. Cambridge, MA: Harvard University Press.

Burris, B. (1983). *No room at the top*. New York: Praeger.

Burris, V. (1983, August). The social and political consequences of overeducation. *American Sociological Review, 48,* 454–467.

Clark, B. (1962). *Educating the expert society*. San Francisco: Chandler.

Coleman, J. S., Campbell, E. Q., Hobson, C. J., McPartland, J., Mood, A. M., Weinfeld, F. D., & York, R. L. (1966). *Equality of educational opportunity*. Washington, DC: Government Printing Office.

Coleman, J. S., & Hoffer, T. (1987). *Public and private schools: The impact of communities*. New York: Basic Books.

Coleman, J. S., Hoffer, T., & Kilgore, S. 1982. *High school achievement: Public, Catholic and private schools compared*. New York: Basic Books.

Collins, R. (1971). Functional and conflict theories of educational opportunity. *Harvard Educational Review, 38,* 7–32.

Collins, R. (1975). *Conflict sociology: Toward an explanatory science*. New York: Academic Press.

Collins, R. (1977). Some comparative principles of educational stratification. *Harvard Educational Review, 47,* 1–27.

Delamont, S. (1989). *Knowledgeable women: Structuralism and the reproduction of elites*. New York: Routledge & Kegan Paul.

Dougherty, K. (1987, April). The effects of community colleges: Aid or hindrance to socioeconomic attainment? *Sociology of Education, 60,* 86–103.

Dougherty, K. (1988, Summer). Educational policymaking and the relative autonomy of the state: The case of occupational education in the community college. *Sociological Forum, 3,* 400–432.

Featherman, D. L., & Hauser, R. M. (1978). *Opportunity and change*. New York: Academic Press.

Freeman, R. (1976). *The overeducated American*. New York: Academic Press.

Hauser, R., & Featherman, D. (1976). Equality of schooling: Trends and prospects. *Sociology of Education, 49,* 99–119.

Jencks, C. S., Smith, M., Acland, H., Bane, M. J., Cohen, D., Gintis, H., Heyns, B., & Michelson, S. (1972). *Inequality*. New York: Basic Books.

Jencks, C., Bartlett, S., Corcoran, M., Crouse, J., Eaglesfield, D., Jackson, G., McClelland, K., Mueser, P., Olneck, M., Schwartz, J., Ward, S., & Williams, J. (1979). *Who gets ahead?* New York: Basic Books.

Kirp, D. L. (1982). *Just schools: The idea of racial equality in American education*. Berkeley, CA: University of California Press.

Lavin, D. E., & Alba, R. D. (1981). *Right versus privilege: The open admissions experiment at the City University of New York*. New York: The Free Press.

Persell, C. H. (1977). *Education and inequality*. New York: The Free Press.

Pincus, F. L. (1980). The false promise of community colleges. *Harvard Educational Review, 50*, 332–360.

Sewell, W., & Hauser, R. M. (1974). *Education, occupation, and earnings*. New York: Academic Press.

Sewell, W., & Hauser, R. M. (1976). Causes and consequences of higher education: Modes of the status attainment process. In W. H. Sewell, R. M. Hauser, and D. L. Featherman (Eds.), *Schooling and achievement in American society*. New York: Academic Press.

Sexton, P. C. (1961). *Education and income*. New York: Viking.

Silberman, C. (1969). *Crisis in the classroom*. New York: Random House.

CHAPTER 9

# Explanations of
# Educational Inequality

In Chapter 8, we explored unequal educational outcomes among various groups in U.S. society. The data suggest that there are significant differences in educational achievement and attainment based on social class, race, gender, and other ascriptive characteristics. Further, such unequal outcomes call into question the country's ideology of equality of educational opportunity and the ethos that schooling provides an important mechanism for social mobility. Although the data indicate that there has been mobility for individuals and that schooling has become increasingly tied to the labor market as a credentialing process in the twentieth century, they do not support the democratic-liberal faith that schooling provides mobility for entire groups. In fact, the data indicate that the relationship between family background and economic outcomes has been fairly consistent in the twentieth century, with family background exerting a powerful effect on both educational achievement and attainment and economic outcomes.

Given the persistent inequalities of educational outcomes—especially those based on race, class, and gender (although as we noted in the previous chapter, social class remains the most powerful factor in explaining educational inequalities)—the next step is to explain these unequal outcomes of the schooling process. In a society that is at least ideologically committed to the eradication of educational inequality, why do these differences continue to persist, often in the face of explicit social policies aimed at their elimination?

In this chapter, we will review the complex explanations of the problem. As you will see, there are numerous conflicting theories of educational inequality. We will present an overview of each and then offer our own multidimensional approach to understanding this most difficult situation. Let us note at the outset that there are no simple explanations and no simple solutions, despite experts' claims to the contrary. More often than not, the literature on educational inequality is filled with ideological explanations devoid of evidence. It is incumbent, however, to sift through the polemics and examine the research in order to reach reasonable conclusions. Given the complexity of the problem, this is no easy task; given the enormity and gravity of the problem, there is no choice but to continue to attempt to solve it.

## EXPLANATIONS OF EDUCATIONAL INEQUALITY

The two major sociological theories of education provide a general understanding of the problem, although from very different directions. Both theories are also concerned about the existence of profound and persistent inequalities, albeit from different vantage points. Functionalists believe that the role of schools is to provide a fair and meritocratic selection process for sorting out the best and brightest individuals, regardless of family background. The functionalist vision of a just society is one where individual talent and hard work based on universal principles of evaluation are more important than ascriptive characteristics based on particularistic methods of evaluation.

Functionalists expect that the schooling process will produce unequal results, but these results ought to be based on individual differences between students, not on group differences. Thus, although there is a persistent relationship between family background and educational outcomes, this does not in and of itself mean that the system fails to provide equality of opportunity. It is possible that even with equality of opportunity there could be these patterns of unequal results, although most functionalists would agree that this is highly unlikely. Therefore, functionalists believe that unequal educational outcomes are the result, in part, of unequal educational opportunities. Thus, for functionalists, it is imperative to understand the sources of educational inequality so as to ensure the elimination of structural barriers to educational success and provide all groups a fair chance to compete in the educational marketplace. This perspective has been the foundation of liberal educational policy in the United States since the 1960s.

Conflict theorists are not in the least bit surprised by the data. Given that conflict theorists believe that the role of schooling is to reproduce rather than eliminate inequality, the fact that educational outcomes are to a large degree based on family background is fully consistent with this perspective. Nonetheless, conflict theorists are also concerned with inequality and its eradication. Whereas functionalists focus on the attempts to provide equality of opportunity and to ensure a meritocratic system, conflict theorists are concerned with both equality of opportunity and results. That is, conflict theorists, who usually fall into the more radical political category, do not believe equality of opportunity is a sufficient goal.

A system that could guarantee equitable and fair treatment to all would not necessarily produce equal results, as individual differences (rather than group differences) would still play an important role in creating significant inequalities. Although most radicals do not believe complete equality of results is possible or even desirable, they do want to reduce significantly the degree of educational, social, and economic inequalities. Thus, conflict theorists call for more radical measures to reduce inequality; also, they are far more skeptical than functionalists that the problem can be solved.

Despite these differences, both functionalists and conflict theorists agree that understanding educational inequality is a difficult task. Further, it is clear that the third sociological approach, interactionist theory, is necessary to grasp fully the problem. Interactionism suggests that one must understand how people within institutions such as families and schools interact on a daily basis in order to comprehend the factors explaining academic success and failure. Thus, in addition to studying empirical data on school outcomes, which often explains what happens, one must also look into the lives and worlds of families and schools in order to understand why it happens. Many of the research studies of educational inequality that are discussed in this chapter use an interactionist approach based on field work in order to examine what goes on in families and schools.

The next step is to explain race-, class-, and gender-based inequalities of educational attainment and achievement. Researchers have posed two different sets of explanations. The first is centered on factors outside of the school, such as the family, the community, the culture of the group, the peer group, and the individual student. These explanations are often termed *student-centered* (Dougherty & Hammack, 1990, p. 334) or *extra-school* (Hurn, 1993, p. 161) *explanations.* The second is centered on factors within the school, such as teachers and teaching methods, curriculum, ability grouping and curriculum tracking, school climate, and teacher expectations. These explanations are often termed *school-centered* (Dougherty & Hammack, 1990, p. 334) or *within-school* (Hurn, 1993, p. 162) *explanations.*

Although there is merit in both approaches, the dichotomy between what are inexorably linked spheres is somewhat shortsighted. As Hurn (1993, pp. 161–162) has pointed out, functionalists tend to support extra-school explanations because these provide support for the view that the schooling process is somewhat meritocratic and that educational inequalities are caused by factors outside the schooling process. Conflict theorists, although not denying the deleterious impact of extra-school factors such as poverty, believe that schools play an important role in reproducing the problems. The attempt to pigeon hole the explanation into one explanatory system denies the connection between schooling and other societal institutions.

We prefer a more multidimensional approach, such as the one outlined by Persell (1977), which argues that educational inequality is the product of the relationship between societal, institutional, interactional, and intrapsychic variables. Thus, in order to understand education and inequality, one must explore not only what goes on within society and its institutions (such as the family and the school) but also the connections between them and their effects on individuals and groups. In the following sections, we outline the major student-centered and school-centered explanations and then propose a more multidimensional synthesis of these explanations.

Before we begin, it is important to discuss briefly the interconnection between race, class, gender, and ethnicity. As we noted in Chapter 8, individuals have more than one ascriptive status. For example, in terms of gender, men and women belong to different social classes, races, and come from different ethnic groups. In terms of race and ethnicity, members of different racial and ethnic groups may belong to different socioeconomic classes. Thus, there are differences in educational attainment and achievement between working-class and middle-class women or men, between working-class and middle-class blacks or whites, and between different ethnic groups based on social class position.

Sociological research on educational outcomes attempts to separate the independent effects of these variables, although their relationship is often difficult to distinguish. It is clear, however, that although gender, race, and ethnicity have independent effects, and that women, African Americans, and other ethnic groups are often negatively affected by societal and school processes, social class background has the most powerful effect on educational achievement and attainment. This is not to say that women or African Americans as groups may not be disadvantaged in schools, independent of social class background—only that social class appears to be the more powerful explanatory variable in explaining educational attainment and achievement.

On the one hand, given the powerful relationship between social class and educational attainment and achievement, much of the sociological research on educational outcomes has focused on class issues. On the other hand, given the significant relationship between social class and race, the problems of African-Americans achievement, and the important political movements aimed at ameliorating conditions of African-American poverty and improving African-American educational performance, this research has also focused on the relationship between race and education. In the following sections, we do not treat issues of race and class separately. Rather, we look at research that sometimes examines race as a separate category, sometimes looks at class as a separate category, and sometimes looks at them together. The following discussion assumes that groups that do not fare well in school do so because of their subordinate position in society, with race, class, gender, and ethnicity important components of a group's position. As the bulk of research concentrates on race and class, the following discussion concentrates on these studies.

We are not implying that gender and ethnicity are unimportant. A growing body of literature is interested in the educational performance of different ethnic groups, including Asians, Italians, Latinos, and others (Doran & Weffer, 1992; Wong-Fillmore & Valdez, 1986). Additionally, the problems faced by students whose first language is not English are increasingly the subject of educational research (Hakuta & Garcia, 1989; Thornburg & Karp, 1992; Wong-Fillmore & Valdez, 1986). The following discussions of student-centered and school-centered explanations, although not directly related to particular ethnic groups, assumes that the student- and school-related processes that affect working class and black students also affect other ethnic groups in a similar manner.

The research on gender and education is crucial for understanding how schooling affects particular groups (American Association of University Women, 1992). Unlike the research on ethnicity, this research cannot be easily subsumed under the student- or school-centered rubric. As we noted in Chapter 8, although there are some differences in the educational attainment and achievement of men and women, these differences are less than those based on race and class. Women do better in the humanities and men do better in math and science. However, the key difference is not in education but rather in economic outcomes, with women, despite somewhat equal levels of education doing significantly less well economically. Part of the reason for this is related to labor market issues and gender discrimination in the workplace. Some of it is due to the different occupational choices made by men and women, with traditionally female positions rewarded less well than those occupied by men. Why women select different career paths, many of which pay less well than those selected by men, is an important question. It can be examined through the research on gender and education, which looks specifically at the ways schools socialize men and women differently.

Whereas much of the research on education and inequality focuses on the cognitive outcomes of schooling and concentrates on educational attainment and achievement, research on gender and education also focuses on the noncognitive outcomes of schooling. Thus, this research looks at the ways in which schooling affects the way in which men and women come to view themselves, their roles, and society. Feminist scholarship on schooling examines questions of unequal opportunity for women, the differential socialization processes for boys and girls in schools, and the ways in which the hidden curriculum unequally affects women. Although feminists argue that these differential socialization patterns begin in the family and that girls bring cultural differences to the school, the bulk of educational research focuses on school-related processes. Hence, in the subsequent discussions of student-centered and school-centered explanations, we discuss gender inequalities under the school-centered rubric.

## STUDENT-CENTERED EXPLANATIONS

In the 1960s, sociologists of education interested in educational inequality often worked from a set of liberal political and policy assumptions about why students from lower socioeconomic backgrounds often did less well in school than students from higher socioeconomic backgrounds. The conventional wisdom of the time suggested that economically disadvantaged students attended inferior schools—schools that spent less money on each student, schools that spent less money on materials and extracurricular activities, and schools that had inferior teachers. The argument continued that if school differences and financing were responsible for the problem, then the solution was simply to pump resources and money into schools with children from lower socioeconomic backgrounds.

A number of research studies in the 1960s and 1970s demonstrated, however, that the conventional liberal wisdom was far too simplistic and that solutions were far more complex. Coleman and colleagues (1966), in *Equality of Educational Opportunity,* commonly referred to as the Coleman Report, argued that school differences were not the most significant explanatory variable for the lower educational achievement of working-class and nonwhite students. Rather, the report suggested, it was the differences among the groups of students that had a greater impact on educational performance. Additionally, research by Jencks and colleagues (1972) indicated that the differences between schools in privileged areas and in economically disadvantaged areas had been exaggerated. Moreover, where significant differences did exist, they did not sufficiently explain the inequalities of educational performance.

This research suggested that there were far more significant differences in academic performance among students in the same school than among students in different schools. This latter finding on what is termed *within-school differences* (as opposed to between-school differences) does not rule out the possibility that schools affect educational inequality, as it is possible that differences in the school such as ability grouping and curriculum tracking may explain these differences. Nevertheless, the research by Coleman and by Jencks casted doubt on the claim that differences between schools explained the performance gap among students from different socioeconomic or racial backgrounds. We will return to the question of school differences later in this chapter, but for now, it is important to discuss the consequences of these findings.

If school differences and financing did not explain unequal educational performance, then perhaps the schools themselves were not the most important factor. Based on the Coleman Report, educational researchers and policy makers concluded that the reason students from lower socioeconomic backgrounds did less well in school had more to do with the students themselves, their families, their neighborhood and communities, their culture, and perhaps even their genetic makeup. These student-centered explanations became dominant in the 1960s and 1970s and are still highly controversial and politically charged.

### Genetic Differences

The most controversial student-centered explanation is the genetic or biological argument. From a sociological and anthropological perspective, biological explanations of human behavior are viewed as limited because social scientists believe that environmental and social factors are largely responsible for human behavior. Recent advances in the understanding of mental illnesses such as schizophrenia, however, suggest that there may be biochemical and genetic causes. This research indicates that although social and psychological factors are crucial, biological factors cannot be ruled out entirely. Having said this, the question remains as to whether there is evidence to support the argument that differences in school performance among groups of students are due to genetic differences among these groups, particularly in intelligence.

The argument that unequal educational performance by working class and nonwhite students is due to genetic differences in intelligence was offered by psychologist Arthur Jensen in a highly controversial article in the *Harvard Educational Review* (1969). Jensen indicated that compensatory programs (i.e., programs aimed at improving the educational performance of disadvantaged students) were doomed to failure because they were aimed at changing social and environmental factors, when the root of the problem was biological. Jensen, based on sophisticated statistical analyses, argued that African Americans, genetically, are less intelligent than whites and therefore do less well in school, where intelligence is an important component of educational success. Given these data and his conclusions, Jensen was pessimistic about the likelihood that the academic performance of African Americans could be substantially improved.

Hurn (1993, pp. 142–152) provided a detailed and balanced assessment of the IQ controversy. Given the sensitivity of the subject, more often than not, the debate about Jensen's work consisted of polemical attacks accusing him of being a racist and dismissed his claim that there is a biological basis of intelligence, rather than carefully considering his arguments. Hurn demonstrated through a careful analysis of Jensen's thesis that although there is evidence that a genetic component to human intelligence exists, and that although a small percentage of the social class differences in intelligence may be attributed to genetic factors, the most significant factor affecting intelligence is social. Moreover, he argued that there is no persuasive evidence that social class and racial differences in intelligence are due to genetic factors. Additionally, Hurn and others have indicated that these differences in intelligence are in part due to the cultural bias of IQ test questions, the conditions under which they are given, and cultural and family differences (Bowles & Gintis, 1976, Chapter 4; Kamin, 1974; Persell, 1977, pp. 58–75).

Given the weakness of the genetic argument, how does one explain unequal educational performance by working-class and nonwhite students? As we stated earlier, as a result of the Coleman and Jencks studies, researchers looked to the family and the culture of the students for answers. Cultural deprivation and cultural difference theories have been two related approaches. Although these theories are more widely accepted by social scientists, because they view social and cultural factors as essential, they have been no less controversial.

## Cultural Deprivation Theories

In light of the Coleman Report's findings that school differences and resources did not adequately explain unequal performance by working-class and nonwhite students, some educational researchers argued that these students came to school without the requisite intellectual and social skills necessary for school success. Cultural deprivation theory, popularized in the 1960s, suggests that working-class and nonwhite families often lack the cultural resources, such as books and other educational stimuli, and thus arrive at school at a significant disadvantage.

Moreover, drawing on the thesis advanced by anthropologist Oscar Lewis (1966) about poverty in Mexico, cultural deprivation theorists assert that the poor have a deprived culture—one that lacks the value system of middle-class culture. According to this perspective, middle-class culture values hard work and initiative, the delay of immediate gratification for future reward, and the importance of schooling as a means to future success. The culture of poverty eschews delayed gratification for immediate reward, rejects hard work and initiative as a means to success, and does not view schooling as the means to social mobility. According to cultural deprivation theorists such as Deutsch (1964), this deprivation results in educationally disadvantaged students who achieve poorly because they have not been raised to acquire the skills and dispositions required for satisfactory academic achievement (Dougherty & Hammack, 1990, p 341).

Based on this etiology, policy makers sought to develop programs aimed not at the schools but rather at the family environment of working-class and nonwhite students. Compensatory education programs such as Project Head Start—a preschool intervention program for educationally and economically disadvantaged students—are based on the assumption that because of the cultural and familial deprivation faced by poor students, the schools must provide an environment that makes up for lost time. If these students are not prepared for school at home, then it is the role of the preschool to provide the necessary foundation for learning. Further, programs such as Head Start attempt to involve parents in their children's schooling and to help them develop parenting and literacy skills necessary for their children's academic development.

Cultural deprivation theory was attacked vociferously in the 1960s and 1970s by social scientists who believed it to be paternalistic at best and racist at worst. Critics argue that it removes the responsibility for school success and failure from schools and teachers and places it on families. Further, they suggest that it blames the victims of poverty for the effects of poverty rather than placing the blame squarely where it belongs: on the social and economic processes that produce poverty (Baratz & Baratz, 1970; Dougherty & Hammack, 1990, p. 341; Ryan, 1971).

Another criticism of cultural deprivation theory concerned the relative failure of many of the compensatory education programs that were based on its assumptions about why disadvantaged children have lower levels of achievement than more advantaged children. Although Project Head Start has received mixed evaluations (with early findings somewhat negative and later research providing more positive results; cf. Weikert & Schweinhart, 1984), compensatory programs, as a whole, have not improved significantly the academic performance of disadvantaged students. Given these criticisms and the weakness of the geneticist argument, a third student-centered explanation emerged: cultural difference theory.

### Cultural Difference Theories

Cultural difference theorists agree that there are cultural and family differences between working-class and nonwhite students and white middle-class students. Working-class and nonwhite students may indeed arrive at school with different cultural dispositions and without the skills and attitudes required by the schools. This is not due to deficiencies in their home life but rather to being part of an oppressed minority. The key difference in this perspective is that although cultural difference theorists acknowledge the impact of student differences, they do not blame working-class and nonwhite families for educational problems. Rather, they attribute cultural differences to social forces such as poverty, racism, discrimination, and unequal life chances.

There are a number of different varieties of cultural difference theory. First, researchers such as anthropologist John Ogbu (1978, 1979, 1987) argue that African-American children do less well in school because they adapt to their op-pressed position in the class and caste structure. Ogbu argued that there is a "job ceiling" for African Americans in the United States, as there is for similar caste-like minorities in other countries, and that African-American families and schools social-ize their children to deal with their inferior life chances rather than encourage them to internalize those values and skills necessary for positions that will not be open to them. Although this is a complex, and at times a hidden, process, the results are lower educational attainment and performance.

Ogbu's later work (Fordham & Ogbu, 1986) suggests that school success requires that African-American students deny their own cultural identities and accept the dominant culture of the schools, which is a white middle-class model. African-American students thus have the "burden of acting white" in order to succeed. This explanation, as we will see later in this chapter, rejects the argument that school-centered explanations are unimportant, and proposes the interaction of school and student variables to explain educational achievement. The view that there are cultural differences between the culture of the school and the culture of working-class and nonwhite students has resulted in calls for changes in school curriculum and pedagogy to more adequately represent the cultures of minority children. As we stated in Chapter 7, the demand for multicultural curricula is rooted in the belief that the schools need to reflect the cultures of all the students who attend, not just the culture of dominant social groups.

Ogbu's macrosociological perspective is similar to those of Bowles and Gintis (1976), whose correspondence theory suggests that working-class students adapt to the unequal aspects of the class structure, and to Bourdieu and Passeron (1977) and Bernstein (1977), whose theories point out the ways in which class and cultural differences are reflected in the schools. Bernstein, in particular, has often been accused of being a cultural deprivation theorist because of his theory that working-class students in England have a different language and communication code, which disadvantages them in the schools. Bernstein (1990) has consistently denied that working-class language is deficient. Rather, he has stated that cultural and class differences are a product of an unequal economic system and that the schools reward middle-class communication codes, not working-class codes. This viewpoint is a complex one, as it sees educational inequality as a product of the relationships between the economic system, the family, and the schools, with cultural differences turned into deficits by the schooling process. As with Ogbu's theories, Bernstein's theory insists on looking at the schools as sources of educational inequality, not just the culture or families of working-class students.

A second type of cultural difference theory sees working-class and nonwhite students as resisting the dominant culture of the schools. From this point of view, these students reject the white middle-class culture of academic success and embrace a different, often antischool culture—one that is opposed to the culture of schooling as it currently exists. Research by Willis (1981) on working-class boys in England shows that these students explicitly reject middle-class values and enthusiastically embrace a working-class culture, which eschews the values of schooling. They consciously reject schooling and resist academic success. This resistance results in dropping out of school and into the world of work—that is, the world of the factory floor, which they romanticize as the proper place for men.

A recent study of suburban life in the New York-New Jersey metropolitan area (Gaines, 1991) documents the antischool culture of working-class suburban adolescents, for whom heavy metal, rock and roll music, and "souped-up" automobiles are the symbols of adolescent culture, with the academic life of schooling consciously rejected and scorned. According to this type of cultural difference theory, these cultural norms are not inferior to middle-class norms, only different. Thus, the fact that society and its schools demand middle-class cultural norms places these students at a distinct disadvantage. Cultural difference theorists, such as Ogbu, suggest that subordinate groups often see little reason to embrace the culture of schooling, as they do not believe it will have value for them. Given the labor market barriers to these groups, Ogbu has argued that this type of resistance may in fact be a form of cultural adaptation to the realities of economic life.

The problem with cultural difference theory, according to Hurn (1993, pp. 154–155), is that it is too culturally relativistic. That is, in its insistence that all cultures are equally valid and that all values and norms are acceptable in the context of the culture that generated them, cultural difference theorists too often deny cultural problems and dysfunction. Although it is fair to acknowledge that cultural deprivation theorists are often ethnocentric and biased, and that the culture of schooling often alienates students from working-class and nonwhite families, it is apparent that cultural patterns may negatively affect school performance. That these patterns are often caused by social and economic forces does not eliminate them nor reduce their negative impact on academic achievement. As Hurn (1993, p. 154) stated:

> The claim that lower-class environments are not deficient in their provision of resources for intellectual growth but reflect differential valuations of ideal family forms is also problematic. While we may grant some of the characterizations of lower-class family life as pathological are ethnocentric and insensitive to cultural differences, much research has shown that poverty and unemployment make it extremely difficult for lower-class families to maintain relationships *they define* as satisfactory. Among poor black families, for example, over 50% of the households are headed by women, and illegitimacy rates exceed 60 percent. There is little evidence that blacks regard such families as desirable, and indeed there is increasing evidence that in the 1980s the black community began to define this situation as a crisis in the black family. The causes of that crisis undoubtedly lie in the legacy of discrimination and in poverty and unemployment. But it is hard to deny that the instability of family life in many lower-class black households makes for an unpropitious environment for the development of intellectual skills.

Lemann (1991), in his journalistic history of the black migration from the Mississippi Delta to Chicago in the post-World War II years, chronicled the cycles of poverty, hopelessness, and despair that mark life in the public housing projects of Chicago. Although he argued that economic transformations and conditions are the root causes of poverty, and that racism and discrimination exacerbate the problems, he nonetheless pointed out that the culture of the projects—with their rampant violence, drug abuse, and hopelessness—are part of the problem. Although it is important not to blame the poor for their situation and to understand that what Lemann described is a result of poverty, it is equally important to acknowledge that such life-styles should not be celebrated as "resistance." Rather, as Lemann noted, public policy must simultaneously address the elimination of the social and economic conditions responsible for poverty and the behaviors that serve to reproduce it.

It is important to transcend the often emotional and political arguments that accompany discussions of cultural deprivation and differences. Too often, those who point to the negative impact of cultural differences on academic achievement are accused of class and racial bias, when such ethnocentrism is not part of their analysis. Clearly, the poor should not be blamed for their problems, as the causes of poverty are more social and economic then they are cultural. Neither should the cultural differences related to school success and failure be denied. The key is to move past the ideological and to eliminate the social and educational barriers to school success for working-class and nonwhite students. Perhaps more importantly, one must recognize that unequal educational achievement cannot be explained by looking at students and their families alone; one must need to also look at the schools themselves.

## SCHOOL-CENTERED EXPLANATIONS

Earlier in this chapter, we reviewed the early research of Coleman and of Jencks on the relationship between school quality and resources and unequal academic attainment. Although their research questioned the conventional wisdom that between-school differences are the key factor in explaining differences in student performance between groups, it did not exclude the possibility that schools have significant effects on students. Although Coleman's early work concluded that student differences were more important than school differences, a conclusion that his subsequent work on public and private schools rejects (Coleman, Hoffer, & Kilgore, 1982; Coleman & Hoffer, 1987), and Jencks concluded that school effects were minimal, both researchers found that there are significant within-school differences that suggested schools may indeed make a difference.

For example, how does one explain differences in academic performance among groups of students within the same school? A completely individualistic explanation states that these differences are the result of individual differences in intelligence or initiative. Another student-centered explanation sees these differences as the result of student differences prior to entering school. School-centered explanations, however, suggest that school processes are central to understanding unequal educational performance. In the 1980s, educational researchers examined carefully the myriad processes within schools that explain the sources of unequal academic achievement. This school-centered research focused on both between- and within-school processes.

### School Financing

Jonathan Kozol (1991), in his muckraking book *Savage Inequalities,* compared public schools in affluent suburbs with public schools in poor inner cities. He documented the vast differences in funding between affluent and poor districts and called for equalization in school financing (see Tables 9–1 and 9–2). In order to understand why these inequalities exist, it is important to understand the way in which public schools are financed in the United States.

Public schools are financed through a combination of revenues from local, state, and federal sources. However, the majority of funds come from state and local taxes, with local property taxes a significant source. Property taxes are based on the value of property in local communities and therefore is a proportional tax. Since property values are significantly higher in more affluent communities, these commu-

TABLE 9–1
**School Funding in the Chicago Area (Figures for the 1988–1989 School Year)**

| School or District | Spending Per Pupil |
|---|---|
| Niles Township High School | $9,371 |
| New Trier High School | $8,823 |
| Glencoe (elementary and junior high schools) | $7,363 |
| Winnetka (elementary and junior high schools) | $7,059 |
| Wilmette (elementary and junior high schools) | $6,009 |
| Chicago (average of all grade levels) | $5,265 |

*Source:* Chicago Panel on School Policy and Finance. From *Savage Inequalities* by Jonathan Kozol. Copyright © 1991 by Jonathan Kozol. Reprinted by permission of Crown Publishers, Inc.

TABLE 9–2
**School Funding in the New Jersey Area (Figures for the 1988–1989 School Year)**

| District | Spending Per Pupil |
|---|---|
| Princeton | $7,725 |
| Summit | $7,275 |
| West Orange | $6,505 |
| Cherry Hill | $5,981 |
| Jersey City | $4,566 |
| East Orange | $4,457 |
| Paterson | $4,422 |
| Camden | $3,538 |

*Source:* Educational Law Center, Newark, New Jersey. From *Savage Inequalities* by Jonathan Kozol. Copyright © 1991 by Jonathan Kozol. Reprinted by permission of Crown Publishers, Inc.

nities are able to raise significantly more money for schools through this form of taxation than poorer communities with lower property values. Additionally, since families in more affluent communities have higher incomes, they pay proportionately less of their incomes for their higher school taxes.

Thus, more affluent communities are able to provide more per-pupil spending than poorer districts, often at a proportionately less burdensome rate than in poorer communities. This unequal funding has been the subject of considerable legal attack by communities that argue that funding based on local property taxes is discriminatory under the Equal Protection Clause of the Fourteenth Amendment and that it denies equality of opportunity.

In *Serrano* v. *Priest* (1971), the California Supreme Court ruled the system of unequal school financing between wealthy and poor districts unconstitutional. It did not, however, declare the use of property taxes for school funding illegal. Five other state courts (in Arizona, Minnesota, New Jersey, Texas, and Wyoming) rendered similar rulings within the next year. However, in 1973, the U.S. Supreme Court in *San Antonio (Texas) Independent School District* v. *Rodriquez* reversed a lower-court ruling and upheld the use of local property taxes as the basis for school funding. In a 5–4 opinion, the Court ruled that this method of funding, although unjust, was not unconstitutional. Justice Thurgood Marshall, in a dissenting opinion, stated that the decision represented a move away from a commitment to equality of opportunity (Johnson, 1991, p. 308).

Although the Supreme Court decision has made it unlikely that the federal government will intervene in local financing of public schools, individual states have taken on the responsibility of attempting to decrease inequalities in school financing. The Kentucky, Texas, Arkansas, California, Connecticut, Montana, New Jersey, Washington, West Virginia, and Wyoming state courts have ruled against their states' system of school financing. The Kentucky decision called for a shift to state funding of schools to ensure equality of educational opportunity. In the future, it appears more states will begin to use state funding to close the gap between rich and poor districts. The use of foundation state aid programs, which seeks to make sure all districts receive a minimum standard of funding, with more state aid going to poorer districts in order to enable poorer districts to meet this minimum level, is one way of providing equality of opportunity. Although wealthier districts are still able to go above this minimum by taxing themselves at higher rates through property taxes, the use of foundation aid programs, at the very least, attempts to guarantee that all districts have the minimum necessary to provide a quality education (Johnson, 1991, pp. 314–320).

The use of federal aid to equalize school funding is a controversial issue. Proponents argue that such aid has occurred historically, as in the Elementary and Secondary Education Act of 1965. They also argue that it is the fairest and most progressive system of school financing, as it would guarantee equality of opportunity regardless of residence. Advocates of a federal system of financing, such as Kozol (1991), believe that schools should be financed through federal income taxes. Critics, however, believe that, under the Tenth Amendment to the Constitution, education is a state and local matter and that federal financing would threaten local decision making.

It is clear that the present reliance on local property taxes and state aid has not reduced inequalities of financing. Thus, children from lower socioeconomic backgrounds do not receive equality of opportunity, at least in terms of funding. Although, as we note in the next sections, differences in academic achievement among students from different social classes cannot be understood in terms of funding alone, there is a moral as well as educational question at issue. Even if, as some researchers suggest (e.g., see Jencks, 1972), equalization of funding would not reduce inequalities of achievement among groups, is it fair that some students have significantly more money spent on them than others?

Critics of school financing believe equalization is a moral imperative, but there is not widespread agreement on this matter. For example, when New York Governor Mario Cuomo, faced with severe budgetary shortfalls during the recession in 1991, cut state aid to education more severely in affluent suburbs than in poorer cities, such as New York City, the hue and cry in the suburbs was extraordinary. Affluent suburban districts—faced with dramatic reductions in state aid, which resulted in teacher layoffs and cutbacks in services—argued that such proportionate cutbacks threatened their ability to maintain their academic excellence. Governor Cuomo responded that state aid should be cut in districts spending sometimes over twice as much per pupil than in city districts. Thus, the question of funding is not a moral issue alone; it is a political issue, as different communities struggle to give their children what they consider the best possible education. In doing so, however, critics maintain that affluent communities continue to defend their advantages over poorer communities.

Although the question of the morality of unequal school financing is an important one, its effects on unequal achievement is equally important. There is disagreement over the extent to which school financing affects unequal academic achievement, but it is clear that school factors other than financing have an important impact on achievement. In the next sections, we explore some of these factors.

**Effective School Research**

The findings of Coleman and Jencks that differences in school resources and quality do not adequately explain between-school differences in academic achievement was viewed by teachers as a mixed blessing. On the one hand, if student differences are more important than school differences, then teachers cannot be blamed for the lower academic performance of nonwhite and working-class students. On the other hand, if schools' effects are not significant, then schools and, more specifically, teachers can do little to make a positive difference. Although Jencks's admonition that societal change was necessary to improve schools may have made teachers feel less directly responsible for problems that were often beyond their control, it also left teachers with a sense of hopelessness that there was little if anything they could do to improve schooling from inside the schools. Critics of the student-centered findings went further. They argued that this research took the responsibility away from schools and teachers and placed it on communities and families. Common sense, they believed, suggested that there were differences between good and bad schools, and between good and incompetent teachers. These differences certainly had to have some effects on students. The difficult empirical task, however, is to untangle the ways in which school processes affect student learning.

The concern with unequal educational performance of nonwhite and working-class students is at the heart of such inquiry. The finding that within-school differences are as or more significant than between-school differences raised questions about the common-sense argument that students from lower socioeconomic backgrounds do poorly simply because they attend inferior schools. Ronald Edmonds (1979), an African-American former school superintendent and Harvard professor, suggested that comparing schools in different socioeconomic communities was only part of the puzzle. He argued that researchers needed to compare schools within lower socioeconomic communities as well. If all schools in such neighborhoods produce low educational outcomes, and these lower outcomes could not be explained in terms of school differences in comparison to schools in higher socioeconomic communities, then the student-centered findings could be supported. Conversely, if there are significant differences in student performance between schools within lower socioeconomic neighborhoods, then there have to be school effects. That is, how is it possible that homogeneous groups of students (i.e., in terms of race and socioeconomic class) in a lower socioeconomic community perform differently depending on the school that they attend? Student-centered explanations would suggest that the factors outside the schools that affect nonwhite and working-class students are the same in different schools within the same neighborhood. Thus, if students from the same racial and socioeconomic backgrounds attending different schools within the same community perform at significantly different rates, then something within the schools themselves must be affecting student performance.

Based on this logic, Edmonds and other effective school researchers (Brookover et al., 1979; Austin & Garber, 1985) examined schools that produced unusually positive academic results given what would be expected, based on the socioeconomic composition of the school and/or schools that are unusually effective in general. *The effective school literature,* as it is termed, suggests that there are characteristics of unusually effective schools that help to explain why their students achieve academically. These characteristics include the following:

- A climate of high expectations for students by teachers and administrators
- Strong and effective leadership by a principal or school head
- Accountability processes for students and teachers
- The monitoring of student learning
- A high degree of instructional time on task, where teachers spend a great deal of their time teaching and students spend a great deal of their time learning
- Flexibility for teachers and administrators to experiment and adapt to new situations and problems (Stedman, 1987).

These phenomena are more likely found in effective schools than ineffective ones, independent of the demographic composition of the students in the school. Given the differences between students in schools in lower and higher socioeconomic neighborhoods, these findings may suggest that there are a higher number of schools with these characteristics in higher socioeconomic communities. Or, given the extra-school factors in these neighborhoods, it is easier for schools in higher socioeconomic communities to develop such characteristics within their schools. More importantly, theses findings suggest that there are things that schools can do to positively affect student achievement in lower socioeconomic communities.

The effective school research suggests that there are school-centered processes that help to explain unequal educational achievement by different groups of students. It supports the later work of Coleman and his colleagues (Coleman, Hoffer, & Kilgore, 1982; Coleman & Hoffer, 1987) that argues that Catholic schools produce significantly better levels of academic achievement because of their more rigorous academic curriculum and higher academic expectations. Ironically, Coleman has thus moved full circle from his earlier work, which stated that students—not schools—were the most significant explanatory variable, to his recent work, which states that schools make a significant difference independent of the students who attend. Critics of Coleman's recent work (see Chapter 8), however, suggest that he has insufficiently controlled for student and parental effects and that such extra-school differences may be more important than the differences between public and Catholic schools. What these ongoing debates indicate is that school and student effects cannot be isolated and that the interaction between these factors must be addressed more completely. We will return to this point later in this chapter.

Although the effective school literature has attracted much support from policy makers and is often cited in the educational reform literature as the key to school improvement (Stedman, 1987), the road from research to implementation is not a clear one. The effective school researchers do not provide clear findings on implementation, nor do they provide answers to how effective schools are created. Additionally, some critics of the effective school movement argue that its definition of effective schools is based on narrow and traditional measures of academic achievement, such as standardized test scores, and that such a perspective defines educational success from a traditional back-to-basics perspective. Such a view may result in school reform that emphasizes success on standardized tests and overlooks other nontraditional and progressive measures of school success, which may emphasize artistic, creative, and noncognitive goals as well (cf. Cuban, 1983; Dougherty & Hammack, 1991, p. 339; Stedman, 1985, 1987).

### Between-School Differences: Curriculum and Pedagogic Practices

The effective school research points to how differences in what is often termed *school climates* affect academic performance. Much of this research looked at differences between schools in inner-city, lower socioeconomic neighborhoods in order to demonstrate that schools can make a difference in these communities. Although there are problems with the research, most researchers agree that its findings support the argument that schools do affect educational outcomes, at times, independent of extra-school factors.

Nonetheless, one is still faced with the task of explaining why a larger proportion of students who attend schools in higher socioeconomic communities achieve well in school. Is it because a larger proportion of schools in these communities have school climates conducive to positive academic achievement? This is a difficult question and the data are insufficient to support unequivocally such a claim. A number of theorists, however, argue that there are significant differences between the culture and climate of schools in lower socioeconomic and higher socioeconomic communities.

Bernstein (1990), examining the situation in England, suggested that schools in working-class neighborhoods are far more likely to have authoritarian and teacher-directed pedagogic practices and to have a vocationally or social efficiency curriculum at the secondary level. Schools in middle-class communities are more likely to have less authoritarian and more student-centered pedagogic practices and to have a humanistic liberal arts college preparatory curriculum at the secondary level. Upper-class students are more likely to attend elite private (in England, they are called public schools) schools, with authoritarian pedagogic practices and a classical-humanistic college preparatory curriculum at the secondary level. Bernstein's theory is similar to Bowles and Gintis's view that the type of schooling corresponds to the social class of students in a particular school, with such differences a vehicle for socializing students from different social class backgrounds to their different places in society.

Although Bernstein's work is theoretical and needs further empirical support, especially as it relates to U.S. education, there is a growing research literature that supports the existence of class-based school differences. Rist's (1970, 1973) work on urban schools, Fine's (1991) ethnography of urban school dropouts, MacLeod's (1987) description of urban schooling, Cookson and Persell's (1985) analysis of elite boarding schools, Powell, Farrar, and Cohen's (1985) descriptions of U.S. secondary schools, and Lightfoot's (1985) portraits of urban, suburban, and elite high schools all document important class-related differences in school climate, curriculum, and pedagogic practices. Moreover, recent journalistic portraits—including Freedman's (1990) description of a New York City High School, Kidder's (1989) discussion of a Massachusetts elementary school, and Sachar's (1991) portrait of a New York City middle school—further support the existence of these differences.

What this research does explain is why these differences exist and precisely how they affect the different academic achievement of their students. Do schools reflect differences in student cultures that exist prior to entry into school, thus supporting student-centered explanations? Or do students respond to the different curricula, pedagogic practices, and expectations that exist in different types of schools? Finally, is there sufficient evidence to support the argument that differences in academic achievement are caused by the differences in curricula, pedagogic practices, and expectations in the different schools? These are important questions. Unfortunately, there is conflicting evidence concerning these overall conclusions. There is, however, reason to conclude that these school differences are part of the complex explanation of unequal educational achievement.

For example, a high school student at a "select 16" boarding school, such as Groton, St. Paul's, Hotchkiss, or Andover (for a complete list of the select 16, see Cookson & Persell, 1985), attends a school with a large campus in a bucolic country-like setting. His or her parents pay a hefty tuition (over $10,000 per year) to support small class size, extracurricular activities, the latest in technological and curricular innovations, and support services, including counseling, tutoring, and college advisement. A high school student in an upper middle-class suburb attends a school with many of these features, although he or she lives at home, not at school. His or her parents pay high school taxes to support the level of funding necessary to provide these types of services. A high school student in a poor urban neighborhood attends a school that is often overcrowded, with large classes, a student/counselor ratio of sometimes 400 to 1, and without the latest in technology and curricula innovations.

In his book *Savage Inequalities* (1991), Jonathan Kozol portrayed these significant differences in per-student spending between suburban and urban schools. Cookson, Persell, and Catsambis (1992) documented the achievement differences between boarding schools, private day and parochial schools, and public schools. Although sociologists of education differ as to whether these achievement differences are caused by school differences, independent of student background factors, school differences must play a significant role.

The 17-year-old sitting on the ninth green on the Hotchkiss Golf Course, looking at the fall foliage on the rolling hills of Connecticut, sees a very different set of possibilities than the 17-year-old sitting on the schoolyard at Seward Park High School in New York City (the subject of Freedman's book *Small Victories*). Of course, these different life chances begin with their different class backgrounds, but their different school environments teach them to dream a different set of dreams. Research on the relationship between schooling and life expectations (Cicourel & Kitsuse, 1963; MacLeod, 1987; Ogbu, 1978; Rosenbaum, 1976) suggests that schooling can elevate or limit student aspirations about the future. It seems obvious that these two students receive very different sets of aspirations from their schooling—aspirations that more often than not translate into educational achievement, college choices, and eventual occupational destinations. Whether or not schooling is the causal factor is beside the point—that it is part of the process seems evident.

### Within-School Differences: Curriculum and Ability Grouping

As we have stated, there are not only significant differences in educational achievement between schools but within schools as well. The fact that different groups of students in the same schools perform very differently suggests that there may be school characteristics affecting these outcomes. As we argued in Chapter 7, ability grouping and curriculum grouping (often referred to as *tracking by ability* or *curriculum* tracking) is an important organizational component of U.S. schooling.

At the elementary school level, students are divided into reading groups and separate classes based on teacher recommendations, standardized test scores, and sometimes ascriptive characteristics such as race, class, or gender. For the most part, elementary students receive a similar curriculum in these different groups, but it may be taught at a different pace, or the teachers in the various groups may have different expectations for the different students. At the secondary school level, students are divided both by ability and curriculum, with different groups of students often receiving considerably different types of education within the same school.

There is considerable debate among educators and researchers about the necessity, effects, and efficacy of tracking. From a functionalist perspective, tracking is viewed as an important mechanism by which to separate students based on ability and to ensure that the "best and brightest" receive the type of education required to prepare them for society's most essential positions. For functionalists, the important thing is to ensure that track placement is fair and meritocratic—that is, based on ability and hard work rather than ascriptive variables. Conflict theorists, conversely, suggest that tracking is a mechanism for separating groups, often based on ascriptive characteristics, and that it is an important mechanism in reproducing inequalities.

Debates concerning the pedagogical necessity of ability and curriculum grouping abound. Many teachers and administrators argue that heterogeneous groups are far more difficult to teach and result in teaching to the middle. This results in losing those with lower abilities and boring those with higher abilities. Critics of tracking (Oakes, 1985; Sadovnik, 1991) suggest that homogeneous grouping results in unequal education for different groups, with differences in academic outcomes often due to the differences in school climate, expectations, pedagogic practices, and curriculum between tracks.

Echoing this view, Albert Shanker (1991) stated that education in the United States assumes that students in the lower tracks are not capable of doing academic work and thus schools do not offer them an academically challenging curriculum. When these students do not perform well on examinations measuring their skills and knowledge, it confirms those expectations. The problem, Shanker suggested, is that students cannot learn what they have not been taught. Further, he pointed out that these students are capable of far more than teachers realize, and suggested that if teachers demanded and expected more, students would meet the raised expectations.

Much of the debate concerning tracking is emotional and ideological. Moreover, proponents of each view often lack sound empirical evidence to support their claims. It is important, then, to explore what the research states about ability and curriculum grouping by asking four important questions. First, is there evidence to support the claim that there are significant differences between tracks? Second, are there significant differences in educational attainment by students in different tracks? Third, are track placements based on discriminatory practices based on ascriptive characteristics or are they based on meritocratic selection mechanisms? Fourth, do the differences in the tracks explain the differences in academic attainment between tracks?

With respect to differences between tracks, many researchers (Oakes, 1985; Sadovnik, 1991) stated that there are significant differences in the curricula and pedagogic practices of secondary school curriculum groups. Oakes (1985) suggested that the lower tracks are far more likely to have didactic, teacher-directed practices, with rote learning and fact-based evaluation. Higher tracks are more likely to have more dialectical, student-centered practices, with discussion and thinking-based evaluation. These differences hold even when the tracks are based on ability rather than curriculum (i.e., when students in different ability tracks learn the same material it is usually taught in a very different manner in the lower tracks). When the tracking is based on different curricula, students in different curriculum groups receive essentially different educations within the same school.

With respect to the effects of tracking and track placement, tracking has a significant effect on educational attainment at both the elementary and secondary levels. Although the effects appear to be larger for elementary school ability grouping than for high school tracking, most researchers agree that tracking affects educational attainment and achievement, independent of student characteristics (Alexander & Cook, 1982; Oakes, 1985). Additionally, track placement is associated with student race and social characteristics, with working-class and nonwhite students more likely to be assigned to lower tracks (Alexander & Cook, 1982; Dreeben & Gamoran, 1986; Hallinan, 1984; Rosenbaum, 1980a, 1980b). There is insufficient evidence, however, to prove that track placement is based on discriminatory rather than meritocratic practices.

Although some researchers (Oakes, 1985) argue that the race and social class based composition of tracks is evidence of discrimination, Hurn (1993, pp. 165–167) has contended that high school tracking placement, as well as its effects, is a far more complex process. He suggested that the evidence on track placement and outcomes is mixed, but that, on the whole, track placement is based more on previous ability and aspirations than on discriminatory practices. Although this may suggest that student characteristics prior to schooling or to high school placement are important factors, it also suggests that ability is an important part of high school track assignment. Hurn pointed out, however, that high school track placement may be dependent on elementary school processes, including ability grouping and teacher expectations, which may be far less meritocratic.

Research on the self-fulfilling prophecy of teacher expectations (Rist, 1970; Rosenthal & Jacobson, 1968) and of elementary school ability groups and reading groups (Eder, 1981; Felmlee & Eder, 1983; McDermott, 1977) point to the impact of teacher expectations and ability grouping on student aspirations and achievement at the elementary school level. Persell (1977), in her review of the teacher expectations literature, argued that teacher perceptions of students and their abilities have an impact on what is taught, how it is taught, and, ultimately student performance. Although more research is needed to determine clearly the extent to which these different expectations are based on ascriptive rather than meritocratic factors, there is reason to believe that such processes are not entirely meritocratic (Rist, 1970).

Finally, research indicates that differences in tracks helps to explain the different academic achievement of students in different tracks. Some researchers argue that differences in the amount of instruction are responsible for these differences (Barr & Dreeben, 1983; Dreeben & Gamoran, 1986). Others point to differences in the quality of instruction (McDermott, 1977; Oakes, 1985; Persell, 1977). It seems clear that differences in the curriculum and pedagogic practices between tracks are partly responsible for the different academic achievement of students in different tracks. Given that more working-class and nonwhite students are placed in the lower tracks, it is evident that such school-related practices have a significant effect on their lower academic achievement. What is not entirely clear is the degree to which such placement is unfair and discriminatory or meritocratically based on ability or on characteristics such as ability and aspirations brought by students to the school. This brings you full circle to the question of student-centered versus school-centered explanations. As we noted above, neither one, by itself, is sufficient to explain unequal educational performance. What is needed is a more integrated and multidimensional approach.

### Gender and Schooling

In October 1991, during the confirmation hearing of Supreme Court Justice nominee Clarence Thomas, Anita Hill, a law professor at the University of Oklahoma, charged that Judge Thomas sexually harassed her when he was her supervisor at the Department of Education and later at the EEOC (the Equal Employment Opportunity Commission). The charges and subsequent Senate Judiciary Committee hearings on the allegations pointed to significant differences between how men and women see the world. When the all-male, 14-member committee originally voted to pass the nomination onto the Senate without investigating Professor Hill's charges, women throughout the country were outraged, charging that "men just don't get it" (meaning that they do not take sexual harassment seriously). This episode pointed to a much larger question: If men and women see the world differently, why does this occur? Feminist scholarship on gender differences, in general, and gender and schooling, in particular, has concentrated on this issue.

Although the feminist movement in the United States dates back at least to the mid-nineteenth century (cf. Leach, 1980), the second wave of feminism began in the 1960s. Influenced by the French feminist Simone de Beauvoir (1952) and reacting to the narrowly defined gender roles of the 1950s, feminists in the 1960s and 1970s—including Betty Friedan, Gloria Steinem, Ellen Willis, Germaine Greer, and Kate Millett—challenged the view that biology is destiny. Vivian Gornick (1978), in her poignant essay "The Next Great Moment in History Is Theirs," argued that differences between men and women are cultural, not biological, and that women deserve equality in the public and private spheres of life (the family and the workplace). Thus, the feminist movement challenged unequal treatment of women in all aspects of society and worked actively to change both attitudes and laws that limited the life chances of women.

Feminist scholarship on schooling has attempted to understand the ways in which the schools limit the educational and life chances of women. It has focused on achievement differences (Fennema, 1974, Sadker & Sadker, 1985), on women and school administration (Shakeshaft, 1986, 1987), on the history of coeducation (Tyack & Hansot, 1990), on the relationship between pedagogy and attitudes and knowledge (Belenky, Clinchy, Goldberger & Tarule, 1986), and other related issues. A significant aspect of this literature concerns gender differences in how men and women see the world, their cultural causes, and the role of schools in perpetuating or eliminating them.

Carol Gilligan, a psychologist at Harvard's Graduate School of Education, has been one of the most influential feminist scholars working in the area of gender differences. In her book, *In a Different Voice* (1982), she criticized the view asserted by the psychologist Lawrence Kohlberg that there is a developmental hierarchy in moral decision making. Kohlberg placed a justice orientation to moral reasoning (based on universal principles) on a higher plane than a caring orientation (based on interpersonal feelings). Gilligan argued that women are more likely to adopt a caring orientation, in part because they are socialized to do so, and that Kohlberg's hierarchical categories judged women unfairly. She continued that women do reason in a different voice and that this female voice as an important component of the human experience should not be devalued. Gilligan's work pointed to the differences and their relation to gender socialization and how society rewards men for "male" behavior and negatively affects women for "female" behavior.

Gilligan's work has been extremely controversial among feminists. Many scholars have adopted her concept of caring as a part of female psychology and argue that the schools devalue connectedness and caring in favor of male behaviors such as competition (Martin, 1987; Noddings, 1984). Many feminists argue that schools should revise their curricula and pedagogic practices to emphasize caring and connectedness (Belenky et al., 1986; Laird, 1989). Other feminists (Epstein, 1990) are troubled by the conservative implications of Gilligan's work, which they argue reinforces traditional gender differences by attributing behaviors as typically female and male. The argument that women are more caring and connected and men more competitive and intellectual may reproduce sexist stereotypes that historically justified the domestic roles of women. These feminists believe that traditional male and female characteristics are part of the full range of human possibilities and that schools should socialize both boys and girls to be caring and connected.

Despite these differences, feminists agree that schooling often limits the educational opportunities and life chances of women in a number of ways. For example, boys and girls are socialized differently through a variety of school processes. First, curriculum materials portray men's and women's roles often in stereotypical and traditional ways (Hitchcock & Tompkins, 1987). Second, the traditional curriculum, according to Bennett and LeCompte (1990) "silences women" by omitting significant aspects of women's history and women's lives from discussion. As with other groups calling for multicultural curriculum, feminists call for a more gender-fair curriculum. Third, the hidden curriculum reinforces traditional gender roles and expectations through classroom organization, instructional practices, and classroom interactions (Bennett & LeCompte, 1990, pp. 234–237). For example, research demonstrates that males dominate classroom discussion (Brophy & Good, 1970; Martin, 1972), receive more attention from teachers (Lippitt & Gold, 1959; LaFrance, 1985, Sikes, 1971), and that teachers are more likely to assist males with a task but to do it for female students (Sadker & Sadker, 1985).

Fourth, the organization of schools reinforces gender roles and gender inequality. For example, the fact that women are far more likely to teach elementary grades and men secondary grades gives the message to children that women teach children and men teach ideas. The fact that men are far more likely to be administrators, despite recent advances in this area, reinforces the view that men hold positions of authority. Fifth, research on single-sex education and coeducation indicates that females do better academically in single-sex schools, where the school philosophy often stresses the processes leading to female academic success (Shakeshaft, 1986; Tyack & Hansot, 1990). These unequal processes help to explain both gender differences in attitudes and academic achievement.

Given the role schools play in reproducing gender inequalities, feminists argue that school organization, curriculum, and pedagogic practices need to be changed to more adequately address the needs of females. For example, Gilligan's recent study of the Emma Willard School (Gilligan et al., 1990), a private girls school in Troy, New York, concludes that by adolescence, girls receive an education that devalues their inner voice and limits their opportunities. That this occurs in a single-sex school devoted to the education of females suggests that females face more significant problems of educational opportunity in coeducational institutions.

## DO SCHOOLS REPRODUCE INEQUALITY?

The research on educational inequality, as you have read, is quite complex and perplexing. There is a significant difference of opinion as to the role of the school in affecting student performance, with school-centered explanations stressing the role of schools and student-centered explanations stressing the importance of what students bring to school. Additionally, the research is conflicting concerning the central hypotheses of functionalism and conflict theory. Some researchers believe that the schools unfairly perpetuate social inequalities and thus confirm conflict theorists' belief that schools advantage the dominant groups in society. Other researchers believe that there is insufficient evidence to support much of conflict theory, at least in regard to school processes, and that some of the evidence supports the functionalist view that school selection processes are meritocratic (Hurn, 1993).

How does one reconcile these apparent contradictions? First, we suggest that school-centered and student-centered explanations are not diametrically opposed, but rather need to be incorporated into a multidimensional theory of education and inequality. Second, we suggest that although there is evidence to support some of the functionalist's hypotheses, on the whole, there is more evidence to support conflict theorists' claim that schools help to reproduce inequality. Schools are only part of this process, and must be seen within the context of a larger set of institutional forces affecting social stratification.

Persell's (1977) model for understanding education and inequality, presented in Chapter 8, outlines the relationship between four levels of sociological analysis: the societal level, the institutional level, the interactional level, and the intrapsychic level. The social stratification system, at the societal level, produces structures of domination and societal level ideologies. The structures of domination affect the institutions within a society, including the family, the schools, the churches and synagogues, the media, and others. The important point is that different social groups, based on their position in the societal hierarchy, have different institutional experiences, and are affected in different ways by the social structure. Thus, families from lower socioeconomic backgrounds face different problems and have different life chances than families from higher socioeconomic backgrounds. Much of the student-centered literature focuses on these processes. Children from different classes also attend different types of schools, which often vary in terms of school climate, quality, and outcomes. Much of the school-centered literature focuses on these processes.

The relationships between families and schools at the institutional level, and what goes on within schools at the interactional levels, are not isolated from each other but are dialectically intertwined. Clearly, students from lower socioeconomic backgrounds face significantly different problems in their communities due to factors such as racism, poverty, and other societal and institutional processes. To argue whether they are different or deficient is beside the point; that they negatively impact on children is the point. Children from lower socioeconomic backgrounds thus have significantly lower life chances before they enter schools. Once they enter, they often enter schools that are inferior and have significantly less funding, and encounter school processes that limit their educational chances. That the evidence does not overwhelmingly support the view that school funding and climate are independently responsible for their lower achievement does not eliminate these as part of the problem. It only means that there are other nonschool variables that also affect educational performance. It is clear that at the intrapsychic level, students from different social class backgrounds leave school with different educational outcomes, both cognitive (in terms of learning) and noncognitive (in terms of values and self-esteem). Research on within- and between-school differences demonstrate how school processes may affect such outcomes.

Student-centered theories suggest that these unequal outcomes are the result of differences at the societal and institutional levels, but that families and communities are more important than schools. School-centered theories stress the importance of schooling in reproducing inequality. Persell's (1977) model suggests that society, communities, families, and schools cannot be separated from each other. Societal forces unequally affect families and schools. The result is a complex process through which students from lower socioeconomic backgrounds have lower levels of educational attainment and achievement.

Research that attempts to connect the four levels of sociological analysis is needed to more clearly understand the role of schooling in the reproduction of inequality. A recent study by Annette Lareau (1989) on social class differences in the relationship between family and school documents the importance of both family and schools. It also demonstrates how the differences in schooling for working-class and middle-class students is an important factor in unequal outcomes. Using Bourdieu's concept of cultural capital (the cultural symbols and resources a group has), Lareau demonstrated that those with cultural capital have significant advantages in the schooling process. More ethnographic research of this type—which explores the processes within schools, families, and communities, and their relationship to educational outcomes—is needed.

Do schools reproduce inequality? Based on the evidence reviewed in this chapter, our conclusion is they do not, solely by themselves. Schools are part of a larger complex process in which social inequalities are transmitted across generations. Although there is evidence of social mobility for individuals through schooling and of a degree of meritocracy within schools, there is insufficient evidence to support the functionalist argument that schools are a means for the meritocratic selection of individuals based on talent and hard work. Rather, there is more powerful evidence to support the conflict view that schools are part of the process through which dominant groups maintain their advantages.

In the following articles, the factors explaining educational inequality are explored. In the first selection, "Building 860," Christian Neira provides a poignant analysis of a student's struggle with issues of race and schooling. Written when he was a high school student, Neira discusses the difficult social psychological conflicts that minority students face in order to succeed academically. Neira describes his feelings of anomie as he is required to live in two worlds and often feels that he belongs in neither. This article nicely illustrates the work of Fordham and Ogbu (1986) discussed in this chapter.

The second article, "Females + Mathematics = A Complex Equation," written by educational researcher Karen Karp, provides an overview of the explanations for gender differences in mathematics achievements. Based on the available research, Karp recommends a number of policies to address discrimination against women in the field of mathematics and argues that change must begin in teacher education programs and in elementary schools.

The third article, "Keeping Track, Part 1: The Policy and Practice of Curriculum Inequality," written by educational researcher Jeannie Oakes, argues against curriculum tracking and ability grouping. Oakes, one of the strongest advocates of heterogeneous grouping, examines a number of myths that support tracking and proposes its elimination.

The fourth article, "Social Class Differences in Family-School Relationships: The Importance of Cultural Capital," written by sociologist Annette Lareau, analyzes the relationship between family and school. Applying Pierre Bourdieu's concept of cultural capital, Lareau argues that middle-class parents, who possess more cultural capital than working-class parents, have distinct advantages in advancing their children's educational achievement. Based on an ethnographic study of two schools, one with working-class children and one with middle-class children, Lareau explores how each group of families interacts with their children's schools. She concludes that family differences between working-class and middle-class parents are part of the reason why middle-class children are more successful in school.

# Building 860

## CHRISTIAN NEIRA

When trying to live in two different worlds, one is in peril of not belonging to either of them. One is left in a state of confusion. The morals, behavior, thinking, and perspective of the world of a New York City housing project are radically different from those of an elite preparatory school in the same city. Being put in the position of changing one's character every morning and afternoon to adapt to two different worlds endangers one's identity.

I remember one incident during high school that demonstrates the tightrope that I walked. I was coming out of my home when I saw one of my neighbors also leaving for school. While waiting for the elevator, we began to talk. I was dressed in compliance with the dress code of my school: tie and jacket. She told me she went to Joan of Arc, the public junior high school across the street from my school. I told her I was dressed like this because I went to the Trinity School. Her expression was one of deep shock and pity. She asked, "How do you survive?" I first thought she meant how did I survive living in the projects, but later that day in school I came to the realization that she meant to ask how I survived at the preparatory school.

Each of the two cultures considered me a foreigner, one who did not belong. Where my allegiance resided was their question. Neither world fully understood me because these two cultures almost never meet, and when they meet on the street, violence and suspicion are their common langugage.

### THE WEEK

Monday morning. It begins with a distant rumbling sound that intensifies as it approaches. The walls begin to vibrate. The sound reaches a cresendo of steel against steel as the New York City subway rolls by my window. I look at the graffiti-covered train as it passes, and I remember the kid at school whose parents are art collectors and collect graffiti paintings. The worst vibrations occur when two subways pass simultaneously. The only benefit of having an elevated train so close by is that it is a most effective alarm clock on a Monday morning.

There are three locks and a chain on my apartment door. As I open the door, the wind rushes in from the hallway, and with it comes the odor of rotten food. Outside, the hall is barely five feet wide, not enough space for two people to walk along side by side. The ceiling always leaks and pieces of paint and plaster sometimes fail on you as you walk along. The hall was recently painted, painted by someone with a spray paint can, that is. He left his street name painted on the floor.

As I walk toward the elevators I can only pray that they will be working this morning. One has been out since Saturday. I look through the hole in the elevator door to see if any cables are moving, the indicator that the elevator is working. After a few minutes of waiting for any signs, I resign myself to taking the stairs. Waiting any longer is futile.

The door to the stairs scrapes the floor as I try to push it open; it is held in place by only one hinge. Something is blocking the door

*Source:* Neira, Christian, "Building 860," *Harvard Educational Review,* 58:3, pp. 337–342. Copyright © 1988 by the President and Fellows of Harvard College. All rights reserved.

from swinging open. As I squeeze through the opening, the odor of discarded food, plastic wrappers, and cans strikes me in the face. I quickly turn away in disgust and run down the stairs.

The best way to get down the stairs is to run, but it is not the safest way. Taking the stairs is like plunging into the darkness of a cave hoping to emerge at the other end. There are no lights; the bulbs have either burned out or the sockets simply do not work. As you run down you have to be careful not to lose your balance on the crack vials that litter the floor.

On the first floor I see a mother with a stroller waiting for the elevator. As I push the front door open and emerge onto the street, I yell to her that the elevators aren't working. My friend Mike is already waiting for me at the train station.

Monday lunch. The usual bunch of us sit together. The only thing we all have in common is that we eat lunch together. Some of us have shared experiences; others in the group have experiences and backgrounds that are foreign.

The discussions on Mondays start with Jonathan Swaine III telling the rest of us about his weekend. It is all very predictable, something about a country house somewhere. I never pay much attention to his stories because they do not seem real and tangible to me. They are very much a part of his life, but the stories of weekend country houses are not meaningful to me. I don't think he tells us his weekend stories to impress us; he must have gotten the impression long before that his stories had no effect on the rest of us in either a positive or negative way. He sits with us because he wants to learn from our experiences, which are different from his own. We are a "good experience" that somehow reveals to him a different world. He takes advantage of the "diversity" of the school to have an "interesting experience."

Ragavendra is supposed to give Jonathan that unique experience. The name Ragavendra was Americanized into Rags by the teachers. Since reading *The Autobiography of Makolcom X*, Rags has become a fervent Indian nationalist. He tells us that he did not do anything exciting over the weekend. "The usual," he said. Translated this means that he spent the weekend working as a stock boy at the small bodega (grocery store) only three blocks from where I live.

Rags lives just north of me. I once visited his home. It is a five-story tenement building next to a vacant lot. There were kids having a snowball fight in the lot; they would hide behind piles of discarded tires and abandoned cars. Another group of kids climbed a dumpster and jumped onto an old box spring that they used as a trampoline to fly into the sky.

To enter Rags's home you had to walk through the kitchen. There were four large pots of boiling water giving off heat, and the oven was turned to broil. The landlord refused to give any steam, saying that the boiler was broken. The tenants had retaliated with a rent strike, but were being served with eviction notices. A white sheet hung outside the window of the apartment, emblazoned with the words, "SUPPORT OUR RENT STRIKE."

The next person down the table is my friend Mike, who waits for me every morning at the train station. He spends his weekends and some week nights patrolling the buildings of the Frederick Douglass Housing Projects. A group of tenants wear jackets that read on the back, "Tenant Patrol." They set up a desk in the front lobby of a building which has no lock on the front door and try to ensure that only tenants enter the building. There are more than two dozen buildings in the Douglass Projects, and their efforts are, to a large degree, futile. No amount of time or effort could ensure any degree of safety to the people who enter these buildings.

No lunch group like ours would be complete without a person who desperately needs to be around people very different yet similar to himself. His real name is Eduardo Fernandez, but he wants people to call him Edward. I compromise and call him Ed. His mother is on the school's Board of Trustees and his father is a bank executive. They grew up in El Barrio (Spanish Harlem), but now live in a penthouse on Fifth Avenue. In many ways, Ed's parents' success is what Mike, Rags, and I hope to duplicate. Yet we fear Edward; he has what Rags once called the "oreo disease." Trying to hide his real name is only a small part of the confusion he has about his cultural background. He would never call himself Latino, but he knows he cannot call himself a WASP. His parents shelter him so much from the environment that they grew up in that he is reduced to hearing about El Barrio over the lunch table. Ed gropes to understand his Latino background but at the same time denies it, trivializing it in order to move within the WASP culture of the school.

By the time the conversation reaches me, lunch is almost over, so I simply tell them I gardened. There is a neighborhood community garden on what was once the site of a dope house that the city tore down. So, in the minds of city officials the problem was resolved, but the rubble of the building was left in the lot. The community finally cleared the lot and established a garden on the site. It was planted with flowers and assorted plants. Still, the garden is not a pretty sight. Cardboard, pieces of plywood, and a chain-linked fence serve as a fence around the lot. The bricks that once littered the lot are used for pathways through the garden. Tires are used to hold up some plants.

One section is devoted to vegetables. Urban kids who have never seen the plants that vegetables come from always try to guess what each plant produces. Once, one boy pointed to a plant and said with a great deal of authority, "That's a pickle plant!" An old-er girl snapped back, "No, no, dummy, there's no such thing as a pickle plant. It's a tomato plant."

One section of the garden is devoted to food and medicinal herbs. Señora Rosa works in the herb section; she is the "country doctor" of the community. After people have tried countless doctors and their ailments persist, they consult Señora Rosa. The patient makes an offering (usually money) to Señora Rosa's statue of the Virgin Mary, and she prescribes the necessary herbs. The herb section also serves as the community bulletin board; people gather there to pick the herbs Señora Rosa recommends and to exchange neighborhood gossip.

Monday afternoon. There is a large crowd in front of my building as I approach. No one can get into the building because the front door is locked. Management decided to put a lock on the door because residents had complained that people could just walk in off the street. The problem was that management had forgotten to give anyone the key to the lock. In every group, someone has a bright idea. One kid reaches for the fire hose and uses the metal part to break the glass part of the door, reaches in, and opens the door.

Now a second wait begins, the wait for the elevator. One of them is rumored to be working so everyone waits in anticipation. Everyone tries to listen for the sound of chains rattling that indicates the elevator is moving. The waiting crowd grows, as more people enter, using the new doorknob. After what seems like an interminable wait, the elevator reaches the first floor. Before anyone can get off, the crowd presses forward. Three boys file out. One man in the waiting crowd accuses them of holding up the elevator. They snap back, telling the old man to mind his own business.

Close to fifteen people file into the completely dark elevator. The light bulb is missing. We all take a breath of air before the door swings shut. Our bodies are pressed so close together that no one can move. At every stop, everyone must file out to let someone off and then file back in. By counting the glimpses of light that reflect off other people's faces, I count the number of floors passed.

Tuesday night. Outside on the street are voices yelling at each other over the noise of their boom-box radio. Someone from the building yells at them to go away; it is two in the morning. The yelling and music continue, only louder. After a few minutes, I see a bottle sailing through the air. It came from above me and I live on the eleventh floor. The bottle crashes on one of the yelling men, and I say to myself, "Good hit!"

A couple of hours later while I am writing an English paper, I hear the fire alarm go off. I run toward the living room and see smoke coming through the cracks in the front door. Outside, the hallway is filled with people and smoke. I run to call the fire department. After I give the operator my address, the first question she asks is whether I'm calling from the projects. "Yes, yes," I scream into the receiver, just, hurry—there's a fire in the building!"

By the time the fire department arrives, we have extinguished the fire in the garbage chute. People passed buckets of water and poured them down the chute. The garbage had been backed up to the fifth floor and had caught on fire. The entire scene reminded me of a nineteenth-century bucket brigade.

Wednesday English class. I recount last night to my English teacher because I do not have my creative writing assignment. He simply stares at me, neither in surprise nor disbelief. He is clueless; he does not know how to judge my story. No amount of training in preparatory schools has equipped him with the tools to evaluate this excuse. The rest of the class files into the room, and they begin to read out loud the stories they had written the night before. One story keeps ringing in my mind:

This was one of the scariest experiences of my life. I was walking along 72nd and Park Avenue heading downtown. I stopped at the curb to wait for the light to change. On my left there appeared three guys about my age. I continued to walk along and crossed towards Fifth. I looked back and realized that those same three guys were following me. I started to walk a little faster, then run, but they were still following me. On 66th and Fifth one of the guys grabbed me from behind. I turned around and looked at this greasy, hairy, slimy Rican right in the eyes.

My chest tightens. The entire class is looking straight into Mike's eyes—the Puerto Rican in the class. There is a long, tense pause and only Mike can break the silence. He says, "Oh, was that you we got? Sorry."

There is a laughter of relief.

Thursday afternoon. By the end of the day the incident in English class has spread throughout the school. The story and reaction are slightly different in every version I hear. One version has Mike picking up his desk and throwing it across the room.

Rags and I walk home together. We retell the story over and over again, laughing at the incident in the beginning but becoming more and more angry with each retelling. "That's what they think of Blacks and Latinos. They have no other image," he says. "The only contact they have with any Black or Latino is as their doorman or their housecleaner. Then you have people like Edward that, instead of being a positive image of a Chicano, is wrapped up in trying to be a WASP. A double-stuffed oreo is what he is! The rest of us are there to legitimize their White institution. You know the building they are building across the street from the school? Ten years ago the school sued the city not to build a low-income building on the lot. Now the school has gotten its way; they are building a luxury building on the lot. So, 'to improve relations with the neighborhood' they let the kids in the community center use the pool, and they let in a handful of Blacks and Latinos to add color to the place."

As we approach home, Rags and I start to laugh again at the story; there is not much of anything else we can do. We stop in front of the garden to see if anything has grown. From behind me I hear an echoing noise and then some screams. Before I can figure out that the noises I hear are gun shots, I am pushed to the ground. All I can do is hold my bookbag tightly over my head. My face is buried in Rags's back as we both crouch behind a car not knowing where the noises are coming from. One man kneeling beside me yells in my ear that there is a pusher shooting madly to the air in front of 860.

"I will never get home," I think to myself, "860 is my building." After a few noiseless minutes, people start to run toward their buildings and up the stairs.

A couple of hours later when I am trying to get some schoolwork done, I look at my Social Studies paper topic: "In light of our discussion on the rights and protections afforded to citizens by the Constitution, discuss the question of the 'right' of the government to make certain drugs illegal and whether these drugs should be legalized." I tear up the paper in disgust.

Friday night. I get off the crosstown bus on 96th and start to walk down Fifth. As I approach the building on 88th, the door swings open and the doorman asks if I am here for Edward's party.

"Right, for Eduardo's party," I reply.

He directs me to the elevator on the left. The elevator is already waiting for me. On the way up I begin to talk to the elevator man; his name is Señor Manuel. I know him from other visits I have made and because he is the husband of Señora Rosa. We talk about how the garden is growing this year and how it needs a fence. The lights on the elevator panel finally reach PH. The elevator door opens onto another door. There is no hall-

way to walk, just another door. Inside, the entire school is having a party.

In need of some air, I walk onto the terrace. Mike is leaning against the wall looking out toward the lighted skyline and over Central Park. We do not say much for a while. Then he asks, "What you think of the story yesterday? I mean, you think I said the right thing?"

I look across the park uptown toward the group of buildings where we live. They are easily differentiated from the other buildings if you know what to look for.

"What else was I suppose to say? If I hit the guy like I wanted, out I go. One less Puerto Rican in the school is not going to bother them. These people have no sense that we exist in that school. No matter what they do or say we are simply nameless bodies that walk the halls. No name. No character. It is beyond the stage where they don't want us there; now they simply are oblivious to our presence. We only figure in their minds when we are called upon to agree that their notions of us are the right ones.

On the way home, we walk across Central Park in silence. The scenery changes very quickly when you walk uptown. We reach my building. I push the door open; the lock has been taken off, and pieces of glass are still on the floor. Ms. Johnson is waiting in front of the elevators. She is in a wheelchair.

"I've been waiting for the elevators for more than an hour and I can't get home," she says.

Mike gets into the elevator and presses all the buttons. It does not move. "Maybe if we call the cops they can do something," I say. "A woman that was here earlier called but they haven't come. Housing cops never come," she says. "Well, it's close to midnight and we can't leave her here," Mike says to me. Mike needs to prove something to himself tonight.

Before I know what I have gotten myself into we are carrying Ms. Johnson up the stairs, all twenty flights. It takes us over three hours to carry Ms. Johnson in her wheelchair. She never stops talking during those three hours. She tells us that she is going to City College and studying to become a social worker. Mike and I can barely talk as we concentrate on moving up the stairs.

## A CLOSING THOUGHT

Poised between two different worlds, I have learned that the emotional power of some experiences can never be conveyed to another. Outsiders can only begin to appreciate that which is foreign to them when they realize that they will never fully understand.

# Females + Mathematics = A Complex Equation

## KAREN KARP

The well-known British author, Margaret Drabble, reflecting on her own recollections of mathematics instruction, stated:

> I dropped mathematics at 12, through some freak in the syllabus.... I cannot deny that I dropped math with a sigh of relief, for I had always loathed it, always felt uncomprehending even while getting tolerable marks, didn't like subjects I wasn't good at, and had no notion of this subject's appeal or significance.
>
> The reason, I imagine, was that, like most girls I had been badly taught from the beginning: I am not really as innumerate as I pretend, and suspect there is little wrong with the basic equipment but I shall never know.
>
> ...And that effectively, though I did not appreciate it at the time, closed most careers and half of culture to me forever. (1975, p. 16)

Margaret Drabble's story is not unique. The fact is that many women in all walks of life could relate episodes of their skillful navigation around mathematics coursework during their years of schooling. Some report these tales with a twinge of regret, while others, possibly as a defense mechanism, take perverse pride in using humor to diminish the significance of these events. Regardless of their interpretation, the reality of mathematics avoidance is that women are often bound by the ensuing limitations on their professional qualifications, and may be barred from careers requiring mathematical knowledge.

## PROBLEM

Despite voluminous research efforts on gender issues in education over the past 20 years, stubborn patterns of inequitable practices and beliefs continue to persist. Although there has been some measurable progress, the challenge to overcome chronic inequities is formidable. Even though discrimination on the basis of sex in any federally funded educational program became illegal in 1972, the initial promise of Title IX legislation has fallen short of expectations. Charged with eliminating sex bias, creating equal opportunities, encouraging females to enter male-dominated careers (with a hope that a reduction of pay differential would follow), and given the funding to support such activities, schools began to enact piecemeal remedies. Yet, recent data reveal the following:

- Some 70 percent of all females in vocational high schools study traditionally female fields, thereby avoiding careers that involve mathematics, science, and technology (National Commission on Working Women, 1989).
- Females are still outscored by males by an average of 45 points on the mathematics component of the SAT (Educational Testing Service 1992).
- Females in the workforce earn only a fraction of the salaries of males (U.S. Department of Education, 1992), unless

This article was written expressly for this book and is used with permission from the author.

they have earned eight or more mathematics credits in college (Adelman, 1991).

These statistics raise issues about school practices and stimulate particular inquiries as to why the improvement of females' mathematics performance has proceeded at such an uneven pace.

One researcher refers to mathematics as the "critical filter" (Sells, 1978), for any student entering college with less than the full complement of high school mathematics classes can suffer the *de facto* elimination of 82 potential career paths (Toronto Board of Education, 1989). This fact is especially compelling when linked with the recognition that we live in a time when all five of America's best jobs for the 1990s relate directly to mathematics (Krantz, 1988). That is, when the variables of salary, stress, working conditions, and lifetime security are considered, the following five occupations emerge as the most promising: (1) actuary, (2) computer programmer, (3) computer systems analyst, (4) mathematician, and (5) statistician. Thus, when data stating that two to three times as many males as females take physics, chemistry, and advanced mathematics are correlated with the reality that males comprise more than 90 percent of the employment force in professions relating to mathematics and science, the results are no longer surprising. In actuality, most females are confined to a range of professions that are, in general, poorly paid.

Another barrier in the complex intersection of schooling and future career goals is the Scholastic Aptitude Test: "In a world where test scores translate into scholarships and admission to college, and college in turn leads to high-paying jobs, the failure of high school girls to score as well as boys on college-entrance examinations has led to widespread concern" (Goleman, 1987 p. 42). Although recent research has established that gender differences in spatial and mathematical ability have all but been eliminated, differential performance on the mathematics portion of the scholastic aptitude test lingers as a painful exception (Linn & Hyde, 1989).

In the period between 1982 and 1993, females scored an average of 46 points less than males on the SAT mathematics section. For example, in 1993, males outscored females by 502 to 457 on the SAT-M (College Board, 1993). Although the scores of both males and females increase in linear correspondence with the number of years of mathematics they have taken, surprisingly the greatest gap occurs between the select cohorts of male and female students who have had more than four years of mathematics coursework.

In addition, in the population of students designated as "high scorers" (having scores between 750 and 800) the male to female ratio as reported in 1992–1993 is approximately 4 to 1. In this case, small differences in scores translate into serious consequences, with females at risk of losing out academically through rejection from competitive postsecondary institutions; financially, through scholarships that are bound directly or indirectly to the SAT-M score (until New York State's granting of Regents and Empire State Scholarships solely on the basis of SAT scores was ruled unconstitutional, males captured 72 percent of the awards); and psychologically, as female students are more apt than males to deem the SAT as an accurate assessment of their intelligence, leaving them without the confidence to apply to colleges requesting higher SAT scores.

In contrast to SAT-M results, the grades high school females earn in class are comparable to or in some cases higher than those of males. This dichotomy between classroom performance and summative testing results has enormous impact on female students as well as the public mind, for the results of national testing, not student report cards, are what is shared in public forums, thereby reinforcing images of inadequate performance.

Despite outstanding academic records, fewer females are admitted to the most prestigious colleges and universities as a result of SAT-M scores. This archaic situation continues to exist despite an awareness that testing materials may be patently unfair to females. Certain common testing practices such as biased problem contexts and sexist language have been so often and so consistently shown to discriminate against females that knowledge of them is public; however, many of these patterns still exist.

In evaluating 74 different psychological and educational test items for gender-related content, references to males outnumbered those to females 2 to 1. On items in which people of accomplishment were described, males outnumbered females 8 to 1 (Selkow, 1984). In response, the Educational Testing Service (ETS) has been vigilant in attempting to eliminate overt and subtle biases in their testing instruments. They have utilized elaborate and complex statistical analyses to locate and eliminate gender bias in either problem context or content that may favor one group over another.

Regardless of changes in testing materials, males may have an advantage over females in their speed of response. SAT preparation courses commonly claim to boost overall scores by teaching students to make rapid assessments of problems and then produce quick guesses rather than employ lengthy computations (Robinson & Katzman, 1986). Indeed, if males are more confident in their mathematics ability, as research reports, then they may be more inclined to trust intuitive thinking and holistic examinations of problems. On the other hand, females who have frequently found themselves rewarded for rule-compliance behavior, might be less likely to employ swift inspections of problems and revert to lengthy but reliable formulas.

The tendency is for males to exhibit more confidence in their mathematics abilities than females, even when both groups perform equally well (Linn & Hyde, 1989). This confidence gap is only one explanation commonly used to account for females' performance in mathematics. The following sections examine some other factors and discuss possible means for fostering improved mathematics performance in female students.

## BIOLOGICAL FACTORS

In 1980, Benbow and Stanley conducted what initially seemed to be critical research supporting the genetic inferiority of females in terms of mathematics ability. In an effort to control for previous methodological concerns regarding differential course-taking behaviors of males and females, they administered the SAT mathematics component to gifted seventh- and eighth-graders presumably at a point where they had all taken the same mathematics courses. The results suggested "huge and significant differences" favoring males over females. The researchers concluded that males had superior innate mathematics ability and that this ability naturally shaped the selection of advanced mathematics courses.

According to the study, there were about 13 male math geniuses in seventh grade for every female. In general, females were described as not being able to understand the material and, as a consequence, "women would be better off accepting the differences" (Benbow, 1980, p. 1235). Unfortunately, only after this study received tremendous publicity and media attention did other researchers move to the forefront with questions and serious concerns regarding the methods and conclusions of the investigation (Alexander & Pallas, 1983; Egelman, Alper, Leibowitz, Beckwith, Levine, & Leeds, 1981).

These researchers demanded more details as to how Benbow and Stanley equated SAT-M performance with innate mathematics ability, how they reconciled the inherent bias against females in the testing instrument, what impact the overwhelmingly large percentage of males in the sample had on the results, how the socioeconomic status of the students may have skewed outcomes (most came from family backgrounds where financial support for a summer program for gifted students was possible), how the findings of research with a highly select sample could be generalized to an entire population, and whether the schooling experience up to that point had in reality been the same for males and females. The answers raised serious doubts. Although the Benbow and Stanley study originally heralded the belief that there were causative biological factors, the early support this hypothesis garnered has disappeared.

Another biogenetic theory relating to brain lateralization has also attracted interest. In the maturing human fetus, exposure to the male sex hormone, testosterone, slows development of the left hemisphere of the brain. As a result, the right hemisphere is thought to compensate by increasing dominance and enhancing the components of intelligence under its control (i.e., spatial sense) (Ramey, 1987). Most believe that these developmental differences exist, but direct linkages to mathematical abilities has not been proven.

Declining differences between males and females in both mathematics and spatial skills suggest that a biological causation is not probable (Halpern, 1989). In the words of Rosenthal and Rubin (1982), such changes in gender differences are happening "faster than the gene can travel" (p. 711). Few researchers today would posit that biogenetic theories provide a worthwhile explanation for gender differences in mathematics ability. Most would concur instead with the premise that gender expectations and differential performance remain enmeshed in environmental and cultural variables.

## DIFFERENTIAL ABILITY

Rather than an observed continuity of poor performance, researchers identify a discontinuity in females' mathematics achievement. Usually no performance differences are identified until the age of 10 (Dossey, Mullis, Lindquist, & Chambers, 1988) but, interestingly, when differences are found in the early years, they are inclined to favor females (Brandon, Newton, & Hammond, 1987). In the middle school years, data reveals a mixture of results, but during the high school years differences in favor of males are common (Carpenter, Lindquist, Mathews, & Silver, 1983; NAEP, 1990; Ramist & Arbeiter, 1986).

One area of disparate ability that initially attracted a good share of attention was differences in spatial ability. A recent meta-analysis reveals that these differences are declining to the point where they no longer exist (Linn & Hyde, 1989).

One domain where differences are still marked is in the skill component of mental rotation, which is the ability to flip and turn a geometric figure in space (Thomas & Kail, 1991). These differences are seemingly in speed rather than accuracy, which may suggest that practice will impact favorably on improving this ability (Gallagher & Johnson, 1992). Although measured variance in performance may be slight or even nil, we must be cautious in dismissing this area as rectified, as females' mathematics ability seems to be more inexorably linked to spatial abilities.

Fortunately, spatial skills have proven to respond well to training (Linn & Hyde, 1989; Baenninger & Newcombe, 1989, Ben-Chaim, Lappan, & Houang, 1988). Baenninger and Newcombe further question why such training in spatial skills is omitted from the regular school curriculum if significant improvement has been demonstrated by both genders when such practice is provided. We must ask why there are so many intervention programs for reading problems (which are mainly populated by male students) and yet such little attention devoted to the remediation of spatial skills. Frequently, female students must manifest greater deficiencies than males prior to receiving special services (Vogel, 1990).

## SCHOOL EFFECTS

Researchers overwhelmingly report that mathematics learning is largely a function of mathematics teaching (Coleman, 1975; Corran & Walkerdine, 1981; Fennema, 1990; Karp, 1991). Although mathematics terms may be used outside of school, the classroom remains the central site for instruction. Yet, school is clearly a place of uneven opportunities for females. A recent comprehensive report undertaken by the American Association for University Women Foundation states that their research findings debunk "another myth—that boys and girls receive equal education. The wealth of statistical evidence must convince even the most skeptical that gender bias in our schools is shortchanging girls—and compromising our country" (McKee, 1992 p. Al). Over the years, researchers have identified that the "shortchanging" females experience unfolds in various forms.

## CLASSROOM INTERACTIONS

Sadker and Sadker found that "at all grade levels, in all communities (urban, suburban and rural) and in all subject areas, boys dominated classroom communication. Boys participated in more interactions than girls did, this participation becoming greater as the year went on" (1985, p. 165). Males receive more verbal contact with teachers, both positive and negative (Spendor, 1982). They are

called on more frequently, asked more complex and open-ended questions, and are more often engaged in inquiries that involve abstract reasoning (Jones, 1989).

Conversely, interactions between teachers and female students often include rewards for following rules, conformity, neatness, silence, and appearance. For instance, while observing in a nursery school classroom in England, Walden and Walkerdine (1985) observed two students approach the teacher with a drawing. One was told, "Well done, John, that's a good drawing"; the other was told, "You do look pretty today, Alice." Females are asked more basic recall questions and are often given correct answers when they cannot produce them. Serbin and O'Leary (1975) found that teachers are more likely to encourage learned helplessness by performing a task for a female student who is having difficulty but will give males eight times more information on how to solve the problem themselves. Thus, the crux of the problem regarding disparities between treatment of males and females in classroom discourse lies in the content of student-teacher interactions rather than the number of interactions.

## PARENT EXPECTATIONS

Consistent with stereotypical expectations from the past, a recent investigation yielded the predictable results that parents of males held more positive beliefs regarding their child's mathematics performance and more frequently identified the need for their child to continue in upper-level mathematics than parents of females (Eccles, Flanagan, Goldsmith, Jacobs, Jayaratne, Wigfield, & Yee, 1987). This finding is surprising when the researchers' description of their sample reveals that male and female students were precisely matched for equivalent performance on both formal mathematics tests and in classroom grades. Parents of a subset of the females in the study rated their daughters' abilities in language arts as higher than their mathematics abilities, even though their daughters had identical grades in both subjects. Parents of males with identical grades in these subjects gave a higher rating to their sons' mathematical abilities.

Some researchers suggest that parental influence is a more potent factor in impacting mathematics performance than originally thought (Campbell & Mandel, 1990). Therefore, it seems likely that males and females would be swayed by their parents' expectations and the way their parents reinforce specific achievements over others.

In a study examining the United States, Japan, and China, Stevenson (1987) found that differential parental expectations were evidenced as early as the first grade. For example, both children and their mothers tended to believe that males had superior mathematics ability and that females excelled in reading. Even prior to entering first grade, Japanese females said they preferred reading, while males stated that they preferred mathematics. Although enormous differences in mathematics achievement were identified among the countries, interestingly, only a few significant gender differences in performance were reported but numerous gender differences in attitude toward mathematics (males having more positive attitudes) were identified.

Subtle messages sent by parents to children may be an element in the trend for females to not perform as well in mathematics in the higher grades and for them to opt out of advanced mathematics and mathematically oriented careers.

## GENDER ROLE SOCIALIZATION FACTORS

Gender role socialization factors encompass a variety of behaviors, feelings, attitudes, and interests designated by society as appropriate for females or males. They are learned through interactions with parents, peers, teachers, books, toys, and the media. In addition, participation in social events and encounters with social institutions shape the child's reality.

Sometimes, pressures for children to conform to social definitions of suitable behavior for their sex are great. Even from the moment after a baby's birth where "Is the baby a boy or girl?" is the most commonly asked question (Inton-Peterson & Reddel, 1984), patterns for orchestrating the world around the child as male oriented or female oriented begin. When given an opportunity to play with a baby, adults have engaged in different activities, depending on whether they were told the infant was a male or a female (Will, Self, & Datan, 1976).

Similarly, the first playthings purchased often reflect societal beliefs. Males are frequently supplied with objects that encourage moving, building, and taking things apart and putting them back together. They are apt to be taught at a very young age how to catch a ball and keep score. On the other hand, females are inclined to be given toys that involve relationships with people. Therefore, when males and females first enter school, socialization patterns previously established in the home promote the continuation of play with items and settings that are familiar. In this way, through what is described as the "practice component," the children avoid classroom activities about which they are unfamiliar or less confident (Greenberg, 1985). Hence, the role established in the home environment takes on increased potency.

After exposure to conventional societal expectations, males tend to "judge themselves by what they are able to do" and females "portray their worth in terms of their physical appearance" (Harris & Pickle, 1992, p. 12). This culture-bound, systematic conditioning of humans into patterns of performance is referred to as the "social construction of gender." Undoubtedly, these are the most complex variables to consider as well as the most difficult to unravel. Yet, change in this domain has the potential to generate the greatest effect.

## CURRICULUM

Both in content and in organization, curriculum explicitly and implicitly reflects culture. Critical sociologists (e.g., Apple, 1979) have considered the "hidden curriculum" of schools as including the nonacademic but significant outcomes of schooling that are rarely explicitly expressed. These are often assumptions that underlie what is taught and often result in the replication of culture, class and gender expectations. Although linkages between the school's culture and society are expected, critical sociologists ask why access to educational experiences differs for some groups and why some individuals are able to resist such forces?

For example, in many classrooms the methodology frequently incorporates debate, argument, and challenge, all of which center around the drive to win (Belenky, Clinchy, Goldberger, & Tarule, 1986; Lewis, 1991; Tannen, 1992). Yet, initially through informal groupings and now more formally through structuring by teachers, the ever-increasing incorporation of cooperative learning groups in mathematics sends messages contrary to the usual competitive model. Cooperative learning attempts to balance members' contributions while increasing the focus on group dynamics and encouraging cohesiveness. Females have consistently responded more favorably, through measured increases in academic performance, to the use of cooperative groupings (as compared to competitive) (Peterson & Fennema, 1985; Goldberg, 1988). Perhaps this propensity to function well in groupings that combine academic growth with the development of relationships relates to the development of the "ethic of care" (Gilligan, 1982; Noddings,

1992), which may be a passive form of resistance to traditional mathematics lessons.

## DIRECTIONS FOR THE FUTURE

Given what is known about cultural and environmental variables, the examination must shift to actions that educators can take to reduce or eliminate these obstacles. One collaborative effort, funded by the Ford Foundation and charged with the improvement of mathematics education nationwide, has generated propositions to assist agents of change. They are:

1. Expect high achievement and hold high expectations for all students, particularly those who have been previously underrepresented. Assume everyone can meet with success and develop instructional strategies that will build students' confidence in learning mathematics.
2. Provide access to mathematical concepts, real-world applications, and linkages to students' cultural frameworks.
3. Move away from dependence on standardized tests to more authentic formats that align the learning and assessment processes. Improved observation skills will enable teachers to formally analyze what happens in their classroom during mathematics instruction. Forms of data collection, such as interviewing students and having students keep journals about their experiences in mathematics, promise to reveal much that would not be evident from previous types of assessment, mostly tests.
4. Develop pre-service and in-service teachers' abilities through better preparation in effective methods to teach mathematics. Teachers need to be made familiar with research on equity issues as they relate to classroom teaching practices.
5. Develop pre-service and in-service teachers' knowledge of mathematics curriculum, particularly in light of the recent development of national standards in mathematics.
6. Create a supportive environment for efforts relating to school restructuring, including

increased teacher input in curricular decisions, allocation of resources, and selection
of appropriate professional development
activities. (1991, pp. 5–6)

In the discussion that follows, more specific elements that overlap several of the Urban Collaborative's recommendations and
suggest other routes to pursue are examined
in greater depth. Educational institutions
should be responsive to needed support systems for females, the creation of positive
learning environments, the promise of alternative models of assessment, revised paradigms of teacher education, and the necessity
for administrators to be educated on equity
issues.

## SUPPORT SYSTEMS

Female students who have entered the fields
of mathematics, science, and technology repeatedly report the crucial impact their
teachers' encouragement had on their career
choices. Occasionally, these women have indicated that support came from women who
were working in the field and acted as role
models. These were connections commonly
made through special summer school or after-school programs for females with interests in mathematics and science (AAUW,
1992). Such programs were crucial in building the confidence of young females. This
confidence is critical because, as females'
confidence in their mathematics ability dwin-
dles, so does their performance. The all-fe-
male cohorts assembled for these programs
also reduce the isolation often expressed by
female students with a predilection to mathematics. Such opportunities to identify others
with like interests initiate subsequent support
structures and networks.

Guidance counselors need to be an integral part of the support system for females.
Many have now received in-service training

in equity issues and are therefore less likely
to steer females away from upper-level
mathematics courses (even if their cumulative average might go down). In the past,
counselors were frequently guilty of this
"coercive inducement" (Isaacson, 1988)
wherein females make choices "because of a
system of rewards and approvals which act
as inducements and which are so powerful
that they come to be a kind of coercion" (p.
17).

## METHODOLOGY AND THE CLASSROOM LEARNING ENVIRONMENT

The fundamental template of mathematics
instruction must face the necessity for alter-
ations. The recent standards envisioned and
developed by the National Council of Teachers of Mathematics (1989, 1990) in both
curriculum and methodology promise to be a
paradigm of inclusive instruction. The suggested avoidance of lock-step applications of
procedures and the recommended incorporation of understanding, estimation, testing for
reasonableness, and identification of patterns
are attempts to provide all students with
power in mathematics. A positive learning
environment can be employed to build confidence and problem-solving abilities through
discussion of strategies and thinking processes, demonstrations that mathematics is relevant, nurturing of cooperative efforts, and
emphasis on more authentic assessment
models. Mathematics teachers at all levels
must renounce teaching methods that encourage learned helplessness in students
(Karp, 1991).

Research reported by AAUW (1992) suggests that when teachers become aware of
their gender biases, they are willing to
change. Therefore, teachers require the kind
of in-service and pre-service training that will
keep them apprised of the current theories

and suggested practices in promoting gender equity. This knowledge can result in an increased alertness to gender bias and stereotyping in textbooks, software, audiovisual materials, and course titles, as well as choices of speakers, field trips, and mentoring or job shadowing programs.

Additionally, teachers must terminate the silence in school environments when students or faculty demonstrate behaviors that are biased or discriminatory. Such passive behaviors further entrench attitudes and actions that are harmful to those who are subjected to them. Only active confrontation can encourage the awareness and attitudinal change necessary to promote fairness to all groups. Institutions of teacher education have the responsibility of preparing teachers to assume leadership roles when faced with these challenges.

## TEACHER EDUCATION

In 1980, Sadker and Sadker evaluated the three best-selling texts in mathematics education and found that they did not contain any content related to either gender differences or the contributions of women to mathematics. In a more recent examination of 25 extant texts in mathematics education, which included the three most popular texts (as reported in Pedersen, Beal, Connelly, Klespis, Leitzel, & Tayeh, 1991), similar patterns of invisibility exist (Karp, forthcoming). Only four of the texts made specific mention of gender-related equity issues or techniques that could be incorporated to improve the performance of female students. Although one text had comprehensive coverage, with 21 pages exploring research on gender differences, the other texts each had less than 2 pages of information. Sadker and Sadker stated that pre-service teaching candidates "are being prepared with textbooks more likely to promote and reinforce sex bias than to re-

duce and eliminate such prejudice" (1980, p. 550).

Apparently not much has changed. Current texts provide future teachers with neither the recent research on the issues nor the curricular resources and methodologies to combat sexism or encourage the models proven to be most successful with females. "Teacher education in most institutions of higher learning reinforces the already existing sexist attitudes of many undergraduates" (O'Reilly & Borman, 1984 p. 110) .

To end the reproduction of teachers who are unaware of the challenges engendered by gender inequities in mathematics education, teacher education programs need to aggressively respond. As already implemented by professors of elementary mathematics education courses, readings and discussions on equity issues can and should be supplementary components to any textbook that does not provide adequate information. More importantly, professors must model methods and discourse that are likely to nurture the same gender-balanced behaviors in their students.

## ASSESSMENT

Culture-practice theorists examine the gender differences question from another lens. They weigh heavily the value of examining "context specificity," an assumption that constitutes the framework of this theory. They suggest that when the context in which a problem is posed is relevant to the culture of the individual, previous differences in cognition cease to be identified (Laboratory of Comparative Human Cognition, 1983). For example, Liberian children were given a group of geometric shapes and asked to group them according to an attribute of their choice. When they were unable to accomplish this task successfully, they were deemed weak in classification skills. Instead, when they were asked to group rice, they demonstrated skill in this ability far beyond the performance of American participants (Irwin, Schafer, & Feiden, 1974).

The question, thus, becomes: In what contexts other than those traditionally used in school settings can females best display their mathematics skills? Answers may lie in the diverse options presented by alternative forms of assessing mathematical ability. Formats such as portfolios, performance tasks, or interviews may provide the best forum for unveiling the mathematics skills females possess.

## SCHOOL RESTRUCTURING AND ADMINISTRATION

In addition to the dissemination of awareness information to teachers, administrators need to acquire fine-tuned observation skills that encourage sensitivity to gender inequities (Schmuck & Schubert, 1986). Yet, in particular, women administrators have to be seen as more than just focusing on gender-related issues to avoid losing their job (Shakeshaft, 1987). Shakeshaft (1990) further suggests that her research findings confirm that women's ways of managing are aligned with research on effective schools and that schools and educational administration programs should be restructured to profit from females' strengths.

To best organize a school restructuring effort that includes equity concerns on its agenda, educational institutions should conduct formal assessments of gender equity. From basic statistics on course enrollments and participation in extracurricular activities to elaborate observational evaluations, patterns of inequities need to be identified. The ensuing analyses might result in the development and implementation of administrative and curricular policies to ensure equity in classroom interactions and curricula and school management. As a first step, knowledge about equity laws and research that

counteracts sex biases might be reflected in the comments and suggestions generated by supervisors' observations of lessons.

## CONCLUSION

Schools remain sources of cultural reproduction; therefore, awareness of student's developing roles and values is critical. By tolerating an environment of gender bias, females and males are exposed to behaviors and attitudes that corrupt their overall growth.

Males who excel over females in this environment constitute a small percentage. Not enough students of either gender attain the high levels of mathematics thinking realized by students in other nations. Fortunately, there is not a zero-sum relationship to the nurturing of females' mathematics abilities. Classroom strategies that create an environment where females can be successful do not disadvantage males and in many instances have been beneficial to them. Gender inequities do not just harm females; they impact on everyone.

The answers we seek in creating an environment that encourages females to welcome mathematical experiences and consider possible careers in the discipline are still being generated. In fact, we may need to think of other questions. The key may lie in the more subtle or complex constructs we have not yet investigated, such as those referred to by Tyack and Hansot (1988) when they suggest the "need to be aware of the importance of the dog that did not bark" (p. 34).

## REFERENCES

Adelman, C. (1991). *Women at thirtysomething: Paradoxes of attainment.* Washington, DC: U.S. Department of Education.

Alexander, K., & Pallas, A. (1983). Reply to Benbow and Stanley. *American Educational Research Journal, 20,* 475–477.

American Association of University Women. (1992). *How schools shortchange girls.* Washington, DC: AAUW Educational Foundation and National Education Association.

Apple, M. (1979). *Ideology and curriculum.* London: Routledge & Kegan Paul.

Baenninger, M., & Newcombe, N. (1989). The role of experience in spatial test performance: A meta-analysis. *Sex Roles, 20,* 327–344.

Belenky, M., Clinchy, B., Goldberger, N., & Tarule, J. (1986). *Women's ways of knowing: The development of self, voice, and mind.* New York: Basic Books.

Benbow, C. (1980). In G. B. Kolata, Math and sex: Are girls born with less ability? *Science, 210,* 1234–1235.

Benbow, C., & Stanley, J. (1980). Sex differences in mathematical ability: Fact or artifact? *Science, 210,* 1262–1264.

Ben-Chaim, D., Lappan, G., & Houang, R. (1988). The effect of instruction on spatial visualization skills of middle school boys and girls. *American Educational Research Journal, 25,* 51–71.

Brandon, P., Newton, B. , & Hammond, O. (1987). Children's mathematics achievement in Hawaii: Sex differences favoring girls. *American Educational Research Journal, 24,* 437–461.

Carpenter, P., Lindquist, M., Mathews, W., & Silver, E. (1983). Results of the third NAEP mathematics assessment: Secondary school. *Mathematics Teacher, 76,* 652–659.

Campbell, J., & Mandel, F. (1990). *Sexism is alive and well in Japan.* Paper presented at the Annual Meeting of the American Educational Research Association, San Francisco.

Coleman, J. (1975). Methods and results in the IEA studies of effects of school on learning. *Review of Educational Research, 45* (3), 335–386.

College Board. (1993). *1993 Profile of SAT and Achievement Test Takers.* Princeton, NJ: College Entrance Examination Board.

Conlan, G. (1990). Text and context reading comprehension and the mechanics of meaning. *College Board Review, 157,* 18–25.

Dossey, J., Mullis, I., Lindquist, M., & Chambers, D. (1988). *The Mathematics report card: Are we measuring up? Trends and achievement based on the 1986 national assessment.* Princeton, NJ: Educational Testing Service.

Drabble, M. (1975, August 5). Interview. *The Guardian,* p. 16. London.

Eccles, J., Flanagan, C., Goldsmith, R., Jacobs, J., Jayaratne, T., Wigfield, A., & Yee, D. (1987). *Parents as socializers of achievement attitudes.* Paper presented at the Society for Research in Child Development, Baltimore.

Educational Testing Service. (1992, February 26). Correspondence with N. Burton.

Egelman, E., Alper, J., Leibowitz, L., Beckwith, J., Levine, R., & Leeds, A. (1981). Letter to the editor. *Science, 212,* 116.

Fennema, E. (1990). Justice, equity, and mathematics education. In E. Fennema & G. Leder (Eds.), *Mathematics and Gender* (pp. 1–9). New York: Teachers College Press.

Gallagher, S., & Johnson, E. (1992). The effects of time limits on performance of mental rotations by gifted adolescents. *Gifted Child Quarterly, 36* (1), 19–22.

Gilligan, C. (1982). *In a different voice.* Cambridge, MA: Harvard University Press.

Goldberg, K. (1988, April 27). Among girls, Ethic of caring may stifle classroom competiveness, study shows. *Education Week, 1,* 24.

Goleman, D. (1987, August 2). Girls and math: Is biology really destiny? *New York Times: Educational Supplement,* 42–46.

Greenberg, S. (1985). Educational equity in early childhood environments. In S. Klein (Ed.), *Handbook for Achieving Sex Equity Through Education.* Baltimore: Johns Hopkins University Press.

Halpern, D. (1989). The disappearance of cognitive gender differences: What you see depends on where you live. *American Psychologist, 44,* 1156–1157.

Harris, M., & Pickle, J. (1992). Creating an equitable environment: Gender equity in Lincoln, Nebraska. *The Educational Forum, 57* (1), 12–17.

Intons-Peterson, M., & Reddel, M. (1984). What do people ask about a neonate? *Developmental Psychology, 20* (3), 358–359.

Irwin, M., Schafer, G., & Feiden, C. (1974). Emic and unfamiliar category sorting of Mano farmers and U.S. undergraduates. *Journal of Cross-Cultural Psychology, 5* (4), 407–423.

Isaacson, Z. (1988). Of course you could be an engineer, dear, but wouldn't you rather be a nurse or teacher or secretary? In P. Ernest (Ed.), *The Social Context of Mathematics Teaching* (pp. 17–25). Exeter, UK: Exeter University Publishing.

Jones, G. (1989). Gender bias in classroom interactions. *Contemporary Education, 60,* 216–222.

Karp, K. (1991). Elementary school teachers' attitudes toward mathematics: The impact on students' autonomous learning skills. *School Science and Mathematics, 91* (6), 265–270.

Karp, K. (forthcoming). Mathematics and science education texts: Do they examine the issue of gender equity?

Krantz, L. (1988). *The jobs rated almanac.* New York: Ballantine Books.

Laboratory of Comparative Human Cognition. (1983). Culture and cognitive development. In P. Mussen & W. Kessen (Eds.), *Handbook of child psychology (4th ed.) Volume I: History, theory, and methods* (pp. 295–356). New York: Wiley and Sons.

Lewis, A. (1991). Taking women seriously. *Phi Delta Kappan, 73* (4), 268–269.

Linn, M., & Hyde, J. (1989). Gender mathematics, and science. *Educational Researcher, 12,* 17–19, 22–27.

McKee, A. (1992, February 12). In S. Chira, Bias against girls is found rife in schools, with lasting damage. *New York Times,* pp. Al, A23.

National Commission on Working Women. (1989). *Women, work and the future.* Washington, DC: Wider Opportunities for Women.

National Council of Teachers of Mathematics. 1989. *Curriculum and Evaluation Standards.* Reston, VA: NCTM.

National Council of Teachers of Mathematics. (1990). *Professional Teaching Standards.* Reston, VA: NCTM.

Noddings, N. (1992). The gender issue. *Educational Leadership, 49* (4), 65–70.

O'Reilly, P., & Borman, K. (1984). Sexism and sex discrimination in education. *Theory into Practice, 23* (2), 110–116.

Pedersen, K., Beal, S., Connelly, R., Klespis, M. Leitzel, J., & Tayeh, C. (1991). *How is mathematics education reform affecting teacher education programs?* Presentation at the National Council of Supervisors of Mathematics, New Orleans.

Peterson, R., & Fennema, E. (1985). Effective teaching, student engagement in classroom activity, and sex-differences in learning mathematics. *American Educational Research Journal 22,* 309–335.

Ramey, E. (1987). *Sex hormones and science ability.* Paper presented at the Annual Meeting of the National Science Teachers' Association, Washington, DC.

Ramist, L., & Arbeiter, S. (1986). *Profiles of college-bound seniors: 1985.* New York: College Entrance Examination Board.

Robinson, A., & Katzman, J. (1986). *Cracking the system.* New York: Villard.

Rosenthal, R., & Rubin, D. (1982). Further meta-analytic procedures for assessing cognitive gender differences. *Journal of Educational Psychology, 74,* 708–712.

Sadker, M., & Sadker, D. (1980). Sexism in teacher education texts. *Harvard Educational Review, 50,* 36–46.

Sadker, M., Sadker, D., & Klein, S. (1991). The issue of gender in elementary and secondary education. In G. Grant (Ed.), *Review of the Research in Education, 17,* 269–334. Washington, DC: American Educational Research Association.

Schmuck, P., & Schubert, J. (1986). *Women administrators' views on sex equity: Exploring issues of information, identity, and integration.* Paper presented at the annual meeting of the American Education Research Association, Washington, DC.

Selkow, P. (1984). *Assessing sex bias in testing: A review of the issues and evaluations of 74 psychological and educational tests.* Westport, CT: Greenwood.

Sells, L. (1978). Mathematics—A critical filter. *The Science Teacher, 45,* 28–29.

Serbin, L., & O'Leary, K. (1975 December). How nursery schools teach girls to shut up. *Psychology Today, 55.*

Shakeshaft, C. (1987). *Women in educational administration.* Newbury Park, CA: Sage.

Shakeshaft, C. (1990). Administrative preparation for equity. In H. P. Baptiste, H. C. Waxman, J. Walker de Felix, & J. E. Anderson (Eds.), *Leadership, equity, and school effectiveness* (pp. 213–223). Newbury Park, CA: Sage.

Spendor, D. (1982). *Invisible women: The schooling scandal.* London: Writers and Readers.

Stevenson, H. (1987). America's math problems. *Educational Leadership, 45 (2),* 4–10.

Tannen, D. (1991). How men and women use language differently in their lives and in the classroom. *Education Digest, 57* (6), 3–4.

Thomas, H., & Kail, R. (1991). Sex differences in speed of mental rotation and the X-linked genetic hypothesis. *Intelligence, 15* (1), 17–31.

Toronto Board of Education. (1989). *Dropping math? Say good-bye to 82 jobs.* Toronto, Canada: Mathematics Department of the Toronto Board of Education.

Tyack, D., & Hansot, E. (1988). Silence and policy talk: Historical puzzles about gender and education. *Educational Researcher,* 33–41.

U.S. Department of Education. (1992). *Digest of education statistics.* Washington, DC: Office of Educational Research and Improvement.

Urban Mathematics Collaborative. (1991). Math equity in the classroom: A vision of reform from the urban mathematics collaboratives. *Women's Educational Equity Act Digest.* Newton, MA: Women's Educational Equity Act Publishing Center.

Vogel, S. (1990). Gender difference in intelligence, language, visual-motor abilities, and academic achievement in students with learning disabilities: A review of the literature. *Journal of Learning Disabilities, 23,* 44–52.

Will, J., Self, P., & Datan, N. (1976). Maternal behavior and perceived sex of infant. *American Journal of Orthopsychiatry, 46* (1), 135–139.

# Keeping Track, Part 1: The Policy and Practice of Curriculum Inequality

## JEANNIE OAKES

The idea of educational equality has fallen from favor. In the 1980s policy makers, school practitioners, and the public have turned their attention instead to what many consider a competing goal: excellence. Attempts to "equalize" schooling in the Sixties and Seventies have been judged extravagant and naive. Worse, critics imply that those well-meant efforts to correct inequality may have compromised the central mission of the schools: teaching academics well. And current critics warn that, given the precarious position of the United States in the global competition for economic, technological, and military superiority, we can no longer sacrifice the quality of our schools to social goals. This view promotes the judicious spending of limited educational resources in ways that will produce the greatest return on "human capital." Phrased in these economic terms, special provisions for underachieving poor and minority students become a bad investment. In short, equality is out; academic excellence is in.

On the other hand, many people still argue vociferously that the distinction between promoting excellence and providing equality is false, that one cannot be achieved without the other. Unfortunately, whether "tight-fisted" conservatives or "fuzzy-headed" liberals are in the ascendancy, the heat of the rhetoric surrounding the argument largely obscures a more serious problem: the possibility that the unquestioned *assumptions* that drive school practice and the *basic features of schools* may themselves lock schools into patterns that make it difficult to achieve *either* excellence *or* equality.

The practice of tracking in secondary schools illustrates this possibility and provides evidence of how schools, even as they voice commitment to equality and excellence, organize and deliver curriculum in ways that advance neither. Nearly all schools track students. Because tracking enables schools to provide educational treatments matched to particular groups of students, it is believed to promote higher achievement for all students under conditions of equal educational opportunity. However, rather than promoting higher achievement, tracking contributes to mediocre schooling for *most* secondary students. And because it places the greatest obstacles to achievement in the path of those children least advantaged in American society—poor and minority children— tracking forces schools to play an active role in perpetuating social and economic inequalities as well. Evidence about the influence of tracking on student outcomes and analyses of how tracking affects the day-to-day school experiences of young people support the argument that such basic elements of schooling can *prevent* rather than *promote* educational goals.

## WHAT IS TRACKING?

Tracking is the practice of dividing students into separate classes for high-, average-, and low-achievers; it lays out different curriculum

*Source:* "Keeping Track, Part 1: The Policy and Practice of Curriculum Inequality" by Jeannie Oakes. *Phi Delta Kappan*, September 1986. Reprinted by permission of Dr. Jeannie Oakes.

paths for students headed for college and for those who are bound directly for the workplace. In most senior high schools, students are assigned to one or another *curriculum track* that lays out sequences of courses for college-preparatory, vocational, or general track students. Junior and senior high schools also make use of *ability grouping*—that is, they divide academic subjects (typically English, mathematics, science, and social studies) into classes geared to different "levels" for students of different abilities. In many high schools these two systems overlap, as schools provide college-preparatory, general, and vocational sequences of courses and also practice ability grouping in academic subjects. More likely than not, the student in the vocational curriculum track will be in one of the lower ability groups. Because similar overlapping exists for college-bound students, the distinction between the two types of tracking is sometimes difficult to assess.

But tracking does not proceed as neatly as the description above implies. Both curriculum tracking and ability grouping vary from school to school in the number of subjects that are tracked, in the number of levels provided, and in the ways in which students are placed. Moreover, tracking is confounded by the inflexibilities and idiosyncrasies of "master schedules," which can create unplanned tracking, generate further variations among tracking systems, and affect the courses taken by individual students as well. Elective subjects, such as art and home economics, sometimes become low-track classes because college-preparatory students rarely have time in their schedules to take them; required classes, such as drivers' training, health, or physical education, though they are intended to be heterogeneous, become tracked when the requirements of other courses that *are* tracked keep students together for large portions of the day.

Despite these variations, tracking has common and predictable characteristics:

- The intellectual performance of students is judged, and these judgments determine placement with particular groups.
- Classes and tracks are labeled according to the performance levels of the students in them (e.g., advanced, average, remedial) or according to students' postsecondary destinations (e.g., college-preparatory, vocational).
- The curriculum and instruction in various tracks are tailored to the perceived needs and abilities of the students assigned to them.
- The groups that are formed are not merely a collection of different but equally-valued instructional groups. They form a hierarchy, with the most advanced tracks (and the students in them) seen as being on top.
- Students in various tracks and ability levels experience school in very different ways.

## UNDERLYING ASSUMPTIONS

First, and clearly most important, teachers and administrators generally assume that tracking promotes overall student achievement—that is, that the academic needs of all students will be better met when they learn in groups with similar capabilities or prior levels of achievement. Given the inevitable diversity of student populations, tracking is seen as the best way to address individual needs and to cope with individual differences. This assumption stems from a view of human capabilities that includes the belief that students' capacities to master schoolwork are so disparate that they require different and separate schooling experiences. The extreme position contends that some students cannot learn at all.

A second assumption that underlies tracking is that less-capable students will suffer emotional as well as educational damage from daily classroom contact and competition with their brighter peers. Lowered self-concepts and negative attitudes toward learning are widely considered to be consequences of mixed-ability grouping for slower learners. It is also widely assumed that students can be placed in tracks and groups both accurately and fairly. And finally, most teachers and administrators contend that tracking greatly eases the teaching task and is, perhaps, the *only* way to manage student differences.

## THE RECORD OF TRACKING

Students clearly differ when they enter secondary schools, and these differences just as clearly influence learning. But separating students to better accommodate these differences appears to be neither necessary, effective, nor appropriate.

### Does Tracking Work?

At the risk of oversimplifying a complex body of research literature, it is safe to conclude that *there is little evidence to support any of the assumptions about tracking.* The effects of tracking on student outcomes have been widely investigated, and the bulk of this work *does not* support commonly-held beliefs that tracking increases student learning. Nor does the evidence support tracking as a way to improve students' attitudes about themselves or about schooling.[1] Although existing tracking systems *appear* to provide advantages for students who are placed in the top tracks, the literature suggests that students at all ability levels can achieve at least as well in heterogeneous classrooms.

Students who are *not* in top tracks—a group that includes about 60% of senior high school students—suffer clear and consistent disadvantages from tracking. Among students identified as average or slow, tracking often appears to retard academic progress. Indeed, one study documented the fact that the lowered I.Q. scores of senior high school students followed their placement in low tracks.[2] Students who are placed in vocational tracks do not even seem to reap any benefits in the job market. Indeed, graduates of vocational programs may be less employable and, when they do find jobs, may earn lower wages than other high school graduates.[3]

Most tracking research does not support the assumption that slow students suffer emotional strains when enrolled in mixed-ability classes. Often the opposite result has been found. Rather than helping students feel more comfortable about themselves, tracking can reduce self-esteem, lower aspirations, and foster negative attitudes toward school. Some studies have also concluded that tracking leads low-track students to misbehave and eventually to drop out altogether.[4]

The net effect of tracking is to exaggerate the initial differences among students rather than to provide the means to better accommodate them. For example, studies show that senior high school students who are initially similar in background and prior achievement become *increasingly* different in achievement and future aspirations when they are placed in different tracks.[5] Moreover, this effect is likely to be cumulative over most of the students' school careers, since track placements tend to remain fixed. Students placed in low-ability groups in elementary school are likely to continue in these groups in middle school or junior high school; in senior high school these students are typically placed in non-college-preparatory tracks. Studies that have documented increased gaps between initially comparable high school students placed in different tracks probably capture only a fraction of this effect.

### Is Tracking Fair?

Compounding the lack of empirical evidence to support tracking as a way to enhance student outcomes are compelling arguments that favor exposing all students to a common curriculum, *even if differences among them prevent all students from benefiting equally.* These arguments counter both the assumption that tracking can be carried out "fairly" and the view that tracking is a legitimate means to ease the task of teaching.

Central to the issue of fairness is the well-established link between track placements and student background characteristics. Poor and minority youngsters (principally black and Hispanic) are disproportionately placed in tracks for low-ability or non-college-bound students. By the same token, minority students are consistently underrepresented in programs for the gifted and talented. In addition, differentiation by race and class occurs within vocational tracks, with blacks and Hispanics more frequently enrolled in programs that train students for the lowest-level occupations (e.g., building maintenance, commercial sewing, and institutional care). These differences in placement by race and social class appear regardless of whether test scores, counselor and teacher recommendations, or student and parent choices are used as the basis for placement.[6]

Even if these track placements are ostensibly based on merit—that is, determined by prior school achievement rather than by race, class, or student choice—they usually come to signify judgments about supposedly fixed abilities. We might find appropriate the disproportionate placements of poor and minority students in low-track classes if these youngsters were, in fact, known to be innately less capable of learning than middle- and upper-middle-class whites. But that is not the case. Or we might think of these track placements as appropriate *if* they served to remediate the obvious educational deficiencies that many poor and minority students exhibit. If being in a low track prepared disadvantaged students for success in higher tracks and opened future educational opportunities to them, we would not question the need for tracking. However, this rarely happens.

The assumption that tracking makes teaching easier pales in importance when held up against the abundant evidence of the general ineffectiveness of tracking and the disproportionate harm it works on poor and minority students. But even if this were not the case, the assumption that tracking makes teaching easier would stand up *only if* the tracks were made up of truly homogeneous groups. In fact, they are not. Even within tracks, the variability of students' learning speed, cognitive style, interest, effort, and aptitude for various tasks is often considerable. Tracking simply masks the fact that instruction for any group of 20 to 35 people requires considerable variety in instructional strategies, tasks, materials, feedback, and guidance. It also requires multiple criteria for success and a variety of rewards. Unfortunately, for many schools and teachers, tracking deflects attention from these instructional realities. When instruction fails, the problem is too often attributed to the child or perhaps to a "wrong placement." The fact that tracking *may* make teaching easier for some teachers should not cloud our judgment about whether that teaching is best for any group of students—whatever their abilities.

Finally, a profound ethical concern emerges from all the above. In the words of educational philosopher Gary Fenstermacher, "[U]sing individual differences in aptitude, ability, or interest as the basis for curricular variation denies students equal access to the knowledge and understanding available to humankind." He continues, "[I]t is possible that some students may not benefit equally from unrestricted access to knowledge, but this fact does not entitle us to control access in ways that effectively prohibit all students from encountering what Dewey called 'the funded capital of civilization.'"[7] Surely educators do not intend any such unfairness when by tracking they seek to accommodate differences among students.

## WHY SUCH DISAPPOINTING EFFECTS?

As those of us who were working with John Goodlad on A Study of Schooling began to analyze the extensive set of data we had gathered about 38 schools across the U.S., we wanted to find out more about tracking.[8] We wanted to gather specific information about the knowledge and skills that students were taught in tracked classes, about the learning activities they experienced, about the ways in which teachers managed instruction, about the classroom relationships, and about how involved students were in their learning. By studying tracked classes directly and asking over and over whether such classes differed, we hoped to begin to understand why the effects of tracking have been so disappointing for so many students. We wanted to be able to raise some reasonable hypotheses about the ways in which the good intentions of practitioners seem to go wrong.

We selected a representative group of 300 English and mathematics classes. We chose those subjects because they are most often tracked and because nearly all secondary students take them. Our sample included relatively equal numbers of high-, average-, low-, and mixed-ability groups. We had a great deal of information about these classes because teachers and students had completed extensive questionaires, teachers had been interviewed, and teachers had put together packages of materials about their classes, including lists of the topics and skills they taught, the textbooks they used, and the ways in which the evaluated student learning. Many teachers also gave us sample lesson plans, worksheets, and tests. Trained observers recorded what students and teachers were doing and documented their interactions.

The data gathered on these classes provided some clear and consistent insights. In the three areas we studied—curriculum content, instructional quality, and classroom climate—we found remarkable and disturbing differences between classes in different tracks. These included important discrepancies in student access to knowledge, in their classroom instructional opportunities, and in their classroom learning environments.

### Access to Knowledge

In both English and math classes, we found that students had access to considerably different types of knowledge and had opportunities to develop quite different intellectual skills. For example, students in high-track English classes were exposed to content that can be called "high-status knowledge." This included topics and skills that are required for college. High-track students studied both classic and modern fiction. They learned the characteristics of literary genres and analyzed the elements of good narrative writing. These students were expected to write thematic essays and reports of library research, and they learned vocabulary that would boost their scores on college entrance exams. It was the high-track students in our sample who had the most opportunities to think critically or to solve interesting problems.

Low-track English classes, on the other hand, rarely, if ever, encountered similar types of knowledge. Nor were they expected to learn the same skills. Instruction in basic reading skills held a prominent place in low-track classes, and these skills were taught mostly through workbooks, kits, and "young adult" fiction. Students wrote simple paragraphs, completed worksheets on English usage, and practiced filling out applications for jobs and other kinds of forms. Their learning tasks were largely restricted to memorization or low-level comprehension.

The differences in mathematics content followed much the same pattern. High-track classes focused primarily on mathematical concepts; low-track classes stressed basic computational skills and math facts.

These differences are not merely curricular adaptations to individual needs, though they are certainly thought of as such. Differences in access to knowledge have important long-term social and educational consequences as well. For example, low-track students are probably prevented from *ever* encountering at school the knowledge our society values most. Much of the curriculum of low-track classes was likely to lock students into a continuing series of such bottom-level placements because important concepts and skills were neglected. Thus these students were denied the knowledge that would enable them to move successfully into higher-track classes.

## Opportunities to Learn

We also looked at two classroom conditions known to influence how much students will learn: instructional time and teaching quality. The marked differences we found in our data consistently showed that students in higher tracks had better classroom opportunities. For example, all our data on classroom time pointed to the same conclusion: students in high tracks get more; students in low tracks get less. Teachers of high-track classes set aside more class time for learning, and our observers found that more actual class time was spent on learning activities. High-track students were also expected to spend more time doing homework, fewer high-track students were observed to be off-task during class activities, and more of them told us that learning took up most of their class time, rather than discipline problems, socializing, or class routines.

Instruction in high-track classes more often included a whole range of teacher behav-iors likely to enhance learning. High-track teachers were more enthusiastic, and their instruction was clearer. They used strong criticism or ridicule less frequently than did teachers of low-track classes. Classroom tasks were more various and more highly organized in high-track classes, and grades were more relevant to student learning.

These differences in learning opportunities portray a fundamental irony of schooling: those students who need more time to learn appear to be getting less; those students who have the most difficulty learning are being exposed least to the sort of teaching that best facilitates learning.

## Classroom Climate

We were interested in studying classroom climates in various tracks because we were convinced that supportive relationships and positive feelings in class are more than just nice accompaniments to learning. When teachers and students trust one another, classroom time and energy are freed for teaching and learning. Without this trust, students spend a great deal of time and energy establishing less productive relationships with others and interfering with the teacher's instructional agenda; teachers spend their time and energy trying to maintain control. In such classes, less learning is likely to occur.

The data from A Study of Schooling permitted us to investigate three important aspects of classroom environments: relationships between teachers and students, relationships among the students themselves, and the intensity of student involvement in learning. Once again, we discovered a distressing pattern of advantages for high-track classes and disadvantages for low-track classes. In high-track classes students thought that their teachers were more concerned about them and less punitive. Teachers in high-track classes spent less time on student behavior, and they more often encouraged their students to become independent, questioning, critical thinkers. In low-track classes teachers were seen as less concerned and more punitive. Teachers in low-track classes emphasized matters of discipline and behavior, and they often listed such things as "following directions," "respecting my position," "punctuality," and "learning to take a direct order" as among the five most important things they wanted their class to learn during the year.

We found similar differences in the relationships that students established with one another in class. Students in low-track classes agreed far more often that "students in this class are unfriendly to me" or that "I often feel left out of class activities." They said that their classes were interrupted by problems and by arguing in class. Generally, they seemed to like each other less. Not surprisingly, given these differences in relationships, students in high-track classes appeared to be much more involved in their classswork. Students in low-track classes were more apathetic and indicated more often that they didn't care about what went on or that failing didn't bother most of their classmates.

In these data, we found once again a pattern of classroom experience that seems to enhance the possibilities of learning for those students already disposed to do well—that is, those in high-track classes. We saw even more clearly a pattern of classroom experience likely to inhibit the learning of those in the bottom tracks. As with access to knowledge and opportunities to learn, we found that those who most needed support from a positive, nurturing environment got the least.

Although these data do show clear instructional advantages for high-achieving students and clear disadvantages for their low-achieving peers, other data from our work suggest that the quality of the experience of *average* students falls somewhere between these two extremes. Average students, too, were deprived of the best circumstances

schools have to offer, though their classes were typically more like those of high-track students. Taken together, these findings begin to suggest *why* students who are not in the top tracks are likely to suffer because of their placements: their education is of considerably lower quality.

It would be a serious mistake to interpret these data as the "inevitable" outcome of the differences in the students who populate the various tracks. Many of the mixed-ability classes in our study showed that high-quality experiences are very possible in classes that include all types of students. But neither should we attribute these differences to consciously mean-spirited or blatantly discriminatory actions by schoolpeople. Obviously, the content teachers decide to teach and the ways in which they teach it are greatly influenced by the students with whom they interact. And it is unlikely that students are passive participants in tracking processes. It seems more likely that students' achievements, attitudes, interests, perceptions of themselves, and behaviors (growing increasingly disparate over time) help produce some of the effects of tracking. Thus groups of students who, by conventional wisdom, seem less able and less eager to learn are very likely to affect a teacher's ability or even willingness to provide the best possible learning opportunities. The obvious conclusion about the effects of these track-specific differences on the ability of the schools to achieve academic excellence is that students who are exposed to less content and lower-quality teaching are unlikely to get the full benefit out of their schooling. Yet this less-fruitful experience seems to be the norm when average- and low-achieving students are grouped together for instruction.

I believe that these data reveal frightening patterns of curricular inequality. Although these patterns would be disturbing under any circumstances (and though many white, suburban schools consign a good number of their students to mediocre experiences in low-ability and general-track classes), they become particularly distressing in light of the prevailing pattern of placing disproportionate numbers of poor and minority students in the lowest-track classes. A self-fulfilling prophecy can be seen to work at the institutional level to prevent schools from providing equal educational opportunity. Tracking appears to teach and reinforce the notion that those not defined as the best are *expected* to do less well. Few students and teachers can defy those expectations.

## TRACKING, EQUALITY, AND EXCELLENCE

Tracking is assumed to promote educational excellence because it enables schools to provide students with the curriculum and instruction they need to maximize their potential and achieve excellence on their own terms. But the evidence about tracking suggests the contrary. Certainly students bring differences with them to school, but, by tracking, schools help to widen rather than narrow these differences. Students who are judged to be different from one another are separated into different classes and then provided knowledge, opportunities to learn, and classroom environments that are vastly different. Many of the students in top tracks (only about 40% of high-schoolers) do benefit from the advantages they receive in their classes. But, in their quest for higher standards and superior academic performance, schools seem to have locked themselves into a structure that may *unnecessarily* buy the achievement of a few at the expense of many. Such a structure provides but a shaky foundation for excellence.

At the same time, the evidence about tracking calls into question the widely held view that schools provide students who have the "right stuff" with a neutral environment in which they can rise to the top (with "special" classes providing an extra boost to those who might need it). Everywhere we turn we find that the differentiated structure of schools throws up barriers to achievement for poor and minority students. Measures of talent clearly seem to work against them, which leads to their disproportionate placement in groups identified as slow. Once there, their achievement seems to be further inhibited by the type of knowledge they are taught and by the quality of the learning opportunities they are afforded. Moreover, the social and psychological dimensions of classes at the bottom of the hierarchy of schooling seem to restrict their chances for school success even further.

Good intentions, including those of advocates of "excellence" and of "equity," characterize the rhetoric of schooling. Tracking, because it is usually taken to be a neutral practice and a part of the mechanics of schooling, has escaped the attention of those who mean well. But by failing to scrutinize the effects of tracking, schools unwittingly subvert their well-meant efforts to promote academic excellence and to provide conditions that will enable all students to achieve it.

## ENDNOTES

1. Some recent reviews of studies on the effects of tracking include: Robert C. Calfee and Roger Brown, "Grouping Students for Instruction," in *Classroom Management* (Chicago: 78th Yearbook of the National Society for the Study of Education, University of Chicago Press, 1979); Dominick Esposito, "Homogeneous and Heterogeneous Ability gouping: Principal Findings and Implications for Evaluating and Designing More Effective Educational Environments," *Review of Educational Research,* vol. 43, 1973, pp. 163–79; Jeannie Oakes, "Tracking: A Contextual Perspective on How Schools Structure Differences," *Education Psychologist,* in press; Caroline H. Persell, *Education and Inequality: The Roots and Results of Statification in Ameri-*

*can's Schools* (New York: Free Press, 1977); and James E. Rosenbaum, "The Social Implications of Educational Grouping," in David C. Berliner, ed., *Review of Research in Education, Vol. 8* (Washington, D.C.: American Educational Research Association, 1980), pp. 361–401.

2. James E. Rosenbaum, *Making Inequality: The Hidden Curriculm of High School Tracking* (New York: Wiley, 1976).

3. See, for example, David Stern et al., *One Million Hours a Day: Vocational Education in California Public Secondary Schools* (Berkeley: Report to the California Policy Seminar, University of California School of Education, 1985).

4. Rosenbaum, "The Social Implications..." and William E. Shafer and Carol Olexa, *Tracking and Opportunity* (Scranton, Pa.: Chandler, 1971).

5. Karl A. and Edward L. McDill, "Selection and Allocation Within Schools: Some Causes and Consequences of Curriculum Place-ment," *American Sociological Review,* vol. 41, 1976, pp. 969–80; Karl A. Alexander, Martha Cook, and Edward L. McDill, "Curriculum Tracking and Educational Stratification: Some Further Evidence," *American Sociological Review*, vol. 43, 1978, pp. 47–66; and Donald A. Rock et al., *Study of Excellence in High School Education: Longitudinal Study, 1980–82* (Princeton, NJ.: Educational Testing Service, Final Report, 1985).

6. Persell, *Education and Inequality...*; and Jeannie Oakes, *Keeping Track: How Schools Structure Inequality* (New Haven, Conn.: Yale University Press, 1985).

7. Gary D Fenstermacher, "Introduction," in Gary D Fenstermacher and John I. Goodlad, eds., *Individual Differences and the Common Curriculum* (Chicago: 82nd Yearbook of the National Society for the Study of Education, University of Chicago Press. 1983), p. 3.

8. John I. Goodlad, *A Place Called School* (New York: McGraw-Hill, 1984).

# Social Class Differences in Family-School Relationships: The Importance of Cultural Capital

## ANNETTE LAREAU

The influence of family background on children's educational experiences has a curious place within the field of sociology of education. On the one hand, the issue has dominated the field. Wielding increasingly sophisticated methodological tools, social scientists have worked to document, elaborate, and replicate the influence of family background on educational life chances (Jencks et al. 1972; Marjoribanks 1979). On the other hand, until recently, research on this issue focused primarily on educational *outcomes;* very little attention was given to the *processes* through which these educational patterns are created and reproduced.

Over the past fifteen years, important strides have been made in our understanding of social processes inside the school. Ethnographic research has shown that classroom learning is reflexive and interactive and that language in the classroom draws unevenly from the sociolinguistic experiences of children at home (Bernstein 1975, 1982; Cook-Gumperez 1973; Heath 1982, 1983; Labov 1972; Diaz, Moll, and Mehan 1986; Mehan and Griffin 1980). Studies of the curriculum, the hidden curriculum, the social organization of the classroom, and the authority relationships between teachers and students have also suggested ways in which school processes contribute to social reproduction (Aggleton and Whitty 1985; Anyon 1981; Apple 1979; Erickson and Mohatt 1982; Gearing and Epstein 1982; Gaskell 1985; Taylor 1984; Valli 1985; Wilcox 1977, 1982).

Surprisingly, relatively little of this research has focused on parental involvement in schooling. Yet, quantitative studies suggest that parental behavior can be a crucial determinant of educational performance (Epstein 1984; Marjoribanks 1979). In addition, increasing parental participation in education has become a priority for educators, who believe it promotes educational achievement (Berger 1983; Seeley 1984; National Education Association 1985; Robinson 1985; Trelease 1982; Leichter 1979).

Those studies that have examined parental involvement in education generally take one of three major conceptual approaches to understanding variations in levels of parental participation. Some researchers subscribe to the culture-of-poverty thesis, which states that lower-class culture has distinct values and forms of social organization. Although their interpretations vary, most of these researchers suggest that lower-class and working-class families do not value education as highly as middle-class families (Deutsch 1967). Other analysts trace unequal levels of parental involvement in schooling back to the educational institutions themselves. Some accuse schools of institutional discrimination, claiming that they make middle-class families feel more welcome than working-class and lower-class families (Lightfoot 1978; Ogbu 1974). In an Australian study of home-school relationships, for example, Connell et al. (1982) argue that working-class parents are "frozen out" of schools.

*Source: Sociology of Education* (April 1987): 73–85. Reprinted by permission of the American Sociological Association.

Others maintain that institutional differentiation, particularly the role of teacher leadership, is a critical determinant of parental involvement in schooling (Epstein and Becker 1982; Becker and Epstein 1982).

A third perspective for understanding varying levels of parental involvement in schooling draws on the work of Bourdieu and the concept of cultural capital. Bourdieu (1977a, 1977b; Bourdieu and Passeron 1977) argues that schools draw unevenly on the social and cultural resources of members of the society. For example, schools utilize particular linguistic structures, authority patterns, and types of curricula; children from higher social locations enter schools already familiar with these social arrangements. Bourdieu maintains that the cultural experiences in the home facilitate children's adjustment to school and academic achievement, thereby transforming cultural resources into what he calls cultural capital (Bourdieu 1977a, 1977b).

This perspective points to the structure of schooling and to family life and the dispositions of individuals (what Bourdieu calls habitus [1977b, 1981]) to understand different levels of parental participation in schooling. The standards of schools are not neutral; their requests for parental involvement may be laden with the social and cultural experiences of intellectual and economic elites. Bourdieu does not examine the question of parental participation in schooling, but his analysis points to the importance of class and class cultures in facilitating or impeding children's (or parents') negotiation of the process of schooling (also see Baker and Stevenson 1986; Connell et al. 1982; Joffee 1977; Ogbu 1974; Rist 1978; McPherson 1972; Gracey 1972; Wilcox 1977, 1982).

In this paper I argue that class-related cultural factors shape parents' compliance with teachers' requests for parental participation in schooling. I pose two major questions. First, what do schools ask of parents in the educational experience of young children?

Are there important variations in teachers' expectations of parental involvement in elementary schooling? Second, how do parents respond to schools' requests? In particular, how does social class influence the process through which parents participate in their children's schooling? The analysis and conclusions are based on an intensive study of home-school relationships of children in the first and second grades of a white working-class school and an upper-middle-class school.

I begin the discussion with a very brief review of historical variations in home-school relationships. Then, I describe the research sites and methodology. In the third section, I examine teachers' views of family involvement in schooling. This is followed by a description of family-school interactions in the working-class and middle-class communities. Finally, I analyze the factors contributing to social class variations in home-school relationships and review the implications for future research.

## HISTORICAL VARIATIONS IN FAMILY-SCHOOL RELATIONSHIPS

Families and schools are dynamic institutions: both have changed markedly in the last two centuries. Not surprisingly, family-school interactions have shifted as well. Over time, there has been a steady increase in the level of parental involvement in schooling. At least three major stages of family-school interaction can be identified. In the first period, parents in rural areas provided food and shelter for the teacher. Children's education and family life were intertwined, although parents evidently were not involved in the formal aspects of other children's cognitive development (Overstreet and Overstreet 1949). In the second period, marked by the rise of mass schooling, parents provided political and economic support for the selection and maintenance of school sites.

Parents were involved in school activities and classroom activities, but again, they were not fundamentally involved in their children's cognitive development (Butterworth 1928; Hymes 1953; National Congress of Parents and Teachers 1944). In the third and current period, parents have increased their efforts to reinforce the curriculum and promote cognitive development at home. In addition, parents have played a growing role in monitoring their children's educational development, particularly in special education programs, and have moved into the classroom as volunteers (Berger 1983; Levy, Meltsner, and Wildavsky 1974; Mehan, Hertweck, and Meihls 1986).

These changes in family-school interactions do not represent a linear progression. Nor is there only one form of relationship at any given time. Many factors—e.g., parents' educational attainment, the amount of nonwork time parents can invest in their children's schooling—affect the kind and degree of parental involvement. Family-school relationships are socially constructed and are historically variable. Homeschool partnerships, in which parents are involved in the cognitive development of their children, currently seem to be the dominant model, but there are many possible types of family-school relationships (Baker and Stevenson 1986). As in other social relationships, family-school interactions carry the imprint of the larger social context: Acceptance of a particular type of family-school relationship emerges as the result of social processes.

These aspects of family-school relationships are routinely neglected in social scientists' discussions of parental involvement (Epstein 1983, 1984; Seeley 1984). When home-school relationships are evaluated exclusively in terms of parental behavior, critical questions are neither asked nor answered. The standards of the schools must be viewed as problematic, and further, the researcher must ask what kinds of social resources are useful in complying with these standards.

## RESEARCH METHODOLOGY

The research presented here involved participant-observation of two first-grade classrooms located in two different communities. Also, in-depth interviews of parents, teachers, and principals were conducted while the children were in first and second grade. Following other studies of social class differences in family life (Rubin 1976; Kohn 1977), I chose a white working-class community and a professional middle-class community. I sought a working-class community in which a majority of the parents were high school graduates or dropouts, employed in skilled or semiskilled occupations, paid an hourly wage, and periodically unemployed. For the professional middle-class school, I sought a community in which a majority of the parents were college graduates and professionals who had strong career opportunities and who were less vulnerable to changes in the economy. The two communities described here met these criteria.

Colton School (fictitious name) is located in a working-class community. Most of the parents of Colton students are employed in semiskilled or unskilled occupations (see Table 1). School personnel report that most of

**TABLE 1**
**The Percentages of Parents in Each Occupational Category, by School**

| Occupation | Colton | Prescott |
|---|---|---|
| Professionals, executives, managers | 1 | 60 |
| Semiprofessionals, sales, clerical workers, and technicians | 11 | 30 |
| Skilled and semiskilled workers | 51 | 9 |
| Unskilled workers (and welfare recipients) | 23 | 1 |
| Unknown | 20 | — |

*Source:* California Department of Education 1983.
*Note:* The figures for Prescott school are based on the principal's estimation of the school population.

the parents have a high school education; many are high school dropouts. The school has about 450 students in kindergarten, first grade, and second grade. Slightly over one half of the children are white, one third are Hispanic, and the remainder are black or Asian, especially recent Vietnamese immigrants. About one half of the children qualify for free lunches under federal guidelines.

Prescott School (fictitious name) is in an upper-middle-class suburban community about 30 minutes from Colton. Most of the parents of Prescott students are professionals (Table 1). Both parents in the family are likely to be college graduates, and many of the children's fathers have advanced degrees. The school enrolls about 300 students from kindergarten to fifth grade. Virtually all the students are white, and the school does not offer a lunch program, although the Parents' Club sponsors a Hot Dog Day once a month.

For a six-month period, January to June 1982, I visited one first-grade classroom at each school. My visits averaged once or twice a week per school and lasted around two hours. During this time, I observed the classroom and acted as a volunteer in the class, passing out paper and helping the children with math and spelling problems.

At the end of the school year, I selected six children in each class for further study. The children were selected on the basis of reading-group membership; a boy and a girl were selected from the high, medium, and low reading groups. To prevent the confounding effects of race, I chose only white children. I interviewed one single mother in each school; the remaining households had two parents. In both of the schools, three of the mothers worked full time or part time, and three were at home full time. All of the Colton mothers, however, had worked in recent years, when their children were younger. The Prescott mothers had worked prior to the birth of their children but had not been in the labor force since that time.

When the children finished first grade, I interviewed their mothers individually. When they finished second grade, I interviewed their mothers for a second time, and in separate sessions, I interviewed most of their fathers. I also interviewed the first- and second-grade teachers, the school principals, and a resource specialist at one of the schools. All the interviews were semistructured and lasted about two hours. The interviews were tape recorded, and all participants were promised confidentiality.

## TEACHERS' REQUESTS FOR PARENTAL INVOLVEMENT

The research examined the formal requests from the teachers and school administrators asking parents to participate in schooling, particularly surrounding the issue of achievement. It also studied the quality of interaction between teachers and parents on the school site. Although there were some variations among the teachers in their utilization of parents in the classrooms, all promoted parental involvement and all believed there was a strong relationship between parental involvement (particularly reading to children) and academic performance. At both schools, the definition of the ideal family-school relationship was the same: a partnership in which family life and school life are integrated.

In the course of the school year, teachers in both schools actively promoted parental involvement in schooling in several ways. For example, newsletters were used to notify families of school events and to invite them to attend. Teachers also reminded children verbally about school events to which parents had been invited and encouraged the children to bring their parents to classroom and schoolwide events.

In their interactions with parents, educators urged parents to read to their children.

The principal at Prescott school, for example, told the parents at Back to School Night that they should consider reading the child's homework. In every class at Colton school, there was a Read at Home Program, in which the teacher kept track of the number of hours a child read to an adult at home or was read to by a sibling or adult. A chart posted in the classroom marked hours of reading in 15-minute intervals. A child could choose a free book after eight hours of reading at home. This emphasis on reading also surfaced in the routine interactions between parents and teachers and between teachers and children. In the classroom, the teachers suggested that children check out library books, read to their parents, or have their parents read to them at home. At parent-teacher conferences, teachers suggested that parents read to their child at home. In one 20-minute parent-teacher conference, for example, the teacher mentioned five times the importance of reading to the child at home.

Other requests of parents were made as well. Teachers encouraged parents to communicate any concerns they had about their child. In their meetings with parents, teachers also expressed a desire for parents to review and reinforce the material learned in class (e.g., to help their children learn their spelling words). Generally, teachers at both schools believed that the relationship between parental involvement and academic performance was important, and they used a variety of approaches to encourage parents to participate in education.

Teachers and administrators spoke of being "partners" with parents, and they stressed the need to maintain good communication, but it was clear that they desired parents to defer to their professional expertise. For example, a first-grade teacher at Prescott did not believe in assigning homework to the children and did not appreciate parents communicating their displeasure with the policy by complaining repeatedly to the principal. Nor did principals welcome parents' opinions that a teacher was a bad teacher and should be fired. Teachers wanted parents to support them, or as they put it, to "back them up."

Although generally persuaded that parental involvement was positive for educational growth, some teachers, particularly in the upper-middle-class school, were ambivalent about some types of parental involvement in schooling. The Prescott teachers were very concerned that some parents placed too much pressure on their children. Parental involvement could become counterproductive when it increased the child's anxiety level and produced negative learning experiences. As one Prescott teacher put it,

> It depends on the parent. Sometimes it can be helpful, sometimes it creates too much pressure. Sometimes they learn things wrong. It is better for them to leave the basics alone…and take them to museums, do science, and other enrichment activities.

As Becker and Epstein (1982) have found, there was some variation among the teachers in the degree to which they took leadership roles in promoting parental involvement in schooling, particularly in the area of classroom volunteers. Although all the teachers in the study requested parents to volunteer and had parents in the classroom, there were other teachers in the school who used parents more extensively. Teachers also varied in how they judged parents. While the extreme cases were clear, the teachers sometimes disagreed about how supportive parents were or about how much pressure they were putting on their children. For example, the first-grade teacher at Prescott thought one boy's father placed too much pressure on him, but the second-grade teacher judged the family to be supportive and helpful. Thus, there were variations in teachers' styles as well as in the way they implemented the model of home-school partnerships.

This study does not, however, support the thesis that the different levels of parental involvement can be traced to institutional differentiation or institutional discrimination, i.e., to teachers' pursuit of different kinds of relationships with working-class and middle-class families (Connell et al. 1982; Epstein and Becker 1982). All of the first- and second-grade teachers in the study made similar requests to parents. In both schools, teachers made clear and repeated efforts to promote parental involvement in the educational process.

## Educational Consequences of Family-School Relationships

Parents who agreed with the administrators' and teachers' definition of partnership appeared to offer an educational advantage to their children; parents who turned over the responsibility of education to the professional could negatively affect their child's schooling.

Teachers' methods of presenting, teaching, and assessing subject matter were based on a structure that presumed parents would help children at home. At Colton, for example, spelling words were given out on Monday and students were repeatedly encouraged to practice the words at home with their parents before the test on Friday. Teachers noticed which children had practiced at home and which children had not and believed it influenced their performance.

This help at home was particularly important for low achievers. At Prescott, teachers encouraged parents of low achievers to work with them at home. In one case, a girl missed her spelling lessons because she had to meet with the reading resource teacher. Rather than fall behind in spelling, she and her mother did her spelling at home through most of the year. Colton teachers also tried to involve parents in the education of low achievers. One Colton teacher arranged a special conference at a student's home and requested that the parents urge the student to practice reading at home. The teacher complained that the girl didn't "get that much help at home." The teacher believed that if the parents had taken an active role in schooling, the child would have been promoted rather than retained.

In other instances, the initiative to help children at home came from parents. For example, at Prescott, one mother noticed while volunteering in the classroom that her son was somewhat behind in his spelling. At her request, she and her son worked on his spelling every day after school for about a month, until he had advanced to the lesson that most of the class was on. Prior to the mother's actions, the boy was in the bottom third of the class in spelling. He was not, however, failing spelling, and it was unlikely that the teacher would have requested the parent to take an active role. After the mother and son worked at home, he was in the top third of the class in his spelling work. The teacher was very impressed by these efforts and believed that the mother's active involvement in schooling had a positive effect on her son's performance:

> She is very supportive, very committed. If she didn't work in the class [volunteering] her boys wouldn't do too well. They are not brilliant at all. But they are going to do well. She is just going to see that they are going to get a good foundation. A child like that would flounder if you let him.

Not all parental involvement in schooling was so positive, however. There is a dark side to the partnership, which is not usually addressed in the literature aimed at increasing parental participation in education (Epstein and Becker 1982; Seeley 1984). Particularly in the upper-middle-class school, teachers complained of the pressure parents placed on teachers and children for academic performance. One mother reported that her son had been stealing small objects early in first grade, a pattern the pediatrician and the mother attributed to the boy's "frustration level" in schooling. A girl in the lowest reading group began developing stomach aches during the reading period in first grade. Teachers at Prescott mentioned numerous cases in which parental involvement was unhelpful. In these cases, parents had usually challenged the professional expertise of the teachers.

Generally, however, the teachers believed that the relationship between parental participation and school performance was positive. These results provide indications that teachers take *parental performance* in schooling very seriously. Teachers recall which parents participate and which parents fail to participate in schooling. They believe that their requests of parents are reasonable and that all parents, regardless of social position, can help their children in first and second grade.

## PARENTS' INVOLVEMENT IN SCHOOLING

Although teachers at both schools expressed a desire for parental participation in schooling, the amount of contact varied significantly between the sites. The response of parents to teachers' requests was much higher at the upper-middle-class school than at the working-class school.

### Attendance at School Events

As Table 2 shows, the level of attendance at formal school events was significantly higher at Prescott than at Colton. Virtually all Prescott parents attended the parent-teacher conferences in the fall and spring, but only 60 percent of Colton parents attended. Attendance at Open House was almost three times higher at Prescott than at Colton.

**TABLE 2**

**Percentage of Parents Participating in School Activities, by School, First Grade Only, 1981–1982**

| Activity | Colton ($n = 34$) | Prescott ($n = 28$) |
|---|---|---|
| Parent-teacher conferences | 60 | 100 |
| Open house | 35 | 96 |
| Volunteering in classroom | 3 | 43 |

The difference between the two schools was apparent not only in the quantity of interaction but in the quality of interaction. Although teachers at both schools asked parents to communicate any concerns they had about their children, Colton parents rarely initiated contact with teachers. When Colton parents did contact the school, they frequently raised nonacademic issues, such as lunchboxes, bus schedules, and playground activities. One of the biggest complaints, for example, was that children had only 15 minutes to eat lunch and that slower eaters were often unable to finish.

At Colton, the interactions between parents and teachers were stiff and awkward. The parents often showed signs of discomfort: nervous shifting, blushing, stuttering, sweating, and generally looking ill at ease. During the Open House, parents wandered around the room looking at the children's pictures. Many of the parents did not speak with the teacher during their visit. When they did, the interaction tended to be short, rather formal, and serious. The teacher asked the parents if they had seen all of their children's work, and she checked to see that all of the children had shown their desk and folder of papers to their parents. The classrooms at Colton often contained only about 10 adults at a time, and the rooms were noticeably quiet.

At Prescott, the interactions between parents and teachers were more frequent, more centered around academic matters, and much less formal. Parents often wrote notes to the teacher, telephoned the teacher at school, or dropped by during the day to discuss a problem. These interactions often centered around the child's academic progress; many Prescott parents monitored their children's education and requested additional resources for them if there were problems. Parents, for example, asked that children be signed up to see the reading resource teacher, be tested by the school psychologist, or be enrolled in the gifted program. Parents also asked for homework for their children or for materials that they could complete at home with their children.

The ease with which Prescott parents contacted the school was also apparent at formal school events. At the Open House, almost all of the parents talked to the teacher or to the teacher's aide; these conversations were often long and were punctuated by jokes and questions. Also, many of the parents were friends with other parents in the class, so there was quite a bit of interaction between families. In inviting me to the Open House, the teacher described the event as a "cocktail party without cocktails." The room did indeed have the noisy, crowded, and animated atmosphere of a cocktail party.

In sum, Colton parents were reluctant to contact the school, tended to intervene over nonacademic matters, and were uncomfortable in their interactions in the school. In contrast, although Prescott parents varied in the level of supervision and scrutiny they gave their child's schooling, they frequently contacted teachers to discuss their child's academic progress.

Parents' attendance at school activities and their contact with teachers enabled the teachers to directly assess parents' compliance with requests for involvement. However, Prescott teachers had difficulty estimating the number of children whose parents read to them at home regularly. The teachers believed that a majority of children were read to several

times per week and that many children spent time reading to themselves. Among the six families interviewed, all of the parents said that they read to their children almost every day, usually before bedtime. Colton teachers used the Read at Home Program to evaluate the amount of reading that took place at home. During the participant- observation period, only three or four children in the class of 34 brought back slips every day or every few days demonstrating that they had read at home for it least 15 minutes. Some children checked out books and brought back slips less frequently. The majority of the class earned only two books in the program, indicating that they had read at home an average of 16 hours during the 180 days of school, or between two and four minutes a day.

The Read at Home Program was actively promoted by Colton teachers. Children were brought to the front of the class for applause every time they earned a book, and the teachers encouraged children to check out books and read at home. Nevertheless, in the interviews, only half of the parents said that they read to their children every day; the remainder read to their children much more irregularly. Colton parents clearly did not read to their children as often as the upper-middle-class parents at Prescott.

In addition, Prescott parents played a more active role in reinforcing and monitoring the school work of their children. Colton parents were asked by teachers to help review and reinforce the material at school, particularly spelling words. Though a few parents worked with their children, Colton teachers were disappointed in the response. Colton parents were also unfamiliar with the school's curriculum and with the specific educational problems of their children. Parents of children with learning disabilities, for example, knew only that their children's grades "weren't up to par" or that their children "didn't do too well" in school. Moreover these parents were unaware of the teacher's specific efforts to improve their child's performance.

Prescott parents, on the other hand, carefully followed their children's curriculum. They often showed children the practical applications of the knowledge they gained at school, made up games that strengthened and elaborated children's recently acquired knowledge, and reviewed the material presented in class with their children. Parents of low achievers and children with learning problems were particularly vigorous in these efforts and made daily efforts to work with children at home. Parents knew their child's specific problems and knew what the teacher was doing to strengthen their child's performance. Parents' efforts on behalf of their children were closely coordinated with the school program.

There were some variations in parents' response to teachers' requests in the two school communities. Notably, two of the Colton parents (who appeared to be upwardly mobile) actively read to their children at home, closely reviewed their children's school work, and emphasized the importance of educational success. The teachers were very impressed by the behavior of these parents and by the relatively high academic performance of their children. At Prescott, parents differed in how critically they assessed the school and in their propensity to intervene in their children's schooling. For example, some parents said that they "felt sorry for teachers" and believed that other parents in the community were too demanding. The child's number of siblings, birth order, and temperament also shaped parental intervention in schooling. There was some variation in the role of fathers, although in both schools, mothers had the primary responsibility for schooling.

There were important differences, then, in the way in which Colton and Prescott parents responded to teachers' requests for participation. These patterns suggest that the relationship between families and schools was *independent* in the working-class school, and *interdependent* in the middle-class school.

## FACTORS STRUCTURING PARENTS' PARTICIPATION

Interviews and observations of parents suggested that a variety of factors influenced parents' participation in schooling. Parents' educational capabilities, their view of the appropriate division of labor between teachers and parents, the information they had about their children's schooling, and the time, money, and other material resources available in the home all mediated parents' involvement in schooling

### Educational Capabilities

Parents at Colton and Prescott had different levels of educational attainment. Most Colton parents were high school graduates or high school dropouts. Most were married and had their first child shortly after high school. They generally had difficulties in school as children; several of the fathers, for example, had been held back in elementary school. In interviews, they expressed doubts about their educational capabilities and indicated that they depended on the teacher to educate their children. As one mother stated,

> I know that when she gets into the higher grades, I know I won't be able to help her, math especially, unless I take a refresher course myself.... So I feel that it is the teacher's job to help her as much as possible to understand it, because I know that I won't be able to.

Another mother, commenting on her overall lack of educational skills, remarked that reading preschool books to her young son had improved her reading skills:

I graduated from high school and could fill out [job] applications, but when I was nineteen and married my husband, I didn't know how to look up a word in the dictionary. When I started reading to Johnny, I found that *my* reading improved.

Observations of Colton parents at the school site and in interviews confirmed that parents' educational skills were often wanting. Prescott parents' educational skills, on the other hand, were strong. Most were college graduates and many had advanced degrees.

Parents in the two communities also divided up the responsibility between home and school in different ways. Colton parents regarded teachers as "educated people." They turned over the responsibility for education to the teacher, whom they viewed as a professional. As one mother put it,

My job is here at home. My job is to raise him, to teach him manners, get him dressed and get him to school, to make sure that he is happy. Now her [the teacher's] part, the school's part, is to teach him to learn. Hopefully, someday he'll be able to use all of that. That is what I think is their part, to teach him to read, the writing, any kind of schooling.

Education is seen as a discrete process that takes place on the school grounds, under the direction of a teacher. This mother's role is to get her son to school; once there, his teacher will "teach him to learn."

This mother was aware that her son's teacher wanted him to practice reading at home, but neither she nor her husband read to their son regularly. The mother's view of reading was analogous to her view of work. She sent her children to school to learn for six hours a day and expected that they could leave their schooling (i.e., their work) behind them at the school site, unless they had been given homework. She believed that her seven-year-old boy's afternoons and evenings were time for him to play. In this context, her son's reading at home was similar to riding his bike or to playing with his truck. The mother did not believe that her child's academic progress depended upon his activities at home. Instead, she saw a separation of spheres.

Other parents had a different conception of their role in schooling. They believed education was a shared responsibility: They were *partners* with teachers in promoting their children's academic progress. As one mother stated,

I see the school as being a very strong instructional force, more so than we are here at home. I guess that I am comfortable with that, from what I have seen. It is a three-to-one ratio or something, where out of a possible four, he is getting three quarters of what he needs from the school, and then a quarter of it from here. Maybe it would be better if our influence was stronger, but I am afraid that in this day and age it is not possible to do any more than that even if you wanted to.

Prescott parents wanted to be involved in their child's educational process in an important way. In dividing up the responsibility for education, they described the relationship between parents and teachers as a relationship between equals, and they believed that they possessed similar or superior educational skills and prestige. One Prescott father discussed his relationship with teachers in this way:

I don't think of teachers as more educated than me or in a higher position than me. I don't have any sense of hierarchy. I am not higher than them, and they are not higher than me. We are equals. We are reciprocals. So if I have a problem I will talk to them. I have a sense of decorum. I wouldn't go busting into a classroom and say something.... They are not working for me, but they also aren't doing something I couldn't do. It is more a question of a division of labor.

Prescott parents had not only better educational skills and higher occupational status than Colton parents but also more disposable income and more flexible work schedules. These material resources entered into the family-school relationships. Some Colton mothers, for example, had to make a series of complicated arrangements for transportation and child care to attend a school event held in the middle of the afternoon. Prescott parents, on the other hand, had two cars and sufficient resources to hire babysitters and housecleaners. In addition, Prescott parents generally had much greater flexibility in their work schedules than Colton parents. Material resources also influenced the educational purchases parents made. Colton parents reported that most of the books they bought for their children came from the flea market. Prescott parents had the financial flexibility to purchase new books if they desired, and many of the parents of low achievers hired tutors for their children during the summer months.

### Information about Schooling

Colton parents had only limited information about most aspects of their children's experience at school; what they did know, they learned primarily from their children. For example, the Colton mothers knew the names of the child's teacher and the teacher's aide, the location of the classroom on the school grounds, and the name of the janitor, and they were familiar with the Read at Home Program. They did not know details of the school or of classroom interaction. The amount of information Colton parents had did not seem to vary by how much contact they had with the school.

In the middle-class community, parents had extensive information about classroom and school life. For example, in addition to knowing the names of their child's current classroom teacher and teacher's aide, the mother knew the names and academic reputations of most of the other teachers in the

school. The mothers also knew the academic rankings of children in the class (e.g., the best boy and girl in math, the best boy and girl in reading). Most of the mothers knew the composition of their child's reading group, the math and spelling packet the child was working on, and the specific academic problems to which the child was being exposed (e.g., adding single-digit numbers). Other details of the classroom experience were also widely known, including the names of children receiving the services of the reading resource specialist, occupational therapist, and special education teacher. Although a few fathers had very specific information about the school, most depended on their wives to collect and store this information. The fathers were, however, generally apprised of the reputations of teachers and the dissatisfactions that some parents had with particular teachers.

Much of the observed difference between the schools in parents' information about schooling may be traced to differences in family life, particularly in social networks and childrearing patterns. Prescott families saw relatively little of their relatives; instead, many parents socialized with other parents in the school community Colton parents generally had very close ties with relatives in the area, seeing siblings or parents three times per week or more. Colton parents had virtually no social contact with other parents in the school, even when the families lived on the same street. The social networks of the middle-class parents provided them with additional sources of information about their child's school experience; the networks of working-class parents did not (see Bott 1971; Litwack and Szeleny 1971).

The childrearing patterns of the two groups also differed, particularly in the leisure time activities they encouraged. At Colton, children's after-school activities were informal: bike riding, snake hunting, watching television, playing with neighbor children, and helping parents with younger siblings.

Prescott children were enrolled in formal socialization activities, including swimming lessons, soccer, art and crafts lessons, karate lessons, and gymnastics. All the children in the classroom were enrolled in at least one after-school activity, and many were busy every afternoon with a lesson or structured experience. The parents took their children to and from these activities. Many stayed to watch the lesson, thus providing another opportunity to meet and interact with other Prescott parents. Discussions about schools, teachers' reputations, and academic progress were frequent. For many parents, these interactions were a major source of information about their children's schooling, and parents believed that the discussions had an important effect on the way in which they approached their children's schooling.

## DISCUSSION

Teachers in both schools interpreted parental involvement as a reflection of the value parents placed on their children's educational success (see Deutsch 1967; Strodbeck 1958). As the principal at Prescott commented,

> This particular community is one with a very strong interest in its schools. It is a wonderful situation in which to work. Education is very important to the parents and they back that up with an interest in volunteering. This view that education is important helps kids as well. If parents value schooling and think it is important, then kids take it seriously.

The teachers and the principal at Colton placed a similar interpretation on the lack of parental participation at the school. Speaking of the parents, the principal remarked,

> They don't value education because they don't have much of one themselves. [Since] they don't value education as much as they could, they don't put those values and expectations on their kids.

Interviews and observations of parents told a different story, however. Parents in both communities valued educational success; all wanted their children to do well in school, and all saw themselves as supporting and helping their children achieve success at school. Middle and working-class parents' aspirations differed only in the level of achievement they hoped their children would attain. Several Colton parents were high school dropouts and bitterly regretted their failure to get a diploma. As one mother said, "I desperately want her to graduate. If she can do that, that will satisfy me." All of the Prescott parents hoped that their children would get a college diploma, and many spoke of the importance of an advanced degree.

Although the educational values of the two groups of parents did not differ, the ways in which they promoted educational success did. In the working-class community, parents turned over the responsibility for education to the teacher. Just as they depended on doctors to heal their children, they depended on teachers to educate them. In the middle-class community, however, parents saw education as a shared enterprise and scrutinized, monitored, and supplemented the school experience of their children. Prescott parents read to their children, initiated contact with teachers, and attended school events more often than Colton parents.

Generally, the evidence demonstrates that the level of parental involvement is linked to the class position of the parents and to the social and cultural resources that social class yields in American society. By definition, the educational status and material resources of parents increase with social class. These resources were observed to influence parental participation in schooling in the Prescott and Colton communities. The working-class parents had poor educational skills, relatively lower occupational prestige than teachers, and limited time and disposable income to supplement and intervene in their children's schooling. The middle-class parents, on the other hand, had educational skills and occupational prestige that matched or surpassed that of teachers: they also had the necessary economic resources to manage the child care, transportation, and time required to meet with teachers, to hire tutors, and to become intensely involved in their childrens' schooling.

These differences in social, cultural, and economic resources between the two sets of parents help explain differences in their responses to a variety of teacher requests to participate in schooling. For example, when asked to read to their children and to help them at home with school work, Colton parents were reluctant to comply because they felt that their educational skills were inadequate for these tasks. Prescott parents, with their superior educational skills, felt more comfortable helping their children in these areas. Parents at Colton and Prescott also differed in their perceptions of the appropriate relationship between parents and teachers. Prescott parents conceived of schooling as a partnership in which parents have the right and the responsibility to raise issues of their choosing and even to criticize teachers. Colton parents' inferior educational level and occupational prestige reinforced their trust in and dependence on the professional expertise of educators. The relatively high occupational position of Prescott parents contributed to their view of teachers as equals.[1] Prescott parents occasionally had more confidence in their right to monitor and to criticize teachers. Their occupational prestige levels may have helped both build this confidence and demystify the status of the teacher as a professional.

Finally, more straightforward economic differences between the middle- and working-class parents are evident in their different responses to requests to attend school events. Attendance at parent-teacher conferences, particularly those held in the afternoon, requires transportation, child care arrangements, and flexibility at the workplace—all more likely to be available to Prescott parents than to Colton parents.

The literature on family life indicates that social class is associated with differences in social networks, leisure time, and childrearing activities (Bott 1971; Kohn 1977; Rubin 1976). The observations in this study confirm these associations and, in addition, indicate that social class differences in family life (or class cultures) have implications for family-school relationships. Middle-class culture provides parents with more information about schooling and promotes social ties among parents in the school community. This furthers the interdependence between home and school. Working-class culture, on the other hand, emphasizes kinship and promotes independence between the spheres of family life and schooling.

Because both schools promote a family-school relationship that solicits parental involvement in schooling and that promotes an interdependence between family and school, the class position and the class culture of middle-class families yield a social profit not available to working-class families. In particular, middle-class culture provides parents with more information about schooling and also builds social networks among parents in the school community. Parents use this information to build a family-school relationship congruent with the schools' definition of appropriate behavior. For example, they may request additional educational resources for their children, monitor the behavior of the teacher, share costs of a tutor with other interested parents, and consult with other parents and teachers about their children's educational experience.

It is important to stress that if the schools were to promote a different type of family-school relationship, the class culture of middle-class parents might not yield a social profit. The data do not reveal that the social relations of middle-class culture are intrinsically better than the social relations of working-class culture. Nor can it be said that the family-school relationships in the middle-class are objectively better for children than those in the working class. Instead, the social profitability of middle-class arrangements is tied to the schools' definition of the proper family-school relationship.

Future research on parental participation in education should take as problematic the standards that schools establish for parental involvement in schooling and should focus on the role of class cultures in facilitating and impeding compliance with these standards. In addition, research might profitably examine the role of social class in structuring the conflict between the universalistic concerns of the teacher and the particularistic agenda of parents (Waller 1932; McPherson 1972). Parents and teachers may be "natural enemies" (Waller 1932) and may face enduring problems of negotiating "boundaries" between their "territories" (Lightfoot 1978). Social class appears to influence the educational, status, monetary, and informational resources that each side brings to that conflict.

### Family-School Relationships and Cultural Capital

These results suggest that social class position and class culture become a form of cultural capital in the school setting (Bourdieu 1977a; Bourdieu and Passeron 1977). Although working-class and middle-class parents share a desire for their children's educational success in first and second grade, social location leads them to construct different pathways for realizing that success. Working-class parents' method—dependence on the teacher to educate their child—may have been the dominant method of promoting school success in earlier periods within the middle class. Today, however, teachers actively solicit parents' participation in education. Middle-class parents, in supervising, monitoring, and overseeing the educational

experience of their children, behave in ways that mirror the requests of schools. This appears to provide middle-class children with educational advantages over working-class children.

The behavior of parents in this regard is not fully determined by their social location. There are variations within as well as between social classes. Still, parents approach the family-school relationship with different sets of social resources. Schools ask for very specific types of behavior from all parents, regardless of their social class. Not all cultural resources are equally valuable, however, for complying with schools' requests. The resources tied directly to social class (e.g., education, prestige, income) and certain patterns of family life (e.g., kinship ties, socialization patterns, leisure activities) seem to play a large role in facilitating the participation of parents in schools. Other aspects of class and class cultures, including religion and taste in music, art, food, and furniture (Bourdieu 1984) appear to play a smaller role in structuring the behavior of parents, children, and teachers in the family-school relationship. (These aspects of class cultures might, of course, influence other dimensions of schooling.)

These findings underline the importance of studying the significance of cultural capital within a social context. In recent years, Bourdieu has been criticized for being overly deterministic in his analysis of the role of cultural capital in shaping outcomes (Giroux 1983; Connell et al. 1982). Connell et al., for example, argue that cultural capital

> practically obliterates the person who is actually the main constructor of the home/school relationship. The student is treated mainly as a bearer of cultural capital, a bundle of abilities, knowledges and attitudes furnished by parents. [p. 188]

Moreover, Bourdieu has focused almost exclusively on the social profits stemming from high culture. Although he is quite clear about the arbitrary character of culture, his emphasis on the value of high culture could be misinterpreted. His research on cultural capital of elites may be construed as suggesting that the culture of elites is intrinsically more valuable than that of the working class. In this regard, the concept of cultural capital is potentially vulnerable to the same criticisms that have been directed at the notion of the culture of poverty (Valentine 1968).

This study highlights the need for more extensive research in the area of cultural capital. It would be particularly useful for future research to take into account historical variations in definitions of culture capital. Family-school relationships have changed over time; what constitutes cultural capital at one point in time may or may not persist in a future period. Historical studies help reveal the way in which cultural resources of social groups are unevenly valued in a society; these studies help illustrate the dynamic character of these value judgments. Historical work on definitions of cultural capital can also shed light on the arbitrariness of the current social standards.

In addition, research on cultural capital could fruitfully expand its focus to include more social groups. The research on high culture (Bourdieu 1977*a*, 1977*b*; DiMaggio and Useem 1982; Cookson and Persell 1985) has made a useful contribution to the field (see also Lamont and Lareau 1987). This study, however, suggests that middle-class families have cultural resources that become a form of cultural capital in specific settings. In moving beyond studies of elites, it might be useful to recognize that all social groups have cultural capital and that some forms of this capital are valued more highly by the dominant institutions at particular historical moments. As Samuel Kaplan (pers. comm. 1986) points out, members of the working class have cultural capital as well, but it is only rarely recognized by dominant social institutions. During World War II, for example, the dangerous and difficult task of the marksman was usually filled by working-class youths; only rarely was it assigned to a college boy. Marksman skills and, more generally, compliance with the expectations of supervising officers are important in the military. Here, the childrearing values of working-class parents (e.g., obedience, conformity) may advantage working-class youths; the values of middle-class families (e.g., self-direction, autonomy, and pemissiveness) may disadvantage middle-class youth (Kohn 1977; Kohn and Schooler 1983).

## IMPLICATIONS FOR FURTHER RESEARCH

Educators and policymakers may seek to increase parental involvement in schooling by boosting the educational capabilities and information resources of parents. For sociologists interested in family, schools, and social stratification, a somewhat different task is in order. Families and schools, and family-school relationships, are critical links in the process of social reproduction. For most children (but not all), social class is a major predictor of educational and occupational achievement. Schools, particularly elementary and secondary schools, play a crucial role in this process of social reproduction; they sort students into social categories that award credentials and opportunities for mobility (Collins 1979, 1981*c*). We know relatively little about the stages of this process.

The concept of cultural capital may help by turning our attention to the structure of opportunity and to the way in which individuals proceed through that structure (see also Collins 1981*a*, 1981*b*; Knorr-Cetina and Cicourel 1981). Moreover, the concept does not overlook the importance of the role of the individual in constructing a biography within a social structure. Class provides social and cultural resources, but these resources must be invested or activated to become a form of cultural capital. Analyzing the role of cultural capital in structuring family-school relationships, particularly parental participation in education, provides a rich setting for analyzing the linkages between micro and macro levels of analysis.

## ENDNOTE

1. Some Prescott parents, however, did report that they felt intimidated by a teacher on some occasions.

## REFERENCES

Aggleton, Peter J., and Geoff Whitty. 1985. "Rebels Without a Cause? Socialization and Subcultural Style Among the Children of the New Middle Classes." *Sociology of Education* 58:60–72.

Anyon, Jean. 1981. "Social Class and School Knowledge." *Curriculum Inquiry* 11:1–42.

Apple, Michael W. 1979. *Ideology and Curriculum*. London: Routledge and Kegan Paul.

Baker, David, and David Stevenson. 1986. "Mothers' Strategies for School Achievement: Managing the Transition to High School." *Sociology of Education* 59:156–66.

Becker, Henry Jay, and Joyce L. Epstein. 1982. "Parent Involvement: A Survey of Teacher Practices." *Elementary School Journal* 83: 85–102.

Berger, Eugenia H. 1983. *Beyond the Classroom: Parents as Partners in Education.* St. Louis: C. V. Mosby.

Bernstein, Basil. 1975. *Class, Codes and Control.* Vol. 3. London: Routledge and Kegan Paul.

_____. 1982. "Codes, Modalities and the Process of Cultural Reproduction: A Model." Pp. 304–55 in *Cultural and Economic Reproduction in Education,* edited by Michael W. Apple. London: Routledge and Kegan Paul.

Bott, Elizabeth. 1971. *Family and Social Networks.* New York: Free Press.

Bourdieu, Pierre, 1977a. "Cultural Reproduction and Social Reproduction." Pp. 487–511 in *Power and Ideology in Education,* edited by J. Karabel and A. H. Halsey. New York: Oxford University Press.

_____. 1977b. *Outline of a Theory of Practice.* Cambridge: Cambridge University Press.

_____. 1981. "Men and Machines." Pp. 304–17 in *Advances in Social Theory: Toward an Integration of Micro- and Macro-Sociologies,* edited by K. Knorr-Cetina and A. V. Cicourel. Boston, Routledge and Kegan Paul.

_____. 1984. *Distinction: A Social Critique of the Judgment of Taste.* Translated by Richard Nice. Cambridge, MA: Harvard University Press.

Bourdieu, Pierre, and Jean-Claude Passeron. 1977. *Reproduction in Education, Society and Culture.* Translated by Richard Nice. Beverly Hills: Sage.

Butterworth, Julian E. 1928. *The Parent-Teacher Association and Its Work.* New York: Macmillan.

California Department of Education. 1983. *California Assessment Program 1981–1982.* Sacramento: California Department of Education.

Collins, Randall. 1979. *The Credential Society.* New York: Academic Press.

_____. 1981a. "Micro-Translation as a Theory-Building Strategy." Pp. 81–108 in *Advances in Social Theory: Toward an Integration of Micro- and Macro-Sociologies,* edited by K. Knorr-Cenna and A. V. Cicourel. Boston: Routledge and Kegan Paul.

_____. 1981b. "On the Micro-Foundations of Macro-Sociology." *American Journal of Sociology* 86:984–1014.

_____. 1981c. *Sociology Since Midcentury: Essays in Theory Cumulation.* New York: Academic Press.

Connell, R. W., D. J. Ashendon, S. Kessler, and G. W. Dowsett. 1982. *Making the Difference: Schools, Families and Social Division.* Sydney: George Allen and Urwin.

Cook-Gumperez, Jenny. 1973. *Social Control and Socialization: A Study of Class Difference in the Language of Maternal Control.* Boston: Routledge and Kegan Paul.

Cookson, Peter W., Jr., and Caroline H. Persell. 1985. *Preparing for Power: America's Elite Boarding Schools.* New York: Basic Books.

Deutsch, Martin. 1967. "The Disadvantaged Child and the Learning Process." Pp. 39–58 in *The Disadvantaged Child*, edited by M. Deutsch. New York: Basic Books.

Diaz, Stephan, Luis C. Moll, and Hugh Mehan. 1986. "Sociocultural Resources in Instruction: A Context-Specific Approach." Pp. 187–230 in *Beyond Language: Social and Cultural Factors in Schooling Language Minority Students*, edited by the Bilingual Education Office. Los Angeles: California State University, Evaluation, Dissemination, and Assessment Center.

DiMaggio, Paul, and Michael Useem. 1982. "The Arts in Cultural Reproduction." Pp. 181–201 in *Cultural and Economic Reproduction in Education*, edited by Michael W. Apple. London: Routledge and Kegan Paul.

Epstein, Joyce. 1983. "Effect on Parents of Teacher Practices of Parent Involvement." Report No. 346. Baltimore: Johns Hopkins University, Center for the Social Organization of Schools.

_____. 1984. "Effects of Teacher Practices and Parent Involvement on Student Achievement." Paper presented at the annual meetings of the American Educational Research Association, New Orleans.

Epstein, Joyce, and Henry Jay Becker. 1982. "Teachers' Reported Practices of Parent involvement: Problems and Possibilities." *Elementary School Journal* 83:103–13.

Erickson, Frederick, and Gerald Mohatt. 1982. "Cultural Organization of Participation Structures in Two Classrooms of Indian Students." Pp. 132–75 in *Doing the Ethnography of Schooling*, edited by G. Spindler. New York: Holt, Rinehart and Winston.

Gaskell, Jane. 1985. "Course Enrollment in the High School: The Perspective of Working-Class Females." *Sociology of Education* 58: 48–59.

Gearing, Frederick, and Paul Epstein. 1982. "Learning to Wait: An Ethnographic Probe into the Operation of an Item of Hidden Curriculum." Pp. 240–67 in *Doing the Ethnography of Schooling*, edited by G. Spindler. New York: Holt, Rinehart and Winston.

Giroux, Henry A. 1983. *Theory and Resistance in Education*. South Hadley, MA: Bergin and Harvey.

Gracey, Harry L. 1972. *Curriculum or Craftsmanship*. Chicago: University of Chicago Press.

Heath, Shirley B. 1982. "Questioning at Home and at School: A Comparative Study." Pp. 102–31 in *Doing the Ethnography of Schooling*, edited by G. Spindler. New York: Holt, Rinehart and Winston.

_____. 1983. *Ways with Words*. London: Cambridge University Press.

Hymes, James L., Jr. 1953. *Effective Home-School Relations*. New York: Prentice-Hall.

Jencks, Christopher et al. 1972. *Inequality*. New York: Basic Books.

Joffee, Carol. 1977. *Friendly Intruders*. Berkeley: University of California Press.

Knorr-Cetina, Karin, and Aaron V. Cicourel. 1981. *Advances in Social Theory: Toward an Integration of Micro- and Macro-Sociologies*. Boston: Routledge and Kegan Paul.

Kohn, Melvin L. 1977. *Class and Conformity*. Chicago: University of Chicago Press.

Kohn, Melvin L., and Carmi Schooler. 1983. *Work and Personality: An Inquiry into the Impact of Social Stratification*. Norwood, NJ: Ablex.

Labov, William. 1972. *Sociolinguistic Patterns*. Philadelphia: University of Pennsylvania Press.

Lamont, Michele, and Annette Lareau. 1987. "Cultural Capital in American Research: Problems and Possibilities." Working Paper No. 9. Chicago: Center for Psychosocial Studies.

Leichter, Hope Jensen. 1979. "Families and Communities as Educators: Some Concepts of Relationships." Pp. 3–94 in *Families and Communities as Educators*, edited by H. J. Leichter. New York: Teachers College Press.

Levy, Frank, Arnold J. Meltsner, and Aaron Wildavsky. 1974. *Urban Outcomes*. Berkeley: University of California Press.

Lightfoot, Sara Lawrence. 1978. *Worlds Apart*. New York: Basic Books.

Litwack, Eugene, and I. Szeleny. 1971. "Kinship and Other Primary Groups." Pp. 149–63 in

*Sociology of the Family,* edited by M. Anderson. Middlesex, England: Penguin.

Majoribanks, Kevin. 1979. *Families and Their Learning Environments: An Empirical Analysis.* London: Routledge and Kegan Paul.

McPherson, Gertrude H. 1972. *Small Town Teacher.* Cambridge, MA: Harvard University Press.

Mehan, Hugh, and Peg Griffin. 1980. "Socialization: The View from Classroom Interactions." *Social Inquiry* 50:357–98.

Mehan, Hugh, Alma L. Hertweck, and J. L. Meihls. 1986. *Handicapping the Handicapped.* Stanford: Stanford University Press.

National Congress of Parents and Teachers. 1944. *The Parent-Teacher Organization, Its Origins and Development.* Chicago: National Congress of Parents and Teachers.

National Education Association. 1985. "Teacher-Parent Partnership Program, 1984–1985 Status Report." Unpublished paper. Washington, DC: National Education Association.

Ogbu, John. 1974. *The Next Generation.* New York: Academic Press.

Overstreet, Harry, and Bonaro Overstreet. 1949. *Where Children Come First.* Chicago: National Congress of Parents and Teachers.

Rist, Ray C. 1978. *The Invisible Children.* Cambridge, MA: Harvard University Press.

Robinson, Sharon. 1985. "Teacher-Parent Cooperation." Paper presented at the annual meetings of the American Educational Research Association, Chicago.

Rubin, Lillian B. 1976. *Worlds of Pain.* New York: Basic Books.

Seeley, David. 1984. "Home-School Partnership." *Phi Delta Kappan* 65:383–93.

Strodbeck, F. L. 1958. "Family Interaction, Values, and Achievement." Pp. 131–91 in *Talent and Society,* edited by D. D. McClelland. New York: Van Nostrand.

Taylor, Sandra. 1984. "Reproduction and Contradiction in Schooling: The Case of Commercial Studies." *British Journal of Sociology of Education* 5:3–18.

Trelease, James. 1982. *The Read-Aloud Handbook.* New York: Penguin.

Valentine, Charles A. 1968. *Culture and Poverty.* Chicago: University of Chicago Press.

Valli, Linda. 1985. "Office Education Students and the Meaning of Work." *Issues in Education* 3:31–44.

Waller, Willard. 1932. *The Socioiogy of Teaching.* New York: Wiley.

Wilcox, Kathleen A. 1977. "Schooling and Socialization for Work Roles." Ph.D. diss., Harvard University.

_____. 1982. "Differential Socialization in the Classroom: Implications for Equal Opportunity." Pp. 269–309 in *Doing the Ethnography of Schooling,* edited by G. Spindler. New York: Holt, Rinehart and Winston.

## CHAPTER 9 REFERENCES

Alexander, K., & Cook, M. (1982). Curriculum and coursework. *American Sociological review, 47,* 626–640.

American Association of University Women. (1992). *How schools shortchange girls.* Washington, DC: AAUW Educational Foundation and National Education Association.

Austin, G. R., & Garber, H. (Eds). (1985). *Research on exemplary schools.* Orlando, FL: Academic Press.

Baratz, S. S., & Baratz, J. C. (1970). Early childhood intervention: The social science base of institutional racism. *Harvard Educational Review, 40,* 29–50.

Barr, R., & Dreeben, R. (1983). *How schools work.* Chicago: University of Chicago Press.

Belenky, M. F., Clinchy , B. M., Goldberger, N. R., & Tarule, J. M. (1986). *Women's ways of knowing: The development of self, voice, and mind.* New York: Basic Books.

Bennett, K. P., & LeCompte, M. D. (1990). *How schools work.* New York: Longman.

Bernstein, B. (1977). *Class, codes and control. Vol. III: Towards a theory of educational transmission.* London: Routledge & Kegan Paul.

Bernstein, B. (1990). *The structuring of pedagogic discourse: Vol. 4 of Class, codes and control.* London: Routledge.

Bourdieu, P., & Passeron, J. C. (1977). *Reproduction in society, culture and education.* Beverly Hills, CA: Sage.

Bowles, S., & Gintis. H. (1976). *Schooling in capitalist America: Educational reform and the contradictions of economic life.* New York: Basic Books.

Brookover, W., et al. (1979). *School social systems and student achievement: Schools can make a difference.* New York: Praeger.

Brookover, W., et al. (1982). *Creating effective schools: An inservice program for enhancing school learning climate and achievement.* Holmes Beach, FL: Learning Publications.

Brophy, J. E. , & Good, T. L. (1970). Teachers' communication of differential expectations for children's classroom performance: Some behavioral data. *Journal of Educational Psychology, 61,* 365–374.

Cicourel A. V., & Kitsuse, J. I. (1963). *The educational decision-makers.* New York: Bobbs-Merrill.

Coleman, J. S., et al. (1966). *Equality of educational opportunity.* Washington, DC: U.S. Government.

Coleman, J. S., & Hoffer, T. (1987). *Public and private schools: The impact of communities.* New York: Basic Books.

Coleman, J. S., Hoffer, T., & Kilgore, S. (1982). *High school achievement.* New York: Basic Books.

Cookson, P. W., Jr., & Persell, C. H. (1985). *Preparing for power: America's elite boarding schools.* New York: Basic Books.

Cookson, P. W., Jr., Persell, C. H., & Catsambis, S. (1992). Differential asset conversion: Class and gendered pathways to selective colleges. *Sociology of Education, 65,* 208–225.

Cuban, L. (1983, June). Effective schools: A friendly but cautionary note. *Phi Delta Kappan 64,* 695–696.

de Beauvoir, S. (1989). *The second sex.* New York: Random House. (Original work published 1952)

Deutsch, M., et al. (1964). *The disadvantaged child*. New York: Basic Books.

Doran, B., & Weffer, W. (1992). Immigrant aspirations, high school process and academic outcomes. *American Education Research Journal, 29* (1), 163–181.

Dougherty, K., & Hammack, F. (1990). *Education and society*. New York: Harcourt Brace Jovanovich.

Dreeben, R., & Gamoran, A. (1986). Race, instruction, and learning. *American Sociological Review, 51,* 660–669.

Eder, D. (1981, July). Ability grouping as a self-fulfilling prophecy: A micro-analysis of teacher- student interaction. *Sociology of Education, 54,* 151–162.

Edmonds, R. (1979). Effective schools for the urban poor. *Educational Leadership, 37* (1), 5–24.

Epstein, C. F. (1990). *Deceptive distinctions: Sex, gender and the social order*. New Haven, CT: Yale University Press.

Felmlee, D., & Eder, D. (1983, April). Contextual effects in the classroom: The impact of ability groups on student attention. *Sociology of Education, 56,* 77–78.

Fennema, E. (1974). Mathematics learning and the sexes: A review. *Journal for Research in Mathematics Education 5,* 126–139.

Fennema, E., & Leder, G. (1990). Mathematics and gender. New York: Teachers College Press.

Fine, M. (1991). *Framing dropouts: Notes on the politics of an urban public high school*. Albany: State University of New York Press.

Fordham, S., & Ogbu, J. (1986). Black students' school success: Coping with the "burden" of "acting white." *The Urban Review, 18 (3),* 176–206.

Freedman, S. G. (1990). *Small victories*. New York: Harper Collins.

Gaines, D. (1991). *Teenage wasteland: Suburbia's dead end kids*. New York: Pantheon.

Gilligan, C. (1982). *In a different voice*. Cambridge, MA: Harvard University Press.

Gilligan, C., et al. (1990). *Making connections: The relational worlds of adolescent girls at Emma Willard School*. Cambridge, MA: Harvard University Press.

Gornick, V. (1978). The next great moment in history is theirs. In A. R. Sadovnik et al. (Eds.), *Exploring society* (pp. 260–266). New York: Harper and Row, 1987.

Hakuta, K., & Garcia, E. (1989). Bilingualism and education. *American Psychologist, 53,* 374–379.

Hallinan, M. (1984). Summary and implications. In P. Peterson, L. C. Wilkinson, & M. Hallinan (Eds.), *The social context of instruction* (pp. 229–240). New York: Academic Press.

Hitchcock, M. E., & Tompkins., G. E. (1987). Are basal reading textbooks still sexist? *The Reading Teacher, 41,* 288–292.

Hurn, C. J. (1993). *The limits and possibilities of schooling* (3rd ed.). Boston: Allyn and Bacon.

Jencks, C., et al. (1972). *Inequality*. New York: Basic Books.

Jensen, A. (1969). How much can we boost I.Q. and scholastic achievement? *Harvard Educational Review, 39,* 1–23.

Johnson, J. (1991). *Introduction to the foundations of American education* (8th ed.). Boston: Allyn and Bacon.

Kamin, L. (1974). *The science and politics of I.Q.* Potomac, MD: Erlbaum.

Kidder, T. (1989). *Among schoolchildren.* Boston: Houghton Mifflin.

Kozol, J. (1991). *Savage inequalities.* New York: Crown.

LaFrance, M. (1985). The school of hard knocks: Nonverbal sexism in the classroom. *Theory Into Practice, 24,* 40–44.

Laird, S. (1989). Reforming "Women's true profession": A case for "Feminist pedagogy" in teacher education? *Harvard Educational Review, 58* (4), 449–463.

Lareau, A. (1989). *Home advantage: Social class and parental intervention in elementary education.* London: Falmer.

Leach, W. (1980). *True love and perfect union: The feminist reform of sex and society.* New York: Basic Books.

Lemann, N. (1991). *The promised land.* New York: Vintage.

Lewis, O. (1966). The culture of poverty. *Scientific American, 215,* 19–25.

Lightfoot, S. (1985). *The good high school.* New York: Basic Books.

Lippitt, R., & Gold, M. (1959). Classroom social structure as a mental health problem. *Journal of Social Issues, 15,* 40–49.

MacLeod, J. (1987). *Ain't no making it: Leveled aspirations in a low-income neighborhood.* Boulder: Western Press.

Martin, J. R. (1987). Reforming teacher education, rethinking liberal education. *Teachers College Record, 88,* 406–409.

Martin, R. (1972). Student sex and behavior as determinants of the type and frequency of teacher-student contacts. *Journal of School Psychology, 10,* 339–347.

McDermott, R. P. (1977). Social relations as contexts for learning. *Harvard Educational Review, 47,* 198–213.

Noddings, N. (1984). *Caring: A feminine approach to ethics and moral education.* Berkeley, CA: University of California Press.

Oakes, J. (1985). *Keeping track: How schools structure inequality.* New Haven, CT: Yale University Press.

Ogbu, J. (1978). *Minority education and caste.* New York: Academic Press.

Ogbu, J. (1979). Social stratification and the socialization of competence. *Anthropology and Education Quarterly, 10* (1).

Ogbu, J. (1987). Variability in minority school performance: A problem in search of an explanation. *Anthropology and Education Quarterly, 18,* 312–334.

Persell, C. H. (1977). *Education and inequality: The roots and results of stratification in America's schools.* New York: The Free Press.

Powell, A. G., Farrar, E., & Cohen, D. K. (1985). *The shopping mall high school: Winners and losers in the educational marketplace.* Boston: Houghton Mifflin.

Rist, R. C. (1970). Student social class and teacher expectations: The self-fulfilling prophecy in ghetto education. *Harvard Educational Review, 40,* 411–451.

Rist, R. C. (1973). *The urban school: A factory for failure.* Cambridge, MA: MIT Press.

Rosenbaum, J. (1976). *Making inequality.* New York: Wiley.

Rosenbaum, J. (1980a). Social implications of educational grouping. In D. Berliner (Ed.), *Review of research in education* (pp. 361–401). Washington, DC: American Educational Research Association.

Rosenbaum, J. (1980b). Track misperceptions and frustrated college plans. *Sociology of Education, 53,* 74–87.

Rosenthal, R., & Jacobson, L. (1968). *Pygmalion in the classroom.* New York: Holt, Rinehart and Winston.

Ryan, W. (1971). *Blaming the victim.* New York: Random House.

Sachar, E. (1991). *Shut up and let the lady teach.* New York: Poseidon Press.

Sadker, M. P., & Sadker, D. M. (1985, March). Sexism in the schoolroom of the '80's. *Psychology Today,* 54–57.

Sadovnik, A. R. (1991). Derailing high school tracking: One beginning. *Pathways, 7*(2), 4–8.

Shakeshaft, C. (1986). A gender at risk. *Phi Delta Kappan, 67,* 449–503.

Shakeshaft, C. (1987). *Women in educational administration.* Newbury Park, CA: Sage.

Shanker, A. (1991). Lecture at Adelphi University. October.

Sikes, J. (1971). *Differential behavior of male and female teachers with male and female students.* Unpublished Doctoral Dissertation, University of Texas, Austin.

Stedman, L. C. (1985). A new look at the effective schools literature. *Urban Education, 20,* 295–326.

Stedman, L. C. (1987). It's time we changed the effective schools formula. *Phi Delta Kappan, 69,* 215–224.

Thornburg, D., & Karp, K. S. (1992). Lessons learned: Mathematics + science + higher order thinking × second language learning = ? *Journal of Language Minority Students, 10,* 159–184.

Tyack, D., & Hansot, E. (1990). *Learning together.* New Haven, CT: Yale University Press.

Weikert, D., & Schweinhart, L. J. (1984). *Changed lives: The effects of the Perry Preschool Program on youths through age 19.* Ypsilanti, MI: High Scope.

Willis, P. (1981). *Learning to labor: How working class kids get working class jobs.* New York: Columbia University Press.

Wong-Fillmore, L., & Valdez, C. (1986). Teaching bilingual children. In M. Wittrock (Ed.), *Handbook of research on Teaching* (3rd ed.). New York: Macmillan.


## SUGGESTED READINGS

Alexander, K., & Cook, M. (1982). Curriculum and coursework. *American Sociological Review, 47,* 626–640.

American Association of University Women. (1992). *How schools shortchange girls.* Washington, DC: Author.

Austin, G. R., & Garber, H. (Eds.). (1984). *Research on exemplary schools.* Orlando, FL: Academic Press.

Baratz, S. S., & Baratz, J. C. (1970). Early childhood intervention: The social science base of institutional racism. *Harvard Educational Review, 40,* 29–50.

Barr, R., & Dreeben, R. (1983). *How schools work.* Chicago: University of Chicago Press.

Belenky, M. F., Clinchy, B. M., Goldberger, N. R., & Tarule, J. M. (1986). *Women's ways of knowing: The development of self, voice, and mind.* New York: Basic Books.

Bernstein, B. (1974–1976). *Class, codes, and control.* 3 vols. London: Routledge and Kegan Paul.

Bernstein, B. (1977). *Class, codes and control. Vol. III: Towards a theory of educational transmission* (revised). London: Routledge & Kegan Paul.

Bernstein, B. (1990). *The structuring of pedagogic discourse: Vol. 4 of Class, codes and control.* London: Routledge.

Bloom, B. S., Davis, A., & Hess, R. (1965). *Compensatory education for cultural deprivation.* New York: Holt.

Bourdieu, P., & Passeron, J.-C. (1977). *Reproduction in society, culture and education.* Beverly Hills, CA: Sage.

Bowles, S., & Gintis, H. (1976). *Schooling in capitalist America: Educational reform and the contradictions of economic life.* New York: Basic Books.

Brookover, W., Beady, C., Flood, P., Schweitzer, J., & Wisenbaker, J. (1979). *School social systems and student achievement.* New York: Praeger.

Chall, J. S., Jacobs, V. A., & Baldwin L. E. (1990). *The reading crisis: Why poor children fall behind.* Cambridge, MA: Harvard University Press.

Cicourel, A. V., & Kitsuse, J. I. (1963). *The educational decision-makers.* New York: Bobbs-Merrill.

Clark, R. (1983). *Family life and school achievement: Why poor black children succeed or fail.* Chicago: University of Chicago Press.

Coleman, J. S., et al. (1966). *Equality of educational opportunity.* Washington, DC: U.S. Government.

Coleman, J. S., & Hoffer, T. (1987). *Public and private schools: The impact of communities.* New York: Basic Books.

Coleman, J. S., Hoffer, T., & Kilgore, S. (1982). *High school achievement.* New York: Basic Books.

Cookson, P. W., Jr., & Persell, C. H. (1985). *Preparing for power: America's elite boarding schools.* New York: Basic Books.

Cuban, L. (1983). Effective schools: A friendly but cautionary note. *Phi Delta Kappan, 64,* 695–6996.

Cusick, P A. (1983). *The egalitarian ideal and the American high school.* New York: Longman.

Delamont, S. (1989). *Knowledgeable women: Structuralism and the reproduction of elites.* New York: Routledge & Kegan Paul.

Deutsch, M. et al. (1964). *The disadvantaged child.* New York: Basic Books.

Dreeben, R., & Gamoran, A. (1986). Race, instruction, and learning. *American Sociological Review, 51,* 660–669.

Eder, D. (1981). Ability grouping as a self-fulfilling prophecy. *Sociology of Education, 54,* 151–162.

Edmonds, R. (1979). Effective schools for the urban poor. *Educational Leadership, 37* (1),5–24.

Epstein, C. F. (1990). *Deceptive distinctions: Sex, gender and the social order.* New Haven, CT: Yale University Press.

Fine, M. (1990). *Framing dropouts: Notes on the politics of an urban public high school.* Albany, NY: State University of New York Press.

Fordham, S., & Ogbu, J. U. (1986). Black students' school success: Coping with the "burden" of "acting white." *The Urban Review, 18* (3), 176–206.

Gamoran, A. (1986). Instructional and institutional effects of ability groupings. *Sociology of Education, 59,* 185–198.

Gamoran, A., & Berends, M. (1987). The effects of stratification in secondary schools: A synthesis of survey and ethnographic research. *Review of Educational Research, 57,* 415–437.

Gamoran, A., & Mare, R. D. (1989). Secondary school tracking and educational inequality: Compensation, reinforcement, or neutrality? *American Journal of Sociology, 94* (5), 1146–1183.

Gibson, M., & Ogbu, J. (1991). *Minority status and schooling: A comparative study.* New York: Garland.

Gilligan, C. (1982). *In a different voice.* Cambridge, MA: Harvard University Press.

Hernstein, R. J. (1973). *IQ in the meritocracy.* Boston: Little, Brown.

Heyns, B. (1978). *Summer learning and the effects of schooling.* New York: Academic Press.

Hoffer, T., Greeley, A. M., Coleman, J. S. (1985, April). Achievement growth in public and Catholic schools. *Sociology of Education, 58,* 74–97.

Jencks, C. S., Smith, M., Acland, H., Bane, M. J., Cohen, D., Gintis, H., Heyns, B., & Michelson, S. (1972). *Inequality.* New York: Basic Books.

Jencks, C. S., Bartlett, S., Corcoran, M., Crouse, J., Eaglesfield, D., Jackson, G., McClelland, K., Mueser, P., Olneck, M., Schwartz, J., Ward, S., Williams. J. (1979). *Who gets ahead?* New York: Basic Books.

Jensen, A. (1969). How much can we boost I.Q. and scholastic achhievement? *Harvard Educational Review, 39,* 1–23.

Kamin, L. (1974). *The science and politics of I.Q.* Potomac, MD: Erlbaum.

Karabel, J. (1972). Community colleges and social stratification. *Harvard Educational Review, 42,* 521–562.

Labov, W. (1970). The logic of non-standard English. In F. Williams (Ed.), *Language and poverty,* (pp. 153–189). Chicago: Markham.

Lareau, A. (1989). *Home advantage: Social class and parental intervention in elementary education.* London: Falmer.

Lee, V. E., & Bryk, A. S. (1988). Curriculum tracking as mediating the social distribution of high school achievement. *Sociology of Education, 61,* 78–94.

Lewis, O. (1965, October). The culture of poverty. *Scientific American 215,* 19–25.

McDermott, R. P. (1977). Social relations as contexts for learning in school. *Harvard Educational Review, 47,* 198–213.

McLeod, J. (1987). *Ain't no makin' it: Leveled aspirations in a low-income neighborhood.* Boulder, CO: Westview Press.

Mosteller, F., & Moynihan, D. P. (1972). *On equality of educational opportunity.* New York: Vintage Books.

Natriello, G., (Ed.). (1986). *School Dropouts: Patterns and policies.* New York: Teachers College Press.

Natriello, G., McDill, E. L., & Pallas, A. (1990). *Schooling disadvantaged children: Racing against catastrophe.* New York: Teachers College Press.

Oakes, J. (1985). *Keeping track: How schools structure inequality.* New Haven, CT: Yale University Press.

Ogbu, J. (1978). *Minority education and caste*. New York: Academic Press.

Ogbu, J. (1987). Variability in minority school performance: A problem in search of an explanation. *Anthropology and Educational Quarterly, 18,* 312–335.

Pallas, A. M., Entwisle, D. R., Alexander, K. L., & Cadigan, D. (1987). Children who do exceptionally well in first grade. *Sociology of Education, 60,* 257–271.

Persell, C. H. (1977). *Education and inequality: The roots and results of stratification in America's schools*. New York: The Free Press.

Pinar, W. F., (Ed.). (1988). *Contemporary curriculum discourses*. Scottsdale, AZ: Gorsuch Scarisbrick.

Rist, R. C. (1970). Student social class and teacher expectations: The self-fulfilling prophecy in ghetto education." *Harvard Educational Review, 40,* 411–451.

Rist, R. C., (1973). *The urban school: A factory for failure*. Cambridge, MA: MIT Press.

Rosenbaum, J. (1976). *Making inequality*. New York: Wiley.

Rosenbaum, J. (1980a). Social implications of educational grouping. In D. Berliner (Ed.), *Review of Research in Education* (pp. 361–401). Washington, DC: American Educational Research Association.

Rosenbaum, J. (1980b). Track misperceptions and frustrated college plans. *Sociology of Education, 53,* 74–87.

Rowan, B., & Miracle, A. (1983). Systems of ability grouping and the stratification of achievement in elementary school. *Sociology of Education, 56,* 133–144.

Rutter, M., et al. (1979). *Fifteen thousand hours*. London: Open Books.

Ryan, W. (1969). *Blaming the victim*. New York. Vintage Books.

Scarr, S., & Weinberg, R. A. (1978). The influence of "family background" on intellectual attainment. *American Sociological Review, 43,* 674–692.

Schorr, L. B., & Schorr, D. (1989). *Within our reach: Breaking the cycle of disadvantage*. New York: Doubleday.

Schwartz, F. (1981). Supporting or subverting learning: peer group patterns in four tracked schools. *Anthropology and Education Quarterly, 12,* 99–121.

Slavin, R. E. (1988, September). Synthesis of research on grouping in elementary and secondary schools. *Educational Leadership, 46* 67–77.

Sowell, T. (1977). New light on the black I.Q. controversy. *New York Times Magazine,* March 27, 56–63.

Stedman, L. (1985). A new look at the effective schools literature. *Urban Education, 20,* 295–326.

Stedman, L. (1987, November). It's time we changed the effective schools formula. *Phi Delta Kappan, 69,* 215–224.

Tyack, D., & Hansot, E. (1990). *Learning together*. New Haven, CT: Yale University Press.

Valentine, C. A. (1968). *Culture and poverty: Critique and counter proposals*. Chicago: University of Chicago Press.

Valentine, C. A. (1975). Deficit, difference and bicultural models of Afro-American behavior. In "Challenging the myths: The schools, the blacks and the poor." *Harvard Educational Review* (Reprint Series No. 5), 1–21.

Weikart, D., & Schweinhart, L. J. (1984). *Changed lives: The effects of the Perry Preschool Program on youths through age 19*. Ypsilanti, MI: High Scope.

Willis, P. (1981). *Learning to labor: How working class kids get working class jobs.* New York: Columbia University Press.

Wilson, W. J. (1987). *The truly disadvantaged: The inner city, the underclass, and public policy.* Chicago: University of Chicago Press.

Zigler, E. F., & Muenchow, S. (1992). *Head start: The inside story of America's most successful educational experiment.* New York: Basic Books.

Zigler, E., & Valentine, J. (Eds.). (1979). *Project head start: A legacy of the war on poverty.* New York: The Free Press.

Zweigenhaft, R. L., & Domhoff, G. W. (1991). *Blacks in the white establishment? A study of race and class in America.* New Haven, CT: Yale University Press.

# Educational Reform
# and School Improvement

In Chapter 2, we presented conservative, liberal, and radical perspectives on educational problems. Throughout this book, we have examined a number of educational problems from the foundations perspective. This chapter looks at the most significant educational problems and the role of teachers and schools in solving them. To what extent do teachers and schools make a difference? To what degree can they make a difference? Most importantly, to what extent are teachers and schools limited in their ability to solve educational and social problems, without significant changes outside the schools?

In Chapter 1, we presented the stories of two teachers. The first, memorialized by former *New York Times* education writer Fred Hechinger, was a beloved teacher who made a significant impact on the lives of her students. The second, a veteran teacher in an urban school district, retired from teaching because of the difficult problems she faced. We asked to what extent to the structural problems faced by teachers limit their ability to affect meaningful change and, conversely, to what degree do talented, enthusiastic, and excellent teachers have the ability to affect educational change in spite of the significant problems that they face. Although there is no easy answer to this question, it is clear that teachers work within social and organizational environments that indeed have profound effects on them and often limit their ability to affect meaningful change. It is also clear that teachers can and do make a difference, often in spite of what may seem like intractable problems.

Thus, although teachers can and do make a difference, the research indicates that solutions to educational problems cannot rely on the talent, energy, and hard work of teachers alone, but must reform the social and organizational conditions of schooling (Sizer, 1992). Before we examine ways in which educational reforms have attempted to do this, let us first look at some examples of how individual teachers make a difference.

## EFFECTIVE TEACHERS

Jessica Siegel taught high school English and journalism at Seward Park High School, on New York City's lower east side, for 10 years. Samuel Freedman's *Small Victories* (1990) poignantly chronicles Jessica's struggles, triumphs, and defeats as she attempted to teach her students, most of them poor and immigrants, to value an education and to make their dreams a reality. Teaching in a neighborhood long a haven for immigrants and their children—first for East European Jews and Italians at the turn of the century, and now for Asians, Dominicans, and other Latinos—Jessica battles against the effects of poverty, drugs, gangs, homelessness, family violence and abuse, and language difficulties to give her students an opportunity to succeed in school and in life.

As the advisor to the Seward Park student newspaper, she uses journalism as a vehicle to involve students in the learning experience. Freedman captures the daily struggles, the long hours, and the selfless dedication of a teacher committed to making a difference in the lives of her students. He also captures the bureaucratic nonsense, the petty collegial jealousies, the social problems, and the school conditions that make success difficult, if not impossible. Jessica encourages students to go to college, she helps them with their applications, and she even drives them to college interviews. For every student she helps succeed and who gets into college, there are many others with talent and dreams who do not graduate.

After 10 years of heroic and successful teaching, Jessica decides to leave teaching and return to her first career as a journalist. In part, she leaves because she wants to be a journalist; in part, she leaves because to be a successful teacher required too much personal sacrifice, with too little reward. Freedman's book portrays the limits and possibilities of good teaching—that teachers like Jessica make an important difference, but that without reform of schools, teachers like Jessica may leave teaching. In her review of the book, Johnson (1991, p.184) stated:

> Freedman leaves us with admiration for Jessica Siegel, respect for many of her colleagues, compassion for her students, anger at a seemingly impersonal school bureaucracy, and remorse for a society that values cash more than children.... Yet it is clear that much more can be done to support exemplary teachers like Jessica Siegel. The moral of *Small Victories* is sobering and unequivocal: If we do not change schools to support good teaching, many good teachers will leave schools.

The film *Stand and Deliver* chronicles the work of Jaime Escalante at Garfield High School in East Los Angeles, a poor neighborhood of African Americans, Mexican Americans, and other Latinos. Jaime Escalante refuses to accept the stereotype that students from low-income neighborhoods cannot succeed at high-level academic work. He came to Garfield as a computer teacher after a successful career as a computer analyst in the corporate world and immediately instituted an Advanced Placement (AP) Calculus program, despite the objections of the chairperson of the

Mathematics Department, a woman who did not want to set the students up for failure.

*Stand and Deliver* portrays the heroic efforts of Jaime Escalante to teach his student advanced mathematics. He demonstrates what positive expectations can do and how hard work and dedication on the part of teachers and students can often overcome the pernicious effects of poverty, racism, and social problems. Despite a shortage of materials, the accusation of the Educational Testing Service (ETS) that his students cheated on the AP test (according to ETS, because they had many of the same wrong answers; according to Jaime Escalante, because they did too well for students from their backgrounds), and numerous personal hurdles that students had to overcome, all 18 students passed the AP examination the first year of the program. Within four years, over 85 students passed the AP calculus examination.

*Stand and Deliver* demonstrates a number of important points. First, a talented and dedicated teacher can make a difference. Second, if teachers expect all students to learn and excel, they can and do. Third, it is possible to institutionalize the effective teaching of one teacher into an overall school philosophy, as Garfield High School had to do in order to serve as many students as it now does. Despite these positive lessons, however, there has been a tendency to romanticize the work of Jaime Escalante, or worse to use his success as an example that all that is necessary to improve schools in low-income neighborhoods is to raise expectations. The fact is that although Jaime Escalante did make a difference, students at schools like Garfield High School still have significantly fewer opportunities than students at more affluent high schools. Furthermore, teachers like Jaime Escalante cannot eliminate the negative effects of poverty and other social problems.

These two stories of wonderful teachers can be supplemented by your own recollections of wonderful teachers who have influenced your lives. Unfortunately, they can also be countered by your own stories of terrible teachers and ineffective schools. Our point in telling these stories is to indicate that, as teachers, you can make a difference. However, they also demonstrate that wonderful teachers alone cannot ameliorate societal and school problems, and that wonderful teachers in ineffective schools are severely limited in what they can accomplish. The foundations perspective enlightens one to the importance of changing structures, not just individuals, if the educational system is to improve. For the past decade, there have been a number of significant reform efforts aimed at doing just this. The following section explores some of these efforts.

## EDUCATIONAL REFORM IN THE 1980s*

Dougherty (1990) suggested that the reforms of the 1980s were dominated by what he terms "centrist conservativism." In contrast to the new right's call for a complete reversal of the liberal reforms of the 1960s and 1970s, and the left's belief that

---

*"Educational Reform in the 1980s" and "Educational Reforms in the 1980s: Major Themes" are adapted from Susan F. Semel, Peter W. Cookson, Jr., and Alan R. Sadovnik, "United States," in Peter W. Cookson, Jr., Alan R. Sadovnik, and Susan F. Semel (Eds.), *International Handbook of Educational Reform* (pp. 453–469). © 1992 by Peter W. Cookson, Jr., Alan R. Sadovnik, and Susan F. Semel. Westport, CT: Greenwood Press, 1992, an imprint of Greenwood Publishing Group, Inc., Westport, CT. Reprinted with permission.

educational problems reflect the inherent dilemmas of capitalism, centrist conservatives believed that "education is crucial to the basic interests of society, whether
economic competitiveness, military preparedness, or cultural transmission" (Dougherty, 1990, p. 3). Additionally, a common theme in the major reports on educational
reform was that the U.S. schools were beset by significant problems with the decline
in academic standards and preparation resulting in a threat to national economic and
intellectual competitiveness.

The educational reforms of the 1980s consisted of two waves of reform
(Bacharach, 1990; Passow, 1989). The first wave, marked by the reports of the early
and mid-1980s and the educational initiatives directly responding to them, were
concerned primarily with the issues of accountability and achievement (Dougherty,
1990, p. 3). Responding to the call for increased academic achievement, many states
increased graduation requirements, toughened curriculum mandates, and increased
the use of standardized test scores to measure student achievement.

By the mid to late 1980s, however, it became increasingly clear that such top-
down reform would be ineffective in dealing with the schools' myriad problems.
Although raising achievement standards for students and implementing accountability measures for evaluating teachers had some positive effects, many (including the
National Governors Association, which took a leading role in reform), believed that
educational reform had to do more than provide changes in evaluation procedures.
The second wave of reform, then, was targeted at the structure and processes of the
schools themselves, placing far more control in the hands of local schools, teachers,
and communities. Whereas the first wave was highly centralized at the state level, the
second wave was more decentralized to the local and school levels. What they had in
common, however, was what the Governors Conference emphasized as the "triple
theme of achievement, assessment, and accountability" (Bacharach, 1990, p. 8).

Despite the second wave's insistence that locally based reforms were central to
success, many critics (including teacher organizations and unions) argued that the
reforms were highly bureaucratic and aimed primarily at assessment procedures.
Significant reforms, they suggested, had to emphasize both changes within schools
and changes that involved teachers, students, and parents as part of the reform
process, not merely as objects of it. Toward the latter part of the 1980s, reforms that
emphasized teacher empowerment, school-based management, and school choice
became the most important ones under consideration.

To summarize, the first wave of reform reports stressed the need for increased
educational excellence though increased educational standards and a reversal of the
rising tide of mediocrity. Passow (1989, p. 16) stated the following themes as
essential to the first wave of educational reform:

1. The need to attain the twin goals of excellence and equity
2. The need to clarify educational goals, unburdening schools from responsibilities
   they cannot or should not fill
3. The need to develop a common core curriculum (not unlike the standard college-
   bound curriculum) with few or no electives, little or no curricular differentiation,
   but only pedagogical differentiation
4. The need to eliminate tracking programs so that students could tackle the common
   core courses in a common curriculum in different ways

5. The need for major changes in vocational education: in the student populations served, the curricula provided, and the sites of such education if offered
6. The need for education to teach about technology, including computer literacy, and to become involved in the technological revolution
7. The need to "increase both the duration and intensity of academic learning," lengthening the school day and the school year
8. The need to recruit, train, and retain more academically able teachers, to improve the quality of teaching, and to upgrade the professional working life of teachers
9. The need redefine the principal's role and put the "principal squarely in charge of educational quality in each school"
10. The need to forge new partnerships between corporations, business, and the schools

Typifying the second wave of educational reform were the recommendations of the State Governor's Conference. Governor Lamar Alexander, in *Time for Results: The Governor's 1991 Report on Education* (1986), summarized the Governor's Association's year-long analysis of a variety of issues, including teaching, leadership and management, parental involvement and choice, readiness, technology, school facilities, and college quality, with (among others) the following recommendations:

1. Now is the time to work out a fair, affordable Career Ladder salary system that recognizes real differences in function, competence, and performance of teachers.
2. States should create leadership programs for school leaders.
3. Parents should have more choice in the public schools their children attend.
4. The nation—and the states and local districts—need report cards about results, and about what students know and can do.
5. School districts and schools that do not make the grade should be declared bankrupt, taken over by the state, and reorganized.
6. It makes no sense to keep closed half a year the school buildings in which America has invested a quarter of a trillion dollars while we are undereducated and overcrowded.
7. States should work with four- and five-year-olds from poor families to help them get ready for school and decrease the chances that they will drop out later.
8. Better use of technologies through proper planning and training for use of videodiscs, computers, and robotics is an important way to give teachers more time to teach.
9. States should insist that colleges assess what students actually learn while in college. (cited in Passow, 1989, p.23)

During both waves of educational reform, there were a number of programs and initiatives that received considerable attention. Among these are school choice, school-business partnerships, school-based management, the effective school movement, and reform of teacher education. The following sections discuss these in more detail.

## School Choice

During the 1980s, many educational researchers and policy analysts indicated that most public schools were failing in terms of student achievement, discipline, and morality. At the same period, some researchers were investigating private schools and concluding that they were more effective learning environments than public schools. Private schools were reputed to be accountable, efficient, and safe. Moreover, the work of Coleman, Hoffer, and Kilgore (1982) seemed to prove that private school students learned more than their public school counterparts. Other research on *magnet schools* (schools with special curricula and student bodies) seemed to indicate that public schools that operated independently of the public school bureaucracy were happier, healthier, and more academically productive than zone schools where students were required to attend based on their residence.

As the decade came to a close, some researchers reasoned that magnet schools and private schools were superior to neighborhood public schools because schools of choice reflected the desires and needs of their constituents and were thus sensitive to change. For several decades, the idea of school choice had been on the fringes of the educational policy world in the form of voucher proposals. Essentially, voucher proponents argued that if families, rather than schools, were funded, it would allow for greater parental choice and participation. Moreover, by voting with their dollars, parents would reward good schools and punish bad schools. A voucher system, in effect, would deregulate the public school system. That a voucher system might also privatize the public school system was a muted issue.

By the late 1980s, however, school choice was at the forefront of the educational reform movement. Presidents Reagan and Bush supported choice and one influential White House report enumerated a number of reasons why choice was the right reform for the times (Paulu, 1989). In essence, choice was a panacea that was nonbureaucratic, inexpensive, and fundamentally egalitarian because it allowed market forces to shape school policy rather than subjecting educators to the heavy hand of the educational bureaucracy. A very influential book by John E. Chubb and Terry M. Moe, *Politics, Markets, and America's Schools* (1990), seemed to provide empirical evidence that unregulated school choice policies, in and of themselves, would produce a structural reform in U.S. education.

Congressional support for greater school choice has been expressed in a bill that was passed by the House of Representatives in the summer of 1990 that, among other things, provides direct federal support for open enrollment experiments. Needless to say, all this political activity has stirred up a great deal of controversy and confusion. Choice is controversial because it is deeply political and rests on a set of assumptions about educational marketplaces and private schools that are questionable. It is confusing because choice is a rubric that covers a wide variety of policies that are quite different, except that they include an element of student and parental choice. Next, we briefly touch on some of the major types of school choice plans that have been recently implemented in the United States (see Cookson, 1993, for a complete discussion).

*Intersectional* choice plans include public and private schools. Very recently, for example, the city of Milwaukee provided grants of $2,500 to students who attended private neighborhood academies. The inclusion of private schools in choice plans has stirred a great deal of debate among policy makers because there are fundamental issues of constitutionality and equity inherent in any public policy that transfers funds from the public sector to the private sector. In the United States, there is a constitutionally protected division between church and state that forbids the establishment of any state religion and thus forbids state support of any particular religion. Because the overwhelming number of private schools in the United States are religiously affiliated, this issue is critical. Additionally, equity issues arise from the fact that some private schools are believed to contribute to the maintenance of social inequalities. The most elite secondary schools in the United States, for instance, are private. A public policy that would transfer funds to these schools would clearly raise issues of equal educational opportunity.

Intrasectional school choice policies include only public schools. States, such as Minnesota, permit students to attend school in any public school district in the state, so long as the nonresident school district is willing, has space, and the transfer does not upset racial balance. Statewide choice plans, such as Minnesota's, have been considered by a number of other states. Most choice plans, however, are more limited geographically. The most common form of intrasectional choice plans permit students to attend schools outside of their community school district. These interdistrict choice plans commonly allow urban students to cross district lines and attend suburban schools and vice versa. In St. Louis, for example, minority students from the inner city are able to attend suburban schools that are located in relatively affluent white neighborhoods. In theory, students from the suburbs are supposed to be drawn into the inner city by some outstanding magnet schools, but, in fact, only a handful of white students have traveled into the inner city to attend school.

*Intradistrict* choice plans refer to any option available to students within a given public school district. These options range from a choice of curriculum within a particular school to allowing students to attend any school in the district. One particular intradistrict choice plan that has gained a great deal of recognition is *controlled choice*. In this type of plan, students choose a school anywhere in a district or within some zones within a district. The key to this policy is that student choices are not allowed to upset racial balances. In effect, some students may not be able to enroll in their first choice schools if it would mean increased districtwide racial segregation. Often, other factors are also taken into consideration, such as whether or not an applicant has a sibling already in his or her school of choice. There are several successful controlled choice districts in the United States, including Cambridge (Massachusetts), Montclair (New Jersey), and in District 4 located in the borough of Manhattan in New York City. District 4 also allows students outside its boundaries to attend schools within the district, thus combining intradistrict and interdistrict features.

Boston recently initiated a controlled choice plan that may serve as a test of whether or not these types of plans can be successfully implemented on a citywide basis. According to Charles L. Glenn, executive director of the Office of Educational Equity in the Massachusetts Department of Education, the choice plan in Boston appears to be operationally successful, although "vulnerable schools" (i.e., those with declining student populations) need extra assistance to remain open and to provide services to the students who attend them. According to Glenn (1991, p. 43), "Public school choice will not produce overnight miracles, and the Boston experience—like that of Soviet-bloc economies—shows how very difficult it can be to reform an entrenched institution with a monopoly position and a tradition of top-down decision making."

Clearly, it is too early to tell whether school choice will lead to the revitalization of public education in the United States. It may well be that choice is a method of school improvement, but cannot by itself resolve many of the fundamental problems associated with public education. Moreover, choice plans usually involve complex and volatile issues of constitutionality, equity, and feasibility. For instance, how will already impoverished school districts pay for the increased transportation costs required by many choice plans? In sum, there is evidence that school choice can lead to improvement in individual schools, but there is little convincing evidence that choice will result in the overall improvement of U.S. education.

## School-Business Partnerships

During the 1980s, business leaders became increasingly concerned that the nation's schools were not producing the kinds of graduates necessary for a revitalization of the U.S. economy. Several school-business partnerships were formed, the most notable of which was the Boston Compact begun in 1982. These partnerships have been formed in other cities. For instance, in 1991, the Committee to Support Philadelphia Public Schools pledged management assistance and training to the Philadelphia School District to restructure and implement a site-based management plan. In return, the city promised that by 1995 it would raise the test scores of its graduates and improve grade promotion rates. Other school-business partnerships include scholarships for poor students to attend college and programs where businesses "adopt" a school.

However, despite the considerable publicity that surrounds these partnerships, the fact is that in the 1980s, only 1.5 percent of corporate giving was to public primary and secondary public schools (Reich, 1991, p. 43). In fact, corporate and business support for public schools has fallen dramatically since the 1970s. School-business partnerships have attracted considerable media attention, but there is little convincing evidence that they have significantly improved schools or that, as a means of reform, school-business partnerships will address the fundamental problems facing U.S. education.

## School-Based Management and Teacher Empowerment

In part, the history of education in the United States can be characterized as a struggle between the rivaling traditions of decentralization and centralization. Generally, the educational system, as a whole, is decentralized because the ultimate authority for educational policy rests with the individual states and not with the federal government. Yet, within states and school districts, there has been a long-term tendency to centralize decision making in state agencies, elected and appointed school boards, and superintendents' offices. Throughout the 1980s, there were repeated calls for the exercise of local and community authority in educational decision making. After all, the argument runs, who knows best what the children in any one particular school need—administrators and teachers or state and local bureaucrats?

School-based management is a decentralizing policy that has captured the imagination of many U.S. educators and much of the public. Joseph Fernandez, former New York City's schools chancellor, for instance, is a powerful advocate for school-based management because it enables those who interact with students every day to oversee budgets and set curricula most relevant to the needs of students. He believes in giving schools more decision-making discretion "because generally they will make better decisions" (*Time Magazine,* July 2, 1990).

Major school-based management reforms have been put in place in New York City; Dade County, Florida; San Diego, California; Rochester, New York; Louisville, Kentucky; and Chicago, Illinois. Perhaps the most dramatic of these reforms has been in Chicago, where locally elected councils—composed of six parents, two community residents, two teachers, and the principal—have been put in charge of each of the city's 541 public schools. Although all of the legal issues surrounding this reform have not been settled, there is little doubt that school-based management reforms will continue to enjoy support among many policy makers, some teachers, and some local communities.

The notion that local decision making will automatically make schools better learning environments and more collegial may ignore some of the problems implicit in extreme decentralization. For example, how can the tension between providing teachers with more decision-making authority while simultaneously providing for administrative action and initiative be resolved? There is considerable research that suggests that principals play a key role in creating effective schools.

Moreover, some actions that may be required to make schools more effective may run counter to teachers' desires or self-perceived interests. If teachers and parents are to successfully formulate and implement policy, they need to be given training and related technical assistance. And unless teachers are given substantial amounts of time to plan, implement, monitor, and change their initiatives, there is little reason to expect that school-based reforms will be successful. This issue is becoming more acute in states where budgetary shortfalls have resulted in teacher layoffs and increased teaching workloads. Finally, school-based management requires that some rules and regulations be waived by federal, state, and local authorities as well as teachers' unions. To some extent, these negotiations may mean that school-based reforms may be slowly and partially implemented, and thus their effectiveness may be diminished.

Clearly, school-based management implies teacher empowerment. Without providing teachers with the professional opportunities and responsibilities that come with decision making, many school-level reforms will wither. Yet, what does *teacher empowerment* really mean? How much power should teachers have in policy making and how much power do teachers want? It is becoming increasingly common for principals to establish faculty councils or committees that, in effect, administer the school. These committees and councils may have actual power or they may be thought of more in an advisory capacity.

It is far too early to tell if the teacher empowerment movement will reshape the authority systems within elementary and secondary schools in the United States. In particular, if there is no basic redefinition of teachers' roles within schools, there is little likelihood that teachers will have the opportunity, time, or support to implement change. It is not entirely clear that all teachers want to be policy makers. Definitions of professional responsibilities are not universally agreed upon. Undoubtedly, each school and school district will arrive at a definition of what constitutes teachers' roles and responsibilities in the coming decade. In some schools and school districts, teachers may gain real authority, while in others, principals and superintendents may retain most of the decision-making power. However, if the movement toward school-based management continues, it is likely that teachers will be increasingly empowered and given authority to make professional decisions regarding school management, school curriculum, and pedagogy.

## The Effective School Movement

In response to *A Nation at Risk* and other reports criticizing the effectiveness of U.S. public schools, the school effectiveness movement emerged and suggested that there were characteristics in good schools that could be used as models for improving educational effectiveness. The late Ron Edmonds, one of the early leaders of this movement, argued that educational reform and improvement must consider problems of both equity and quality. Based on Edmonds's work on effective schools for disadvantaged students (Edmonds, 1979), research on school effectiveness sought to identify the characteristics of effective schools (Brookover et al., 1979, 1982).

The school effectiveness research points out five key factors that define successful schools: (1) high expectations for all students, and staff acceptance of responsibility for student learning; (2) instructional leadership on the part of the principal; (3) a safe and orderly environment conducive to learning; (4) a clear and focused mission concerning instructional goals shared by the staff; and (5) frequent monitoring of student progress (Gartner & Lipset, 1987, p. 389).

Based on these principles, school effectiveness researchers and reformers focused their attention on both the content and process of education. First, some critics of present educational practices argued that the nation's schools paid too little attention to the traditional curriculum and that students learned very little subject matter. From Powell, Cohen, and Ferrar's *Shopping Mall High School* (1985) to Ravitch and Finn's *What Do Our Seventeen Year Olds Know?* (1987), U.S. schools were portrayed as having lost their sense of what knowledge is important, and therefore left students with very little sense of the value of knowledge.

Recent popular critiques, including E. D. Hirsch's *Cultural Literacy* (1987) and Allan Bloom's *The Closing of the American Mind* (1987), although the subject of passionate criticism, also portrayed a school system that, in their view, had failed to teach a systematic common body of culturally valuable knowledge. The debate over the usefulness of such knowledge, the Eurocentric and Western bias of the authors, and other criticisms, although important, is not central to this chapter. What is significant, however, is that such criticisms have resulted in an increasing emphasis both on what should be taught and how it should be taught. Thus, much of the school effectiveness movement places a primary emphasis on teaching, teacher effectiveness, and learning, not in terms of the process of learning but in terms of the outcomes of learning.

According to Cuban (1984), the school effectiveness movement recommendations on teaching, teacher effectiveness, and learning are based on research findings concerning the factors that positively affect student achievement. For example, the following teacher factors, according to the effective school research, correlate favorably with student test scores on standardized tests in reading and math:

1. Teacher focuses clearly on academic goals.
2. Teacher concentrates on allotting the instructional period to instructional tasks (time on task).
3. Teacher presents information clearly, organizing by explaining, outlining, reviewing, and covers subject matter extensively.
4. Teacher monitors student progress toward instructional objectives, selecting materials and arranging methods to increase student success.
5. Teacher feedback is quick and targeted on content of instructional tasks. (Cuban, 1984, p. 266)

Based on these research findings, the school effectiveness movement sought to develop scientific models for ensuring better teaching (defined as behaviors responding to the preceding correlations) and the supervision of teachers to ensure increased student achievement. The best example of the attempt to create a rational-scientific pedagogy is the work of Madeline Hunter, one of the most popular figures in school administrative circles. According to Hunter (1982), although teaching is both an art and a science, the scientific model is essential to effective schools and teaching is a manifestation of science because:

1. Identifiable cause-effect relationships exist between teaching and learning.
2. Those relationships hold for all teaching and learning regardless of content, age, and socioeconomic and ethnic characteristics of the learner.
3. Although many of these relationships were identified in the static purity and potential sterility of the research laboratory, those relationships seem to hold in the dynamics inherent in the vitality of a functioning classroom.
4. Those relationships are stated in terms of probability, not certainty.
5. The deliberate, intuitive, or inadvertent use of those cause-effect relationships can be observed and documented in the process of teaching.
6. The principles derived from those relationships should also be incorporated in the process of planning and evaluated before and after teaching.
7. The science of teaching can be taught and predictably learned by most professionals who are willing to expend the required effort.

Although Hunter conceded that "effective teaching also can be an art that goes beyond proficiency," the core of her work emphasizes a science of teaching that revolves around content decisions, learner behavior decisions, teacher behaviors, and the design of effective lessons. Thus, Hunter's model, much like B. F. Skinner's (1971) call for a technology of behavior, proposes a technology of teaching—one that reduces the act of teaching into a series of categories, decisions, steps, and types.

Although there is some merit to the attempt to rationalize educational practice based on research findings, the bureaucratic-rational model that underlies this science of teaching is often misguided and distorted by its becoming an end, rather than a means to and end. Most importantly, this model ignores important realities of teaching and learning, as well as the relationship between schools and other external institutional and societal forces.

## Teacher Education

The emergence and development of teacher education as an educational problem was a response to the initial debates concerning the failure of the schools (Labaree, 1992a, 1992b). If the schools were not working properly, then teachers and teaching—perhaps the most important piece in the puzzle—had to be looked at critically. In addition, teacher organizations such as the National Education Association (NEA) and the American Federation of Teachers (AFT), fearing the scapegoating of their members, took an active role in raising the debate as the opportunity to both recognize and improve the problematic conditions under which, from their perspective, most of their members work.

Finally, if teachers and teaching were indeed part of the problem, then perhaps the education and training of teachers was a good starting point for analysis. Thus, teacher education and schools and colleges of education, long the object of critical scrutiny within universities, became the subject of intensive national investigation. By 1986, at least five major reports (by the National Commission on Excellence in Teacher Education, The California Commission on the Teaching Profession, The Holmes Group, The Southern Regional Education Board, and the Carnegie Report of the Task Force on Teaching as a Profession) outlined major problems in teacher education and the professional lives of teachers, and proposed a large-scale overhaul of the system that prepares teachers. Although the reports differed in some respects, there was widespread agreement about the nature of the problem. The debate revolved around three major points:

1. The perceived lack of rigor and intellectual demands in teacher education programs
2. The need to attract and retain competent teacher candidates
3. The necessity to reorganize the academic and professional components of teacher education programs at both the baccalaureate and post baccalaureate levels (Teacher Education Project, 1986).

Although all five reports contributed to the ongoing discussions, the Carnegie and Holmes reports attracted the most public response and became symbolic of the teacher education reform movement. (Perhaps this was because they represented two of the major interest groups in teacher education; in the case of Carnegie, major political and educational leaders, and for Holmes, the Deans of Education from the major research universities.) Therefore, the next section will analyze the Carnegie and Holmes reports as representative of the current attempts to improve the training of teachers (see Labaree, 1992a, 1992b, for a detailed discussion).

The Carnegie Report, entitled *A Nation Prepared: Teachers for the 21st Century* (1986) and prepared by its Task Force on Teaching as a Profession (including representatives from corporations, the NEA and AFT, school writers and administrators, legislators, the Governor of New Jersey, and a Dean of Education of a major research university), focused on the necessity of educational quality for a competitive U.S. economy, and the value of education in a democratic political system. Building on the critique offered by *A Nation at Risk,* the Carnegie Report suggested that improvements in teacher education were necessary preconditions for improvements in education.

In addition to this underlying democratic-liberal model of education, the report argued that the decline in traditional low wage jobs in the U.S. economy and the corresponding increase in high-technology and service positions would require the schools to better prepare its students for this "new" economic reality. In this regard, also, the Carnegie Report stressed the centrality of better prepared teachers to meet the challenges of the twenty-first century. Echoing this political-economic perspective, the report stated:

> If our standard of living is to be maintained, if the growth of a permanent underclass is to be averted, if democracy is to function effectively into the next century, our schools must graduate the vast majority of their students with achievement levels long thought possible for only the privileged few. The American mass education system, designed in the early part of the century for a mass production economy, will not succeed unless it not only raises but redefines the essential standards of excellence and strives to make quality and equality of opportunity compatible with each other. (1986, p. 3)

In order to accomplish these democratic-liberal goals, the Carnegie Report (1986, p. 3) called for "sweeping changes in educational policy," which would include the restructuring of schools and the teaching profession, the elimination of the undergraduate education major, the recruitment of minorities into the teaching profession, and the increase of standards in teacher education and in teaching.

The Holmes Group, on the other hand, avoided explicit political-economic goals, but focused on the relationship between university-based teacher education, the professional lives of teachers, and the structure of the schools themselves. Arguing that their role as teacher educators gave a unique and also perhaps subjective perception of these issues, the Holmes Report, entitled *Tomorrow's Teachers* (1986), outlined a set of five goals and proposals for the improvement of teacher education. Michael Sedlak, one of the original coauthors of the report, introduced his brief summary of the document by stressing that "the Holmes Group is dedicated not just to the improvement of teacher education but to the construction of a genuine profession of teaching" (1987, p. 315). The goals of the report included raising the intellectual soundness of teacher education, creating career ladders for teachers, developing entry-level requirements into the profession, linking schools of education at the university level to schools, and improving schools for students and teachers.

Despite differences in tone and some minor differences in emphasis, both the Carnegie and Holmes Reports focus on the same general concerns. First, they agree that overall problems in education cannot be solved without corresponding changes in teacher education. Second, teacher education programs must be upgraded in terms of their intellectual rigor and focus, their need to emphasize the liberal arts, their need to eliminate undergraduate teacher education programs and, like other professions (i.e., psychology, social work, law, medicine), move professional training and certification to the graduate level. Third, rigorous standards of entry into the profession must be implemented, and systematic examinations to monitor such entry must be developed. Fourth, university teacher education programs and schools must be connected in a more systematic and cooperative manner. Fifth, career ladders that recognize differences in knowledge, skill, and commitment must be created for teachers. Sixth, necessary changes must be made in the schools and the professional lives of teachers in order to attract and retain the most competent candidates for the profession.

John Goodlad, in *Teachers for Our Nation's Schools* (1990), proposed a radical transformation of the way teachers are prepared, requiring an overhaul of university-based teacher preparation. Echoing many of the recommendations of the Carnegie Commission and the Holmes Group on school-university cooperation, Goodlad stressed the importance of rewarding teacher-educators for their work, rather than relegating them, as is currently the case, to the bottom rung of the university status hierarchy.

Representative of the second wave of educational reforms, the effective school movement's recommendations, as well as those of the Carnegie and Holmes reports, emphasized the processes of teaching and learning, the school environment, and especially the need to improve the professional lives and status of teachers.

## EDUCATIONAL REFORM IN THE 1980s: MAJOR THEMES

Bacharach (1990, pp. 415–430) suggested that U.S. educational reform in the 1980s may be understood in terms of five central themes or questions:

1. The reform of actors and their roles
2. Excellence or equity?
3. Redefining good education for a new century
4. Toward an education marketplace: Choice or greater inequality?
5. Reconceptualizing the role of the teacher

### The Reform of Actors and Their Roles

In the 1980s, the major reform actors shifted from the federal to the state to the local levels. From the outset, the federal government, through the Department of Education, attempted to balance its ideological belief that education is not a federal governmental matter, with its commitment to providing the impetus for change. First, through its influential report, *A Nation At Risk* written during the tenure of Secretary Terrel Bell, and second, through his successor William Bennett's use of his office as a "bully pulpit," the U.S. Department of Education played a significant role in keeping the pressure on states and localities to improve educational results, which for Secretary Bennett defined the goals of educational reform.

The first wave of reforms involved the states becoming the primary level of educational reform. Through the setting of tougher standards and the implementation of new standardized testing procedures, educational reform became centralized to the state level (Honig, 1990; Passow, 1990). As many critics began to point out the problematic and, at times, contradictory nature of these rational-bureaucratic processes, the second wave of reforms began to target the local and school levels as the appropriate venues for improvement, and administrators, teachers, and parents were targeted as the appropriate actors.

Bacharach (1990, p. 418) pointed out that many discussions of school reform refer to top-down or bottom-up reforms as either-ors, as if these are mutually exclusive options. He cautioned that the lessons of the 1980s portend that only through an overall reform process that integrates the many levels of reform (federal, state, local, school) and the diverse actors (governors, legislators, administrators, teachers, parents, and students) will meaningful reform have the opportunity to succeed.

## Excellence and Equity

From the outset of the reforms of the 1980s, the tensions between excellence and equity have been a central concern. Although, as Passow (1989, p. 16) pointed out, "Excellence became a shibboleth of the reform movement," many writers were equally concerned with how the new tougher standards would affect students already disadvantaged because of unequal educational opportunities (Boyer, 1990; Apple, 1990; Cuban, 1990). Whereas the first wave of reforms were explicitly tied to the excellence side of the equation, the second wave of reforms were more often concerned with the need to balance the objectives of equity. Many of the reform proposals of this period—including magnet schools, the effective school movement, public school choice, and school restructuring—all, at least in part, addressed the need to create schools that work for all students. Although many critics of proposals such as school choice asserted they would increase, not decrease, nonetheless, inequality during the second-wave equity issues, began to emerge as vitally important.

At the core of the discussion about these issues are fundamentally differing views of the goals of education. On the one hand, the conservatives, as exemplified by the Heritage Foundation (see Pincus, 1985), stressed the role of schools from a functionalist perspective. From this perspective, the role of the schools is to provide a sorting mechanism to select and educate the "best and the brightest" to fill the functionally essential positions in society. To do this effectively requires that educational funding be geared to programs that ensure high standards. On the other hand, liberals and others to the political left stressed the importance of serving the educational needs of all students, and warned of the deleterious effects on the already disadvantaged of raising standards. Although there have been no easy answers to these complicated questions, it is safe to say that the reforms of the 1980s, at least ideologically, were concerned with balancing excellence and equity. In practice, however, this balance has been far from a reality.

## The Redefinition of Good Education

As in previous periods of U.S. educational reform, the 1980s were concerned with the definition of what constitutes a good education. Just as in the progressive era of the first part of the twentieth century, educational reformers debated the question:

Should all children receive the same education or should the schools provide different types of education for different students? Additionally, the question of what constitutes the type of education necessary for the increasing technological demands of the twenty-first century became a critical issue of the decade.

Interestingly, it was centrist conservatives such as E. D. Hirsch (1987) and Ravitch and Finn (1987) who seized the offensive in these debates. Arguing that the progressive reforms of the twentieth century had resulted in the decline of traditional knowledge (defined as Western), they called for a return to a liberal arts curriculum for all students. By inserting the concern for equity into the call for action, they seized the left's own platform; additionally, by criticizing progressive education, they sought to combine the dual demands for excellence and equity. Although the left would criticize this centrist conservative position for its ethnocentric Western bias (and call for a more multicultural curriculum), the centrist conservatives effectively dominated the curriculum discourse by taking what they saw as the "moral high ground."

Whereas these curriculum debates were essentially about what should be taught to students within the liberal arts tradition, another aspect of the debates concerned the role of education in preparing students for life and the world of work. Although a major theme of many of the reports concerned the relationship between education and economic competitiveness, it was not clear throughout the decade exactly what constituted the proper role of the school.

Many business leaders, including David Kearns of Xerox Corporation, called for closer linkages between school and corporations. Others, such as Robert Reich (1990), pointed out that fundamental changes in the global economy would necessitate workers who can be creative, imaginative, and flexible, and that schools would have to change accordingly. Still others, such as Michael Apple (1990), suggested that the new global economy would reduce the number of jobs requiring such intellectual and analytical dispositions, and that the contradiction of the reforms of the 1980s was the increased emphasis on critical and analytical thinking in a world where the largest number of new jobs would not require them. Finally, others, such as Mary Futrell (1990) and Dianne Ravitch (1985), returned to the notion that education had to prepare students for civic responsibility and an education "that prepares them not only for a life of work but for a life of worth" (Futrell, 1990, p. 423).

Clearly, the debate about what constitutes a good education for the twenty-first century, although a central philosophical concern of the 1980s, is nowhere close to resolution. Perhaps, as Ravitch (1985) pointed out, because Americans have had little consensus about the goals of education, they have been unable to create an educational system with a unified set of objectives.

## The Creation of an Educational Marketplace

The question of school choice became the burning issue of the late 1980s. Supported by both conservatives and some liberals, given national exposure by Chubb and Moe's (1990) controversial book *Politics, Markets, and America's Schools,* and supported by elected officials as diverse as President Bush and Milwaukee African-American city councilwoman Polly Williams, school choice programs have been seen by many as the most effective mechanism for school improvement. Although many agree that reforms that are aimed at the schools themselves, and at the school bureaucracy in particular, are likely to be more effective than those that simply make top-down mandates, critics, such as Cookson (1991), pointed out that the free market strategy is not likely to produce the educational panacea forecasted. Given the vicissitudes of the free market and the ways in which it will likely be more advantageous to the economically advantaged, Cookson cautioned against unrealistic optimism.

By the close of the 1980s, the question of whether school choice programs would improve education for all students or increase educational inequality was left unanswered. As the choice programs become the popular reform of the 1990s, however, educational researchers will have the opportunity to assess empirically the important answer to this question.

## Redefining the Role of the Teacher

The first wave of reform in the 1980s attempted to reduce uncertainty in the classroom and thus sought to increase bureaucratic controls on teacher behavior. Through tightened bureaucratic control, it was thought that the standardization of teaching would result in increased student achievement. As it became increasingly clear that these efforts often were counterproductive, as they led to the deskilling of the teaching profession and teachers mindlessly teaching to tests, the second wave of reforms sought to redefine the role of teachers as professionals. The Holmes (1986) and Carnegie (1986) reports both proposed radical reforms in teacher education and the professional lives of teachers. Stressing career ladders, a national board for professional standards, and cooperation between universities and schools, among other things, these reports sought to professionalize rather than deskill teachers. Other reforms of this period, including teacher empowerment and school-based management, sought to make teachers essential actors in the reform process.

As the decade drew to a close, the conflict between two differing models of school administration—the bureaucratic and the professional (Bacharach, 1990, p. 427)—was still unresolved. The former dominated the first wave of reformers; the latter dominated the second wave. As the 1990s proceed, this conflict will surely remain as central to ongoing reform efforts.

The 1980s were a decade of momentous debate about education and considerable efforts at school improvement. As Passow (1989, p. 37) pointed out, the fact that educational issues became so fundamental to the nation, and that the emphasis in the second wave was on pedagogy, curriculum, teachers as professionals, school organization, and school improvement, was reason for some optimism. However, as many of the best criticisms of U.S. education such as Boyer's (1983) on high schools, Sizer's (1985) on school structure and process, and McNeil's (1988) on the contradictions of reform, pointed out, educational improvement requires more than ideological rhetoric; it requires fundamental school restructuring.

So far—despite some efforts such as Sizer's imaginative *Coalition of Essential Schools,* a nationally implemented school restructuring effort, and the action research of the National Center for Restructuring Education, Schools and Teaching

(NCREST) (headed by Linda Darling-Hammond and Ann Lieberman, two Teachers College, Columbia University professors)—the nation's schools appear resistant to structural change. This should not come as a surprise, as Sarason (1982) has suggested the culture of the school has always been difficult to alter. Perhaps, more importantly, school improvement cannot occur without societal reforms as well. Nonetheless, at the very least, the 1980s represented a period of national soul searching about complex educational problems.

## EDUCATION IN THE 1990s

By the early 1990s, it was still unclear as to whether school reforms would begin to produce some of the improvements they promised. In 1990, President Bush—with the support of the National Governor's Association—announced six national goals for U.S. education:

- Goal 1: By the year 2000, all children will start school ready to learn.
- Goal 2: By the year 2000, the high school graduation rate will increase to at least 90 percent.
- Goal 3: By the year 2000, American students will leave grades 4, 8, and 12 having demonstrated competency in challenging subject matter, including English, mathematics, science, history, and geography, and every school in America will ensure that all students learn to use their minds well, so they may be prepared for responsible citizenship, further learning, and productive employment in our modern economy.
- Goal 4: By the year 2000, U.S. students will be first in the world in mathematics and science achievement.
- Goal 5: By the year 2000, every adult American will be literate and will possess the skills necessary to compete in a global economy and exercise the rights and responsibilities of citizenship.
- Goal 6: By the year 2000, every school in America will be free of drugs and violence and will offer a disciplined environment conducive to learning. (*Education Week,* 1990, pp. 16–17)

Until 1993, President Bush's educational reform proposal *America 2000,* based on these national goals, was in the implementation stage. *America 2000* built on four related themes:

- Creating better and more accountable schools for today's students;
- Creating a New Generation of American Schools for tomorrow's students;
- Transforming America into a nation of students; and
- Making our communities places where learning will happen. (The White House, 1991)

Within each of the objectives, *America 2000* proposed a number of specific goals:

- Creating better and more accountable schools for today's students:
  1. World Class Standards in Five Core Subjects (English, mathematics, science, history, and geography).

2. A system of voluntary national examinations.
3. Schools as the site of reform.
4. Providing and promoting school choice.
5. Promoting outstanding leadership by teachers and principals.
- Creating a New Generation of American Schools for tomorrow's students:
  1. The development of Research and Development teams, funded by the business community, to develop these schools.
  2. The creation of at least 535 New American Schools that "break the mold" of existing school designs.
  3. The development of leadership at all levels, federal, state, and local.
  4. The commitment of families and children devoted to learning.
- Transforming America into a nation of students:
  1. Strengthening the nation's education effort for yesterday's students, today's workers.
  2. Establishing standards for job skills and knowledge.
  3. Creating business and community skill clinics.
  4. Enhancing job training opportunities.
  5. Mobilizing a "nation of students," by transforming a "Nation at Risk" into a "Nation of Students."
- Making our communities places where learning will happen:
  1. Developing greater parental involvement.
  2. Enhancing program effectiveness for children and communities.

When President Clinton was elected in November 1992, he already had a great deal of experience as an educational reformer. As Governor of Arkansas, he led a statewide campaign for teacher accountability, higher academic standards for students, and public school choice. In the late 1980s, he was Chair of the National Governor's Association and led the governors in establishing a national agenda for educational improvement. As president, Clinton has promised to revitalize education and to pay close attention to issues of equity and community service. To this end, he initiated legislation for national service and legislation that would make college student loans easier to obtain and at a lower interest level. The "Goals 2000" bill formally recognizes the national goals and provides a framework for what is referred to as "systemic" reform. Systemic reform is the coordination of reform efforts at the local, state, and federal levels. It is top-down support for bottom-up reform. An important component to systemic reform is the creation of national standards; panels of experts are currently creating content standards, performance standards, and new forms of assessment. A key issue in the development of national standards is the degree to which government is responsible for providing students with equal opportunities to learn if they are to be held to high standards. The reauthorization of the Elementary and Secondary Education Act will be an opportunity for the Clinton administration to fulfill its promise for greater education equity because the ESEA is the federal government's largest compensatory education program. Funding for the ESEA in 1994 is approximately $9 billion. While the educational reforms proposed by President Clinton are significant, we believe that genuine reform must include issues of teacher empowerment, diversity, and creating schools that are communities. In the next section, we propose a more systematic approach to educational reform.

## A THEORY OF EDUCATIONAL PROBLEMS AND REFORMS

In Chapters 1 and 2, we examined a number of pressing educational problems and the ways in which conservatives, liberals, and radicals defined and approached them. Throughout the book, we have looked at how anthropologists, historians, philosophers, political scientists, sociologists, and educators have analyzed a variety of issues and problems.

For the past decade, the dominant political definition of educational problems has been a conservative one, with the crisis in education defined in terms of the decline of standards and authority, and the putative mediocrity of American schools and students. From the *Nation at Risk* report in 1983 through President George Bush's educational reform proposal *America 2000* in 1991, the question of how to improve schools has centered on definitions of academic excellence. Although we certainly believe there is some merit to the conservative claims about the need to raise standards for all American students, the preoccupation with excellence has unfortunately obscured other significant educational problems, most particularly those related to issues of equity.

Furthermore, the emphasis on standards has defined educational problems narrowly, looking primarily on the intellectual and skills function of schooling to the exclusion of the social and psychological functions. Schools, in addition to teaching children skills and knowledge, also should provide students from all backgrounds the opportunity to succeed in U.S. society, as well as to develop their individual potential. The Deweyan conception that schools should have integrative, developmental, and egalitarian functions has been lost in the past decade, with the latter two almost fully overlooked.

Thus, school improvement ought to be aimed at all three aspects of schooling. In the *integrative realm,* schools do need to improve their effectiveness in teaching basic skills and knowledge. Although the conservative claim that the decline in educational standards is the cause of U.S. economic decline is overstated, the nation's students too often graduate from high school without the requisite skills or knowledge for postsecondary education. In part, this is due to the erosion of the academic function of schooling in the twentieth century and the belief that all students cannot handle an academically rigorous curriculum. On the one hand, to the extent that curriculum tracking and ability grouping has limited access to an academic curriculum to working-class and nonwhite students, the erosion of standards has been significantly undemocratic. On the other hand, since academic standards and performance appear to have declined across social class, race, gender, and ethnic lines, the problem of mediocrity is a problem for U.S. education in general.

Where we part company with conservatives is with regard to their preoccupation with standards as the most significant educational problem and with their emphasis on academic standards as either ends in themselves or as they relate to technological and economic imperatives. The reason a society should want a literate and skilled citizenry is not just because these traits are necessary for the economic system. They are also, as Dewey argued, the cornerstone of a democracy, where intelligent and informed citizens take an active role in their community. Thus, education is not an end in and of itself but is instrumental in the life of a democratic society.

In the *developmental realm,* schools need to become more humane institutions where students develop as complete human beings. The conservative emphasis on academic standards and the life of the mind is too shortsighted. Although the life of the mind is important, so too is the life of the heart. Schools need to emphasize, as well, values such as caring, compassion, and cooperation, as feminist educators have correctly pointed out (Laird, 1989, Noddings, 1984). Moreover, schools ought to be places that nurture the creative and spiritual (spiritual need not connote religious) lives of children and enable them to develop a thirst for active learning and creative endeavor. In far too many of our nation's schools, student creativity and imagination is stifled rather than developed.

What is wrong with U.S. schools in this regard is not new. It has been the subject of criticism from Dewey's progressive call for child-centered schools that would emphasize community and development, to the romantic progressive critiques of schooling in the 1960s as authoritarian and stifling, to current calls for educational reform from a variety of individuals and groups. All of these emphasize the need to create schools to educate children in all aspects of life—the social, psychological, emotional, moral, and creative—not just the intellectual. These efforts have included feminist educators with their concern with caring and cooperation, holistic educators with their concern for creative and spiritual dimensions, radical educators with their concern with transformative and liberating dimensions, and progressive educators with their concern for community, democracy, and the need to connect students' lives to the curriculum. These educators encompass both the liberal and radical political spectrum and continue to define educational problems more broadly than do conservatives, and to define solutions that are aimed at making schools places where children want to be.

Perhaps the most overlooked aspect of schooling during the past decade of conservative ascendancy has been the *egalitarian realm* of schooling. Although many of the reports on the crisis in education have stressed the need to balance equity and excellence, the role of schooling in providing equality of opportunity and possibilities for social mobility have taken a backseat. As we argued in Chapters 8 and 9, inequalities of educational opportunity and achievement have remained persistent problems. Jonathan Kozol, in his book *Savage Inequalities* (1991), pointed to the profound inequalities in funding between schools in poor urban areas and affluent suburban districts. In a muckraking style, Kozol placed the issue of equity back on the nation's front burner and demonstrated how current conditions belie the democratic and egalitarian ethos of American schooling.

In a report on Kozol's book, *Time Magazine* (October 14, 1991) chronicled the political controversies over unequal funding of public schools based on property taxes. Although many child advocacy groups have called for the elimination of property taxes in educational financing because they are an advantage to affluent neighborhoods with higher property values, there is often strong opposition from parents in affluent neighborhoods against a "Robin Hood" plan, which would redistribute funds from affluent to poor districts. Kozol, who is interviewed in the article, stated that it is not that affluent parents do not care in the abstract about poor children, but that in the concrete they care more about giving their own children the best education they can afford. They believe that their tax dollars should support their own schools and that redistribution would lead to across-the-board mediocrity.

Although these conflicts point to the sharp divisions and perhaps ambivalence Americans feel about equity issues, they also point out the difficulty of ameliorating problems of educational inequality. Nonetheless, the fact seems clear that as the twenty-first century approaches, the divisions between rich and poor and in the schooling they receive is becoming more glaring than ever. The solutions to these problems will not be easy, and certainly cannot be addressed through school reform alone, but it is apparent that the issue of equity has been relegated to the back burner for too long. Thus, efforts at school improvement must consider equity issues as central to their agenda.

What we are suggesting is that educational reform needs to be aimed at creating schools that teach students the basic skills and knowledge necessary in a technological society—where students have the opportunity to develop their emotional, spiritual, moral, and creative lives; where concern and respect for others is a guiding principle; where caring, cooperation, and community are stressed; where students from different social classes, races, genders, and ethnic groups have equality of opportunity; and where inequalities of class, race, gender, and ethnicity are substantially reduced. These goals, which have been the cornerstone of progressive education for almost a century, are goals that progressives (both liberals and radicals) have too often felt obliged to apologize for, as they have been viewed as either politically naive or utopian. They are neither, although they certainly will be difficult to achieve.

At the beginning of this chapter, we discussed some effective teachers and suggested that effective teaching is necessary but not sufficient to solve educational problems. Without reforms aimed at societal problems, many educational dilemmas will remain unsolved. At the school level, unless schools are restructured to support good teaching and learning, teachers will continue to swim upstream against the current of school improvement.

There are, however, examples of schools that are succeeding. Central Park East Secondary School (CPESS) is a school in East Harlem, which is part of the Center for Collaborative Education (CCE) in New York City. The Center consists of elementary, middle, and high schools and is affiliated with the Coalition for Essential Schools. CPESS is a progressive urban public secondary school that subscribes to the CCE's 12 principles of education:

- Schools that are small and personalized in size
- A unified course of study for all students
- A focus on helping young people use their minds well
- An in-depth, intradisciplinary curriculum respectful of the diverse heritages that encompass our society
- Active learning with student-as-worker/student-as-citizen and teacher-as-coach
- Student evaluation by performance-based assessment methods
- A school tone of unanxious expectation, trust, and decency
- Family involvement, trust, and respect
- Collaborative decision making and governance
- Choice
- Racial, ethnic, economic, and intellectual diversity
- Budget allocations targeting time for collective planning

Under the leadership of Deborah Meier and a committed and talented faculty, CPESS has provided an alternative to the failing comprehensive high schools for urban students. Fine (1991) used CPESS to demonstrate the possibilities for change and described it "as an example of what can be" (p. 215).

We began this book with the conviction that the foundations perspective (i.e., the use of the politics, history, sociology, and philosophy of education) is an important tool in understanding and solving educational problems. Throughout the book, through text and readings, we have provided an analysis of many educational problems and a look at some of the proposed solutions. We end it with the conviction that teachers can make a difference, that schools can and must be restructured, and that the types of reforms discussed here are possible. They will not happen, however, unless people make them happen. School improvement is thus a political act. As prospective teachers and teachers, you must be a part of the ongoing struggle to improve our nation's schools. As Maxine Greene (1988, p. 23) stated:

> [I am] not the first to try to reawaken the consciousness of possibility...or to seek a vision of education that brings together the need for wide-awakeness with the hunger for community, the desire to know with the wish to understand, the desire to feel with the passion to see. I am aware of the ambivalences with respect to equality and justice as well. Fundamentally, perhaps, I am conscious of the tragic dimension in every human life. Tragedy, however, discloses and challenges; often it provides images of men and women on the verge. We may have reached a moment in our history when teaching and learning, if they are to happen meaningfully, must happen on the verge. Confronting a void, confronting nothingness, we may be able to empower the young to create and re-create a common world—and, in cherishing it, in renewing it, discover what it signifies to be free.

We believe that as teachers, you will have the opportunity to contribute to the improvement of this nation's schools. As we have attempted to indicate throughout this book, solutions to educational problems are by no means easy, as the problems are complex and multidimensional. Teachers, alone, will not solve these problems. However, they must be part of the solution. We encourage you to accept the challenge.

The following articles examine issues relating to educational reform and school improvement. The first article, "Reinventing Teaching," written by educator Deborah Meier, analyzes the changes that will be required in schools to assure that good teaching can take place. Based on her ground-breaking work as principal of Central Park East Secondary School in East Harlem, New York City, Meier proposes significant changes in the structure of schools and underscores the importance of good teaching.

The second article, "Better Schools," written by educator Theodore Sizer, proposes significant changes in the structure, organization, and practices of U.S. schools. Sizer, the head of the Coalition of Essential Schools (of which Central Park East Secondary School is a part), has directed a national school reform effort based on these principles.

# Reinventing Teaching

## DEBORAH MEIER

Since I began teaching, some twenty-five years ago, I have changed the way I think about what it means to be a good teacher. Today it is clear that since we need a new kind of school to do a new kind of job, we need a new kind of teacher, too.

The schools we need require different habits of work and habits of mind on the part of teachers—a kind of professionalism within the classroom few teachers were expected to exhibit before. In addition, to get from where we are now to where we need to be will require teachers to play a substantially different role within their schools as well as in public discourse. Teachers need to relearn what it means to be good in-school practitioners, while also becoming more articulate and self-confident spokespeople for the difficult and often anxiety-producing changes schools are expected to undertake. If teachers are not able to join in leading such changes, the changes will not take place. Politicians and policymakers at all levels may institute vast new legislated reforms; but without the understanding, support, and input of teachers, they will end up in the same dead end as such past reforms as "new math" or "open ed." For all the big brave talk, they will be rhetorical and cosmetic, and after a time they will wither away.

Four experiences over the past twenty-five years have influenced my thinking and led me to this conclusion. The first (and latest) is my experience on the National Board for Professional Teaching Standards, which has spent the past three years trying to define the qualities of excellent teaching. The effort we have spent has been well worth it (whether trying to test for it will be as successful I am not yet sure). The National Board has done a superb job of trying to describe the complex set of knowledge and skills that an experienced "master" of teaching must possess. It is a daunting description, but it tells us little about what might go into the making of such a teacher or how such a teacher can be an agent and shaper of the reforms the National Board argues must go hand-in-hand with such an upgraded concept of the profession. I urge you to read it over carefully: It is an important starting place.[1]

The other three experiences that have gradually shaped my thinking on this subject began, not surprisingly, with my own early experiences as a student—my elementary, secondary, and college education. My fortunate and favored personal history had the advantage of making me acutely aware of what distinguished America's best from its worst schools. It was, as a result, not until I started teaching in the Chicago public schools in my early thirties that I experienced what it meant to be treated with disrespect, both personally and intellectually. It was in the role of schoolteacher, not student, that I first had such an experience, and it hit me like a ton of bricks.

The next formative experience was working in the school system, as a kindergarten and Head Start teacher, then as a teacher "trainer," and finally as a teacher director and principal trying to shape a school environment. Twenty-five years of experience in urban public schools has not numbed me, but it has made me aware of the constraints on change, of the enormous difficulties under

*Source: Teachers College Record,* Volume 93, Number 4, Summer 1992. Copyright © by Teachers College, Columbia University. Reprinted by permission.

which my colleagues work, our students learn, and their parents labor—difficulties that are profound, long-standing, and deeply imbedded in our system and our mind set.

Finally, my recent work with the Coalition of Essential Schools, in seeking ways to force-feed changes in a whole interrelated set of entrenched school practices, has required **me** to think about larger social policy questions as they affect school reform: How can we use "top-down" reform to influence what, in the end, must be "bottom-up" change?

In all these years, surprisingly, I have not spent a lot of time thinking about how schools of education could assist in this task of school reform. They never fit into my bottom-up or top-down agenda. Since I have thought about a lot of issues, this may take some explaining. It has probably been a by-product of the fact that I did not enter teaching through that route, nor have many of the teachers whose work I have known best. Perhaps it has also been influenced by the fact that while I was always a "good student," I have never enjoyed "student-hood." Unlike many of my friends, I have never taken a formal course voluntarily since I got my M.A. thirty-five years ago. Finally, I will admit that the courses I did have to take in education were not a sample of the best that could be found, but generally of the worst.

Above and beyond my personal educational history, and based on literally hundreds of in-depth experiences with new teachers, I have yet to see the best or worst schools of education exert much influence. The so-called better schools often attract "better" students, but it is hard for me to see what value has been added. The dominant educational impact—99 percent—had already happened. I am referring to the cumulative influence of their own schooling.

The lessons drawn from sixteen or more years of school experience as a student remain largely intact and dictate the way most people handle their role as teachers. This is hardly surprising. Many of those who enter teaching hope to do unto others what the teachers they knew and loved did unto them. In a few cases—and I tend to have a fondness, however short-lived, for these exceptions—teaching as a career attracts young people who did not like their schooling or were not naturally successful at it. They hope that as teachers they might be able to do unto others what they wished their teachers had done for them. They have come into teaching to change practice, not perpetuate it—to break a tradition, not carry it on. But such teachers often leave teaching quickly, when they discover that their students do not love them for being different, less authoritarian, more genial, smarter. They often leave with new ideas about what is wrong with "these" kids or the evils and stupidity ties of their fellow teachers—the ones who stayed. Some people, fortunatley, enter teaching at a later age, not fresh out of school. They bring to their jobs a wider range of experience, and are accustomed to different kinds of institutional arrangements and ways of relating to colleagues. Sometimes they even come to teaching after they have had children, and if they are lucky, at least one of their children has not found school so easy. They are not quite so quick to judge parents at fault, and may have a special personal empathy for school losers. But in most cases the constraints of the job, plus old habits and a kind of societal nostalgia for what school "used to be like," make teachers part of the broader inertia that makes fundamental change hard to implement.

In short: The habits of schooling are deep, powerful, and hard to budge. No public institution is more deeply entrenched in habitual behavior than schools—and for good reason. Aside from our many years of direct experience as students, we have books, movies, television shows, advertisments, and myriad other activities, games, and symbols that reinforce our view of what school is "supposed" to be. Our everyday language and metaphors are built on a kind of prototype of schoolhouse and classroom, with all its authoritarian,   filling-up-the-empty-vessel, rote-learning assumptions.

For example, the other night I watched a semi-documentary entitled "Yearbook." It purported to depict the life of a school by following a group of seniors during their last year in high school. We watch, with a kind of false nostalgia, the senior year so few of us truly had but believe we should have had: the selection of cheerleaders and homecoming queens in the fall, the pains of dating, the sports fields, the trivia of home economics classes, and so forth. There is not even a momentary bow to the intellectual purposes of high school. At Central Park East schools, we laugh sometimes about how our own students (and even our own children), many of whom have never attended any school but ours, still play "pretend school" in a traditional way—lining up the desks, and yelling at the children. Our Central Park East Secondary School (CPESS) high school students complain about not having lockers—that is where true high school life takes place, the absence of bells, passing time, proms, and so forth. They view these as essential rites of passage. My four-year-old granddaughter loves playing school with me—but I am required to be the mean principal who does awful things to bad children. She cannot wait until she gets to such a real school.

It is no easier to change such habits, built around age-old metaphors about teaching and learning, about getting ahead, than it is to change our personal habits (like giving up smoking), or our seemingly ingrained primitive ideas about the physical universe. It is current wisdom to recognize that despite all the correct information offered in physics and astronomy courses, including laboratory experiences and visits to the planetarium, the average citizen's real-life view of the universe remains amazingly heliocentric at best (and geocentric, if not New York-centric, at

worst). We pile new theories on top of old conceptions rooted in childhood experience, language, and symbols, and they are absorbed in some odd commonsensical way. The sky remains up, as does the North Pole; we imagine looking up at the moon and therefore assume that the men on the moon must look down to see the Earth; we know that the moon is very far away—about halfway to Mars or Venus. This is now old-hat theory, yet few schools are successful in getting their students to see the world in post-Copernican terms. Habit and everyday common sense rule. So why should it be any different when it comes to teaching adults how to teach?

Until we are ready to engage students in a far different form of pedagogy, with far greater in-depth exploration, such commonsense habits will not be overcome in physics classes. Our graduates may be able to recite more modern ideas, but their understanding will remain paper-thin and school-bound. That may suffice for physics, because few have to base their future practices on a different view of the universe. In everyday life, in fact, the old pre-Copernican view works quite well.

So too with education courses, and pedagogical theories. As in physics, our habitual view of teaching as telling and learning as remembering is hard to dislodge. The difference is, of course, that we expect would-be teachers to overcome such views and then act on the basis of their new wisdom. We pretend that this can be so, despite the fact that we know that teaching, more than virtually any field (aside from parenting, perhaps), depends on quick instinctive habits, behaviors, and deeply held ways of seeing and valuing. Teachers are confronted with literally hundreds of decisions and unmonitored responses every hour they work, which cannot be mediated by cool calculation. Nothing is more unsettling in the presence of real-live students in real-live classrooms than an uncertain teacher, searching for the right response. A doctor can examine patients slowly and carefully, and look up the answers in books before being required to commit to action. Not so a teacher.

In short, we come to be teachers knowing all about teaching. We have been exposed to more teaching and teachers than to any other single phenomenon. Most of us have spent more time with teachers than with our parents. To make matters worse, what we learn from our parents in a more informal pedagogy is rarely even thought of as having been taught. In fact, the more "naturally" and "readily" we learn something, the less credit we give to those who taught us. Furthermore, our first exposure to teaching is done under the frequently scornful eye of experienced teachers who are quick to put down the green ambitions of innovators, whose early innovations are likely to be dismal failures.

If teaching and schooling are so entrenched, if our habits are so deeply rooted and so hard to change, is there no hope for school reform? The answer will depend on how serious we are about the need to change, and how long we are willing to stick with the effort to effect it.

At present, there is not a lot of evidence of a serious will to change. There is a desire, for sure, for youngsters to "do better," for much better results—especially on competitive test scores. But it should surprise no one, given the above analysis, that most people think improvement is a matter of all those involved trying harder—or even returning to former more didactic ways, which presumably we have mistakenly abandoned. Lots of people want parents and teachers to be more like they used to be in the good old days—if mothers would just stay home and teachers would just assign more homework, and so forth. More demanding, tougher, and more dedicated teachers might restore the high standards many of the critics suggest. Let the students face the consequences. Some suggest these nostrums will not work given the nature of "kids today" and some wonder about whether "those" children (read "non-

white") are really able to meet high standards. But few see the problem the way the members of prestigious task forces do: as creating a different system to do a different job. Thus, the will thoroughly to restructure the institutions themselves, with all this implies in terms of resources for basic research and development, for massively retraining the educational work force, has little public backing.

Many things must be done if we are to alter this bleak picture. At the heart of it is the question of how teachers can be changed—even what it means to "retrain" the educational work force. The change that must take place among the work force involves three tough tasks: changing how teachers view teaching and learning, developing new habits to go with that new cognitive understanding, and simultaneously developing new habits of work—habits that are collegial and public in nature, not solo and private as has been the custom in teaching. Such changes cannot be "taught" in the best-designed retraining program and then imported into classroom practice. What is entailed is changing the daily experiences of teachers, substituting experiences that will require them to engage in new practices and support them in doing so.

If it were possible to escape the issue by somehow inculcating the next generation with a different set of habits, thus bypassing both teachers and their parents, it would be an attractive idea. Otherwise, this is a kind of pulling-oneself-up-by-the-bootstraps problem. Every revolutionary ideology comes up against this same conundrum and, historically, most revolutionaries think they can resolve it only by totalitarian measures. Some try removing children from their families, sowing suspicion between generations, forcing prescriptive ideological training from infancy on up, or creating a network of "big brothers." They hope thus to breed a new generation that leaps over the weaknesses of the present misguided and corrupted generation. In a milder form, most school reform efforts are not so different in conception. It is the familiar design that rests on hopes for teacher-proof curriculum, reform by testing and monitoring, by penalties and threats. They will have no more luck.

One cannot impose such change—not because it is immoral or unpleasant, but because it does not work. And the price paid for trying to wipe out the past by fiat is enormous. Benign schemes for trying to do the same thing fail just as the obviously malign ones do. This is not surprising. It is illogical to imagine that we can produce thoughtful and critical thinkers by rote imposition or that we can build strong intellectual understanding through required amnesia. If the logic of it fails to impress, years and years of failed efforts to do so ought to. It is, at the very least, a great waste of time, a diversion of energy and resources that we can ill afford. We cannot pass on to a new generation that which we do not ourselves possess. That is the conundrum, the seemingly impossible paradox.

How might we approach such a riddle? We can change the schools so as to promote thoughtful and critical practices on the part of teacher practitioners, and in ways that undercut any need for teachers themselves to become lobbyists against change. Teachers must lead the way toward their own liberation.

Teachers were force-marched to the promised land of "new math," and the results should be a warning. Impatience for rapid improvement in math education following *Sputnik* produced a dud—and today, thirty years later, we are once again trying to introduce just such a math education. Had we been more patient thirty years ago we would be thirty years ahead of the game now.

The only route possible requires involving all parties to education in the process of reinventing schooling. Not, please note, revolution or reform, but reinvention is required. It is our mind set that needs changing, and the institutional arrangements that either support or impede the new mind set. However, you do not and should not fool with people's minds loosely. It requires the utmost respect, a stance that is not easy for us to assume. The changes needed are not changes in the solo acts teachers perform inside their classrooms, hard as that might be to accomplish. We are talking about creating a very different school culture, a new set of relationships and ideas. We are talking about changes that will affect not just teachers (although without them it is pointless), but also their constituents—parents and children. Given enough time—if we are not in too much of a hurry; if we allow for lapses and half-measures, and do not give up—we might begin to see changes. It is through collective co-ownership of new designs for schooling, in an atmosphere that allows for reflective examination and reshaping based on experience, that something new might emerge.

We can change teachers only by changing the environment in which teaching takes place. Teaching can be changed only by reinventing the institutions within which teaching takes place—schools. Reinvention has to be done by those who will be stuck in the reinvented schools. It cannot be force-fed—not to teachers, nor to parents and children. All three constituents can sabotage the best-laid plans. While parents and children will put up with some dissonance and anxiety, the mismatch between what they expect and what they experience cannot be ignored or evaded. Their willingness to participate in change is critical. While such willingness can be encouraged by various public policies, a thoroughly "converted" and committed faculty is a must.

When school people visit CPESS they often dismiss our achievements—which I believe to be modest compared with the achievements that lie ahead of us—on the basis that we, after all, had the opportunity to start from scratch, whereas they must reform an existing huge, sluggish institution, only some of whose members want to change. If we had your freedom, they suggest, we too could produce Central Park East's successes. I think they are right, so I suggest they be given precisely the same freedom we have had. That is what public policy can create.

Our visitors argue that we have the advantage of having a student and parent body who chose to come to our school. I propose that all schools be given precisely the same freedom: a student and parent body of those who choose to come to their school. (Note that by "school" I do not necessarily mean a building. A single building can contain many such reinvented schools of choice.) Visitors argue that we had a chance to select our staff, from among those who agree with us. It is much easier to carry out a collective policy when people agree on the policy, they complain. We propose that all schools should have this same freedom. Professionals should work in a school that they want to work in because they share its assumptions. Visitors complain that our work is not replicable because we have been given the freedom to organize our day, select our curriculum, and design our forms of assessment in the way we think best—and to change them whenever we find they do not work. We propose that all other schools be offered the same freedom, along with the same responsibilities we have accepted.

If these are the four freedoms that you envy, we tell our visitors, why not demand the same for yourselves? But you have to want such freedom and you have to accept the responsibility that goes with it. It will be exhausting, even at times frustrating. The thing we keep telling our colleagues in other schools is that it surely will not lead to "burnout"—because people burn out when they are treated like appliances. This kind of teaching and schooling is, in contrast, never dehumanizing. It rests on intense human interaction and involvement.

You can only change people's habits, at best, when they have strong reasons to want to change and an environment conducive to it. That is the first requirement. For teachers, this means sufficient support from those they depend on—schools boards, administrators, parents—to take some risky first steps. They need, furthermore, the luxury of being able to waste money on ideas that will not work, rather than feeling obliged to pretend that everything they do is successful. They need access to expertise without promising to follow expert advice. They need time. They need more time in a daily weekly, monthly sense—to reflect, examine, redo. They also need recognition of the other kind of time—the years it will take to see it through. These are the conditions we know work whenever we are really in a hurry to do something difficult: cure cancer, go to the moon, invent new technologies, or win a war.

The greater the desire for change on the part of teachers, parents, and children, the less it will cost. Unpaid volunteer armies can defend their homeland better than highly trained and equipped mercenary troops. Very eager and driven reformers are ready to exploit themselves, putting in endless hours and sleepless nights—although they often also exhaust themselves too soon. But the more timid, the less eager, the less confident and self-motivated, the more ideal the circumstances must be before we get the necessary sustained effort. Money (for extra personnel, financial incentives, paid time, equipment) compensates for zeal. We will not get large-scale school reform in the United States if we count only on zealots, but we would be foolish indeed not to promote such zeal, and give such ardent reformers the room and space to work their hearts out as we build up credibility for more ambitious national efforts.

The job of those in policymaking positions who want to improve the quality of teachers must be to change the conditions of teaching. They must offer incentives for change, and above all the resources (in this case the key is well-designed staff development time) to enable teachers to learn from their changed conditions. Unlike most industries, we cannot retool by closing down the factories and sending all the workers back to school. We need to do everything at once. It is driving while changing the tires, not to mention the transmission system.

Our schools must be labs for learning about learning. Only such labs can teach both children and their teachers simultaneously. They must create a passion for learning, not only among children, but also among their teachers. Both have become "passion-impaired." In the words of Ginny Stiles, a kindergarten teacher at Reek Elementary School in Wisconsin, "It's my job to find the passion, to open eyes and weave a web of intrigue and surprise." Indeed, she notes, too many teachers have themselves become what she calls passion-impaired. The motivator par our excellence is our heart's desire, our taste for "the having of wonderful ideas," as Eleanor Duckworth calls it.[2] How better to impart such ideas than by engaging in the having of wonderful ideas oneself?

If I could choose five qualities to look for in prospective teachers they would be: (1) a self-conscious reflectiveness about how they themselves learn and, maybe even more, how and when they do not learn; (2) a sympathy toward others, an appreciation of their differences, an ability to imagine their "otherness"; (3) a willingness to engage in, better yet a taste for, collaborative work; (4) a desire to have others to share some of one's own interests; and (5) a lot of perseverance, energy, and devotion to getting things right.

Since we cannot count on finding enough teachers who already possess all five qualities, we need to create the kind of schools that will draw out these qualities. Of course, when I say we need schools that will encourage such characteristics, I include liberal arts colleges and schools of education as well as schools for children and adolescents. Nothing we have discovered lately about how the brain works is uniquely true for children versus adults, or would-be teachers versus

would-be anything else. The kind of education that is best for teachers is one that is best for learners in all subjects and domains.

We will change American education only insofar as we make all our schools educationally inspiring and intellectually challenging for teachers, not just students. It is not enough to worry about some decontextualized quality called teacher "morale" or "job satisfaction." Those words, like "self-esteem," are not stand-alones. Neither happy teachers nor happy students are our goal. What we need is a particular kind of job satisfaction that has as its anchor intellectual growth. The school itself must be intellectually stimulating—organized to make it hard for teachers to remain unthoughtful. High teacher (or student) morale needs to be viewed as a by-product of the wonderful ideas that are being examined under the most challenging circumstances. During our first year at CPESS we went around muttering under our breath that our job was not to make the children happy but to make them strong. That goes for teacher education too.

Mindlessness as a habit may drive employers crazy, but it is a habit we have too often fostered in schools. The habit of failing back on excuses—"I had to," "that's the way it's supposed to be"—can be rooted out only by major surgery. It will be painful, and it will not all come out at once. Expecting teachers to take responsibility for the success of the whole school requires that they begin to accept responsibility for their own as well as their colleagues' teaching—surely no overnight task. At the very least, one must imagine schools in which teachers are in frequent conversation with each other about their work, have easy and necessary access to each other's classrooms, take it for granted that they should comment on each other's work, and have the time to develop common standards for student work. They need frequent and easy access to the kind of give-and-take with professionals from allied fields that is the mark of a true professional. They need opportunities to speak and write publicly about their work, attend conferences, read professional journals, and discuss something besides what they are going to do on Monday. There must be some kind of combination of discomfiture and support—focused always on what does and does not have an impact on children's learning.

What would be the role in such schools of administration and supervision? I do not think the answer is yet in regarding the nature of school governance best suited to faculty growth. Insofar as the faculty are prevented from blaming others for their problems, they are more likely to look to their own practice. So some form of work-place democracy is essential, but there are numerous possible candidates for the form and style that best frees teachers to work together on professional matters. What is certain is that this kind of collegiality works best in settings that are sufficiently small and intimate so that self-governance and staff-development schemes do not exhaust teachers' energies or divert them from their central task.

There are doubtless many models of how a university faculty could work with such restructured schools. It is easy to see how they could play critical roles, probably involving far less emphasis on running full-time education programs for would-be teachers. Most of the models I can envisage would take place primarily around the work site itself, although school people (like other professionals) need opportunities to "get away" from time to time for more distanced reflections, sometimes with people other than those they daily contend with. "Distance" can become an advantage. That goes for the distance that the university faculty bring to the work site, and the distance that teachers can experience when they go away from their work site. I can envisage countless ways in which an empowered and self-confident school faculty could use the expertise of university people. For example, university faculty could teach occasional mini-courses to children under careful-

ly observed and even videotaped conditions; they could meet with faculty to examine curriculum in their fields of expertise; they could observe classes and act as friendly critics; they could videotape instructional settings for teachers and act as guides in looking them over; they could read student papers and discuss ways to support better writing; they could lead reading groups on issues of pedagogical or school reform; they could give lectures on issues the faculty as a whole wants to learn more about, including lectures on particular literary texts, historical disputes, or mathematical discoveries, not just pedagogy; they could recommend important readings or circulate articles relevant to each school's situation. They could include "school teachers" of history in professional historical associations, acknowledging them in the brother- and sisterhood of historains. And, of course, they could teach differently in their own courses.

Above all, our university colleagues can commit themselves to the equally difficult task or taking teaching and learning seriously in their own institutions, to reinventing universities as educational institutions. They can observe each other, consider why and how their students are or are not learning what they intend to be teaching. They can provide models of a lively intellectual community for their students. They can team teach, creating courses that are contentious so that students are forced to deal with different viewpoints, make judgments between them, consider evidence, and ask questions.

Psycholinguist Frank Smith tells a story about a lecture he gave, attacking courses on "thinking skills." After the meeting, the superintendent of schools came up to him and said that he was in a quandary. The week before another speaker had presented just the opposite viewpoint. What should he do, he asked Smith. Well, said Smith, we cannot both be right can we? So you will just have to think about it and then make your own decision. That is what thinking is all about.

The world of schools has habituated us not only to teach children that there is always one "right" answer, but to think that way ourselves. Even where we have taken the giant step of considering that how we teach is worthy of serious intellectual thought, we rarely think about the impact the institutional arrangement of teaching and learning has on our lives and on the lives of our students. We do not imagine that thinking about that is part of our job as teacher educators.

Colleges and universities, not just public elementary and secondary schools, bear considerable responsibility for having given the vast majority of those we send out into schools as teachers the same mis-messsage that Frank Smith's superintendent labors under. The vast majority of those who enter teaching attended colleges that also rewarded mindlessness and rote learning. The thing that is wrong with prescriptive teaching is not that it does not "work"—it does work. It produces just the kind of miseducated people that society may once have been looking for, or in any case not seriously minded. But for the kind of educational purposes that are now being demanded, such mindlessness will not do.

Since the public at large plays such an important role in decisions about education, perhaps the only specific education requirement that all colleges should have is one directed at all its students, not just those considering teaching as a career. Reflecting on learning, becoming more sensitive to how human beings in general learn as well as how each of us individually learns—as well as addressing issues of schools as institutions—would be foundation courses at least as appropriate, if not more so, for liberal arts students as for would-be teachers. Maybe Ed 101 should be mandatory for all students, or its content woven into all courses.

The Central Park East schools were created, invented if you will, with all these considerations, plus a few more, in mind. They were efforts to imagine the kind of collegial setting in which adults could and would learn side by side with their students. We sought to create an intellectually transformative environment, a culture of mutual respect for others, a set of habits of mind that foster inquiry as well as responsibility. We based our work on some simple principles, familiar enough to those who work with young children, but less familiar to those who work with adolescents or adults. We started with the premise that there is far more in common between a five-year-old, a fifteen-year-old, and a fifty-year-old than there are differences. Our common humanity means we learn in much the same way. That was, in fact, our first principle. Good kindergarten practice is probably on target at any age, including the age of teachers.

For example, we knew that five-year-olds learn best when they feel relatively safe—physically as well as psychically. (Young children need to feel comfortable about going to the bathroom, for example. How about teenagers? How about teachers?) Feeling safe includes trusting at least some of those "in charge," not to mention being able to predict with some degree of accuracy how the place works. The same is true for adults. For young children we know it also means that parents need to see the school as safe so that they can reassure their children that "those people are okay," "you can trust them to care for you," "they are not our enemies." It turns out that this is also critical for the development of fifteen-year-olds. They too suffer if they come to school carrying wary or hostile warnings from their families. The appropriate rebellion of adolescence cannot be carried out successfully in a setting in which the adults may truly be seen as dangerous. Healthy "testing out" rests on a basic trust that there are adults prepared to set limits. Is it so different at fifty? Do we not need a work place that is safe, predictable, and on our side, if we expect to do our best work?

A second principle, one at the heart of the Coalition of Essential Schools' "Nine Basic

Principles," can be put succinctly: You cannot teach well if you do not know your students well. That means size and scale are critical. Even prisons, or army units, are not as huge, impersonal, and anonymous as many schools for young children, not to mention the average American high school. It is not just children who suffer from this depersonalization of work; adults do too. All but a few stars become lookers-on, admirers, or wallflowers, not active participants.

Our third principle is an old familiar one: You cannot use the coach or expert well if he or she is also judge and high executioner. As my son explained to me one day when I was trying to convince him to ask his teacher to explain something to him, "Mom, you don't understand. The last person in the world who I'd let know what I don't understand is my teacher." Schooling becomes a vast game in which teachers try to trick students into revealing their ignorance while students try to trick teachers into thinking they are not ignorant. Getting a good grade, after all, is getting the teacher to think you know more than you do. Is it so different for teachers, whose only source of help and support is precisely the person who rates and rules them? The metaphor "teacher as coach" is full of possibilities not only for the relationship between adults and children, but in all teaching/learning settings.

A fourth principle for an efficient learning environment is that we learn best when we are in a position to make sense of things—especially to make sense of things we are interested in. Human beings are by nature meaning-makers, trying to put the puzzle together. From the moment of birth until our death this is our preeminent mode. Schools rarely capitalize on it. A nursery school teacher uses the room itself to create interest and curiosity. She carefully sets up the environment so that it invites questions; and she spends her time moving about the room, prodding, inquiring, changing materials and tools so that curiosity is kept lively and current. She creates dissonances as well as harmonies; she creates confusion as well as serenity. Contradictions are accepted as natural. By the time students reach high school we have stripped the environment bare, and lessons are dry and "clear cut." No high school teacher (and surely not a college professor) worthy of her salt assumes the actual physical setting of the classroom is a relevant part of her job. The typical explanation for why we teach what we do is that it is required at the next grade level—or, at best, that it is required on a state-mandated exam. Teaching becomes simplified, focusing more and more on test-taking skill. Nor do teachers view the courses they are required to take to get a license or upgrade their status much differently. Teachers' own interests are often irrelevant, or sneaked into a high school schedule. A teacher with a love for physics and expertise in the field may teach biology because that is what is "needed." No wonder that the phrase "It's academic" means it is irrelevant.

Fifth, human beings by nature are social, interactive learners. We check out our ideas, argue with authors, bounce issues back and forth, ask friends to read our early drafts, talk together after seeing a movie, pass on books we have loved, attend meetings and argue out our ideas, share stories and gossip that extends our understanding of ourselves and others. Talk lies at the heart of our lives. This kind of exchange is never allowed in school, nor modeled there—not between children, nor between adults. Monthly faculty meetings are no better imitations of true discussion than the average so-called classroom discussion. The most powerful motivation for becoming learned—that we might influence others—is purposely removed from students and their teachers. No one among the powerful policymakers wonders, as they imagine the perfect curriculum, what it means to teach a subject year after year, based on someone else's design. We organize schools as though the ideal were an institution impervious to human touch.

If we intend dramatically to improve the education of American children we need to invent very different environments for them. Teachers must be challenged to invent schools they would like to teach in, organized around the principles of learning that we know matter. That is the simple idea we put into practice at Central Park East.

What did we do? First, children stay with teachers for two years, so it is worth getting to know each other well—students, their families, and the teacher. Even high school students do not move around every forty-five minutes, do not change courses in midyear, and stay with the same faculty for two years. There are no pull-outs, and no seven-period days. In the high school most students see no more than two to three different teachers a day, including an advisor who spends an hour a day with a small group of his or her own fifteen advisees. Furthermore, each teacher teaches an interdisciplinary course: literature and history or math and science, for example.

A typical class is long enough (often two hours) to include whole-class seminars, small-group work, independent study, and one-on-one coaching by teachers and fellow students. Students do their writing and reading in school, not just as homework, so they can get feedback and insight into how to read and write more effectively. Teachers, furthermore, teach in collaborative settings; four to five teachers work in physically contiguous rooms and with the same set of students so that they can easily make decisions, alter plans, rearrange schedules, regroup students, share ideas, and observe each other at work.

Decisions are made as close to each teacher's own classroom setting as possible, although all decisions are ultimately the responsibility of the whole staff. The decisions are not merely on minor matters—length of classes or the number of field trips. The teachers collectively decide on content, pedagogy, and assessment as well. They teach what they think matters. The "whole staff" is not enormous—none of our Central Park

East schools is larger than about 450 students, most are 200 to 300. That means a faculty that can sit in a circle in one room and get a chance to hear each other. Governance is simple. There are virtually no permanent standing committees. Finally, we work together to develop assessment systems for our students, their families, ourselves, and the broader public—systems that represent our values and beliefs in as direct a manner as possible. When we are asked "Does it work?" we have had a voice in deciding what "work" means. Our forms of assessment are constantly open to public review and what is open is direct evidence: Observers may visit our classrooms, read our students' work, examine our scoring grids, look at samples of graduation-level portfolios. We even invite experts to review our work and our students' performances, as a way to sharpen our insights and check our potentially overgenerous hearts.

The result: Our students succeed in far greater measure than their socioeconomic, ethnic, and racial background and prior academic skills would predict. We have not closed the gap between rich and poor, we have not sent all our graduates to prestigious colleges, nor made enough difference to ensure that none will fall through the cracks of the larger society. But in a city in which nearly half of all students fail to complete high school, about 90 percent of those who attend Central Park East schools do complete high school, even after only four to six years in our elementary schools. While the fact that half of those who graduate from our elementary schools go on to college is a promising piece of data, the numbers are much higher for those who attend our secondary school. We hope, over time, to prove that their capacity to stick it out in college and hold good jobs and be strong citizens will be even more convincing. Whether they leave us at twelve or eighteen, they are far better able to join society as productive and socially useful citizens than are their counterparts.

It is not enough. It never will be. But the fact that schools cannot do the job alone is a far cry from claiming that schools cannot do their job better if they take seriously what they know about teaching and learning and practice it at every age and grade level. Period.

Just as our student body is not exceptional, but reflects the general population of New York City schools, our faculty are by no means exceptionally well educated, more learned than the average teacher in New York City, and certainly no more experienced. Many had virtually no prior experience as teachers and some had taken no courses in teaching. Many started as interns with us, spending their first year in low-paid assistant teaching roles. Some came from other schools where they had been good but not exceptional teachers (the most exceptional often build comfortable niches for themselves and are hard to woo away). But they all came with a willingness to learn from each other, although often vulnerable, prickly, and defensive, and they have all grown incredibly in the process of becoming better teachers. Today many speak about our work all over the country, something we consciously committed ourselves as a faculty to help each other learn to do. Others write about our work, again something we have helped each other learn to do. They see themselves first as the teachers of a particular group of youngsters, but then also see themselves as the governing body of a school and the carriers of an idea.

My colleague Ann Bussis claims that teaching is not so complex as to verge on the impossible or to defy conception at an abstract level, but it does defy concrete prescriptions for action—there is neither prescription for action nor a checklist for observation to assure intelligent and responsive teaching. All that can be offered is a guiding theory and abundant examples.

That is what schools must help us develop—guiding ideas and abundant examples, and then the opportunity to put such guiding ideas into practice and to learn from our abundant examples. It is hoped that someday, not too far in the future, we will have abundant enough examples of what such reinvented schools might be like for them to become the norm.

In summary, if we want schools for the twenty-first century to resemble schools of the twentieth century, we can afford to tinker a little and leave the structure pretty much intact. Then teacher-training institutions need only follow suit, tinkering too. But if we want the least of our citizens to know and be able to do the kinds of things that only those lucky few at the top of the ladder have ever achieved before, then we need to begin a slow and steady revolution in how and what teachers must know and know how to do. To do this means we have to learn how to drive while changing not only the tire but the whole mechanism! Impossible? No, but very, very hard. The place it will happen is in the schools themselves—not the schools as we now know them, but reinvented schools created by school people and their communities. And it does not come with guarantees.

A version of this article was presented as the DeGarmo Lecture for the Sociey of Professors of Education at the annual meeting of the American Educational Research Association, April 4, 1991 in Chicago.

## ENDNOTES

1. National Board for Professional Teaching Standards, "What Teachers Should Know and Be Able to Do," in *Toward High and Rigorous Standards for the Teaching Profession. Initial Policies for the National Board for Professional Teaching Standards* (Detroit: NBPTS, 1991), pp. 13–32.
2. Eleanor Duckworth, *"The Having of Wonderful Ideas" and Other Essays on Teaching and Learning* (New York: Teachers College Press, 1987).

# Better Schools

## THEODORE SIZER

There are five imperatives for better schools:

1. Give room to teachers and students to work and learn in their own, appropriate ways.
2. Insist that students clearly exhibit mastery of their school work.
3. Get the incentives right, for students and for teachers.
4. Focus the students' work on the use of their minds.
5. Keep the structure simple and thus flexible.

*Giving teachers and students room* to take full advantage of the variety among them implies that there must be substantial authority in each school. For most public and diocesan Catholic school systems, this means the decentralization of power from central headquarters to individual schools. For state authorities, it demands the forswearing of detailed regulations for how schools should be operated. It calls for the authorities to trust teachers and principals—and believe that the more trust one places in them, the more their response will justify that trust. This trust can be tempered by judicious accreditation systems, as long as these do not reinfect the schools with the blight of standardized required practice.

The purpose of decentralized authority is to allow teachers and principals to adapt their schools to the needs, learning styles, and learning rates of their particular students. The temptation in every school will be to move toward orderly standardization: such is the instinct, it seems, of Americans, so used as we

are to depending on structure. Good schools will have to resist this appeal of standardization nation: the particular needs of each student should be the only measure of how a school gets on with its business. Greater authority is an incentive for teachers, one that will attract and hold the kind of adults which high schools absolutely need on their staffs.

The requirement for *exhibitions of mastery* forces both students and teachers to focus on the substance of schooling. It gives the state, the parents, prospective employers, and the adolescents themselves a real reading of what a student can do. It is the only sensible basis for accountability.

Effective exhibitions will be complicated to construct and time-consuming to administer. To be fair, they need to be flexible: not all students show themselves off well in the same way. They cannot, then, merely be standardized, machine-graded, paper-and-pencil tests.

The process of constructing and overseeing these exhibitions can be threatening, because it will force teachers to see and to deal with the gaps and redundancies that arise from the traditional curriculum. Teachers find it safe to work in the privacy of their classrooms, delivering the credits their courses bestow on each student. A commonly constructed exhibition invades this privacy—a step that is as necessary as it may be intimidating.[1]

The existence of specific exhibitions is itself a strong *incentive* for both students and teachers. Exhibitions clarify ends. The student knows what she or he has to do in order to progress and graduate. If pursuit of that high school graduation diploma is voluntary, the adolescent is left on his or her own; the games attendant on compulsory attendance can no longer be used as excuses. To the young person who has met the minimal competencies in literary, numerary, and civic understanding, the high school says, Here is what our diploma means; join us and we'll help you master the knowledge it represents, but the work is basically yours to do. The challenge of such an arrangement is powerful. There is self-esteem to be gained from being the key worker, and if wise teachers appropriately adjust the study to the pace of each student, success will breed success. The personalization inherent in such adjusted pacing is also rewarding; it signals to the student that he or she is important as an individual.

Not all adolescents will find any one school setting congenial. Some students respond well to judicious prodding. Others wilt under it, but flourish in gentler places. The claim for personalization extends to a variety of school settings (separate schools or schools-within-schools), and the opportunity for choice among them itself is a spur to energy. Loyalty roots only with difficulty, if at all, in places forced on us; commitment readily follows from, free choice.

The focus of high school should be on *the use of the mind*. Although young citizens need to learn about and be exposed to many sides of life, the mind is central, and the school is the principal institution that society has for assisting adolescents in its use. High schools cannot be comprehensive and should not try to be comprehensive; there are some aspects of an adolescent's life in which a school has no right to intrude, and helping students to use their minds well is a large enough assignment, in any case.

The only way to learn to think well and usefully is by practice. The way a teacher assists this learning is by coaching. What a student chooses or is asked to think about is

important, obviously, but secondary to the skills of observing and imaginatively using knowledge. A self-propelled learner is the goal of a school, and teachers should insist that students habitually learn on their own. Teacher-delivered knowledge that is never used is temporary.

Issues concerning values inevitably arise in every school, and learning to use one's mind involves making decisions of conduct and belief. How one uses one's mind, and how one accordingly behaves, raise questions about character: Is this fair? Is it thoughtful? Is it generous? Is it *decent*? Schools should not teach merely pure thinking; they must also promote thoughtfulness, at core the qualities of decency. Schools should accept that obligation, not only because it is important, but because it is inescapable. A school *will* affect its students' character, willy-nilly. It should do so carefully, in a principled way.

Personalization of learning and instruction requires a flexible school structure. A flexible structure implies *a simple structure*. A school day segmented into seven or eight time units, each with its own set of imperatives, is almost impossible to bend. A curriculum represented by six or seven autonomous subjects quickly freezes hard: if each gets what its teacher feels is its due, all lose substantial freedom. Furthermore, such a fractionated and specialized set of subjects distorts knowledge for young minds; a simpler, more cogent organization of subject matter is wise.

Any effort to simplify the curriculum will be as threatening to teachers as will be the creation of general graduation exhibitions. We have been trained in our specializations, and we step outside them with trepidation. Our university mentors may often mock these forays, too; for many of them "specialization" and "standards" are synonymous—a false equation, but one that they will nonetheless scathingly defend. Reconstituting the shape of the curriculum—strengthening it by simplifying it and making it cogent to adolescents—will be a lonely, politically rocky effort.

Fortunately, each of these five imperatives governs the work of one or another existing school. There is no novelty here. However, pressing them ahead *together* would be novel, a school reconstruction effort of considerable scope and risk.

We hope that many schools will find one or more of these imperatives persuasive enough to push them vigorously. We also hope that some will have the courage to embrace them all, simultaneously. We need new model schools, ones resting on imperatives, like these five, that appear to serve well modern conditions and adolescents. The imperatives interlock, and as they are engineered into practical forms, their interconnection will become a source of strength—and of efficiency. The financial costs of better schools can be justified if the pretentious practices of comprehensiveness are stalwartly eliminated.

Better schools will come when better structures are built. Those structures have no inherent merit, however: their sole function will be to provide apt and nurturing conditions that will attract students and teachers and make their work together worthwhile and efficient.

## A PARALYSIS OF IMAGINATION

Hackles rise when recipes for changing school system structures are offered. From the Ocean Hill–Brownsville controversy in New York City to proposals for tuition vouchers, controversy seems inevitable. The issues instantly become ideological, it seems, paralyzing our imaginations.

Educators, so often criticized, are defensive. That most self-styled school reformers are not nor have ever been practicing high school teachers or administrators adds insult to injury. Educators may well ask, How

would lawyers react if the rest of us handed them prescriptions for legal reform? It is no surprise that school people are instinctively resistant to change. Like a large flywheel spinning at great speed, the traditional hierarchical bureaucracy has a headlong momentum. Suggestions for changes in the process—such as holding serious faculty meetings and empowering teachers to adapt their schools to the local circumstances they collectively identify—undermine the predictable sureties that systems require. It is easier for central authority to mandate fifty-four thousand minutes per year than to give discretion to local groups. The specificities of schooling and the seemingly endless requirements of standardized practice strangle not only learning, but also the imaginations of educators and politicians.

Behind top-down regulation lies a distrust of American teachers. The argument is simple: the fate of an adolescent cannot be left in the hands of a semicompetent adult, however well-meaning. So supervise and carefully control that teacher and, by necessary bureaucratic extension, *all* teachers. However, proud people rarely join professions that heavily monitor them. Being trusted is the elixir of commitment. Unless we trust some teachers (and are prepared to live with the political cat fights that will ensue from making what are ultimately subjective judgments as to who those "some teachers" are), we will only get more semicompetent people in the profession. Eventually, hierarchical bureaucracy will be totally self-validating: virtually all teachers will be semicompetent, and thus nothing but top-down control will be tolerable. America is now well on the way to this state of affairs.

Today, there is a sizable core of fine teachers and administrators in our schools. They are often demoralized, but they could, if empowered, lead a renaissance of American high schools: their numbers are large enough. But they need the trust of those in political power. Unfortunately, they have difficulty even getting these people's attention.

One hears much skepticism about reform by means of models like those I favor. The approach has not worked in the past, it has been said with some justification. It could work, though, if money were redirected to back it up, as has been shown by social revolutions from Medicare to higher education after the passage of the G.I. Bill of Rights to schooling for the handicapped. The pressures of successful models can be powerful, even if slow in their effect.[2]

The public's most troubling skepticism is about adolescents. Teenagers are a throwaway generation, and they resent it. It is not for nothing that no age group has a higher crime rate. What Vera Randall has called that "terrible, mocking smile of adulthood"[3] is not lost on young people; inexperienced, they choose to act as though they deserved the mockery. Their awkwardness, particularly their sexual fumbling, is exploited with old folk's sweaty-palmed glee, and the young people flock to *Porky* and then *Porky II* to find out what show biz thinks growing up is all about. When there is a reaction to all this, it is a patronizing one. Let our children be children, it says. They want structure, it argues. They want us to direct them. In practice, these somewhat sensible notions get exaggerated; they become overkill.

We stereotype adolescents in other ways. In spite of the rhetoric to the contrary, they are largely tracked by social class and gender. Too few adults really believe that poor kids or minority kids can make it. Don't educate them to use their minds, the conventional wisdom goes, because they aren't interested, and anyway, we do them a big service by preparing them for (semiskilled) jobs. The possibility that turned-off kids can be turned around, that young women can see a world beyond the pep squad, that poor kids, imaginatively taught, will respond to academic abstractions, remains vividly alive only to that band of teachers and principals in the schools which is making those things happen. America writ large does not believe it possible.

Horace Smith and his ablest colleagues may be the key to better high schools, but it is respected adolescents who will shape them. America must take its young more seriously, not out of some resurgence of 1960s' chic, where the Word from the Kids was considered the Real Truth, but out of simple human courtesy and recognition that adolescents do have power, power that can be influenced to serve decent and constructive ends. This power can only grow person by person—each tender life substaining the assaults of the universe, to paraphrase James Agee again.[4] High school must not be party to those assaults.

James Bryant Conant once said that for any recommendation to be taken seriously, it had to have a number attached.[5] He was a master at this process, arguing in *The American High School Today* that no English teacher should have more than a hundred students or guidance counselor more than three hundred clients or senior high school fewer than a hundred seniors. I hope he was wrong, because the problems of contemporary American high schools and the opportunities within the schools' grasp often do not lend themselves easily to quantification. The hours per week of homework and credits per year of courses are important, but nonetheless secondary to issues of attitude, to the subtle, confusing, controversial humanness that infuses every school. Give me, a student, a teacher who inspires me to learn on my own, and the brica-a-brac of schoolkeeping—the course labels, the regulations, the regularities, the rituals—will cease to have much importance. And give me, a teacher, hungry pupils, and I'll teach them in a tumbledown warehouse, and they will learn.

Inspiration, hunger: these are the qualities that drive good schools. The best we educational planners can do is to create the most likely conditions for them to flourish, and then get out of their way.

# AFTERWORD: AN EXPERIMENT FOR HORACE

With luck, a book is an important fragment in a continuing thoughtful conversation. A volume on secondary education like *Horace's Compromise* is an organized argument made at a particular moment. Publication spawns reaction to that argument; and time passes, altering (though often subtly) the context in which high schools, and the arguments for their improvement, reside. This paperback edition is a reprint of my first statement on Horace's compromises, but it is also, through this Afterword, part of a continuing conversation about high schools, about adolescents and their learning.

*Horace's Compromise* was part of a blizzard of reports and manifestos on education that swirled through America from April 1983 through the end of 1984. If there was a common theme among them, it was concern over the uneven quality of secondary education afforded young citizens. The remedies suggested were largely systemic, calling for an increase in regulation from central authorities, but some observers, such as John Goodlad, Ernest Boyer, Joe Nathan, Mortimer Adler, Seymour Sarason, and those of us in A Study of High Schools, puzzled over the obvious inefficiencies of the basic structure of schools. Merely greasing the existing gears might not accomplish very much, some of us wrote. For example, would insisting that a teacher like Horace assign more writing to his pupils help much, when he is responsible for 120 to 180 students at once? Hardly, our Study concluded, as the mere arithmetic of the minutes required for him to read, comment upon, and "correct" these papers bluntly testifies. Would adding time to the school day and school year help? Perhaps. But unless the genial incoherence of so much of Mark's day is lessened, little will show for this new investment. The weaknesses of the high school lie deeper, in how it is organized and in the attitudes of those who work there. As long as Melissa dodges and Steve Brody fakes it, the stubborn hold of mediocrity will persist, whatever the regulators impose.

Accordingly, we called attention to the structure of schools and urged a fresh challenge to the assumptions that shape it. The "time" spent in school ("four years of English") should not be the system's coinage, its unit of measurement, we argued. People learn at different rates, and substantive accomplishment should be the only product on which the school places importance. Age-grading, while bureaucratically neat, hurts children, we insisted, as some youngsters develop more rapidly than others. Take young people where they are, we counseled, and move them forward as efficiently as possible. How they compare with age-mates is a matter of secondary importance.

Simplify the school day, we said, if for no other reason than to lessen the frantic, colorful, wasteful rush over "knowledge" that a seven- or eight-period day requires. A curriculum of many courses, taken in rapid succession, has only the political virtue of accommodating numerous subjects that compete for students' time; as an educating system it creates incoherence and promotes superficiality. When challenged at this, we pointed out that no other serious educating institutions—those in business or the military, for example—have ever copied the frenetic eclecticism of the high school day, for the obvious reason that it is inefficient.

Less is more, we said. Thoroughness counts more than coverage. Make the routines simpler so that the inevitable complexity caused by the differences among individual students can be addressed. Above all, get the teacher's load down to a tolerable level. Don't force Horace to make compromises that cripple his students' opportunity to learn.

The readers of *Horace* who agreed, more or less, with its central theme almost always pressed a particular question, cast in a number of ways, usually in accusing or skeptical language. So the existing structure is ill designed, they would say; but how can it be improved, practically? Does anyone really want it changed? What are *you* going to do about it? In a word, as a practical and political matter, *can* Horace be uncompromised?

The answer is yes, very likely so. We must experiment with changes in the ways high schools keep. We must try to change the compromises, in actual schools. Let us see if the "five imperatives for better schools" can find real form, see if the nitty-gritty details of daily schoolkeeping can be shaped by principles more sensible and sensitive than those often now in practice.

Of course we must be humble and patient in attempting this. Schools are complicated and traditional institutions, and they easily resist all sorts of well-intentioned efforts at reform. Furthermore, many Americans may not want change, for to accept the need for it is an admission of error, however unintended. Such an admission is painful, and, accordingly, many find persisting with a status quo that they privately know is flawed to be the better part of valor. A public relations campaign is easier to stage than a serious attempt to reform schools—and, alas, the education establishment today is full of hype on behalf of things as they are. Challenge, in the eyes of some, is traitorous. In spite of this doleful reality, an attempt at restructuring is still worth making. Indeed, not to try would be truly traitorous, a failure to act to improve the education of children when we know that improvement is urgently needed.

For us, the key general questions are obvious. Can a new design for schools improve their quality—the standard of students' learning, the decency of students' life at school, the effectiveness and joy for teachers and principals and other schoolpeople? Can such a design, which will necessarily be comprehensive, be installed, as a *practical* matter? Can it be adopted, even in experimental

form, as a *political* matter? That is, will enough people, somewhere, want it enough to risk it, nurture it, be honest with it, give it time? Is there money available to buy the teachers' and principals' after-school hours to plan and test and replan? Can designs be both true to some common standards and at the same time respectful of local traditions and of each faculty's need for a deep sense of ownership of its own school?

In response to these questions a number of schoolpeople have joined us, agreeing to band together their schools, which corporately share some principles and appear to have the political, practical, and financial support to play these principles out, however substantial the required restructuring might be. These institutions, together with Brown University and with the continuing sponsorship of the National Association of Secondary School Principals and the National Association of Independent Schools, have created the Coalition of Essential Schools, which will experiment with ways to reduce the compromises schoolpeople and students must now make. The Coalition of Essential Schools is based at Brown University (Box 1938, Brown University, Providence, Rhode Island 02912) and has initial generous support from the Carnegie Corporation of New York, the Danforth Foundation, the Charles E. Culpeper Foundation, the Exxon Education Foundation, and the Edward John Noble Foundation.

The Coalition has no model to "plug in," no program to "install." Models and programs, to have sustenance and integrity, must arise independently out of their communities and schools. What the Coalition has in common is a set of nine principles, as insistent as they are largely general:

**1.** *Focus.*   The school should focus on helping adolescents learn to use their minds well. Schools should not attempt to be "comprehensive" if such a claim is made at the expense of the school's central intellectual purpose. That is, Essential Schools should not attempt to provide an unrealistically wide range of academic, vocational, extracurricular, and social services for adolescents.

**2.** *Simple goals.*   The school's goals should be simple: that each student master a limited number of centrally important skills and areas of knowledge. While these skills and areas will, to varying degrees, reflect the traditional academic disciplines, the program's design should be shaped by the intellectual and imaginative powers and competencies that students need, rather than by "subjects" as conventionally defined.   That is, students' school experience should not be molded by the existing complex and often dysfunctional system of isolated departments, "credit hours" delivered in packages called English, social studies, science, and the rest. Less is more. Curricular decisions should be guided by the aim of student mastery and achievement rather than by an effort to "cover content."

**3.** *Universal goals.*   The school's goals should be universal, while the means to these goals will vary as the students themselves vary. School practice should be tailor-made to meet the needs of every group or class of adolescents.

**4.** *Personalization.*   Teaching and learning should be personalized to the maximum feasible extent. Efforts should be directed toward a goal that no teacher have direct responsibility for more than eighty students. To allow for personalization, decisions about the details of the course of study, the use of students' and teachers' time, and the choice of teaching materials and specific pedagogies must be unreservedly placed in the hands of the principal and staff.

**5.** *Student-as-worker.*   The governing practical metaphor of the school should be student-as-worker, rather than the more familiar teacher-as-deliverer-of-instructional-services. Accordingly, a prominent pedagogy will be

coaching, to provoke students to learn how to learn, and thus to teach themselves.

**6.** *Diploma by exhibition.*   Students entering secondary school studies are those who are committed to the school's purposes and who can show competence in language, elementary mathematics, and basic civics. Students of traditional high school age who are not yet at appropriate levels of competence to enter secondary school studies will be provided intensive remedial work to assist them quickly to meet these standards. The diploma should be awarded upon a successful final demonstration of mastery for graduation—an "exhibition." This exhibition by the student of his or her grasp of the central skills and knowledge of the school's program should be jointly administered by the faculty and by higher authorities: the exhibition represents the latter's primary and proper influence over the school's program. As the diploma is awarded when earned, the school's program proceeds with no strict age-grading and with no system of "credits earned" by "time spent" in class. The emphasis is shifted to the students' demonstration that they can do important things.

**7.** *Attitude.*   The tone of the school should explicitly and self-consciously stress values of unanxious expectation ("I won't threaten you but I expect much of you"), of trust (until abused), and of decency (the values of fairness, generosity, and tolerance). Incentives appropriate to the school's particular students and teachers should be emphasized, and parents should be treated as essential collaborators.

**8.** *Staff.*   The principal and teachers should perceive themselves as generalists first (teachers and scholars in general education) and specialists second (experts in only one particular discipline). Staff should expect multiple obligations (teacher-counselor-manager) and feel a sense of commitment to the entire school.

**9.** *Budget.*   Ultimate administrative and budget targets should include, in addition to total student loads per teacher of eighty or fewer pupils, substantial time for collective planning by teachers, competitive salaries for staff, and an ultimate per pupil cost not to exceed that at traditional schools by more than 10 percent. To accomplish this, administrative plans will inevitably have to show the phased reduction or elimination of some services now provided to students in many traditional comprehensive secondary schools.

These principles, and *Horace's Compromise,* have provoked many good questions, mostly from schoolpeople.

*What's new here? What you're suggesting here is as old as McGuffey. Why, in my school ...*

Yes, nothing we're suggesting here in these principles is new. All nine find successful expression somewhere. What *is* a bit new, however, is putting them all together. Piecemeal reform is no reform.

*Don't these principles smack of the 1960s, with all their preaching about treating kids "individually"? We tried all that and it didn't work.*

Yes, some of these ideas are reminiscent of the 1960s—and of the 1780s too, when "exhibitions" for graduation were routinely expected. We hope to take the best from several eras, including the recent past: from the sixties, the special concern for individual differences and the special needs of the poor, and from the late seventies and early eighties, the concern for quality, for demonstrable achievement, for standards. We believe the priorities of the late 1970s cannot, in fact, find fruition without adopting some of those of the 1960s, and vice versa. Personalization of schooling and common standards go hand-in-glove; one without the other won't make it, as we have discovered.

*Will anyone take seriously these radical ideas of yours? You want to tip the cart over.*

My critique and the plans of the Coalition are the result of common sense and experience. What *is* truly radical, however, is the idea that serious intellectual activity can go on in rushed fifty-five minute snippets, seven in a row. It *is* radical to think that even an able, devoted teacher can help the intellectual development of more than one hundred youngsters simultaneously. It *is* radical to think that a large corps of devoted, full-time teachers will evolve just because we say it must, when we both pay teachers a fraction of what they are worth and patronize them with regulation from on high. It *is* radical to think that time spent (thirty-six thousand minutes per year) is the most important variable in learning. If you want truly radical ideas—radical in the sense of extreme—there they are, *deep in current practice.* On the other hand, if you use "radical" in its less familiar sense of going back to first principles, then we happily embrace the label.

*What of standards? The Coalition's nine principles, and* Horace's Compromise, *are awfully vague on them.*

We accept that criticism, but beg for patience. True standards of intellect—even those of a restless, noisy adolescent—do not lend themselves wholly to quickly collected, precise, standard measurement. We need to devise clusters of instruments (to use a bloodless but apt word) to probe our students' ability to think resourcefully about important things. Indeed, we need time to reflect deeply on what we mean by "think resourcefully" and what we feel are the most "important things." The Coalition will get more specific as our work unfolds. Design of "exhibitions"—the culminating exercise in high school—is a first priority.

*That's a waffle. We already have tests. Let's use them.*

Yes, let's use them. Carefully. And honestly accept the fact that some well-regarded tests, such as the Scholastic Aptitude Tests of the College Board (SATs), have severe limitations, ones well understood by their designers but ill recognized by the public at large. Furthermore, mastery—a word often used in *Horace's Compromise*—can be reduced by some to narrow, easily quantified scores. Adolescents, whose education should involve the claims of intuition, imagination, and subtlety, are not well served by such reductive measures of learning.

Yes, we know that it is no better to end with that assertion than it is to wind up with standards defined merely as rank in high school class, SAT scores, or class attendance, It sounds evasive. However, we will work to get beyond what you see as a waffle. Just give us time, and sympathy.

*If the "exhibition" is what gets a student a diploma, what happens if he or she can "pass" it without having attended school?*

Exhibitions—"performance" diplomas—open a Pandora's Box, I know. But open it we should; school *attendance* isn't what education is all about, *learning* is. If exhibitions weaken the argument for compulsory schooling, so be it—as long as a student's ultimate performance is of high standard.

*That teacher-pupil ratio—one to eighty. It's impractical without greatly increased expenditures. Get realistic!*

The work load, of high school teachers will not decline without new compromises—ones such as teaching two subjects to 80 students rather than one to 160. Or narrowing the curriculum. Or expecting a larger percentage of the adults in a school building to teach students, and to teach them well, than is now often the case. Yes, the load *can* be brought down, if people are willing to reconsider some of our cherished assumptions about the structures of secondary schooling.

*As I said, be realistic!*

The status quo—the sum of Horace's compromises—is demonstrably unrealistic. The existing school structure clearly serves many students poorly. However, I know that the realism to which you are referring is found in certification laws, union contracts, and tradition. But realism is also found in students who are drifting anonymously through a friendly but soft school program. That's *our* realism. Yes, changing rules and attitudes and doing things differently will be difficult—but these factors are susceptible to change. The learning of a largely neglected student (however much that student enjoys that neglect) is not going to change unless we do; that fact is the ultimate realism. Some school authorities accept this, painful though the implications are. We'll work with them and hope that their honesty and courage are contagious.

*What of the course of study? You are as vague about the curriculum as you are about standards.*

As the Coalition schools converge upon the substance of the final "exhibition" for graduation, this will become clearer. A careful survey of the four areas outlined in *Horace's Compromise*—Inquiry and Expression, Mathematics and Science, Literature and the Arts, and History and Philosophy—will soon be under way. But care should be taken to remember both that the details of any curriculum must reflect the community and the students served and that any "course of study" represents only one point on the triangle of student, teacher, and subject. Alter any one and the others shift—or the triangle breaks.

*Give me an example.*

Let me give you an extreme one, one represented by the Charles Gross of whom I wrote in *Horace's Compromise*. In the vocational school class I described, his ultimate goals were the general intellectual training of his students and their ability to express themselves. The way he got their attention was through his course on electricity; without this, most of the students would be truant. But the details of electrical work—procedures with devices and materials that would soon be obsolete in a rapidly changing industry—were secondary. What was foremost was Gross's effort to get his students to be constructively thoughtful about their work and able to verbalize that thought. "What would happen, Billy, if you switched that circuit in (some different way)?" he'd ask. The young man would point, and Gross would assert,

"Billy, I'm blind. You have to tell me." So Billy would work at telling Mr. Gross clearly the results of his (to put it pompously but accurately) hypothetico-deductive reasoning. Only with such prowess, Gross knew, could Billy and the other low-income minority kids make it in society. Mr. Gross was, very simply, teaching "Inquiry and Expression" in a powerful way *in the form and setting required by his pupils.* Other teachers would head toward the same goal over very different paths. (It should also be noted that Gross's total student load was 50, the maximum allowed for vocational-technical schools receiving federal funds in his community. If Charles Gross were expected to teach 175 students, the load of his colleagues teaching in the "academic" areas, he'd quit.)

*But I thought you were opposed to vocational education!*

I'm opposed to schooling that focuses narrowly on particular job training. I'm for general education, but arranged so as to attract and to hold pupils. If hands-on skill experience is a route to general intellectual prowess, that's fine with me. There is no One Best Curriculum, and there can never be, if school is to be effective. Students—inconveniently, perhaps—differ. So, then, must the ways to help them learn differ, even if there are common standards for the learning that is ultimately exhibited. Common ends, then, and diverse means.

*So couldn't foreign languages be taught in school? You seem to be opposed to them, too.*

I'm all for the study of a foreign tongue in American schools, most especially if that tongue is English. My point is not to *mandate* foreign language instruction. For example, a fifteen-year-old Anglo youngster who can barely read or write English should not be asked now to learn French too. Concentrate on English.

This is not at all to denigrate the importance of a second language. Indeed, an *ideal* school would be wholly bilingual: all ultimately can deeply benefit from a multilingual

experience. My view here, however, merely states a priority today forced on schools where conditions are not ideal.

*And physical education?*

I'm all for physical education, but not for Physical Education as it is currently pursued in many schools, as I argued in *Horace's Compromise.* I'm also for competitive sports—which are different in important respects from Physical Education. Many schools "hold" their pupils because of sports; but all too many of those pupils play Melissa as well as basketball. That is, they cop out of their academic education.

"School spirit" driven by athletics is educationally meaningless unless that spirit is somehow ultimately directed to the principal purposes of the school. That can be done, and sometimes is. However, the sports tail often wags the academic dog.

*Isn't your program, so focused on the "intellect," very elitist, and dull in addition?*

It is elitist only if one thinks that using one's mind resourcefully is the preserve of some special minority group. Our view is that it is the right of every citizen and the ultimate bulwark of democracy. A populace that is difficult to con is a people who will prosper in decent ways—such is the democratic faith. Learning to use one's mind well need not be a dusty academic exercise, devoid of connection to one's world and not fun at all. Learning is both joyless and useless when it is prescribed in mindless ways; but in the hands of a Sister Michael or a Charles Gross or a Fred Curtis it is not. The trick (again) is to respect the triangle—the chemistry of a *particular* teacher with *particular* students engaged on *a particular* subject. The first two shape the third, and vice versa.

*That's romantic nonsense. The Fred Curtises of the world are rare. And many kids really want a practical education, to go to work and not to college.*

Fred Curtis is rare, but not so rare as conventional wisdom implies. Get teaching conditions right, and Americans will discover thousands of Curtises it never knew it had. Organize sensible inservice programs, get the incentives right for teachers to engage in them, and even more will emerge. The people are already there, in most schools.

As for those students who "want a practical education": There is a self-fulfilling prophecy here. The kids who fail at school say they want something different, so we accommodate them. Our response, then, isn't more vigorous or more imaginative teaching for these students in the subjects they are failing: we sidestep that difficult prospect by rationalizing that these students have "different needs" from youngsters who are learning to read Hemingway and do algebra. So, we conclude, make them hewers of wood and drawers of water.

The fact remains that these students are the very ones who need *more* "academic" education, not less. And they need legitimate success at it. If they don't get it, or are denied it, they will not be able to function with even a modicum of freedom in modern society.

The fact that most of the students who are presumed to want something else are from lower-income groups adds to the outrage. There is blatant class discrimination in how schools "meet individual needs." An intellectual education is every citizen's right and need, and schools must learn to provide it. Giving up on a child's mind is simply unacceptable.

*O.K. But what do you do with the ninth-grader who can't read?*

You invest heavily—almost exclusively—in teaching how to read. Get her or him (Dennis, for instance) to have some success. If this implies one-on-one tutoring, as many literacy programs have shown, ways must be found. If a school is not saddled with strict "class" structure (ninth grade, tenth grade, and so on), one can bring this youngster along with his age-mates some of the time; that is, the pre-high school study that Dennis needs may take place in the high school building, where social mates readily mingle.

But he must be helped on his basic studies—and he must not be handed a monster textbook that he cannot read and for which he is somehow held accountable. When he has met the three preconditions for entering high school-level studies—literacy, numeracy, and civic understanding, as outlined in *Horace's Compromise*—he can be brought along, accelerated if possible. Above all, he must be both nurtured (we'll help you) and told the truth (you cannot read). This takes time and resources—the essential place for "compensatory" funding from state and federal sources. And it takes great sensitivity on the part of teachers to help Dennis keep his self-respect.

*What of the student who is so adept a scholar that he or she passes the high school exhibition at age fourteen?*

If such a student passes the exhibition but needs to stay in school with his or her age-mates, a broadened program is possible—a third language, a second science, and so forth. Part-time attendance at a local college is a possibility. Most schools that we've visited handle this problem well, usually with help from higher education—certainly better than they cope with the problem represented by Dennis.

*What of the social services now provided by schools—the hot lunches, counseling, medical care, and the rest? Do you jettison all this in the cause of an "intellectual" education?*

Yes and no. Yes, when the services are redundant with those provided at home. No, when home isn't home, when the school must substitute as parent, parent-of-last-resort. But the services thus provided must be seen as *additional* to basic educational services. Too often today they *replace* educational services, as funds are not available for both. This is sadly ironic, as the students who need social services are often the very students who require the most intensive educational service. If social services are needed, then, and can be efficiently provided through the school's systems, let this provision be added to the existing program while not undermining its essential core.

In addition, let us not confuse such social services or educational services with "social" service of publicly-paid-for parties. When the Junior Prom dominates the life of students and teachers for two weeks prior to the event, one knows that priorities are awry.

*Won't students resent the narrowing of their options that is inevitable in an Essential School? Electives are seen by most as their absolute right. A school with no choices for them to make will be opposed by its students.*

Initially, yes. But everyone, including the students, must go back to the beginning, to the reasons for electives in the first place. Their genesis was not so much a response to student freedom of choice as it was to accommodate student differences—different interests, aptitudes, skills. The hope was that everyone would be appropriately "placed" and successful there. (Most of us like what we're successful at.)

However, there are things in this world which are so important that we must learn them, whether we like them or not. The culture doesn't forgive us if we say we don't "like" to become literate; it merely shuts the door in our face. What is essential must be grasped, and the task of an Essential School is to adapt—to *personalize*—its program so that each student, or small group of students, can "elect" the means to that essential end, however discouraging the goal may at first appear. We're back to Charles Gross's class again: his ends there were common to all in an Essential School, but his means were tailored to his students. Pupils may "choose" among differing means and teachers may devise varying means. But the ends, albeit generally stated, remain the same.

*Will the students buy this?*

Eventually. They will like legitimate personalization. However, many will resist other aspects of an Essential School, particularly its emphasis on student-as-worker and on graduation on the basis of performance. The op-

portunity to get a diploma even when one dodges, like Melissa, or barters, as was the case in Steve Brody's class, will vanish. Some kids won't like the demise of these easy options to the work of real learning.

*How does the emerging research on brain functioning and neuropsychology, on different learning styles affect your ideas?*

The research so far clearly shows the astonishing complexity of the process of learning and the great variability among individuals. While no one yet should say with assurance precisely how to apply the findings of this research to practice, at least one general implication is demonstrably clear: schools must be personalized to the maximum feasible extent. Kids differ, one from the other, profoundly; and while we should make the best of the commonalities, we must accommodate and capitalize on those differences. Standardized practice—that panacea of so much of the contemporary reform movement—runs in precisely the opposite direction, lamentably.

*But doesn't personalized instruction put a new and heavy load on teachers, an expectation for extraordinary judgment about the learning style of each youngster?*

Yes, inescapably. It would be nice if there were One Best Method of schooling, but that is not to be. The variety among pupils is inconvenient, but we're stuck with it. So we'll have to trust teachers.

*We can't. The profession is too weak.*

We must; there isn't any alternative. The profession must be radically strengthened. Horace mustn't compromise in the ways he is forced to now. And teachers must be given the privilege of autonomy and the compliment of accountability to an unprecedented degree—if we are to take the implications of the new research seriously.

To repeat: the existing teaching force has substantial strength. We must empower and enhance the abler folk within it. Our experiment absolutely depends on able teachers. To plan otherwise is to give up.

*There isn't money for all this reform.*

Perhaps. We believe that we can use our existing resources better—assuming that we have the political will to change priorities. In any event, the Coalition assumes that not much more money will be available for high school education, certainly not more than 10 percent over existing per pupil expenditures, assuming inflation. Our effort, therefore, takes this financial restriction as a given.

*What you want is threatening for parents. How will you get their support? Will they buy in if they think it may put their children's college chances at risk?*

We insist that our Essential School program is experimental; no parent or student should have to take part. At the same time, we must persuade parents that our approach is sensible, more so than the status quo. We must also gain the understanding and endorsement of university leaders, as they are the best people to reassure parents of college-bound youngsters. Most colleges will applaud any school that awards its diploma only on the basis of the exhibition of substantial accomplishment; college admissions officers are as exasperated as anyone else with the current credit-collecting system that masks mastery.

*How will you evaluate the work of the Coalition?*

Slowly. First, by the staff members of each school themselves. They will quickly know what's awry, and can try to correct it. Second, by sensitive outside review, much as the better accreditation efforts are conducted. And, finally, by the performance of the students and the constructive stability of the faculties that teach them. We'll be as precise as possible, while recognizing that precision is neither possible nor wise in some areas of our business.

*What is the state's or central office's role?*

To support school-level work and the premise that diversity among schools is a virtue. To give principals real authority. To give the Coalition schools all possible and appropriate freedom. To give advice, and not to get upset when not all of it is taken. To give money where it is needed. To protect the experiment from those who unfairly expect quick results or whose turf is being (wisely) invaded. To have high expectations, and to be specific and honest about them. To ask probing, informed questions. To assist, sensitively, in the administration of exhibitions, as this is the place where ultimate accountability resides.

*But no one cares.*

Yes, too many don't care, even parents.

Few citizens really know what's going on in their schools. They settle for the familiar form and ignore the substance. The businessman who would neither copy any part of the high school's routine or structure for his own firm's training programs nor tolerate for his employees the work conditions that are standard in schools sanctimoniously takes part in pep rallies for the schools. The college professor who on principle would not stand for close state regulation of her classes of freshmen blithely endorses tight control on twelfth-grade instruction, and even assists central authorities with that standardized regulation. Hypocrisy? Not really. Just indifference. And the unwillingness to think hard and honestly about the process of education.

Perhaps the country is as docile as many of its children, wedded over twenty-two hours per week to the authority of the television set, where Johnny Carson, in contrast with Sister Michael, neither sees the yawn nor hears the scream. We seem happy to deny the complexity of learning, and are satisfied with simple remedies to the obvious ills of the schools. And perhaps Americans don't want question-askers, people who want answers. Perhaps, in sum, the unchallenging mindlessness of so much of the status quo is truly acceptable: it doesn't make waves.

But perhaps we—all of us—are better than that. That is the belief of those of us in the Coalition. Our new project, guided by that belief, tries to make an essential intellectual education joyful and accessible to all.

## ENDNOTES

1. Two such approaches were developed at Phillips Academy during the 1970s—a so-called Competence Course, in reading and expression, within the English department, and a History Qualification Test, and course patterns that flowed from its findings, by history and social studies teachers. Students are expected to take the Competence Course until they master it; it is a prerequisite to courses in literature for all students of whatever age. The HQT assists the history department in the placement of students among a variety of courses and guides the department's chairperson in the assignment of faculty. Both of these programs—and they are but two of many found at a variety of thoughtful public and private schools—are complicated and require constant adjustment. While they serve most students well, the exceptions need special arrangements. The Competence Course resulted in a textbook: *The Competence Handbook,* revised edition (Wellesley, Massachusetts: Independent School Press, 1982).

2. See Hampel, *American High Schools Since 1940.*

3. Vera Randall, "Waiting for Tim," in Thomas West Gregory, *Adolescence in Literature* (New York: Longman, 1978), p. 64.

4. From *Let Us Now Praise Famous Men,* as quoted by Robert Coles, *Children of Crisis: A Study of Courage and Fear* (Boston: Little, Brown, 1964), p. 381.

5. Personal conversation with Mr. Conant, 1972.

## CHAPTER 10 REFERENCES

Alexandar, L. (1986). Chairman's summary. In *time for results: The governor's report on education.* National Governor's Association Center for Policy Research and Analysis. Washington, DC: National Governor's Association.

Apple, M. (1990). What reform talk does: Creating new inequalities. In S. Bacharach (Ed.), *Educational reform: Making sense of it all* (pp. 155–164). Boston: Allyn and Bacon.

Bacharach, S. (1990). *Educational reform: Making sense of it all.* Boston: Allyn and Bacon.

Bloom, A. (1987). *The closing of the American mind.* New York: Simon and Schuster.

Boyer, E. (1983). *High school.* New York: Harper and Row.

Boyer, E. (1990). The new agenda for the nation's schools. In S. Bacharach. (Ed.), *Education reform: Making sense of it all* (pp.30–38). Boston: Allyn and Bacon.

Brookover, W., et al. (1979). *School social systems and student achievement: Schools can make a difference.* New York: Praeger.

Brookover, W., et al. (1982). *Creating effective schools: An inservice program for enhancing school learning climate and achievement.* Holmes Beach, FL: Learning Publications.

Carnegie Task Force on Teaching as a Profession. (1986). *A nation prepared: Teachers for the 21st century.* Washington, DC: Carnegie Forum on Education and the Economy.

Chubb, J. E., & Moe, T. M. (1990). *Politics, markets, and America's schools.* Washington, DC: Brookings Institution.

Coleman, J., Hoffer, T., & Kilgore, S. (1982). *High school achievement.* New York: Basic Books.

Cookson, P. W., Jr. (1991). Politics, markets, and America's schools: A review. *Teacher College Record, 93,* 156–160.

Cookson, P. W., Jr. (1993). *Contested ground: School choice and the struggle for the soul of American education.* New Haven, CT: Yale University Press.

Cuban, L. (1984). *How teachers taught: Constancy and change in American classrooms, 1890–1980.* New York: Longman.

Cuban, L. (1990). Why do some reforms persist. In S. Bacharach (Ed.), *Education reform: Making sense of it all.* Boston: Allyn and Bacon.

Dougherty, K. (1990). *Quality, equality, and politics: The political sources of the current school reform wave.* Paper presented at the Annual Meeting of the American Sociological Association.

Edmonds, R. (1979). Effective schools for the urban poor. *Educational Leadership, 37* (1), 5–24.

*Education Week.* (1990, March 7). Text of statement of goals adopted by the governors. *Education Week, 9,* 16–17.

Fine, M. (1991). *Framing dropouts.* Albany, NY: SUNY Press.

Freedman, S. G. (1990). *Small victories.* New York: Harper and Row.

Futrell, M. H. (1990). Redefining national security: New directions for education reform. In S. Bacharach (Ed.), *Education reform: Making sense of it all* (pp. 259–268). Boston: Allyn and Bacon.

Gartner, A., & Lipsky, D. K. (1987). Beyond special education: Toward a quality system for all students. *Harvard Educational Review, 57,* 367–395.

Glenn, C. L. (1991). Will Boston be the proof of the choice pudding. *Educational Leadership, 48*, 41–43.

Goodlad, J. (1990). *Teachers for our nation's schools.* San Francisco: Jossey-Bass.

Greene, M. (1988). *The dialectic of freedom.* New York: Teachers College Press.

Hirsch, E. D. (1987). *Cultural literacy.* Boston: Houghton Mifflin.

Holmes Group. (1986). *Tomorrow's teachers.* East Lansing, MI: Holmes Group.

Honig, B. (1990). The key to reform: Sustaining and expanding upon initial success. In S. Bacharach (Ed.), *Education reform: Making sense of it all* (pp. 52–56). Boston: Allyn and Bacon.

Hunter, M. (1982). *Mastery teaching.* El Segundo, CA: TIP Publications.

Johnson, S. M. (1991). Review of *Small victories* by Samuel G. Freedman. *Teachers College Record, 93* (1), 180–184.

Kozol, J. (1991). *Savage inequalities.* New York: Crown.

Labaree, D. F. (1992a). Doing good, doing science: The Holmes group reports and the rhetorics of educational reform. *Teachers College Record, 93* (4), 628–640.

Labaree, D. F. (1992b). Power, knowledge, and the rationalization of teaching: A genealogy of the movement to professionalize teaching. *Harvard Educational Review, 62* (2), 123–155.

Laird, S. (1989). Reforming "women's true profession": A case for "feminist pedagogy" in teacher education? *Harvard Educational Review, 58* (4), 449–463.

McNeil, L. M. (1988). *Contradictions of control: School structure and school knowledge.* New York: Routledge, Chapman and Hall.

National Commision on Excellence in Education. (1983). *A nation at risk.* Washington, DC: U.S. Government Printing Office.

Noddings, N. (1984). *Caring: A feminine approach to ethics and moral education.* Berkeley: University of California Press.

Passow, A. H. (1989). Present and future directions in school reform. In T. Sergiovanni & J. Moore (Eds.), *Schooling for tomorrow* (pp. 13–39). Boston: Allyn and Bacon.

Paulu, N. (1989). *Improving schools and empowering parents: Choice in American education.* Washington, DC: U.S. Government Printing Office.

Pincus, F. L. (1985). From equity to excellence: The rebirth of educational conservatism. In B. Gross and R. Gross (Eds.), *The great school debate* (pp. 329–344). New York: Simon and Schuster.

Powell, A., Cohen, D., & Ferrar, E. (1985). *The shopping mall high school.* Boston: Houghton Mifflin.

Ravitch, D. (1985). *The schools we deserve.* New York: Basic Books.

Ravitch, D., & Finn C. E. (1987). *What do our seventeen year olds know?* New York: Basic Books.

Reich, R. B. (1991, January 20.) Succession of the successful. *The New York Times Magazine,* pp. 42–45.

Reich, R. B. (1990). Education and the next economy. In S. Bacharach (Ed.), *Education reform: Making sense of it all* (pp.194–212). Boston: Allyn and Bacon.

Sarason, S. B. (1982). *The culture of the school and the problem of change.* Boston: Allyn and Bacon.

Sedlak, M. (1987). Tomorrow's teachers: The essential arguments of the Holmes Group Report. *Teachers College Record, 88* (3), 314–325.

Sizer, T. R. (1985). *Horace's compromise.* Boston: Houghton Mifflin.

Sizer, T. R. (1992). *Horace's school.* Boston: Houghton Mifflin.

Skinner, B. F. (1971). *Beyond freedom and dignity.* New York: Bantam.

Teacher Education Project. (1986). A compilation of the major recommendations of teacher education. Washington, DC: National Educational Project.

*Time Magazine.* (1991). Do poor kids deserve poor schools, October 14, pp. 60–61.

U.S. Government. (1991). *America 2000.* Washington, DC: The White House.

## SUGGESTED READINGS

Adler, M. (1982). *The paideia proposal: An educational manifesto.* New York: Macmillan.

Adler, M. (1990). *Reforming education: The opening of the American mind.* New York: Macmillan.

Bacharach, S. (1990). *Educational reform: Making sense of it all.* Boston: Allyn and Bacon.

Bennett, W. J. (1984). *To reclaim a legacy.* Washington, DC: National Endowment for the Humanities.

Boyer, E. (1983). *High school.* New York: Harper and Row.

Carnegie Task Force on Teaching as a Profession. (1986). *A nation prepared: Teachers for the 21st century.* Washington, DC: Carnegie Forum on Education and the Economy.

Chubb, J. E., & Moe, T. E. (1990). *Politics, markets, and America's schools.* Washington, DC: Brookings Institution.

Cookson, P. W., Jr., (1993). *Contested ground: School choice and the struggle for the soul of American education.* New Haven, CT: Yale University Press.

Education Commission of the States. (1983). *Action for excellence: A comprehensive plan to improve our nation's schools.* Denver, CO: Author. (ERIC ED 235 588)

Fine, M. (1991). *Framing dropouts.* Albany, NY: SUNY Press.

Freedman, S. G. (1990). Small victories. New York: Harper and Row.

Goodlad, J. (1990). *Teachers for our nation's schools.* San Francisco: Jossey-Bass.

Hess, G. A., Jr. (1991) *School restructuring, Chicago style.* Newbury Park, CA: Corwin Press.

Holmes Group, The. (1983). *Tomorrow's schools.* East Lansing, MI: Author.

Holmes Group, The. (1986). *Tomorrow's teachers.* East Lansing, MI: Author.

Kingston, P. W. (1986, Fall). Theory at risk: Accounting for the excellence movement. *Sociological Forum, 1,* 632–656.

Maeroff, G. I. (1988). *The empowerment of teacher: Overcoming the crisis of confidence.* New York: Teachers College Press.

National Commision on Excellence in Education. (1983). *A nation at risk.* Washington DC: U.S. Government Printing Office.

Powell, A. G., Farrar, E., & Cohen, D. K. (1985). *The shopping mall high school: Winners and losers in the educational marketplace.* Boston: Houghton Mifflin.

Sarason, S. B. (1982). *The culture of the school and the problem of change.* Boston: Allyn and Bacon.

Sizer, T. R. (1985). *Horace's compromise.* Boston: Houghton Mifflin.

Sizer, T. R. 1992. *Horace's school.* Boston: Houghton Mifflin.

Twentieth Century Fund Task Force on Federal Elementary and Secondary Education Policy. (1983). *Making the grade.* New York: Author. (ERIC ED 233 112).

William T. Grant Foundation Commission on Work, Family, and Citizenship. (1988). *The forgotten half: Pathways to success for America's youth and young families.* Washington, DC: William T. Grant Foundation.

# Index

Ability grouping, 322–24, 325, 486. *See also* Tracking
within-school differences due to, 456–58
Abstract empiricism, 189–91, 327
Academic freedom, 293–94
Academic track. *See* Tracking
Access to knowledge, tracking and, 489–90
ACE-CIRP, 413
Achievement. *See* Attainment, economic; Attainment, educational; Attainment, occupational; Outcomes, educational
Achievement ideology, 141
Action, moral, 235
Action research, 192
Activism, constituent, 62
Addams, Jane, 76, 114
Adler, Mortimer, 201, 561
Administration
attention to gender-related issues, 480
models of school, 537
Adolescents, public's skepticism about, 560
Advanced Placement (AP) Exams, 406n14
Advantage, struggle for, 163
Advisors, college, 400–401
African Americans. *See also* Race
cultural differences theory and, 446–47, 448
education in South, 84
equality of opportunity and, 83–84
public education for, 74–75
in racially mixed schools, 151–52

slaves, 71–72
AIDs, 294
Alexander, Benjamin, 43
Alexander, Lamar, 41, 525
Alexander the Great, 202
Alienation of students, 149–50
Allender, Jerome S., 192
"Almond Trees, The" (Camus), 227
American Association for University Women Foundation, 475
American Dream, perspectives on, 33–34
American Federation of Teachers (AFT), 532
*American High School Today, The* (Conant), 560
*America 2000*, 538–39, 540
*Antigone*, 222
Antiintellectualism, 127
Antoinette, Marie, 206
*Any Person, Any Study*, 55
Apple, Michael W., 212, 326, 327–41, 536
Aquinas, Thomas, 202, 203
Aristotle, 201–2, 203, 204, 351n2
Arons, Stephen, 43
Ascriptive status, 442
Ashby, Eric, 55
Assessment, 11–12. *See also* Tests and testing
competency-based, 205
of teachers, 283–84
Associational groups, 162
Association for the Advancement of Progressive Education, 112
Assumptions of sociologists, background, 189, 192
Attainment, economic

community college education and, 417–20
educational attainment and, 375–77
Attainment, educational. *See also* Outcomes, educational
community college education and, 413–17, 420–27
economic achievement and, 375–77
measuring, 383
parental, 503–5
percentage of (1869–1965), 157
private schooling and, 384–86
race and, 370, 442
social background and, 104–6, 144–45, 155
twofold nature of crisis of, 60
variables affecting high school, 382
Attainment, occupational, 155
social origins and, 161
Attitude
Coalition of Essential Schools on, 563
effects of schooling on, 144–45
Attractiveness, teacher's expectations and, 180
Augustine, St., 200
Authentic evaluation, 281
Authority
characteristics of, 268–69
in classroom, 321
conceptions of source of, 35–36
decentralized, 557
decline of, 31
defined, 268
school organization and, 268–70
of teachers, 110

Autonomy of teachers, 266
Axiology, 198

Babbitt, Irving, 46
Bacharach, Samuel, 534, 535
Bachelor's degrees, attainment by
    community college students,
    416–17, 420–27
Back to basics movement, 32
Bacon, Francis, 202, 203, 205,
    206
Baenninger, M., 474
Bailyn, Bernard, 67
"Banking" education, 338
Banks, James, 205
Bank Street School, 307
Barnard, Chester I., 272n18
Barnard, Henry, 89
Bartering in elite college
    admissions, 378, 393–409
Barzun, Jacques, 355
Bastian, Anne, 37, 59–63
Beacon Hill school, 204
Beecher, Catherine Esther, 74
Behavior modification, 110
Bell, Terrel, 48, 87, 534
Benbow, C., 473–74
Bennett, Tony, 334–35
Bennett, William, 87, 91, 92, 201,
    305, 336, 534
Berg, Ivar, 377
Bernard, Thomas, 116
Bernstein, Basil, 144, 190, 304,
    447, 454–55
Bestor, Arthur, 47, 81, 312
Bethell, Tom, 62
"Better Schools" (Sizer), 543,
    557–70
Between-school differences, 449,
    452, 454–56
"Bill for the More General
    Diffusion of Knowledge,"
    69–70
Black, Theodore, 43
"Black Student's Reflection on
    Public and Private Schools, A"
    (Perry), 378, 387–91
Bloom, Allan, 18, 47, 50, 53, 530
Boarding schools, elite, 396–409
Bobbitt, Franklin, 78
Book banning, 313
Boston, desegregation conflicts in,
    85
Boston Compact, 528
Bourdieu, Pierre, 463, 496, 508–9
Bowles, Samuel, 33, 91, 93–94,
    95–121, 142, 212, 447, 455
Boyer, Ernest, 42, 49, 561
Brain lateralization, biogenetic
    theory relating to, 474
Brameld, Theodore, 207
Brazelton, T. Berry, 288–89
Brint, Steven, 91

British Civil Service, 162
British schools, tracking in, 180
Brogan, D.W., 47
"Broken Promises: School Reform
    in Retrospect" (Bowles &
    Gintis), 93–94, 95–121
Brown University, 562
*Brown* v. *Board of Education of
    Topeka*, 84, 290
Bruere, Henry, 76
Bruner, Jerome, 15
Bryan, William Jennings, 312
Buber, Martin, 210, 211, 224
Budget, Coalition of Essential
    Schools on, 563–64
"Building a New Agenda" (Bastian,
    Fruchter, Gittel, Greer, &
    Haskins), 37, 59–63
"Building 860" (Neira), 462,
    465–70
Bureaucracies, 142, 254
Bureaucratic model of school
    administration, 537
Bureaucratic-rational model of
    teaching, 531–32
Burnout, teacher, 257, 291
Bush, George W., 25, 245, 311,
    526, 536, 538, 540
Business administration schools,
    160, 165
Business elite, 167–68
    composition of, 161
Business executives, 167
"Business methods" in schools,
    113–14
Business-school partnerships, 528
Busing, 374
Bussis, Ann, 556

Callahan, Raymond E., 113
Cameron, J.M., 131
Camus, Albert, 221, 225, 227
Capital, cultural, 143, 317–18,
    462, 463, 496
    family-school relationship and,
    508–10
Capitalism, 24, 25–26, 103
    Marx's critique of, 142
    radical critique of, 212–13
    top-down control of social life
    under, 115
Cardinal Principles of Secondary
    Education, 79, 305–6
Careerists, 149
Career paths, mathematics and,
    472
Caring orientation, 459
Carnegie, Andrew, 75, 95
Carnegie Commission, 55
Carnegie Foundation for the
    Advancement of Teaching, 79,
    95
Carnegie Report, 532–33, 534, 537

Carnegie Task Force, 18
Casals, Pablo, 226
*Case Worker, The* (Konrad), 222
Caste stratification, 367
Catholics, 73, 163
Catholic schools, 190, 247, 375,
    381, 384–86, 453
Center for Collaborative Education
    (CCE) in New York City, 542
Center for Educational Renewal,
    260
Centralization, size and degree of,
    245–46
Central Park East Secondary School
    (CPESS), 542–43, 547,
    549–50, 553
    principles guiding, 553–55
Centrist conservatism, 523–24, 536
Certification, teacher, 297n38
Change, conflict and, 255
"Chartering and Bartering: Elite
    Education and Social
    Reproduction" (Persell &
    Cookson, Jr.), 378, 393–409
Chicago, IL
    culture of public housing projects
    of, 448
    school-based management
    reforms in, 529
    school funding in, 450
Child abuse and neglect, 296n12
    teachers' responsibilities to
    report, 294
*Child and the Curriculum, The*
    (Dewey), 76
Childrearing patterns, social class
    and, 505–6
Children
    "latchkey," 289
    poverty among, 288–89, 296n7
"Children of the Rainbow," 314
*Children out of School in America*,
    52
Children's Defense Fund, 51–52
Chiswick, Barry, 106
Choice programs, 8–9, 88, 152,
    381, 525–28, 536–37
Christ, as transformative model and
    storyteller, 349
Chubb, John E., 526, 536
Citizenship, 126
City and Country School, 307
City Technology Colleges (U.K.),
    250
City University of New York, 86
Civic motive for education, 69–70
Civilization, decline of, 31
Civil religion, 146
Civil rights movement, 81, 84
Class, social. *See* Social class
Class-reproduction views, 411–13,
    427. *See also* Reproduction,
    social

Classroom
  authority in, 321
  gender and communication in, 475
  open, 82
  physical setting of, 554
  sociology of interactions in, 138
Classroom environment
  methodology and, 478–79
  personal development and, 108–9
  tracking and, 490–92
Class stratification, 367–68
Class structure, 103, 150
Class struggle, 213
Climate. *See also* Environment
  of classroom, tracking and, 490–92
  of school, 454
Clinton, Bill, 539
*Closing of the American Mind, The* (Bloom), 50, 92, 530
"Closing the Rift between Scholarship and Practice: The Need to Revitalize Educational Research" (Cookson, Jr.), 153–54, 189–96
Coalition of Essential Schools, 537, 546, 562–70
  on curriculum, 565–67
  principles of, 542, 553–54, 562–64
Cobb, Stanwood, 112
Coeducation, 355
Cohen, David, 79, 80, 530
Cohen, Judith H., 261, 287–99
Coleman, James S., 43, 85, 86, 190, 372–75, 443, 444, 449, 452, 453–54
Coleman Report, 372–74, 443, 444, 445
Collaborative research, 191–92
College(s). *See also* Community colleges
  attendance in, 124–25
  elite, 166
  entrance requirements for, 40–41
  income and attendance in, 105
  Ivy League, admissions into, 378, 393–409
  responsibilities of, 53–54
*College: The Undergraduate Experience in America,* 49
College advisors, 400–401
Collins, Randall, 143, 153, 155–74, 376–77
Colonial education, 67, 68–72
Columbia University, 314
Comer, James, 8
Committee of Ten, 79, 305
Committee to Support Philadelphia Public Schools, 528

*Common Ground* (Lukas), 85
Common School Era, 72–75, 80, 89
Common schools, 247
Communism, collapse of, 26–27
Community colleges, 379, 411–34
  class-reproduction views of, 411–13, 427
  dropout rates in, 421–22
  economic attainment and, 417–20
  educational attainment and, 413–17, 420–27
  functionalist views of, 411, 412–13, 427
  lack of residential facilities in, 422
  transfers to four-year colleges, 422–27
Community-level reform, 62–63
*Compelling Belief* (Arons), 43
Compensatory education, 8, 11, 86, 445–46
  economic payoff to, 107
Competency tests, 205, 282
*Complex Roles of the Teacher: An Ecological Perspective* (Heck & Williams), 257
Compulsory education
  laws on, 77, 78
  technology and, 271n9
Computers, 190
Conant, James Bryant, 83, 560
Confidence gap in mathematics, gender and, 473
Conflict(s)
  change and, 255
  over curriculum, 310, 312–13
  power and, 34–35
Conflict perspectives, 213. *See also* Radical perspectives
  on curriculum, 317–19
  on educational inequality, 440–41
  on education as status culture, 164
  neo-Weberian, 318
  on selection in organizations, 162
  on society-school relationship, 141–43
  status groups and, 162–64
  struggle for advantage and, 163–64
  tests of, 164–68
Connell, R.W., 508
Consciousness, reproduction of, 317–18
Conservatism
  centrist, 523–24, 536
  resurgence of, 328–29, 336–37
Conservative perspectives, 24–25, 27

  on definition of educational problems, 30–31
  on education and the American Dream, 33–34
  on history of education, 91–92
  on policy and reform, 32
  on reforms of 1960s and 1970s, 87
  on role of school, 28, 29
  on social efficiency curriculum, 306
  on unequal educational performance, 30
Constituent activism, 62
Content-process interrelationship, 255
Contest mobility, 146, 169
Contradictions of control, 259, 284–85
*Contradictions of Control: School Structure and School Knowledge* (McNeil), 277
"Contradictions of Reform" (McNeil), 261, 275–86
Control
  contradictions of, 259, 284–85
  teaching and, 258
Controlled choice, 527
Cookson, P.W., Jr., 537
Cooper, James Fenimore, 46
Cooperative learning, 477
Copperman, Paul, 47, 49, 52–53
Core curriculum, 10–11, 314
Correspondence theory, 447
Council for Basic Education, 128
Counseling of parents by teachers, 287, 288
Counts, George, 207, 308
Creationism, 312
Creativity, IQ and, 110–11
Credentialism, 143
Credentials, 377, 378
  income and, 146
Cremin, Lawrence A., 21, 23, 36, 45–57, 76, 82, 89–90, 113, 208–9
Crises in education, 2, 260
  sociology of education and, 153–54
  twofold nature of, 60
  urban, 6–9
*Crisis in the Classroom* (Silberman), 82
Critical curriculum theory, 304, 308
Critical literacy, 17–19
Critical pedagogy, 33
Cuban, Larry, 82, 530
Cubberly, Ellwood, 89
Cultural capital, 143, 317–18, 462, 463, 496
  family-school relationship and, 508–10

Cultural deprivation theories, 445–46, 448
Cultural differences theories, 446–49
Cultural incorporation, politics of, 334–39
Cultural literacy, 30, 205
*Cultural Literacy* (Hirsch), 92, 530
Cultural politics, 326, 327–41
Cultural reproduction theorists, 143
Culture(s)
  curricula as expressions of, 147–48
  dominant, 334–35
  employer, 166
  ethnic, 170*n*4
  oppositional, 335
  school-group, 166
  of schools, 253–56, 274, 549–50
  status, 164
  student, 149–50
  subordinate, 231
  WASP, 165
*Culture of Narcissism* (Lasch), 13
Culture of poverty, 445, 495
Cuomo, Mario, 452
Current performance, teacher expectations and, 180–81
Curriculum, 303–26
  AIDs and, 294
  appropriate content of, 313–14
  between-school differences in, 454–56
  Coalition of Essential Schools on, 565–67
  conflicts over, 310, 312–13
  conflict theorist perspectives on, 317–19
  core, 10–11, 314
  critical curriculum theory, 304, 308
  developmentalist, 307–8
  Dewey on, 220
  discipline-centered, 210
  effects of, 324–25
  existentialist, 211
  of expanding environments, 210
  as expression of culture, 147–48
  functionalist perspectives on, 316–17
  Great Books, 201
  hidden, 315–16, 317, 460, 477
  high school, in 1890s, 78–80
  history and philosophy of, 304–9
  humanist, 304–5, 308, 311
  idealist, 201
  inequality in, 485–93
  influences on policy making, 310–12
  integrative core, 308–9
  mission of education and, 292

  multicultural, 314
  neo-Marxist view of, 215
  parental values and, 314
  phenomenologist, 211
  policy disagreements about, 10–11
  politics of, 309–15
  power and, 310
  pragmatist, 209–10
  proficiency-based, 275–76, 281–83
  realist, 205
  scientific management of, 306
  sex education, 294
  simplification of, 561
  social efficiency, 305–7, 308, 311, 322
  social meliorist, 308
  sociological approach to, 304
  sociology of, 315–19
  stratification of, 322–24
  thematic core, 309
  traditional, 303–4, 321
  utilitarian components of, 69
  "watered down," 10
  workplace skills and, 318–19
Curriculum design, scientific approach to, 78
Curriculum placement (grouping), 11, 306, 322–24, 325, 486. *See also* Tracking
  within-school differences due to, 456–58
Curti, Merle, 67, 89

Dalton School, 307
Dame schools, 70
*Dare the Schools Build a New Social Order?* (Counts), 308
Darling-Hammond, Linda, 538
Darrow, Clarence, 312
Darwin, Charles, 206
Darwinism, social, 24
*Death at an Early Age* (Kozol), 82
Decentralized authority, 557
Decision making, joint, 295
*De facto* segregation, 85, 246
  inequality and, 151–52
Defensive teaching, 277, 279–80
*Deformation professionelle,* 189–90
Delinquency, juvenile, 183, 297n19
Democracy
  educated citizenry and, 540
  in educational theory, 96–101
*Democracy and Education* (Dewey), 208
*Democratic Education* (Gutmann), 35–36
Democratic-liberal perspective on history of education, 89–90
"Democratic school," 97, 115

Democratic schooling, case for, 60
Democratic socialism, 25–27
Democratic state viewpoint, 36
Descartes, Rene, 200
Desegregation, 84–85, 290
Developmental function of education. *See* Personal development
Developmentalist curriculum, 307–8
"Development cases," 403
Deviance, labeling theory of, 176–78
Dewey, Alice Chapman, 207
Dewey, John, 15, 112, 333, 541
  developmentalist curriculum and, 307
  on goal of education, 320–21
  on the Golden Rule, 226–27
  liberal-democratic perspective of, 25, 97–98, 114–15
  pragmatism and, 205, 206–7
  on restructuring schools, 76–77
  on social corrective value of education, 99–101
  social meliorist curriculum and, 308
Dialectic, 15, 200
  of freedom, 208
Dialectical method, 320
Dialectical notion of human agency, 233
Didactic method, 320
Diploma by exhibition of mastery, 563
Discipline-centered curriculum, 210
Discipline in schools, personal development and, 108, 110
Discrimination. *See also* Gender; Race
  gender, 152–53, 354–56
  tracking and, 457–58
Division of labor, hierarchical, 115
*Doll's House* (Ibsen), 226
Dominant culture, 334–35
Dominated reading of text, 338
"Double-schooling" phenomenon, 252
Dougherty, Kevin, 91, 379, 411–34, 523
Drabble, Margaret, 471
Dreeben, Robert, 316
"Drive for Excellence: Moving Towards a Public Consensus, The" (Finn, Jr.), 36, 39–44
Dropout rate(s), 51
  of community college students, 421–22
  of community college transfers, 424–27
  in urban schools, 6, 7
Drug abuse, 289

Duckworth, Eleanor, 551
Durkheim, Emile, 141, 190, 208, 316

Eastern Europe, 26
Economic development, education and level of, 158–59
Economic purposes of education, 23
Economy
  elitism and, 61
  market, 24, 25
  of schools and colleges, 44
Edmonds, Ronald, 145, 373, 452–53, 530
Education, 1–20
  assessment issues in, 11–12
  crises in, 2, 6–9, 260
  decline of literacy and, 9–11
  defined, 21–22
  experiential voice of teachers and, 17–19
  foundations of, 13
  foundations perspective, 12–19
  history of, 13–14
  philosophy of, 14–15
  poles of teaching experience, 2–5
  politics of, 15–16
  purposes of, 22, 23
  reform movements in, 1–2
  schooling vs., 21–22
  sociology of, 16–17
  of teachers, 18–19
  universal, 46–47
  urban, 6–9
Education, Department of, 245, 534
*Education, Politics and the State* (Salter & Tapper), 191
Education Acts (1870, 1944) (U.K.), 249
Educational marketplace, 536–37. *See also* School choice
Educational Reform Act (1988) (U.K.), 249–50
Educational Testing Service (ETS), 473
*Education and Jobs: The Great Training Robbery* (Berg), 377
*Education and Sociology* (Durkheim), 141
Education for All Handicapped Children Act (EAHCA), 290
"Education for Life Adjustment" movement, 80
Educators, professional, 312
Edwards, Jonathan, 108
Effective schools
  characteristics of, 453
  literature on, 453–54
Effective schools movement, 8, 11, 12, 32, 60, 145, 530–32

"Effects of Community Colleges: Aid Or Hindrance to Socialeconomic Attainment" (Dougherty), 379, 411–34
Efficient management, ideology of, 113
Egalitarian function of education, 97–98, 101–7. *See also* Equality of opportunity; Inequality
  improving, 541–42
*Eighteenth Brumaire of Louis Bonaparte, The* (Marx), 13
Eisenhower, Dwight D., 84–85
Elementary and Secondary Education Act of 1965, 81, 451, 539
Elementary education in Puritan New England, 70
Elementary school, 246–47
Eliot, Charles, 79
Elite education, social/class reproduction and, 378, 393–409
Elites, 163
  business, 161, 167–68
Elitism, economy and, 61
Elliot, Charles W., 112
Elliott, John, 191
Ellsberg, Daniel, 226
Emancipation, resistance theories and, 233, 235
Emerson, Ralph Waldo, 72–73, 95
*Emile* (Rousseau), 74, 206
Emma Willard School, 460
Empiricism, 16
  abstract, 189–91, 327
Employer culture, school-group culture and, 166
Employment
  educational requirements for, 155–56
  effects of schooling on, 145–46
Empowerment of teachers, 17–19, 88, 529–30
Engels, Frederick, 212
Engineers, employment-education linkage and, 167
English, standard, 369
Enrollment
  open, 86
  optional (voucher system), 60
Entrance requirements, college and university, 40–41
Environment, 206. *See also* Classroom environment
  academic achievement and, 384
  curriculum of expanding, 210
  of magnet schools, 279
  principles for effective, 553–55
  school organization and, 266–68
"Epistemic" tradition. *See* Mimetic tradition

Epistemology, 198
*Equality of Educational Opportunity* (Coleman et al.), 85, 86, 443, 444, 445
Equality of opportunity, 32–33, 82–87, 102–3, 140. *See also* Outcomes, educational
  belief in, 365
  education's power to promote, 100–101
  excellence vs., 485, 535–38
  race and, 83
  social stratification and, 366–71, 378
Equal Protection Clause of Fourth Amendment, 451
Erickson, Donald, 247
Escalante, Jaime, 522–23
Estate stratification, 367
Ethics of tracking, 488–89
Ethnic cultures, functional differences in, 170*n*4
Ethnicity
  educational achievement and attainment and, 442
  status groups and, 163–64
  teacher's expectations and, 180
Evaluation
  authentic, 281
  teacher, determinants of, 179–80
Events, parental attendance at, 501–3
Evolution, 312
*Evolution of Educational Thought* (Durkheim), 141
Excellence, equity vs., 485, 535–38
Executives, business, 167
Exhibition of mastery, requirement of, 557, 563
Existentialism, 210–12
Expanding environments, curriculum of, 210
Expectations
  parent, gender and, 475–76
  schooling and, 456
  of teacher, 148–49, 175, 178–81, 458
  tracking and, 457
Experience, 206
  teaching, poles of, 2–5
Experimentalism, 207
Expertise, methodological and substantive, 349
Extra-school explanations of inequality. *See* Student-centered explanations of educational inequality

Fairness of tracking, 488–89
Family
  academic achievement and, 384
  educator's view of, 109

Family-school relationship
   cultural capital and, 508–10
   educational consequences of,
      500–501
   historical variations in, 496–97
   independence vs.
      interdependence, 503, 507
   social class differences in,
      495–512
Family state viewpoint, 35
Faubus, Orval, 85
Featherstone, Joseph, 82
Federal government
   aid to equalize school funding,
      451
   educational policy making by,
      245
Feedback loop, 346
"Females + Mathematics = A
   Complex Equation" (Karp),
   462, 471–83
Feminist movement, 459–60
Feminist theorists, 214, 215, 321
Fenstermacher, Gary, 488
Ferguson, Adam, 114
Fernandez, Joseph, 314, 528–29
Ferrar, E., 530
Financial aid for community college
      transfers, 426
Financing of schools, 7, 449–52,
   541
Finn, Chester E., Jr., 10, 11, 36,
   39–44, 91, 92, 205, 530, 536
First Industrial Revolution, 75
Flanders, Ned, 138
Flexible school structure, 558
Flexner, Abraham, 46
Foreign language teaching,
   Coalition of Essential Schools
   on, 566
"Forgetting the Questions: The
   Problem of Educational
   Reform" (Ravitch), 94,
   123–31
Foundations perspective, 12–19,
   543
   defined, 12–13
   experiential voice of teachers and,
      17–19
   historical component of, 13–14
   multidisciplinary and
      interdisciplinary approach of,
      17
   philosophical component of,
      14–15
   political component of, 15–16
   sociological component of,
      16–17
Fourth Amendment, Equal
   Protection Clause of, 451
*Frames of Mind* (Gardner), 54
France, school organization in, 250

Franciscan schools, 190
Franklin, Benjamin, 69
Freedman, Samuel, 522
Freedom
   academic, 293–94
   dialectic of, 208
Freidman, Milton, 24
Freire, Paulo, 110, 212, 308
Fruchter, Norm, 37, 59–63
"Functional and Conflict Theories
   of Educational Stratification"
   (Collins), 153, 155–74
Functionalist perspectives
   on community colleges, 411,
      412–13, 427
   on curriculum, 316–17
   on educational inequality, 440,
      441
   inadequacy of, 160–62
   on job candidate selection,
      160–62
   on society-school relationship,
      140–41
   technical-function theory,
      156–60, 162, 167
Funding, disparate impact of,
   297n27
Futrell, Mary, 536

Gagnon, Paul, 205
Gardner, David P., 48
Gardner, Howard, 54, 210
Garrity, Arthur, 85
Gender
   discrimination, 152–53, 354–56
   economic opportunity and, 107
   educational achievement and
      attainment and, 442–43
   educational outcomes and,
      370–71
   elite college admission and,
      406n10
   mathematics and, 370–71,
      471–83
   noncognitive outcomes of
      schooling and, 443
   parent expectations and, 475–76
   schooling and, 458–60
   socialization and, 443, 460
Gender role socialization, 476–77
Genetic differences, 444–45
   mathematics skill and, 473–74
GI Bill of Rights, 82–83, 124–25
Gilligan, Carol, 459–60
Gintis, Herbert, 91, 93–94,
   95–121, 142, 212, 447, 455
Giroux, Henry, 212
Gittel, Marilyn, 37, 59–63
Glenn, Charles L., 527
Goals of education, 563
   Dewey on, 320–21
   under existentialism, 211

under idealism, 200
under neo-Marxism, 214
under phenomenology, 211
under pragmatism, 207–9
under realism, 204
variety of, 263
Goals of organizations, 263–64,
   271n3
Goals 2000 legislation, 11
Golden, John, 76
Golden Rule, 226–27
Good, Platonic concept of the, 200
Goodlad, John, 51, 52, 256, 260,
   489, 534, 561
Gornick, Vivian, 459
Goslin, Willard, 313
Governance of school, 244–45
Grading, personal development
   and, 110–12
Graham, Bob, 42
Graham, Patricia, 275
Graham Down, A., 330
Grammar, sexist, 355
*Grandes ecoles,* 250
Great Books curriculum, 201
Great Britain
   school organization in, 249–50
   tracking in, 180
"Great debate, the," (U.K.) 81
Greene, Maxine, 208, 210, 215–16,
   221–28, 308, 543
Greer, Colin, 37, 59–63
Griffin, Susan, 356
Gross, Beatrice, 82
Gross, Charles, 565–66, 568
Gross, Ronald, 82
Growth through education, 208–9
Gutmann, Amy, 22

Habitual view of teaching, 546–48
Haley, Margaret, 333
Hall, G. Stanley, 77, 79, 112
Hall, Stuart, 336
Halsey, 190–91
*Hamlet* (Shakespeare), 222
Hammond, Jay, 42
Handicapped children,
   mainstreaming of, 290
Hare, Sharon E., 191–92
Harlan, John Marshall, 83–84
"Harvard Test of Inflected
   Acquisition," 179
Haskins, Kenneth, 37, 59–63
"Hawthorne effect," 271n7
*Hazelwood School District* v.
   *Kuhlmeier,* 293
Head Start, 86, 125, 445–46
Hechinger, Fred, 4, 521
Heck, S.F., 257
Heffner, Richard, 50
Hegel, George Wilhelm Friedrich,
   200

Heidegger, Martin, 210
Helplessness, learned, 475
Herbert Spencer Education Club, 46
Heritage Foundation, 535
Hermeneutics, 211
Herrnstein, Richard, 114
Hidden curriculum, 315–16, 317, 460, 477
Higher education
  compensatory, 86
  liberal reforms of, 86
High school, 246
  learning rate in, 383
  public, 78–80
  variables affecting achievement in, 382
*High School Achievement: Public, Catholic and Private Schools Compared* (Coleman, Hoffer, & Kilgore), 374
High School and Beyond (HSB) study, 381–82, 383
  tests used in, 383
Hill, Anita, 458
Hirsch, E.D., Jr., 11, 18, 91, 92, 205, 530, 536
Historical change, 168–69
History of education, 13–14, 67–136
  colonial era, 67, 68–72
  Common School Era, 72–75
  conservative perspective on, 91–92
  curriculum, 304–9
  democratic-liberal perspective on, 89–90
  post World War II era (1945–1980), 80–87
  radical revisionist perspective on, 90–91
  reaction to reform in 1980s and 1990s, 87–88
  urbanization and the progressive impetus, 75–80
Hodgkinson, Harold, 153
Hoffer, Thomas, 190, 374
Hofstadter, Richard, 76, 80
Hogan, David, 90
Holland, John L., 111
Holmes Group, 18, 533
Holmes Report, 533–34, 537
Homosexuality, 314
*Horace's Compromise* (Sizer), 256, 561, 564, 565, 567
*How Teachers Taught* (Cuban), 82
Human agency
  dialectical notion of, 233
  reproduction theories and, 230–31
  resistance theories and, 230–31, 233, 236

Humanist curriculum, 304–5, 308, 311
Humanistic research, 192
Hunter, Madeleine, 531
Hurn, C.J., 441, 445, 448, 457–58
Hutchins, Robert Maynard, 46, 47, 81, 83
Hylla, Erich, 47

Ibsen, Henryk, 226
Idealism, 199–201
Ideology, 213
  achievement, 141
  of efficient management, 113
  reproduction of dominant, 229
*Illiterate America* (Kozol), 10
Imagination, sociological, 5–6, 153
  threat to, 190
Immigrants, burden placed on schools by, 289
*In a Different Voice* (Gilligan), 459–60
Incentives for students and teachers, 557–58
Incidental learnings, 351
Income
  college attendance and, 105
  credentials and, 146
  distribution of, 106–7, 367
  social class and, 150
  social stratification and, 368–69
Independence vs. interdependence between family and school, 503, 507
Indian College, 72
Individuals, effects of schooling on, 144–47. *See also* Personal development
  employment, 145–46
  knowledge and attitudes, 144–45
  mobility, 146–47
Inductive reasoning, 206
Industrialization, 142
Industrial Revolution, 72, 75
Inequality, 125, 150–53
  *de facto* segregation and, 151–52
  gender, 152–53
  inadequacy of schools and, 151
  in income, 105–7
  perpetuation of, 460–63
Inequality, educational, 439–63. *See also* Tracking
  in curriculum, 485–93
  Jeffersonian two-track educational system and, 103
  school-centered explanations of, 441, 449–60
  social background and, 104–6
  student-centered explanations of, 441, 443–49
  theories explaining, 440–43

"Inferences from Studies of Public/ Private School Differences" (Witte), 378, 381–86
Informal (hidden) curriculum, 315–16, 317, 460, 477
Information about schooling, parents' access to, 505–6
Inglis, Fred, 329
Instructional reform, 61
Instructional time, tracking and, 490
Instruction methods
  existentialist, 211
  idealist, 201
  neo-Marxist, 214–15
  phenomenologist, 211
  pragmatist, 209
  realist, 204–5
Instrumentalism, 207
Integrative core curriculum, 308–9
Integrative function of education, 97–98, 540
*Integrity in the College Curriculum,* 49
Intellectual purposes of schooling, 22, 23
Intellectuals, 149
  transformative, 214
Intelligence, genetic differences in, 444–45
Interactional theories of society-school relationship, 143–44
Interaction Analysis Scale, 138
Interactionist perspective, 175
  on educational inequality, 441
International Association for the Evaluation of Educational Achievement (IAEEA), 9
Internships, teaching, 295
Intersectional choice plans, 526–27
Intradistrict choice plan, 527
Invisible pedagogy, 321
IQ, creativity and, 110–11
Ivy League college admissions, 378, 393–409

Jackson, Philip, 319–20, 326, 343–52
Jacobson, L., 182
James, William, 112, 205
Japan
  school organization in, 252
  textbook controversy in, 331
Jaspers, Karl, 210
Jefferson, Thomas, 69–70, 103
Jencks, Christopher, 385–86, 443, 444, 449, 452
Jensen, Arthur, 114, 444–45
Jesuit schools, 190
Job-related stress, 291
Jobs, over-education for available, 158. *See also* Employment

Job skills, 158–59
Johnson, Lyndon B., 25, 85, 95–96, 125
Johnson, S.M., 522
Joint decision making, 295
"Jug and mug" approach, 110
Juku (study institution, Japan), 252
Junior high school, 246
Juvenile delinquency, 183, 297n19

Kanawha County, West Virginia, 329, 331
Kant, Immanuel, 200
Kaplan, Samuel, 409
Karabel, Jerome, 91, 190–91
Karier, Clarence, 90
Karp, Karen, 462, 471–83
Katz, Michael, 90
Kearns, David, 536
"Keeping Track, Part 1: The Policy and Practice of Curriculum Inequality" (Oakes), 462, 485–93
Kennedy, John F., 25, 85
Keynes, John Maynard, 25
Kierkegaard, Soren, 210, 211, 226
Kilgore, Sally, 190, 374
Kindergarten, 246–47
Kings, philosopher, 35, 200
Kliebard, H.M., 304
Knowledge
    effects of schooling on, 144–45
    mimetic tradition and, 344–46
    official, 328–30
    tracking and access to, 489–90
    transformative tradition and, 346–47
Kohl, Herbert, 82
Kohlberg, Lawrence, 459
Konrad, George, 222
Kozol, Jonathan, 10, 82, 449, 455, 541
Kuehnle, Anne, 348
Kuhn, Thomas, 114

Labeling as rite of passage, 183
Labeling theory, 175–88
    of deviance, 176–78
    self-fulfilling prophecy and, 181–85
    teacher expectation and, 178–81
Labor, hierarchical division of, 115
Laboratory School at the University of Chicago, 76–77, 207
Labor unions, 213
La Follette, Robert, 76
Lareau, Annette, 462, 463, 495–512
Larsen, Yvonne W., 48
Lasch, Christopher, 13
Laski, Harold, 47
"Latchkey" children, 289

Latin Grammar School, 70
Law(s)
    compulsory education, 77, 78
    Old Deluder, 68–69
    role expansion and role ambiguity and, 293–94
Lawyers, employment-education linkage and, 167
Learned helplessness, 475
Learning
    cooperative, 477
    incidental, 351
    passion for, 551
    personalization of, 558, 563, 568
Learning environment, principles for efficient, 553–55
Learning rate in high school, 383
Legal pressures, teachers' role expansion and, 289–91
Lemann, N., 448
Lewin, Kurt, 191
Lewis, Oscar, 445
Liberal education, 130–31
Liberal educational reform, critique of, 114–17
Liberal perspectives, 24, 25, 27
    basic strategy underlying, 96
    on definition of educational problems, 31
    democratic-liberal perspective, 89–90
    "democratic school," 97, 115
    on education and the American Dream, 34
    on functions of education, 97–98
    on policy and reform, 32
    on role of school, 28–29
    "technocratic-meritocratic," 97, 98–100, 101, 115–17
    on unequal educational performance, 30
Lieberman, Ann, 538
Life Adjustment Education, 47, 209
Life arithmetic, 366, 367
Life chances, 377–78
Life expectations, schooling and, 456
Life outcomes, 366–71
Lightfoot, Sara, 54
Literacy
    critical, 17–19
    cultural, 30, 205
    decline of, 9–11
Litigation, school-related, 292
Little Rock, Arkansas, 84–85
Livesey, Francis, 46
Locke, John, 35, 202, 203–4, 205, 206
Logic, Aristotelian, 202
Lortie, Dan, 259
Lower class, 150

Lower middle class, 150
Lukas, J. Anthony, 85
Luke, Allan, 337
Lyon, Mary, 74

McCarthy, Joseph, 312
McCarthyism, 312–13
Macdonald, Dwight, 50
McNeil, Linda M., 259, 261, 275–86
Magnet schools, 8, 275, 277–81, 374, 526
    centralized school reforms and, 278
    course content of, 279–81
    environment of, 279
    proficiency-based curricula and, 275–76, 281–83
Mainstreaming, 290
Male, George, 250
Management
    school-based, 59, 88, 260, 295, 528–30
    scientific, 306
*Man and His Changing World* (Rugg), 330
Mann, Horace, 73, 89, 99, 103, 366
Marcuse, Herbert, 233
Market economy, 24, 25
Marketplace, education, 536–37. *See also* School choice
Marshall, Thurgood, 451
Martyna, Wendy, 355
Marx, Karl, 13, 26, 142, 212–13, 229
Mastery, exhibition of, 557, 563
Mathematics
    gender and, 370–71, 471–83
    "new math," 549
    teacher education in, 479
Meier, Deborah, 8, 542, 545–56
Meritocracy, 60–61, 97, 98–100, 101, 115–17, 316. *See also* Equality of opportunity
    GI Bill and, 83
Merit pay concept, 59
Merleau-Ponty, Maurice, 210
Metaphysics, 198
Methodological expertise, 349
Metz, Mary Haywood, 261, 263–74
Middle class
    family-school relationship in, 497–510
    rejection of norms of, 447–48
Middle colonies, education in, 71
Middle school, 246
Mill, James, 96
Mill, John Stuart, 35
Mills, C. Wright, 5–6, 18, 327

Milwaukee, intersectional choice plan in, 526
"Mimetic and Transformative: Alternative Outlooks on Teaching, The" (Jackson), 326, 343–52
Mimetic tradition, 320, 321, 326, 344–46, 349
    concept of knowledge in, 344–45
    transmission of knowledge in, 345–46
Mincer, Jacob, 106
Mind, focus on use of, 558, 562–63
Minnesota, intrasectional school choice plan in, 527
Minority students, 6–7. *See also* Ethnicity; Inequality; Race
Minority teachers, lack of, 9
Mission, curriculum and, 292
Mobility, 368–69, 377–78
    boarding school attendance and, 400, 404
    contest, 146, 169
    educational, 366
    effects of schooling on, 146–47
    social, 366
    sponsored, 146
Modeling, personal, 349
Moe, Terry M., 526, 536
Moral education, 252
*Moral Education* (Durkheim), 141
Morality, transformative tradition and, 349, 350–51
Moral life, 215–16, 221–28
Moral order, authority and, 268, 269–70
Moral reasoning, 459
Moral responsibility, 272n16
Morgan, Janet, 293–94
Mount Holyoke College, 74
Multiculturalism, 92, 314
Multidimensional approach to explaining educational inequality, 441
"My Pedagogic Creed" (Dewey), 76, 215, 217–20
Mystification, 277, 279–80

Nader, Ralph, 128
Narrative, use of, 349
Nassaw, David, 93
Nathan, Joe, 561
National Association for the Advancement of Colored People (NAACP), 84
National Association of Independent Schools, 562
National Association of Secondary School Principals, 562
National Board for Professional Teaching Standards, 545

National Center for Restructuring Education, Schools and Teaching (NCREST), 537–38
National Commission on Excellence in Education, 42–43, 45–46, 48, 49, 51, 87
National Education Association (NEA), 79, 128, 532
National Governor's Association, 524, 538
National Longitudinal Survey of Labor Market Experience (NLSLME), 413
National Longitudinal Survey of the High School Class of 1972 (NLS–72), 413
National standards, 539
National Task Force on Education for Economic Growth, 42
*Nation at Risk, A*, 11, 45–46, 47, 48, 49, 87, 141, 530, 533, 534, 540
*Nation Prepared: Teachers for the 21st Century, A* (Carnegie Report), 532–33, 534
Native Americans, 67
    formal schooling for, 72
Natural selection, 206
Negotiated reading of text, 338
Neill, A.S., 82, 307
Neira, Christian, 462, 465–70
Nelson High School, 277
Neo-Marxism, 215–15, 317
Neo-Thomism, 203
Neo-Weberian conflict theory, 318
Networks
    "old school tie," 170
    transmission of privilege through, 395
Newcombe, N., 474
New Deal era, 25
*New England Primer*, 70, 73
New England Puritan communities, 70, 108–9
New Jersey, school funding in, 450
Newmann, Fred, 281
"New math," 549
New Right, 328
New scholasticism, 189–91
New sociology of education, 304
New York City schools, 291
Normal school (teacher training school), 73
Normative control emphasis, 165–66, 167
Norms, 226–27
    violations of, 176

Oakes, Jeannie, 11, 191–92, 457, 462, 485–93
Oberlin Collegiate Institute, 74
Occupational achievement, 155

    social origins and, 161
Occupational placement, education as mechanism of, 164–66
Occupation-education linkage, variations in, 166–68
Official knowledge, politics of, 328–30
Ogbu, John, 446–47
"Old school tie" networks, 170
Old World, 68
"On Understanding the Processes of Schooling: The Contributions of Labeling Theory" (Rist), 153, 175–88
Open classroom, 82
Open enrollment, 86
"Openness," degree of, 246–47
Operation Head Start, 86, 125, 445–46
Opportunities to learn, tracking and, 490
Opportunity, equality of, 32–33, 82–87, 102–3, 140. *See also* Outcomes, educational
    belief in, 365
    education's power to promote, 100–101
    excellence vs., 485
    race and, 83
    social stratification and, 366–71, 378
Oppositional behavior, 233–34, 235
Oppositional cultures, 335
Oppositional reading of text, 338
Optional enrollment (voucher), issue, 60
Order
    maintenance of, 264
    moral, authority and, 268, 269–70
    students' attacks upon, 266–67
Organizational politics, 16
Organizational prominence, 167
"Organizational Tensions and Authority in Public Schools" (Metz), 261, 263–74
Organization of schools, 244–53
    authority, 268–70
    degree of "openness," 246–47
    environment and, 266–68
    in former Soviet Union, 250–51
    in France, 250
    goals and, 263–64
    governance, 244–45
    in Great Britain, 249–50
    in Japan, 252
    outcomes and, 371–75, 378
    private schools, 247–48
    size and degree of centralization, 245–46

structure, 265–66
student composition, 246
technology and, 264–65, 266, 267
Organizations, goals of, 263–64, 271n3
Outcomes, educational, 365–437
    calculating, 366–71
    Coleman study of (1966), 372–74
    Coleman study of (1982), 374–75
    economic achievement and, 375–77
    gender and, 370–71
    race and, 107, 370, 442
    school differences and, 371–75
    social class and, 104–6, 144–45, 155, 369–70, 378, 442
Outcomes, life, 366–71

Packard, Frederick, 46
*Paideia Proposal* (Adler), 43, 201
Parental involvement in education
    attendance at school events, 501–3
    factors structuring, 503–6
    social class differences in, 495–512
    teachers' requests for, 498–501
Parents
    curriculum and values of, 314
    gender and expectations of, 475–76
    teachers' counseling of, 287, 288
Parsons, Talcott, 316
Passion for learning, 551
Passow, A.H., 524, 535
Peabody, Robert, 272n17
Pedagogy, 319–22. *See also* Teaching
    between-school differences in, 454–56
    critical, 33
    differences between tracks in, 458
    invisible, 321
    progressive, 306
    visible, 321–22
Peer groups, student, 149–50, 373
Performance, educational
    during early 1980s, 52–53
    measuring, 160–61
    political perspectives on, 30
    power and standards of, 161
    teacher expectations and, 179–81
Persell, Caroline Hodges, 441, 458, 461, 462
Personal development, 97–98, 107–14, 116
    classroom environment and, 108–9

creativity, 111–12
discipline in schools and, 108, 10
grading and, 110–12
improving, 541
Progressivism and, 112–14
Personalization of teaching and learning, 558, 563, 568
Personal modeling, 349
Personnel. *See* Staff, staffing; Teacher(s)
Perspectives, 24. *See also* Political perspectives
Phenomenology, 210–12
Philadelphia School District, 528
Philosopher kings, 35, 200
Philosophy of education, 14–15, 197–241
    curriculum, 304–9
    defined, 198
    existentialism and phenomenology, 210–12
    idealism, 199–201
    neo-Marxism, 212–15
    perspective of, 197–98
    pragmatism, 205–10
    realism, 201–5
    teaching, 319–22
Physical education, Coalition of Essential Schools on, 566
Physical setting of classroom, 554
Piaget, Jean, 307
Pierce, George Sanders, 205
Placement. *See also* Tracking
    curriculum, 306
    occupational, 164–66
*Plague, The* (Camus), 222
Plato, 35, 199–200, 201, 202, 204, 350
Platonic philosophy, 199
*Plessy* v. *Ferguson,* 83–84
Policy(ies)
    on literacy, 10–11
    political perspectives on, 31–33
    state textbook-adoption, 331
    on urban education, 7–8
Policy making
    curriculum, 310–12
    by federal government, 245
Political correctness, 315
Political perspectives, 23–34
    on American Dream, 33–34
    conservative, 24–25, 27
    definition of educational problems and, 30–31
    liberal, 24, 25, 27
    on policy and reform, 31–33
    radical, 24, 25–27
    on role of school, 28–30
    traditional and progressive visions, 27–28
    on unequal educational performance, 30

Political purposes of schooling, 22, 23
*Politics, Markets, and America's Schools* (Chubb and Moe), 526, 536
Politics of education, 15–16, 34–36
    cultural, 326, 327–41
    cultural incorporation, 334–39
    curriculum, 309–15
    official knowledge, 328–30
    progressive coalition, 63
    school cultures and, 253–54
Poor, universal education and the, 102
Popular education. *See* Universal education
*Popular Education and Its Discontents* (Cremin), 89
"Popular Schooling" (Cremin), 36, 45–57
Postmodernist theories of education, 214, 215
Poverty, 125
    among children, 296n7
    cultural deprivation theory and, 445–46
    culture of, 445, 495
    expansion of teachers' role and, 288–89
    urban, 6
Powell, Arthur, 530
Power
    as basis for selection in organizations, 162
    conflicts and, 34–35
    curriculum and, 310
    dual concept of, 332
    models of, 310
    relations of, 15–16, 141
    resistance theories and, 233
    standards of performance and, 161
    struggle for, 163
*Practice of Teaching, The* (Jackson), 319–20
Pragmatism, 205–10
    curriculum under, 209–10
    of Dewey, 207
    goal of education under, 207–9
    instruction methods under, 209
    role of teacher under, 209
Prestige, struggle for, 163
Primary deviant, 177–78
Principal, 254
*Principia Mathematica* (Russell & Whitehead), 204
Principles, 226–27
Prior achievement
    future academic achievement and, 384
    teacher evaluations and, 179–80
Prisons, 266

Private school, 165
  bartering and chartering for elite
    college admissions in, 378,
    393–409
  conflicts over curriculum in, 310
  included in school choice plans,
    526–27
  organization of, 247–48
  public schools compared with,
    374, 378, 381–91
  student achievement and,
    384–86
Privatization of school, 32
Privilege, transmission through
  networks, 395
Process-content interrelationship,
  255
Productivity, level of education and,
  158
Professional educators, 312
Professionalization of teachers, 178,
  244, 259–61, 285, 295, 545
Professional model of school
  administration, 537
Programmatic issues in urban
  education, 8–9
Progressive coalition politics, 63
Progressivism, 75–82, 207, 209
  pedagogical, 306
  personal development and,
    112–14
  reform under, 62, 75–82
  romantic, 307
  visions of, 27–28
Project Head Start, 86, 125, 45–46
Proletariat, 142
Promotion, minimum performance
  requirements for, 11
Property taxes, school financing
  through, 449–51, 541
"Proposals Related to the
  Education of Youth in
  Pennsylvania" (Franklin), 69
Prosser, Charles, 80
Protagoras, 343
Protestants, 163
Publications, student, 293
Public education
  for African Americans, 74–75
  opposition to, 73–74
  for women, 74–75
Public school
  conflicts over curriculum in,
    310
  high school, 78–80
  private schools compared with,
    374, 378, 381–91
  WASP culture and, 165
Puritans, New England, 108–9
Putney School, 307
*Pygmalion in the Classroom*
  (Rosenthal & Jacobson), 182

Quality with equality argument,
  32
Queens, philosopher, 35

Race
  cultural deprivation theories and,
    445–46, 448
  cultural differences theories and,
    446–49
  differences in intelligence and,
    444–45
  educational outcomes and, 107,
    370, 442
  equality of opportunity and, 83
  public school-private school
    differences and, 387–91
  student composition by, 246
  teacher's expectations and, 180
  tracking and, 457–58, 488, 492
Radical perspectives, 24, 25–27, 318
  on definition of educational
    problems, 31
  on education and the American
    Dream, 34
  on history of education, 90–91
  on policy and reform, 32–33
  reproduction and resistance in,
    216, 229–37
  on role of school, 29, 30
  on social efficiency curriculum,
    306–7
  on unequal educational
    performance, 30
Randall, Vera, 560
Rape, 355–56
Ravitch, Diane, 11, 18, 29, 78,
  91–92, 93, 94, 123–31, 205,
  209, 530, 536
Reagan, Ronald, 25, 245, 526
Realism, 201–5
Recession, economic, 44
Reform(s), 1–2, 521–43. *See also*
  Coalition of Essential Schools;
  History of education
  of actors and their roles, 534–35
  centralized, 278, 282–83
  in college and university entrance
    requirements, 40–41
  community-level, 62–63
  contradictions of, 261, 275–86
  effective school movement, 8, 11,
    12, 32, 60, 145, 530–32
  effective teachers and, 522–23
  excellence-equity tension and,
    535–38
  first wave of, 524–25
  in former Soviet Union, 251
  functional view of, 141
  in Great Britain, 249–50
  imperatives for better schools,
    557–59
  instructional, 61

  in intellectual norms for school
    teachers, 41
  major themes of, 534–35
  on national level, 42–43
  in 1980s, 87–88, 523–35
  in 1990s, 87–88, 538–39
  political perspectives on, 31–33
  Progressive, 62, 75–82
  reinvention of teaching, 545–56
  rise of common school and,
    72–75
  school-based management and
    teacher empowerment, 528–30
  school-business partnerships, 528
  school choice, 8–9, 88, 152, 381,
    525–28, 536–37
  in school improvement strategies,
    41–42
  second wave of, 525
  social shifts and, 43
  in standards of achievement,
    39–40
  systemic, 539
  in teacher assessment, 283–84
  teacher education, 532–34
  theory of educational problems
    and, 540–43
  traditional-progressive cycles of,
    80–82
Regulation, top-down, 559–60
Reich, Robert, 536
"Reinventing Teaching" (Meier),
  543, 545–56
Religion
  formal instruction and, 68–69
  founding of schools and, 164–65
  instruction in, 347
  private schools and, 247–48
Remedial services, 86
Reminiscence, doctrine of, 201
Remunerative control emphasis,
  165
Reproduction, social, 377–78
  community college education
    and, 411–13, 427
  of consciousness, 317–18
  elite education and, 378,
    393–409
  forms of, 229–30
  radical perspectives on, 216,
    229–37
  through traditional curriculum,
    321
"Reproduction and Resistance in
  Radical Theories of Schooling"
  (Giroux), 216, 229–37
Reproduction theories, 214, 216,
  229–37
  critique of, 230
  human agency and, 230–31
Research
  action, 192

collaborative, 191–92
effective school, 452–54
humanistic, 192
new directions in, 191–93
revitalization of, 189–96
Residential segregation, 246
Resistance theories, 214, 216, 229–37
assumptions of, 231, 233
emancipation and, 233, 235
human agency and, 230–31, 233, 236
meaning of "resistance," 232
oppositional behavior and, 233–34, 235
power and, 233
theoretical flaws of, 232
value of, 234–36
Responsibility(ies)
moral, 272n16
of schools and colleges, 53–54
Revisionist perspective. *See* Radical perspectives
Ribich, Thomas, 106–7
Rice, Joseph Mayer, 108
Rich, Adrienne, 326, 353–58
Rickover, Hyman, 47
Riis, Jacob, 125
Rist, Ray C., 153, 175–88
Rite of passage, labeling as, 183
Roberts, Benjamin, 75
Rockefeller, John D., 75
Role(s) of teacher
under existentialism, 211
expansion of, 287–99
under idealism, 200–201
under neo-Marxism, 214
under phenomenology, 211
under pragmatism, 209
under realism, 204
reconceptualizing, 537–38
Role-strain, 148
Roman Catholics, 73
Roman Catholic schools, 190, 247, 375, 381, 384–86, 453
Romantic progressivism, 307
Roosevelt, Franklin Delano, 25
Rosenthal, R., 182
Ross, Edward A., 109
Rossides, Daniel, 366
Rousseau, Jean-Jacques, 74, 205, 206
Rugg, Harold, 308, 313, 330
Rush, Benjamin, 108
Russell, Bertrand, 202, 204

Sadker, D., 475, 479
Sadker, M., 475, 479
Sadler, Sir Michael, 47
Safety of schools, 553
Saint John's University, 201
Salter, Brian, 191

*San Antonio (Texas) Independent School District* v. *Rodriquez,* 451
Sarason, Seymour, 257–58, 538, 561
Sartre, Jean Paul, 210–11
Satisficing, 160
SAT (Scholastic Achievement Test) scores, 399
decline in, 9–10, 127–28
gender and math scores, 472
SAT (Scholastic Aptitude Test), 564
*Savage Inequalities* (Kozol), 449, 455, 541
Scholasticism, new, 189–91
School(s). *See also* Catholic schools; Organization of schools; Private school; Public school
academic achievement and composition of, 384
culture of, 253–56, 274, 549–50
Dewey on, 218–19
educational outcomes and differences in, 371–75
elite, 166
financing of, 7, 449–52, 541
immigrants in, 289
magnet, 374
privatization of, 32
structure of, 265–66, 276–77
support systems in, 295
*School and Society, The* (Dewey), 76
School-based management, 59, 88, 260, 295, 528–30
School-business partnerships, 528
School-centered explanations of educational inequality, 441, 449–60
between-school differences, 449, 452, 454–56
effective school research, 452–54
gender and schooling, 458–60
school financing, 449–52
within-school differences, 444, 449, 452, 456–58
School choice, 8–9, 88, 152, 381, 525–28, 536–37
School climates, 454
School environment. *See* Environment
School-group culture, employer culture and, 166
School improvement strategies, reforms in, 41–42
Schooling
education vs., 21–22
non-cognitive effects of, 325
purposes of, 22–23
*Schooling in Capitalist America* (Bowles & Gintis), 94, 142
School privatization, 32

School restructuring effort for gender equity, 480
School-society relationship, 139–44
conflict theories, 141–43
functional theories, 140–41
interactional theories, 143–44
theoretical perspectives on, 140
"Schools of Tomorrow...Today" project, 255
School system
expansion of, 168
selectivity of, 248
Schultz, Alfred, 221
Scientific management of curriculum, 306
Scientific models of teaching, 531–32
Scopes, John, 312
Scopes Trial, 312
Secondary deviant, 177–78
Secondary education
private schools, 165
in Puritan New England, 70
Second Industrial Revolution, 75
Sedlak, Michael, 533
SEEK Program, 353–54
Segregation, 6–8, 84–85
*de facto,* 85, 151–52, 246
residential, 246
Selective traditional textbooks, 329
Selectivity of school system, 248
Self-esteem, tracking and, 487
Self-fulfilling prophecy, 148, 175
labeling theory and, 181–85
of teacher expectations, 458
tracking and, 492
"Separate but equal" doctrine, 83–84
*Serrano* v. *Priest,* 451
Sewall, Gilbert, 43
Sex education, 294
Sexist grammar, 355
Shady Hill School, 307
Shanker, Albert, 457
*Shopping Mall High School* (Powell, Cohen, & Ferrar), 530
Siegel, Jessica, 522
Silberman, Charles S., 82, 108, 112
Simple school structure, 558
Single-sex schools, 460
Sirotnik, Kenneth A., 191–92
Sizer, Theodore, 42, 281, 537, 543, 557–70
Skills
curriculum and, 318–19
job, 158–59
vocational, 159–60
Skinner, B.F., 531
Slaves, African-American, 71–72
*Small Victories* (Freedman), 522
Smith, Adam, 24, 100
Smith, Frank, 552–53

Smith, Horace, 560
Smith, Marshall, 52
Smith, Mortimer, 81
Snow, C.P., 192
Snyder, Jimmy (the Greek), 293
Sobel, Thomas, 293–94, 314
Social class
   between-school differences and,
      454–56
   childrearing patterns and, 505–6
   cultural deprivation theories and,
      445–46, 448
   cultural differences theories and,
      446–49
   curriculum stratification and, 322
   differences in intelligence and,
      445
   educational outcomes and,
      104–6, 144–45, 155, 369–70,
      378, 442
   family-school relationship and,
      495–512
   Ivy League admission and,
      399–400
   norms of academic success and,
      422
   status groups and, 163–64
   teacher expectations and, 181
   tracking and, 457–58, 488, 492
"Social Class Differences in Family-
   School Relationships: The
   Importance of Cultural
   Capital" (Lareau), 463,
   495–512
Social control
   deviance and, 177
   education as means of, 101–2
   top-down, under capitalism,
      115
Social Darwinism, 24
Social efficiency curriculum, 305–7,
   308, 311, 322
Social imperatives, educational
   responses to, 61
Socialism, 142, 213
   democratic, 25–27
Socialization, 23, 139
   gender and, 443, 460
   gender role, 476–77
Social life, Dewey on, 219–20
Social meliorist curriculum, 308
Social origins
   attainment and, 155
   occupational success and, 161
Social policy, education as tool of,
   95–96
Social processes, demystification of,
   191
Social purposes of schooling, 23
Social stratification, 6–7, 366–67
   forms of, 367–68
   income and, 368–69

Social stratification. *See*
   Stratification
Society, expansion of teachers' role
   and, 288–89
Society-school relationship, 139–44
   conflict theories, 141–43
   functional theories, 140–41
   interactional theories, 143–44
   theoretical perspectives on, 140
Socioeconomic status (SES),
   academic attainment and, 6–7.
   *See also* Social class
Sociologese, 191
Sociological analysis, relationship
   between four levels of, 461–62
Sociological-economic perspective,
   dominance of, 128–29
Sociological imagination, 5–6, 153,
   190
*Sociological Imagination, The*
   (Mills), 5–6
Sociologists, background
   assumptions of, 189, 192
Sociology of education, 16–17,
   137–96
   classroom interactions, 138
   current educational crisis and,
      153–54
   curriculum, 315–19
   effects of schooling on
      individuals, 144–47
   inequality, 150–53
   new, 304
   research agenda of, 189
   inside schools, 147–50
   school-society relationship,
      139–44
   sociology of, 190–91
   uses for teachers, 138–39
*Sociology of Teaching, The* (Waller),
   142–43
Socrates, 199, 349, 350
Socratic method, 350
"Soft" suasion, 349
South, education in the
   of African Americans, 84
   in colonial period, 71–72
Soviet Union, former, 26
   school organization in, 250–51
Spatial ability, differences in,
   474–75
Sponsored mobility, 146
Spring, Joel, 90
*Sputnik*, 81
Staff, staffing. *See also* Teacher(s)
   Coalition of Essential Schools on,
      563
   urban education crisis and, 8
*Stand and Deliver* (film), 522–23
Standard English, 369
Standardized testing, 53, 306
   decline in scores on, 9–10

Standards, 60, 564
   of achievement, reforms in,
      39–40
   decline of, 30, 127–28
   emphasis on, 540
   national, 539
   of performance, power and,
      161
   policy disagreements about,
      10–11
Stanford University, 314
Stanley, J., 473–74
State of families viewpoint, 35
State of individuals viewpoint,
   35–36
State textbook-adoption policies,
   331
Status, teacher evaluation and
   social, 179, 180
Status-attainment models, 394
Status-attainment process, 368–69
Status culture, 142
   education as, 164
Status groups, 162–64
Status group struggle, 143
Stedman, Lawrence, 52
Stiles, Ginny, 551
Story, Joseph, 109
*Straight Talk about American
   Education* (Black), 43
Stratification, 6–7, 150, 366–71
   of curriculum, 322–24
   forms of, 367–68
   functional and conflict theories
      of, 153, 155–74
   by gender, 370–71
   income and, 368–69
   by race, 370
   by social class, 369–70, 378
Stress, job-related, 291
Strivers, 149
Structure of schools
   contradictions in, 276–77
   spatial and temporal, 265–66
Struggle for advantage, 163
*Struggle for the American
   Curriculum: 1893–1958, The*
   (Kliebard), 304
Student(s)
   academic achievement and
      background characteristics of,
      384
   alienation of, 149–50
   attacks upon order, 266–67
   composition of, 246
   peer groups of, 149–50
   in poverty, 288–89
   relationships between, tracking
      and, 491
   resistance by, 235
   women, 353–58
   working-class, 231

Student-as-worker, 563
Student-centered explanations of
    educational inequality, 441,
    443–49
  cultural deprivation theories,
    445–46, 448
  cultural differences theories,
    446–49
  genetic differences, 444–45
Student publications, 293
Student-teacher ratio, 245
"Study institution" (juku), 252
Study of High Schools, A, 561
Subcultures, student, 149
Subjective approach to research,
    192
Subordinate cultures, 231
Substantive expertise, 349
Successful schools, factors defining,
    530. *See also* Effective schools
    movement
*Summerhill* (Neill), 82
Sumner, William Graham, 24
Support systems
  in schools, 295
  for women in mathematics,
    478
Syllogism, 202–3
Systemic reform, 539

*Tabula rasa*, 203, 206
"Taking Women Students
    Seriously" (Rich), 326, 353–58
Tapper, Ted, 191
Taylor, Frederick Winslow, 77,
    114, 306
Teacher(s)
  assessment of, 283–84
  authority of, 110
  autonomy of, 266
  community-college, 422
  counseling of parents by, 287,
    288
  demographic characteristics of,
    256
  distrust of American, 559
  educational reform and effective,
    522–23
  empowerment of, 17–19, 88,
    529–30
  as factor in effectiveness of
    schools, 531
  interactions with students by
    gender, 475
  minority, lack of, 9
  professionalization of, 178, 244,
    259–61, 285, 295, 545
  qualifications of, 257
  qualities to look for in
    prospective, 551
  reforms in intellectual norms for,
    41

  requests for parental
    involvement, 498–501
  roles of. *See* Role(s) of teacher
  schools as inspiring and
    challenging for, 551–52
  textbook selection by, 333
  uses of sociology for, 138–39
  values of, 224
  women, 357
Teacher behavior, sociology of,
    148–49
Teacher burnout, 257, 291
Teacher certification, 297n38
Teacher education, 18–19, 299n73,
    532–34, 546, 553
  crisis in, 260
  in mathematics, 479
Teacher empowerment, 88, 529–30
Teacher evaluations, determinants
    of, 179–80
Teacher expectations
  labeling theory and, 178–81
  origins of, 175
  self-fulfilling prophecy of, 458
  student achievement and,
    148–49
*Teachers for Our Nation's Schools*
    (Goodlad), 534
Teacher-student ratio, 245
Teacher-student relationship,
    tracking and, 490–91
Teacher training school (normal
    school), 73
Teaching
  defensive, 277, 279–80
  habitual view of, 546–48
  mimetic, 320, 321, 326, 344–46,
    349
  nature of, 257–58
  personalization of, 558, 563, 568
  philosophy of, 319–22
  reinvention of, 545–56
  scientific models of, 531–32
  transformative, 320–21, 326,
    346–51
Teaching internships, 295
Teaching quality, tracking and, 490
Team building, 255
Technical-function theory, 156–60,
    162, 167
"Technocratic-meritocratic" school,
    97, 98–100, 101, 115–17
Technological change, 167
Technology
  compulsory education and,
    271n9
  in educational theory, 96–101
  expansion of education and,
    168–69
  school organization and, 264–65,
    266, 267
  of teaching, 531

Television, 126
Tenth Amendment, 451
Test of General Ability (TOGA),
    179
Tests and testing
  competency, 205, 282
  dispute over, 128
  HSB, 383
  standardized, 9–10, 53, 306
"Text and Cultural Politics, The"
    (Apple), 326, 327–41
Textbooks
  conservative resurgence and,
    328–29, 336–37
  as economic commodities,
    330–31
  as instruments of regulation and
    exploitation, 332–33
  "official knowledge" in, 328–30
  responses to, 338
  selection of, 313, 329–30, 333
  selective traditional, 329
  state adoption policies, 331
Thatcher, Margaret, 249
Thematic core curriculum, 309
Theory, definition of, 140
*36 Children* (Kohl), 82
Thomas, Clarence, 458
Thomas, W.I., 181
Thoreau, Henry David, 221
Thorndike, Edward L., 77, 79
*Time for Results: The Governor's
    1991 Report on Education*
    (Alexander), 525
Tocqueville, Alexis de, 46
*Tomorrow's Teachers* (Holmes
    Report), 533–34
Top-down regulation, 559–60
*To Reclaim a Legacy*, 48, 49
"Tournament selection," 147, 369
Town school, 70
Tracking, 151, 384, 394, 456–58,
    485–92
  in British schools, 180
  characteristics of, 486
  curriculum, 11, 322–24, 325
  defining, 485–86
  race and, 457–58, 488, 492
  reasons for disappointing effects
    of, 489–92
  record of, 487–89
  underlying assumptions of,
    486–87
Traditional curriculum, 303–4, 321
Traditional reform, 80–82
Traditional visions of education,
    27–28
Transformative intellectual, 214
Transformative tradition, 320–21,
    326, 346–51
  concept of knowledge in, 346–47
  exemplars of, 349–50

modes of operation in, 348–49
moral and philosophic, 350–51
*Troubled Crusade, The* (Ravitch),
    91, 92
Trow, Martin, 55
Troy Female Seminary, 74
Truth, Platonic search for, 199
Twentieth Century Fund, 48
Two-track educational system, 103

Unconnected (student type), 149
Underclass, 150
Unintended consequences,
    phenomenon of, 351
Unions
    labor, 213
    teachers', 123
United Federation of Teachers
    (UFT), 294
U.S. education, national goals for,
    538–39
U.S. Supreme Court, on school
    financing, 451
Universal education, 49–50
    the poor and, 102
    as radical ideal, 51, 52
    technocratic-meritocratic
        perspective on, 99
University faculty working with
    restructured schools, 552
University of Chicago, 314
Upper class, 150
Upper middle class, 150
Urban education
    crisis in, 6–9
    inequalities and, 151
Urbanization, 75–80, 142, 208
Utilitarianism in education, 69

Values
    decline of, 31

educational, social class and,
    506
parental, 314
of teachers, 224
Vanderbilt, Cornelius, 75
*Varieties of Religious Experience*
    (James), 205
Verbal abuse of women, 356
Visible pedagogy, 321–22
Vocational education, 209, 487
    Coalition of Essential Schools on,
        566
Vocational skills, 159–60
Voltaire, 332
Voucher (optional enrollment)
    issue, 60, 526

Wage costs, 171$n$8
Wage returns, 158
Wald, Lillian, 76
Waller, Willard, 142–43, 253
War on Poverty, 106–7
Warren, Earl, 84
WASP culture, public school system
    and, 165
Wealth, struggle for, 163
Weber, Max, 142, 155, 163, 184,
    254, 272$n$18
Welfare state, 213
Westway Project, 310
*What Do Our Seventeen Year Olds
    Know?* (Ravitch & Finn), 10,
    530
"What Is a Teachers's Job?: An
    Examination of the Social and
    Legal Causes of Role
    Expansion and Its
    Consequences" (Cohen), 261,
    287–99
Whitehead, Alfred North, 112,
    137, 202, 204

Whole-language movement, 307–8,
    309
Wicker, Tom, 355
"Wide awakeness," education as,
    214
"Wide-Awakeness and the Moral
    Life" (Greene), 215–16,
    221–28
Willard, Emma Hart, 74
Williams, C.R., 257
Williams, Polly, 536
Williams, Raymond, 329
Willis, Paul, 229, 447
Winter, Governer, 42
Within-school differences, 444,
    449, 452, 456–58
Within-school explanations of
    inequality. *See* School-centered
    explanations of educational
    inequality
Witte, John F., 378, 381–86
Women
    mathematics and, 471–83
    public education for, 74–75
    verbal abuse of, 356
Women students, 353–58
Women teachers, 357
Work, dehumanizing conditions of,
    100
Working class, family-school
    relationship in, 497–510
Working-class students, 231
Work performance, measuring,
    160–61
Workplace skills, curriculum and,
    318–19
Wrigley, Julia, 90

Young, Michael F.D., 304
Yucaipa, California, 329, 331